D1552604

# JOHANNINE THEOLOGY

## THE GOSPEL,
## THE EPISTLES
### *and the*
## APOCALYPSE

PAUL A. RAINBOW

IVP Academic

An imprint of InterVarsity Press
Downers Grove, Illinois

Apollos
Nottingham, England

InterVarsity Press
P.O. Box 1400, Downers Grove, IL 60515-1426,, USA
World Wide Web: www.ivpress.com
Email: email@ivpress.com

APOLLOS (an imprint of Inter-Varsity Press, England)
Norton Street, Nottingham NG7 3HR, England
ivpbooks.com
ivp@ivpbooks.com

InterVarsity Press® is the book-publishing division of InterVarsity Christian Fellowship/USA®, a movement of students and faculty active on campus at hundreds of universities, colleges and schools of nursing in the United States of America, and a member movement of the International Fellowship of Evangelical Students. For information about local and regional activities, write Public Relations Dept., InterVarsity Christian Fellowship/USA, 6400 Schroeder Rd., P.O. Box 7895, Madison, WI 53707-7895, or visit the IVCF website at www.intervarsity.org.

Cover design: David Fassett
Interior design: Beth McGill
Images: St. John the Evangelist: St. John the Evangelist at Patmos, from the Mystic Marriage of St. Catherine Triptych
        by Hans Memling, at the Memling Museum, Bruges, Belgium. The Bridgeman Art Library
        cross illustration: © FONG_KWONG_CHO/iStockphoto

ISBN 978-0-8308-4056-4 (print)
ISBN 978-0-8308-9650-9 (digital)

Printed in the United States of America ∞

**Library of Congress Cataloging-in-Publication Data**

Rainbow, Paul A. (Paul Andrew)
  Johannine theology : the gospel, the Epistles and the Apocalypse / Paul A. Rainbow.
    pages cm
  Includes bibliographical references and index.
  ISBN 978-0-8308-4056-4 (hardcover : alk. paper)
  1. Bible. John—Theology. 2. Bible. Epistles of John—Theology. 3. Bible. Revelation—Theology. I. Title.
  BS2601.R35 2014
  226.5'06—dc23

                                                                      2014022815

| P | 24 | 23 | 22 | 21 | 20 | 19 | 18 | 17 | 16 | 15 | 14 | 13 | 12 | 11 | 10 | 9 | 8 | 7 | 6 | 5 | 4 | 3 | 2 | 1 |
|---|----|----|----|----|----|----|----|----|----|----|----|----|----|----|----|---|---|---|---|---|---|---|---|---|
| Y | 34 | 33 | 32 | 31 | 30 | 29 | 28 | 27 | 26 | 25 | 24 | 23 | 22 | 21 | 20 | 19 | 18 | 17 | 16 | 15 | 14 | | | |

Mentoris acris J. V. Dahms memor

# CONTENTS

# PREFACE

As far as I am aware, this volume is the only English-language textbook on John's theology that aims to be both critical and comprehensive. It is critical in that I have tried to be aware of the basis and extent of our knowledge, given the problems inherent in the use of ancient human documents. It is comprehensive in that it includes all the books of the New Testament ascribed to John: the Gospel, the three Epistles and the Apocalypse (the book of Revelation).

By no means are Johannine specialists in agreement that sound criticism allows a comprehensive approach in that sense. Not all believe that John wrote even one of these books. In mainline scholarship the number of hypothetical hands that shaped the Gospel alone keeps growing. Some suppose that each of the three Epistles had a different author, and that the John who wrote the Apocalypse was a fifth (at least!). Even conservative scholars nowadays are less strident in defending the apostolic authorship of the Apocalypse than were their predecessors of a previous generation, and some have gone mute. In harking back to the old solution, I claim no more than to testify to what I myself see—come what may in reviews.

About the steady, mighty river of learned publications on the Johannine literature C. K. Barrett spoke with candor for many when he wrote, "Probably no one has read it all; I know I have not."[1] That was back in 1975, before annual output more than doubled to what it is today. Selection is imperative. I have concentrated on works that have proved seminal, become classic or been especially influential and on journal articles and serial monographs since the turn of the third millennium.

Anyone who delves into the theology of John finds the subject inexhaustible.

---

[1]C. K. Barrett, foreword to *John: Witness and Theologian*, by John Painter (London: SPCK, 1975), p. ix.

No matter how one shapes the material, the result is but a sketch that captures certain aspects. I have done my best, through prayer and thoughtful labor, to capture some key aspects. Whether the result is serviceable to those seeking further insight into John's writings is for them to judge.

# ACKNOWLEDGMENTS

ALL SCRIPTURE QUOTATIONS ARE initially based on *The Holy Bible: Revised Standard Version* (second edition; copyright 1972 by the Division of Christian Education of the National Council of the Churches of Christ in the United States of America), even in cases where the author has taken it upon himself to alter one or more words to bring out nuances of the original Hebrew or Greek text. So numerous are these cases that it would have been pedantic and burdensome to indicate every one. But the author wishes to acknowledge his debt in the preponderance of cases where the wording is identical to the RSV.

# ABBREVIATIONS

## General

| | |
|---|---|
| // | parallel text(s) |
| § | section |
| ca. | circa |
| cf. | compare |
| chap(s). | chapter(s) |
| e.g. | for example |
| esp. | especially |
| etc. | and the rest |
| ET | English translation |
| fol. | folio |
| Gk. | Greek |
| Heb. | Hebrew |
| ibid. | in the same source |
| idem | by the same author(s) |
| i.e. | that is |
| Lat. | Latin |
| lit. | literally |
| MS(S) | manuscript(s) |
| no(s). | number(s) |
| par(s). | parallel(s) |
| p(p). | page(s) |
| v(v). | verse(s) |

## Ancient Texts, Types and Version

| | |
|---|---|
| LXX | Septuagint |
| MT | Masoretic Text |

## Modern Editions

| | |
|---|---|
| UBS⁴ | *The Greek New Testament*, United Bible Societies, 4th edition |

## MODERN VERSIONS

| | |
|---|---|
| NAB | New American Bible |
| RSV | Revised Standard Version |

## APOCRYPHA AND SEPTUAGINT

| | |
|---|---|
| 1-4 Kgdms | 1-4 Kingdoms |
| 1-4 Macc | 1-4 Maccabees |
| Sir | Sirach |
| Tob | Tobit |
| Wis | Wisdom of Solomon |

## OLD TESTAMENT PSEUDEPIGRAPHA

| | |
|---|---|
| *2 Bar.* | *2 Baruch (Syriac Apocalypse)* |
| *1 En.* | *1 Enoch (Ethiopic Apocalypse)* |
| *4 Ezra* | *1 Ezra* |
| *Let. Arist.* | *Letter of Aristeas* |
| *Pss. Sol.* | *Psalms of Solomon* |
| *T. Ash.* | *Testament of Asher* |
| *T. Dan.* | *Testament of Dan* |

## DEAD SEA SCROLLS

| | |
|---|---|
| CD-A | *Damascus Document*[a] |
| CD-B | *Damascus Document*[b] |
| 1QpHab | *1QPesher to Habakkuk* |
| 1QS | *1QRule of the Community* |
| 4Q398 (4QMMT[e]) | *4QHalakhic Letter*[e] |

## MISHNAH AND TALMUD

| | |
|---|---|
| *b.* | Babylonian Talmud |
| *m.* | Mishnah |
| *y.* | Jerusalem Talmud |

| | |
|---|---|
| *ʿAbod. Zar.* | *ʿAbodah Zarah* |
| *ʾAbot* | *ʾAbot* |
| *Bek.* | *Bekorot* |
| *Ber.* | *Berakot* |
| *Beṣah* | *Beṣah* |

| | |
|---|---|
| B. Meṣ'ia | Baba Meṣ'ia |
| 'Ed. | 'Eduyyot |
| Demai | Demai |
| Ḥag. | Ḥagigah |
| Ḥul. | Ḥullin |
| Kelim | Kelim |
| Ketub. | Ketubbot |
| Mak. | Makkot |
| Menaḥ. | Menaḥot |
| Mo'ed Qaṭ. | Mo'ed Qaṭan |
| Ned. | Nedarim |
| Nid. | Niddah |
| 'Ohal. | 'Ohalot |
| Parah | Parah |
| Pe'ah | Pe'ah |
| Pesaḥ. | Pesaḥim |
| Qidd. | Qiddušin |
| Šabb. | Šabbat |
| Sanh. | Sanhedrin |
| Šeb. | Šebi'it |
| Šeqal. | Šeqalim |
| Soṭah | Soṭah |
| Sukkah | Sukkah |
| Ta'an. | Ta'anit |
| Tamid | Tamid |
| Ṭehar. | Ṭeharot |
| Yad. | Yadaim |
| Yebam. | Yebamot |
| Zebaḥ. | Zebaḥim |

## OTHER RABBINIC WORKS

| | |
|---|---|
| Mek. | Mekilta |
| Rab. | Rabbah (+ biblical book) |
| Sipra | Sipra |

## APOSTOLIC FATHERS

| | |
|---|---|
| *Barn.* | *Barnabas* |
| *2 Clem.* | *2 Clement* |
| *Did.* | *Didache* |
| Herm. *Sim.* | Shepherd of Hermas, *Similitude* |
| Ign. *Smyrn.* | Ignatius, *To the Smyrnaeans* |
| Ign. *Trall.* | Ignatius, *To the Trallians* |

## NEW TESTAMENT APOCRYPHA AND PSEUDEPIGRAPHA

| | |
|---|---|
| *Prot. Jas.* | *Protevangelium of James* |

## GREEK AND LATIN WORKS

Aristotle
| | |
|---|---|
| *Eth. nic.* | *Ethica nichomachea (Nichomachean Ethics)* |
| *Pol.* | *Politica (Politics)* |

Augustine
| | |
|---|---|
| *Corrept.* | *De correptione et gratia (Admonition and Grace)* |
| *Grat.* | *De gratia et libero arbitrio (Grace and Free Will)* |
| *Praed.* | *De praedestinatione sanctorum (The Predestination of the Saints)* |
| *Tract. Ev. Jo.* | *In Evangelium Johannis tractatus (Tractates on the Gospel of John)* |
| *Trin.* | *De Trinitate (On the Trinity)* |

Clement of Alexandria
| | |
|---|---|
| *Quis div.* | *Quis dives salvetur (Salvation of the Rich)* |
| *Strom.* | *Stromata (Miscellanies)* |

Cyril of Alexandria
| | |
|---|---|
| *Comm. Jo.* | *Commentarium in Evangelium Johannes (Commentary on the Gospel of John)* |

Epiphanius
| | |
|---|---|
| *Pan.* | *Panarion (Adversus haereses) (Refutation of All Heresies)* |

Eusebius
| | |
|---|---|
| *Hist. eccl.* | *Historia ecclesiastica (Ecclesiastical History)* |

Hippolytus
| | |
|---|---|
| *Trad. ap.* | *Traditio apostolica (Apostolic Tradition)* |

Irenaeus
    *Haer.*            *Adversus haereses (Against Heresies)*

Jerome
    *Vir. ill.*          *De viris illustribus*

Josephus
    *Ag. Ap.*         *Against Apion*
    *Ant.*              *Jewish Antiquities*
    *J.W.*              *Jewish War*
    *Life*               *The Life*

Justin
    *1 Apol.*         *Apologia i (First Apology)*
    *Dial.*            *Dialogus cum Tryphone (Dialogue with Trypho)*

Juvenal
    *Sat.*              *Satirae (Satires)*

Minucius Felix
    *Oct.*              *Octavius*

Philo
    *Abr.*              *De Abrahamo (On the Life of Abraham)*
    *Agr.*              *De agricultura (On Agriculture)*
    *Alleg. Interp.*   *Legum allegoriae (Allegorical Interpretation)*
    *Cher.*            *De cherubim (On the Cherubim)*
    *Conf.*            *De confusione linguarum (On the Confusion of Tongues)*
    *Congr.*          *De congressu eruditionis gratia (On the Preliminary Studies)*
    *Decal.*          *De decalogo (On the Decalogue)*
    *Det.*              *Quod deterius potiori insidari soleat (That the Worse Attacks the Better)*
    *Deus*            *Quod Deus sit immutabilis (That God Is Unchangeable)*
    *Ebr.*              *De ebriatate (On Drunkenness)*
    *Fug.*              *De fuga et inventione (On Flight and Finding)*
    *Her.*             *Quis rerum divinarum heres sit (Who Is the Heir?)*
    *Legat.*          *Legatio ad Gaium (On the Embassy to Gaius)*
    *Migr.*           *De migratione Abrahami (On the Migration of Abraham)*
    *Mos.*            *De vita Mosis (On the Life of Moses)*
    *Mut.*            *De mutatione nominum (On the Change of Names)*
    *Opif.*            *De opificio mundi (On the Creation of the World)*
    *Plant.*           *De plantatione (On Planting)*

| | |
|---|---|
| *Praem.* | *De praemiis et poenis (On Rewards and Punishments)* |
| *QE* | *Quaestiones et solutiones in Exodum (Questions and Answers on Exodus)* |
| *QG* | *Quaestiones et solutiones in Genesin (Questions and Answers on Genesis)* |
| *Sacr.* | *De sacrificiis Abelis et Caini (On the Sacrifices of Cain and Abel)* |
| *Sobr.* | *De sobrietate (On Sobriety)* |
| *Somn.* | *De somniis (On Dreams)* |
| | *Spec.  De specialibus legibus (On the Special Laws)* |
| | *Virt.  De virtutibus (On the Virtues)* |

Tacitus

| | |
|---|---|
| *Ann.* | *Annales (Annals)* |
| *Hist.* | *Historiae (Histories)* |

Tertullian

| | |
|---|---|
| *Apol.* | *Apologeticus (Apology)* |
| *Cor.* | *De corona militis (The Crown)* |
| *Marc.* | *Adversus Marcionem (Against Marcion)* |
| *Praescr.* | *De praescriptione haereticorum (Prescription Against Heretics)* |

Varro

| | |
|---|---|
| *Rust.* | *De re rustica (On Agriculture)* |

## S<small>ECONDARY</small> S<small>OURCES</small>

| | |
|---|---|
| AB | Anchor Bible |
| *ABD* | *Anchor Bible Dictionary.* Edited by D. N. Freedman. 6 vols. New York, 1992 |
| ABG | Arbeiten zur Bibel und ihrer Geschichte |
| *ABR* | *Australian Biblical Review* |
| ABRL | Anchor Bible Reference Library |
| *ACR* | *Australasian Catholic Record* |
| *AcT* | *Acta theological* |
| ACTR | Ashgate Contemporary Thinkers on Religion: Collected Works |
| *AcTS* | *Acta theologica supplementum* |
| AGJU | Arbeiten zur Geschichte des antiken Judentums und des Urchristentums |

| | |
|---|---|
| AnBib | Analecta biblica |
| ANCT | Ashgate New Critical Thinking in Religion, Theology, and Biblical Studies |
| *Ang* | *Angelicum* |
| *APB* | *Acta Patristica et Byzantina* |
| *ASE* | *Annali di storia dell'esegesi* |
| ATANT | Abhandlungen zur Theologie des Alten und Neuen Testaments |
| *ATJ* | *Ashland Theological Journal* |
| *AUSS* | *Andrews University Seminary Studies* |
| AWRBR | Aus der Welt der Religion: Biblische Reihe |
| AzTh | Arbeiten zur Theologie |
| *BAR* | *Biblical Archaeology Review* |
| BBB | Bonner biblische Beiträge |
| BBC | Blackwell Bible Commentaries |
| *BBET* | *Beiträge zur biblischen Exegese und Theologie* |
| *BBR* | *Bulletin for Biblical Research* |
| BDAG | Bauer, W., F. Danker, W. F. Arndt, and F. W. Gingrich. *Greek-English Lexicon of the New Testament and Other Early Christian Literature.* 3rd ed. Chicago, 1999 |
| BETL | Bibliotheca ephemeridum theologicarum lovaniensium |
| BG | Biblische Gestalten |
| BGBE | Beiträge zur Geschichte der biblischen Exegese |
| *Bib* | *Biblica* |
| *BibInt* | *Biblical Interpretation* |
| BibTS | Biblical Tools and Studies |
| BIS | Biblical Interpretation Series |
| *BJRL* | *Bulletin of the John Rylands University Library of Manchester* |
| BJS | Brown Judaic Studies |
| *BK* | *Bibel und Kirche* |
| *BL* | *Bibel und Liturgie* |
| *BLE* | *Bulletin de littérature ecclésiastique* |
| *BN* | *Biblische Notizen* |
| *BR* | *Biblical Research* |
| *BSac* | *Bibliotheca sacra* |

| | |
|---|---|
| BSR | Biblioteca di scienze religiose |
| BT | *The Bible Translator* |
| BTB | *Biblical Theology Bulletin* |
| BTNT | Biblical Theology of the New Testament |
| BTS | Biblische-theologische Studien |
| BTTB | Bibliothèque de théologie: Théologie biblique |
| BU | Biblische Untersuchungen |
| BWANT | Beiträge zur Wissenschaft vom Alten und Neuen Testament |
| BZ | *Biblische Zeitschrift* |
| BZNW | Beihefte zur Zeitschrift für die neutestamentliche Wissenschaft |
| CahRB | Cahiers de la Revue biblique |
| CahT | Cahiers théologiques |
| CBET | Contributions to Biblical Exegesis and Theology |
| CBQ | *Catholic Biblical Quarterly* |
| CBQMS | Catholic Biblical Quarterly Monograph Series |
| CC | *Cross Currents* |
| CEP | Contemporary Evangelical Perspectives |
| CH | *Church History* |
| Chm | *Churchman* |
| CIS | Copenhagen International Seminar |
| CivCat | *Civiltà Cattolica* |
| COL | Christian Origins Library |
| ConBNT | Coniectanea biblica: New Testament Series |
| ConJ | *Concordia Journal* |
| COQG | Christian Origins and the Question of God |
| CS | *Chicago Studies* |
| CSB | Collana studi biblici |
| CTQ | *Concordia Theological Quarterly* |
| CurBR | *Currents in Biblical Research* |
| CurTM | *Currents in Theology and Mission* |
| CV | *Communio viatorum* |
| DBSJ | *Detroit Baptist Seminary Journal* |
| DRev | *Downside Review* |
| EBib | Études bibliques |
| EC | *Early Christianity* |

| | |
|---|---|
| ECC | Eerdmans Critical Commentary |
| *Eccl* | *Ecclesiology* |
| EH | Europäische Hochschulschriften |
| *Enc* | *Encounter* |
| ESEC | Emory Studies in Early Christianity |
| *EstBib* | *Estudios bíblicos* |
| ESW | Ecumenical Studies in Worship |
| *ETL* | *Ephemerides theologicae lovanienses* |
| *ETR* | *Etudues théologique et religieuses* |
| *EV* | *Esprit et vie* |
| *EvQ* | *Evangelical Quarterly* |
| *ExAud* | *Ex auditu* |
| *ExpTim* | *Expository Times* |
| FAT | Forschungen zum Alten Testament |
| FB | Forschung zur Bibel |
| FBBS | Facet Books: Biblical Series |
| *FilNeot* | *Filología Neotestamentaria* |
| *FoiVie* | *Foi et vie* |
| FOP | Faith and Order Papers |
| FreiTS | Freiburger theologische Studien |
| FRLANT | Forschungen zur Religion und Literatur des Alten und Neuen Testaments |
| FrTS | Frankfurter theologische Studien |
| GD | Gorgias Dissertations |
| *GL* | *Geist und Leben* |
| GNS | Good News Studies |
| *Greg* | *Gregorianum* |
| HBS | Herders biblische Studien |
| HNT | Handbuch zum Neuen Testament |
| *Hor* | *Horizons* |
| *HTR* | *Harvard Theological Review* |
| HUT | Hermeneutische Untersuchungen zur Theologie |
| *HvTSt* | *Hervormde teologiese studies* |
| *IBS* | *Irish Biblical Studies* |
| ICC | International Critical Commentary |
| *IKaZ* | *Internationale katholische Zeitschrift* |

| | |
|---|---|
| *Int* | *Interpretation* |
| IRT | Issues in Religion and Theology |
| *JATS* | *Journal of the Adventist Theological Society* |
| *JBL* | *Journal of Biblical Literature* |
| *JBTh* | *Jahrbuch für biblische Theologie* |
| JCH | Jewish and Christian Heritage |
| *JETS* | *Journal of the Evangelical Theological Society* |
| *JGRCJ* | *Journal of Greco-Roman Christianity and Judaism* |
| JPTSup | Journal of Pentecostal Theology: Supplement Series |
| *JR* | *Journal of Religion* |
| *JSHJ* | *Journal for the Study of the Historical Jesus* |
| JSJSup | Supplements to the Journal for the Study of Judaism |
| *JSNT* | *Journal for the Study of the New Testament* |
| JSNTSup | Journal for the Study of the New Testament: Supplement Series |
| *JSOT* | *Journal for the Study of the Old Testament* |
| *JTI* | *Journal of Theological Interpretation* |
| *JTS* | *Journal of Theological Studies* |
| *KD* | *Kerygma und Dogma* |
| LB | Lire la Bible |
| LBT | Library of Biblical Theology |
| LCL | Loeb Classical Library |
| LD | Lectio divina |
| LEC | Library of Early Christianity |
| LHD | Library of History and Doctrine |
| LN | Louw, Johannes P., and Eugene A. Nida. *Greek-English Lexicon of the New Testament: Based on Semantic Domains.* 2 vols. New York, 1989 |
| LNTS | Library of New Testament Studies |
| LSSTS | Det Laerde Selskabs Skrifter: Teologiske Skrifter |
| LTPM | Louvain Theological and Pastoral Monographs |
| MBPS | Mellen Biblical Press Series |
| MNTC | Moffatt New Testament Commentary |
| MNTS | McMaster New Testament Studies |
| MR | Macrosociology of Religion |
| *MS* | *Marian Studies* |

| | |
|---|---|
| NACSBT | NAC Studies in Bible and Theology |
| NCB | New Century Bible |
| *Neot* | *Neotestamentica* |
| NET | Neutestamentliche Entwürfe zur Theologie |
| NICNT | New International Commentary on the New Testament |
| *NIDNTT* | *New International Dictionary of New Testament Theology.* Edited by C. Brown. 4 vols. Grand Rapids, 1997-1985 |
| NIGTC | New International Greek Testament Commentary |
| *NKGWG* | *Nachrichten von der Königlichen Gesellschaft der Wissenschaft zu Göttingen: Philologische-historische Klasse* |
| *NovT* | *Novum Testamentum* |
| NovTSup | Supplements to Novum Testamentum |
| NSBT | New Studies in Biblical Theology |
| NST | Nouvelle série théologique |
| NTAbh | Neutestamentliche Abhandlungen |
| NTOA | Novum Testamentum et Orbis Antiquus |
| NTL | New Testament Library |
| NTM | New Testament Monographs |
| *NTR* | *New Theology Review* |
| *NTS* | *New Testament Studies* |
| NTT | New Testament Theology |
| OtSt | Oudtestamentische studiën |
| PBM | Paternoster Biblical Monographs |
| PBTM | Paternoster Biblical and Theological Monographs |
| PD | Parole de Dieu |
| PG | Patrologia graeca [= Patrologiae cursus completes: Series graeca]. Edited by J.-P. Migne. 162 vols. Paris, 1857-1886 |
| PHSR | Prentice-Hall Studies in Religion |
| *PIBA* | *Proceedings of the Irish Biblical Association* |
| PL | Preacher's Library |
| POTTS | Pittsburgh Original Texts and Translations Series |
| *ProEccl* | *Pro ecclesia* |
| *PRSt* | *Perspectives in Religious Studies* |
| PTMS | Princeton Theological Monograph Series |
| QD | Quaestiones disputatae |
| *RB* | *Revue biblique* |

| | |
|---|---|
| *RevExp* | *Review and Expositor* |
| *RevistB* | *Revista biblica* |
| RHPR | *Revue d'histoire et de philosophie religieuses* |
| RSPT | *Revue des sciences philosophiques et théologiques* |
| *RRef* | *La revue réformée* |
| RSR | *Recherches de science religieuse* |
| R*Thom* | *Revue thomiste* |
| RTL | *Revue de théologique de Louvain* |
| RTP | *Revue de théologie et de philosophie* |
| RTR | *Reformed Theological Review* |
| SB | *Sémiotique et Bible* |
| SBB | Stuttgarter biblische Beiträge |
| SBEC | Studies in the Bible and Early Christianity |
| SBL | Studies in Biblical Literature |
| SBLAB | Society of Biblical Literature Academia Biblica |
| SBLDS | Society of Biblical Literature Dissertation Series |
| SBLECL | Society of Biblical Literature Early Christianity and Its Literature |
| SBLEJL | Society of Biblical Literature Early Judaism and Its Literature |
| SBLMS | Society of Biblical Literature Monograph Series |
| SBLSBS | Society of Biblical Literature Sources for Biblical Study |
| SBLSymS | Society of Biblical Literature Symposium Series |
| SBS | Stuttgarter Bibelstudien |
| SBT | Studies in Biblical Theology |
| SCC | Studies in Creative Criticism |
| *ScEs* | *Science et esprit* |
| SCJ | *Stone-Campbell Journal* |
| SEÅ | *Svensk exegetisk årsbok* |
| SEBS | Scholars' Editions in Biblical Studies |
| SIMSVD | Studia Instituti Missiologici Societas Verbi Divini |
| SJ | Studies in Judaism |
| SJET | *Scottish Journal of Evangelical Theology* |
| SJLA | Studies in Judaism in Late Antiquity |
| SJT | *Scottish Journal of Theology* |
| SK | *Skrif en kerk* |
| SNTSMS | Society for New Testament Studies Monograph Series |

| | |
|---|---|
| SNTSU | *Studien zum Neuen Testament und seiner Umwelt* |
| SNTW | Studies of the New Testament and Its World |
| SP | Sacra Pagina |
| SPhilAnn | *Studia philonica Annual* |
| SPIB | Scripta Pontificii Instituti Biblici |
| SPNT | Studies on Personalities of the New Testament |
| SRB | Supplementi alla Rivista biblica |
| SS | *Sacra Scripta* |
| StPatr | *Studia patristica* |
| StPB | Studia post-biblica |
| SubBi | Subsidia biblica |
| SVTQ | *St. Vladimir's Theological Quarterly* |
| TANZ | Texte und Arbeiten zum neutestamentlichen Zeitalter |
| TBei | *Theologische Beiträge* |
| TCAAS | Transactions of the Connecticut Academy of Arts and Sciences |
| TD | Theologische Dissertationen |
| TDNT | *Theological Dictionary of the New Testament*. Edited by G. Kittel and G. Friedrich. Translated by G. W. Bromiley. 10 vols. Grand Rapids, 1964-1976 |
| Teol | *Teología* |
| TGl | *Theologie und Glaube* |
| TGST | Tesi gregoriana: Serie teologia |
| Them | *Themelios* |
| THKNT | Theologischer Handkommentar zum Neuen Testament |
| ThTo | *Theology Today* |
| TJ | *Trinity Journal* |
| TNTC | Tyndale New Testament Commentaries |
| TP | *Theologie und Philosophie* |
| TRev | *Theologische Revue* |
| TS | *Theological Studies* |
| TTKi | *Tidsskrift for Teologi og Kirke* |
| TTS | Theologische Texte und Studien |
| TTZ | *Trier theologische Zeitschrift* |
| TUGAL | Texte und Untersuchungen zur Geschichte der altchristlichen Literatur |

| | |
|---|---|
| *TynBul* | *Tyndale Bulletin* |
| TZ | *Theologische Zeitschrift* |
| UNT | *Untersuchungen zum Neuen Testament* |
| VC | *Vigiliae christianae* |
| *VerbEccl* | *Verbum et Ecclesia* |
| VF | *Verkündigung und Forschung* |
| VGTB | Van Gorcum's theologische bibliotheek |
| VR | *Vox reformata* |
| VT | *Vetus Testamentum* |
| WBC | Word Biblical Commentary |
| *WeslTJ* | *Wesleyan Theological Journal* |
| WF | Wege der Forschung |
| WMANT | Wissenschaftliche Monographien zum Alten und Neuen Testament |
| *WTJ* | *Westminster Theological Journal* |
| WUL | World University Library |
| WUNT | Wissenschaftliche Untersuchungen zum Neuen Testament |
| *WW* | *Word and World* |
| ZAW | *Zeitschrift für die alttestamentliche Wissenschaft* |
| ZKT | *Zeitschrift für katholische Theologie* |
| ZNT | *Zeitschrift für Neues Testament* |
| ZNW | *Zeitschrift für die neutestamentliche Wissenschaft und die Kunde der älteren Kirche* |
| ZS | Zacchaeus Studies |
| ZTK | *Zeitschrift für Theologie und Kirche* |

# INTRODUCTION

O F AUTHORS WHOSE WRITINGS MAKE UP the New Testament, John was the last, leaving his legacy toward the end of the first Christian century. By this time the meaning of the Christ-event had mellowed for around seventy years in the mind of one who had had close dealings with Jesus and with most of the key leaders of the mother church in Jerusalem. John is the one who contemplates most deeply the eternal communion of the divine Father, Son and Spirit among themselves, a loving fellowship to which God's self-disclosure invites humankind. "Not surprisingly," therefore, "John is often treated as the pinnacle of the development of New Testament theology."[1] During the next five centuries John's language was fodder for patristic discussions about the triunity of God and about the union of the divine and the human in our Lord's person.[2] In countless other ways as well John's writings have fertilized Christian self-understanding.[3] Alone among the four Evangelists John enjoys the title of "the Theologian."[4]

---

[1]D. Moody Smith, *The Theology of the Gospel of John* (NTT; Cambridge: Cambridge University Press, 1995), p. 57. In agreement is Jörg Frey, "Die johanneische Theologie als Klimax der neutestamentlichen Theologie," *ZTK* 107 (2010): 448-78.

[2]Maurice F. Wiles, *The Spiritual Gospel: The Interpretation of the Fourth Gospel in the Early Church* (Cambridge: University Press, 1960); T. E. Pollard, *Johannine Christology and the Early Church* (SNTSMS 13; London: Cambridge University Press, 1970); Elaine H. Pagels, *The Johannine Gospel in Gnostic Exegesis: Heracleon's Commentary on John* (SBLMS 17; Nashville: Abingdon, 1973); Charles E. Hill, *The Johannine Corpus in the Early Church* (Oxford: Oxford University Press, 2004); Kyle Keefer, *The Branches of the Gospel of John: The Reception of the Fourth Gospel in the Early Church* (LNTS 332; London: T & T Clark, 2006); Tuomas Rasimus, ed., *The Legacy of John: Second-Century Reception of the Fourth Gospel* (NovTSup 132; Leiden: Brill, 2010).

[3]For example, Dorothy Lee, "In the Spirit of Truth: Worship and Prayer in the Gospel of John and the Early Fathers," *VC* 58 (2004): 277-97; April D. DeConick, *Voices of the Mystics: Early Christian Discourse in the Gospels of John and Thomas and Other Ancient Christian Literature* (JSNTSup 157; Sheffield: Sheffield Academic Press, 2001).

[4]Many Eastern Orthodox churches are so dedicated. For example, there is the Church of St. John the Theologian near Ephesus, on Ayasoluk Hill in Selçuk, built in the sixth century by order of Emperor

## JOHANNINE THEOLOGY

The present volume sets forth the Johannine theology according to the relations among the divine persons (Father, Son, Holy Spirit) and the world made up of its various constituents. This is not the only possible way to lay out the matter. Proposals for how to do biblical theology, and Johannine theology in particular, are manifold.

*Biblical theology: Nature and problems.* Insofar as biblical theology focuses on the oeuvre of a canonical author, it seeks to configure that author's ideas, in contrast to exegesis, which expounds texts. But biblical, in contrast to systematic, theology sticks to terms, concepts and accents peculiar to the author in the author's own time and setting.

This task raises problems of method. How, when the connections are rarely explicit, can we be sure to connect the author's ideas in the way the author would? What guide have we for ranking ideas by generality, centrality or weight when fundamental concepts may show up in only a very few places? How can we determine an author's presuppositions if the author never fully expresses them anywhere, even though parts may jut to the surface here and there like tips of an iceberg? How are we to discover the coherence of ideas with one another when the texts convey only select aspects relevant for particular situations? Although these questions and others are not yet settled to the satisfaction of all,[5] the human mind strives toward integration. So biblical theologizing must go on even as the discipline seeks criteria for legitimacy and rigor.

*Historical-theological approach based on the Jewish matrix?* One entrance into New Testament theology might be to move from Judaism to early Christianity. Judaism of the late Second Temple period was the matrix that gave birth to the religion of Jesus and his first followers. Early Judaism, though perhaps more an orthopraxy ("right practice") than an orthodoxy, was founded on four tenets: (1) there is but one God, in contrast to pagan polytheism;[6] (2) there is

---

Justinian. Also famous is the Monastery of St. John the Theologian on the acme of the island of Patmos overlooking the village of Chora, a monastery founded in 1088 by Ioannis Christodoulos, today housing a library of over a thousand precious manuscripts.

[5]Among many publications on biblical theology of the New Testament, one may get an overview of the methodological problems by consulting Gerhard F. Hasel, *New Testament Theology: Basic Issues in the Current Debate* (Grand Rapids: Eerdmans, 1978); I. Howard Marshall, *New Testament Theology: Many Witnesses, One Gospel* (Downers Grove, IL: InterVarsity Press, 2004), pp. 17-48.

[6]On the antiquity and uses of the Shema—Deuteronomy 6:4-9 together with related passages, recited by Jewish males twice a day as required by the oral law—see Emil Schürer, *The History of the Jewish People in the Age of Jesus Christ (175 B.C.-A.D. 135)* (rev. and ed. Geza Vermes, Fergus Millar and

one people of God, constituted by God's call of Abraham and his descendants (2 *Bar.* 48:23b-24a); (3) there is one covenant between God and Israel, made possible by atoning sacrifices and couched in the stipulations of Torah (Ex 24:7-8);[7] (4) and there will be one end for the world, God's final kingdom (2 *Bar.* 85:14[-15]; *Amidah*, Benediction 14).

Each of these beliefs underwent transformation as Christians absorbed the impact of Christ's coming. (1) God's unity constrained Christian understanding of God's Son and Spirit. Because monotheism could not be compromised, the divine Son and Spirit had to be identified with the unique and incommunicable deity. (2) That believing Gentiles were accepted into the church without circumcision did not blur the line that separated God's unique people from the pagan world. (3) A new covenant predicted by the prophets was ratified by Jesus' blood and requires faith that issues into obedience to God's will. The standard of Christian conduct is, at its moral and spiritual core, identical to that of the Mosaic covenant, even if Jewish rituals are not enjoined on Gentiles. (4) God has inaugurated his future kingdom by exalting Jesus to his right hand and will consummate it by sending Christ again to judge the living and the dead.[8]

Monotheism was the bedrock of Judaism. The apostolic church followed suit in compressing its deepest-held beliefs into various formulas based on the predicate "one" (Mt 23:8-10; 1 Cor 8:4-6; Rom 3:29-30; Eph 4:4-6; 1 Tim 2:5-6). Significantly, Mark Appold finds the Gospel of John outstanding in the number of its unity-formulations in the areas of Christology, soteriology and ecclesiology (Jn 10:16, 30; 11:52; 17:11, 21-23).[9] Since the seminal minds of the New Testament canon—Jesus, Paul, John—were Jewish, any adequate account of New Testament theology must show how those minds strove to articulate a divine Christology while keeping monotheism in the forefront of their thought.

Analysis of this sort sheds light on the theology common to all the New Testament authors. Of a piece with Judaism are John's root beliefs concerning God, humankind, sin, the world and salvation history. The Christ-event put its stamp on a two-stage eschatology that John shares with the other apostles.

Martin Goodman; 3 vols. in 4; Edinburgh: T & T Clark, 1973–1987), 2:454-55. The Shema is the creed of Judaism. Mark 12:28-34 shows that Jesus valued this passage.
[7]N. T. Wright combines "one people" and "one covenant" under the term "election" (*The New Testament and the People of God* [COQG 1; Minneapolis: Fortress, 1992], chap. 9).
[8]N. T. Wright sketches an approach to Pauline theology along these lines in *Paul: In Fresh Perspective* (Minneapolis: Fortress, 2005), pp. 83-153.
[9]Mark L. Appold, *The Oneness Motif in the Fourth Gospel: Motif Analysis and Exegetical Probe into the Theology of John* (WUNT 2/1; Tübingen: Mohr Siebeck, 1976), esp. pp. 261-94.

But further description is needed to take into account what is characteristic of him individually.

*Topical approach?* In addition to unresolved methodological issues of New Testament theology in general, John's writings present special problems. He expresses thoughts not in logical order but through a meditative interweaving of key words and themes, constantly repeated in fresh, kaleidescopic patterns. John's interest in a given topic we must gauge not by finding a rich paragraph but by noting scattered references throughout his writings. Hardly any two of his numerous brief, nontechnical phrases are identical, and each is connected with other ideas in its own context. His ruminative method invites an approach that compares text with text topically. But the only thorough way to explore his ideas is to study each term, concept, or theme in relation to all the others, and that is impracticable.[10]

*Literary-theological approach?* A more workable alternative is to start with literary-theological readings of the individual books in the Johannine corpus. Andreas Köstenberger, in his massive *Theology of John's Gospel and Letters*, after using a quarter of his space on introductory matters (pp. 35-174), devotes more than another quarter to a survey of the Gospel narrative and the Epistles (pp. 175-272), before he plows through the material again looking at major themes (pp. 273-546).[11] His commitment to a narrative approach requires even the thematic portion to break down each theme according to linear sections of the books where it appears. An advantage of this tactic is that it reads the big ideas straight out of the literature by theological exegesis and thus cannot stray far from the author's own arrangement of thoughts. A drawback, besides repetition, is that the ideas remain unsystematized.[12]

---

[10]"It is impossible to treat his great ideas individually and successively. Every effort to bring a certain portion into the light necessarily directs our attention to the whole" (W. K. Grossouw, "Christian Spirituality in John," in *A Companion to John: Readings in Johannine Theology [John's Gospel and Epistles]* [ed. Michael J. Taylor; New York: Alba House, 1970], p. 214).

[11]Andreas J. Köstenberger, *A Theology of John's Gospel and Letters: The Word, the Christ, the Son of God* (BTNT; Grand Rapids: Zondervan, 2009).

[12]In the thematic section unit titles are still determined largely by literary categories such as "The End," focusing on John 20:30-31 (chap. 7); "The Beginning," focusing on John 1:1-18 (chaps. 8–12); "The Middle," focusing on John 13:1-3 (chaps. 13–15). As a result, the topic of Jesus' messiahship (chap. 7) is widely separated from the theology of the cross (chap. 14), the Trinity (chap. 9) precedes salvation history (chap. 10), the Johannine love ethic (chap. 13) is separated from the mission theology (chap. 15), the chapter on creation and new creation falls toward the middle instead of flanking the other topics (chap. 8), and the motif of the cosmic trial gets a chapter of its own as though it were a theological locus (chap. 11).

*Organization around personal entities.* Another approach, followed here, is to organize John's ideas by the main characters around whom they revolve. The Johannine universe is essentially personal; it consists of persons divine and human and their relationships.[13]

In the Gospel the witness of the Son to the world concerning his relationship to the Father dominates the first twelve chapters. John 13–17 highlights the impending gift of the Spirit, himself a partner of the Father and the Son, to the community of disciples as "another paraclete" (Jn 14:16) in succession to Christ. In the passion account (Jn 18–19) the world crucifies Christ. In the closing chapters (Jn 20–21), Jesus convinces the disciples of his resurrection and ascent to the Father and bequeaths to them the Spirit to carry on his witness to the world. The main characters are God, world (including "the Jews" and the "ruler of this world"), Son, Spirit and believers (individually related to Christ; also corporately related to Christ or to the world).[14]

The Johannine Epistles contain references to more or less the same entities: the Father, the Son, the "anointing which you received from him" (1 Jn 2:27) or "the Spirit of God" (1 Jn 4:2), the community that has remained loyal to the author ("the elder" with his "little children"), and the world (of which a movement of schismatic heretics have shown themselves to be a part).[15]

Only slightly more elaborate is the bill of characters in the Apocalypse. Representing the divine triad are the One sitting on the throne of heaven, the Lamb and the Spirit of the prophets. Symbolizing the church are the seven churches, sometimes viewed in continuity with Israel and sometimes portrayed as an international and multilinguistic throng with prophetic, sacerdotal and royal

---

[13]"It is indeed true that this great theologian did make our communion with Christ and God the central point in his thinking" (Rudolf Schnackenburg, "Christian Morality According to John," in Taylor, *Companion to John*, p. 202).

[14]Comparable analyses with only slightly varied divisions are found in Royce Gordon Gruenler, *The Trinity in the Gospel of John: A Thematic Commentary on the Fourth Gospel* (Grand Rapids: Baker Books, 1986); Philip B. Harner, *Relation Analysis of the Fourth Gospel: A Study in Reader-Response Criticism* (Lewiston, NY: Mellen, 1993); Ron Kangas, "A Panoramic View of the Gospel of John," *Affirmation & Critique* 9 (2004): 8-25; Udo Schnelle, "Trinitarisches Denken im Johannesevangelium," in *Israel und seine Heilstraditionen im Johannesevangelium: Festgabe für Johannes Beutler SJ zum 70. Geburtstag* (ed. Michael Labahn, Klaus Scholtissek and Angelika Strotmann; Paderborn: Schöningh, 2004), pp. 367-86; Craig R. Koester, *The Word of Life: A Theology of John's Gospel* (Grand Rapids: Eerdmans, 2008).

[15]Fernando F. Segovia, *Love Relationships in the Johannine Tradition: Agapē/Agapan in I John and the Fourth Gospel* (SBLDS 58; Chico, CA: Scholars Press, 1982); Enno Edzard Popkes, *Die Theologie der Liebe Gottes in den johanneischen Schriften: Zur Semantik der Liebe und zum Motivkreis des Dualismus* (WUNT 2/197; Tübingen: Mohr Siebeck, 2005).

functions. The world consists of antagonists that mimic the roles of the persons in the Trinity—the dragon, the beast, the false prophet—together with all dwellers on earth who are deceived by them. Diametrically opposed destinies of Lady Babylon and of Lady Jerusalem underscore the polarity between the world and the church.

This analysis yields a theology of persons and their relationships.[16] The community of disciples taken out of the world are first the object of the saving activity of the Father and the Son and then, imbued with the Spirit, are taken up into a working partnership with the divine Trinity to make known God's love to a world that remains in darkness. Most of the components are present, explicitly or implicitly, in the opening of 1 John: "That which we have seen and heard we proclaim to you also, so that you may have fellowship with us; and our fellowship is with the Father and with his Son Jesus Christ" (1 Jn 1:3).

Accordingly, the following chapters will explore Johannine thought by concentrating on God the Father (chap. 2), the world-system (chap. 3), God's self-revelation in the Son (chaps. 4–5), the Spirit-Paraclete (6), the believer united to the risen Christ (chaps. 7–8), and believers in relation to one another (chap. 9) and to the world (chap. 10).

## STATE OF THE QUESTION

Despite John's importance as the one who summed up the apostles' message and laid much of the foundation of church dogmatics, a comprehensive survey of the Johannine theology is wanting in current English-speaking New Testament scholarship.[17] Since roughly 1850 criticism has occupied itself with preliminary questions concerning the religio-historical genesis, authorship, edi-

---

[16]A disadvantage is that certain theological topics, such as John's view of Scripture, his concepts of truth and of love, and his eschatology, get distributed among the chapters.

[17]The excellent tome by Yale professor George Stevens, which was, to his knowledge, a first attempt of its sort, is long out of date: George B. Stevens, *The Johannine Theology: A Study of the Doctrinal Contents of the Gospels and Epistles of the Apostle John* (New York: Scribner, 1894). Also illuminating but now dated is W. F. Howard, *Christianity According to St. John* (London: Duckworth, 1943). Valuable insights can be gleaned from Edwin Kenneth Lee, *The Religious Thought of St. John* (London: SPCK, 1962); Joseph Crehan, *The Theology of St. John* (New York: Sheed & Ward, 1965); D. George Vanderlip, *Christianity According to John* (Philadelphia: Westminster, 1975); and especially the collected articles in Taylor, *Companion to John*. Not all will be persuaded of the dispensationalist accents in W. Robert Cook, *The Theology of John* (Chicago: Moody, 1979). More recently, Smith, *Theology*, is critical and thoughtful but brief and covers only the Gospel; Koester, *Word of Life*, is fuller but again focuses on the Gospel; even Köstenberger, *Theology*, like most of the publications above, omits the Apocalypse.

tions and sociological character of these documents.[18] Insights into select Johannine themes and ideas are scattered in an ever-swelling mass of publications, but an overview remains a desideratum. To remedy this lack is one aim of this volume.

**Rudolf Bultmann.** The most influential synthesis of the mid-twentieth century was done by Rudolf Bultmann.[19] Bultmann offered a masterly sketch of some major concepts of the Fourth Gospel under the keynote "revelation." His discussions of the Johannine concepts of the world, of the division of the human race by the divine revealer's coming, and of faith are incisive.

But many now concur that "every answer Bultmann gives to the really important questions he raises—is wrong."[20] Bultmann relied on a questionable reconstruction of a Gnostic revealer myth to explain John's Christology.[21] Hypercriticism bound him to a radically dissected and rearranged Fourth Gospel in isolation from the Epistles and the Apocalypse.[22] And his hermeneutical program of existentialist demythologization imposed a focus that left but a torso of John's thought. No scholar without a strong agenda would deny that John is aware of salvation history, or wonder whether for him the devil is "a

[18]For reviews of scholarship, see Sean P. Kealy, *John's Gospel and the History of Biblical Interpretation* (2 vols.; MBPS 60A, 60B; Lewiston NY: Mellen, 2002); John Ashton, *Understanding the Fourth Gospel* (Oxford: Clarendon, 1991), pp. 3-117; W. F. Howard, *The Fourth Gospel in Recent Criticism and Interpretation* (ed. C. K. Barrett; 4th ed.; London: Epworth, 1955); Robert Kysar, *The Fourth Evangelist and His Gospel: An Examination of Contemporary Scholarship* (Minneapolis: Augsburg, 1975); Klaus Scholtissek, "The Johannine Gospel in Recent Research," in *The Face of New Testament Studies: A Survey of Recent Research* (ed. Scot McKnight and Grant Osborne; Grand Rapids: Eerdmans, 2004), pp. 444-72; Tom Thatcher, ed., *What We Have Heard from the Beginning: The Past, Present, and Future of Johannine Studies* (Waco, TX: Baylor University Press, 2007); Paul N. Anderson, "Beyond the Shade of the Oak Tree: The Recent Growth of Johannine Studies," *ExpTim* 119 (2008): 365-73.

[19]Rudolf Bultmann, "The Eschatology of the Gospel of John," in *Faith and Understanding* (ed. Robert W. Funk; trans. Louise Pettibone Smith; New York: Harper & Row, 1969), pp. 165-83; idem, *The Gospel of John: A Commentary* (ed. R. W. N. Hoare and J. K. Riches; trans. G. R. Beasley-Murray; Philadelphia: Westminster, 1971); idem, *Theology of the New Testament* (trans. Kendrick Grobel; 2 vols.; New York: Scribner, 1951–1955), 2:3-92.

[20]Ashton, *Understanding*, p. 45. See also D. Moody Smith, "Johannine Studies Since Bultmann," *WW* 21 (2001): 343-51.

[21]Note the cautionary remarks in Robert M. Grant, *Gnosticism: A Source Book of Heretical Writings from the Early Christian Period* (New York: Harper, 1961); Carsten Colpe, *Die religionsgeschichtliche Schule: Darstellung und Kritik ihres Bildes vom gnostischen Erlösermythus* (FRLANT 60; Göttingen: Vandenhoeck & Ruprecht, 1961); Edwin M. Yamauchi, *Pre-Christian Gnosticism: A Survey of the Proposed Evidences* (Grand Rapids: Eerdmans, 1973).

[22]For critique, see Eugen Ruckstuhl, *Die literarische Einheit des Johannesevangeliums: Der gegenwärtige Stand der einschlägigen Forschungen* (2nd ed.; NTOA 5; Freiburg: Universitätsverlag; Göttingen: Vandenhoeck & Ruprecht, 1987).

reality," or reduce his cosmological opposition between good and evil to a "dualism of decision," or systematically remand every passage that cuts against the grain of the interpreter's theological commitments to a posited "ecclesiastical redactor," or organize Johannine theology around individual human faith while ignoring its Old Testament roots and its interest in the trinitarian persons.[23] Building on Bultmann and others, we can advance by starting from a saner critical base and allowing the fullness of John's thought to emerge in John's own categories.

*Johannine Christianity?* From about 1970 Johannine specialists began to abandon Bultmann's paradigm in favor of another. The discovery of a unique Jewish-Christian community whose history and traditions supposedly produced the Johannine literature was the work of many contributors.[24] Curious features of that corpus seemed to make sense when set in the light of a reconstructed series of social ruptures that would have left relics layer by editorial layer. According to this postulate, a group of Jews devoted to Jesus separated or suffered expulsion from their parent synagogues (the event behind the Gospel), had strife with at least one rival Christian group holding a different Christology and ethics (1–3 John), and stood apart from the pagan environment of Asia (the Apocalypse). The movement became increasingly sectarian on all fronts. To bolster their fragile identity they stressed Jesus' divine authority (e.g., Jn 5:18) and otherness (Jn 8:23), they engaged in anti-Jewish polemics (Jn 8:42-44), defined Jesus' saviorhood in exclusive terms (Jn 14:6), claimed to be over-

---

[23]Bultmann, *Theology*, 2:v, 8, 17, 21.

[24]Seminal works were Wayne A. Meeks, *The Prophet-King: Moses Traditions and the Johannine Christology* (NovTSup 14; Leiden: Brill, 1967); idem, "The Man from Heaven in Johannine Sectarianism," *JBL* 91 (1972): 44-72; J. Louis Martyn, *History and Theology in the Fourth Gospel* (2nd ed.; Nashville: Abingdon, 1979); R. Alan Culpepper, *The Johannine School: An Evaluation of the Johannine-School Hypothesis Based on an Investigation of the Nature of Ancient Schools* (SBLDS 26; Missoula, MT: Scholars Press, 1975); Oscar Cullmann, *The Johannine Circle* (trans. John Bowden; Philadelphia: Westminster, 1976); Robert Kysar, "Community and Gospel: Vectors in Fourth Gospel Criticism," *Int* 31 (1977): 355-66; Raymond E. Brown, *The Community of the Beloved Disciple: The Life, Loves, and Hates of an Individual Church in New Testament Times* (New York: Paulist Press, 1979). By the 1980s, a large cadre of scholars shared a common outline of the sectarian community and its history, and some spoke of a consensus, or even of an assured result: Klaus Wengst, *Bedrängte Gemeinde und verherrlichter Christus: Der historische Ort des Johannesevangeliums als Schlüssel zu seiner Interpretation* (BTS 5; Neukirchen-Vluyn: Neukirchner, 1981); D. Moody Smith, "Johannine Christianity," in *Johannine Christianity: Essays on Its Setting, Sources, and Theology* (Columbia: University of South Carolina Press, 1984), pp. 1-36; idem, "The Contribution of J. Louis Martyn to the Understanding of the Gospel of John," in *The Conversation Continues: Studies in Paul and John* (ed. Robert T. Fortna and Beverly R. Gaventa; Nashville: Abingdon, 1990), pp. 275-94; David Rensberger, *Johannine Faith and Liberating Community* (Philadelphia: Westminster, 1988), pp. 1-36.

comers against impossible odds (Jn 16:33), and construed reality starkly as a contest between light and darkness (Jn 1:5).

For some time now the Johannine community hypothesis has been showing signs of strain.[25] Influential though it is, it rests on a tissue of assumptions, none of which is proven. A global axiom of radical biblical criticism is that New Testament documents manipulate facts of history for theological ends.[26] It is taken for granted that the first generation(s) of Christians comprised not the united church of the book of Acts but rather a sprawling congeries of conflicting movements;[27] that each of our Gospels is the distillate of an urban church whose interests shaped (or created) oral traditions about Jesus;[28] that the Johannine community was eccentric[29] and, like the sectaries at Qumran, a more or less sequestered group with unique values and traditions;[30] that it was on a trajectory toward Gnosticism;[31] and that statements within the Johannine corpus pitted against one another (rather than allowed to qualify one another) mark editors with inconsistent points of view or successive stages in the development of the Johannine community (rather than John's dialectical way of presenting complex thoughts). This last is a chosen method of interpretation, as unverifiable as it is invincible.

---

[25]According to Köstenberger (*Theology*, pp. 56-60), leading proponents began to jump off the bandwagon in the 2000s as it faced up to its burden of proof. But it persists in the minds of many New Testament scholars, such as M. J. J. Menken, "Envoys of God's Envoy: On the Johannine Communities," *PIBA* 23 (2000): 45-60; Jürgen Becker, *Johanneisches Christentum: Seine Geschichte und Theologie im Überblick* (Tübingen: Mohr Siebeck, 2004); Allen Dwight Callahan, *A Love Supreme: A History of the Johannine Tradition* (Minneapolis: Fortress, 2005).

[26]Scholars who respect John's integrity counter that historical problems in John's Gospel exist in the eye of critics who bring a certain set of presuppositions to bear, not necessarily in the texts themselves. See Craig L. Blomberg, *The Historical Reliability of John's Gospel: Issues and Commentary* (Downers Grove, IL: InterVarsity Press, 2002).

[27]Walter Bauer and his followers greatly exaggerated the multiple origins of early Christianity. See Walter Bauer, *Orthodoxy and Heresy in Earliest Christianity* (Philadelphia: Fortress, 1971 [1934]). For withering evaluation, see Thomas A. Robinson, *The Bauer Thesis Examined: The Geography of Heresy in the Early Christian Church* (Lewiston, NY: Mellen, 1988); Arland J. Hultgren, *The Rise of Normative Christianity* (Minneapolis: Fortress, 1994).

[28]For critiques of this assumption, see Martin Hengel, *Die johanneische Frage: Ein Lösungsversuch* (WUNT 67; Tübingen: Mohr Siebeck, 1993); Samuel Byrskog, *Story as History—History as Story: The Gospel Tradition in the Context of Ancient Oral History* (WUNT 123; Tübingen: Mohr Siebeck, 2000); Richard Bauckham, ed., *The Gospels for All Christians: Rethinking the Gospel Audiences* (Grand Rapids: Eerdmans, 1998); idem, *Jesus and the Eyewitnesses: The Gospels as Eyewitness Testimony* (Grand Rapids: Eerdmans, 2006).

[29]This assumption attributes idiosyncrasies of the author(s) to a whole community.

[30]Questioned by Bauckham, *Gospels*; Paul N. Anderson, *The Fourth Gospel and the Quest for Jesus: Modern Foundations Reconsidered* (LNTS 321; London: T & T Clark, 2006).

[31]Refuted by Hill, *Johannine Corpus*.

A distinctive Johannine stream in early Christianity was absent from secondary literature prior to 1970 because it is invisible in our sources for the period (the book of Acts, Irenaeus, Tertullian, Eusebius). It did not come into full view until the nest of assumptions just named had accumulated in New Testament criticism. The present volume neither builds on nor seeks to overthrow the reigning paradigm; it proceeds from an independent assessment of probabilities concerning the author of this literature and his place in the church.

## THE JOHANNINE LITERATURE: NATURE AND PURPOSES

The Fourth Gospel, like Matthew, Mark, and Luke, tells the story of Jesus' ministry from the time of John the Baptist to Jesus' glorification and sending of his followers into the world. A prologue lays out the main themes: the divine origin and essence of God's only-begotten one, who as the life and light of the human race became flesh to reveal the Father (Jn 1:1-18).[32] The subsequent narrative unfolds its theology according to Jesus' earthly career. In the first half Jesus testifies to the world about his unique relation to the Father and is met for the most part with incomprehension and unbelief (Jn 1:19–12:50).[33] Then, having prepared the small band of his followers for his return to the Father (Jn 13–17),[34]

---

[32]Form critics regarded John 1:1-18 as virtually an independent composition, going back to a preexisting hymn amplified by the author or a prior editor (e.g., Rudolf Bultmann, "The History of Religions Background of the Prologue to the Gospel of John," in *The Interpretation of John* [ed. John Ashton; IRT 9; Philadelphia: Fortress, 1986], pp. 18-35). But as it stands, it opens the narrative of the Gospel (cf. Jn 1:6-8, 15 on John the Baptist, referred to in Jn 1:30) and so is integral with what follows. See Peder Borgen, "The Prologue of John—as Exposition of the Old Testament," in *Philo, John, and Paul: New Perspectives on Judaism and Early Christianity* (BJS 131; Atlanta: Scholars Press, 1987), pp. 75-101; P. J. Williams, "Not the Prologue of John," *JSNT* 33 (2011): 375-86.

[33]Textual considerations tell against the originality of the unit about the woman taken in adultery (Jn 7:53–8:11). See Chris Keith, "Recent and Previous Research on the *Pericope Adulterae* (John 7:53–8:11)," *CurBR* 6 (2008): 377-404. It may well be regarded as belonging to the New Testament canon, even if not part of John's Gospel. See A. D. Baum, "Hat die Perikope von der Ehebrecherin (Joh 7,53–8,11) kanonische Autorität? Ein interkonfessioneller Zugang," *TBei* 43 (2012): 7-20.

[34]John 13–17; 21:15-23, assuming the salvation of Jesus's disciples ("you are clean," ὑμεῖς καθαροί ἐστε [Jn 13:10]), have to do with pneumatology linked with the ethic of love, ecclesiology and mission. Jesus' discourses to his own are hard to summarize. The ecclesiology is stamped by the concept of the body of disciples as the object of God's love in its fullness. John 13:1 is programmatic, John 17:26 a summary. The verb "to love" (ἀγαπᾶν) suddenly becomes frequent. After being used only seven times in John 1–12 (and with Christ as subject only in Jn 11:5), "to love" occurs no fewer than twenty-nine times in John 13–21, with Christ as subject and his disciples as objects nine times. John 13–17, having the character of a testament looking ahead to Jesus' death and departure (Jn 13:1, 31-33; 14:1, 4, 27-31; 16:4-7, 16-22, 28-33; 17:1-5), assumes that the church will be left in the world (Jn 13:1; 17:11-13) and details the provisions that Jesus makes for it in his absence. After washing them (Jn 13:1-11 [a prefiguration of his death]), he bequeathes them the Spirit (Jn 14:16-20, 23, 25-26; 15:26; 16:7-15; 20:22); commandments to keep (Jn 13:12-17, 34-35; 14:15, 21-24; 15:10, 12-17; cf. 21:19,

he lays down his life for them and takes it up again (Jn 18–20). An epilogue (Jn 21) mirrors the prologue and rounds off the whole.[35] The author appeals to the widest possible range of readers with a view to their believing that Jesus is the Son of God, in whom is life (Jn 20:30-31). In places the wording seems sharply pointed to counter either adherence of some to a lingering Baptist sect (Jn 1:8; 3:22-30),[36] or Jewish nomism centered on Moses' ascent of Mount Sinai (Jn 3:13), or official Jewish rejection of Jesus (Jn 9:22; 12:42; 16:1-4), or proto-Gnosticism (Jn 1:14; 6:53-58). But these accents are subordinate to an overall purpose, which is to draw people of all sorts to Jesus.[37]

A trilogy of Johannine letters appears to have been delivered on a single occasion by the hand of Demetrius (3 Jn 12).[38] The one known as 3 John is a personal letter to Gaius, a householder. It praises Gaius for bucking a bid for control by Diotrephes, apparently an overseer of a house church in the same town. In 2 John the words of the "elder" convey greetings from one local church ("the children of your elect sister") to a second, probably in another city ("to the elect lady and her children"). In 1 John, a longer tract, there is no conventional epistolary opening or closing matter, and it seems to be a homily meant to reach a larger circle of churches.[39] Both 1 John and 2 John express a pastoral concern to reassure the faithful who remain in the primitive Christian tradition, after some teachers or prophets from their midst have made an exit.[40]

---

22); promises, of their future presence with him (Jn 13:36; 14:2-3, 21-22; 17:24), of answered prayers (Jn 14:13-14; 15:7, 16; 16:23-27), and of persecutions (Jn 13:18-30; 15:18–16:4; 17:14-16); and a commission to bear witness to him and bear fruit (Jn 13:20; 14:12; 15:1-11, 16, 27; cf. 20:21-23). On the literary unity of this body of material, see L. Scott Kellum, *The Unity of the Farewell Discourse: The Literary Integrity of John 13:31–16:33* (JSNTSup 256; London: T & T Clark, 2004).

[35]Many critics regard John 21 as an appendix added by an editor, but a strong case can be made for a deliberate correspondence between the prologue (Jn 1:1-18) and the epilogue (Jn 21). See Bauckham, *Eyewitnesses*, pp. 364-69; Giuseppe Segalla, "Un epilogo necessario (*Gv* 21)," *Teol* 31 (2006): 514-33.

[36]Wilhelm Baldensperger, *Der Prolog des vierten Evangeliums: Sein polemisch-apologetischer Zweck* (Freiburg: Mohr, 1898); Christoph G. Müller, "Der Zeuge und das Licht: Joh 1,1–4,3 und das Darstellungsprinzip der σύγκρισις," *Bib* 84 (2003): 479-509.

[37]Rudolf Schnackenburg, *The Gospel According to St. John* (trans. Kevin Smyth et al.; 3 vols.; New York: Herder & Herder; Seabury; Crossroad, 1968–1982), 1:165-72; Raymond E. Brown, *An Introduction to the Gospel of John* (ed. Francis J. Moloney; ABRL; New York: Doubleday, 2003), pp. 151-88.

[38]Although 3 John is not a "letter of recommendation," it does contain a commendation of Demetrius, who therefore probably was its bearer. For a contrary view, see Luca Marulli, "A Letter of Recommendation? A Closer Look at Third John's 'Rhetorical Argumentation,'" *Bib* 90 (2009): 203-23.

[39]On the oral/auditory features, see Russ Dudrey, "1 John and the Public Reading of Scripture," *SCJ* 6 (2003): 235-55.

[40]Stephen Rockwell, "Assurance as the Interpretative Key to Understanding the Message of 1 John," *RTR* 69 (2010): 17-33.

They went spouting doctrinal innovations about Christ, probably of a Docetic nature and fostering a licentious lifestyle.[41] John's Epistles counter their impact by reinforcing the three cardinal values of truth, righteousness and love.[42] The trio of letters corresponds to three distinct levels of ecclesiastical organization: house church (3 John), urban fellowship (2 John) and regional web of churches (1 John).[43]

The Apocalypse is a Christian prophecy dressed in the form of a letter but stylistically in the vein of Jewish apocalypses. It was sent to the churches of western Asia Minor at a time when they were under social pressure to adopt the Roman values of wealth, power and pleasure. It applies florid apocalyptic imagery, adapted from all over the Hebrew Scriptures,[44] to referents in John's contemporary environment.[45] The prophet calls on the churches to persevere in recognizing the One who sits on the throne in heaven and the Lamb, who shares it, to whom alone worship and obedience are due, even if such fidelity

---

[41]Though the language leaves room for other possibilities, the emphasis on the tangibility of the word of life in 1 John 1:1-3 and the warnings in 1 John 4:2; 2 John 7 seem to have in view a denial that the divine Logos became truly incarnate. Cerinthus taught that the Christ was a spirit who descended on the man Jesus at his baptism and flew away before the crucifixion (Irenaeus, *Haer.* 1.26.1). While John's antagonism toward him is clear only in a patristic anecdote (Irenaeus, *Haer.* 3.3.4), to interpret 1 John 5:6 against a Cerinthian background makes luminous sense of an otherwise obscure verse. Most scholars think that the secessionists are proto-Gnostics. Typical of the majority past and present are Georg Strecker, *The Johannine Letters: A Commentary on 1, 2, and 3 John* (ed. Harold W. Attridge; trans. Linda M. Maloney; Hermeneia; Minneapolis: Fortress, 1996), pp. 69-76; Wolfram Uebele, *"Viele Verführer sind in die Welt ausgegangen": Die Gegner in den Briefen des Ignatius von Antiochien und in den Johannesbriefen* (BWANT 151; Stuttgart: Kohlhammer, 2001). A minority have taken the secessionists to be Jews who never believed in Jesus, or Jewish Christians who renounced their belief that Jesus is the Messiah. See, for example, J. C. O'Neill, *The Puzzle of 1 John: A New Examination of Origins* (London: SPCK, 1966); Terry Griffith, *Keep Yourselves from Idols: A New Look at 1 John* (JSNTSup 233; London: Sheffield Academic Press, 2002); Daniel R. Streett, *They Went Out from Us: The Identity of the Opponents in First John* (BZNW 177; Berlin: de Gruyter, 2011). Difficult though it is to pin down the exact nature of the false teaching of the opponents, few doubt that there was an historical movement behind the Johannine construct of them; contra Hansjörg Schmid, *Gegner im 1. Johannesbrief? Zu Konstruktion und Selbstreferenz im johanneischen Sinnsystem* (BWANT 159; Stuttgart: Kohlhammer, 2002); idem, "How to Read the First Epistle of John Non-Polemically," *Bib* 85 (2004): 24-41.

[42]J. Ramsey Michaels, "Reflections on the Three Epistles of John," in Taylor, *Companion to John*, pp. 257-71.

[43]Note an identical relationship among Philemon, Colossians and Ephesians, carried by Tychicus with Onesimus, which could have served as John's model for the trilogy.

[44]G. K. Beale, *John's Use of the Old Testament in Revelation* (JSNTSup 166; Sheffield: Sheffield Academic Press, 1998); David Mathewson, "Assessing Old Testament Allusions in the Book of Revelation," *EvQ* 75 (2003): 311-25.

[45]Paul A. Rainbow, *The Pith of the Apocalypse: Essential Message and Principles for Interpretation* (Eugene, OR: Wipf & Stock, 2008), pp. 13-27, 61-66.

should result in martyrdom during this present age. Full of intricate literary patterns, a simple general structure is discernible: a prologue (Apoc 1:1-11), a disclosure of Christ in glory leading into seven oracles for the churches (Apoc 1:9–3:21), an invitation up to the heavenly throne room leading into seven recapitulatory visions of the destiny of the world (Apoc 4:1–22:9),[46] and an epilogue mirroring the themes of the prologue (Apoc 22:6-21).[47]

## AUTHORSHIP

Until roughly 1800 the leading lights of the church held these books to have a single author, John, one of the twelve apostles, son of Zebedee and brother of James. This ancient opinion rested on secure grounds. Many critics still subscribe to it in spite of doubts that have made headway in the scholarly community since the European Enlightenment.[48] This is not the place for a full review of the question of authorship, but the main lines of the discussion may be set forth.

*John's Gospel: Internal clues.* An eyewitness of Jesus' ministry is behind the Fourth Gospel. "We have beheld his glory" (Jn 1:14). "He who saw it has borne witness—his testimony is true, and he knows that he tells the truth" (Jn 19:35).[49] He is an individual ("I suppose" [Jn 21:25]) and is the writer (ὁ γράψας ταῦτα [Jn 21:24]). He identifies himself as "the disciple Jesus loved" (Jn 21:20),[50] a claim

---

[46]The visions are of seven seals (Apoc 6:1–8:4), seven trumpets (Apoc 8:6–11:19), combat joined (Apoc 12:1–15:4), seven bowls (Apoc 15:5–16:21), Lady Babylon (Apoc 17:1–19:10), combat resolved (Apoc 19:11–21:8), Lady Jerusalem (Apoc 21:9–22:9).

[47]On the basic literary structure, see Rainbow, *Pith*, chapter 3. For other analyses indicating the great complexity of the work, see Marko Jauhiainen, "Recapitulation and Chronological Progression in John's Apocalypse: Towards a New Perspective," *NTS* 49 (2003): 543-59; Alan S. Bandy, "The Layers of the Apocalypse: An Integrative Approach to Revelation's Macrostructure," *JSNT* 31 (2009): 469-99.

[48]In the case of the Fourth Gospel, doubts about the apostolic authorship, first voiced tentatively by Richard Simon (1695), began to gain a hearing only after 1800, and only in Germany. See Andreas J. Köstenberger, "Early Doubts of the Apostolic Authorship of the Fourth Gospel in the History of Modern Biblical Criticism," in *Studies on John and Gender: A Decade of Scholarship* (SBL 38; New York: Peter Lang, 2001), pp. 17-47.

[49]Ashton (*Understanding*, p. 438) calls this "the obvious reading" of these verses, in a comment directed against Bultmann. It applies just as well to the argumentative windings of Andrew T. Lincoln ("The Beloved Disciple as Eyewitness and the Fourth Gospel as Witness," *JSNT* 85 [2002]: 3-26), who finds in these claims only a literary device on the part of the narrator. In critique of Lincoln, Bauckham (*Eyewitnesses*, pp. 384-411) upholds the claim of the Fourth Evangelist to be a "witness." A thoroughgoing collection of eyewitness features found throughout the Gospel is offered in Leon Morris, *Studies in the Fourth Gospel* (Grand Rapids: Eerdmans, 1969), pp. 139-214.

[50]Howard M. Jackson, "Ancient Self-Referential Conventions and Their Implications for the Authorship and Integrity of the Gospel of John," *JTS* 50 (1999): 1-34; Bauckham, *Eyewitnesses*, pp. 358-83. In no way does this phrase claim that he held a special place in Jesus' affections. An author who

attested by the community that he serves ("we know that his testimony is true" [Jn 21:24]). He reclined close to Jesus' breast at the Last Supper (Jn 13:23; 21:20) and conveyed Peter's query (Jn 13:23-25), Peter also being in a position of privilege at Jesus' other side. So among Jesus' disciples the disciple in question must have belonged to the most honored and intimate circle. Jesus on the cross entrusted him with the care of Jesus' mother (Jn 19:26-27). The Beloved Disciple preceded Peter to the empty tomb (Jn 20:2-8), and he was one of four unnamed disciples who ate breakfast with the resurrected Lord, two of whom were Zebedee's sons (Jn 21:2).

His nearness to Jesus at the supper indicates that he was one of the inner three among the Twelve, whom we know from Mark's Gospel to have been Peter, James and John (Mk 5:37; 9:2; 13:3; 14:33). Of those, James and Peter were dead before the Fourth Gospel was written (Acts 12:2 [A.D. 41/42]; Jn 21:18-19). His coupling with Peter is paralleled by John in the book of Acts (Acts 3:1-11; 4:13, 19; 8:14). It would be natural for Jesus in dying to entrust his mother to a disciple who was a cousin.[51] As B. F. Westcott argued in a cogent case that is often overlooked, these facts zero in on John.[52]

**Clues in the Johannine Epistles.** Likewise the author of the three letters has the self-consciousness of an apostle. He beheld and touched Jesus in the flesh and counts himself a member of that foundational band who proclaim their experiences of the incarnate life to other believers (1 Jn 1:1-4). He refers to himself as an "elder" (2 Jn 1; 3 Jn 1) and to his readers as "dear children" (seven times in 1 John). Pastors of local churches, such as Diotrephes, have a duty to acknowledge him (3 Jn 9) because he exercises leadership at an intercongregational level through delegates who circulate on his behalf (3 Jn 10).

**Evidence of the Apocalypse.** Only in the Apocalypse does the author give his name as "John" (Apoc 1:1, 4, 9; 22:8). Critics who doubt whether this John

---

withholds his name, pointing to Jesus' wondrous love even for him as the only really significant fact about himself, is self-effacing.

[51]Assuming "his mother's sister" (Jn 19:25) to be Salome (Mk 15:40), "the mother of the sons of Zebedee" (Mt 27:56). On the plausibility of this identification, see J. A. T. Robinson, *The Priority of John* (ed. J. F. Coakley; London: SCM Press, 1985), pp. 119-22.

[52]B. F. Westcott, *The Gospel According to St. John: The Greek Text with Introduction and Notes* (2 vols. in 1; Grand Rapids: Eerdmans, 1954), pp. ix-lix. Updated versions of Westcott's argument in dialogue with critical scholarship of the twentieth century are given in Arthur C. Headlam, *The Fourth Gospel as History* (Oxford: Blackwell, 1948), pp. 32-70; H. P. V. Nunn, *The Authorship of the Fourth Gospel* (Eton: Alden & Blackwell, 1952); Morris, *Studies*, pp. 215-80; Robinson, *Priority*, pp. 93-122; Henri J. Cazelles, "Johannes: Ein Sohn des Zebedäus, 'Priester' und Apostel," *IKaZ* 31 (2002): 479-84.

was the apostle nevertheless accept the name. Here he appears as a prophet (Apoc 1:3; 10:11; 22:7, 9, 10, 18, 19) whose person and authority are so well known to the churches of Asia, to whom the book is addressed as an encyclical, that he need not identify himself more closely. That he refers to "the apostles of the Lamb" in the third person (Apoc 21:14) no more excludes him from that group than does "the sons of Zebedee" (Jn 21:2) from that pair. The island of Patmos, where he was at the time of his visions (Apoc 1:9), lies thirty-seven miles west-southwest of Miletus, a location consistent with traditions that place the apostle in the area of Ephesus, thirty miles north of Miletus, toward the end of his career.

***Relation of John's Gospel to his Epistles.*** Until the twentieth century virtually all commentators recognized the affinity of the Gospel and the Epistles, and of the Epistles with one another, in language, style and motifs.[53] In recent decades increasing numbers question the identity of authorship of these pieces, urging nuances of phrase and concept.[54] Others leave the matter undecided.[55] But the grounds on which authorial unity commends itself remain intact.[56] As we might expect from an author who never repeats himself verbatim, there are indeed many small differences of expression and of theo-

---

[53]Recent literary criticism has added only niceties to the shrewd analysis of Dionysius of Alexandria, preserved in Eusebius, *Hist. eccl.* 7.25.17-21, 24-25. For full lists of similarities and differences in vocabulary and idea, see A. E. Brooke, *A Critical and Exegetical Commentary on the Johannine Epistles* (ICC; New York: Scribner, 1912), pp. i-xix, 235-42; Robert Law, *The Tests of Life: A Study of the First Epistle of St. John* (3rd ed.; Edinburgh: T & T Clark, 1914), pp. 339-59.

[54]C. H. Dodd, "The First Epistle of John and the Fourth Gospel," *BJRL* 21 (1937): 129-56; idem, *The Johannine Epistles* (MNTC; New York: Harper, 1946), pp. xlvii-lxxi; Rudolf Bultmann, *The Johannine Epistles* (ed. Robert W. Funk; trans. R. Philip O'Hara, Lane C. McGaughy and Robert W. Funk; Hermeneia; Philadelphia: Fortress, 1973); Raymond E. Brown, *The Epistles of John: Translated, with Introduction, Commentary, and Notes* (AB 30; Garden City, NY: Doubleday, 1982), pp. 14-35; Stephen S. Smalley, *1-3 John* (WBC 51; Waco, TX: Word, 1984), p. xxii; Strecker, *Johannine Letters*, pp. xxxv-xlii; John Painter, *1, 2, and 3 John* (SP 18; Collegeville, MN: Liturgical Press, 2002), pp. 60-73; Judith Lieu, *I, II, and III John: A Commentary* (NTL; Louisville: Westminster John Knox, 2008), pp. 3, 239-40.

[55]I. Howard Marshall, *The Epistles of John* (NICNT; Grand Rapids: Eerdmans, 1978), pp. 31-41; Rudolf Schnackenburg, *The Johannine Epistles: Introduction and Commentary* (trans. Reginald Fuller and Ilse Fuller; New York: Crossroad, 1992), pp. 6-11, 34-38.

[56]C. H. Dodd's arguments are answered effectively and in detail by W. F. Howard, "The Common Authorship of the Johannine Gospel and Epistles," *JTS* 48 (1947): 12-25. Summarizing opinion in continental Europe in 1973, Werner Kümmel found "no adequate reason for assuming that I John was written by someone other than the author of the Gospel of John" and considered the differences in 2 John and 3 John "too trivial to make probable the assumption of different authors" (*Introduction to the New Testament* [trans. Howard Clark Kee; rev. ed.; London: SCM Press, 1975], pp. 445, 450). Köstenberger evaluates the misgivings of Dodd, Bultmann and some others in the last forty years, and concludes, "John remains convincingly the best candidate" (*Theology*, pp. 72-79, 86-93).

logical emphasis between the Gospel and the Epistles, due to the nature, purpose and situation of each.[57]

***Relation of the Apocalypse to the other Johannine books.*** The Apocalypse warrants more discussion. Everything about it—apocalyptic ethos, Semitic interference in the language, imagery from the Hebrew Scriptures, knowledge of the temple cultus—indicates that the author was a Palestinian Jew who had settled in Asia.[58] Yet few today ascribe it to the author of the Gospel and the Epistles, since it differs considerably in diction and outlook.[59] To some, its Greek seems barbarous. Its orientation toward the future stands in contrast to the Gospel's stress on eternal life in the present, and its lurid portrayals of divine vengeance likewise run against the Johannine dictum that God is love.

Theological differences can be overplayed, however. The Gospel has in it more of the future, and the Apocalypse more of the present, than some have allowed.[60] In the Gospel salvation is from the looming judgment of the world (e.g., Jn 3:16, 18, 36), while the Christ of the Apocalypse declares his jealous love for his people (Apoc 1:5; 3:9).

Care is needed to assess to what extent language and style bear on the matter of authorship. Written artifacts vary, of course, in vocabulary level, in the complexity of grammatical constructions, and in their use of stylistic devices. Disparity often does point to different authors, but not necessarily, for a number of factors can influence the way or ways a person writes.

---

[57]Brown (*Epistles of John*, pp. 25-28, 97-100) summarizes some of the main differences. They are wholly explicable in light of the factors named, without Brown's hyperanalytical theory about the development of Johannine Christianity, which multiplies John into at least three authors in an evolving tradition (Jesus—tradition—Beloved Disciple—tradition—Evangelist—tradition—Gnosticizing secessionists versus the author of the Epistles, who reclaimed Johannine traditions earlier than the Fourth Gospel).

[58]David E. Aune, *Revelation* (3 vols.; WBC 52A, 52B, 52C; Dallas: Word, 1997–1998), 1:xlix-l.

[59]The classic list of differences in language and idea comes from Dionysius of Alexandria according to Eusebius, *Hist. eccl.* 7.25.8-27. For more differences, see R. H. Charles, *A Critical and Exegetical Commentary on the Revelation of St. John* (2 vols.; ICC; New York: Scribner, 1920), 1:xxix-xxxvii.

[60]On the apocalyptic schema in John's Gospel, note for starters John 5:28-29; 6:39-40, 44, 54; 14:3; 17:24; 21:22. A growing consensus sees the eschatological images of the Apocalypse as referring to persons and institutions of the author's day. For example, the beast symbolizes Roman imperial power; the false prophet, priests of the imperial cult in Asia; Lady Babylon, the attractions of Roman society, economy and culture around the turn of the century; the battle of Armageddon, the clash of pro-Roman ideology with the truth of the gospel of Jesus Christ; the millennial reign, God's vindication of Christian martyrs and the reversal of their fortunes. Viewed in that way, the Apocalypse arguably has a more elaborate "realized eschatology" than does the Gospel.

For one thing, an author can adopt a style deliberately. Luke, for example, imitates narrative portions of the Septuagint in the opening chapters of his Gospel. Tacitus too wrote in several styles.[61] Most of the peculiarities and solecisms in the Apocalypse have a rationale, which usually is to signal evocations of the Old Testament.[62]

Comparisons within a given genre can be telling, as between the letters of Paul and that to the Hebrews. But in the New Testament the Johannine is the only corpus that encompasses several genres (gospel, homily, letter, apocalypse).[63] Having no other example to serve as a control, who would dare say how much variance in language, style or theological emphasis might be manifest in the work of single, versatile writer?[64]

Also clouding the picture is the fact that Aramaic speakers such as Peter and John from the Palestinian working class with little formal education (Acts 4:13) would have required the service of a secretary to draft a piece for publication in Greek. How likely is it that the same helper accompanied them from place to place? Amanuenses often enjoyed considerable latitude in crafting words before submitting the final product to the author for approval.[65] Some variations within a corpus may be due to them.

---

[61]A case in point is Tacitus's *Dialogus de oratoribus*. Written in neo-Ciceronian style, it "offers so sharp a contrast to the later manner of Tacitus that its authenticity was early called in question, first by Peter Rhenanus, then by Justus Lipsius, with the full weight of his great name. Only in 1911 were the doubts dispelled by Lange's discovery that a letter from Pliny to Tacitus alludes unmistakably to the Dialogue" (John Jackson, introduction to *Tactitus: Histories, Books IV-V; Annals, Books I-III* [LCL 249; Cambridge MA: Harvard University Press, 1931], pp. 230-31).

[62]G. K. Beale, *The Book of Revelation: A Commentary on the Greek Text* (NIGTC; Grand Rapids: Eerdmans; Carlisle: Paternoster, 1999), pp. 100 103. On the peculiar language, see Charles, *Revelation*, pp. cxvii-clix; Aune, *Revelation*, 1:clx-ccxi. There are many Semitisms and Septuagintalisms, the significance of which is debated. See Gerard Mussies, *The Morphology of Koine Greek as Used in the Apocalypse of St. John: A Study in Bilingualism* (NovTSup 27; Leiden: Brill, 1971); Steven Thompson, *The Apocalypse and Semitic Syntax* (SNTSMS 52; Cambridge: Cambridge University Press, 1985); Stanley E. Porter, "The Language of the Apocalypse in Recent Discussion," *NTS* 35 (1989): 582-603; Daryl D. Schmidt, "Semitisms and Septuagintalisms in the Book of Revelation," *NTS* 37 (1991): 592-603; Beale, *Revelation*, pp. 100-107. Some broken grammatical patterns can be explained as part of the deliberate structuring of the material. See Iwan M. Whiteley, "An Explanation for the Anacoloutha in the Book of Revelation," *FilNeot* 20 (2007): 33-50.

[63]Matthew, Mark and Luke wrote only biographical or historical narratives; Paul, James, Peter and Jude wrote only letters; Hebrews seems to be a sermon ("this word of exhortation" [Heb 13:22]).

[64]To take a modern example, C. S. Lewis left a legacy in many genres. Were his corpus to be subjected to the level of hairsplitting that biblical critics apply to canonical documents, how many authors might the examination produce?

[65]On the roles played by amanuenses in Greco-Roman antiquity, see E. Randolph Richards, *Paul and First-Century Letter Writing: Secretaries, Composition and Collection* (Downers Grove, IL: InterVarsity Press, 2004), pp. 64-79.

A factor of another kind in discussions about authorship, one that can operate on participants subconsciously, is the social aspect of knowledge. What others say has a formative impact on one's opinions. For a century and a half after the Johannine writings were published not one father of the church raised a scruple about the Apocalypse based on language or style, even though they spoke Greek as their native language, some had had formal training in rhetoric, and the lengthy controversy with the Gnostics trained their antennae to detect spurious books. When the lone voice of Dionysius of Alexandria denied the Apocalypse to the apostle, he wore a dogmatic motive on his sleeve.[66] His negative judgment did not prevail. A century later the church included the book in the New Testament canon. If a predisposition to admit whatever might plausibly be apostolic could explain the patristic consensus, might social pressure likewise explain pervasive skepticism concerning apostolic authorship among academics since the rise of biblical criticism?

Considerations of language and style are in fact woolly enough to allow for divergent conclusions about the authorship. Based on this criterion alone, neither upholders nor doubters of John the apostle can make a case strong enough definitively to exclude the other.

For what it is worth, the Apocalypse is written in short, simple, straightforward clauses usually strung together with the word "and" (καί) in paratactic rather than subordinate constructions.[67] In these respects the grammar is like that of Matthew, Mark and John and differs from Luke, Paul and Hebrews. The limited vocabulary, consisting of 916 Greek words of which 128 (13.97%) occur just once in the New Testament, is comparable to that of John's Gospel (1,011 words, with 114 *hapax legomena*, or 11.27%),[68] even though the list of *hapax legomena* in the Apocalypse is quite distinct from that of John's Gospel,[69] as one would expect for different subject matter. Like Mark, John and 1-3 John, the Apocalypse shows no literary pretensions (over against Luke-Acts, Hebrews, James, 1 Peter, 2 Peter). In these basic aspects of style the Apocalypse is more

---

[66]That motive was to oppose the excesses of a particular millenarian sect. According to Gerhard Maier, Dionysius's criticism was targeted at church politics and transparently dogmatic in motivation (*Die Johannesoffenbarung und die Kirche* [WUNT 25; Tübingen: Mohr Siebeck, 1981], p. 107).

[67]Aune, *Revelation*, 1:cxci-cxcv.

[68]In contrast, Acts uses 2,038 words, of which 478 (23.45%) are *hapax legomena*. Paul's Epistles draw on 2,648 words, of which 795 (30.02%) are *hapax legomena*.

[69]The statistics are given in Aune, *Revelation*, 1:ccvii-ccxi.

similar to John's Gospel and Epistles than it is to the other corpora of the New Testament.[70] Even critics who find more than one author typically posit a common tradition.

The array of points of contact is impressive. Otto Böcher compares the Apocalypse with the other Johannine books with respect to unique points of Christology,[71] ecclesiology[72] and eschatology.[73] We might add characteristic lexical choices (ἀληθινός; γεννᾶν; σφάζειν; τηρεῖν ἐντολάς); "I am" predications (Apoc 1:17; 2:23; 21:6; 22:13, 16);[74] a tendency to think of the Spirit concretely as indwelling and acting through the church, and of the church imbued with the Spirit as a fellowship partner with the Father and the Son; the antichrist figure; elevation of the symbolic number "seven" to a structural role.[75]

Yet more telling than surface traits are mental dispositions: a sense of the ideal embodied in the particular; penetration to central truths;[76] narrowing down to a small number of main characters and themes;[77] ruminative development of thoughts by cyclical variations having a constantly shifting

---

[70]Comparisons focusing on specific phenomena, such as the use of Greek particles, neither confirm nor clearly exclude common authorship. See Vern S. Poythress, "Johannine Authorship and the Use of Intersentence Conjunctions in the Book of Revelation," *WTJ* 47 (1985): 329-36.

[71]Oneness of the Son with the Father; *logos*; "lamb"; "shepherd"; "judge"; "overcoming" (νικᾶν).

[72]Church as true Israel composed of Jews and Gentiles, and as bride of the messianic bridegroom; Christians as children of the daughter of Zion, and as "sheep," "lambs," "victors," witnesses.

[73]The present as the time of the end; visions of angels; eschatological war; chiliasm; world Sabbath; judgment and punishment with fire; heavenly city; paradise with water and bread of life. See Otto Böcher, "Johanneisches in der Apokalypse des Johannes," *NTS* 27 (1981): 310-21. Böcher bows to the judgment of most scholars, distances himself from common authorship, and regards the likenesses therefore as "surprising." Does he exemplify the magnetic pull of prevailing opinion in the guild?

[74]Karl Kundsin, "Charakter und Ursprung der johanneischen Reden," *Latvijas Universitates Raksti (Acta Universitatis Latviensis): Teologijas Fakultates Serija* 1, no. 4 (1939): 268-84.

[75]For more comprehensive comparisons of the language and theology of the Fourth Gospel and the Apocalypse, see Jörg Frey, "Erwägungen zum Verhältnis der Johannesapokalypse zu den übrigen Schriften im Corpus Johanneum," in Hengel, *Die johanneische Frage*, pp. 326-429; André Heinze, *Johannesapokalypse und johanneische Schriften: Forschungs- und traditionsgeschichtliche Untersuchungen* (BWANT 142; Stuttgart: Kohlhammer, 1998); Craig S. Keener, *The Gospel of John: A Commentary* (2 vols.; Peabody, MA: Hendrickson, 2003), 1:126-39. These scholars find the similarities impressive. Frey (p. 428) thinks the Gospel and Revelation are connected to the figure of John at least in part. Keener (p. 138) concludes that common authorship is "not impossible."

[76]"This peculiarity of thought, which centralizes ideas in their logical source or ground, is pervading and fundamental in the writings of John" (Stevens, *Johannine Theology*, p. 6). "The theological lines are more sharply drawn, the view is deeper, the thoughts simplified but directed to what is essential and permanent" (Schnackenburg, "Christian Morality," p. 188).

[77]"Compressed into a few fundamental realities" (Grossouw, "Christian Spirituality," p. 214).

texture of thematic elements;[78] varied word choices;[79] construal of reality in sharp polarities; an eye for symbols;[80] a tendency to tap the Old Testament thematically or to quote it paraphrastically rather than word for word; delight in artistic patterns;[81] prophetic consciousness;[82] indebtedness to apocalyptic;[83] prominence of trinitarianism and vivid picture language for the relations among members of the divine Trinity. May not choice of genre and the nature of the subject matter go far toward explaining what remains peculiar to the Apocalypse?

Many ostensibly "literary" judgments are at bottom theologically bent. Dionysius of Alexandria distanced the millennial vision from the apostle, as we saw, to undermine a crass misuse of it. Martin Luther, in his 1522 "Preface to the Revelation of St. John," considered that "Christ is neither taught nor known in it," by which Luther usually meant that a given book was unclear about justification by faith and talked more than he liked about the role of works in

---

[78]Gilbert van Belle, "Repetition, Variation and Amplification: Thomas Popp's Recent Contribution on Johannine Style," *ETL* 79 (2003): 166-78; Gilbert van Belle, Michael Labahn and Pieter Maritz, eds., *Repetitions and Variations in the Fourth Gospel: Style, Text, Interpretation* (BETL 223; Leuven: Peeters, 2009).

[79]Edwin D. Freed, "Variations in the Language and Thought of John," *ZNW* 55 (1964): 167-97; Morris, *Studies*, pp. 293-319.

[80]John's use of symbolism has been studied heavily. For recent studies on the Gospel, see René Kieffer, *Le monde symbolique de Saint Jean* (LD 137; Paris: Cerf, 1989); Ulrich Busse, *Das Johannesevangelium: Bildlichkeit, Diskurs und Ritual; Mit einer Bibliographie über den Zeitraum 1986-1998* (BETL 162; Leuven: Leuven University Press, 2002); Craig R. Koester, *Symbolism in the Fourth Gospel: Meaning, Mystery, Community* (2nd ed.; Minneapolis: Fortress, 2003); Ruben Zimmermann, *Christologie der Bilder im Johannesevangelium: Die Christopoetik des vierten Evangeliums unter besonderer Berücksichtigung von Joh 10* (WUNT 171; Tübingen: Mohr Siebeck, 2004); Jörg Frey, Jan G. van der Watt and Ruben Zimmermann, eds., *Imagery in the Gospel of John: Terms, Forms, Themes, and Theology of Johannine Figurative Language* (WUNT 200; Tübingen: Mohr Siebeck, 2006); on the Apocalypse, see Jörg Frey, "Die Bildersprache der Johannesapokalypse," *ZTK* 98 (2001): 161-85; Lynn R. Huber, *Like a Bride Adorned: Reading Metaphor in John's Apocalypse* (ESEC 10; London: T & T Clark, 2007).

[81]For the Gospel, see R. Alan Culpepper, *Anatomy of the Fourth Gospel: A Study in Literary Design* (Philadelphia: Fortress, 1983); Mark W. G. Stibbe, *John as Storyteller: Narrative Criticism and the Fourth Gospel* (SNTSMS 73; Cambridge University Press, 1992), pp. 13-22; idem, "Telling the Father's Story: The Gospel of John as Narrative Theology," in *Challenging Perspectives on the Gospel of John* (ed. John Lierman; WUNT 2/219; Tübingen: Mohr Siebeck, 2006), pp. 170-93; Jeffrey Lloyd Staley, *The Print's First Kiss: A Rhetorical Investigation of the Implied Reader in the Fourth Gospel* (SBLDS 82; Atlanta: Scholars Press, 1988); Gunnar H. Østenstad, *Patterns of Redemption in the Fourth Gospel: An Experiment in Structural Analysis* (SBEC 38; Lewiston, NY: Mellen, 1998); Wayne Brouwer, *The Literary Development of John 13-17: A Chiastic Reading* (SBLDS 182; Atlanta: Society of Biblical Literature, 2000). Not all the patterns discerned by these scholars are convincing, but many readers share the impression that patterns are there to be discovered.

[82]Ashton, *Understanding*, pp. 181-93.

[83]Ibid., pp. 383-406.

salvation.[84] Jewish apocalyptic literature with its supernatural elements was not to the taste of J. S. Semler and other early practitioners of the historical-critical method. Nor did it square with Bultmann's existentialism. May it be repulsion at the message of the Apocalypse, not literary sensitivity, that prompts many to deny it to the author of the Johannine Gospel?

***Reception of the corpus by the Fathers.*** Patristic tradition univocally attributes the Johannine corpus to John.[85] Justin, who spent time at Ephesus in A.D. 135, states point-blank that the prophecy of Christ's thousand years in Jerusalem was made by "a certain man with us, whose name was John, one of the apostles of Christ" (*Dial.* 81.4). Irenaeus, who heard Polycarp reminisce about John, adds, "That was seen no very long time since, but almost in our own day, towards the end of Domitian's reign [i.e., ca. A.D. 95]" (*Haer.* 5.30.3). As far as the Apocalypse is concerned, "There is no book of the entire New Testament whose external attestation can compare . . . in nearness, clearness, definiteness, and positiveness of statement."[86] The personal authority of the author of the Apocalypse and of the Epistles is congruent with plentiful and sound early traditions to the effect that John migrated from Jerusalem to settle in Asia near Ephesus toward the end of the century, where he supervised churches.[87]

---

[84]Martin Luther, *Word and Sacrament I*, vol. 35 of *Luther's Works* (ed. Theodore Bachmann; Philadelphia: Fortress, 1960), p. 399.

[85]Dionysius is the exception that proves the rule, since he consciously set himself against the tradition.

[86]Benjamin W. Bacon, *The Making of the New Testament*, pp. 190-91, quoted in Leon Morris, *The Revelation of St. John* (TNTC; Grand Rapids: Eerdmans, 1969), p. 27. Bacon nevertheless did not accept the tradition. The ancient testimonies are collected in Robert H. Mounce, *The Book of Revelation* (NICNT; Grand Rapids: Eerdmans, 1998), pp. 11-12.

[87]Justin, *Dial.* 81.4 ("there was a certain man with us" [at Ephesus]). Eusebius cites the following sources: Papias, bishop of Hierapolis, early second century (*Hist. eccl.* 3.39.1); Irenaeus, harking back to "all the clergy in Asia who came in contact with John" (*Hist. eccl.* 3.23.1-4); Polycarp, bishop of Smyrna, died ca. 155/156 (*Hist. eccl.* 4.14.6; 5.24.16); Polycrates, bishop of Ephesus, ca. 190 (*Hist. eccl.* 3.32.3; 5.24.3); Clement of Alexandria (*Hist. eccl.* 3.23.5-19); and Origen (*Hist. eccl.* 3.1.1). The apocryphal *Acts of John* sets John in Ephesus passim, as does the Syriac *History of John, the Son of Zebedee* (William Wright, *Apocryphal Acts of the Apostles: Edited from Syriac Manuscripts in the British Museum and Other Libraries* [2 vols.; London: Williams & Norgate, 1871], 2:3-60). J. A. T. Robinson, on surveying the data, concludes, "In the ancient tradition of the church there is simply no alternative to Ephesus as the place of writing [of John's Gospel]. . . . This is a case where the external evidence is uncontested and is supported by whatever indications there are from the internal" (*Priority*, pp. 46-47 [his discussion is on pp. 45-48]). Sjef van Tilborg, using recently edited and published epigraphic data, has shown how many aspects of John's Gospel would have resonated in first-century Ephesus (*Reading John in Ephesus* [NovTSup 83; Leiden: Brill, 1996]). On the Ephesian provenance, see also Ulrich B. Müller, "Die Heimat des Johannesevangeliums," *ZNW* 97 (2006): 44-63; Lance Byron Richey, *Roman Imperial Ideology and the Gospel of John* (CBQMS 43; Washington, DC: Catholic Biblical Association of America, 2007); Warren Carter, *John and Empire: Initial Explorations* (London: T & T Clark, 2008).

Eusebius collected statements from catholic fathers concerning the authorship of the Gospel,[88] at least the first of the three Epistles,[89] and the Apocalypse.[90] This body of ancient ecclesiastical testimony is augmented by a considerable number of Gnostic and apocryphal writers.[91]

Justin's note dates from within forty years of the apostle's death and stems from the very city of John's tomb, Ephesus. Irenaeus's report has a very old source indeed, heard by him not more than a generation after the lifetime of the apostle, in a chain of transmission of only three links.[92] Clement's information also goes back to disciples and protégés of John in Asia.[93] These were men of the late first and early second centuries whose lifespans overlapped with John's, who interacted with him personally, who had direct knowledge that he wrote these books in that place. The sources are multiple, independent and convergent. For the century and a half and more that followed John's death the patristic church knew of no contrary claim concerning the author of this body of literature. Several Fathers of the second century treat the Johannine writings as a united corpus from a single authoritative person, using a passage from one part to help interpret a passage from another.[94] If any traditions deserve to be taken seriously by historians, these do.[95]

*Biblical criticism since the European Enlightenment.* Nevertheless, criticism

---

[88]The "tradition" in Eusebius, *Hist. eccl.* 3.24.1-2, 8, 11 has points in common with a parallel story in the Muratorian Canon, lines 10-16. The Muratorian Canon is conveniently available in Edgar Hennecke, *New Testament Apocrypha* (ed. Wilhelm Schneemelcher; trans. and ed. R. McL. Wilson; 2 vols.; Philadelphia: Westminster, 1963), 1:42-45. For John Zebedee as the author, Eusebius cites Irenaeus (*Hist. eccl.* 5.8.4), Clement of Alexandria (*Hist. eccl.* 6.14.5-7), and Dionysius of Alexandria (*Hist. eccl.* 7.25.7).

[89]General opinion up to Eusebius's time: *Hist. eccl.* 3.24.17-18; Dionysius of Alexandria: *Hist. eccl.* 7.25.7.

[90]Eusebius (*Hist. eccl.* 3.18.3) quotes from Irenaeus. Irenaeus himself refers to "those men who saw John face to face" (*Haer.* 5.30.1), with whom Irenaeus must have had contact while he was living in Asia. General opinion about the Apocalypse was later divided, according to Eusebius, *Hist. eccl.* 3.24.18.

[91]Documented in J. B. Lightfoot, *Biblical Essays* (Grand Rapids: Baker Books, 1979), pp. 45-122; Westcott, *St. John*, pp. lix-lxvii; Leon Morris, *The Gospel According to John* (NICNT; Grand Rapids: Eerdmans, 1971), pp. 21-30; Keener, *John*, 1:91-100. All traditions about John are gathered and sifted in R. Alan Culpepper, *John, the Son of Zebedee: The Life of a Legend* (SPNT; Columbia: University of South Carolina Press, 1994).

[92]John—Polycarp—Irenaeus (Irenaeus's letter *To Florinus* in Eusebius, *Hist. eccl.* 5.20.4-8; the same chain of transmission is also evident in Irenaeus's letter *To Victor* in Eusebius, *Hist. eccl.* 5.24.14-17).

[93]Clement of Alexandria, *Quis div.* 42, quoted by Eusebius starting at *Hist. eccl.* 3.23.5.

[94]Hill, *Johannine Corpus*, pp. 449-64.

[95]For a fine summary and appraisal of the traditions about John, see Theodore Zahn, *Introduction to the New Testament* (trans. John Moore Trout et al.; 3 vols.; New York: Scribner, 1909), 3:174-206.

rightly spares no tradition, however credible, from testing. Pious legends and misinformation sprouted early.[96] Strictly speaking, the Johannine Gospel and Letters are anonymous. Patristic accounts pointing to apostolic authorship are by no means so irrefragable as to forestall speculation about alternative figures.

Other options have been canvassed. Could the disciple whom Jesus loved have been a member of the household of Lazarus,[97] or doubting Thomas,[98] or an unknown eyewitness of Jesus' ministry?[99] Does he represent one or more unidentified exponents of the apostle in the next generation?[100] Is he one of a circle of charismatic leaders after the apostle's death?[101] The latter type of solution is sometimes combined with the hypothesis of a Johannine community that produced the literature.[102] But thus far none of these proposals has won a following among scholars, for indeed none emerges from the data of the books themselves as naturally as John does.

***John the Elder of Ephesus?*** Perhaps the most widely debated alternative is a John of Ephesus, whom Eusebius tried to distinguish from the apostle and whose shadowy figure has fired the imaginations of a number of modern critics.[103]

Eusebius (*Hist. eccl.* 3.39.5-7) gives his interpretation of a paragraph that he quotes from Papias, bishop of Hierapolis in the early decades of the second century.

> Papias: "And I shall not hesitate to append to the interpretations all that I ever learnt well from the presbyters and remember well, for of their truth I am confident. For unlike most I did not rejoice in them who say much, but in them who teach the truth, nor in them who recount the commandments of others, but in

---

[96]For example, Irenaeus (*Haer.* 2.22.5-6), on the authority of Asian elders who were conversant with John, maintains with equal vehemence that Jesus died at over forty years old. This seems very unlikely.

[97]Stibbe, *John as Storyteller*; Ben Witherington III, *John's Wisdom: A Commentary on the Fourth Gospel* (Louisville: Westminster John Knox, 1995).

[98]James H. Charlesworth, *The Beloved Disciple: Whose Witness Validates the Gospel of John?* (Valley Forge, PA: Trinity Press International, 1995).

[99]Richard Bauckham, *The Testimony of the Beloved Disciple: Narrative, History, and Theology in the Gospel of John* (Grand Rapids: Baker Academic, 2007).

[100]Stephen S. Smalley, *John: Evangelist and Interpreter* (Exeter: Paternoster, 1978), p. 81; G. R. Beasley-Murray, *John* (WBC 36; Waco, TX: Word, 1987), p. lxxv; Brown, *Introduction to the Gospel of John*, pp. 189-99.

[101]Udo Schnelle, *Das Evangelium nach Johannes* (THKNT; Leipzig: Evangelische Verlagsanstalt, 1998), pp. 1-27.

[102]Raymond E. Brown, *An Introduction to the New Testament* (ABRL; New York: Doubleday, 1997), pp. 373-76.

[103]B. H. Streeter, *The Primitive Church* (London: Macmillan, 1929), pp. 89-97; Martin Hengel, *The Johannine Question* (Philadelphia: Trinity Press International, 1990); Richard Bauckham, "Papias and Polycrates on the Origin of the Fourth Gospel," *JTS* 44 (1993): 24-69.

them who repeated those given to the faith by the Lord and derived from truth itself; but if ever anyone came who had followed the presbyters, I inquired into the words of the presbyters [τῶν πρεσβυτέρων], what Andrew or Peter or Philip or Thomas or James or John or Matthew had said [εἶπεν], and what Aristion and the presbyter [ὁ πρεσβύτερος] John, the Lord's disciples, were saying [λέγουσιν]. For I did not suppose that information from books would help me so much as the word of a living and abiding voice." (Eusebius, *Hist. eccl.* 3.39.3-4)[104]

Eusebius woodenly descries here a second John, who belongs "outside the number of the Apostles" (*Hist. eccl.* 3.39.5). But that Papias meant that is quite improbable, seeing that Papias merely distinguishes between what the apostles, whom he calls "presbyters," had said in the remoter past, and what two select disciples of Jesus were still saying while Papias (ca. 60-130) was a young man, when John the son of Zebedee (ca. 10-100) was yet alive. Papias naturally put him in a different category from the apostles who had died. Eusebius also cites the presence of two tombs of John at Ephesus (*Hist. eccl.* 3.39.6), but that fact does not require two Johns.

In addition, Eusebius quotes at length the extract from Dionysius, bishop of Alexandria (died ca. 264), in which he set out to prove that the author of the Apocalypse was a John other than the apostle (*Hist. eccl.* 7.25). But to repeat, Dionysius was opposing a millenarian sect centered in Arsinoe that based some of their strange beliefs on the Apocalypse. He had a motive for denying its apostolicity and casting about for some other John. There is no shred of evidence that a John of Ephesus, as distinct from John the apostle, ever existed.[105]

**Conclusion: John the son of Zebedee.** On the question of authorship there seems little reason to be swayed by the prevalence of excessive caution in academe rather than by the internal evidence of the books supported by the Fathers. Although the primary data are not so forceful as to compel assent, they are solid and are congruent with the tradition.

If theological coherence becomes apparent, this will add to the points in favor of John's authorship. It is neither possible nor necessary to settle the au-

---

[104]Translation by Kirsopp Lake in the Loeb edition.

[105]On this tidbit of Papias, see Robinson, *Priority*, pp. 101-4; D. A. Carson and Douglas J. Moo, *An Introduction to the New Testament* (2nd ed.; Grand Rapids: Zondervan, 2005), pp. 233-35; Randar Tasmuth, "Authority, Authorship, and Apostolicity as a Part of the Johannine Question: The Role of Papias in the Search for the Authoritative Author of the Gospel of John," *ConJ* 33 (2007): 26-42. For an incisive evaluation of Bauckham's pleas in favor of "John the Elder," see Andreas J. Köstenberger and Stephen O. Stout, "'The Disciple Jesus Loved': Witness, Author, Apostle—A Response to Richard Bauckham's *Jesus and the Eyewitnesses*," *BBR* 18 (2008): 209-31.

thorial question to the satisfaction of all antecedently to a theological comparison. To segregate the documents and caricature their differences could skew the theological picture as badly, should they have emanated from a single mind, as to coordinate the documents would do, should they be from a plurality of minds. The attribution to John, allowing for some editorial help, fits the data better than any alternative. Therefore my working hypothesis will be that the Johannine literature, including the Apocalypse, more probably than not stems from a single mind.[106]

***Occasion for writing.*** The event that prompted John to write his Gospel is plainly recorded in several patristic sources. "His fellow-disciples and bishops urged him" (Muratorian Canon, line 10). "John, last of all, conscious that the outward facts had been set forth in the Gospels, was urged on by his disciples, and, divinely moved by the Spirit, composed a spiritual Gospel" (Clement of Alexandria, in Eusebius, *Hist. eccl.* 6.14.7). "The apostle John was asked to relate in his own gospel" (Eusebius, *Hist. eccl.* 3.24.11). From the final verses of the epilogue to the Fourth Gospel we get a snapshot of a venerable figure who had long survived the other apostles to attain iconic status. The very devotees who testified to his truth (Jn 21:24) must have realized that they had a precious opportunity to capture his memoirs for posterity.[107] This makes John's Gospel the least occasional of his writings.

He wrote it, he himself tells us, to draw people to Jesus (Jn 20:31). Of course, it reflects its time and place as well as the issues of community self-definition and polemic in which he and the churches that he served became embroiled. Today many scholars who have set aside the witness of antiquity to the authorship are perplexed and frustrated that the Gospel of John does not more readily yield up the secrets of its origins. Can a religio-historical search that brackets out what can be known of the author make progress? John's distinctive

---

[106]With Harnack, Schlatter, Zahn, Preisker, Feine, Stauffer, Lohmeyer, Morris, Mounce. So also F.-M. Braun, *Jean le théologien* (4 vols.; EBib; Paris: Gabalda, 1959–1972); Donald Guthrie, *New Testament Introduction* (3rd ed.; Downers Grove, IL: InterVarsity Press, 1970), pp. 934-39; Giorgio Marcato, "Ricerche sulla 'Scuola Giovannea,'" *Ang* 75 (1998): 305-31; Carson and Moo, *Introduction*, pp. 700-707; Wolfgang Fenske, *Der Lieblingsjünger: Das Geheimnis um Johannes* (BG 16; Leipzig: Evangelische Verlagsanstalt, 2007).

[107]It is possible to date the composition of John's Gospel prior to A.D. 70, and some fine critical scholars do so (J. A. T. Robinson, *Redating the New Testament* [London: SCM Press, 1976], pp. 254-85; Klaus Berger, *Im Anfang war Johannes: Datierung und Theologie des vierten Evangeliums* [2nd ed.; Stuttgart: Gütersloher, 2003]), but there is no strong reason to resist the impression created by John 21:23-24 that it was later in John's lifetime rather than earlier.

language and conceptions are due mostly to the genius of John.[108]

If it was indeed John whose mind suffuses this literature, then what we know about him will help us find a path through the critical issues that remain to be considered.

## STAGES OF COMPOSITION

It was not John himself, but a voice from his church, who penned the commendation in John 21:24: "We know that his testimony is true." Just before that, the disciple whom Jesus loved claims to be the very person "who wrote these things" (ὁ γράψας ταῦτα), and just afterwards he lets slip an unmistakably singular "I suppose" (Jn 21:25). To what extent, then, may the final form of the material be due to (an)other(s) who may have acted in the role(s) of secretary, editor(s) or creative traditors? The question is fair, but we have no basis on which to seek an answer. According to the Muratorian Canon (lines 10-16), the writing of John's Gospel was a group effort with John taking responsibility. As for internal clues, the Gospel presents plenty of little quirks and puzzles that could be vestiges of notes now lost or of more than one draft over time.[109] Yet B. H. Streeter is worth quoting: "The critic's pretence that he can unravel the process is grotesque. As well hope to start with a string of sausages and reconstruct the pig."[110] With all due respect for the brilliance that some bring to bear on attempts to detect behind the Gospel literary precursors,[111] editorial stages,[112]

---

[108]P.-H. Menoud, "L'originalité de la pensée joh.," *RTP* 28 (1940): 233-61. For a similar judgment about the Epistles (though uncommitted to authorship by John), see Schnackenburg, *Johannine Epistles*, pp. 24-34. He notes that we should not "overlook the strongest factor in Johannine theology, the genial, God-illumined, religious personality of the author" (p. 34).

[109]Eduard Schwartz, "Aporien im vierten Evangelium," *NKGWG*, part 1 (1907): 342-72; part 2 (1908): 115-48; part 3 (1908): 149-88; part 4 (1908): 497-650; F. Warburton Lewis, *Disarrangements in the Fourth Gospel* (Cambridge: Cambridge University Press, 1910).

[110]B. H. Streeter, *The Four Gospels: A Study of Origins* (London: Macmillan, 1924), p. 377.

[111]Following in Bultmann's train, Robert T. Fortna, *The Gospel of Signs: A Reconstruction of the Narrative Source Underlying the Fourth Gospel* (SNTSMS 11; London: Cambridge University Press, 1970); idem, *The Fourth Gospel and Its Predecessor: From Narrative Source to Present Gospel* (Philadelphia: Fortress, 1988); Smith, *Johannine Christianity*, pp. 37-93; Urban C. von Wahlde, *The Earliest Version of John's Gospel: Recovering the Gospel of Signs* (Wilmington, DE: Michael Glazier, 1989). For rebuttal, see Gilbert van Belle, *The Signs Source in the Fourth Gospel: Historical Survey and Critical Evaluation of the Semeia Hypothesis* (trans. Peter J. Judge; BETL 116; Leuven: Peeters, 1994).

[112]Esp. Raymond E. Brown, *The Gospel According to John: Introduction, Translation, and Notes* (2 vols.; AB 29, 29A; Garden City, NY: Doubleday, 1966-1970), 1:xxxiv-xxxix; idem, *Community*; idem, *Introduction to the Gospel of John*, pp. 40-69; Barnabas Lindars, *Behind the Fourth Gospel* (SCC 3; London: SPCK, 1971); idem, *The Gospel of John* (NCB; London: Marshall, Morgan & Scott, 1972), pp. 46-54; Howard M. Teeple, *The Literary Origin of the Gospel of John* (Evanston, IL: Religion and Ethics Institute, 1974); Ashton, *Understanding*, pp. 160-377; Herman C. Waetjen, *The Gospel of the Beloved Dis-*

or *relectures* of a maturing gospel tradition,[113] is it not ironic that jurors whose uncompromising standards of proof reject sufficiently secure traditions about John the son of Zebedee will turn around and amass tomes trying to squeeze theories from the almost total dearth of information that we have about unknown authors and redactors?[114] As J. A. T. Robinson sagely observes, the end product, with its artful arrangement and homogeneity of style, looks more like an author's unpolished manuscript than it does a motley collage of several editors.[115] Since our objective is to understand John's theology, we are on firm ground if we start where he ended: the final form of the canonical text.

In what order John composed the five books that make up his corpus is not to be learned from the data that we have. We must proceed without that knowledge.

## The Synoptic Gospels and the Gospel of John

That the Fourth Gospel pursues a line of its own is plain to anyone who compares it with the Synoptic Gospels (Matthew, Mark, Luke). All four share the same outline and many details in varied order. Geographically, the movement is from Galilee, where Jesus teaches and heals, to Jerusalem, where he is crucified and reappears to his disciples.

---

ciple: *A Work in Two Editions* (London: T & T Clark, 2005); Urban C. von Wahlde, *The Gospel and Letters of John* (3 vols.; ECC; Grand Rapids: Eerdmans, 2010). This approach continues to inform many narrower studies by entrants into the guild of New Testament scholarship, such as Konrad Haldimann, *Rekonstruktion und Entfaltung: Exegetische Untersuchungen zu Joh 15 und 16* (BZNW 104; Berlin: de Gruyter, 2000). But by and large the last two decades of the twentieth century saw a decisive swing away from an analytic approach and toward one that seeks the meaning of the present form of the text. See Klaus Scholtissek, "Johannes auslegen I: Forschungsgeschichtliche und methodische Reflexionen," *SNTSU* 24 (1999): 35-84; idem, "Johannes auslegen II: Methodische, hermeneutische und einleitungswissenschaftliche Reflexionen," *SNTSU* 25 (2000): 98-140; idem, "Eine Renaissance des Evangeliums nach Johannes: Aktuelle Perspektiven der exegetischen Forschung," *TRev* 97 (2001): 267-88; Udo Schnelle, "Recent Views of John's Gospel," *WW* 21 (2001): 486-90.

[113] Andreas Dettwiler, *Die Gegenwart des Erhöhten: Eine exegetische Studie zu den johanneischen Abschiedsreden (Joh 13,31–16,33) unter besonderer Berücksichtigung ihres Relecture-Charakters* (FRLANT 169; Göttingen: Vandenhoeck & Ruprecht, 1995); Johannes Rinke, *Kerygma und Autopsie: Der christologische Disput als Spiegel johanneischer Gemeindegeschichte* (HBS 12; Freiburg: Herder, 1997); Klaus Scholtissek, "Relecture—Zu einem neu entdeckten Programmwort der Schriftauslegung," *BL* 70 (1997): 309-15; idem, "Relecture und Réécriture: Neue Paradigmen zu Methode und Inhalt der Johannesauslegung aufgewiesen am Prolog 1,1-18 und der ersten Abschiedsrede 13,31–14,31," *TP* 75 (2000): 1-29; Jean Zumstein, *Kreative Erinnerung: Relecture und Auslegung im Johannesevangelium* (ATANT 84; Zürich: Theologischer Verlag Zürich, 2004); François Vouga, "Erinnerung an Jesus im Johannesevangelium," *ZNT* 10 (2007): 28-37.

[114] Ashton speaks in a different connection of "the readiness with which scholars, not being supermen, follow one another down culs-de-sac, *Sackgassen*, and the blindest of blind alleys" (*Understanding*, p. 275).

[115] Robinson, *Priority*, pp. 17-18.

But John has no parallels to some key incidents. In John's Gospel there is no explicit account of Jesus' baptism (only of the Baptist's testimony about the descent of the dove [Jn 1:32-34]), no record of Jesus' itinerant proclamation of the kingdom of God, of most of the parables and miracles done in Galilee, of Peter's confession at Caesarea Philippi, of the transfiguration, of the classic trio of passion predictions, of the way to Jerusalem and the teachings on discipleship, of the Olivet Discourse, or of the institution of the Eucharist. The Synoptic theme of the "messianic secret" appears in John in but one unit (Jn 7:3-10). When John does share Synoptic material, the location in John can be surprising, as in the case of the cleansing of the temple, which John alone places toward the beginning (Jn 2:13-16).[116] Often, instead of a Synoptic event John has another having a similar gist.[117]

In the first part of John's Gospel, which corresponds broadly to the Synoptic Galilean ministry (Jn 2:1–11:16),[118] John's account runs parallel to the Synoptic at only two points: where Jesus heals an official's son at Capernaum (Jn 4:46-54),[119] and where Jesus feeds the five thousand followed by his walking on the lake (Jn 6:1-21). Otherwise, John devotes almost two-thirds of this space to Jesus' interactions with people not in Galilee but in Jerusalem (Jn 2:13–4:3; 5; 7:10–10:39) and in Sychar of Samaria (Jn 4:4-43). Although the healing of an invalid on a Sabbath (Jn 5:1-9) and the opening of a blind man's eyes on a Sabbath (Jn 9:1-14) are the sort of things that Jesus does in the Synoptics, in John both happen in Jerusalem.

Nothing in the Synoptic Gospels corresponds to the many messianic identifications of Jesus that punctuate the Fourth Gospel (Jn 1:41, 49; 4:26; 6:15; 7:25-27, 31, 41-42; 9:37; 11:25-27). Only in John does Jesus turn water to wine and raise Lazarus from the dead, the first and last of his signs. Instead of pithy sayings embedded in anecdotes, the Jesus of the Fourth Gospel delivers lengthy discourses or engages in dialogues about his identity and soteriological benefits

---

[116]Robinson (*Priority*, pp. 127-31) defends John's chronology, pointing not least to the specific year suggested by John 2:20 (A.D. 27). Since either the Synoptic Gospels or John could have a topical reason for the placement of the story, the question can remain open. See Blomberg, *Historical Reliability*, pp. 87-91.

[117]For example, compare Matthew 16:16 with John 6:68-69; Matthew 16:18 with John 1:42; Matthew 16:24-26 with John 12:24-26.

[118]Galilee is the point of return: John 1:43; 2:1, 12; 4:3, 43-46, 54; 6:1, 17; 7:1-9.

[119]Although, it is uncertain whether this is another version of the same story found in Matthew 8:5-13 // Luke 7:1-10.

to followers—in the style, moreover, of the narrator (Jn 3; 5; 6; 7–8; 10; 12).[120] Competition between the disciples of John the Baptist and those of Jesus is recorded only here (Jn 3:22-30), as is the Jerusalem-based synagogue ban on Jews confessing Jesus to be the Messiah (Jn 9:22; 12:42). The Farewell Discourses are special to John (Jn 14–17). Even the passion account has unique events: soldiers falling to the ground in the garden of the arrest, a hearing before Annas, Pilate's "Behold the man," the seamless tunic, the handing on of Jesus' mother, the piercing of Jesus' side. The postresurrection reports have no parallels, as is true of each of the Gospels.

How to assess John's differences from the Synoptics yet overlaps with them has been discussed at length.[121] Throughout the nineteenth century and well into the twentieth there was a consensus that John knew and used one or more of the others. This began to change with Percival Gardner-Smith,[122] after which the position quickly became dominant that John made no direct use of any of our other canonical Gospels but rather drew from independent streams of oral tradition.[123] To this view C. H. Dodd gave monumental expression.[124] Frans Neirynck and C. K. Barrett, among other leading critics, resisted it.[125] Following the 26th Biblical Colloquium at Louvain in 1975, however, the newer consensus itself began to fracture,[126] and by the 39th Colloquium in 1990 winds were blowing in all directions, at least in continental Europe.[127] Three major commentaries published in 1998 by Ludger Schenke, Udo Schnelle, and Ulrich Wilckens espoused John's broad dependence on at least one of the Synoptic

---

[120]Christoph Demke, "Das Evangelium der Dialoge: Hermeneutische und methodologische Beobachtungen zur Interpretation des Johannesevangeliums," *ZTK* 97 (2000): 164-82.

[121]Fine histories of the problem are provided in Jozef Blinzler, *Johannes und die Synoptiker: Ein Forschungsbericht* (SBS 5; Stuttgart: Katholisches Bibelwerk, 1965); D. Moody Smith, *John Among the Gospels: The Relationship in Twentieth-Century Research* (Minneapolis: Fortress, 1992).

[122]Percival Gardner-Smith, *Saint John and the Synoptic Gospels* (Cambridge: Cambridge University Press, 1938).

[123]For example, Bent Noack, *Zur johanneischen Tradition: Beiträge zur Kritik an der literarkritischen Analyse des vierten Evangeliums* (LSSTS 3; Copenhagen: Rosenkilde & Bagger, 1954).

[124]C. H. Dodd, *Historical Tradition in the Fourth Gospel* (Cambridge: Cambridge University Press, 1963). Dodd thought that John used traditions just as primitive and valuable as those behind Mark.

[125]C. K. Barrett, "John and the Synoptic Gospels," *ExpTim* 85 (1974): 228-33; idem, *The Gospel According to St. John* (2nd ed.; Philadelphia: Westminster, 1978), pp. 42-45; Frans Neirynck, *Jean et les Synoptiques: Examen critique de l'exégèse de M.-É. Boismard* (BETL 49; Leuven: Leuven University Press, 1979).

[126]Marinus de Jonge, ed., *L'Évangile de Jean: Sources, rédaction, théologie* (BETL 44; Gembloux: Duculot, 1977).

[127]Adelbert Denaux, ed., *John and the Synoptics* (BETL 101; Leuven: Leuven University Press, 1992).

Gospels.[128] Exactly how to characterize the relationship remains unclear.[129]

Had John known nothing of any of the earlier Gospels, we are left to explain how he conceived of writing a Gospel, and how he and other Evangelists before him stumbled onto the same subgenre, with the exact main components, independently. Unexplained allusions in the Fourth Gospel assume hearers' prior knowledge that John the Baptist baptized Jesus (Jn 1:32) and later was imprisoned (Jn 3:24), that Jesus appointed twelve apostles (Jn 6:67-71; 20:24), that Mary anointed Jesus and wiped his feet with her hair (Jn 11:2), that Jesus was tried under Caiaphas (Jn 18:24, 28).[130] A few Synoptic sayings of Jesus have a Johannine ring (e.g., the *Jubelruf* ["cry of joy"], Mt 11:25-27 // Lk 10:21-22). Conversely, John often presents the equivalent of Synoptic content in his own way (e.g., compare Jn 12:25 with Mt 10:39; Mk 8:35; Lk 9:24).[131] To read the Fourth Gospel with a background knowledge of the Synoptic Gospels adds a depth of understanding.[132] Could this be what John intends?

John was, with Peter, James and the rest of the twelve, prominent among those who "gave their testimony to the resurrection of the Lord Jesus" in the Jerusalem community (Acts 4:33). He, with the other apostles, remained in the

---

[128]See also Ismo Dunderberg, "Johannine Anomalies and the Synoptics," in *New Readings in John: Literary and Theological Perspectives; Essays from the Scandinavian Conference on the Fourth Gospel in Aarhus 1997* (ed. Johannes Nissen and Siegfried Pedersen; Sheffield: Sheffield Academic Press, 1999), pp. 108-25; Michael Labahn and Manfred Lang, "Johannes und die Synoptiker: Positionen und Impulse seit 1990," in *Kontexte des Johannesevangeliums: Das vierte Evangelium in religions- und traditionsgeschichtlicher Perspektive* (ed. Jörg Frey and Udo Schnelle; WUNT 175; Tübingen: Mohr Siebeck, 2004), pp. 443-15; Stefan Schreiber, "Kannte Johannes die Synoptiker? Zur aktuellen Diskussion," *VF* 51 (2006): 7-24; Hartwig Thyen, "Das Johannesevangelium als literarisches Werk und Buch der Heiligen Schrift," *ZNW* 12 (2009): 54-61.

[129]Mark A. Matson, *In Dialogue with Another Gospel? The Influence of the Fourth Gospel on the Passion Narrative of the Gospel of Luke* (SBLDS 178; Atlanta: Society of Biblical Literature, 2001); Peter Leander Hofrichter, ed., *Für und wider die Priorität des Johannesevangeliums: Symposion in Salzburg am 10. März 2000* (TTS 9; Hildesheim: Olms, 2002); Rainer Riesner, "Versuchung und Verklärung (Lukas 4,1-13; 9,28-36; 10,17-20; 22,39-53 und Johannes 12,20-36)," *TBei* 33 (2002): 197-207; Ian D. Mackay, *John's Relationship with Mark: An Analysis of John 6 in the Light of Mark 6-8* (WUNT 2/182; Tübingen: Mohr Siebeck, 2004); Philipp F. Bartholomä, "John 5,31-47 and the Teaching of Jesus in the Synoptics: A Comparative Approach," *Bib* 92 (2011): 368-91; Benjamin E. Reynolds, "The Johannine Son of Man and the Historical Jesus: Shall Ever the Twain Meet? John 9.35 as a Test Case," *JSHJ* 9 (2011): 230-42.

[130]Richard Bauckham, "John for Readers of Mark," in Bauckham, *Gospels*, pp. 147-71.

[131]Howard, *Fourth Gospel*, pp. 213-27, 306-9; Dodd, *Historical Tradition*, pp. 313-420; Michael Theobald, *Herrenworte im Johannesevangelium* (HBS 34; Freiburg: Herder, 2002), pp. 60-199; Roland Bergmeier, "Die Bedeutung der Synoptiker für das johanneische Zeugnisthema: Mit einem Anhang zum Perfekt-Gebrauch im vierten Evangelium," *NTS* 52 (2006): 458-83.

[132]Tobias Nicklas, "Die johanneische 'Tempelreinigung' (John 2,12-22) für Leser der Synoptiker," *TP* 80 (2005): 1-16.

city when many Jewish Christians were dispersed (Acts 8:1, 14). John served as a "pillar" of the church and guardian of the evangel (Gal 2:9). As one who himself contributed to the hammering out of the oral tradition behind the Synoptic Gospels, he could scarcely have been unaware of at least the central narrative now preserved in the triple tradition material, even if he never saw a final edition of Matthew, Mark or Luke. If he did, he would have noted how each (or any) of them filled out the skeleton, and he would have had precedent all the more for producing his own version. His purpose would have been neither to fill in any perceived gaps nor to correct, much less to polemicize against or to supersede, the received records of the Jesus tradition,[133] but instead to offer an account based on personal recollections, in many respects complementary and confirmatory to theirs, but standing on its own merits.[134]

## John and Judaism

Apostolic authorship sheds light on the vexed question of the religio-historical milieu of the Johannine corpus. John demonstrates a more exact knowledge of Palestinian places, customs and social conditions than any other Evangelist.[135] In fact, his writings mention incidental details of the southwestern quarter of old Jerusalem, where traditions of the early Christians are concentrated.[136] His very language points to his Palestinian origin.[137] If the author was a fisherman of Galilee (Jn 21:7) who was known to the high priest in Jerusalem (Jn 18:15),[138]

---

[133]This last is the thesis of Hans Windisch, *Johannes und die Synoptiker: Wollte der vierte Evangelist die älteren Evangelien ergänzen oder ersetzen?* (UNT 12; Leipzig: Hinrichs, 1926).

[134]Morris, *Studies*, pp. 15-63; Robinson, *Priority*.

[135]On all these points one may still profit from Lightfoot, *Biblical Essays*, pp. 1-44, 123-98. For updates, see W. F. Albright, "Recent Discoveries in Palestine and the Gospel of John," in *The Background of the New Testament and Its Eschatology: In Honour of Charles Harold Dodd* (ed. W. D. Davies and David Daube; Cambridge: Cambridge University Press, 1954), pp. 153-71; John McRay, *Archaeology and the New Testament* (Grand Rapids: Baker Books, 1991), pp. 114-19, 186-92; James H. Charlesworth, "The Historical Jesus in the Fourth Gospel: A Paradigm Shift?" *JSHJ* 8 (2010): 3-46. Further on social conditions of Palestine, see Timothy J. M. Ling, *The Judaean Poor and the Fourth Gospel* (SNTSMS 136; Cambridge: Cambridge University Press, 2006), esp. pp. 146-216.

[136]Robinson, *Priority*, pp. 48-67.

[137]E. C. Colwell cautioned against indiscipline in identifying Semitisms in John's Greek: *The Greek of the Fourth Gospel: A Study of Its Aramaisms in the Light of Hellenistic Greek* (Chicago: University of Chicago Press, 1931). But on John's language and other personal peculiarities, note G. D. Kilpatrick, "What John Tells Us about John," in *Studies in John: Presented to Professor J. N. Sevenster on the Occasion of His Seventieth Birthday* (NovTSup 24; Leiden: Brill, 1970), pp. 75-87.

[138]The traditional site in Jerusalem of the home of the Zebedee family is an arched structure at the Café of the Columns (Kahwat el Umdan) near the bazaars on David Street in the southwestern part of the city, not far from the house of Caiaphas (John Wenham, *Easter Enigma* [CEP; Grand Rapids: Academie Books, 1984], pp. 14-16). The late medieval *Historia passionis Domini* quotes a lost

we can set aside any suggestion that the primary religious influence on John came from an erudite philosophical Judaism (as represented by Philo or the Wisdom of Solomon), the Hermetic literature of Egypt, incipient Gnosticism, or a Palestinian gnosis that developed into Mandaism.[139]

Parallels between the Fourth Gospel and the lately discovered Qumran scrolls impressed researchers in the mid-twentieth century.[140] Some proposed that the seedbed of Johannine "sectarianism" could have been circles of heterodox, perhaps Gnosticizing, Jews already at the fringes of Pharisaic-rabbinic influence even before they embraced Christianity.[141] But scholarship has barely scratched the most likely religious environment of all: common Palestinian Judaism defined by the Pharisean interpretation of the Hebrew Scriptures.[142]

---

*Gospel of the Nazareans* as saying that John "had often brought fish to the palace of the high priests Annas and Caiaphas" (Hennecke, *New Testament Apocrypha*, 1:152). How this statement, if true, might shed light on otherwise puzzling facts in John's Gospel is shown by Robinson (*Priority*, pp. 116-17). Other explanations of how John could have been known to the high priest are that his father, Zebedee, had once lived near the temple (Prochorus's prologue to the *Acts of John*, Vatican Gr. 654, fol. 88v), or that after his father's death John sold the family property in Galilee and used the proceeds to acquire land in the priestly quarter of Jerusalem (Hippolytus of Thebes, "Syntagmate chronologico" [A.D. 980], in *PG* 117:1032-33, 1037, 1052; Epiphanius the Monk, *Life of the Virgin* [A.D. 1015] 18, 20, in *PG* 120:208-9). See Culpepper, *Son of Zebedee*, pp. 61-63, 174-75. None of the medieval sources is reliable, but neither is a personal connection of some sort between John and the priestly family intrinsically implausible.

[139]All are compassed in C. H. Dodd, *The Interpretation of the Fourth Gospel* (Cambridge: Cambridge University Press, 1953), pp. 10-129. Dodd leaned toward the Hermetic explanation.

[140]Raymond E. Brown, "The Qumran Scrolls and the Johannine Gospel and Epistles," *CBQ* 17 (1955): 403-19, 559-74; idem, *John*, 1:cxxii-cxxv; Otto Böcher, *Der johanneische Dualismus im Zusammenhang des nachbiblischen Judentums* (Gütersloh: Mohn, 1965); Herbert Braun, *Qumran und das Neue Testament* (2 vols.; Tübingen: Mohr Siebeck, 1966); James H. Charlesworth, ed., *John and the Dead Sea Scrolls* (COL; New York: Crossroad, 1972); Mary L. Coloe and Tom Thatcher, eds., *John, Qumran, and the Dead Sea Scrolls: Sixty Years of Discovery and Debate* (SBLEJL 32; Atlanta: Society of Biblical Literature, 2011). But for the view that Qumran has little to offer for comparative studies with John's writings, see Jörg Frey, "Licht aus den Höhlen? Der 'johanneische Dualismus' und die Texte von Qumran," in *Kontexte des Johannesevangeliums: Das vierte Evangelium in religions- und traditionsgeschichtlicher Perspektive* (ed. Jörg Frey and Udo Schnelle; WUNT 175; Tübingen: Mohr Siebeck, 2004), pp. 117-203.

[141]For example, Smith, "Johannine Christianity"; Ashton, *Understanding*, pp. 124-59. Palestinian Merkabah mysticism continues to be explored as a possible influence on John. See Jey J. Kanagaraj, *"Mysticism" in the Gospel of John: An Inquiry into Its Background* (JSNTSup 158; Sheffield: Sheffield Academic Press, 1998).

[142]Until quite recently almost the only significant work to pursue this line was Adolf Schlatter, "Die Sprache und Heimat des vierten Evangelisten (1902)," in *Johannes und sein Evangelium* (ed. Karl H. Rengstorf; WF 82; Darmstadt: Wissenschaftliche Buchgesellschaft, 1973), pp. 28-201. Schlatter, like Strack and Billerbeck, wrote before critical study of the rabbinic compilations got under way and made, we now judge, injudicious use of some of these materials to illustrate the Pharisaism of the first century. But his intuition was correct. The learned commentary of Odeberg explores possible rabbinic parallels. Methodologically chastened but narrowly focused is John Christopher

From the fact that John can call the authorities either "the Pharisees" or "the Jews" indifferently (note Jn 1:19, 24; 7:32, 35; 9:13-18), we may infer that the Judaism he remembers was influenced in large part by the Pharisees. This is in keeping with Josephus's contemporary statements that the Pharisees swayed the populace (*Ant.* 13.298; 18.15).[143]

The Judaism of the Fourth Gospel—the heritage of the author and of his characters—approximates that of the sages, sometimes on quite technical points. Jesus taught in synagogues (Jn 6:59; 18:20). He and his followers were loyal, for they were troubled at being expelled (Jn 9:22; 12:42; 16:2). He and his Jewish interlocutors shared the highest possible view of the inspiration and divine authority of the Scriptures (Jn 5:39; 10:35). "To search" (ἐραυνᾶν) them (Jn 5:39; 7:52), a phrase attested only in John among New Testament writings, was an activity known to the Tannaim as "midrash" (from שׁרד, "seek, be intent on").[144] There are correspondences in phraseology between the Johannine writings and *Targum Isaiah*.[145]

The boast of the descendants of Abraham (Jn 8:33, 39) assumes that Abraham stood firm (*m. ʾAbot* 5:3) and can bequeath merits to succeeding generations of Israelites (*m. ʿEd.* 2:9; *Mek.* 4, I 216 to Ex 14:15). Moses' name comes up twice as many times in the Gospel of John (13×) as in Matthew, the latter widely regarded as a Gospel for Jewish-Christians (7×). According to John, Jesus' opponents held up Jesus against Moses as the proven teacher of Judaism (Jn 9:28-29; cf. *m. Soṭah* 1:9; *Mek.* 1, I 169 to Ex 13:17).

---

Thomas, "The Fourth Gospel and Rabbinic Judaism," *ZNW* 82 (1991): 159-82. Klaus Wengst, building on *Bedrängte Gemeinde* in his commentary *Das Johannesevangelium* (2 vols; THKNT 4; Stuttgart: Kohlhammer, 2000–2001), sets the Gospel of John against a rabbinic background. Also giving due attention to Pharisaic-rabbinic Judaism (in the context of other Hellenistic writings) are the independent commentaries by Barrett, *St. John*, and Keener, *John*.

[143]That Josephus's assertion is not far off the mark is supported by his own decision, as an ambitious young man, to associate with the Pharisees though he was of priestly stock (*Life* 12). They enjoyed a high reputation as models of piety (e.g., Mt 5:20; 23:2; Lk 18:9-12) and so are prominent in the Synoptic Gospels. The apostle Paul considered his former membership of the Pharisee party a boast (Phil 3:5; cf. Acts 23:6; 26:5). The importance of the Pharisees in the Fourth Gospel confirms Josephus. Adherence to a radical criticism made the early Jacob Neusner, Anthony Saldarini and others excessively skeptical of Josephus and of the New Testament on this point. For a more tempered critical approach, see Martin Hengel and Roland Deines, "E. P. Sanders' 'Common Judaism,' Jesus, and the Pharisees," *JTS* 46 (1995): 1-70.

[144]Also John shares homiletic techniques with the midrashim. See Peder Borgen, *Bread from Heaven: An Exegetical Study of the Concept of Manna in the Gospel of John and the Writings of Philo* (NovTSup 10; Leiden: Brill, 1965); idem, *Philo, John, and Paul: New Perspectives on Judaism and Early Christianity* (BJS 131; Atlanta: Scholars Press, 1987), pp. 75-204.

[145]John L. Ronning, "The *Targum of Isaiah* and the Johannine Literature," *WTJ* 69 (2007): 247-78.

John more than matches Matthew in the frequency at which he mentions the Scriptures (ἡ γραφή, αἱ γραφαί: 4× in Matthew, 12× in John), the Torah (νόμος: 9× in Matthew, 13× in John) and the Passover (4× in Matthew, 10× in John). John regards the law of Moses as the great gift of God's grace and love (Jn 1:17; cf. *m.* ʾ*Abot* 3:15),[146] considers that it outweighs all the prophets together (Jn 1:45; 5:45-46; cf. *Exod. Rab.* 42:8),[147] and takes over metaphors for the law ("bread," "water," "light," "life") into his presentation of Jesus.[148] Together with a positive valuation of the Mosaic law, we find in John's writings a complete lack of polemics against practical devotion to it.[149] John makes more frequent use of the phrase "to keep the commandments" (τηρεῖν ἐντολάς) than the other New Testament authors combined (Jn 14:15, 21; 15:10 [2×]; 1 Jn 2:3, 4; 3:22, 24; 5:3; Apoc 12:17; 14:12).[150] Arguing from the legitimacy of circumcising on the Sabbath, to making a whole man well (Jn 7:23), Jesus invoked the rabbinic rule of *qal wahomer* ("from the less to the greater").[151] The question of the crowd, "What must we do to be doing the works of God?" (Jn 6:28) and Jesus' reply (Jn 6:28-29) reflect a nomistic usage of "labor" and "work" (cf. Jn 4:34; 6:27; 17:4) found in Palestinian Judaism (see 4Q398 14-17 II, 3; cf. Rom 2:20; Gal 2:16) and in the rabbis (e.g., *m.* ʾ*Abot* 1:3; 2:8, 14; 3:12, 16; 4:10).

There are two ages: this world (Jn 8:23; 12:25) and the world to come (*m. Peʾah* 1:1; cf. *m. Sanh.* 10:1). Messianic concepts in the atmosphere ranged from the expectation of an earthly king (Jn 6:15; cf. *Pss. Sol.* 17) to the view that the Messiah will originate in heaven and abide forever (Jn 7:27; 12:34; cf. *4 Ezra* 13; *1 En.* 37–71). A final resurrection of the righteous (Jn 5:21, 29; 6:40; 11:24) was a belief held by the Pharisees (Acts 23:8; Josephus, *J. W.* 2.163; *Ant.* 18.14).

John's Pharisees are conscious of a distinction between themselves and the crowd who are ignorant of the law (Jn 7:47-49; cf. *m. Demai* 2:3; 3:4; *m. Ḥag.* 2:7;

---

[146]Note also the prayer *Ahabah Rabbah.*

[147]On the principle that a whole can be named by its outstanding part, John sometimes follows the rabbinic practice of referring to the Scriptures, including the prophets and the psalms, as "the law" (Jn 10:34 [Ps 82:6]; 12:34 [Ps 110:4; Is 9:6; Dan 7:14]; 15:25 [Ps 35:19; 69:4]).

[148]Severino Pancaro, *The Law in the Fourth Gospel: The Torah and the Gospel, Moses and Jesus, Judaism and Christianity According to John* (NovTSup 42; Leiden: Brill, 1975), pp. 452-87.

[149]Martin Vahrenhorst, "Johannes und die Tora: Überlegungen zur Bedeutung der Tora im Johannesevangelium," *KD* 54 (2008): 14-36.

[150]Elsewhere only Matthew 19:17; 1 Timothy 6:14; but compare also Mark 7:9 (παράδοσιν); Acts 15:5 (νόμον Μωϋσέως); James 2:10 (νόμον). On the metamorphosis of terms for "keeping the law" (τὸ θέλημα/ἔργον τοῦ θεοῦ ποιεῖν, τηρεῖν τὸν λόγον τὰς ἐντολάς) in John, see Pancaro, *Law*, pp. 367-451.

[151]For example, *m. Yebam.* 8:3; *m. Zebaḥ.* 12:3; *m. Ḥul.* 2:7; *m. Bek.* 1:1.

*m. Ṭehar.* 10:1). Their interest in seeing signs (Jn 3:2) is characteristic of the period (Mt 12:39; 16:1; Jn 11:47; 1 Cor 1:22). The concept of Jesus as God's sent one (Jn 4:34 and passim) seems related to the rabbinic maxim "A man's agent is like to himself" (*m. Ber.* 5:5). A "figure" (παροιμία) in Jesus' speech (Jn 10:6; 16:25, 29) is equivalent to a rabbinic *mashal*. Jesus, when reappearing to his disciples after death, brought the usual greeting of *shalom*, "peace" (Jn 20:19, 21, 26; cf. 14:27).

For ritual purification, Jesus' neighbors in Cana stored water in jars of stone (Jn 2:6) as being less amenable to defilement than leather (*m. Kelim* 5:11; *m. Beṣah* 2:2-3; *m. Parah* 3:2). Jews of Judea would not share utensils with Samaritans (Jn 4:9; *m. Ber.* 8:8; *m. Demai* 3:4; *m. Nid.* 4:1; *m. Šeb.* 8:10). A woman was not to talk with a man in a public place (Jn 4:27; *m. Ketub.* 1:8; 7:6). To carry a load from one domain to another on the Sabbath (Jn 5:9-10) was impermissible (*m. Šabb.* 7:2; 11:1-2), as were symbolic gestures of a healer (Jn 9:6; *m. Šabb.* 7:2; 22:5-6). The requirement to perform a circumcision on the eighth day had already been judged to override Sabbath restrictions (Jn 7:22-23; *m. Šabb.* 18:3; 19:1-3; *m. Ned.* 3:11). A suspect did not count as one of the two or three witnesses in his or her own favor (Jn 5:31-47; 8:13; *m. Yebam.* 15:1-2; *m. Ketub.* 1:6-9), although a defendant could present a case and argue for acquittal (Jn 7:51; *m. Sanh.* 5:4).

On coming in from the street, one was to wash hands and feet before eating (Jn 13:8-9; Mk 7:1-5; *m. Yad.* 3:1-2). Temple officials might not enter a Roman praetorium lest they incur ceremonial impurity (Jn 18:28; *m. ʿAbod. Zar.* 1:1-2; *m. ʾOhal.* 18:7-9). Probably the reason why bystanders offered the crucified Jesus a drink on a sprig of hyssop (Jn 19:29) was that he was sufficiently near dying to raise concern about their being defiled in the act (*m. ʾOhal.* 1:1). The linen cloths and spices wrapped about Jesus' corpse were those required by Jewish burial custom (Jn 19:40). The body was deposited in a newly hewn tomb nearby (Jn 19:41) because digging a tomb niche was not permitted during mid-festival (*m. Moʾed Qaṭ.* 1:6). Yet disposal of the dead was always a matter of urgency (*m. B. Meṣʿia* 6:1), even apart from an impending Sabbath day (Jn 19:42). On Easter morning the author hesitated to enter Jesus' tomb, expecting it to convey uncleanness (Jn 20:5; cf. *m. Ṭehar.* 4:5). To set forth the full significance of Jesus, the Fourth Gospel draws upon the meanings of several Jewish festivals: Passover (Jn 2:13; 6:4; 11:55), Tabernacles (Jn 7:2)—complete with the traditional setting ablaze of lights at night (cf. Jn 8:12; *m. Sukkah* 5:2) and the pouring of water (cf. Jn 7:37; *m. Šeqal.* 6:3; *m. Sukkah* 4:1, 9), neither

of which is mandated by Scripture—and Hanukkah (Jn 10:22), which was
added to the calendar only from the Maccabean period (1 Macc 4:59).[152]

Major ideas of Palestinian Judaism—Biblicism, nomism, two ages, messianism, resurrection, judgment—thus combine with concerns for ritual purity
and Sabbath and festival observance typical of the Pharisees.[153] This is the
sphere that formed John's worldview radically.

Living in the midst of a Jewish populace influenced by the Pharisees could
not in itself have generated the contours of John's thought. What he wrote received impetus from Jesus and took on coloring in the cosmopolitan setting of
Hellenized and Romanized greater Ephesus. But only by observing proper
limits can the religio-historical enterprise, with its fixation on the explanatory
power of the cultural environment, avoid reducing the genesis of Johannine
Christianity to a syncretistic conflux. From a historical perspective, everyday
Jewish piety of the first century A.D. was the germinal ground.

If the author was Jewish to his bones, there will be a presumption against
answering positively the post-Holocaust question of possible anti-Semitism or
anti-Judaism in the Fourth Gospel.[154] John took his place in the long line of
Hebrew prophets who castigated Israel, neither for their ethnicity nor for their
performance of Torah, but for lack of respose to God's accredited messengers.
On one point, and one only, does John denounce his co-religionists: their intransigence toward God's climactic self-revelation in Christ. For this he blames
"the Jews" and not specifically "the scribes," "the Pharisees," "the elders" or "the
chief priests" because, by the time of writing, attitudes toward Jesus taken up
by the leaders during Jesus' ministry had won the day among the rank and file
(Mt 16:5-12; 21:23-27; 27:41-43; Lk 7:30; Jn 9:22; 12:42).

## HISTORY AND THEOLOGY IN THE FOURTH GOSPEL

John presents his Gospel with bold avowals that it is his "witness" or "testimony"
to the truth about Jesus (Jn 19:35; 21:24; cf. 1 Jn 1:2; 4:2).[155] The family of words that

---

[152]Gale A. Yee, *Jewish Feasts and the Gospel of John* (ZS; Wilmington, DE: Michael Glazier, 1989).

[153]Jacob Neusner, *Judaism: The Evidence of the Mishnah* (Chicago: University of Chicago Press, 1981),
pp. 45-75.

[154]For a collection of representative essays on the problem, see Reimund Bieringer, Didier Pollefeyt
and Frederique Vandecasteele-Vanneuville, eds., *Anti-Judaism and the Fourth Gospel: Papers of the
Leuven Colloquium, 2000* (JCH 1; Assen: Van Gorcum, 2001).

[155]Thomas Söding, "Die Wahrheit des Evangeliums: Anmerkungen zur johanneischen Hermeneutik,"
*ETL* 77 (2001): 318-55. Alexander Jensen thinks that John struggled for language in which to articulate Christian claims (*John's Gospel as Witness: The Development of the Early Christian Language*

he uses (root μαρτυρ-) finds its natural setting in courts of law; what he has to say invites cross-investigation, and he expects it to stand.[156] His writing conforms to standards of Roman historiography.[157] The signs that he has selected for inclusion in the Gospel are meant to lead a discerning reader to believe (Jn 20:30-31). If the story seems more than usually laden with doctrinal import—what some biblical critics have called "mythology"—that is because John is fully convinced that "the Word became flesh" (Jn 1:14). Earthly things bore eternal verities.[158] Deity took up residence in the incarnate one and revealed itself in the empirical realm where John, among others, heard, saw and touched it (Jn 1:14; 1 Jn 1:1).

***Historical factuality sacrificed for theology?*** To what extent John might have skewed historical facts to enhance his theological portrayal of Jesus has exercised wary minds only since the early nineteenth century, when a number of leading figures in Germany agreed among themselves that the exent was considerable.[159] The pitting of theology against history was a twist of European rationalism. G. E. Lessing (1729–1781) spoke of a "nasty ditch," an unbridgeable gulf. Historians work with probabilities, he observed, not certainties. On the contingencies of history, so the argument goes, necessary truths cannot rest secure; out of finite premises eternal truth cannot derive; from mere experience we can never arrive at certainty about God. Biblical narrative must either tell the facts and fail to uncover the divine, leaving us agnostic, or violate the ground rules of objective historiography.

If we set out from a strict, anthropological starting point, this logic is unassailable, and indeed nobody is more keenly aware than John that no human being has ever seen God (Jn 1:18; 5:37; 6:46; 1 Jn 4:12). But John's thought does not rise from below; it is receptive to God's revelation from above. At issue is

---

*of Faith* [ANCT; Aldershot: Ashgate, 2004]). Lutz Simon argues that both Peter and the disciple whom Jesus loved function side by side in the Gospel as guarantors of the tradition (*Petrus und der Lieblingsjünger im Johannesevangelium: Amt und Autorität* [EH 23/498; Frankfurt: Peter Lang, 1994]).

[156]Bauckham, *Eyewitnesses*, pp. 385-86.

[157]Richard Bauckham, "Historiographical Characteristics of the Gospel of John," *NTS* 53 (2007): 17-36.

[158]Johannine spirituality is "universal, precisely so far as it is not enclosed by concrete, accidental circumstances. . . . The evangelist is constantly anxious to have the timeless element shine through the historical situation" (Grossouw, "Christian Spirituality," p. 214).

[159]Watershed publications included Karl Gottlieb Bretschneider, *Probabilia de evangelii et epistolarum Joannis, Apostoli, indole et origine* (Leipzig: Sumtibus Jo. Ambros. Barthii, 1820); David Friedrich Strauss, *Das Leben Jesu, kritisch bearbeitet* (2 vols.; Tübingen: Osiander, 1835–1836); Ferdinand Christian Baur, *Kritische Untersuchungen über die kanonischen Evangelien, ihr Verhältniss zu einander, ihren Charakter und Ursprung* (Tübingen: Verlag Fues, 1847). A similar outlook continues today in Maurice Casey, *Is John's Gospel True?* (London: Routledge, 1996).

not whether the world can transcend itself to achieve knowledge of the eternal, but whether God would use what he made as the vehicle of self-disclosure to his own creatures. That decision is for God to make. What God decided, John would urge, is evident from the entire course of God's dealings with the Hebrew nation, culminating in the sending of his Son.

The Gospel genre is a special kind of biography structured according to the primitive Christian kerygma, combining reports of Jesus' teaching and actions with a passion, burial and resurrection account.[160] Does the kerygma of the Fourth Gospel correspond in any meaningful way to Jesus as he was?

Not everything in the narrative is kerygmatic. Some incidental details bear no theological freight (e.g., "tenth hour" [Jn 1:39]; "there they stayed for a few days" [Jn 2:12]; "Jews do not use with Samaritans" [Jn 4:9]; "by the Sheep Gate a pool, in Hebrew called Beth-zatha" [Jn 5:2]; "a town called Ephraim—there he stayed" [Jn 11:54]). The motives that John attributes to those who engineered Jesus' crucifixion smack of psychological reality (Jn 11:47-50). The christological content of the Gospel goes beyond anything in Judaism and so meets the authenticity test of religio-historical "dissimilarity." It puzzled the author more than once before he became convinced of it (e.g., Jn 2:22; 12:16; 20:9), so by the same criterion the author's imagination is excluded as its source. Had we only the Fourth Gospel to go by, it would appear to be an account of a singular personality by someone who was won over by him. Could not the subject of the portrait have stamped his image on the portrait?[161]

In comparison with the Christ of the Synoptic Gospels—the only measure we have—the Johannine Son of God stands somewhat apart. For example, is the climactic seventh sign, the resuscitation of Lazarus still in graveclothes, believable? If so, why did the Synoptic tradition not include such a forceful piece of evidence? Did Jesus the Galilean preacher deliver anything like the extended Johannine dialogues and monologues, rich in lofty claims about the Son's ineffable origin and destiny—couched in the unmistakable literary style of the Evangelist? How much historical value can criticism recognize in this material?

As for Jesus' signs, John would have no truck with Ernst Troeltsch's (1865-

[160]David E. Aune, *The New Testament in Its Literary Environment* (LEC; Philadelphia: Westminster, 1987), pp. 17-76; R. A. Burridge, *What Are the Gospels? A Comparison with Greco-Roman Biography* (SNTSMS 70; Cambridge: Cambridge University Press, 1992).

[161]"What could have been used as a basis of such expansion or exposition must have been of such a kind as to inspire precisely to such expansion or exposition" (Anders Ekenberg, "The Fourth Gospel and the History of Jesus," *CV* 44 [2002]: 189).

1923) dictum that history by definition excludes the supernatural. Try telling a man who has personally observed not one miracle but many, on too many occasions to enumerate (Jn 20:30; 21:35), that miracles are impossible—or at least, as David Hume pled, that their probability is contrary to all human experience—and the witness will turn away and bless those who, without having seen for themselves, accept the firm testimony of those who were there (Jn 20:29). It is only a question of whether the testimony comes from people who are trustworthy. If God breathed life into Adam at the creation, and is going to raise all the dead at the end of the age, as Jesus taught (Jn 6:40; 11:24-26; cf. Mt 22:29-32), what is to hinder God from restoring an individual during this present age? Is not the attestation of his Son that the world may find in him eternal life (Jn 20:31) a sufficient reason for doing so?

The calling forth of the deceased Lazarus is by no means unique. The Synoptic Gospels attest to more than one resuscitation (Mt 9:18-19, 23-26;[162] Lk 7:11-17). Jairus's daughter fits nicely into the literary plan of the Synoptic Gospels, which gather miracle reports mainly from Galilee. Lazarus, coming shortly before Jesus' triumphal entry into Jerusalem, encapsulates John's theme of Jesus as the life. One might as well ask why others do not record the Lukan incident at Nain as why John alone notes Lazarus.[163]

Admittedly, the christological discourses in John serve up a heady fermentation. From them it is hard to extract *ipsissima verba* of Jesus with confidence.[164] On the other hand, leading ideas of the Fourth Gospel often draw out what is implicit in Synoptic nuggets. The Johannine dialogues of Jesus preserve more features of oral communication than the form critics recognized,[165] and some Johannine sayings of Jesus can be shown to meet sensible criteria of authenticity.[166] It is not so much that John has taken flight from sober facts as that

---

[162]The raising of Jairus's daughter is found in the triple tradition: besides Matthew, also in Mark 5:21-24, 35-43; Luke 8:40-42, 49-56. All agree the girl had been dead.

[163]If the Twelve consolidated the Synoptic outline at a time when Lazarus was still a marked man in the vicinity of Jerusalem (Jn 12:10-11), they may have had reason to omit mention of him, a reason that no longer obtained when John wrote in Ephesus.

[164]But see Peter W. Ensor, "The Johannine Sayings of Jesus and the Question of Authenticity," in *Challenging Perspectives on the Gospel of John* (ed. John Lierman; WUNT 2/219; Tübingen: Mohr Siebeck, 2006), pp. 14-33.

[165]Tom Thatcher, *The Riddles of Jesus in John: A Study in Tradition and Folklore* (SBLMS 53; Atlanta: Society of Biblical Literature, 2000).

[166]Peter W. Ensor, *Jesus and His "Works": The Johannine Sayings in Historical Perspective* (WUNT 2/85 Tübingen: Mohr Siebeck, 1996); Linda M. Bridges, "Aphorisms of Jesus in John: An Illustrative Look at John 4.35," *JSHJ* 9 (2011): 207-29.

he has set the kernels, now germinated and grown, into a rounded understanding of Jesus' personage.[167]

Allowing that the sayings material in John is several steps further removed
from stenography than that in the Synoptic Gospels, is this final impression in
the mind of Jesus' most intimate friend of less value for history? Historical
criticism seeks not merely to chronicle, but to explain. The quest of the historical Jesus cannot rest with establishing the tokens that Jesus left behind in
the collective memory of his followers. It wants through them to test hypotheses
about his self-consciousness, his motives, his goals; to arrive at a construal that
unites the raw data. Each Synoptic Gospel preserves Jesus' public logia in a
redactional framework that points the way to their significance; the Johannine
speeches lay out their full and plain import in the sayings themselves. That
there is a difference between the two approaches caused the History of Religions school to posit an evolutionary development in the early church's conception of Jesus, such that the founder became encrusted in an ever thicker
farrago of dogma alien to his self-understanding.[168] A reader who shares John's
perspective will think rather of a deepening of insight on the part of "the disciple whom Jesus loved." Perhaps Jesus' self-understanding found in the Johannine Christology its most kindred and probing articulation.[169] Radical

---

[167]"The author's redactional tendencies are comparable with those discernible in his handling of Old
Testament quotations, and lie in the direction, not so much of creating material 'de novo,' nor of
radically changing the original teaching of Jesus into something quite different, but rather of concentrating on its christologically significant elements, placing originally quite separate motifs
alongside one another in a mutually interpretative way, clarifying previously obscure or ambiguous
elements in the tradition, and generally re-expressing traditional sayings and motifs after his own
manner, though occasionally also preserving sayings in roughly their original form" (Ensor, *Jesus
and His "Works,"* p. 269). See also Paul N. Anderson, Felix Just and Tom Thatcher, eds., *Critical
Appraisals of Critical Views*, vol. 1 of *John, Jesus, and History* (SBLSymS 44; Atlanta: Society of Biblical Literature, 2007); idem, eds., *Aspects of Historicity in the Fourth Gospel*, vol. 2 of *John, Jesus, and
History* (SBLECL 2; Atlanta: Society of Biblical Literature, 2009).
[168]Wilhelm Bousset, *Kyrios Christos: A History of the Belief in Christ from the Beginnings of Christianity
to Irenaeus* (trans. John E. Steely; Nashville: Abingdon, 1970).
[169]Franz Mussner analyzes the Johannine *Sehweise* ("mode of seeing") as a hermeneutical fusion of
two horizons: the tradition about Jesus by a member of the apostolic "we," and the fullness of truth
into which the Paraclete was leading the church toward the end of the century (Jn 16:12-13) as it
wrestled with unforeseen christological questions generated by heretical movements (*The Historical Jesus in the Gospel of St. John* [trans. W. J. O'Hara; QD 19; New York: Herder & Herder, 1967]).
C. K. Barrett observes, "Johannine theology is not so much the imposition of alien forms and
terminology upon primitive Christian thought (though it is expressed partly in new forms and
terminology), as the spontaneous development of primitive Christian thought under the pressure
of inner necessity and the lapse of time" (*St. John*, p. 69). See also Theobald, *Herrenworte*, pp. 600-
618; Tom Thatcher, *Why John Wrote a Gospel: Jesus—Memory—History* (Louisville: Westminster
John Knox, 2006); John Painter, "Memory Holds the Key: The Transformation of Memory in the

critics from Strauss and Baur through Bousset and Bultmann supposed John to have made Jesus out to be something he was not. A criticism whose underlying philosophy is not at odds with the faith of the sources may consider that John came to see clearly who the historical Jesus was. But the latter brand of criticism will keep the Synoptic and the Johannine presentations separate when drawing conclusions about Jesus' public persona and exploring his inner mystery, respectively.

*Two-level readings of the Fourth Gospel.* In one of the most widely received monographs on John's Gospel since Bultmann's commentary, J. Louis Martyn looked at history and theology from another angle. He read the Gospel as a "two-level drama" describing Jesus in his time, but also referring to the author's ecclesiastical community at the end of the century.[170] While the healing of a man born blind belongs to Jesus' ministry (Jn 9:1-7), the threat of expulsion from the synagogue (Jn 9:22; 12:42; 16:2), Martyn suggested, may actually reflect the insertion of a curse on Jewish crypto-Christians into the synagogue liturgy. The Benediction of the Heretics (*Birkat ha-Minim*) was added by the rabbinic academy at Javneh under the leadership of Rabban Gamaliel II between A.D. 80 and 115. Supposedly, the Johannine author makes the tradition about Jesus his own by blending it with his contemporary situation.

A knotty question is whether the aspiring rabbinic movement had yet, in the final third of the first century, garnered authority in synagogues of all Palestine, much less in Asia.[171] In fact, the tense of the verb in John 9:22 (συνετέθειντο, pluperfect) makes it clear the agreement to expel Jesus' disciples was a thing of the past by the time of writing, having been limited to the synagogues of Jerusalem, where the Pharisees had some sway (Jn 9:13, 15-16). No doubt John held Jesus to have

---

Interface of History and Theology of John," in Anderson, Just and Thatcher, *Critical Appraisals*, pp. 229-45.

[170]Martyn, *History and Theology*. For a similar approach, see Wayne A. Meeks, "The Divine Agent and His Counterfeit in Philo and the Fourth Gospel," in *Aspects of Religious Propaganda in Judaism and Early Christianity* (ed. Elisabeth Schüssler Fiorenza; Notre Dame: University of Notre Dame Press, 1976), pp. 43-67; idem, "Man from Heaven." "Mirror" readings of the Fourth Gospel that ransack the document for clues to the sociology of the Johannine "community" have now reached such a pitch that even Jesus' distinctive "I am" sayings can be seen as indirect indications of the community's way of picturing its own identity. See Christian Cebulj, *Ich bin es: Studien zur Identitätsbildung im Johannesevangelium* (SBB 44; Stuttgart: Katholisches Bibelwerk, 2000).

[171]William Horbury, "The Benediction of the Minim and the Early Jewish-Christian Controversy," *JTS* 33 (1982): 19-61; Philip S. Alexander, "The 'Parting of the Ways' from the Perspective of Rabbinic Judaism," in *Jews and Christians: The Parting of the Ways, A.D. 70 to 135* (ed. James D. G. Dunn; WUNT 66; Tübingen: Mohr Siebeck, 1992), pp. 6-11; Raimo Hakola, *Identity Matters: John, the Jews and Jewishness* (NovTSup 118; Leiden: Brill, 2005), pp. 41-74.

continuing relevance, but precisely as the incomparable, unrepeatable God-man who had once laid down his life for the world and had now departed to the Father, not as a literary figure whose story can be stretched and bent for every age.[172]

In regard to the Gospel's life setting, the gradual break between synagogue and church was but one of many factors, and hardly the chief one, in generating the Gospel. Andreas Köstenberger's alternative hypothesis that John wrote in the wake of the destruction of the second temple, presenting Jesus "without peer or rival as the new tabernacle, the new temple, and the new center of worship," unifies a wider band of data.[173] But Köstenberger's hypothesis likewise captures only a part of the picture of Jesus as "Savior of the world" (Jn 4:42). As we noted above, John wrote to advertize Jesus Christ. This subject determines the presentation. John's rhetorical situation can illumine at most secondary accents.

*Superimposition of postresurrection glory onto the earthly ministry?* There is little promise in the notion, constantly repeated in secondary literature, that John portrays Jesus from a standpoint after Easter, if that means that John retrojects Jesus' later glory onto his whole career. This has even been called "the Johannine way of seeing."[174] But John takes pains not to superimpose what came later on what happened earlier. The narrator distinguishes between hazy and clear understanding on the part of Jesus' disciples, before and after his glorification (Jn 2:22; 7:39; 20:9).[175] As in the Synoptic Gospels, the title "Christ" (Μεσσίας or Χριστός) is applied to Jesus by others but is not heard from his own lips during his ministry (except once, in prayer, on the brink of his departure [Jn 17:3]); instead, Jesus usually calls himself either "the Son of Man" (13×), a term absent from the developed Christology of the Johannine Epistles and of the Apocalypse,[176] or "the Son (of God)" (14× [cf. Mt 21:37-38]), a cor-

---

[172]Tobias Hägerland, "John's Gospel: A Two-Level Drama?" *JSNT* 25 (2003): 309-22; Edward W. Klink, "Expulsion from the Synagogue? Rethinking a Johannine Anachronism," *TynBul* 59 (2008): 99-118.

[173]Andreas Köstenberger, "The Destruction of the Second Temple and the Composition of the Fourth Gospel," in *Challenging Perspectives on the Gospel of John* (ed. John Lierman; WUNT 2/219; Tübingen: Mohr Siebeck, 2006), pp. 69-108. Köstenberger develops this hypothesis further in *Theology*, pp. 53-72.

[174]Mussner, *Historical Jesus.*

[175]In the sense that John invites readers to watch Jesus' disciples (including himself during the ministry) struggle toward full understanding, yes, he writes from a postresurrection point of view. See David W. Wead, *The Literary Devices in John's Gospel* (TD 4; Basel: Friedrich Reinhardt Kommissionsverlag, 1970), pp. 1-11.

[176]"As a son of man" occurs in Apocalypse 1:13; 14:14 as a nontitular description of a figure in a vision (cf. Dan 7:13).

ollary of the Synoptic address to his "Father."[177] It is hard to dredge up a single instance of indiscriminate fusion of periods. To be sure, the Johannine Jesus is, prior to his glorification, a union of the divine and the human, the heavenly and the earthly, the above and the below, but not of a former and a latter on the plane of chronology.

**Conclusion.** According to John, then, to know Jesus of Nazareth as he was is to encounter God's supreme self-communication. To come to grips with the history is to be overwhelmed by the reality. John's special material, which is most of it, parallels the Synoptic accounts in kind. His meditative way of conveying the words of Jesus magnifies, clarifies and intensifies the tendency of the Synoptic portrayal of Jesus without incrementing its substance. Far from falsifying history in the interest of theology, John has an eye for small incidentals, not previously captured by other Evangelists, that confirm the same picture of the God-man.

## READERS OF THE FOURTH GOSPEL

John's memories of Jesus went back to Palestine, but his readers lived in western Asia. Until A.D. 70 John ministered in Jerusalem, where the team of leaders included Peter, James the Lord's brother and other apostles (Acts 3–4; 8:14; Gal 2:9). Presumably, John was not free to travel much while caring for Jesus' aging mother (Jn 19:26-27). Upon moving to Ephesus, he took his place in a church that had been founded by Paul some two decades earlier (Acts 19), and that may have claimed Timothy as its first resident bishop (Eusebius, *Hist. eccl.* 3.7.5). When a clutch of doctrinal innovators made their exit, they parted from an ecclesiastical network known for orthodoxy (Apoc 2:2, 6) that stood consciously in the apostolic tradition (1 Jn 2:24; 2 Jn 9).

John addressed himself to an audience made up mostly of Gentiles. Even in the Diaspora, Jews needed no explanation of terms such as "rabbi" or "messiah" (Jn 1:38, 41), though they may have appreciated help with *kepha* (Jn 1:42) or "Siloam" (Jn 9:7); nor were they unaware of the Jewish rites of purification (Jn 2:6), nor were they the ones to whom John would have found it necessary to point out that Passover and Tabernacles were Jewish feasts (Jn 2:13; 6:4; 7:2; 11:55), or that Jews regarded Samaritans as impure (Jn 4:9), or that all Jews came together in the temple (Jn 18:20), or what were the Jewish burial customs (Jn

---

[177]Richard Bauckham, "Messianism According to the Gospel of John," in *Challenging Perspectives on the Gospel of John* (ed. John Lierman; WUNT 2/219; Tübingen: Mohr Siebeck, 2006), pp. 34-68.

19:40). Indeed, John's frequent designation of his compatriots as "the Jews" (68×) is paralleled only in the book of Acts (69×), where the proclamation of Christ to the Gentile world is thematic. John penned his Gospel among Gentiles, who more readily thought of the Pharisees as Jewish than as non-Sadducean or non-Essene.

Since one could not lean on a marketing industry to bring a book to the general public, John's channels of distribution ran through personal contacts and travelers. He wrote for people in the churches that he served, drawing upon material that he had presented orally. He recorded his memoirs to edify fellow believers and to provide them with material that they too could use for evangelistic and apologetic witness. To conclude that John had in his purview primarily believers, but also mission fields beyond them, one need only canvass the contents of the Gospel. By Jesus' testimony to the world (Jn 1–12) faith can be strengthened as well as awakened; conversely, inquirers into Christianity may take an interest in Jesus' special care for his own followers (Jn 13–17). The notorious textual crux in John 20:31, whether the Gospel is meant to awaken faith (ἵνα πιστεύσητε, aorist tense) or to confirm it (ἵνα πιστεύητε, present tense), cannot and need not be decided, as the Gospel serves both purposes.[178]

John was a churchman of catholic breadth. Although the facts about John are sketchy, the outline that they trace is of a career at the very center of the emerging church catholic for the duration of the first century.[179] Yet many scholars today suppose the author(s) of the Johannine corpus played a key role in a sectarian "Johannine community" that was at increasing odds with the rest of the church.[180] How likely is this alternative construct?

Given the vital grid of communications among churches toward the end of the first century, Ephesus being a hub,[181] given John's congenial relations with

---

[178]To muddy the question, a complexive and categorical aorist would differ little in force from a timeless present. On the problem, see D. A. Carson, "Syntactical and Text-Critical Observations on John 20:30-31: One More Round on the Purpose of the Fourth Gospel," *JBL* 124 (2005): 693-714.

[179]See also the much fuller review of John's career toward the beginning of chapter nine below.

[180]For example, Ernst Käsemann, *The Testament of Jesus: A Study of the Gospel of John in the Light of Chapter 17* (trans. Gerhard Krodel; Philadelphia: Fortress, 1968), chaps. 3-4; Meeks, "Man from Heaven"; Segovia, *Love Relationships*; Rensberger, *Johannine Faith*, pp. 135-52. The consensus view is described in Smith, "Johannine Christianity." Note also the excursus on theories of Johannine community history by Francis J. Moloney in Brown, *Introduction to the Gospel of John*, pp. 69-85. Nearer the target is Edward W. Klink (*The Sheep of the Fold: The Audience and Origin of the Gospel of John* [SNTSMS 141; Cambridge: Cambridge University Press, 2007]), who applies Bauckham's general thesis to the Gospel of John.

[181]Bauckham, *Gospels*, esp. pp. 9-70. Bauckham's thesis is further developed in Edward W. Klink, ed.,

many local churches in Asia (Apoc 1–3)[182] and with traveling Christian companions (3 Jn 3, 5-8),[183] given the encyclopedic nature of John's synthesis of earlier Christian traditions oriented to the worldwide Christian community,[184] and given John's expressed convictions about the one (Jn 17:11-26), holy ("saints" [e.g., Apoc 5:8; 8:3-4; 11:2, 18]), catholic (Jn 10:16; Apoc 7:9-12) and apostolic (1 Jn 2:24; 2 Jn 9; Apoc 21:14) church, is it very plausible that John wrote for a sectarian "Johannine community" in retreat from the world and possibly sequestered from the rest of the church?

On the working assumption that John the son of Zebedee, a Palestinian Jew who had been among Jesus' Twelve, wrote the books ascribed to him in the New Testament canon while he was serving as apostolic superintendent of Gentile churches in the metropolitan area of Ephesus toward the end of his life and of the first century, we turn to the task of delineating John's theology of persons.

---

*The Audience of the Gospels: The Origin and Function of the Gospels in Early Christianity* (LNTS 353; London: T & T Clark, 2010).

[182]See also Clement of Alexandria, *Quis div.* 42 (= Eusebius, *Hist. eccl.* 3.23.6).

[183]Among associates who claimed to be Christians, John denounced only heretics of the most crass opinions (1 Jn 2:18-19, 22-23; 4:1, 3) and Diotrephes, who took up an antagonistic stance toward his authority (3 Jn 9-10).

[184]Thomas L. Brodie, *The Quest for the Origin of John's Gospel: A Source-Oriented Approach* (New York: Oxford University Press, 1993), esp. pp. 144-52.

# THE REVELATION OF GOD
# (THE FATHER)

GOD IS THE PERSON FROM WHOM ALL REALITY COMES and to whom it goes, both in the whole Bible and in John's thought. At the center of the Johannine theology is God the Father, specifically the revelation of God's love for the world by sending his Son.

This statement refines certain emphases in New Testament scholarship. Until recently, many leading New Testament scholars judged the preeminent figure in Johannine thought to be Jesus Christ. Few addressed the place of the Father. It went without saying that John inherited his concept of God from the Hebrew Scriptures. He could hardly bypass speaking of God; theism is the basis of the biblical worldview. But his real interest was to set forth God's Son. Now it is increasingly recognized that however accurate it may be to describe John's theology as christocentric, it is, at its deepest level, theocentric.[1]

---

[1]"An essential point about the theology of the Fourth Gospel is that the centre of the picture is not Jesus but the Father. The Fourth Gospel and First Epistle are the great theocentric tracts of the New Testament" (E. M. Sidebottom, *The Christ of the Fourth Gospel in the Light of First-Century Thought* [London: SPCK, 1961], p. 194). "The witness of Jesus is to the Father, and to himself only as the Way to the Father" (Edwin Kenneth Lee, *The Religious Thought of St. John* [London: SPCK, 1962], p. 33). See also George B. Stevens, *The Johannine Theology: A Study of the Doctrinal Contents of the Gospels and Epistles of the Apostle John* (New York: Scribner, 1894), pp. 46-73; Lee, *Religious Thought*, pp. 3-55; W. Robert Cook, *The Theology of John* (Chicago: Moody, 1979), pp. 40-45; C. K. Barrett, "Christocentric or Theocentric? Observations on the Theological Method of the Fourth Gospel," in *Essays on John* (Philadelphia: Westminster, 1982), pp. 1-18; Paul W. Meyer, "'The Father': The Presentation of God in the Fourth Gospel," in *Exploring the Gospel of John: In Honor of D. Moody Smith* (ed. R. Alan Culpepper and C. Clifton Black; Louisville: Westminster John Knox, 1996), pp. 255-73; Birger Olsson, "*Deus Semper Maior?* On God in the Johannine Writings," in *New Readings in John: Literary and Theological Perspectives; Essays from the Scandinavian Conference on the Fourth Gospel in Aarhus 1997* (ed. Johannes Nissen and Siegfried Pedersen; Sheffield: Sheffield Academic Press, 1999), pp. 143-71; Adele Reinhartz, ed., *God the Father in the Gospel of John* (Semeia 85; Atlanta: Society of Biblical

For example, the prologue to the Fourth Gospel highlights the incarnation of the creative divine Logos in Jesus. To speak of Christ as God's Logos sets Christ in the limelight, thus also implying that it is of God that he is the supreme self-revelation. The prologue leads up to the statement that the only-begotten God has explained God (Jn 1:18). Again, the purpose of the Gospel is to persuade readers to confess Jesus as the Christ, the Son of God (Jn 20:31). But that statement raises tacit questions: Who appointed Christ as the means to life? And to whom is such life ordered? Earlier in the Gospel Jesus Christ himself says that the Father sent him, and later that eternal life consists in knowing the only God (Jn 17:3).

An outstanding proponent of Christocentrism was Rudolf Bultmann. The part of Bultmann's *Theology of the New Testament* that covers the Johannine literature has, after an historical introduction, sections on several important themes and concepts, but a chapter or major section on God the Father is lacking.[2] According to Bultmann, the Old Testament has tenuous relevance for the New Testament.[3] He concedes that Jesus preached about the reign of

---

Literature, 1999); Marianne Meye Thompson, *The God of the Gospel of John* (Grand Rapids: Eerdmans, 2001), pp. 1-15; Daniel Rathnakara Sadananda, *The Johannine Exegesis of God: An Exploration Into the Johannine Understanding of God* (BZNW 121; Berlin: de Gruyter, 2004); Mark W. G. Stibbe, "Telling the Father's Story: The Gospel of John as Narrative Theology," in *Challenging Perspectives on the Gospel of John* (ed. John Lierman; WUNT 2/219; Tübingen: Mohr Siebeck, 2006), pp. 170-93; Edith Zingg, *Das Reden von Gott als "Vater" im Johannesevangelium* (HBS 48; Freiburg: Herder, 2006). More than one commentator has observed a shift from a focus on Christ in John's Gospel to the attribution of things such as light and commandments to God in the Epistles. See Raymond E. Brown, *The Epistles of John: Translated, with Introduction, Commentary, and Notes* (AB 30; Garden City, NY: Doubleday, 1982), p. 26; Judith Lieu, *The Second and Third Epistles of John: History and Background* (ed. John Kenneth Riches; SNTW; Edinburgh: T & T Clark, 1986), pp. 198-216. On the theocentricity of 1 John, see Judith Lieu, *The Theology of the Johannine Epistles* (NTT; Cambridge: University Press, 1991), pp. 78-79, 103; C. Clifton Black, "Short Shrift Made Once More," *ThTo* 57 (2000): 386-94. On the Apocalypse, see Carol J. Rotz and Jan A. du Rand, "The One Who Sits on the Throne: Towards a Theory of Theocentric Characterisation According to the Apocalypse of John," *Neot* 33 (1999): 91-111; Thomas Söding, "Gott und das Lamm: Theozentrik und Christologie in der Johannesapokalypse," in *Theologie als Vision: Studien zur Johannes-Offenbarung* (ed. Knut Backhaus; SBS 191; Stuttgart: Katholisches Bibelwerk, 2001), pp. 77-120.

[2]An independent essay by Bultmann on talking about God does little to redress this lack, as it denies that God is an object about which language can assert anything (Rudolf Bultmann, "What Does It Mean to Speak of God?" in *Faith and Understanding* [ed. Robert W. Funk; trans. Louise Pettibone Smith; New York: Harper & Row, 1969], pp. 53-65).

[3]"Rudolf Bultmann presented the theology of the Fourth Gospel without dealing with the attitude to the OT and the history of salvation in the old covenant" (Nils Alstrup Dahl, "The Johannine Church and History," in *Current Issues in New Testament Interpretation: Essays in Honor of Otto A. Piper* [ed. William Klassen and Graydon F. Snyder; PL; London: SCM Press, 1962], p. 124). For a vigorous reaffirmation of the importance of salvation history for John over against Bultmann's denial, see Oscar Cullmann, "L'Évangile johannique et l'histoire du salut," *NTS* 11 (1965): 111-22. "It must be

God, not about his own person. But he regards Jesus' message as only "a presupposition for the theology of the New Testament rather than a part of that theology itself."[4] Not until Jesus, the original "proclaimer," became the theme of the apostles' message, the one "proclaimed" by them, did Christian faith, and thus New Testament theology proper, emerge.[5] This shift came to fruition in the Fourth Gospel, where Jesus fills the stage. Curiously, Jesus insists only on the formal point "that" he reveals God.

> He speaks only of his own person as the Revealer whom God has sent. . . . He
> does not communicate anything, but calls men to himself. . . . All the words of
> Jesus in John are assertions about himself and no definite complex of ideas can
> be stated as their content and claimed to be the 'teaching' of Jesus. . . . Jesus as
> the Revealer of God reveals nothing but that he is the Revealer. . . . John, that is,
> in his Gospel presents only the fact (*das Dass*) of the Revelation without de-
> scribing its content (*ihr Was*).[6]

That God is, however, a theme for John is evident from the statistical occurrence of key terms.

Table 2.1

|            | ὁ θεός | ὁ πατήρ | ὁ κύριος | ὁ οὐρανός | δεῖ |
|------------|--------|---------|----------|-----------|-----|
|            | "God" | "the Father" | "the Lord" | "heaven" | "it is necessary" |
|            | reference to God | reference to God | reference to God | symbol of God | idiom of God's fixed will |
| **Gospel** | 85× | 121× | 4× | 18× | 7× |
| **Epistles** | 67× | 16× | 0× | 0× | 0× |
| **Apocalypse** | 97× | 5× | 14× | 40× | 8× |

Bultmann's illustrious career ended in the middle of the twentieth century,[7] just as some of the next generation of scholars began to observe that God had

---

admitted that Bultmann was not at his best when exploring the scriptural background to the Fourth Gospel. His statement: 'Proof from prophecy plays a scanty role [in the Gospel]' is an unfortunate one" (Anthony Tyrrell Hanson, *The Prophetic Gospel: A Study of John and the Old Testament* [SEBS; Edinburgh: T & T Clark, 1991], p. 248). An international symposium of leading scholars evaluated Bultmann's peculiar denial of the relevance of the Old Testament for Christian theology: Bernhard W. Anderson, ed., *The Old Testament and Christian Faith* (New York: Harper & Row, 1963).

[4]Rudolf Bultmann, *Theology of the New Testament* (trans. Kendrick Grobel; 2 vols.; New York: Scribner, 1951–1955), 1:3.

[5]Ibid., 1:33.

[6]Ibid., 2:4, 41, 63, 66.

[7]Bultmann retired in 1951 and died in 1976.

been "the neglected factor in New Testament theology."[8] Their students in turn launched a wide-ranging inquiry into the relationship between Jewish monotheism and the Christology of the early church.[9] Perhaps Bultmann did not fully weigh the possibility that what he perceived as a lack of content in the message of the Johannine Christ might actually point to the ultimacy of the God who sent him. The Johannine Jesus' transparency corresponds to Jesus' proclamation of God's kingdom in the Synoptic Gospels. Moreover, what specifically Jesus revealed about God is not to be sought in Jesus' teaching alone. For John, God becomes manifest in Jesus' acts, especially in the climactic events at the end of his ministry.[10]

"God is light and in him is no darkness at all." This sentence at the outset of 1 John encapsulates "the message we have heard from him [the incarnate life] and proclaim to you" (1 Jn 1:5), providing a significant commentary on the Fourth Gospel. It points to God as the subject of Jesus' ministry. Light symbolizes superlative truth, righteousness and love—the three values woven together in the letter that follows. Toward the end comes a summary: "The Son of God has come and has given us understanding, to know him who is true" (1 Jn 5:20). According to John, the Son of God came to draw people not to himself ultimately, but to his Father. He wanted us to see that God is wonderful beyond imagining, and to respond with love to God's love.

---

[8]Nils Alstrup Dahl, "The Neglected Factor in New Testament Theology," *Reflection* 73 (1975): 5-8; Leander E. Keck, "Toward the Renewal of New Testament Theology," *NTS* 32 (1986): 362-77.
[9]James D. G. Dunn, "Was Christianity a Monotheistic Faith from the Beginning?" *SJT* 35 (1982): 303-36; Paul A. Rainbow, "Monotheism and Christology in I Corinthians 8.4-6" (D.Phil. thesis; University of Oxford, 1987); Larry W. Hurtado, *One God, One Lord: Early Christian Devotion and Ancient Jewish Monotheism* (Philadelphia: Fortress, 1988); idem, *Lord Jesus Christ: Devotion to Jesus in Earliest Christianity* (Grand Rapids: Eerdmans, 2003); idem, *How on Earth Did Jesus Become a God? Historical Questions About Earliest Devotion to Jesus* (Grand Rapids: Eerdmans, 2005); idem, *God in New Testament Theology* (LBT; Nashville: Abingdon, 2010); N. T. Wright, "Monotheism, Christology and Ethics: 1 Corinthians 8," in *The Climax of the Covenant: Christ and the Law in Pauline Theology* (Minneapolis: Fortress, 1992), pp. 120-36; idem, *The New Testament and the People of God* (COQG 1; Minneapolis: Fortress, 1992), chap. 9; Richard Bauckham, *God Crucified: Monotheism and Christology in the New Testament* (Grand Rapids: Eerdmans, 1998); idem, "Monotheism and Christology in the Gospel of John," in *Contours of Christology in the New Testament* (ed. Richard N. Longenecker; MNTS; Grand Rapids: Eerdmans, 2005), pp. 148-66; Carey C. Newman, James R. Davila and Gladys S. Lewis, eds., *The Jewish Roots of Christological Monotheism: Papers from the St. Andrews Conference on the Historical Origins of the Worship of Jesus* (JSJSup 63; Leiden: Brill, 1999); Loren T. Stuckenbruck and Wendy E. S. North, eds., *Early Jewish and Christian Monotheism* (JSNTSup 263; London: T & T Clark, 2004).
[10]"The story of the earthly life of the Son is the medium through which the Father is revealed" (W. F. Howard, *Christianity According to St. John* [London: Duckworth, 1943], p. 58).

## PROPOSITIONS ABOUT GOD

John presents God through statements rooted in prior revelation, and through narratives of God's latest deeds. It never occurs to John to take up the theoretical problem of the possibility of God's existence, or to set out to prove it, in abstraction from what God himself has said and done. For John (as for the other biblical authors), the inference is sufficient: God has revealed himself, therefore he is.

From the dawn of time God has revealed himself to human beings using human words, by sending messengers to speak "the word(s) of God" recorded in the Scriptures.[11] "The prophets" have been many down through history.[12] With Jews of the first century, to whom Jesus said, "You search the scriptures, because you think that in them you have eternal life" (Jn 5:39), John shares the highest possible view of the divine authorship and verbal inviolability of the enscripturated oracles. "Scripture cannot be broken," says Jesus (Jn 10:35). One dare not tamper with prophetic words (Apoc 22:18-19).[13] That what Scripture says must be true or come to fulfillment is axiomatic.[14] John rarely quotes Scripture verbatim.[15] He prefers to paraphrase, allude to or conflate passages.[16]

---

[11]Jn 3:34; 5:38; 8:47; 10:35; 17:6, 14, 17; 1 Jn 1:10; 2:7, 14; Apoc 1:2, 9; 6:9; 17:17; 19:9, 13; 20:4.

[12]Jn 1:45; 6:45; 8:52-53; Apoc 10:7; 11:18; 16:6; 18:20, 24; 22:6, 9.

[13]G. K. Beale, "Can the Bible Be Completely Inspired by God and Yet Still Contain Errors? A Response to Some Recent 'Evangelical' Proposals," *WTJ* 73 (2011): 1-22.

[14]Jn 2:22; 7:38, 42; 13:18; 17:12; 19:24, 28, 36, 37; 20:9.

[15]From the Johannine books, the editors of the United Bible Societies edition of the Greek New Testament give a list of sixteen citations (UBS⁴, p. 889), all in the Gospel (Jn 1:23; 2:17; 6:31, 45; 10:34; 12:13, 15, 38, 40; 13:18; 15:25; 19:24, 36, 37). To these one may add John 7:38, 42; 12:34; 17:12; 19:28 on the strength of the introductory formulae, though the wording of the citations is free. Material from the Gospel is laid out in Hans Hübner, *Evangelium secundum Iohannem*, vol. 1.2 of *Vetus Testamentum in Novo* (Göttingen: Vandenhoeck & Ruprecht, 2003).

[16]General studies of the use of Scripture in John include Edwin D. Freed, *Old Testament Quotations in the Gospel of John* (NovTSup 11; Leiden: Brill, 1965); Günter Reim, *Studien zum alttestamentlichen Hintergrund des Johannesevangeliums* (SNTSMS 22; Cambridge: Cambridge University Press, 1974); Peder Borgen, "John's Use of the Old Testament, and the Problem of Sources and Traditions," in *Philo, John and Paul: New Perspectives on Judaism and Early Christianity* (BJS 131; Atlanta: Scholars Press, 1987), pp. 145-57; D. A. Carson, "John and the Johannine Epistles," in *It Is Written: Scripture Citing Scripture; Essays in Honour of Barnabas Lindars* (ed. D. A. Carson and H. G. M. Williamson; Cambridge: Cambridge University Press, 1988), pp. 245-64; Martin Hengel, "Die Schriftauslegung des 4. Evangeliums auf dem Hintergrund der urchristlichen Exegese," *JBTh* 4 (1989): 249-88; Hanson, *Prophetic Gospel*; Bruce G. Schuchard, *Scripture Within Scripture: The Interrelationship of Form and Function in the Explicit Old Testament Citations in the Gospel of John* (SBLDS 133; Atlanta: Scholars Press, 1992); Andreas Obermann, *Die christologische Erfüllung der Schrift im Johannesevangelium: Eine Untersuchung zur johanneischen Hermeneutik anhand der Schriftzitate* (WUNT 2/83; Tübingen: Mohr Siebeck, 1996); Claus Westermann, *The Gospel of John in the Light of the Old Testament* (trans. Siegfried S. Schatzmann; Peabody, MA: Hendrickson, 1998); Kirsten Nielsen, "Old Testament Im-

But "the importance of the OT as the primary source for Johannine theology cannot be overstated."[17]

Several lapidary propositions about God stand out in the Johannine corpus: God is spirit (Jn 4:24), God is light (1 Jn 1:5), God is the Alpha and the Omega (Apoc 1:8), and God is love (1 Jn 4:8, 16). It will be convenient to organize what John has to say about God around these statements.

*God is Spirit.* "God is spirit" (Jn 4:24). In the original languages of the Bible the word for "spirit" is "wind" or "breath" (Heb. *rûaḥ*, Gk. *pneuma*). The ancient mind associated the blowing of wind with life: "It is the spirit that gives life . . . the words that I have spoken . . . are spirit and life" (Jn 6:63). The invisible God is living, personal energy. In John 4 the Samaritan woman has asked Jesus whether the place to worship is on Mount Gerizim or in Jerusalem. By calling God "spirit," Jesus emphasizes that God is not confined to either location.[18] This will be the case even if "spirit and truth" in this eschatological context ("the hour is coming, and now is" [Jn 4:23]) also connotes the pouring out of the Holy Spirit to enable authentic worship in the last days.

Nowhere does John define life. He assumes that his readers know of life and death from experience. What is distinctive of God is that he "has life in himself" (Jn 5:26). In so simple a phrase John points to the mind-boggling datum that God depends on no source, support, cause or reason external to himself; that in him life simply is, self-existent, self-sufficient, absolute; that all other modes of life derive from his, are possible because the divine life is their ground; that God in himself is an inexhaustible well of life.[19] In the same vein, God is "he

---

agery in John," in Nissen and Pedersen, *New Readings in John*, pp. 66-82; J.-J. Müller, "Les citations de l'Écriture dans le quatrième Évangile," *FoiVie* 100 (2001): 41-57; J. Kevin Newman, "Certain Old Testament Parallels in St John's Gospel," *DRev* 121 (2003): 211-24; Francis J. Moloney, "The Gospel of John as Scripture," *CBQ* 67 (2005): 454-68. The use of the Old Testament in the Apocalypse is complex and has attracted many studies: Steven Moyise, *The Old Testament in the Book of Revelation* (JSNTSup 115; Sheffield: Sheffield Academic Press, 1995); G. K. Beale, *John's Use of the Old Testament in Revelation* (JSNTSup 166; Sheffield: Sheffield Academic Press, 1998); Steven Moyise, "The Old Testament in the New: A Reply to Greg Beale," *IBS* 21 (1999): 54-58; Paul B. Decock, "The Scriptures in the Book of Revelation," *Neot* 33 (1999): 373-410; Steven Moyise, "Does the Author of Revelation Misappropriate the Scriptures?" *AUSS* 40 (2002): 3-21; idem, "Intertextuality and the Use of Scripture in the Book of Revelation," *Scriptura* 84 (2003): 391-401; idem, "Singing the Song of Moses and the Lamb: John's Dialogical Use of Scripture," *AUSS* 42 (2004): 347-60.

[17]Andreas J. Köstenberger, *A Theology of John's Gospel and Letters: The Word, the Christ, the Son of God* (BTNT; Grand Rapids: Zondervan, 2009), p. 310.

[18]So, rightly, Stevens, *Johannine Theology*, pp. 46-52.

[19]Cook, *Theology of John*, p. 42. In contrast, a human being is "lent" (δεδανεισμένος) spirit; therefore people cannot pass on life to the things that they make (Wis 15:16-17). See Urban C. von Wahlde, "He Has Given to the Son to Have Life in Himself (John 5,26)," *Bib* 85 (2004): 409-12.

who is" (ὁ ὤν [Apoc 1:4, 8]). This phrase is identical to that used in the Septuagint at Exodus 3:14 to translate God's special name, "I am who I am"
(אֶהְיֶה אֲשֶׁר אֶהְיֶה). In the Old Testament story Moses asks God to declare his
name. In the ancient Near East a name was thought to signify the inner nature
of its subject. God's reply is that he is who he is: a wonder defined only by reference to himself and intelligible only to himself. God alone can grasp who
God is. Implied are the givenness of God's existence, his untrammelled freedom
to do as he wills, and, in the context of the exodus, his immutable faithfulness
to his covenant promises. Therefore he is the one "who lives for ever and ever"
(Apoc 4:9-10; 10:6; 15:7), "the living God" (Apoc 7:2).

The refrain "No one has ever seen God" (Jn 1:18; cf. 5:37; 6:46; 1 Jn 4:12, 20)
is the backdrop to the Johannine theology. It lies with God to reveal of himself
to his creatures, for they, being finite and fallen, cannot search him out. No one
born on earth has ascended to heaven (Jn 3:13). These negatives are not meant
to deny that select Israelites were vouchsafed visions of the celestial glory (e.g.,
Ex 24:11; Num 12:8; 1 Kings 22:19; Is 6:1; Ezek 1). John knew that[20] and personally had such an experience (Apoc 4–5). Yet when it comes to depicting
God, John's bare brush strokes in Apocalypse 4 show a studied avoidance of any
feature descriptive of God's person.[21] Side by side with the visionary motif in
the Hebrew Scriptures is another, equally ancient, to the effect that no mortal
can encounter God and live (e.g., Gen 32:30; Ex 33:20; Deut 4:33; Judg 6:22-23;
13:22; Is 6:5). What the few have seen are representations of aspects of the divine
under worldly analogies, not the very essence of deity.

What God is, is a marvel that human language, suited to created things,
cannot convey (Gen 32:29; Ex 3:13-14; Judg 13:17-18). It takes another who is
infinite to plumb the abyss of infinity. Only the Son of God, who is what God
is and lies in the Father's "bosom,"[22] knows him and can speak of him (Jn 1:18;
3:13; 6:46).[23] Unlike the Son, who receives the Father's love and gift of the Spirit
without measure (Jn 3:34), those whom he redeems can receive only "of" (ἐκ)
the riches of the Spirit (1 Jn 4:13). Behind that small preposition looms a

---

[20]Even if he reads the vision of God in Isaiah 6 as a Christophany (Jn 12:38-41)—unless the "glory"
that Isaiah "saw" was that of God's servant in Is 52:13; 53:10-12.

[21]The Greek underlying the phrase "one seated on the throne" (Apoc 4:2 RSV) has only an anarthrous
participle (καθήμενος), putting emphasis on the activity of sitting, not on the one who sits.

[22]The Greek word κόλπος can also have the sense "lap," inviting comparison with the rabbinic picture
of the Torah resting on God's lap before the creation of the world. See Otfried Hofius, "'Der in des
Vaters Schoß ist' Joh 1,18," ZNW 80 (1989): 163-71.

[23]Thompson, God of the Gospel, pp. 101-43.

boundless transcendence. Yet John, living at the dawn of the eschatological era, sees tokens of the veil lifting: God appeared in Jesus (Jn 1:14; 14:7-9),[24] comes to the believing community in the Spirit-Paraclete (Jn 14:16-19), and shows up in their love for one another (1 Jn 4:12). In the renewed creation the taboos will fall away, and God will make himself available to enjoy face to face (1 Jn 3:2; Apoc 22:4).[25]

God subsists eternally beyond space and time. Before he founded the world he was there (Jn 1:1-2; 17:5, 24). Although all the references to "eternal life" in the Gospel and in the First Epistle highlight God's gift of it to human beings, God possesses it to give to others, and so is eternal himself. This presupposition becomes apparent in a few places where God (or the Father) and eternal life are mentioned in direct juxtaposition (Jn 17:3; 1 Jn 1:2; 5:20). John can designate God as the one "who is and who was and who is to come" (Apoc 1:4, 8; 4:8; cf. 11:17; 16:5).

***God is light.*** Besides spirit or life, another key symbol of the divine in John's writings, as in all the major religions, is light. Life and light are related. As in nature the sun powers crop growth and illumines daily activities (Jn 11:9-10), so the divine light energizes life, as we see in the phrase "the light of life" (Jn 8:12). Surrounding the heavenly throne are flashes of gems—jasper (green) and carnelian (red)—and an emerald rainbow (transparent or yellowish green) (Apoc 4:3). This glory will illumine the city of God in the new creation (Apoc 21:23; 22:5). Applied to God in the Johannine writings, however, light points above all to God's goodness. The sentence "God is light and in him is no [οὐκ ἔστιν] darkness at all [σκοτία . . . οὐδεμία]" (1 Jn 1:5) uses a double negative to disavow any shadow of evil in his character. This fact has a bearing on human behavior in a paragraph enjoining that only if we walk in the light and refrain from sin can we have fellowship with him (1 Jn 1:6–2:6). For he testifies of humans that they have sin (1 Jn 1:10), and, as the man whose eyes Jesus has opened knows, God does not listen to sinners but only to those who worship him and do his will (Jn 9:31).[26]

An arresting turn of phrase occurs where John, having just stated that God "is" light (1 Jn 1:5), goes on to describe God as being "in" the light, the model for

---

[24]Erich Zenger, "Gott hat niemand je geschaut (Joh 1,18): Die christliche Gottesrede im Angesicht des Judentums," *BK* 65 (2010): 87-93.

[25]Thus the Augustinian theme of the *visio Dei* stems from John, though there are also parallels in pagan literature and Philo. See Lee, *Religious Thought*, pp. 128-56.

[26]On God as light, see further ibid., pp. 32-38.

our walking in the light (1 Jn 1:7). Are God and light the same thing, or does the light shine on God from above? John seems to distinguish, while assuming the unity of, what God is and what he does, giving priority to the former. God's character shapes his will, not vice versa; John is no voluntarist. "Shall not the Judge of all the earth do right?" (Gen 18:25). "You are great and do wondrous things" (Ps 86:10). "You are good and do good" (Ps 119:68). As human activity must conform to God's commandments (1 Jn 2:3-4), so God is always bathed in his own light. His actions flow from his perfect being.

"God is true" (Jn 3:33; cf. 8:26). This statement stands side by side with affirmations that God's sent one corresponds exactly to God. God is dependable in having sent the Son as his envoy; what Jesus says and does is precisely what God means to reveal of himself. The Hebrew אֱמֶת, often translated "truth," has the connotation, when describing a person, of reliability, continuance, fidelity, and shades over into faithfulness and righteousness. "If we confess our sins, he is faithful [πιστός] and just [δίκαιος] to forgive us our sins" (1 Jn 1:9). We may fully expect God to follow through in doing what he has said he will do for us. "He is righteous [δίκαιος]" (1 Jn 2:29) and so we must abide in Christ lest we be ashamed and shrink from his presence at his coming (cf. Jn 17:25). God's promises are "trustworthy [πιστός = faithful] and true," a rock on which to stand in the present age of deception (Apoc 21:5; 22:6).

"Holy, holy, holy" chant the cherubim who are nearest God's presence, day and night (Apoc 4:8). Holiness is the sum of excellences that set God apart from all contingent reality. His beauty attracts, yet he remains unapproachable, even as bolts of lightning, rumblings, thunder and blazing fire resist domestication while they fascinate (Apoc 4:5). Who will not be struck with fear and glorify his name once he manifests himself (Apoc 15:4)?

**God is the Alpha and the Omega.** "Alpha" and "omega" are the first and last letters of the Greek alphabet. Of all things God is the Alpha and the Omega, the beginning and the end (Apoc 1:8; 21:6). Back of these statements are the claims of Yahweh against false gods of polytheism in the latter part of Isaiah: "I am the first and I am the last" (Is 44:6; cf. 41:4; 43:10; 48:12).

God's acts comprise and direct the whole of history from the creation to the consummation.[27] His first deed was to create the world. The opening phrase of the Fourth Gospel, "In the beginning," takes readers back to Genesis 1:1: "In the

---

[27]Jean Calloud, "Je suis l'alpha et l'oméga: L'Apocalypse à la lettre," *SB* 128 (2007): 23-38.

beginning God created the heavens and the earth." For the Hebrew ברא ("create") John uses the Greek κτίζω; God created "all things" (Apoc 4:11), including heaven, the earth, the sea and the things in them (Apoc 10:6). Related words are κτίσις ("creation" [Apoc 3:14]) and κτίσμα ("creature" [Apoc 5:13]). God is "he who made" (ὁ ποιήσας) these things (Apoc 14:7) and will make them new (Apoc 21:5). In keeping with the Hebrew Scriptures and the Jewish understanding of them, God as creator acted alone, without any helper, assistant or servant, whether subordinately divine or angelic: "I am the LORD, who made all things, who stretched out the heavens alone, who spread out the earth— Who was with me?" (Is 44:24). Nothing in John's writings would qualify that stark claim.[28] If it was "through" the Logos that all things were made (Jn 1:3, 10), John is identifying the Logos with God's utterance each time he said, "Let (there be) . . ." (Gen 1:3, 6, 9, 11, 14, 20, 24, 26). God operated through his own fiat, which served as God's executor to bring the whole of his determinate will, without addition or remainder, into existence.

By virtue of his unique creatorship, God is the sole sovereign of the universe. Maker of heaven and earth (Apoc 10:6; 14:7) and recipient of universal acclaim (Apoc 5:13), he "knows all things" (γινώσκει πάντα [1 Jn 3:20]). The epithet "the Almighty" (ὁ παντοκράτωρ[29]) proclaims his unlimited power throughout the universe. Though he finished his creative work on the seventh day, by sustaining life every day he continues to labor in his own Sabbath rest (Jn 5:17). He is "Lord of the earth" (Apoc 11:4) and the "God of heaven" (Apoc 11:13). No one can receive anything except what is given from above (Jn 3:27; 19:11). That God is "the Almighty" takes graphic form in the image, frequent in the Apocalypse, of a heavenly "throne" exalted above all things (39× in reference to God's throne), a throne that will govern the new creation as well as the present one (Apoc 22:1, 3).

God has a master plan for all time that drives the course of affairs toward the destiny that he has fixed. The apocalyptic imagination presents this concept under the figure of a sealed scroll (Apoc 5–6). Known in all its dates and details to himself only, it is "the mystery of God," bits of which he has announced progressively to his servants the prophets (Apoc 10:7). As "King of the ages" (Apoc 15:3), God has predetermined that certain events "must" (δεῖ) occur (Apoc 1:1; 4:1; 22:6), or are "about to" (μέλλειν) happen (Apoc 1:19). Divinely

---

[28]Bauckham, *God Crucified*, p. 12.
[29]Apoc 1:8; 4:8; 11:17; 15:3; 16:7, 14; 19:6, 15; 21:22.

ordained events include matters large and small: Jesus' outstripping of John the
Baptist in making converts (Jn 3:30), his passing through Samaria (Jn 4:4), Judas's betrayal of Jesus (Jn 6:71; 12:4), Jesus' death (Jn 11:51; 12:33; 18:32) and enthronement (Apoc 12:5), the giving of the Holy Spirit (Jn 7:39; 14:22; 20:22), the
rise of the antichrist (Apoc 17:8, 10; 20:3), the sufferings of the church (Apoc
2:10; 6:11), the tribulation of earth dwellers (Apoc 3:10; 8:13) and the final punishment of God's foes by fire (Apoc 11:5) and by sword (Apoc 13:10).

That being the case, it comes as no suprise that the Fourth Gospel points out
in Jesus' ministry, especially in the closing events, many fulfillments of Scripture.
Jesus' zeal in cleansing the temple (Jn 2:17, quoting Ps 69:9), the unbelief of his
contemporaries (Jn 12:38, quoting Is 53:1) and their unwarranted hatred of him
(Jn 15:25, quoting Ps 35:19 conflated with Ps 69:4), Judas's treachery against Jesus
(Jn 13:18, quoting Ps 41:9; 17:12), the distribution of Jesus' garments by lot among
the soldiers who crucified him (Jn 19:23-24, citing Ps 22:18), his thirst quenched
by vinegar (Jn 19:28, thinking of Ps 69:21), the fact that the Roman soldiers did
not break Jesus' legs when they found him already dead on the cross (Jn 19:31-33,
conflating, in Jn 19:36, Ex 12:46 and Ps 34:20), the piercing of his side with a
lance (Jn 19:34, quoting, in Jn 19:37, Zech 12:10), Jesus' resurrection (Jn 2:22,
probably with some combination of Ps 16:10, Jon 1:16 or Amos 9:11 in mind)—
all took place according to God's will laid down in the Scriptures. Sayings of
Jesus, like Scripture, also demanded fulfillment (Jn 2:21-22, referring to Jn 2:19;
Jn 18:9, referring to Jn 17:12).

As some of the foregoing data indicate, things ordained by God include the
evil as well as the good. A man was born blind, and Lazarus later died, that the
works of God might be shown (Jn 9:3; 11:4). For wicked political motives
Caiaphas recommended a proceeding against Jesus that God had in fact de-
creed, and he spoke better than he knew of Jesus' vicarious role in dying for
others (Jn 11:49-51). At the Last Supper Jesus in effect commissioned Judas to
step out into the night to enact his diabolical scheme (Jn 13:21-30). Jesus told
his disciples in advance of his homegoing and of their afflictions to follow (Jn
14:29; 16:1, 4). Jesus accepted the cup that the Father gave him (Jn 18:11). Martyrdom was in store for Peter (Jn 21:18-19). In the last days satanically inspired
government (the beast) will reduce the godless social and economic engines of
society (the harlot) to ruins according to God's will (γνώμη [Apoc 17:17]). Not
all names are written in the book of life (Apoc 13:8).

Nowhere does John reflect on the philosophical problem of God ordaining things to happen that are opposed to his moral will. John's careful language is consistent with the fact (though John does not make a point of it) that God determines each objective human deed and its impact on the nexus of events but leaves to the human agent the motive for which the agent will be judged.[30] John tacitly maintains that no evil can come about that is not a necessary part of God's grand design, while also holding that there is not the slightest admixture of malice in the radiance of the divine nature (1 Jn 1:5).

**God is love.** With the thesis "God is love," twice put (1 Jn 4:8, 16),[31] John comes as close to a definition of the divine essence as the human mind is capable of.[32] This truth sends out a ray from the impenetrability of the deity. Love that originates in God and is reciprocated by creatures bridges over the ontological and logical gulf between the infinite and the finite. The apophatic method in theology emphasizes the chasm, showing how all metaphors ultimately fail, and tends to a mystical agnosticism. Appropriate though its reticence is, this approach is not the last word because God has declared himself to be love by sending his Son to be the propitiation for sins (1 Jn 4:9-10).

Nowhere does John define love as such. But if God's sending of his Son is the paradigm, we see at once that love in general must be a disposition to give oneself for the sake of another's existence, life and welfare: "God so loved the world that he gave . . ." (Jn 3:16). As we will see below, the Johannine concept of God includes the fact that the Father imparted all that he is to the Son before the foundation of the world (Jn 5:26; 17:24). Since the Father is self-existent, eternal and infinite, so too is the only-begotten Son. Therefore the relationship between the Father and the Son is an eternal one; never was there a time when God did not exist as Father to the Son and simultaneously as Son to the Father. So the act of Father-love and the reciprocal act of Son-love form an eternal

---

[30]Especially instructive in this regard are the multiple perspectives in the Fourth Gospel on Judas's betrayal of Jesus. God ordained it in advance and prophesied it in the Scriptures (Jn 6:71; 12:4; 17:12). Satan put the purpose into Judas's heart (Jn 13:2) and was active in his deed (Jn 13:27). Judas for his own part was the "son of perdition" (Jn 17:12).

[31]Variations: "love is of God" (1 Jn 4:7); "we love because he first loved us" (1 Jn 4:19). These pithy statements in 1 John epitomize a major theme of the Gospel (Jn 3:16; 14:21, 23; 16:27; 17:23).

[32]On divine love in the Fourth Gospel, see André Feuillet, *Le mystère de l'amour divin dans la théologie johannique* (EBib; Paris: Gabalda, 1972); in the Johannine Epistles, Fernando F. Segovia, *Love Relationships in the Johannine Tradition: Agapē/Agapan in I John and the Fourth Gospel* (SBLDS 58; Chico, CA: Scholars Press, 1982); Enno Edzard Popkes, *Die Theologie der Liebe Gottes in den johanneischen Schriften: Zur Semantik der Liebe und zum Motivkreis des Dualismus* (WUNT 2/197; Tübingen: Mohr Siebeck, 2005); in the Apocalypse, Pieter G. R. de Villiers, "Divine and Human Love in the Revelation of John," *APB* 18 (2008): 43-59.

cycle on which the Father-Son relationship is founded. This eternity of love in the divine being answers the question of whether loving is something that God chooses to do or something that flows by a kind of necessity from his nature. No doubt God does choose to love, but this choice cannot be for him an arbitrary decision. No more could God choose not to love than not to exist. Loving is a property of his very being. John says not only "God loves," but also "God is love." What God is, fundamentally and by definition, is love.[33]

Love is by no means a comprehensive revelation of all that God is; but it is a real revelation of his marrow.[34] André Feuillet considers this the apex (*point culminant*) of the revelation of the New Testament.[35] No other quality of the divine character, manifest or hidden, can be incongruent with this. God invites us to move into him in the confidence that every new vista that he opens to us will be coherent with love.

*The one and only God.* This union of utter otherness with sublimest goodness and love, a harmony of all personal virtues in the numinous, metaphysical ground of being, makes God unique and matchless. That there could be more than one infinity possessing the quality of aseity, or that there could be multiple *summae bonorum*, is inconceivable. John is a monotheist of the strictest order. For him, God is "the only God" (Jn 5:44), "the only true God" (Jn 17:3), "he who is true . . . the true God" (1 Jn 5:20), "the living God" (Apoc 7:2); and God's servants confess, "You alone are holy" (Apoc 15:4). John is heir to the message of the Hebrew prophets. "You shall have no other gods before/besides me" (Ex 20:3). "The LORD is God; there is no other besides him" (Deut 4:35; cf. 4:39). "Hear, O Israel: the LORD our God, the LORD is one" (Deut 6:4). "See now that I, even I, am he, and there is no god beside me" (Deut 32:39). "I am the LORD/I am God, and there is no other" (Is 45:5, 6, 14, 18, 22; 46:9; cf. 45:21). Therefore idols are ruled out—"Little children, keep yourselves from idols" (1 Jn 5:21; cf. Apoc 9:20)—as well as their worshipers (εἰδωλολάτραι [Apoc 21:8; 22:15]) and the eating of meat sacrificed to them (εἰδωλόθυτα [Apoc 2:14, 20]). In contrast to idols, the true God is the "living" one (Apoc 4:9-10; 7:2; 10:6; 15:7). Though

---

[33]Stevens, *Johannine Theology*, pp. 52-54, 273-89.
[34]Popkes, *Theologie*, pp. 93-97.
[35]Feuillet, *Mystère*, pp. 179-233. Note also the following statement by Birger Olsson: "The Johannine writings have, then, more than any other writings in the New Testament, brought the love concept into the very center of their understanding of God and a relationship with God" ("*Deus Semper Maior?*" p. 162). See further Jean Zumstein, "Dieu est amour," *FoiVie* 99 (2000): 95-106; Tobias Nicklas, "'Gott ist die Liebe' (1 Joh 4,8b)—1 Joh als Knotenpunkt biblischer Theologie," *BL* 79 (2006): 245-48.

angels bring messages from the beyond (Jn 20:12-13; Apocalypse, passim), God is the authority to whom they report (Apoc 8:2; 11:16). Angels are, alongside of human beings, but fellow servants of God and do not receive worship (Apoc 19:10; 22:8-9). Even as the God of the Old Testament would not allow his glory to be transferred to any graven image (Ex 20:4-5; Is 42:8; 48:11), so God the Father in John's writings is the aboriginal and proper possessor of eternal glory (Jn 17:5, 24).[36]

How John squares his high Christology with such a rigorous monotheism we will explore below. Suffice it for now to observe that Jesus never claims to be a second deity; he shares an identity of being, he is "one" (neuter ἕν), with his Father (Jn 10:30).

## ACTS OF GOD IN HISTORY

John is familiar with the Old Testament saga of God's dealings with Israel. It is the story that leads up to the sending of the Son. Most of the salient points of the Old Testament find mention in the Johannine literature.

From the book of Genesis, John refers to God's act of creation;[37] his purpose that the progeny of Adam and Eve rule the world (Apoc 22:5; cf. Gen 1:26, 28; also Ps 8:6-8; Dan 7:18, 27); the tree of life God planted in the garden of Eden (Apoc 2:7; 22:2, 14, 19; cf. Gen 2:9; 3:22, 24); the serpentine tempter casting doubt on God's word (Jn 8:44; 1 Jn 3:8; Apoc 12:9; 20:2; cf. Gen 3:1-7); Cain hating and slaughtering Abel (1 Jn 3:12; cf. Gen 4:1-8); God's choice of Abraham and his children to be the instrument of blessing for the nations: "Salvation is from the Jews" (Jn 4:22; cf. Gen 12:1-3); God's promise to be the God of Abraham and his offspring (Apoc 21:3, 7; cf. Gen 17:7-8); the requirement of circumcision (Jn 7:22; cf. Gen 17:10-13; also Lev 12:3); Abraham's "rejoicing" at seeing the Messiah's day (Jn 8:56; cf. Gen 17:17-19; 21:3, 6);[38] the rising smoke of Sodom

---

[36]On God as the "true" God in contradistinction to the nothingness of the heathen gods, see Lee, *Religious Thought*, pp. 38-42.

[37]Dan Lioy, *The Search for Ultimate Reality: Intertextuality Between Genesis and Johannine Prologues* (SBL 93; New York: Peter Lang, 2005).

[38]Commentators puzzle over what Old Testament reference is behind John 8:56. For Abraham, the birth of Isaac fulfilled God's promise to bless him and pointed ahead to the ripening of the blessing for the nations through his offspring at the end of days. The name "Isaac" (יִצְחָק) is related to the verb צָחַק ("laugh") at Genesis 17:17, 19, in the context of Abraham's amusement at the idea of giving birth to a son at his advanced age. Later, in Genesis 21:6, where Sarah's joy at the birth is uncontainable, she says that her laughter will infect all who hear of it, of whom her husband was the nearest. Thus Abraham's rejoicing with her at Isaac's nativity was in effect his exultation at all its future implications. Since the Genesis texts just cited mention laughter, they seem a more likely background to the "re-

and Gomorrah when God judged the cities of the plain (Apoc 14:11; cf. Gen 19:28); Jacob's dream at Bethel (Jn 1:51; cf. Gen 28:12); Jacob's gift to Joseph of a field near Sychar in Samaria (Jn 4:5; cf. Gen 33:19; 48:22; also Josh 24:32); the prophetic comparison of Judah to a lion (Apoc 5:5; cf. Gen 49:9-10).

Moses (Ex 2—Deut 34) is mentioned by John more often than any other Old Testament personage (13× in the Gospel, once in the Apocalypse). In this regard, John takes his place firmly in Judaism of the Second Temple era. God's special name revealed to Moses (Ex 3:14) gets expanded into the tripartite title of God in the Apocalypse (Apoc 1:4, 8; 4:8; 11:17; 16:5). The plagues against Egypt (Ex 7–11) inform John's idea of a prophet's powers (Apoc 11:6) and shape his vision of the tests God will bring at the end of the world (Apoc 3:10; 8–9; 16). John knows the Passover (10× in the Gospel) as a memorial feast (Ex 12). Lambs are needed for sacrifices of atonement (Jn 1:29, 36; Apoc 5; cf., e.g., Ex 12:3-6; 29:38-39; Lev 1:10; 3:6-7). Israel's exodus from Egypt (Ex 13–14) serves as a type of the final exodus of God's people from the world-system (Apoc 12:14-16; 15–16).[39] The song of Moses and Miriam (Ex 15) is the model for the tribulation saints' hymn of triumph (Apoc 15:3-4). John alludes to God's provision of manna in the wilderness (Jn 6:31, 49; Apoc 2:17; cf. Ex 16; Num 11).[40] He takes up the charter of Israel, "You shall be to me a kingdom of priests and a holy nation" (Ex 19:6), and applies it to believers in Jesus (Apoc 1:6). Phenomena that accompanied the theophany at Mount Sinai are used by John to depict the divine presence in heaven (Apoc 4:5; 8:5; 11:19; 16:18; cf. Ex 19:16). John characterizes Moses as Israel's lawgiver (Jn 1:17, 45; 5:45-47; 7:19, 22-23; 8:5; 9:28-29) and understands the Mosaic law as an expression of God's grace surpassed only by the sending of the Son (χάριν ἀντὶ χάριτος, "grace in place of grace" [Jn 1:16-17]).[41] John often speaks of God's "commandments" in the plural (Jn 14:15, 21;

---

joiced" in John 8:56 than does Genesis 15:7-21 (caked with Jewish apocalyptic interpretations [e.g., *Apocalypse of Abraham*]), which says nothing about Abraham exulting. For an interpretation of John 8:56 along this latter line, see Dahl, "Johannine Church," p. 134; Martin Hengel, "The Old Testament in the Fourth Gospel," in *The Gospels and the Scriptures of Israel* (ed. Craig A. Evans and W. Richard Stegner; JSNTSup 104; Sheffield: Sheffield Academic Press, 1994), p. 387.

[39]Laslo Gallus, "The Exodus Motif in Revelation 15–16: Its Background and Nature," *AUSS* 46 (2008): 21-43.

[40]See Peder Borgen, *Bread from Heaven: An Exegetical Study of the Concept of Manna in the Gospel of John and the Writings of Philo* (NovTSup 10; Leiden: Brill, 1965); Susan Hylen, *Allusion and Meaning in John 6* (BZNW 137; Berlin: de Gruyter, 2005).

[41]William Loader, "Jesus and the Law in John," in *Theology and Christology in the Fourth Gospel: Essays by Members of the SNTS Johannine Writings Seminar* (ed. Gilbert van Belle, Jan G. van der Watt and P. J. Maritz; BETL 184; Leuven: Leuven University Press, 2005), pp. 135-54; Hartwig Thyen, *Studien*

15:10; 1 Jn 2:3-4; 3:22, 24; 5:2-3; 2 Jn 6; Apoc 12:17; 14:12), and, while he may have at the forefront of his mind the dual love-command—to love God (1 Jn 2:5; 2:15) and to love one's brothers and sisters (1 Jn 2:7; 4:20–5:2)—in fact most of the Ten Commandments are represented in the ethics of the Apocalypse (see chap. 8 below). From the tabernacle of the premonarchic period (Ex 24–31; 35–40), John gets the concept of God "tenting" on earth (Jn 1:14; Apoc 21:3). The ark of the covenant (Ex 25:10-22) represents God's faithfulness to his promises (Apoc 11:19); the precious stones on the high priest's breastpiece, God's election of his people (Apoc 21:12-13; cf. Ex 28:21); the altar of incense, a means of approach to God (Apoc 8:3; 9:13; cf. Ex 30:1-3; Lev 16:12); the cloud that filled the tabernacle, God's holiness (Apoc 15:5, 8; cf. Ex 40:34).

Picking up on a refrain of the book of Leviticus, John holds that God's people are to be "purified," "sanctified" or "holy."[42] The Feast of Tabernacles as a memorial of Israel's liberation foreshadows the freedom from sin given by Jesus (Jn 7:2, 37; 8:31-36; cf. Lev 23:34, 36). God's name is not to be blasphemed (Jn 10:33; 19:7; cf. Lev 24:16).

The head count of the elect in John's Apocalypse (Apoc 7:4-8) looks back to the census in the book of Numbers (Num 1–4; 26). God's instruction to Moses to lift up the bronze serpent in the wilderness foreshadowed the lifting up of the Son of Man (Jn 3:14). The prophecy of a star to come forth out of Jacob (Num 24:17) points to Jesus (Apoc 22:16). In the same way that Balaam taught Balak to undo Israel by seducing them with fornication into idolatry (Num 31:16), so the Nicolaitans entice the church at Pergamum (Apoc 2:14-15, 20).

Only on evidence from two or three independent witnesses may a person be condemned (Jn 8:17; cf. Deut 17:6; 19:15). Deuteronomy 18:15 19 promises a coming prophet like Moses (Jn 1:21, 25; 6:14; 7:40). A hung criminal must be buried before nightfall (Jn 19:31; cf. Deut 21:22-23).[43]

David, the king of Judah out of whose dynasty the Messiah would come (Jn 7:42), John recognizes as an ancestor of Jesus (Apoc 3:7; 5:5; 22:16).[44] From the

---

zum Corpus Iohanneum (WUNT 214; Tübingen: Mohr Siebeck, 2007), pp. 425-28. The preposition ἀντί denotes opposition or substitution, not accumulation. See Christian Blumenthal, "Χάρις ἀντὶ χάριτος (Joh 1,16)," ZNW 92 (2001): 290-94; Alessandro Belano, "Il significato della preposizione ἀντί con particolare riferimento a Gv 1,16," RevistB 57 (2009): 223-29.

[42]Jn 17:17, 19; 1 Jn 3:3; Apoc 22:11; cf. Lev 11:44-45; 19:2; 20:7, 26; 21:8.

[43]Further on echoes of the Pentateuch in John, see Brian Byron, "Non-Explicit Allusions to the Pentateuch in the Gospel of John: Catch-Words for Catechesis on Jewish Basics?" ABR 82 (2005): 335-45.

[44]Ombretta Pisano, La radice e la stirpe di David: Salmi davidici nel libro dell'Apocalisse (TGST 85;

period of the monarchies in Judah and northern Israel, John draws especially on the prophets Elijah (Jn 1:21, 25; Apoc 11:6; cf. 1 Kings 17:1; 18:1; Mal 4:5), Isaiah (Jn 1:23; 6:45; 12:38-39, 41),[45] Jeremiah (Apoc 11:5; cf. Jer 5:14),[46] Ezekiel (Jn 10:1-30; 15:1-10; Apoc 10:8-11; cf. Ezek 3:1-3),[47] Daniel[48] and Zechariah (Jn 12:15; 19:37).[49] Though John names no Hebrew king but David, Ahab's Sidonian wife, Jezebel, serves as a cipher for the false prophetess of Thyatira (Apoc 2:20).

Babylon's hubris against God and violence toward Judah at the time of the exile (2 Kings 24-25; Is 13-14) John recalls by applying her name to the godless society that will oppress the church in the last days (Apoc 14:8; 16:19; 17:5; 18:2, 10, 21).

When Jewish exiles returned to Palestine, their rebuff to the local inhabitants based on the Jews' exclusive relation to God occasioned a rift that lasted into the first century A.D. (Jn 4:9, 20; cf. Ezra 4:1-5).

With other apocalyptically minded Jews of his day, John looked for a new creation (Apoc 21:1; cf. Is 65:17). This will follow a general resurrection, including the righteous and the wicked (Jn 5:28-29; Apoc 20:12-14; cf. Dan 12:2), and a universal judgment[50] in which every person will get "wages" based on what he or she has done (Jn 4:36; 2 Jn 8). An outpouring of God's "wrath" on the unjust will cleanse the world of evil once and for all.[51] Then God will establish his kingdom (Jn 3:3; Apoc 7:17; 11:15, 17; 12:10; 19:6; 21:3-5) in fulfillment

---

Rome: Editrice Pontificia Università Gregoriana, 2002). For possible echoes of the Psalter in John's Gospel, see Margaret Daly-Denton, *David in the Fourth Gospel: The Johannine Reception of the Psalms* (AGJU 47; Leiden: Brill, 2000); Andrew C. Brunson, *Psalm 118 in the Gospel of John: An Intertextual Study on the New Exodus Pattern in the Theology of John* (WUNT 2/158; Tübingen: Mohr Siebeck, 2003).

[45]For the Apocalypse, see Jan Fekkes, *Isaiah and Prophetic Traditions in the Book of Revelation: Visionary Antecedents and Their Development* (JSNTSup 93; Sheffield: JSOT Press, 1994).

[46]See further Kenneth Mulzac, "The 'Fall of Babylon' Motif in the Books of Jeremiah and Revelation," *JATS* 8 (1997): 137-49.

[47]On the many other allusions, see Gary T. Manning, *Echoes of a Prophet: The Use of Ezekiel in the Gospel of John and in Literature of the Second Temple Period* (JSNTSup 270; London: T & T Clark, 2004); Beate Kowalski, *Die Rezeption des Propheten Ezechiel in der Offenbarung des Johannes* (SBB 52; Stuttgart: Katholisches Bibelwerk, 2004); Dieter Sänger, ed., *Das Ezechielbuch in der Johannesoffenbarung* (BTS 76; Neukirchen-Vluyn: Neukirchener Verlag, 2004).

[48]The influence is pervasive in the Apocalypse. See G. K. Beale, *The Use of Daniel in Jewish Apocalyptic Literature and in the Revelation of St. John* (Lanham, MD: University Press of America, 1984); David J. Bryan, "A Comparative Literary Study of Daniel and Revelation: Shaping the End," *JSOT* 79 (1998): 134-35.

[49]Marko Jauhiainen, *The Use of Zechariah in Revelation* (WUNT 2/199; Tübingen: Mohr Siebeck, 2005).

[50]Jn 3:18-21; 12:43; 1 Jn 3:19-21; 4:17; Apoc 6:10, 16-17; 11:18; 14:7; 16:5-7; 18:5, 8, 20; 19:1-10, 15, 17; 20:9, 11-15; cf. Ps 7:6-8; Dan 7:10, 22, 26.

[51]Jn 3:36; Apoc 6:16-17; 11:18; 14:10, 19; 15:1, 7; 16:1, 19; 19:15; cf. Zeph 1.

of the Adamic creation mandate (Apoc 2:7 ["paradise of God"]; 22:1-5). As his creatures offer worship,[52] God will reign over the cosmos forever[53] in glory.[54]

This panorama of the acts of God from the beginning to the end of history John read out of his Hebrew Bible.[55] Far from ignoring, minimizing or side-lining the biblical record, John's proclamation of Jesus Christ presents him as the goal of salvation-history.[56]

## IMPACT OF THE CHRIST EVENT ON OUR KNOWLEDGE OF THE FATHER

With other early Christians, John understood Jesus in the light of this framework. Divine revelation culminated in God's agent, Jesus Christ.[57] By sending him, God has set in motion the irreversible transition from the present age to that which is to come. "The hour is coming, and now is" (Jn 4:23; 5:25). "The darkness is passing away and the true light is already shining" (1 Jn 2:8; cf. 2:17-18).[58] God's Son, appointed as God's deputy to perform God's plan, is the pivot on which the scheme of history turns: "From his fullness [πλήρωμα] have we all received, [final] grace in place of [former] grace. For the law was given through Moses; grace and truth came through Jesus Christ" (Jn 1:16-17).

These last two parallel clauses, without any connective ἀλλά ("but"), em-phasize the continuity between Moses, chief prophet of the Old Testament, and Jesus, supreme revelation of God. What Moses wrote bears witness to God's

---

[52]Jn 4:23-24; Apoc 5:11-14; 7:9-12; 11:15-19; 15:2-4; 19:1-10.

[53]Jn 6:51, 58; 8:35; 12:34; 14:16; Apoc 11:15; 22:5; cf. Ex 15:18.

[54]Jn 17:24; Apoc 19:1, 7; 21:11, 23; 22:5; cf. Num 14:21; Ps 72:19; Is 66:18-19; Hab 2:14.

[55]"When we consider how many allusions, echoes, and implicit references to scripture we have de-tected in this Gospel . . . could we not . . . call John's work 'the prophetic Gospel'? Far more than any of the other three, this Gospel is concerned with scripture and the fulfilment of scripture" (Hanson, *Prophetic Gospel*, pp. 251, 253).

[56]See E. L. Miller, *Salvation-History in the Prologue of John: The Significance of John 1:3-4* (NovTSup 60; Leiden: Brill, 1989), pp. 97-107. Miller rightly highlights the importance of salvation-history in John, even if one is unpersuaded by his exegetical attempt to find it in John 1:1-5. Likewise Hanson: "Salvation history is in the background throughout. . . . Without salvation history John could never have arrived at his all-important concept of the pre-existence of the Word" (*Prophetic Gospel*, p. 242).

[57]M. J. J. Menken, "Observations on the Significance of the Old Testament in the Fourth Gospel," *Neot* 33 (1999): 125-43. Menken poses a false alternative, however, in saying that for John real divine revelation is located exclusively in Jesus Christ and not in the Scriptures.

[58]On the two-stage eschatology that John has in common with other contributors to the New Testa-ment, see Alf Corell, *Consummatum Est: Eschatology and Church in the Gospel of St John* (trans. The Order of the Holy Paraclete; London: SPCK, 1958); David Earl Holwerda, *The Holy Spirit and Es-chatology in the Gospel of John: A Critique of Rudolf Bultman's Present Eschatology* (Grand Rapids: Eerdmans, 1959); Lodewijk van Hartingsveld, *Die Eschatologie des Johannesevangeliums: Eine Aus-einandersetzung mit R. Bultmann* (VGTB 36; Assen: Van Gorcum, 1962); Jörg Frey, *Die johanneische Eschatologie* (3 vols.; WUNT 96, 110, 117; Tübingen: Mohr Siebeck, 1997).

Christ (Jn 5:39, 46). While the prophets looked back to Torah as the definition of God's will for Israel, they also, with Moses, looked forward to him who was to come as Torah's perfect embodiment (Jn 1:45). John interprets the Old Testament as a salvation-historical platform for God's eschatological self-revelation. Moses' writings were never meant to stand on their own in such a way as to judge and negate God's final word (as "the Jews" suppose in Jn 9:28-29); that would be to miss not only God's greatest communication but also the meaning of Torah itself. People's response to Moses and their response to Christ are one and the same. Believing Moses leads to belief in Christ; unbelief toward Christ betrays unbelief toward Moses and toward God (Jn 5:46-47).

This leads to the question of whether in Johannine theology God's self-disclosure in the Son shows the Father himself in a new light.

*God's unity.* It will be fitting to make our way into this large question by taking up first the matter of the unity of God. From the standpoint of Judaism, there is no more fundamental issue. Jews of the Second Temple period held monotheism as their first tenet[59] and proclaimed God's unity energetically in a polytheistic environment.[60] John's record of Jesus' ministry bears witness to the fact that Jesus' claims brought him into conflict with Palestinian authorities who zealously guarded certain aspects of monotheism (Jn 5:17-18; 10:30-39; 19:7). For John the Evangelist, a Jewish Christian living in Ephesus with its cosmopolitan mix of religious ideas, there could be no more pressing question than how Jesus was related to the one God.[61] What meaning did the confession of God's unity retain after John committed himself to the highest possible view of Jesus as the Son of God?

Posed in this way, the question resolves into two, on neither of which is there a scholarly consensus. What did Palestinian Jews of the late Second Temple period mean by their insistence that God is one?[62] And in what sense did John

---

[59]Statements by Jews of the period to the effect that monotheism had a primary place in their faith include *Let. Arist.* 132; Philo, *Decal.* 52, 65; *Spec.* 1.12, 54; 2.166; *Virt.* 180; Mark 12:28-32; Josephus, *Ant.* 3.91; *Ag. Ap.* 2.190-193; and the fact that the Mishnah opens with a chapter about posture for recitation of the Shema (*m. Ber.* 1).

[60]That the Jews got their point across to the pagan world is clear from reports by Gentiles—for example, Tacitus, *Hist.* 5.5; Juvenal, *Sat.* 3.16; 14.96-97. The pagan world found this strident monotheism threatening and offensive. See David Rokeah, *Jews, Pagans and Christians in Conflict* (StPB 33; Jerusalem: Magnes Press, Hebrew University; Leiden: Brill, 1982), p. 210.

[61]Ulrich Wilckens, "Monotheismus und Christologie," *JBTh* 12 (1997): 87-97.

[62]The main points of the debate and much of the secondary literature are summarized in Michael Mach, "Concepts of Jewish Monotheism during the Hellenistic Period," in Newman, Davila and Lewis, *Jewish Roots*, pp. 21-42; Richard Bauckham, "The Throne of God and the Worship of Jesus,"

believe in the deity of God's Son? For the sake of clarity, it is best to postpone full treatment of the latter question until chapter four, on Christology, and to anticipate the result here: John held God's Son to be, along with the Father, a distinct entity in which there subsists the indivisible divine essence.

Jewish primary sources of the period express the kind of monotheism that John would have absorbed from childhood. God is the unique, eternal, transcendent creator of all things, sole governor and judge of the world and its history. Negatively, no created being, however exalted in power and honor—even if accorded titles or adjectives of deity—is worthy of worship; participation in the cultus of any such being, whether celestial or terrestrial, as happened in the rites of pagan polytheism, is illicit.[63] Jewish monotheists could speculate about angels and other supernatural beings under God. Some equated pagan pantheons with angels, others with demons, yet others denied them existence as figments of the human imagination.[64] In an environment where some rulers received divine honors, Jewish apocalyptists and apologists could commend Enoch, Moses and other glorified heroes by letting them bear a divine title or exercise a divine prerogative on God's behalf.[65] But no Jews whom we know of blended these figures with the creator in concept or offered sacrifices to them.[66]

Weighed by this standard, John remains a monotheist. Without compromise he upholds the transmundane nature of the deity over against finite reality, even while conceiving of the Son as existing eternally with the Father (Jn 1:1-2; 17:5, 24). The Son acts not on his own but rather as the Father's executor in the Father's acts of creating the world (Jn 1:3), owning it (Jn 17:10) and raising and judging the dead (Jn 5:21-23). John's writings bear witness to

---

in Newman, Davila and Lewis, *Jewish Roots*, pp. 43-60; William Horbury, "Jewish and Christian Monotheism in the Herodian Age," in Stuckenbruck and North, *Monotheism*, pp. 16-44; Larry W. Hurtado, "First-Century Jewish Monotheism," in *How on Earth?* pp. 111-33; Michael S. Heiser, "Monotheism, Polytheism, Monolatry, or Henotheism? Toward an Assessment of Divine Plurality in the Hebrew Bible," *BBR* 18 (2008): 1-30.

[63]Many of the relevant texts by Jewish writers from the Second Temple period are collected and categorized in Rainbow, "Monotheism and Christology," pp. 22-127. Concepts of divine agency in Jewish monotheism are analyzed in Hurtado, *One God, One Lord*. Looking back on the Hebrew Bible, Michael Heiser ("Monotheism") agrees that Yahweh was "species unique" among the many gods and goddesses that the canonical authors acknowledged, in that he created them, and their powers were contained within his.

[64]Rainbow, "Monotheism and Christology," pp. 27-29; Thompson, *God of the Gospel*, pp. 194-208.

[65]Hurtado, *One God, One Lord*, pp. 51-69.

[66]Rightly emphasizing worship practice as a litmus test of monotheistic belief are Bauckham, "Throne of God," pp. 43-51; Hurtado, "Jewish Monotheism," pp. 121-29.

the fact that the early church offered expressions of worship to Jesus (Jn 9:38; 20:28; cf. Apoc 5:8-14). But Christians did not spread divine honors to created beings generally, for to them the union of the divine Logos with precisely this man was a singularity—even as Jews did not seek God's presence at pagan shrines because the dwelling of his "name" over the cherubim of the ark in Jerusalem was a special dispensation.[67]

To distinguish discrete entities within the divine unity complicates, but need not obscure, the concept of one. John was by no means the first or the only thinker of Jewish heritage to move in this direction. Already in the Hebrew Bible divine qualities are isolated at least in speech: God's glory, face, voice, name, arm, wisdom, justice, truth, righteousness, mercy, power(s), angel, spirit or word may be aspects of his self-manifestation in various circumstances.[68] Whether later reflection on some of these—especially on God's wisdom (Prov 8:22-31; Sir 24; Wis 7–9), word (Philo's Logos; Wis 18:15-16; the *Memra* of the Targumim), spirit—went beyond literary personification to real hypostatization is debated,[69] but it does seem probable in a number of passages in the the early Targumim,[70] in the Wisdom of Solomon[71] and in Philo, to take just a few outstanding examples.[72] That these very writers offered

---

[67]Num 7:89; 1 Sam 4:4; 2 Sam 6:2; 1 Kings 8:27-30; 2 Kings 19:15; 21:7.

[68]Gerhard Pfeifer, *Ursprung und Wesen der Hypostasenvorstellungen im Judentum* (AzTh 31; Stuttgart: Calwer, 1967).

[69]The secondary literature on divine agency in Jewish monotheism is immense. Of the tendency to deny hypostatization, a classic example is George Foot Moore, "Intermediaries in Jewish Theology: Memra, Shekinah, Metatron," *HTR* 15 (1922): 41-85; to affirm it, Helmer Ringgren, *Word and Wisdom: Studies in the Hypostatization of Divine Qualities and Functions in the Ancient Near East* (Lund: Ohlsson, 1947). Robert Hayward sees the *Memra* as more than a circumlocution and less than a hypostasis, being rather a way of describing God's presence with his people centered in the temple (*Divine Name and Presence: The Memra* [Totowa, NJ: Allanheld, Osmun, 1981]).

[70]Daniel Boyarin notes, "In the first century many—perhaps most—Jews held a binitarian view of God.... The more rabbinized of the Targums (Targums *Onkelos* and *Pseudo-Jonathan*) and rabbinic literature itself suppress the use of the term *Memra* quite observably. Indeed, in rabbinic literature, it has disappeared entirely, and in the more rabbinized Targums, it appears much less frequently, suggesting a struggle between the forms of piety that were current in the synagogues and those that were centered in the Houses of Study of the rabbis. This strongly implies that Logos theology was a living current within non-Christian Judaic circles from before the Christian era until well into late antiquity" ("Two Powers in Heaven; or, the Making of a Heresy," in *The Idea of Biblical Interpretation: Essays in Honor of James L. Kugel* [ed. Hindy Najman and Judith H. Newman; JSJSup 83; Leiden: Brill, 2004], pp. 334-35). See also John L. Ronning, *The Jewish Targums and John's Logos Theology* (Peabody, MA: Hendrickson, 2010).

[71]In the Wisdom of Solomon wisdom is a "breath" of God, a "stream" (ἀπόρροια) of his glory, a "ray" (ἀπαύγασμα) of eternal light (Wis 7:25-26); she sits by God's throne, from which she can be sent (Wis 9:4, 6, 10, 17).

[72]For Philo, God and his Logos are "two different things" (πράγματα διαφέροντα) in that God existed

strenuous credos in one God[73] indicates that they posited hypostases within the unity of God's being,[74] not outside it in such a way as to weaken, threaten or compromise monotheism.[75] With a vividness that goes only a hair beyond Philo's language, John envisages interpersonal communion between the eternal Father and Son (e.g., Jn 1:18; 17:24). This conception is consistent with the plural pronominal endings in Genesis 1:26; 3:22, embedded in Israel's monotheistic creation account(s).[76]

---

"before the Logos" (πρὸ τοῦ λόγου [Somn. 1.66; cf. QG 2.62]), and only ignorant folk fail to make the distinction (Somn. 1.239; QG 3.34). God is the "fountain" (πηγή) of the Logos (Det. 82; cf. QG 3.15) and his "father who begot him" (ὁ γεννήσας πατήρ [Plant. 9]). The Logos is God's "firstborn son" (Agr. 51; Conf. 63, 146), "the word of the Cause" (Plant. 20) and God's "instrument" (ὄργανον [Migr. 4-6; cf. Her. 140]) by means of which (δι' οὗ [Cher. 127; Sacr. 8; Spec. 1.81]) or according to which (καθ' ἥν [Conf. 137]) he created all things. The Logos is the place where God stands (Conf. 96; QE 2.39); God dwells in the Logos as in a house (Migr. 4-5). The Logos is God's "viceroy" (ὕπαρχος [Agr. 51; Fug. 111; Somn. 1.241]), "image" (εἰκών [Conf. 97, 147; Fug. 101; Somn. 2.45; Spec. 1.81]), "messenger" (Migr. 174; Her. 205-6), "minister" (ὑπηρέτης [Mut. 87; cf. QG 3.34]), "cup-bearer" (οἰνοχόος [Somn. 2.249]), a "second God" (QG 2.62), "less" than God (ἐλάττων [Somn 2.188]). Wisdom is "the daughter of God" and "occupies a second place" (Fug. 51-52; QG 4.97). Philo also distinguished between God's ruling power ("Lord") and goodness ("God"): Alleg. Interp. 3.73; Cher. 27-28; Sacr. 59-60; Deus 76, 109-10; Plant. 86; Sobr. 55; Her. 166; Mut. 28; Somn. 1.163, 185; Abr. 121; Mos. 2.99; Spec. 1.307; QG 1.57; 2.16, 51, 52, 75; 3.39, 42; 4.2, 8, 30, 53, 87; QE 2.62, 64, 66. This selection of passages omits Philo's intricate theory of other divine powers (e.g., Fug. 94-99; QE 2.68).

[73]See Wisdom of Solomon 12:12-14, 27; 14:12-31; Philo, Opif. 100, 171, 172; Alleg. Interp. 1.44, 51; 2.1-2; 3.180; Cher. 27, 77, 92; Ebr. 109-10; Conf. 41-43, 170-71; Her. 94; Mut. 135; Somn. 1.229; Abr. 70; Spec. 1.54, 67; 3.29; 4.159; Virt. 35, 179; Praem. 40, 123; Legat. 115, 290, 347.

[74]Telling in this regard are Philo's descriptions of God's potencies as "uncircumscribed" (ἀπερίγραφος [Sacr. 59]), "uncreated" (ἀγένητοι [Deus 78]), "not differing from the divine image" (θείας ἀδιαφοροῦν εἰκόνος [Conf. 62]), "indicative of his essence" (QE 2.37). He explicitly identifies God's powers as Platonic "forms" of the divine attributes in Spec. 1.48, 327-29; cf. QG 1.54; 4.1; QE 2.63, 124.

[75]As wrongly construed in Wilhelm Bousset, Die Religion des Judentums im späthellenistischen Zeitalter (ed. Hugo Gressmann; 3rd ed.; HNT 21; Tübingen: Mohr Siebeck, 1926), pp. 302-57. By way of correction, see Daniel Boyarin, "The Gospel of the Memra: Jewish Binitarianism and the Prologue to John," HTR 94 (2001): 243-84.

[76]Early Jews left little commentary on Genesis 1:26 ("Let us make man in our image") or Genesis 3:22 ("The man has become like one of us, knowing good and evil") until Christians took up these verses as prooftexts for the Son's distinction-in-unity from the Father. The Septuagint (late third century B.C.) translates the plurals without elaboration. Jubilees 2:14 paraphrases Genesis 1:26 in such a way as to pass over the grammar, but at Jubilees 3:4 is inserted an analogous "let us make" where the underlying text (Gen 2:18) has none. Pseudo-Philo and the Genesis Apocryphon do not cover Genesis 1-3. Josephus's summary is silent on these points (Ant. 1.32). Prior to the rabbis, only Philo is exercised. Concerning Genesis 1:26, Philo confesses, "The full truth about the cause of this it must needs be that God alone knows" (Opif. 72). He speculates that although God alone created what is excellent in human nature without assistance, he employed subordinates to make what tends to sin (Opif. 72-76; Conf. 168-79; Fug. 67-70; Mut. 30-32). At Genesis 3:22 he admits the plurality but denies that God is addressing his powers (QG 1.54). Nothing is made of Genesis 1:26 or Genesis 3:22 in the New Testament. Among the Apostolic Fathers, 1 Clement quotes Genesis 1:26 only to prove the dignity of man in God's image. First in the Epistle of Barnabas (late

Alongside of this trajectory toward recognizing a richness in the divine nature along binitarian or multitarian lines there may well have been Jews whose confession of one God meant that the divine nature is simple. But they left no trace until a century after the rise of Christianity. Capital charges leveled against Jesus by Palestinian leaders in his day accused him of "blasphemy" (Mk 2:6-7; 14:63-64; Jn 10:34) rather than heresy. John explains their thinking: "You, being a man, make yourself God" (Jn 10:33)—injuring God's honor by overstepping the chasm that divides the divine from the human. In the same way, Philo applied the category of blasphemy to rulers who received divine honors from subjects (*Mut.* 181; *Somn.* 2.130-32; *Legat.* 75, 77, 118). It was opposition to Hellenistic hero cults and to myths of apotheosis in the Greco-Roman world (e.g., Judith; Wis 14:16-21),[77] not to the idea of entities within the Godhead, that made Jews of the first century virulent toward early Christian worship of Jesus.[78] Evidence for unitarianism as the creed of Ju-

---

first to early second century A.D.) we find the plural forms taken to refer to a conversation between God and his Son (*Barn.* 6:12). Not until Justin's *Dialogue* with Trypho the Jew (shortly after A.D. 155) do we have indirect evidence of exegetical interest in these verses on the part of the sages. In chapter 62 Justin rejects three Jewish interpretations: (1) the plural forms are deliberative; (2) God spoke to the elements of earth and similar substances; (3) God spoke to angels. The deliberative explanation of Genesis 1:26 cannot account for the partitive construction in Genesis 3:22 ("as one of us"), which latter context ("to know good and evil") also excludes the inanimate world. Justin and the Jewish teachers agree that the suggestion of angels is heretical, no doubt partly because Scripture always reserves the work of creation to God alone, partly because man is never said to be in the image of angels. Justin concludes that God "conversed with some one who was numerically distinct from Himself, and also a rational Being." See Robert McL. Wilson, "The Early History of the Exegesis of Gen. 1:26," *StPatr* 1 (1957): 420-37. Naturally, neither the sages nor Justin gave serious consideration to the view, popular among modern critics, that these plurals are a relic of polytheistic mythology that the biblical redactor was too dull to edit away. See Gerhard F. Hasel, "The Meaning of 'Let Us' in Gn 1:26," *AUSS* 13 (1975): 58-66; Lyle M. Eslinger, "The Enigmatic Plurals Like 'One of Us' (Genesis i 26, iii 22, and xi 7) in Hyperchronic Perspective," *VT* 56 (2006): 171-84.

[77]For a concise review of how rulers were honored in the Greco-Roman world, see Adela Yarbro Collins, "The Worship of Jesus and the Imperial Cult," in Newman, Davila and Lewis, *Jewish Roots*, pp. 247-57. She uses this information, incautiously in my view, to try to explain the rise of devotion to Jesus in the church.

[78]By looking at the early church through the eyes of its Jewish persecutors, Larry Hurtado ("Early Jewish Opposition to Jesus-Devotion," in *How on Earth?* pp. 152-78) proves his main point that Jesus-devotion began in the first generation. But more evidence is required, and will be hard to come by, to establish his assumption that the countermeasures of the Jews were intended to keep God's unity as such intact. Much less have we evidence for a "charge of ditheism" (John Ashton, *Understanding the Fourth Gospel* [Oxford: Clarendon, 1991], p. 167). "The very category of heresy in Judaism did not exist in the first century or indeed before the rabbinic formation. . . . There is, I submit, no pre-Christian (or even first-century) evidence for" the expulsion of binitarianism as "heretical" (Boyarin, "Two Powers," pp. 333, 334n13).

daism first becomes clear in the second-century rabbinic polemic against "two powers" or simply "powers in heaven."[79]

John, whose mind had been formed in prerabbinic Jewish monotheism, was careful to build into his view of the Father and the Son a number of safeguards to the divine unity. (1) He continued to use titles of deity in the traditional way. (2) Of the Father and the Son he affirmed a perfect identity of being. (3) Insofar as the Son is distinct from the Father, he is not ontologically independent, but begotten of the Father, who remains the sole principle of deity. (4) Nor does the Son operate independently, but always and only as the agent to carry out the Father's will. (5) Devotion is directed to God, though the Son of God is included in that devotion. Let us consider each point separately.

(1) In John's writings, as in the New Testament generally, the traditional title ὁ θεός ("God" with the definite article) denotes the Father. Ancient peoples used the noun "god" to denote any celestial being having superhuman power whom it is prudent for human beings to honor. Jews shared this usage but reserved the definite ὁ θεός for the transcendent creator and consummator of the world.[80] The Septuagint regularly uses the articular ὁ θεός (roughly 2,280×) to translate the Hebrew אֱלֹהִים ("God").[81] Of the 249 occurrences of θεός in the Johannine literature, 90 percent (223) have the article, and most of the others are definite in context, bringing definite uses of θεός to a total of 239/249, or 96 percent.[82] That the reference is to the Father is explicit in places where "God" and "Father" refer to the same one (Jn 5:18; 6:27; 8:41, 54; 2 Jn 3; Apoc 1:6).

---

[79]Carefully documented in Alan F. Segal, *Two Powers in Heaven: Early Rabbinic Reports About Christianity and Gnosticism* (SJLA 25; Leiden: Brill, 1977). On the early rabbinic movement as the watershed that first defined Judaic orthodoxy, see Daniel Boyarin, "A Tale of Two Synods: Nicaea, Yavneh and the Making of Orthodox Judaism," *Exemplaria* 12 (2000): 21-62.

[80]Rainbow, "Monotheism and Christology," pp. 22-30; Thompson, *God of the Gospel*, pp. 17-55.

[81]Analysis of the Septuagintal usage in Murray J. Harris, *Jesus as God: The New Testament Use of Theos in Reference to Jesus* (Grand Rapids: Baker Books, 1992), pp. 22-26.

[82]The article has dropped out of several stock prepositional phrases (ἀπὸ θεοῦ [Jn 3:2; 13:3; 16:30]; ἐκ θεοῦ [Jn 1:13]; ἐν θεῷ [Jn 3:21]; παρὰ θεοῦ [Jn 1:6; 9:16, 33; 2 Jn 3]) and from the genitive construct τέκνα θεοῦ (Jn 1:12; 1 Jn 3:1, 2). At John 6:45 an anarthrous θεός translates the personal name of God (יהוה, "Yahweh") in a quotation of LXX Isaiah 54:13. In John 8:54 the anarthrous θεός is made definite by the possessive ὑμῶν that follows. At John 19:7 υἱὸς θεοῦ is definite by the canon of Apollonius Dyscolus concerning nouns in regimen (Nigel Turner, *Syntax*, vol. 3 of *A Grammar of New Testament Greek*, by James Hope Moulton [Edinburgh: T & T Clark, 1978], p. 180). The collocation of θεός with ζῶν ("[the] living God" [Apoc 7:2]) is a Jewish monotheistic formula (Rainbow, "Monotheism and Christology," p. 45). These sixteen cases of anarthrous θεός are definite. Plurals occur at John 10:34, 35 in an argument that Jesus makes from Psalm 82:6. The remaining instances of anarthrous θεός (Jn 1:1, 18 [2×]; 10:33; 1 Jn 4:12; 2 Jn 9; Apoc 21:3 [textually uncertain], 7) will be treated below.

On the other hand, the Son of God is never designated ὁ θεός.[83]

Moreover, monotheistic formulae are reserved for the Father. Jesus refers to the Father as the "only God" (Jn 5:44; 17:3), and John confesses that he who is true, whose Son is Jesus Christ, is "the true God" (1 Jn 5:20).[84] Therefore Jesus acknowledges the Father to be his God (Jn 20:17; Apoc 1:6; 3:2, 12), and Peter calls Jesus "the Holy One of God" (Jn 6:69). John could hardly have demonstrated more forcefully his conviction that even after the revelation of the Son of God, the Father remains God in the proper sense.

John's use of the other common Old Testament term for deity, κύριος ("Lord"), is more nuanced. In the Septuagint κύριος is the ordinary translation of אֲדֹנָי ("Lord"), the title that expressed God's royal claim to be king of Israel.[85] In a host of verses κύριος also stands for the Tetragrammaton, יהוה, God's special covenantal name, unveiled at the time of Israel's national redemption from Egypt (Ex 6:3). This peculiarity of translation arose from the fact that, according to Jewish custom, אֲדֹנָי or κύριος was substituted orally in public readings to avoid pronouncing the Tetragrammaton. John preserves the original reference to God the Father in three quotations from the Bible in his Gospel (Jn 1:23, quoting Is 40:3; Jn 12:13, quoting Ps 118:26; Jn 12:38 quoting Is 53:1) and in three freely composed sentences in the Apocalypse reflecting biblical style (Apoc 11:4, 15; 15:4). Also in reference to the Father he uses the combination of titles "the Lord God" (κύριος ὁ θεός), found in parts of the Old Testament.[86]

More often in the Gospel κύριος denotes Jesus (36/44×). Usually it is a respectful form of address by a stranger or by Jesus' disciples who regard him as master. But in rare comments by the narrative voice it may take on the connotation of deity (Jn 4:1; 6:23; 9:38; 11:2). It unquestionably has this supreme sense in Thomas's declaration, "My Lord [κύριος] and my God!" (Jn 20:28), and

---

[83]In John 1:1 the Logos receives the predicate θεός without an article. He is μονογενὴς θεός in John 1:18. Jews accuse Jesus of making himself θεός (anarthrous) in John 10:33. In Thomas's acclamation in John 20:28 ὁ θεός μου is vocative rather than titular. None of these verses applies the articular ὁ θεός to the Son of God in an unqualified way.

[84]To give the full picture, we should observe that Jesus Christ stands in juxtaposition to the "only" and "true" God at John 17:3; 1 John 5:20. John is claiming that the exclusive God of the Old Testament has now made the definitive revelation of himself in Jesus Christ, and no one who denies that revelation is in a covenant relationship with that God.

[85]Joseph A. Fitzmyer, "The Semitic Background of the New Testament Kyrios-Title," in A Wandering Aramaean: Collected Aramaic Essays (SBLMS 25; Missoula, MT: Scholars Press, 1979), p. 132.

[86]Apoc 1:8; 4:8; 11:17; 15:3; 16:7; 18:8; 19:6; 21:22; 22:5, 6. Compare ὁ κύριος καὶ ὁ θεὸς ὑμῶν (Apoc 4:11).

in a few places in the Apocalypse (Apoc 11:8; 14:13; 17:14; 19:16; 22:20, 21). Since the Tetragrammaton was God's covenant name, John extends it to the one whom the Father sent into the world to perfect his covenantal relationship to his own. Nevertheless, John does not let go of its former denotation.

(2) In John's language we find an inchoate distinction between God viewed as concrete (ὁ θεός) and the quality that constitutes his essence (θεός).[87] With God the Father, the Son shares the latter. Because in Jewish monotheism deity is a unique category that cannot be transferred, diffused, distributed or shared by more than one being (Is 42:8; Wis 14:21), the Father and the Son are not particulars of a universal, as in Greco-Roman adumbrations of monotheism,[88] but rather are discrete entities having in common a strict identity of being.

Relevant here are the seven (or eight) occurrences of θεός without the article, where stress falls on "the nature and quality of what is expressed by the noun."[89] Both times when John writes, "No one has ever seen God" (Jn 1:18; 1 Jn 4:12), he brings the object θεόν to the head of the sentence and drops the article. The effect is to deny that anyone has beheld what God is in naked reality, even though God has revealed tokens of himself. In the promise in Apocalypse 21:7, "I will be his God [θεός] and he will be my son [υἱός]," omission of the articles for "God" and "son" emphasizes the God-son relationship.[90] When the Jews took up stones upon hearing Jesus' claim that he and his Father were one (thing) (ἕν [Jn 10:30]),[91] they accused him of making himself "God" (anarthrous θεόν [Jn 10:33]). No one supposed that Jesus would presume to displace the God of heaven (ὁ θεός), but they suspected him of eroding the sharp line that separates humanity from deity. These uses of anarthrous θεός denote the divine nature as such. They differ lexically but not in import from more formal

---

[87]On the distinction, which is not carried through formally and consistently by the writers of the New Testament, see Harris, *Jesus as God*, pp. 36-40.

[88]On monotheistic tendencies in Greece, see Rainbow, "Monotheism and Christology," pp. 24-26; Horbury, "Jewish and Christian Monotheism," pp. 27-31.

[89]Maximilian Zerwick, *Biblical Greek, Illustrated by Examples* (ed. Joseph Smith; SPIB 114; Rome: Pontifical Biblical Institute, 1963), §179.

[90]The same will be true of the God-people relationship in Apocalypse 21:3 if we accept the questionable reading "as their God."

[91]Jesus' claim in John 10:30 gives the basis for the concerted operation of Jesus and his Father in holding their sheep in their hands (Jn 10:28-29). The neuter form of "one" points to an identity of being, as the reaction of the Jews and their reason in John 10:33 make clear. But in John 17:22 the neuter ἕν has a different connotation. There it indicates a unity of purpose and love between the Father and the Son, a unity in which Jesus' disciples have a share.

metaphysical vocabulary pointing to the divine φύσις ("nature"),[92] ὑπόστασις ("substance"),[93] οὐσία ("essence, being"),[94] θεότης ("deity")[95] or τὸ θεῖον ("the divine").[96]

It is therefore plain what John is getting at when he writes in the opening verse of the prologue to his Gospel, "In the beginning was the Word, and the Word was with God [πρὸς τὸν θεόν], and the Word was God [θεὸς ἦν]." At the birth of the universe the Logos was in fellowship with the personal God (τὸν θεόν). This was possible because the Logos too was essentially divine. The New English Bible brilliantly captures the exact nuance of the grammar: "The Word dwelt with God, and *what God was*, the Word was" (italics added).[97]

The last verse of the prologue returns to this idea. No one has ever seen God as he is (anarthrous θεόν); the only-begotten God (μονογενὴς θεός)[98]—he who is all that God is (anarthrous θεός) but is differentiated from his Father as the only-begotten possessor of the divine nature (μονογενής)—the one who is in the bosom of the Father, he has made him known (Jn 1:18).

In 2 John 9 this thought is turned against heretics who do not confess Jesus Christ coming in flesh (cf. 2 Jn 7): "Everyone who goes ahead and does not abide in the doctrine of Christ does not have God [θεὸν οὐκ ἔχει]; the one who abides in the doctrine has both the Father and the Son." To abandon the doctrine is to let go of God as he truly is (anarthrous θεόν), existing as Father and Son. Here we see a concrete Father and a concrete Son united in the divine being.

John does not articulate binitarianism using technical terms of Greek ontology as the ecumenical councils would later do.[99] Nevertheless, by those

---

[92] Already in Paul to distinguish between the true God and "beings that by nature are no gods" (Gal 4:8).

[93] Of the divine substance in Hebrews 1:3.

[94] Used in the New Testament only in the sense of the substance of one's property (Lk 15:12, 13). But John's description of God as ὁ ὤν . . . (Apoc 1:4, 8; 4:8; 11:17; 16:5) touches on ontology.

[95] Of the fullness of deity in Colossians 2:9.

[96] Attributed to Paul in his speech on the Areopagus in Acts 17:29.

[97] On the sense of John 1:1, see Harris, *Jesus as God*, pp. 51-71.

[98] There is a textual question whether the phrase "only-begotten [noun?]" in John 1:18 should read θεός, "God" (with P[66] P[75] ℵ B C), or υἱός, "Son" (with A f[1] f[13]). Since the superior cluster of manuscripts supports the conceptually more difficult reading, we need not hesitate to adopt "God" as more likely original. For full analysis of the textual question, see Harris, *Jesus as God*, pp. 74-83. See also Benjamin J. Burkholder, "Considering the Possibility of a Theological Corruption in Joh 1,18 in Light of Its Early Reception," *ZNW* 103 (2012): 64-83.

[99] I use the term "binitarianism" descriptively, not dogmatically. John very often speaks of the Father and the Son side by side and comparatively rarely has a triad including the Spirit. His binitarianism was open to development into trinitarianism.

formulae the patristic church sought to clarify and defend the intricate structure of the idea of God implied in the canonical documents.[100] An advantage of distinguishing between ὁ θεός and θεός as John does, instead of between ὑποστάσεις and οὐσία, or *personae* and *substantia/essentia/natura* as later generations would do, is that John's terminology makes clear the inherence of God's essence in God's person with no hint that the divine being is analyzable into ontic layers. That which subsists in the Father also subsists in the Son; considered abstractly in itself, θεός is incapable of multiplication or of any other kind of becoming. The divine essence is a perfect, infinite monad.

[100]Between about 1850 and 1950 it was widely held by biblical critics and church historians that the New Testament authors were naïve of metaphysics, and the patristic development superimposed upon the content of the Christian faith an influx of Greek concepts. Major representatives of this trend were A. Ritschl (1822–1889), W. Herrmann (1846–1922), A. von Harnack (1851–1930), W. Bousset (1865–1920) and R. Bultmann (1884–1976). This theory rests on a pernicious tendency of German rationalism to split complex unities, such as substance and function, into alternatives and insist on making choice between them. Even if function is to the fore, as it is in biblical modes of speech, it is inseparable from that which functions. The bifurcation is falsified by a mass of biblical facts. On the interrelatedness of religion and metaphysics from a philosophical point of view, see Frank B. Dilley, *Metaphysics and Religious Language* (New York: Columbia University Press, 1964). On the presence of some general metaphysical concepts in the Bible, see Duncan Black Macdonald, *The Hebrew Philosophical Genius: A Vindication* (Princeton, NJ: Princeton University Press, 1936); Claude Tresmontant, "Biblical Metaphysics," *CC* 10 (1960): 229-50. Thorlief Boman demonstrated the similarity of Old Testament to Platonic ontology in *Hebrew Thought Compared with Greek* (trans. Jules L. Moreau; LHD; Philadelphia: Westminster, 1960), esp. pp. 27-73, in spite of some fallacious linguistic arguments noted in James Barr, *The Semantics of Biblical Language* (Glasgow: Oxford University Press, 1961). The Yale scholar George B. Stevens, writing at the height of the reaction among Christian theologians against metaphysics, ably showed that John's doctrine of an "ethical" union of the divine Son and the Father logically presupposes a "metaphysical" union (*Johannine Theology*, pp. 102-27). Lars Hartman cautiously suggests that John's language in several places goes beyond a merely functional mission Christology ("Johannine Jesus-Belief and Monotheism," in *Aspects on the Johannine Literature: Papers Presented at a Conference of Scandinavian New Testament Exegetes at Uppsala, June 16-19, 1986* [ed. Lars Hartman and Birger Olsson; ConBNT 18; Uppsala: Almqvist & Wiksell, 1987], pp. 85-99). Ethelbert Stauffer put it baldly: "The starting-point of Johannine thought is a theological metaphysic.... Hence he starts the Prologue with a saying about Being before he mentions Becoming at all" (*New Testament Theology* [trans. John Marsh; London: SCM Press, 1955], p. 42). D. Moody Smith has written, "Although John does not engage in metaphysical exploration or ontological construction, the kinds of christological controversies that arose later and drew upon his terminology, and seemingly his conceptuality, were not a misrepresentation of John's own purpose and intent, which cannot be adequately dealt with under functionalist or existentialist categories" (*The Theology of the Gospel of John* [NTT; Cambridge: Cambridge University Press, 1995], p. 130). Note also Udo Schnelle's observation that Christ's "action [*Wirken*] is grounded comprehensively in unity with the Father, and only from this unity does he himself obtain his unique dignity, that is, his unity in revelation is rooted in unity of being [*Wesenseinheit*]" ("Trinitarisches Denken im Johannesevangelium," in *Israel und seine Heilstraditionen im Johannesevangelium: Festgabe für Johannes Beutler SJ zum 70. Geburtstag* [ed. Michael Labahn, Klaus Scholtissek and Angelika Strotmann; Paderborn: Schöningh, 2004], p. 377 [my translation]).

(3) Although the Son, like the Father, is θεός, the Son does not possess the divine nature from himself, but from the Father, as God "begotten." Insofar as more than one concrete subject are θεός, the plurality stems from a single principle.

The Father-Son relationship in the Godhead is of special interest to John. A remarkable feature of the Johannine literature is the high frequency of its references to God as Father (142× in all).[101] Along with this there is a spike in the number of references to Jesus as "the Son of God" or "the Son" in the Fourth Gospel (28×).[102] In most contexts where God is denominated "Father," the relationship between him and the Son is in view rather than God's relation to believers or to the human race at large: Jesus Christ is "the Father's Son" (2 Jn 3).[103]

God's paternity of Jesus is unique and unlike any other. In reference to this pair "Father" and "Son" are frequently collocated.[104] God is Jesus' "own" (ἴδιος) Father (Jn 5:18). Again and again Jesus calls him "my" (μου) Father.[105] Father and Son know each other (Jn 10:15), and the Son has unique knowledge of the Father (Jn 1:18; 7:29; 8:26; 15:15; 16:25; 17:25, 26). The Father loves the Son (Jn 3:35; 5:20; 10:17; 15:9-10; 17:23, 24, 26), and the Son loves the Father (Jn 14:31). It is typically as "Father" that God "gives" all things into Jesus' hands, as an earthly father bequeathes an estate to his son.[106] The Father consecrated the Son (Jn 10:36) and sent him into the world (Jn 5:23, 36, 37; 6:44, 57; 8:18; 10:36; 12:49;

---

[101]The breakdown is as follows: Gospel, 121×; Epistles, 16×; Apocalypse, 5×. These figures compare to about a dozen in the whole of the Old Testament; Matthew, 45×; Mark, 5×; Luke, 17×; all thirteen Pauline Epistles together, 42×. For further statistical analysis of the occurrences of "Father" in the Gospel, see Zingg, *Gott Als "Vater,"* pp. 24-28.

[102]Compare with the Synoptic Gospels: Matthew, 13×; Mark, 7×; Luke, 8×.

[103]"God's actions as Father are focused on Jesus himself" (Thompson, *God of the Gospel*, p. 58). Thompson's summary concerns the Gospel, where there are very few exceptions (Jn 8:19, 41-42; 16:27; 20:17). In the Epistles God's fatherhood of believers figures in a number of passages (1 Jn 1:3; 2:1, 13, 15, 16, 24; 3:1; 2 Jn 4), but the relationship between the Father and the Son is still fundamental (1 Jn 1:2, 3; 2:22-24; 4:14; 2 Jn 3 [2×], 9). In the Apocalypse God is invariably the Father of Jesus Christ (αὐτοῦ [Apoc 1:6; 14:1]; μου [Apoc 2:28; 3:5, 21]). Nowhere in the Johannine literature does God's Fatherhood describe him as creator in relation to all people. A different view is taken by Stevens, who, under the influence of the nineteenth-century liberal doctrine of the universal Fatherhood of God and fraternity of humankind, could write, "God, then is the Father of all men," and proceed to strive against the grain of the very passages that he cites as proof (*Johannine Theology*, pp. 70-73). Sounder exegetically is Lee (*Religious Thought*, pp. 42-55), who concludes, "The more richly the idea of God's Fatherhood is developed, so much the more impossible is it to think of it in relation to the world in general" (pp. 52-53).

[104]Jn 3:35; 5:19, 20, 21, 22, 23, 26; 6:40; 10:15; 14:13; 1 Jn 1:3; 2:1, 22, 23, 24; 4:14; 2 Jn 3, 9.

[105]Jn 2:16; 5:17, 43; 6:32, 40; 8:19 [2×], 49, 54; 10:18, 25, 29, 37; 14:2, 7, 20, 21, 23; 15:1, 8, 15, 23, 24; 20:17. Also Jesus' interlocutors call him "your [σου] father" (Jn 8:19).

[106]Jn 3:35; 5:22, 26, 27, 36; 6:37, 39; 10:29; 13:3; 17:2, 6, 7, 8, 9, 22, 24; cf. 16:15; 17:10. Only in John 3:34 is it "God" who gives the Spirit to Jesus.

14:24; 20:21; 1 Jn 4:14). Jesus has received charge from his Father (Jn 10:18; 14:31; 15:10; 18:11), imitates his Father in word (Jn 5:19-20; 8:28, 38; 12:50; 14:24; 15:15) and deed (Jn 5:17; 8:28; 10:25, 32, 37), and honors him (Jn 8:49-50). Jesus has come in the "name" of his Father, meaning that he embodies what has been revealed of God to humankind (Jn 5:43; 10:25). To honor the Son is to honor the Father (Jn 5:23; cf. 15:23; 1 Jn 2:22-24). God the Father has set his "seal" on the Son of Man, meaning that Jesus bears the stamp of God's personal authority (Jn 6:27). To know Jesus is to know the Father (Jn 1:14, 18; 8:19; 14:7-9; cf. 16:3). As the Father glorifies the Son (Jn 8:54; 13:31-32; 17:5, 22, 24), so the Son glorifies the Father (Jn 17:4); Father and Son glorify one another (Jn 17:1), and the Father is glorified in the Son's glory (Jn 10:4; 12:23 with Jn 12:28; 13:31; 14:13). The Father and Jesus are one (Jn 10:30), and they indwell one another (Jn 10:38; 14:10-11, 20; 17:21, 23). Jesus is the exclusive way to the Father (Jn 14:6). God's paternity of Jesus differs in kind from his paternity of Jesus' disciples (Jn 20:17). In the Johannine literature only Jesus is ever designated the "Son" (υἱός) of God; John is careful to call the disciples "children" (τέκνα) of God.

Based on the well-known fact that children bear a family resemblance to their parents, the metaphor of father and son applied to the Godhead conveys two main ideas: homogeneity of nature, and derivation of the second from the first. Since homogeneity follows from identity of being, which we examined in the preceding subsection, here we concentrate on the idea of derivation.

In what sense does John imagine the Son to be derived from the Father? The Son "has life in himself" as does the Father (Jn 5:26), is "that which was from the beginning," "the eternal life which was with the Father" (1 Jn 1:1, 2), and so must be eternally self-existent. This is confirmed by passages that speak of his presence with the Father before the foundation of the world (Jn 1:1-2; 17:5, 24). So we are not to envisage an act of generation in time like a human birth, bringing the Son into being out of nonexistence. Rather, to have life in oneself, to be characterized by aseity, has been "granted" to the Son by the Father (Jn 5:26).[107] This is why the Son has life not "through" the Father as the efficient cause of his existence, in the way the world does (πάντα δι᾽ αὐτοῦ ἐγένετο [Jn

---

[107]This is "clearly an ontological statement. . . . The Son has been given to self-subsist as God self-subsists" (Albert C. Sundberg, "*Isos Tō Theō* Christology in John 5:17-30," *BR* 15 [1970]: 24-25). See also the thoroughgoing exegesis of John 5:26 in Hans-Christian Kammler, *Christologie und Eschatologie: Joh 5,17-30 als Schlüsseltext johanneischer Theologie* (WUNT 126; Tübingen: Mohr Siebeck, 2000), pp. 169-83, confirming the line laid down in patristic exegesis of the passage (e.g., Augustine, *Tract. Ev. Jo.* 22.10).

1:3]), but rather "because of" the Father as his exemplary cause (ζῶ διὰ τὸν πατέρα [Jn 6:57]).[108] It is also why the Son has power, after laying down his life of his own accord, to take it again (Jn 10:17-18).

To be θεός, to have life in oneself, belongs to God alone. It belongs to both the Father and the Son, but it belongs to the Father intrinsically and to the Son by gift. Aseity is of the Father, and he communicates it to the Son. The Father initiated the infinite gift, and the Son received it. What is given does not come into being, change or pass out of existence, for it is the plenitude of life; but an Uncreate whose property it is can donate it to another Uncreate whose property it becomes. Becoming is not found in the divine essence itself; it describes the eternally existing Son's way of coming into possession of it. Were the having of life in oneself the original, independent property of both, there would be not only two eternals, but also two principles, fathers, powers in heaven—two gods. The unidirectional, nonreciprocal communication of the Father's essential being to the Son establishes the Father as the radical unit within the Godhead. It is in this sense—and in what follows from it: the Father is the commissioner and point of orientation for the Son's mission, the one from whom the Son sets out and to whom he returns—that the Father is greater than the Son (Jn 14:28).

For God the Father having begotten the Son, the most straightforward language is found in the second clause of 1 John 5:18. The believer, "the one born of God" (ὁ γεγεννημένος ἐκ τοῦ θεοῦ), does not sin because "he who was born of God" (ὁ γεννηθεὶς ἐκ τοῦ θεοῦ) keeps him or her. The latter participial phrase marks a different subject,[109] as does the introduction of the aorist tense, after the perfect tense has denoted the believer for the ninth consistent time in this epistle. Mention of the Son's begottenness is apt in this context, which, like 1 John 3:9, takes up the matter of sinlessness in a world dominated by the evil one. According to that verse, the reproduction of God's seed (σπέρμα) in one whom he begets makes the offspring unable to sin. However John understands

---

[108]It is inaccurate to say that the Father "gives authority to the Son to have life," or that the Son "receives life from the Father" or "has 'been given' such life by the Father" (Marianne Meye Thompson, "'The Living Father,'" *Semeia* 85 [1999]: 20-21; *God of the Gospel*, 69, 70, 79). This is exactly what the Son denies by claiming to have life in himself. What the Father gave the Son was not life but rather "to have life in himself"—the property to be self-existent as the Father is.

[109]Had John meant the believer to be the subject of the latter clause as well—"the one begotten of God keeps *himself*" (ἑαυτόν, with א Aᶜ K P Ψ 33 81 1739 *al.*)—there would have been no need to name the subject again. John would have written simply, ὁ γεγεννημένος ἐκ τοῦ θεοῦ οὐχ ἁμαρτάνει, ἀλλ' [. . .] τηρεῖ ἑαυτόν (or αὐτόν), "The one born of God does not sin, but . . . keeps himself," where the ellipsis marks the point where I have omitted the second subject that he in fact wrote.

that of believers, it will be true in an eminent degree of God's Son, who is thereby qualified to keep believers from sin. Here the Son's homogeneity in righteousness with the Father is to the fore, not his derivation, nor does 1 John 5:18 invite the reader to contemplate the eternal mystery of the generation as such, but that mystery is bound in the expression that John chooses.

Whether the adjective μονογενής provides further evidence for John's belief in the divine generation, as older translations such as *unigenitus* (Vulgate) and "only begotten" (King James; Douay-Rheims) would indicate, is now widely questioned on linguistic grounds.[110] The element -γενής either signifies "kind" (from γένος) or is linked etymologically to a root for "generation" (γεν, γον). In the latter case, the semantic value was much weakened by the first century, so that μονογενής often means little more than "only (one) of its kind."[111] But in the Greek-speaking environment -γενής could be, and sometimes was, taken to mean "only one born."[112] The question, then, is whether John used the word with this connotation.

Where μονογενής modifies υἱός ("Son" [Jn 3:16, 18; 1 Jn 4:9]) the ending may or may not be potent, and the sense could be "only Son." But in John 1:14 the word stands alone in the phrase ὡς μονογενοῦς παρὰ πατρός, "as of an only [...] from a father." Here -γενής implies a child, one born, as the Revised Standard Version recognizes by translating the bare adjective as "only Son."[113] Even more significantly, at John 1:18 the word occurs as part of the subject of the second

---

[110]In favor of the tradition are Friedrich Büchsel, "μονογενής," *TDNT* 4:737-41; John V. Dahms, "The Johannine Use of *Monogenēs* Reconsidered," *NTS* 29 (1983): 222-32. Representative of the more recent trend of opinion are Dale Moody, "God's Only Son: The Translation of John 3:16 in the Revised Standard Version," *JBL* 72 (1953): 213-19; LN, vol. 1, §58.52; Harris, *Jesus as God*, pp. 84-87; Gerard Pendrick, "Μονογενής," *NTS* 41 (1995): 587-600. BDAG leaves the matter open.

[111]For example, in the LXX μονογενής translates יָחִיד ("only") at Judges 11:34; Psalm 22:20 (LXX 21:21); 25:16 (LXX 24:16); 35:17 (LXX 34:17). The Hebrew adjective does not connote generation. The Johannine use is often understood in this sense. See, for example, Isak J. du Plessis, "Christ as the Only Begotten," in *The Christ of John: Essays on the Christology of the Fourth Gospel; Proceedings of the Fourth Meeting of Die Nuwe-Testamentiese Werkgennskap van Suid-Afrika* (Neotestamentica 2; Potchefstroom, South Africa: Pro Rege, 1971), pp. 22-31.

[112]Büchsel, "μονογενής," p. 738n6; Pendrick, "Μονογενής," pp. 588, 592. These writers point to parallel formations such as διο-γενής ("born of Zeus"), γη-γενής ("earth-born"), εὐ-γενής ("noble, high-born"), and συγ-γενής ("related, kin, sharing the same birth"), where -γενής denotes sharing of nature based on derivation.

[113]In this context παρὰ πατρός refers to the Son's mission, not his filiation within the Trinity. Nevertheless, mention of a father implies that the μονογενής is his only offspring or son, not just an only "one" of some unspecified category. "La filiation est supposée par la mention du 'Père'" (Michèle Morgen, "Le [Fils] monogène dans les écrits johanniques: Évolution des traditions et élaboration rédactionnelle," *NTS* 53 [2007]: 177).

clause, according to the best manuscripts: "No one has ever seen God; [the] μονογενὴς θεός, who is in the bosom of the Father, he has made him known." The phrase in question cannot mean "only God," for the Father is the only God (ὁ μόνος θεός [Jn 5:44; 17:3]), and the Son is never so described. Μονογενής distinguishes this figure from the only God, and so must convey the fuller sense "only-begotten."[114] Within this clause a polarity between the μονογενής God and "the Father" requires a stress on the sonship or begottenness of the former. At least in the context of the prologue to the Fourth Gospel, where the relationship between the Father and his μονογενής is analogous to that between a speaker and the speaker's word (Jn 1:1-2), μονογενής points to the Son as generated.[115] John's point has to do with revelation. God unbegotten is unknowable except through another who, because he is begotten, could fittingly be sent (Jn 1:14), and who, because he is essentially God, can explain him authoritatively, from within.[116]

John, then, adumbrates the doctrine of the eternal generation of the Son. After him Justin, Origen, Athanasius, the Cappadocian Fathers and many others developed the doctrine further.[117] Already in John this idea, along with

---

[114]Some commentators impose a comma: μονογενής, θεός . . . ("[the] only [one], God . . ."), or take μονογενής as a substantival adjective. But this is grammatically impossible. (1) An adjective by itself cannot be the subject of a clause unless it is turned into a substantive by the addition of an article. The proposed interpretation flies in the face of general usage by separating the anarthrous adjective μονογενής from the noun θεός and taking it as a subject in its own right. (2) Μονογενής can be used absolutely where it qualifies no noun, but only in contexts where the implied noun, usually a "son" or "daughter," is clear (Lk 9:38; Jn 1:14; Heb 11:17). Here there is no such clear implication. (3) Indefinite nominative θεός elsewhere is always a predicate (Jn 1:1; 8:54; Apoc 21:7), never a subject. For these reasons, μονογενής and θεός in John 1:18 need each other. Μονογενής makes θεός definite as subject; θεός provides the substantive that μονογενής lacks on its own. Morgen rightly translates, "Monogène Dieu" ("Le Monogène," pp. 177-79).

[115]This was recognized by a shift, already in the period before the Arian controversy, from *unicus* to *unigenitus* "in one or more forms of the Old Latin in all the five passages where it has reference to our Lord, all occurring in St John's writings; and in the Prologue of the Gospel the change took place very early" (F. J. A. Hort, "On ΜΟΝΟΓΕΝΗΣ ΘΕΟΣ. Note D: Unicus *And* Unigenitus *Among the Latins*," in *Two Dissertations* [Cambridge: Macmillan, 1876], p. 50). For *unigenitus* at John 1:14, Hort cites Tertullian, *Against Praxeas* 16; Irenaeus, lat.² (42, 315); Novatian, *On the Trinity* 13; Old Latin MSS b, c, f. On John 1:18 he cites Tertullian, *Against Praxeas* 15; Irenaeus, lat.; Old Latin MSS b, c, e, f. The interplay between λόγος and μονογενής in the Johannine prologue also undergirds the trinitarian conclusion of Emmanuel Durand, "Λόγος, Μονογενής et Υἱός: Quelques implications trinitaires de la christologie johannique," *RSPT* 88 (2004): 93-103.

[116]It is just possible that μονογενής, in an Ephesian environment feeling the impact of the Augustan ideology, may also have served polemically to distinguish the Lord Jesus Christ, the sole ruler who is truly derivative from God, from the Caesars, who falsely claimed mythical descent from Jupiter (Lance Byron Richey, *Roman Imperial Ideology and the Gospel of John* [CBQMS 43; Washington, DC: Catholic Biblical Association of America, 2007], pp. 145-48).

[117]For an exposition of the mature Catholic doctrine of the eternal generation of the Son, see Aloysius

the concept of an essential identity of the Father and the Son, safeguards mono-theism by pointing to the Father as the ultimate ground of unity where a plu-rality is concerned. The Father's total self-donation to the Son may be seen as his supreme and eternal act of love (Jn 1:18 [κόλπος]; 3:35; 17:24) on the basis of which he has granted to the Son all created things as well (Jn 3:35; 13:3; 16:15; 17:7, 10; Apoc 5:7). Thus God's love for the world (Jn 3:16), stupendous though it is, is neither his oldest nor his deepest love, for behind it is a love internal to the Godhead, the Father's love for the Son (Jn 15:9).[118]

(4) The determining will behind the common action of God and his Son is the Father's. According to John's Gospel, the Son did not come into the world on his own initiative but was sent by God (Jn 7:28; 8:42; 13:3; 16:28). Jesus' food is to do his Father's will and complete his Father's work (Jn 4:34). He did not come to do his own will but his Father's (Jn 5:30; 6:38). The Father gave Jesus the work(s) that he is carrying out (Jn 5:36; 17:4). Jesus can do nothing of his own accord but only what he sees the Father doing (Jn 5:19). He judges only as he hears (Jn 5:30). He speaks only as his Father has taught him (Jn 3:11, 32; 7:17; 8:26, 28, 38, 40; 14:10; 15:15). Jesus keeps his Father's word (Jn 8:55).

This total compliance of the Son with the will of God is also a theme of the

---

Janssens, *The Mystery of the Trinity* (Fresno, CA: Academy Library Guild, 1954), pp. 48-60. On the Johannine anchorage for the doctrine, see J. Ernest Davey, *The Jesus of St. John: Historical and Christological Studies in the Fourth Gospel* (London: Lutterworth, 1958), pp. 73-157, summarized in his "Dogmatic Implications of the Foregoing Studies" as follows: "Eternal generation, or con-tinual derivation according to the Father's purposes, is the meaning of Sonship" (p. 164). Note also John V. Dahms, "Isaiah 55:11 and the Gospel of John," *EvQ* 53 (1981): 78-88; idem, "The Genera-tion of the Son," *JETS* 32 (1989): 493-501, esp. pp. 496-97. Maurice F. Wiles ("Eternal Generation," *JTS* 12 [1961]: 284-91) shows how the patristic doctrine developed by fits and starts from Origen to the time of the trinitarian controversies, but he does not go into the question of its congruence with the scriptural norm. For a critique of Wiles and a reaffirmation of the doctrine and of its biblical basis, see Colin E. Gunton, "'And in One Lord Jesus Christ . . . Begotten Not Made,'" in *Father, Son and Holy Spirit: Essays Toward a Fully Trinitarian Theology* (London: T & T Clark, 2003), pp. 58-74. The critical remarks on the doctrine in Robert L. Reymond, *John, Beloved Disciple: A Survey of His Theology* (Fearn: Mentor, 2001), pp. 63-71, are vitiated by a fundamental misunder-standing of it. Neither the church fathers who articulated the idea nor the medieval scholastics can be faulted for holding the error that the divine essence is generated. The Son is generated with respect to sonship only; the divine essence in itself is ingenerate.

[118]"Love must find within the divine Being himself an eternal object for its exercise. If God is the absolute Being, and the universe is not eternal but dependent upon his will, then must the essential nature of God as love find its object and exercise in God himself. This could not be the case if God were absolutely solitary; on the other hand, the conception of love requires the view that there is within his essence some kind of a manifoldness and intercommunion of life. The very nature of love as the outgoing, self-imparting impulse in God, suggests, and even seems to require, some conception of the divine Being which includes the idea of the interrelation of subject and object" (Stevens, *Johannine Theology*, p. 56).

Apocalypse. God gave Jesus Christ the contents of the book as a whole to show to his servants (Apoc 1:1). From the Father the reigning Christ has received messianic authority and power finally to smash the nations (Apoc 2:27). A striking symbol of monotheism shared with Jewish writings of the same milieu is the singular throne that represents God's supreme authority thirty-nine times throughout the book.[119] Jesus Christ is portrayed as sitting with God on his singular throne (Apoc 3:21; 5:6; 7:17; 22:1). To sit with him the Father granted to the Son (Apoc 3:21). From the right hand of the one sitting on the throne the Lamb takes the sealed scroll containing the script of the ages, which he is to enact (Apoc 5:7). In no case does Christ have another throne of his own. That Christ does sit on God's throne indicates his plenary authority as God's viceroy; that the throne is God's reserves heavenly power to a monarchy of the Father.

On this score John is immune from later rabbinic strictures designed to protect the truth that "only God can act independently in the heavenly realm." If the rabbis "were particularly scrupulous to avoid the connotation that any heavenly being could exercise *independent authority*,"[120] John too took pains to avoid that suggestion.

(5) Even where Jesus Christ is accorded devotion alongside of God, God remains its ultimate object. The Christian practice of offering devotion to Jesus together with God had a precedent in the royal court of Judah. Though the king was not regarded as a divine being, he was graced from on high to participate in the exercise of authority over God's people[121] and received honor as God's human regent (Ex 22:28; 1 Chron 28:5; 29:23; 2 Chron 9:8). In that capacity, his subjects did obeisance to him together with God: "And all the assembly blessed the LORD, the God of their ancestors, and bowed their heads and prostrated themselves before the LORD and the king" (1 Chron 29:20). This honorific act was not inconsistent with monotheism. It was an acknowledgment that the king had been granted a position and role within the sphere of God's unique rule.

Jesus, answering the Samaritan woman's query about where people ought to worship, assumes that God the Father is the proper object (Jn 4:21-24). Two individuals in the Fourth Gospel worship Jesus: the blind man whose eyes Jesus

---

[119]Bauckham, "Throne of God," pp. 51-53.
[120]Segal, *Two Powers*, p. 8n8. Note also Shaye J. D. Cohen's comment: "Monotheism was compromised not by the belief in the existence of supernatural powers but by the attribution of independence to them" (*From the Maccabees to the Mishnah* [LEC 7; Philadelphia: Westminster, 1987], p. 84).
[121]2 Sam 14:17, 20; 19:27; 1 Kings 3:28; Ps 89:19-27; Prov 16:10; 20:8; 25:5.

opened (Jn 9:38),[122] and doubting Thomas on seeing Jesus resurrected (Jn 20:28). But it is a teaching of this same Jesus that he seeks the glory of God (Jn 12:28; 15:8; 17:4), not his own (Jn 7:18; 8:50, 54), and that the Father is glorified in the Son (Jn 13:31; 14:13; 17:1).

A special concern of the Apocalypse is to show whom people should worship. An initial doxology to Jesus praises him for presenting those he redeemed "to his God and Father" (Apoc 1:5-6). The tract condemns Greco-Roman idolatry and associated worship practices (Apoc 2:14, 20; 9:20; 21:8; 22:15) and is especially barbed toward the Roman imperial cult (Apoc 2:13; 13; 17).[123] As an antidote, John records his tour of heaven by invitation (Apoc 4:1). There he saw the plan of God that sets the course of history, punctuated by scenes of angels and saints acclaiming God and the Lamb. God as creator is the object of adoration in the introductory throne room scene (Apoc 4). Next the Lamb comes and receives accolades for having been slain (Apoc 5:1-12). As all creatures in heaven and earth join the liturgy, their hymn lifts up both figures, with "him who sits on the throne" in the first place (Apoc 5:13). Another vision reveals a multitude of nations ascribing salvation to God on his throne and to the Lamb, in that order, followed immediately by all angels lauding God alone (Apoc 7:9-12). Yet other frames of heavenly worship focus just on God or his throne (Apoc 11:16-18; 14:2-3; 15:3-4; 16:5-7; 19:1-8). In the book as a whole, God is invariably the center of worship. Though Christ may be worshiped side by side with God, he is never isolated from God as an independent target of praise, nor does praise terminate on Christ without redounding to the glory of God.

Likewise prayer is offered to God. In the Gospel Jesus himself models praying to his Father (Jn 6:11; 11:22, 41-42; 12:28; 14:16; 16:26; 17). Jesus' disciples are to make prayers to the Father "according to his will" (1 Jn 5:14-16) and "in [Jesus'] name" (Jn 14:13-14; 15:16; 16:23, 24, 26). Answers to prayer come down from God (Jn 15:7 [*genēsetai*, a divine passive]; 1 Jn 3:22) or from Jesus acting for the Father's glory (Jn 14:13-14). The Apocalypse pictures the prayers of the saints rising from golden bowls of incense in the presence of God (Apoc 8:3-4), which is also the presence of the Lamb (Apoc 5:8 [but God is mentioned in Apoc 5:13]). The only instance in the Johannine literature of a prayer addressed

---

[122]Martijn Steegen, "To Worship the Johannine 'Son of Man': John 9,38 as Refocusing on the Father," *Bib* 91 (2010): 534-54.

[123]Paul A. Rainbow, *The Pith of the Apocalypse: Essential Message and Principles for Interpretation* (Eugene, OR: Wipf & Stock, 2008), pp. 18-22.

to Jesus is the *maranatha* cry translated into Greek at the end of the Apocalypse: "Come, Lord Jesus!" (cf. 1 Cor 16:22).

In view of these five considerations, John's idea of God stands in continuity with that of prerabbinic Jewish monotheism, from which it drew all its elements. Undoubtedly, when the Son of God was distinguished as a second subject within the unity of the divine, a configuration of monotheism emerged, the full like of which had not been seen. But it was a blooming of commingled tendrils that had been growing in the soil of Judaism for centuries. When the Tannaim and Amoraim later decided to define themselves as unitarians, they chopped away ancient branches of their own heritage.[124]

***Revelation of the Father in the Christ-event.*** By enriching the divine unity, Jesus Christ in the Johannine literature is the focus of every facet of God's revelation of himself, building on the Old Testament. Ultimately, it is God the Father who makes himself known in the Son, in a new situation in which "God must be understood in terms of Jesus."[125] The Johannine perspective on God is stated concisely at the end of the First Epistle: "The Son of God has come and given us understanding, to know him who is true; and we are in him who is true, in his Son Jesus Christ" (1 Jn 5:20). That the God of Israel is the "true God" is a formula of Jewish monotheism (2 Chron 15:3; Jer 10:10; 1 Thess 1:9); therefore "he who is true" refers to God the Father. But we are "in" him who is true precisely in the sense that we are "in his Son Jesus Christ." To be in the Son is to be in the Father; such is the means of abiding in God, because the Father himself is in the Son and the Son in the Father (cf. Jn 17:21). When John goes on to add "This is the true God and eternal life," he can only mean by "this" the Father insofar as he is known in the Son. The true God is the God who has explained himself in christological terms.

Before the foundation of the world there was already a dynamism of fellowship and of love among personal entities in the eternal life of the one God (Jn 1:1-2). This intradivine love was part of the splendor that the Son enjoyed with the Father (Jn 17:5, 24). God was not lonely; he did not undertake to make the universe out of any deficiency of his own. Even as the fecundity of the Father's infinite being must flow outwards to constitute another Eternal in himself, so his generous nature must bestow his own moral and spiritual image on finite being called into existence out of nothing. The lately revealed christological

---

[124]Boyarin, "Two Powers."

[125]C. K. Barrett, *The Gospel According to St. John* (2nd ed.; Philadelphia: Westminster, 1978), p. 99.

face of God shows with a more poignant clarity than ever before that the universe is founded on love.

As we have seen, God remains the creator in John's view (Apoc 4:11; 10:6). He acted "through" the Logos as another bearer of his own divinity (instrumental διά [Jn 1:3, 10]). God in the act of creation had no helper other than Godself—namely, an agent constituted from his own being. The agency of the Logos in no way upstages the role of the Father as primal originator.

As in protology, so in eschatology. The Father raises the dead, even if it is through the Son that he does so (Jn 5:21). Judgment belongs to God, who has given all judgment to the Son (Jn 3:36; 5:22; 12:26; Apoc 3:2, 5). If the throne that represents everlasting rule is that of God and of the Lamb (Apoc 22:1), it is the Father who has granted to Jesus to sit down with him upon it (Apoc 3:21). When all has been fulfilled, God will be shown to have been true to his revealed nature and his covenant (Apoc 11:19; 21:3). God in Johannine theology relinquishes none of his unique prerogatives, least of all where the Father carries them out through the Son.

God is the author of divine revelation and the almighty one whose plan for the universe reveals his glory, acting through Jesus Christ.[126] If he sends the prophets to point to Christ, nevertheless he it is who sends them (Jn 1:6, 33; 12:38, 40; Apoc 1:1), and likewise angels to do his will (Jn 1:51; Apoc 3:5; 8:2; 10:1; 15:6; 18:1). The Scriptures as a whole testify of Jesus, but as the witness of the Father himself they make up the evidence that clinches Jesus' case (Jn 5:37-44).

The reason why the world needs a savior is that God as high judge has passed sentence of death on sin (Jn 5:24, 29; 8:51; 1 Jn 3:14), in the same way that he sent lethal serpents to judge Israel's rebellion in the wilderness so that Moses had to raise a serpent to stem the spreading death (Num 21:4-9; cf. Jn 3:14). God's "wrath" against sin will be carried out in the future (Apoc 6:16-17; 11:18; 14:10, 19; 15:1, 7; 16:1, 19; 19:15; cf. 20:14-15), but it already abides on the world-system and is not lifted except in the case of those who find refuge in the Son (Jn 3:36). So the world is in imminent danger of perishing (Jn 3:16; 6:39; 10:28; 11:50) and is in fact passing away (1 Jn 2:8, 17).

God himself loved the world (Jn 3:16-17; 1 Jn 4:9, 10-11) and planned its redemption. The Father gave to the Son those who are to come to him and be saved through him (Jn 6:37, 65; 17:2, 6, 9, 24), whose names have been written

---

[126]Kobus de Smidt, "A Meta-Theology of ὁ θεός in Revelation 1:1-2," *Neot* 38 (2004): 183-208.

in the heavenly book of life from the foundation of the world (Apoc 13:8; 17:8; 20:12, 15). It was as "the Lamb of God," meaning the Lamb provided by God himself (cf. Gen 22:8, 14), that Jesus appeared (Jn 1:29, 36). By his blood he bought people "for God" (Apoc 5:9), to be firstfruits "to God" (Apoc 14:4). It is God's will that on the last day Jesus raise to life those whom God gave him (Jn 6:39-40). God owns the house over which the Son has disposal (Jn 8:35; 14:2). Redemption, like creation, is the Father's idea. If, in the early worship scenes of the Apocalypse, the work of creation is appropriated to God (Apoc 4:11) and that of redemption to the Lamb (Apoc 5:9-10), yet at a later point we hear, "Salvation belongs to our God who sits upon the throne, and to the Lamb" (Apoc 7:10).

God is the prime mover who set the program of redemption in process. He is the sender of the Son[127] and the one to whom the Son returned having fulfilled his mission (Jn 7:33-36; 13:1, 3; 14:6, 12, 28; 16:5, 10, 17, 28; 17:11, 13; 20:17; Apoc 12:5). God assigned Jesus his "work" (Jn 4:34; 5:36; 17:4). God's will determines that "it is necessary" (δεῖ) for certain things to happen in Jesus' ministry, particularly his death and resurrection (Jn 3:14; 4:4; 9:4; 10:16; 12:34; 20:9). God gave Jesus "commandment" what to do (Jn 10:18; 14:31; 15:10), gave him "authority over all flesh" (Jn 17:2). God measured the span of time within which Jesus had to work (Jn 9:4; 11:9-10; 13:33), God fixed Jesus' "hour" (Jn 2:4; 7:6, 8, 30; 8:20; 12:23, 27; 13:1; 17:1). It is in reference to this mandate that Jesus finally cries, "It is finished" (τετέλεσται [Jn 19:30]).

During the earthly ministry Jesus repeatedly claims his Father as one who bears witness to him (Jn 5:37-44; 8:16-18; 12:28-30; cf. 1 Jn 5:9-11). The Father is the power behind Jesus' signs (Jn 3:2; 6:30-32), the source of Jesus' words and teaching (Jn 3:34; 7:16-17; 8:26, 28, 38, 40, 47; 12:49-50; 14:10, 24; 17:8, 14), the doer of Jesus' works (Jn 10:37-38; 14:10-11). Jesus knows that in his darkest hour, when all his disciples will have abandoned him, he will not be alone, for the Father is with him (Jn 16:32).

Jesus' death has a direct impact on God the Father, which fact John puts in terms of "propitiation" (ἱλασμός). The exact sense of the word was a matter of scrutiny and debate in twentieth-century New Testament scholarship.[128] In John

---

[127]"God" is the subject who sends Jesus (Jn 3:34; 8:42), he "who sent [Jesus]" (Jn 7:29; 12:44-45; 13:20; 15:21); the "Father" is the sender (Jn 17:18, 21, 23, 25; 20:21; 1 Jn 4:14); the Son comes "from God" (Jn 13:3), "from heaven" (Jn 3:31; 6:32-33).

[128]C. H. Dodd ignited the debate by denying what most had thought, that the word in biblical usage has the same sense that it has universally in pagan literature, of averting wrath (*The Bible and the*

it has its usual sense, prevalent and undisputed in nonbiblical Greek, of appeasement or conciliation, as is apparent in 1 John 2:1-2. A child of God who has committed sin needs an "advocate [παράκλητος] with the Father, Jesus Christ the righteous one." That is, such a person needs a counsel for the defense who can go to the aggrieved officer of law and plead his own standing as righteous on behalf of the fallen. Given the fact that God's judgment and wrath form the backcloth to the concept of salvation in the Fourth Gospel and in the Apocalypse, it is hardly out of character for John to use a noun that indicates the removal of God's wrath in his First Epistle. When brought into association with the biblical concept of God, propitiation, like any metaphor, is purged of connotations that it has in human relationships. It is not the buttering up of one turned sore and resentful toward the offender; it is the satisfaction of God's inviolable holiness without which he cannot extend forgiveness with integrity.[129] That this thought of God requiring to be placated is by no means inconsistent with God's loving nature is clear at 1 John 4:10, where God's love is shown precisely in that he sent his Son to be the propitiation for our sins. Indeed, to present the death of Jesus in terms of a divine satisfaction makes it the supreme expression of God's love, for by upholding God's uncompromising holiness it clarifies the extremity to which God went to rescue the unholy (1 Jn 4:9-11, 19). Jesus' expiration on the cross is the image of God's refusal both to relax the moral order and to let the world perish. Here too the Father is supreme.

---

*Greeks* [London: Hodder & Stoughton, 1935], pp. 82-95). Others reaffirmed this semantic content (Leon Morris, *The Apostolic Preaching of the Cross* [3rd ed.; Grand Rapids: Eerdmans, 1965], pp. 144-213; David Hill, *Greek Words and Hebrew Meanings: Studies in the Semantics of Soteriological Terms* [SNTSMS 5; Cambridge: Cambridge University Press, 1967], pp. 23-48) or took up Dodd's side (Norman H. Young, "C. H. Dodd, 'Hilaskesthai' and His Critics," *EvQ* 48 [1976]: 67-78; idem, "'Hilaskesthai' and Related Words in the New Testament," *EvQ* 55 [1983]: 169-76). Thomas Knöppler has extended the scope of the debate by analyzing related expressions and affirms the presence of the concept of propitiation and its importance in most books of the New Testament (*Sühne im Neuen Testament: Studien zum urchristlichen Verständnis der Heilsbedeutung des Todes Jesu* [WMANT 88; Neukirchen-Vluyn: Neukirchener Verlag, 2001]).

[129]"Biblical language avoids the expression of the idea that God is, in his disposition or feeling, averse to forgiveness. . . . The Biblical idea is that the obstacle to forgiveness lies in his essential righteousness which so conditions his grace that without its satisfaction God cannot, in self-consistency, forgive. . . . In heathenism men win the favor of the gods; in Biblical religion God's favor is sovereign and free, but it manifests itself in accord with the whole nature of God; its operation in the forgiveness of sin is conditioned upon the manifestation, at the same time, of the divine displeasure at sin and the assertion of its desert of punishment. God cannot forgive as if he were mere good nature. He can forgive only in accordance with his changeless, essential righteousness, which must be vindicated and satisfied. To effect this vindication and satisfaction is the function of sacrifice or expiation in the Bible" (Stevens, *Johannine Theology*, pp. 183-84).

As in the Old Testament, the divine spirit is the "Spirit of God" (1 Jn 4:2; cf. "seven spirits [of God]" in Apoc 1:4; 4:5; 5:6.). The ascended Son dispenses the Spirit (Jn 15:26), having received the Spirit from God (Jn 1:32; 3:34), and God is the wellspring of the Spirit given to believers (Jn 7:39 [divine passive]; 14:16-17, 26; 15:26; 1 Jn 2:20, 27; 3:24–4:2; 4:13; Apoc 11:11).

Johannine soteriology begins and ends with God the Father.[130] Eternal life consists in knowing the only God and Jesus Christ, whom he sent (Jn 17:3). The Father has promised eternal life (1 Jn 2:25) and sets the requirements for salvation. To be saved, one must do the "work of God," which is to believe in him whom God has sent (Jn 6:28-29); one must keep "his commandment" (Jn 12:50; cf. 1 Jn 3:22-24) or "his commandments" (1 Jn 5:2-3; Apoc 12:17; 14:12), which involve believing in Jesus, loving one another, and doing the truth (2 Jn 4), and one must do "the will of God" (1 Jn 2:17). God is the first and proper object of believing (Jn 14:1). No one can come to Jesus unless drawn to him by the Father (Jn 6:44-45). Those who come to God and to Jesus are "born of God" (Jn 1:13; 1 Jn 3:9-10; 4:7; 5:1, 4, 18) or born "from above" (ἄνωθεν [Jn 3:3]). God adopts believers into his family, and Jesus' disciples become "children of God" (Jn 1:12; 11:52; 1 Jn 2:13; 3:1, 2, 10; 5:2), sharing the divine characteristics of truth (1 Jn 4:4, 6), sinlessness (1 Jn 5:19), indefectibility (2 Jn 2) and goodness (3 Jn 11), and bearing God's very name (Jn 17:11-12; Apoc 14:1). God is the forgiver of sins (1 Jn 1:9; 2:12). God himself undertakes to bring about good deeds in those who come to the light, so that on the day of judgment it may be known that they were wrought in God (Jn 3:21; cf. 1 Jn 3:17). God it is who preserves believers (Jn 10:29; 17:11, 15; Apoc 7:2-3; 9:4; 12:6), tends his vine (Jn 15:1-2), and sanctifies them in truth to the end of the age (Jn 17:17, 19). For their part, while they are to abide in Jesus (Jn 15:4-7), they are also to abide in the Father (1 Jn 2:24; 3:24; 4:15-16). God himself loves the disciples (Jn 14:21, 23; 16:27; 17:23, 26), indwells them (Jn 14:23), and receives their love (1 Jn 2:5, 15). To the Father they direct their prayers (Jn 11:22, 41-42; 12:28; 14:16; 15:16; 16:23-24, 26; 17; 1 Jn 3:22; Apoc 6:10) and their worship (Jn 4:21, 23-24; 5:23; Apoc 5:13-14; 7:11-12; 8:4; 14:2-3; 15:2-4; 19:10). Him they are to glorify (Jn 15:8; Apoc 7:10). It is with the Father and with his Son, Jesus Christ, that the apostles have "fellowship" and invite others to join (1 Jn 1:3). Grace, mercy and peace flow to us from God the Father and from Jesus Christ, the Father's Son (2 Jn 3).

---

[130]José Caba, "La iniciativa del Padre en la historia de la salvación según la teología joanea," *Greg* 87 (2006): 239-61.

Jesus confesses the Father to be greater than all (Jn 10:29), greater than he himself is (Jn 14:28). The Second Person of the Godhead looks up to his Father and calls him "my God" (Jn 20:17; Apoc 3:2, 12). To try to limit these statements to Jesus' temporary state of incarnation, as one stream of orthodoxy in the patristic church did,[131] will not wash. "The Father is greater than I" comes in a context where Jesus is explaining to his incredulous disciples that instead of being sad they ought to be happy for him because he is shortly to return to the Father, from whom he came and to whom he goes (Jn 16:28), to be enfolded once more in his loving embrace and to resume the pretemporal glory that the Father granted him (cf. Jn 1:18; 17:5, 24). Jesus, risen from the dead and about to ascend, calls God "my God," and any doubt about whether the ascended Christ continues to call him "my God" in his state of glory is dispelled when the glorified Lord (Apoc 1:12-20) is the very speaker at Apocalypse 3:2, 12. The Father has granted to the Son to be all that he is and to do all that he does. Therefore it is not in respect of any particular divine attribute, nor of the complete round of them, that the Son acknowledges him superior, but only in having received from him the grant and the commission that follows from it. In that respect, the Father comes first, always has, and always will.[132]

**Conclusion.** John presents the Christ-event as the beginning of the eschatological epiphany of the God of Israel. Because Jesus is the incarnate "God," what is revealed in him of the divine is in direct continuity with the revelation of God in the Hebrew Scriptures. Because Jesus is God "become flesh," the same content is revealed in a new way now at the dawnbreak of the eternal world order. New Testament scholarship rightly recognizes Christology as the "center" of the Johannine theology, but it has not always emphasized that the doctrine of God is the sphere that has such a center: the Christology is inextricable from the theology proper, and serves it.[133] John presents Jesus Christ as conspicuous but penultimate, for he was sent to reveal him who is ultimate, God the Fa-

---

[131]Patristic interpretations of this crux are collected and categorized in B. F. Westcott, *The Gospel According to St. John: The Greek Text with Introduction and Notes* (2 vols. in 1; Grand Rapids: Eerdmans, 1954), pp. 191-96. For a broader summary of the patristic material, see Maurice F. Wiles, *The Spiritual Gospel: The Interpretation of the Fourth Gospel in the Early Church* (Cambridge: University Press, 1960), pp. 120-24.

[132]"As far as human thought can penetrate such a mystery, it is reasonable to 'ground the congruity of the mission' of the Son upon the immanent pre-eminence of the Father" (Westcott, *St. John*, p. 191).

[133]Thompson, *God of the Gospel*, pp. 227-40.

ther.[134] In John's theology of persons and their relationships the Father is the person to whom all others—whether the Son, the Holy Spirit, the world, or those whom God has chosen out of the world—relate.

---

[134]For a glimpse into the reception history of John's concept of God, covering Luther, Calvin, B. F. Westcott, Heinrich Holtzmann, Rudolf Bultmann, and Raymond Brown, see Tord Larsson, *God in the Fourth Gospel: A Hermeneutical Study of the History of Interpretations* (ConBNT 35; Stockholm: Almqvist & Wiksell, 2001).

# THE WORLD

JOHN'S CONCEPT OF THE WORLD, like his view of God, is indebted to the Hebrew Bible and the Judaic tradition. What the Bible teaches about God, creation, angelic beings, humankind, good versus evil, sin and the history of the human race and of the Jewish people in particular forms the worldview within which the good news of Jesus Christ is meaningful. In this chapter we will note the distinctive vocabulary and body of symbols that John uses to refer to these things. We also will focus our attention on points where John's understanding of God's final revelation in Christ puts a fresh spin on long-familiar ideas.

This inquiry takes its departure from passages where John speaks of "the world" (ὁ κόσμος, ὁ αἰών), "all things" (τὰ πάντα), "the earth" (ἡ γῆ) and collocations such as "heaven and earth" (e.g., Apoc 5:3, 13) and "sea and land" (Apoc 10:2).

## THE BEGINNING AND END OF THE WORLD

A basic difference between God and the world is that the world has a beginning and an end. "In the beginning [ἐν ἀρχῇ] . . . all things came into being [πάντα . . . ἐγένετο]" (Jn 1:1, 3). Statements that God's Son "was from the beginning" (1 Jn 1:1; 2:13, 14) assume that for the world, in contrast to the divine Son, there was a beginning.[1] As usual, John points to this fact using a variety of terms.

---

[1]Some have wondered whether "from the beginning" in 1 John 1:1 could refer to the beginning of the gospel proclamation or of the Christian community or era rather than the absolute beginning of the world. That is unlikely. (1) "From the beginning" is a modifier of "that which was," not of the following "which we have heard." Emphasis falls on what existed from the beginning. (2) 1 John 1:2 is a parenthetical repetition of 1 John 1:1 in alternative wording. Here "the eternal life that was with the Father" corresponds to "that which was from the beginning" (1 Jn 1:1). (3) The parallel expression "he who is from the beginning" in 1 John 2:13-14 is undoubtedly cosmic in reference. In other contexts in John's Epistles, of course, "from the beginning" can have an intratemporal reference, whether to the beginning of history (1 Jn 3:8), or of Israel as a covenant people (1 Jn 2:7) or of the church (1 Jn 2:24; 3:11; 2 Jn 5-6).

The world had a "foundation" (καταβολή [Jn 17:24; Apoc 13:8; 17:8]). God "created" (κτίζω [Apoc 4:11; 10:6]) it, so that it is his "creation" (κτίσις [Apoc 3:14]) and consists of his "creatures" (κτίσμα, -ατα [Apoc 5:13; 8:9]). God "made" (ποιεῖν [Apoc 14:7]) heaven and earth.

Did John believe in creation *ex nihilo* ("out of nothing")? Other Jewish authors of the same period affirmed this doctrine more explicitly. In 2 Maccabees 7:28, written about two centuries earlier, we read, "Look at the heaven and the earth and see everything that is in them, and recognize that God did not make them out of things that existed (οὐκ ἐξ ὄντων)." Equally clear is Romans 4:17, from a few decades earlier than John's writings: God "calls into existence the things that do not exist [καλοῦντος τὰ μὴ ὄντα ὡς ὄντα]." In *2 Baruch*, a contemporary work, Baruch prays to God, "O hear me, you who created the earth . . . who in the beginning of the world called that which did not yet exist and they obeyed you" (*2 Bar.* 21:4). These passages are significant, not because John is likely to have read them, but because their authors were Palestinian Jews. They bear witness to a way of reading Genesis that is more widely attested among ancient Jews than is the Greek concept of primordial stuff (ὕλη), found in Philo of Alexandria and the Wisdom of Solomon (Wis 11:17).[2] To John the idea of eternal matter is foreign. A clause in Apocalypse 4:11, "you created all things, and because of your will [θέλημα] they existed [ἦσαν] and were created," agrees with the Gospel prologue: through God's Logos all things without exception "came to be" (ἐγένετο/γέγονεν [Jn 1:3, 10]).[3] Apart from God's will and efficient agency in founding, creating, making all

---

[2]Hebrews 11:3 likewise denies that matter existed before God's creative work, though this document has no direct tie with Palestinian Judaism. It has been questioned whether these and other like passages express belief in *creatio ex nihilo*. See Gerhard May, *Creatio ex Nihilo: The Doctrine of "Creation Out of Nothing" in Early Christian Thought* (trans. A. S. Worrall; Edinburgh: T & T Clark, 1994). May sees no such doctrine until the church's tussle with Middle Platonism and Gnosticism in the second century. But his readings of the evidence are strongly challenged by J. C. O'Neill, "How Early Is the Doctrine of *Creatio ex Nihilo*?" *JTS* 53 (2002): 449-65; Paul Copan and William Lane Craig, *Creation Out of Nothing: A Biblical, Philosophical, and Scientific Exploration* (Grand Rapids: Baker Academic; Leicester: Apollos, 2004), pp. 29-145. Copan and Craig (pp. 97, 107-12) demonstrate the possibility of interpreting even Philo and the Wisdom of Solomon as teaching an initial creation of the ὕλη out of nothing.

[3]So, for John 1:3 (to choose just a few of the most prominent commentators): Rudolf Bultmann, *The Gospel of John: A Commentary* (ed. R. W. N. Hoare and J. K. Riches; trans. G. R. Beasley-Murray; Philadelphia: Westminster, 1971), p. 38; Raymond E. Brown, *The Gospel According to John: Introduction, Translation, and Notes* (2 vols.; AB 29, 29A; Garden City, NY: Doubleday, 1966-1970), 1:8; Rudolf Schnackenburg, *The Gospel According to St. John* (trans. Kevin Smyth et al.; 3 vols.; New York: Herder & Herder; Seabury; Crossroad, 1968-1982), 1:238-39; Klaus Wengst, *Das Johannesevangelium* (2 vols; THKNT 4; Stuttgart: Kohlhammer, 2000-2001), 1:48.

things, the universe did not exist. That amounts to creation out of nothing.

So too the world's end lies in the hand of God. God (with the Son of God) is the Alpha and the Omega (Apoc 1:8; 21:6; 22:13), "the beginning and the end" (ἡ ἀρχὴ καὶ τὸ τέλος [Apoc 21:6; 22:13]). John never speaks of a final cessation of the universe; rather, he knows of blessings that believers will enjoy "forever" (εἰς τὸν αἰῶνα [Jn 4:14; 6:51, 58; 8:35, 51, 52; 10:28; 11:26; 12:34; 13:8; 14:6]), in "a new heaven and new earth" (Apoc 21:1). Apocalyptic passages that portray a future cosmic dissolution (Apoc 6:12-17; 16:18-21; 20:11) look for God's judgment and transformation of the present world order, not for God to discard his first creation and replace it with something else *de novo*.[4] A contrasting verse sees continuity when it says the kingdom of the world is destined to "become" (γενέσθαι) the kingdom of our Lord and of his Christ, who will reign forever (Apoc 11:15).[5] "Whatever God does endures forever" (Eccles 3:14), "like the earth, which he has founded forever" (Ps 78:69). But that it should last incessantly is not an intrinsic property of the world. It lasts only because God upholds it (Jn 5:17).

Johannine thought about the creation is irreconcilable with the devaluation of the world in Gnostic dualism. Gnosticism was a flux of speculative systems that swirled across the Mediterranean basin in the second and third centuries of the Christian era, fed syncretistically by streams from the first century. Some Gnostic teachers considered the world to have been created by an evil archon, others by a merely lesser deity than the one who is ineffable. All shared the view that the original deity and the universe are polar opposites in no fruitful relationship.[6] Every page of the Johannine literature cries out that the world exists because God wanted it to be, and God wants it to enjoy a relationship with him. "God . . . loved the world" (Jn 3:16).[7]

---

[4]Jeannine K. Brown, "Creation's Renewal in the Gospel of John," *CBQ* 72 (2010): 275-90; Jonathan Moo, "Continuity, Discontinuity, and Hope: The Contribution of New Testament Eschatology to a Distinctively Christian Environmental Ethos," *TynBul* 61 (2010): 21-44; Mark B. Stephens, *Annihilation or Renewal? The Meaning and Function of New Creation in the Book of Revelation* (WUNT 2/307; Tübingen: Mohr Siebeck, 2011).

[5]Paul F. Guttesen, *Leaning into the Future: The Kingdom of God in the Theology of Jürgen Moltmann and in the Book of Revelation* (PTMS 117; Eugene, OR: Pickwick, 2009).

[6]Hans Jonas, *The Gnostic Religion: The Message of the Alien God and the Beginnings of Christianity* (2nd ed.; Boston: Beacon, 1963), pp. 42-43, 250-53; W. K. Grossouw, "Christian Spirituality in John," in *A Companion to John: Readings in Johannine Theology (John's Gospel and Epistles)* (ed. Michael J. Taylor; New York: Alba House, 1970), pp. 209-10.

[7]John Painter, "Earth Made Whole: John's Rereading of Genesis," in *Word, Theology, and Community in John* (ed. John Painter, R. Alan Culpepper and Fernando F. Segovia; St. Louis: Chalice, 2002), pp. 65-84.

The world, then, came into being and is kept from passing away by the will of God. It is contingent, dependent on him, finite, temporal, yet he made it and ascribes worth to it.

## LIGHT VERSUS DARKNESS

"And God saw everything that he had made, and behold, it was very good" (Gen 1:31). John's midrash on the creation account summarizes God's gifts in two symbols: life (Gen 2:7) and light (Gen 1:3).[8] The life that is in the Logos enlightens humankind (Jn 1:4, 9). Wherever the light shines, it overcomes the darkness and is not overcome by it (Jn 1:5).

Whence, then, came darkness? In the prologue to the Fourth Gospel, as in Genesis 1, darkness makes a jarring appearance without explanation. If God's nature is light containing no shadow (1 Jn 1:5), if through the Logos he made everything that was made (Jn 1:3),[9] and everything that he made was good, how was there darkness? Surely there was no eternal, metaphysical principle over against God. Surely God did not make evil. The rabbis in their perplexity declared the story of creation to be one of the passages not to be expounded by novices (*m. Ḥag.* 2:1), one of the "matters which He has withheld from His creatures" (*Rab. Gen.* 1:5). Concerning it, Rabbi Eleazar said in the name of Ben Sira, "Do not pry into things too hard for you or examine what is beyond your reach" (*y. Ḥag.* 2:1, 47c).

Genesis 1 and the Johannine prologue have the same opening sequence: first God creates something (Gen 1:1; Jn 1:3),[10] and then darkness is there in the background (Gen 1:2-3; Jn 1:5). Darkness, then, is the antipode not of God or

---

[8]On life and light, see Karl Schelkle, "John's Theology of Man and the World," in *A Companion to John: Readings in Johannine Theology (John's Gospel and Epistles)* (ed. Michael J. Taylor; New York: Alba House, 1970), pp. 127-32.

[9]In spite of the valiant arguments of E. L. Miller (*Salvation-History in the Prologue of John: The Significance of John 1:3-4* [NovTSup 60; Leiden: Brill, 1989]), the words "that was made" (ὃ γέγονεν) belong to the sentence that begins in John 1:3, not to the one that ends in John 1:4. The effect of adding the clause in question to what precedes ("without him was not anything made") is to distinguish the created universe "that was made" from God and his Logos, who were not made, but were in the beginning (Jn 1:1-2). With its "in him was life," John 1:4 launches into a further statement about the uncreated Logos, not about the life or light as such of humankind. John 1:5, on the light shining in the darkness, is still ruminating on Genesis 1:3, not yet on the incarnation, which first comes into view in John 1:9, 14. On the punctuation of John 1:3-4, see Hartwig Thyen, *Studien zum Corpus Iohanneum* (WUNT 214; Tübingen: Mohr Siebeck, 2007), pp. 411-17.

[10]For this way of understanding Genesis 1:1, as opposed to the alternative reading that takes Genesis 1:1-2 as setting the scene for God's creative work to begin only in Genesis 1:3, see Painter, "Earth Made Whole," pp. 68-71.

of his creative working, but rather of what he makes. In the context of the monotheistic creation accounts of the Bible darkness signifies the shadowy edge of what is finite, the nothingness or absence of positive being that lies beyond the boundary of what God makes and constitutes good. In itself it is an entailment of the definition of finitude, not an evil. It becomes a moral and spiritual evil when created beings love it and move toward it and away from the light (Jn 3:19-20), so that they "walk" in darkness (Jn 8:12; 12:35; 1 Jn 1:6; 2:9, 11) or "abide" in it (Jn 12:46) in danger of being engulfed by it (Jn 12:35). "Night" functions in the Gospel as a symbol of self-chosen ignorance of God (Jn 3:2; 9:4; 11:10; 19:39) or of self-chosen perdition (Jn 13:30). In the renewed world there will no longer be night (Apoc 21:25; 22:5). "Blindness" is the state of those who prefer the dark (Jn 9; 1 Jn 2:11). God neither put human beings in darkness nor makes them to enter into darkness, but instead gave them a life that was their original light and continues to illumine every person (Jn 1:4, 9). All things that are came into being by God's will through the Logos and were a fit gift from the Father to the Son (Jn 3:35).[11]

Angels are fellow servants and worshipers of God with humans (Apoc 19:10; 22:9). John no more answers the question of when God made the angels than the rest of the Bible does. On the basis of the Scriptures (esp. Daniel, Zechariah) and of his own apocalyptic experience he shares the belief of the majority of his Jewish contemporaries that angels exist (Jn 12:29).[12] Angels play a minimal role in the Fourth Gospel; Jesus mentions them once as messengers between heaven and earth (Jn 1:51), and Mary Magdalene meets two angels in Jesus' empty tomb after his resurrection (Jn 20:12). There is no reason for angels to appear in the Epistles. The Apocalypse has the most elaborate angelology of any canonical book.

In the Apocalypse we learn of the angelic ranks. Nearest God's throne are the four "living creatures" (Apoc 4:6-8), equivalent to the seraphim of Isaiah (Is 6:2-3) and the cherubim of Ezekiel (Ezek 1:5-25). These four mediate God's rule over all sectors of the creation, as is clear from their likeness to a lion, an ox, a man and an eagle. Next are the seven archangels "who stand before God" (Apoc 8:2) and serve as priests in his temple (Apoc 15:1, 5).[13] Then come the

---

[11]Further on light and darkness as themes of the Fourth Gospel, see Craig R. Koester, *Symbolism in the Fourth Gospel: Meaning, Mystery, Community* (2nd ed.; Minneapolis: Fortress, 2003), pp. 141-73.

[12]Doubt about whether angels exist seems to have been a peculiarity of the party of the Sadducees (Acts 23:8).

[13]John does not integrate the seven archangels of Apocalypse 8–9 into the concentric circles of

twenty-four elders, whose number (corresponding either to twelve patriarchs plus twelve apostles or to the number of priestly courses appointed by David according to 1 Chron 24:7-19) suggests an assignment to watch over the people of God (Apoc 4:4, 10).[14] Finally, there are "myriads of myriads and thousands of thousands" of other angels (Apoc 5:11). One or more appearances of a "mighty" angel in the Apocalypse (Apoc 10:1; 18:2, 21) may be Gabriel, God's "man of might" who brings messages to the faithful (Dan 8:16; 9:21). Michael (Apoc 12:7) is the prince who defends Israel (Dan 10:13, 21; 12:1). Particular angels have power over fire (Apoc 14:18) and over water (Apoc 16:5); we probably can infer the same for earth and air, to complete the four elements of ancient science. Yet other angels are associated with stars (Apoc 1:20; 9:1). Angels, then, are pillars of the cosmic order and guardians of God's people.

Demons are less prominent in the Johannine corpus. The Gospel, unlike the Synoptics, has no account of an exorcism. As in the Synoptic Gospels, Jesus' opponents pin on him the calumny of being demon-possessed (Jn 7:20; 8:48, 52; 10:20-21; cf. Mt 9:34; 11:18; 12:24; Mk 3:22; Lk 7:33; 11:15). He denies the charge, not the reality of demons. Jesus considers Judas to be a devil (Jn 6:70).[15] According to the Apocalypse, idolatrous worship is unknowingly directed to demons (Apoc 9:20), demonic spirits will gather the kings of the world to Armageddon (Apoc 16:14), and demons might populate a desolate waste (Apoc 18:2).

More definite in conception is the king of the demons. By name he is "Abaddon" (Hebrew) or "Apollyon" (Greek, "ruiner" [Apoc 9:11]), "the devil" (Jn 8:44; 13:2; 1 Jn 3:8, 10; Apoc 2:10; 12:9, 12; 20:2, 10), "Satan" (Jn 13:27; Apoc 2:9, 13, 24; 3:9; 12:9; 20:2, 7), "the evil one" (Jn 17:15; 1 Jn 2:13-14; 3:12; 5:18-19) or "he who is in the world" (1 Jn 4:4). His reach is totalitarian. Jesus calls him "the ruler of this world" (Jn 12:31; 14:30; 16:11),[16] the First Epistle says that the whole world lies in him—that is, in his power (1 Jn 5:19)—and the Apocalypse shows him seducing the nations to their destruction (Apoc 16:13-14; 20:8, 10). From the beginning he sinned (1 Jn

---

Apocalypse 4–5. I position them next after the four by hazarding the guess that ascending numbers of angels rank by rank signify descending levels of authority.

[14]Whether the twenty-four elders are angelic or human figures has often been discussed. That they have human features no more makes them human beings than the bestial characteristics of three of the four living creatures make them animals. Their position in the retinue between the four and the myriads of angels classes them among angels, as does their role as guides who stand outside the groups of redeemed human beings whom they explain (Apoc 7:13-14).

[15]André Gagné, "Caractérisation des figures de Satan et de Judas dans le IVᵉ évangile: Stratégie narrative et déploiement des intrigues de conflit," ScEs 55 (2003): 263-84.

[16]Torsten Löfstedt, "The Ruler of This World," SEÅ 74 (2009): 55-79.

3:8) and was a murderer (Jn 8:44). Lies spew from his very character; he is "the father of lies" (Jn 8:44), "the deceiver of the whole world" (Apoc 12:9). From these descriptions he emerges as a personal, spiritual being with moral responsibility under God, one who seeks to undo what God does,[17] above all the Johannine ideals of life and truth.[18] Included within the universe of things created by God, he can only have been good before he went wrong. At one remote time, it is implied, he was in the truth, but "did not stand" (οὐκ ἔστηκεν) in it (Jn 8:44). It is hard to say whether the depiction of him as a celestial dragon whose tail swept down a third of the stars (Apoc 12:3-4) is a timeless symbol of a violent and reckless nature or points to an event near the morning of history that brought about the perversion of fellow angels. Deadly though he is, his peer is Michael the archangel, not God, and Michael is the stronger (Apoc 12:7-9).

Darkness, then, arises only in the created realm, and only as an absence of what God places there. It exists at the finite edge where the light has not come, and it becomes evil only when creatures choose it in preference to the light and thus render themselves guilty.

## THE HUMAN RACE AND SIN

John's richly nuanced usage of "the world" (ὁ κόσμος) conveys his concept of the human race. In the great majority of its 103 occurrences in the Johannine literature[19] the world refers to the world of humanity.[20] Unlike Paul, John's distinctive anthropological accents are not associated with the words "flesh," "body," "soul," "(human) spirit," "heart," "mind," "conscience," or "inner man"— though John uses all but the last two in non-technical ways—but with "(divine) spirit," "life," "freedom," "truth," and "falsehood."[21]

---

[17]Pieter G. R. Villiers, "Prime Evil and Its Many Faces in the Book of Revelation," *Neot* 34 (2000): 57-85.

[18]The Johannine stress on sin as consisting of falsehood and murder is brought out by Jose Ignacio González Faus, "Sin of the World, Light of the World," in *2000: Reality and Hope* (ed. Virgil Elizondo and Jon Sobrino; Concilium 1999/5; London: SCM Press, 1999), pp. 39-49.

[19]The "world" is a characteristic usage of John. Compare Synoptic Gospels and Acts, 15×; Pauline Epistles, 46×; General Epistles (excluding the Johannine), 18×; Johannine literature, 103×; New Testament total, 182×.

[20]In a few places "world" denotes the whole of the creation (Jn 1:9; 17:5, 24; Apoc 11:15; 13:8; 17:8). John 21:35 says that the world is too small to contain what could be written about Jesus. Everywhere else it denotes or involves the world of people. David J. Clark, "The Word *Kosmos* 'World' in John 17," *BT* 50 (1999): 401-6; Stanley B. Marrow, "Κόσμος in John," *CBQ* 64 (2002): 90-102.

[21]Christina Urban, *Das Menschenbild nach dem Johannesevangelium: Grundlagen johanneischer Anthropologie* (WUNT 2/137; Tübingen: Mohr Siebeck, 2001).

A knowledge of the temptation account in Genesis 3 lies back of John's descriptions of the devil as the archdeceiver (Jn 8:44) and "that ancient serpent" (Apoc 12:9; 20:2). But John never speaks of Adam or Eve as representative individuals (cf. Gen 1–5) and has nothing akin to the Pauline Adam/Christ typology. He thinks of the world collectively. God created it at first (e.g., Jn 1:10: "the world came to be through him"), but now it finds itself in danger of perishing and in desperate need of salvation (e.g., Jn 3:16). The world needs a Lamb to take away sin (Jn 1:29); it has offended the Father and needs an advocate to make propitiation (1 Jn 2:2); it is "in [its] sin," and death is certain unless it believes in Jesus (Jn 8:21, 24). There is a sobering use of the generic "man" at John 2:25. Jesus did not entrust himself to the many who were impressed by his signs at the feast, "because he knew all men and needed no one to bear witness of man [περὶ τοῦ ἀνθρώπου]; for he himself knew what was in man [ἐν τῷ ἀνθρώπῳ]." After the creation, at the very beginning of human history, a fall took place, but John does not enlarge on the details.

***Perspectives on sin and sins.*** "Sin" occurs in the Johannine literature either as an abstract singular noun,[22] or, in the plural, in reference to particular acts of sin[23] sometimes these senses are juxtaposed (Jn 8:21, 24; 1 Jn 3:4-5; 5:16-17).[24] Sin is rooted in love for the world apart from its creator, which John characterizes as a love for darkness rather than light (Jn 3:19-20). Since God's light entered into the world through the Torah before it came through Jesus Christ (Jn 1:9, 17), sin may be defined in a Judaic manner as revolt toward Torah, or in a christological manner as rejection of Jesus Christ. John, being a Jew who believes in Jesus, looks at the matter both ways. "None of you keeps the law," said Jesus (Jn 7:19), before warning his hearers that they were in danger of dying in their sin(s) (Jn 8:21, 24). So "every one who commits sin is guilty of lawlessness [ἀνομία]; sin is lawlessness" (1 Jn 3:4). Here speaks John the Jew. Especially in the First Epistle, where professing church members have turned out to deny Jesus by their actions, the emphasis is practical, and Torah is the standard against which one measures human behavior.[25] John follows Jesus in

---

[22]Jn 1:29; 8:21, 34 (2×), 46; 9:41 (2×); 15:22 (2×), 24; 16:8, 9; 1 Jn 1:7, 8; 3:4 (2×), 5, 8, 9; 5:17 (2×).

[23]Jn 8:24 (2×); 9:34; 19:11; 20:23; 1 Jn 1:9 (2×); 2:2, 12; 3:5; 4:10; 5:16 (2×); Apoc 1:5; 18:4, 5.

[24]On the literary treatment of sin in the Fourth Gospel, see Jean Zumstein, "Die Sünde im Johannesevangelium," *ZNW* 12 (2009): 27-35.

[25]The Mosaic commandments lie at the base of John's conception of "lawlessness" (ἀνομία), even if the term also connotes eschatological apostasy (cf. Mt 24:12), as suggested by Judith Lieu, *The Theology of the Johannine Epistles* (NTT; Cambridge: University Press, 1991), pp. 52-53, 61.

distilling the many precepts into the single command to love one's fellows (Mt 22:34-39; 1 Jn 3:23). Failure to love—to hate—is in effect to murder (1 Jn 3:11-15). This is to violate a cardinal value of Torah, with the result that the perpetrator wanders blindly in darkness (1 Jn 2:7-11). Like the prophets of old, John points out specific sins. Lady Babylon is guilty of fornication (Apoc 17:2, 4; 18:3, 9; 19:2), pride (Apoc 18:7-8) and greed for luxuries (Apoc 18:14, 16-17, 19). The vice lists in the Apocalypse reflect the Decalogue, selecting from it issues that were relevant to the churches of Asia in their Romanized environment: idolatry, practice of abominations, sorcery, uncleanness, pollution, acting like dogs, murder, immorality, fornication, lying, practice of falsehood (Apoc 9:20-21; 21:8, 27; 22:15).

But lawless deeds have a deeper cause in the sinner's attitude toward God, of which the index is the attitude toward God's supreme self-statement, his sending of his Son. The world in its darkness hates Jesus (Jn 7:7; 15:18, 23-25). Its sin consists in its unbelief toward Jesus (Jn 16:9).[26] To refuse to believe in Jesus is itself disobedience to God's commandment (1 Jn 3:23) and manifests itself in disobedience to other aspects of God's will (Jn 3:36). Here, in a Gospel written to point the world toward Jesus, is John's Christian voice.

Between the Judaic and the Christian outlooks on sin John sees a fit. Believing in Jesus and adhering to the love norms of the Torah go hand in hand (1 Jn 3:23). God's people are those who "keep his commandments" and also "bear testimony to Jesus" (Apoc 12:17; cf. 14:12). Anyone who recognizes the divine light in the Torah and is willing to perform God's will will acknowledge the divine light come in Jesus (Jn 7:17). Those Jewish leaders who disdained Jesus did so not because they were faithful observers of Torah, but because they were not. They searched the Scriptures without encountering God and had no love for God within them (Jn 5:37-40, 42). Precisely because they were knowledgeable in the Scriptures, they ought to have recognized the Son of God by his words and signs; their very knowledge increased their guilt (Jn 9:41; 15:22, 24).

*Sin as power over the sinner.* The effect of sinning, and especially of persistence in sin, on the mind is to plunge the sinner into the confusion of blindness (1 Jn 2:11). Due to this loss of sight, sin is a state that is easy to enter but impossible to exit. "Everyone who commits sin is a slave to sin," yet in their bondage

---

[26]"Sin is concentrated into the rejection of Christ" (C. K. Barrett, *The Gospel According to St. John* [2nd ed.; Philadelphia: Westminster, 1978], p. 80). See also Rainer Metzner, *Das Verständnis der Sünde im Johannesevangelium* (WUNT 122; Tübingen: Mohr Siebeck, 2000), p. 354.

sinners protest that they are free: "We . . . have never been in bondage to any one. How is it that you say, 'You will be made free'?" (Jn 8:33-34). In their blindness they claim to see: "Some of the Pharisees . . . said to him, 'Are we also blind?'" (Jn 9:40). Thus the deception wrought by the devil on the human race is invincible. Lured into darkness by an appearance of luminosity, sinners suppose that they have found a greater light when in fact their condition is fatal (Jn 8:42-47). Not only do they not believe, but also they can lose the ability to come to faith (Jn 8:43; 12:39). Left to their own devices, they sink ever deeper into a fathomless unreality where they put darkness for light and light for darkness (cf. Is 5:20). So they become impenitent, railing at the just judgment of God until crushed by it (Apoc 9:20-21; 16:11, 21).

Sin's prevailing power over the sinner is a biblical concept that receded in Judaism during the latter part of the Second Temple period, marking a point of difference between rabbinic Judaism and Christianity. The Hebrew Bible contains poignant expressions of human powerlessness over depravity. "All our righteous deeds are like a polluted garment" (Is 64:6). "Behold, their ears are uncircumcised, they cannot listen" (Jer 6:10). "Can the Ethiopian change his skin or the leopard his spots? Then also you can do good who are accustomed to do evil" (Jer 13:23). "Who can say, 'I have made my heart clean; I am pure from my sin'?" (Prov 20:9). This depth of self-consciousness persisted among the Essenes. The author of the *Community Rule* at Qumran was horrified at the perversity of his own heart—"Mankind has no way, and man is unable to establish his steps" (1QS XI, 10)—and so cast himself wholly on God for justification. But among the official temple scribes a more optimistic appraisal of human ability began to make its way, perhaps under the impact of Hellenism. God has left the human being "in the power of his own inclination," so that humans can keep the commandments, reaching out their hand for either life or death as they choose (Sir 15:14-17).[27] Josephus described the Pharisees and the Sadducees as making room in their "philosophies" for varying amounts of interplay between God's will and human free will (*J.W.* 2.162-165; *Ant.* 13.171-173). The *Psalms of Solomon*, emanating from pious circles having much in common with Pharisaism, have the words "Our actions are subject to our own choice and freedom of will, to do right or wrong in the works of our hands" (*Pss. Sol.* 9:4). The book of 2 *Baruch*, on a trajectory toward rab-

---

[27]Martin Hengel, *Judaism and Hellenism: Studies in Their Encounter in Palestine During the Early Hellenistic Period* (trans. John Bowden; 2 vols.; Philadelphia: Fortress, 1974), pp. 140-41.

binism, denies that Adam's sin affected his posterity (2 *Bar.* 54:15, 19). After the
destruction of the Jewish state by Rome in A.D. 70 and the disappearance of
the Jewish parties, this humanizing view established itself. Arthur Marmorstein could epitomize the rabbinic view thus: "Men and women can rise by
positive deeds to such a height of moral beauty, virtue, and accomplishment,
in spite of their natural shortcomings and innate faults, that they are regarded
as meritorious before God."[20]

It was Paul, with his background of intense devotion to Torah, not John, who
after becoming a Christ-follower meditated most profoundly on the utter inability of the Mosaic law to enliven and sanctify sinners dead in their trespasses.
"By works of the law shall no one be justified" (Gal 2:16 [cf. Rom 3:20]). "I
through the law died to the law" (Gal 2:19). "If a law had been given which
could make alive, then righteousness would indeed be by the law. But the
scripture consigned all things to sin" (Gal 3:21-22). The divided self seen in
Romans 7:7-25, delighting in the law of God in one's inmost being but sold
under sin and subverted by it in the flesh, experiences frustration and inevitable defeat in attempts to do the good. This stands in the starkest contrast to
*Pirke 'Abot*, where Rabbi Hillel is quoted as saying, "The more study of the Law,
the more life" (*m. 'Abot* 2:7); and to the view of the Talmud, where God is made
to say, "I created the Law as a drug. As long as you occupy yourselves with the
Law, the *yetzer* [evil inclination] will not rule over you" (*b. Qidd.* 30b).

In comparison with Paul on the law, the brief exchange between Jesus and
the Jews about bondage to sin and freedom from it in John 8:31-36 is but a
kernel. In this conversation the same difference of outlook is at work. Jesus
regards his interlocutors as thralls of sin, though they insist they have never
been slaves to anyone.

Because the world lies in (the) evil (one) (Jn 17:15; 1 Jn 5:19), it neither knows
God (Jn 4:22; 5:37-38; 7:28; 8:19; 15:21; 16:3; 17:25; 1 Jn 3:1, 6; 4:8) nor accepts Jesus'
testimony (Jn 1:10; 3:11, 32; 5:43; 12:48). It no longer sees Jesus (Jn 7:33-36; 8:21-22;
14:19, 22; 16:10), nor can it receive the Spirit of truth (Jn 14:17). Sensing that Jesus'
disciples live in the light, the world, stung by the contrast, hates them (Jn
15:18-25; 17:14; 1 Jn 3:1, 12-13) and persecutes them.[29] Unlike the saints, hu-

---

[28]Arthur Marmorstein, *The Doctrine of Merits in Old Rabbinic Literature* (New York: Ktav, 1968
[1920]), p. 3.
[29]Jn 16:1-4, 20, 22, 32-33; Apoc 1:9; 2:9-10, 13; 6:9-11; 11:7-10; 12:17; 13:7, 10, 15; 14:12-13; 16:6;
17:16; 18:24; 20:4.

mankind is not sealed against the horrendous plagues of the last days (Apoc 9:4). They will follow the dragon, the beast and the false prophet (Apoc 13:4, 7-8, 13-17) and are destined to enter with them into the second death, the lake of fire that burns forever (Apoc 14:9-11; 19:20; 20:10, 15). Even now the world abides in death (Jn 5:24; 1 Jn 3:14-15; 5:12).

## WORLD AS GODLESS SYSTEM

Though created by God, the world, then, has become alienated from him and rages against him. Under "the ruler of this world" (Jn 12:31; 14:30; 16:11) it forms a system that lies prone in evil (1 Jn 5:19). All that is in the world may be captured in three phrases: the lust of the flesh, the lust of the eyes, the boastful pride of life. This array is doomed (1 Jn 2:16-17).

God and the world in this sense are antagonists. The world's antitheistic attitude John designates by the verb "to hate" (μισεῖν). The world hates the light (Jn 3:20), therefore it hates Jesus (Jn 7:7; 15:18, 23-25) and his disciples (Jn 15:18-19; 17:14; 1 Jn 3:13). In hating them it hates the Father (Jn 15:23). John never speaks of God as reciprocating the world's hatred. To the world's hatred, John opposes God's love for the world and his judgment of evil, a just judgment that has struck hard at the buttresses of the world-system and shattered them. God's light shines in the darkness of the world to dispel it (Jn 1:5; 3:19; 8:12; 9:5; 12:46). The Son of God came into the world to bear witness to the truth (Jn 18:37) and thereby "to unravel" (ἵνα λύσῃ) the works of the devil (1 Jn 3:8). Jesus claims to have "conquered" (νενίκηκα) the world (Jn 16:33). A "combat" (πόλεμος) continues between the forces of the world and the Lamb's followers until the end of the age (Apoc 11:7; 12:17; 13:7; 16:14; 19:19; 20:8).

*The two ages.* At the turn of the eras, Jewish and early Christian apocalyptists had a basic eschatology that divided the timeline of world history into two ages: the present age and the one to come.[30] During the present aeon, sin and death hold sway under God's providence; hence we are living in this "evil age" (Gal 1:4). John took over this scheme. "He who hates his life in this world will keep it for eternal life" (Jn 12:25). "The kingdom of the world has become the kingdom of our Lord and of his Christ, and he shall reign for ever and ever" (Apoc 11:15). "Then I saw a new heaven and a new earth; for the first

---

[30]For references and discussion, see Emil Schürer, *The History of the Jewish People in the Age of Jesus Christ (175 B.C.-A.D. 135)* (rev. and ed. Geza Vermes, Fergus Millar and Martin Goodman; 3 vols. in 4; Edinburgh: T & T Clark, 1973–1987), 2:537-38.

heaven and the first earth had passed away" (Apoc 21:1). It is on this large salvation-historical canvas that John's frequent use of the phrase "this world" (ὁ κόσμος οὗτος) has full meaning. The phrase refers to the wicked world-system during the current period of time (Jn 8:23; 9:39; 11:9; 12:25, 31; 13:1; 16:11; 18:36; 1 Jn 4:17).[31]

Symbols as well as terminology highlight the contrast between the ages. This world is to the coming one as water is to wine (Jn 2:1-11); as ordinary water is to living water (Jn 4:10-15); as flesh is to spirit (Jn 3:3-9); as earth is to heaven (Jn 3:12, 31); as worship at geographic centers is to worship in Spirit and truth (Jn 4:20-24); as the eating of food is to doing the will of God (Jn 4:31-34); as giving what is not permanent is to Jesus' bestowal of the Spirit on his disciples forever (Jn 14:27).

One of the most distinctive and remarked characteristics of Johannine thought is this casting of reality into binary oppositions. We have touched on a number of them. God and the sinful world are antithetical, as are Michael/Satan, life/death, light/darkness,[32] truth/falsehood, freedom/slavery, love/hatred, above/below, heaven/earth, good/evil (deeds), spirit/flesh, believing/unbelief, sight/blindness. The world is the sum total of the negative terms of these contrary pairs.[33]

Though Western empiricists studying John may judge his bipolar construal of the moral universe overly stark and simple, we should bear in mind that John is in fact aware of the gradations and ambiguities of human existence. In his Gospel the human characters illustrate neither pure faith nor unbelief, neither steady obedience nor outright disobedience, but are real people whose wills move between extremes.[34] In the Apocalypse Christ's evaluation of each

---

[31]Bultmann erects a false alternative when he says, "In this term, the point is the contrast between the nature of the world and God, not a contrast between the ages" (*Theology of the New Testament* [trans. Kendrick Grobel; 2 vols.; New York: Scribner, 1951–1955], 2:15). "Contrast between the nature of the world and God," yes; but the denial of salvation-history serves Bultmann's individualizing existentialism and distorts John's intent.

[32]Yves-Marie Blanchard, "Lumière et ténèbres dans la tradition johannique," *Transversalités* 85 (2003): 103-17.

[33]On this, Bultmann is insightful: "The concepts light, truth, life, and freedom explain each other: so do the concepts darkness, falsehood, death, and bondage in the contrasting group" (*Theology*, 2:20). Other antitheses are studied in Günter Stemberger, *La symbolique du bien et du mal selon Saint Jean* (PD; Paris: Seuil, 1970); Andreas J. Köstenberger, *A Theology of John's Gospel and Letters: The Word, the Christ, the Son of God* (BTNT; Grand Rapids: Zondervan, 2009), pp. 282-92.

[34]Colleen M. Conway, "Speaking Through Ambiguity: Minor Characters in the Fourth Gospel," *BibInt* 10 (2002): 324-41.

church recognizes both its strong points and its faults (Apoc 2–3). We will be nearer the mark if we consider John an idealist, one whose thought penetrates beyond surface phenomena to principles. Are we quite certain that life and death are not the consequences of decisions between fundamental alternatives?

Secondary literature is peppered with discussions of whether the so-called Johannine dualism[35] has more in common with emerging gnosis or with the Palestinian thought-world represented by the Dead Sea Scrolls.[36] Metaphysical dualism is the belief in two principles of the universe, usually a good and an evil, as in Zoroastrianism. Logically, neither principle can be absolute, since each qualifies the other, but in fact dualists have tended to cling to the hope that the good will gain the upper hand in the tussle of the ages.

John's view is not dualistic in that sense. God is the single principle who made the universe (Jn 1:3), governs it (Jn 19:11), and will judge and rule it (Jn 5:28-29; 12:48). Evil comes of its rebellion against him and has a strict temporal limit (Jn 12:31; 1 Jn 2:17).

This is perhaps clearest in the Apocalypse. Here the solitary "throne" of heaven, emblem of the Father's presence and sovereignty, exists in a realm far above earthly conflicts, brooking no rivalry, unassailable by evil. The course of world history, foreordained by him, moves step by step in the sequence visions of the seals, trumpets and bowls toward its fixed goal. In the titanic combat between the forces of good and of evil the counterpart of the devil is Michael

---

[35]In common usage "dualism" is "a theory or system of thought which recognizes two independent principles" (*New Shorter Oxford English Dictionary* [1993]). Johannine scholars use the term to denote the ethical choice between good and evil options in a moral universe (ethical dualism), the opposition between angels and demons in God's world (cosmic dualism), or a contrast between the present age and the one to come (salvation-historical or eschatological dualism). See Lieu, *Theology*, 80. But there are perhaps more apt designations for all these polarities. Note the critical observations about the term "dualism" in Johannine studies in Otto Schwankl, *Licht und Finsternis: Ein metaphorisches Paradigma in den johanneischen Schriften* (HBS 5; Freiburg: Herder, 1995), pp. 355-61; Stephen C. Barton, "Johannine Dualism and Contemporary Pluralism," in *The Gospel of John and Christian Theology* (ed. Richard Bauckham and Carl Mosser; Grand Rapids: Eerdmans, 2008), pp. 7-10; Miroslav Volf, "Johannine Dualism and Contemporary Pluralism," in Bauckham and Mosser, *John and Christian Theology*, pp. 22-25.

[36]Major publications include Raymond E. Brown, "The Qumran Scrolls and the Johannine Gospel and Epistles," *CBQ* 17 (1955): 403-19, 559-74; Otto Böcher, *Der johanneische Dualismus im Zusammenhang des nachbiblischen Judentums* (Gütersloh: Mohn, 1965); Herbert Braun, *Qumran und das Neue Testament* (2 vols.; Tübingen: Mohr Siebeck, 1966); James H. Charlesworth, "A Critical Comparison of the Dualism in 1QS III,13–IV,26 and the 'Dualism' Contained in the Fourth Gospel," *NTS* 15 (1968–1969): 389-418; John Ashton, *Understanding the Fourth Gospel* (Oxford: Clarendon, 1991), pp. 205-37; Georg Strecker, *The Johannine Letters: A Commentary on 1, 2, and 3 John* (ed. Harold W. Attridge; trans. Linda M. Maloney; Hermeneia; Minneapolis: Fortress, 1996), pp. 26-28.

the archangel, not God himself (Apoc 12; 20). Insofar as God involves himself in the antagonism of the ages, he does so in the person of the Lamb, who shares his throne. This figure, captain of the 144,000 saints, stands in antithesis to the beast, around whom rally all who "dwell on earth" (Apoc 13:16–14:5). The opposition between the righteous and the wicked is grim, but every stage of the battle is part of the divine plan directed from the throne. At no point are the two sides in equilibrium, nor is the eucatastrophe ever in doubt. Finally the triumph of the divine cause is total, and God is revealed as the Alpha and the Omega, whose good purpose comprehended the heights and the depths, who makes all things new, who puts the former things away so that they are no more.

Recognizing that the one God has no rival in John's theology, some prefer to speak of a "modified dualism" wherein God is seen as sovereign over an age-long conflict between subordinate principles of light and darkness.[37] But given that antagonism to God has arisen, in John's view, out of a world that God created in a state of goodness, that evil is a self-twisting of the finite good introduced by the rampant wills of creatures, and that its defeat and disappearance are only a matter of God's timing, the word "dualism" seems out of place and might best be dropped in reference to the Johannine writings.

## FORCES AND INSTITUTIONS OF THE WORLD

People make up the world. People are either "children of God" or "children of the devil" (1 Jn 3:1, 10). Even among Jesus' followers who believed in him (Jn 8:31) some were of their father the devil (Jn 8:38-41, 44). Nowhere does John speculate on how large a numerical proportion of the human race are nonelect, but his terminology gives the impression that they form the vast majority and control the visible institutions of society. "The world knew him not. . . . But to all who received him, who believed in his name, he gave power to become children of God" (Jn 1:10, 12). The world-at-large stands over against a rather modest subset. The "world" hates the few whom Jesus chose out of it (Jn 15:18-19), owns the establishment that will put them out of the synagogues (Jn 16:2-3) and will subject them to tribulation (Jn 16:33). Therefore he prays for them, beleaguered here after his departure (Jn 17:9-19). Jesus' followers can expect the

---

[37]That Qumran and John share this worldview continues to be defended. See John Painter, "Monotheism and Dualism: John and Qumran," in *Theology and Christology in the Fourth Gospel: Essays by Members of the SNTS Johannine Writings Seminar* (ed. Gilbert van Belle, Jan G. van der Watt and P. J. Maritz; BETL 184; Leuven: Leuven University Press, 2005), pp. 225-43.

world to listen to false prophets and not to them (1 Jn 4:5-6). According to the Apocalypse, unbelievers make up "the tribes" (Apoc 1:7), "the nations" (Apoc 11:2, 9-10, 18; 13:7; 14:8; 16:19; 17:15; 18:3, 23; 20:3, 8) and "the destroyers of the earth" (Apoc 11:18)—in other words, all who dwell on earth, everyone whose name is not in the book of life (Apoc 13:8; 17:8). They are symbolized by Lady Babylon (Apoc 17:1–19:10), whose influence extends to kings, merchants, shipmasters, seafarers and sailors (Apoc 18:9, 11, 17). The opposite symbol is Lady Jerusalem, representing the chosen of God (Apoc 12; 21:9–22:9).

Earthly forces arrayed against God are typified in the Apocalypse as a trinity of evil. Aspiring to the divine throne, but effectively checked by Michael the archangel, is the dragon (Apoc 12–13), the ancient Near Eastern chaos monster who, with seven heads (cf. Ps 74:13-14) and ten horns (cf. Dan 7:7) represents the diabolical inspiration behind the Roman power. Over against God's Christ stands the imperial court caricatured as the beast, reflecting the dragon in its heads and horns but offering a parody of Christ by springing back after a mortal wound (Apoc 13:1-10; 17). The witness of the Spirit through the prophetic church is countered by the beastly false prophet who incites earth dwellers to worship the beast and thus symbolizes the officials of the state religion of the empire (Apoc 13:11-18). These three succeed in deceiving and mustering the whole world to Armageddon (Apoc 16:13-16).[38] John's prophetic decrial of Asian society at the end of the first century is thus aimed at its chief spiritual (the dragon), political (the beast) and religious (the false prophet) dimensions, as well as its comprehensive socioeconomic aspect (Lady Babylon).

*The Jews.* Does John use "the Jewish religion" as his specimen of the world, his "example" of "the human will to self-security"?[39] Is John anti-Jewish or anti-Judaistic, as many critics suppose?[40]

John's references to "the Jews" divide between a wistful, backward look that sees his erstwhile Palestinian co-religionists in historical and cultural continuity with the Old Testament people of God, and a resigned, forward look that yields the title of "the Jews" to those Judean leaders whose rejection of Jesus became definitive of Judaism.

---

[38]For further analysis of the dragon, the beast and the false prophet, see Paul A. Rainbow, *The Pith of the Apocalypse: Essential Message and Principles for Interpretation* (Eugene, OR: Wipf & Stock, 2008), pp. 79-82.

[39]Bultmann, *Theology*, 2:27 (see 2:27-32).

[40]Urban C. von Wahlde, "'The Jews' in the Gospel of John: Fifteen Years of Research (1983-1998)," *ETL* 76 (2000): 30-55.

It is ironic that the Fourth Gospel should be so widely regarded as the most anti-Judaistic of the Gospels.[41] John takes obvious pride in his own people's religious heritage. Jesus was Jewish. So was John.[42] "We worship what we know, for salvation is from the Jews," declared Jesus, uniquely in John's Gospel, to a member of a rival group that had contested the centrality of Jerusalem for centuries (Jn 4:22). "Behold, an Israelite indeed, in whom is no guile," is Jesus' sincere commendation of Nathanael (Jn 1:47). Jewish customs come up by the bye without aspersion (Jn 2:6; 3:25; 4:9; 19:31, 40, 42). If the grace that has come in Jesus Christ surpasses the Torah, nevertheless the Torah was the outstanding gift of God's grace in the preeschatological era (Jn 1:16-17) and still beams forth God's truth and justice (Jn 7:19, 23, 51; 8:17; 10:34; 15:25).

The Scriptures of Judaism are indispensable to the Johannine Christology.[43] Taken as a whole, they point to the Messiah (Jn 1:45; 5:39; 12:34). To prove Jesus' messianic status, John shows in the Fourth Gospel how nineteen specific prophecies came to fulfillment.[44] Each feast of the Jewish calendar symbolizes an aspect of Christ (Jn 2:13; 5:1; 6:4; 7:2; 10:22; 11:55). Pilate attaches the royal title "King of the Jews" to Jesus' bloodied person, intending it as an anti-Semitic slur on his accusers but, in John's view, unknowingly pointing to the truth (Jn 18:33, 39; 19:3, 19).

In John's writings there is no criticism of any of the great Jewish institutions. He has respect for the temple (Jn 2:16; 5:14; 7:14, 28; 8:20, 59; 10:23; 18:20) and the priesthood (Jn 1:19).[45] The office of the high priest enjoys a special prophetic charism that overrides the pernicious motive of the incumbent and draws profundity from his ruthless pragmatism (Jn 11:51). In the Apocalypse the temple serves as a positive symbol of heavenly verities.[46] The Sanhedrin is

---

[41]See, for example, the essays collected in Reimund Bieringer, Didier Pollefeyt and Frederique Van-decasteele-Vanneuville, eds., *Anti-Judaism and the Fourth Gospel: Papers of the Leuven Colloquium, 2000* (JCH 1; Assen: Van Gorcum, 2001).

[42]Pierre Grelot, *Les Juifs dans l'évangile selon Jean* (CahRB 34; Paris: Gabalda, 1995), pp. 169-82.

[43]Peder Borgen, "The Old Testament in the Formation of New Testament Theology," in *Philo, John, and Paul: New Perspectives on Judaism and Early Christianity* (BJS 131; Atlanta: Scholars Press, 1987), pp. 159-70.

[44]Jn 1:23; 2:17; 6:31, 45; 7:38, 42; 10:34; 12:13, 15, 34, 38, 40; 13:18; 15:25; 17:12; 19:24, 28, 36, 37.

[45]The chief priests and the high priest appear in the Fourth Gospel, especially in its passion account, as enemies of Jesus who plotted his death, because that is what they did. John, however, is not opposed to the existence of the offices as such. It happens that the scribes find no mention in the Gospel.

[46]Robert A. Briggs, *Jewish Temple Imagery in the Book of Revelation* (SBL 10; New York: Peter Lang, 1999); Simon J. Kistemaker, "The Temple in the Apocalypse," *JETS* 43 (2000): 433-41; Gregory Stevenson, *Power and Place: Temple and Identity in the Book of Revelation* (BZNW 107; Berlin: de

the valid judicial authority with a tradition of justice (Jn 3:1; 7:50-51). Jesus taught in synagogues (Jn 6:59; 18:20). Amid the welter of opinions that Jesus stimulated during his ministry—a plurality that the leaders took increasingly harsh steps to squelch (Jn 7:13; 9:22; 11:47-54; 12:42; 19:38; 20:19)—there were many Jewish people who followed him for a time, who spoke in his favor, or who actually believed in him (Jn 6:60, 66; 7:12, 26, 31, 41; 8:31; 9:16; 10:21; 12:42).

These facts make it untenable that John is antagonistic either toward the Jews as a people or toward the religion of the Hebrew Bible.[47] The sole point on which John distances himself from Jews is their repudiation of Jesus' messiahship and divine sonship.[48] However typical this attitude may be of modern Judaism, John lived during the formative period when Jewish responses to Jesus went from many to one, from open to closed. He regards the result as in no way a necessary consequence of Judaic principles, but rather a gross violation of them.[49]

Gruyter, 2001); John Ben-Daniel and Gloria Ben-Daniel, *The Apocalypse in the Light of the Temple: A New Approach to the Book of Revelation* (Jerusalem: Beit Yochanan, 2003).

[47]For a more comprehensive collection of positive perspectives on Judaism in the Gospel of John, see Johannes Beutler, *Judaism and the Jews in the Gospel of John* (SubBi 30; Rome: Pontifical Biblical Institute, 2006), pp. 7-144.

[48]Manfred Diefenbach observes that John uses "the Jews" to denote a faith conviction that excludes belief in Jesus as the Christ, but his denial that this applies to the real Jews of the first century is indefensible (*Der Konflikt Jesu mit den "Juden": Ein Versuch zur Lösung der johanneischen Antijudaismus-Diskussion mit Hilfe des antikes Handlungsverständnisses* [NTAbh 41; Münster: Aschendorff, 2002]).

[49]A Jewish colleague of mine once quipped that Jews cheerfully disagree among themselves about anything and everything, except that "Jesus is not the messiah." To soften on that point is un-Jewish. In a similar vein, but from a Christian liberal perspective, the editors of an important collection of essays hold that the Fourth Gospel, with its lofty Christology, is "anti-Judaistic" (Reimund Bieringer, Didier Pollefeyt and Frederique Vandecasteele-Vanneuville, "Wrestling with Johannine Anti-Judaism: A Hermeneutical Framework for the Analysis of the Current Debate," in Bieringer, Pollefeyt and Vandecasteele-Vanneuville, *Anti-Judaism*, pp. 3-37). But that is to accede to the same definition of Judaism. John, on the contrary, holds that Judaism gave up its soul when it insisted that Torah and Christ were mutually exclusive alternatives and chose the former. Adele Reinhartz, a Jewish scholar with a special interest in the Johannine writings of the New Testament, summarizes John's basic position: "Jews, like all others, will have eternal life only if they believe Jesus to be the Christ and Son of God." But her next statement, "In taking on this belief, they also leave behind their own community and Jewish identity," prompts the question of why that community should have laid it down so. To her general assessment, "The Fourth Gospel's polemic against the Jews . . . undermines its declaration of God's boundless love for the world," John would doubtless reply that God loves the Jewish people not a whit less than he loves the rest of the world and holds out his Son to them as their savior too—where is the "polemic" in that? See Adele Reinhartz, "'Jews' and Jews in the Fourth Gospel," in Bieringer, Pollefeyt and Vandecasteele-Vanneuville, *Anti-Judaism*, pp. 226-27; idem, "Judaism in the Gospel of John," *Int* 63 (2009): 382-93. At the end of the day, John sees no way that acceptance of Jesus as God's supreme self-revelation and the repudiation thereof could be equally valid—the ideal of relativistic pluralism behind Reinhartz's *Befriending the Beloved Disciple: A Jewish Reading of the Gospel of John* (New York: Continuum, 2001).

When Jesus said, "You are of your father the devil" (Jn 8:44), he pointed to the depth of depravity in the human heart. The statement describes the sinful condition of his immediate addressees, not their ethnicity. Significantly, the group in question had believed in Jesus in some sense (Jn 8:31), though by the end of the dialogue they were ready to stone him (Jn 8:59). That they were children of Abraham (Jn 8:33, 37, 39) only lends poignancy to Jesus' analysis. Not because they were worse than other people, but because they walked in the way of Torah and knew themselves to be virtuous in comparison with others, Jesus' words are telling. Conscious of their privileges, they saw no need for liberation from sin's power or for supernatural birth into eternal life (Jn 8:31-52). Blinded by sin, they had no idea to what extent they were in bondage to it: "Every one who commits sin is a slave to sin" (Jn 8:34). Descendants of Abraham though they were, they stood in need of a savior. While it happens to be the case that this dialogue took place among Jews who were proud of their ancestry (Jesus being one of them), Jewishness is not the main issue, but rather human sinfulness. What Jesus said to them is true of everyone. That he found fault with the moral superstars of his time and place lends his point special force.[50] The aim was to shock them into awareness of their state so that they might repent and believe, negating Jesus' charge.[51]

As presented by John, Jesus' opponents wore a sheen of religion and, in the eyes of a Torah-observant populace, had to frame their objections to him in religious terms even though their real antipathy toward him was personal. Twenty times John names the Pharisees out of the body of "the Jews," usually as enemies of the good, but not always.[52] Although Jewish sects debated questions of halakah among themselves without bloodshed, Jesus lost the Pharisees' support by repeatedly ignoring their rule against healing people on the Sabbath (Jn 5:1-16; 9:1-17) and by shaming them in public for missing the deeper hu-

---

[50]On John 8:44, see further Maria Neubrand, "Das Johannesevangelium und 'die Juden': Antijudaismus im vierten Evangelium," *TGl* 99 (2009): 205-17.

[51]Stephen Motyer, *Your Father the Devil? A New Approach to John and "the Jews"* (PBTM; Carlisle: Paternoster, 1997).

[52]There are exceptions. At John 1:19-24 the Pharisees exercise an appropriate vigilance by looking into the credentials of John the Baptist. Nicodemus was a Pharisee (Jn 3:1) who, moved by curiosity, gave Jesus a private hearing (Jn 3:1-15), pleaded with the council to let Jesus defend himself (Jn 7:50-52), and performed the pious act of helping to bury Jesus (Jn 19:39-42). On Nicodemus, see Raimo Hakola, "The Burden of Ambiguity: Nicodemus and the Social Identity of the Johannine Christians," *NTS* 55 (2009): 438-55. Some Pharisees were dubious whether one who had healed a congenitally blind man could be a sinner (Jn 9:16).

manitarian values behind the biblical statute (Jn 7:22-24; 8:15).[53] In his view, they busied themselves in the Scriptures without perceiving the drift of God's invitation to know and love him (Jn 5:37-47; 8:19, 55). They were elitists (Jn 7:47-49; 9:34). Unable to deny the factuality of signs that everyone could see, they attributed Jesus' claims to demonic madness (Jn 7:20; 8:48-49, 52; 10:20-21)[54] or produced the more plausible charge that he was a blasphemer crossing the line between humanity and deity (Jn 5:18; 10:31-39). Professing to be disciples of Moses, whom they knew God had attested (Jn 9:28-29), they found Jesus' signs meaningless if Jesus showed himself incorrigible in regard to their Sabbath rule (Jn 9:16). Thus they proved deliberately blind (Jn 9:41). But they loved prestige in the eyes of society (Jn 5:44). What stoked their anxiety was Jesus' rapidly expanding popularity with the crowds (Jn 7:31-32; 11:47-48) and their progressive loss of control (Jn 12:19).

Likewise the temple authorities. At bottom, it was no religious commitment that drove their vendetta against Jesus, but rather their realization that he posed a threat to their ability to flay their sheep (Jn 2:14-18; 10:1, 8, 10, 12-13) and to their gubernatorial role as appointees of Rome (Jn 11:47-48).[55] With Caiaphas, they rationalized that in taking Jesus out, they were patriots protecting the nation from Roman reprisal (Jn 11:48).[56] In a striking upset of priorities, temple officials refused to enter the praetorium to keep their ritual purity, even as they conspired to have an innocent man executed (Jn 18:28), of whose criminality they failed to convince the prefect (Jn 18:29-32, 38; 19:6). Their malice toward Jesus was what enabled Pilate to manipulate them, in a deft reversal of their blackmail, into swearing allegiance to Caesar (Jn 19:12-15). According to John, it was arrant defense of personal power masquerading as Jewish piety that sought and secured the crucifixion of Jesus.

---

[53]On these passages, see Severino Pancaro, *The Law in the Fourth Gospel: The Torah and the Gospel, Moses and Jesus, Judaism and Christianity According to John* (NovTSup 42; Leiden: Brill, 1975), pp. 9-52.

[54]This smear persisted to *b. Sanh.* 43a: "On the eve of Passover Yeshu was hanged. For forty days before the execution took place, a herald went forth and cried, 'He is going forth to be stoned because he has practiced sorcery and enticed Israel to apostasy. Any one who can say anything in his favour, let him come forward and plead on his behalf.' But since nothing was brought forward in his favour he was hanged on the eve of Passover" (trans. Jacob Shachter, in *Hebrew-English Edition of the Babylonian Talmud* [ed. Isidore Epstein; new ed.; London: Soncino, 1987]).

[55]Camillus Umoh, *The Plot to Kill Jesus: A Contextual Study of John 11.47-53* (EH 23/696; Frankfurt: Peter Lang, 2000); Lynne Courter Boughton, "The Priestly Perspective of the Johannine Trial Narratives," *RB* 110 (2003): 517-51.

[56]On Caiaphas, see Helen K. Bond, *Caiaphas: Friend of Rome and Judge of Jesus?* (Louisville: Westminster John Knox, 2004). Bond, however, is unnecessarily chary of the Gospels.

That John has in view these self-preserving politico-religious leaders of Judea when "the Jews" serve as a foil to Jesus[57] is most apparent in passages where Jewish common folk do not speak their mind for fear of "the Jews" (Jn 7:13; 9:22).[58] The only "Jews" hostile to Jesus other than the Judean leaders are those in the synagogue at Capernaum who take offense at Jesus' proposal of a heaven-sent messiah who gives his life for the life of the world (Jn 6:41, 52, 60-61). Here too it is not primarily religious scruples, but rather politicization of the messianic hope under the Roman occupation of Galilee (Jn 6:15), that fuels their scorn of Jesus. At this early date we see the rift opening between "the Jews" and the disciples of Jesus. Jesus' disciples were Jewish to the core, yet Jesus put them in a different category from "the Jews": "As I said to the Jews so now I say to you" (Jn 13:33).[59]

If John hates neither Jews as such nor their ancestral religion, why does he so often use the expression "the Jews" to designate Jesus' enemies, without distinguishing the corrupt leaders from the mass of the Jewish people? Simply because in time most Jews followed those leaders, closing their hearts and their religion to Jesus. Those who held the reins in Judea until A.D. 70, and were followed in many respects by the sages at Yavneh who laid the foundations of rabbinic Judaism, were largely successful in propagating a vision of Judaism that had no room for Jesus Christ. It is not to vilify bona fide Jewish seekers after God that John applies the name of "Jews" to a body of rulers who, in that very name, acted in their own worldly interests at the turn of the eras, but rather to clarify that when it came to defining the attitude of an entire people toward Jesus—one's stance toward Christ being, from John's perspective, a matter of eternal life or death—that body's stance fatefully carried the day.[60]

---

[57]"The Jews" has a negative connotation in about half of its occurrences in the Fourth Gospel: John 2:18, 20; 5:10, 15, 16, 18; 7:1, 11, 13, 15, 35; 8:22, 48, 52, 57; 9:18, 22; 10:24, 31, 33; 11:8, 54; 13:33; 18:12, 14, 31, 36, 38; 19:7, 12, 14, 21, 31, 38; 20:19. These comprise thirty-five of the total of seventy-one instances of "the Jews" in the Gospel. For another classification that differs from mine only in the details, see Lars Kierspel, *The Jews and the World in the Fourth Gospel: Parallelism, Function, and Context* (WUNT 2/220; Tübingen: Mohr Siebeck, 2006), pp. 74-75.

[58]On the frequent reference of the phrase elsewhere to the authorities, see Urban C. von Wahlde, "The Johannine 'Jews': A Critical Survey," *NTS* 28 (1982): 33-60; idem, "The Gospel of John and the Presentation of Jews and Judaism," in *Within Context: Essays on Jews and Judaism in the New Testament* (ed. David P. Efroymson, Eugene J. Fisher and Leon Klenicki; Philadelphia: American Interfaith Institute, 1993), pp. 74-75.

[59]This awareness of group identity is apparent as early as Nicodemus's initial approach, where Jesus addresses him as an exponent of the establishment: "We speak of what we know, and bear witness to what we have seen; but you [plural] do not receive our testimony" (Jn 3:11).

[60]Cornelis Bennema, "The Identity and Composition of οἱ Ἰουδαῖοι in the Gospel of John," *TynBul* 60 (2009): 239-63.

John's Gentile readers in western Asia Minor at the end of the century may have been familiar with the opposition of "the Jews" of the Diaspora to the church. John wrote the Apocalypse when some members of local synagogues were informing against Christians to the civic authorities, undermining the cause of Jesus Christ in the same way the Palestinian authorities did during Jesus' lifetime, with sometimes capital consequences for their victims ("unto death" [Apoc 2:10]). John scathingly describes them as those who "say that they are Jews and are not" and calls them the "synagogue of Satan" (Apoc 2:9; 3:9).[61] Only bitterest disappointment with co-religionists not living up to their privileges and promise drew forth such unmincing denunciation.[62] This is not defamation of the sort that we find targeted at Jews from malignant anti-Semites in the Roman environment;[63] it is open-eyed, intra-Jewish, prophetic exposure.[64]

In conclusion, then, John in his Gospel does indeed present "the Jews" as representatives of the world. But he does so owing neither to their ethnicity, which he shared, nor to their religion, which he practiced in his early life and of which he viewed faith in Jesus as the fulfillment. His reason for castigating "the Jews" is the same as his reason for taking aim at others besides Jews. In the figure of Pontius Pilate a climb to raw political power trumped the truth (Jn 18:33-38; 19:12-16). In the Johannine Epistles the world appears in the form of Christian heretics who deny the Father and the Son (1 Jn 2:18-19; 4:1-6; 2 Jn 7). In the Apocalypse the world is a Romanizing paganism that was impinging on the inner life of the churches in Asia Minor (Apoc 2:2, 6, 14-15, 20-24; 3:2-3, 15-17). As with the prophets of Israel and Judah, what John inveighs against is human unbelief and impenitence, wherever and however they show up. "The Jews" are the culprits in the Gospel because theirs happens to have been the society with whom the protagonist, the historical Jesus of Palestine, had to deal.

---

[61]Because Asian Jews of several localities opposed Paul's ministry at midcentury (Acts 13–14; 21:27), the traditional interpretation of Apocalypse 2:9; 3:9 seems likely. See Jan Lambrecht, "Jewish Slander: A Note on Revelation 2,9-10," *ETL* 75 (1999): 421-29. David Frankfurter's argument, irenic enough in the post-Holocaust dialogue between Jews and Christians, that these verses have to do with Jewish members of the church does not convince ("Jews or Not? Reconstructing the 'Other' in Rev 2:9 and 3:9," *HTR* 94 [2001]: 403-25).

[62]Ashton (*Understanding*, pp. 131-59) emphasizes the intrafamilial nature of the polemic between Johannine Christianity and official Judaism.

[63]For documentation of which, see John G. Gager, *The Origins of Anti-Semitism: Attitudes toward Judaism in Pagan and Christian Antiquity* (New York: Oxford University Press, 1983).

[64]Felix Porsch, "'Ihr habt den Teufel zum Vater' (Joh 8,44): Antijudaismus im Johannesevangelium?" *BK* 44 (1989): 50-57; François Vouga, "Antijudaismus im Johannesevangelium?" *TGl* 83 (1993): 81-89; von Wahlde, "Presentation of Jews," pp. 79-81.

## JUDGMENT IN THIS PRESENT EVIL AGE

Not only has the world rejected God, the creator who governs the universe with lovingkindness, it also does not embrace his self-revelation in Jesus intended to rescue it from darkness (Jn 16:9). Therefore it stands even now under eternal condemnation (Jn 3:18; cf. 3:36).

*Unbelief toward Jesus as God's Sent One.* The Johannine literature offers a penetrating analysis of several forms of unbelief and of factors that contribute to it.

(1) Some people reject God's testimony flat-out. "The world knew him not . . . his own people received him not" (Jn 1:10-11 [see also Jn 3:11, 32; 5:38-47; 6:64-66; 10:25-26]). The psychological cause of this pushing away is unwillingness to do God's will (Jn 7:17) combined with acquiescence in the devil's will (Jn 8:44). John has it both ways: unbelief produces disobedience to God (Jn 3:36), and, conversely, addiction to evil deeds stands in the way of coming to know the truth (Jn 7:17). Such persons are chagrined to have their evil deeds shown for what they are (Jn 3:20-21; 7:7). They may even be intolerant and murderous toward those whose doing of the truth casts their deeds in negative relief (Jn 8:39-43, 45-46; 1 Jn 3:12; Apoc 18:24). Socially, this mindset is reinforced by a worldly frame of reference in which people love to get glory from one another rather than from God (Jn 5:41-42, 44; 12:43). The divine cause of unbelief is that its subjects do not belong to God (Jn 8:47) and are not among God's sheep (Jn 10:25-26).

(2) Others take note of Jesus' signs but misconstrue them. They may conclude that Jesus was a teacher sent from God (Jn 2:23-25; 3:1-2, 4, 9-12; 4:44-45). The invalid at the pool by the Sheep Gate showed ingratitude by informing on his healer (Jn 5:14-15). A crowd of Galileans enjoyed Jesus' handout of a meal and decided that he would make a fine king (Jn 6:2, 14-15, 26-27, 30-31, 34). His brothers urged him to make a spectacle of himself at the Feast of Tabernacles (Jn 7:3-5). Some who supposed him to be a prophet went on later to believe (Jn 4:19; 9:17), others apparently did not (Jn 6:14; 7:40). All these recognized the presence of the supernatural in Jesus, but most failed to perceive him as the Logos come as Lamb to put away the world's sin.[65]

(3) Yet a third group believes for a time but fails to abide in the truth. Some Jews who believed in Jesus on hearing his words (Jn 8:30-31a) came in for one

---

[65]On people in the Fourth Gospel who "believed" in Jesus' signs but did not truly believe in his person, see Marinus de Jonge, *Jesus, Stranger from Heaven and Son of God: Jesus Christ and the Christians in Johannine Perspective* (SBLSBS 11; Missoula, MT: Scholars Press, 1977), pp. 31-32.

of the harshest harangues in the Gospel because as dupes of their father the devil they remained in the grip of sin and would not face the fact. Offended that Jesus should claim to give eternal life, being eternal himself, they took up stones to throw at the man in whom they had believed (Jn 8:33-59). Knowing the nature of their believing, Jesus warned that abiding in his word is a condition of true freedom (Jn 8:31b-32). On another occasion some in the church who came to deny the incarnation of the Son of God (1 Jn 2:18-23) departed and thus committed the "sin unto death" (1 Jn 5:16).

Whether the spurning of God's light be blatant or subtle, transparent or buried in the subconscious, it leads through a process of divine hardening to an outright inability to believe (Jn 5:44; 8:43; 12:39). People respond to the light in the sphere of God's working. No sinner, not even one who is eventually converted and comes to faith, has it in himself or herself to believe in Jesus apart from being drawn to him by God (Jn 6:44, 65). There is also a hardening action by which God leaves some to their own choice. God's drawing and his hardening are unlike each other and should not be set in symmetry. "We love, because he first loved us" (1 Jn 4:19): God's love for those who believe is absolutely prior to their love for him. But there is no corresponding statement that some despise God because he first despised them. On the contrary, in the structure of the Fourth Gospel it is at the end, not at the beginning, of Jesus' witness to an unreceptive world (Jn 1–12) that the author introduces a retrospective quotation of Isaiah 6:10 on how God blinded people's eyes and hardened their heart, having just emphasized the world's inexcusability for turning a blind eye to Jesus' signs (Jn 12:37-38). Only after God gave people ample inducements to believe and they did not (Jn 12:37) did he take from them the possibility (Jn 12:39). "Therefore" they could not believe (Jn 12:39-40). How stubbornness can be the ultimate cause of damnation for some while God's sweet persuasion wins others to faith is an unsolved puzzle of systematic theology, but there the data lie.

***Judgment of the world outside of Christ.*** Outside of Jesus Christ, the world is on the way to judgment and destruction. That there will be a final accounting before God is a common theme in the Hebrew Scriptures (e.g., Ps 7:7-8; Joel 3; Dan 7:9-14), in Jewish apocalyptic literature (*1 En.* 90:20-39; *4 Ezra* 7:32-44; *2 Bar.* 24) and in the New Testament (e.g., Mt 25:31-46; Rom 2:6-10; Jas 2:12-13). Passages in all subdivisions of the Johannine literature likewise look for a final assize. Jesus' claim that the Father has given the prerogative of judging to the

Son of Man assumes the full eschatological scenario (Jn 5:21-29). Between Jesus and his critics God "will be the judge" (Jn 8:50). "On the last day" the word that Jesus has spoken will be the judge of those who rejected it (Jn 12:48). Believers need a ground of confidence "for the day of judgment" (1 Jn 4:17). The Apocalypse is replete with images of the coming scrutiny: God's vengeance will come in due course (Apoc 6:10); an angel heralds "the hour of his judgment" (Apoc 14:7); Babylon will be cast down to ruin in a single day (Apoc 18:8, 10); and at the end of the world there appears a great white throne, the dead are brought forth from wherever they lie, and books are opened (Apoc 20:11-15; cf. 11:18; 15:4; 17:1; 19:2, 11).

But in keeping with John's partially realized eschatology, the judgment is already under way as people take up positions toward Jesus Christ.[66] Just before Jesus died, he proclaimed that the judgment was about to take place and the ruler of this world be cast out (Jn 12:31; 16:11). This event plays out visually in the Apocalypse in the form of a celestial combat that resulted in the ousting of the serpentine accuser from heaven by Michael and his angelic host (Apoc 12:7-12). Since that time, every person who disbelieves in the Son of God "is condemned already" (Jn 3:18), and "the wrath of God abides on him" (Jn 3:36).[67]

A world under condemnation is destined to "perish" (Jn 3:16). "The world passes away" (1 Jn 2:8, 17). In the Apocalypse we see numerous images of utter desolation: holy fire thrown on the earth (Apoc 8:5), the destruction of destroyers (Apoc 11:18), a field harvested with a sharp sickle and a winepress trodden (Apoc 14:14-20), the upending of earth's geography and a pelting hailstorm (Apoc 16:20-21), an imploding world war (Apoc 17:16-17), a wilderness populated by foul creatures and a vibrant civilization laid waste (Apoc 18:2, 21-24), a massacre of the kings of the earth with their armies (Apoc 19:21), smoke rising from a lake of fire and brimstone forever (Apoc 14:10-11; 20:10, 15).

## WORLD AS OBJECT OF REDEMPTION

Nevertheless there are many passages in the Johannine corpus where "the world" is the object of God's saving action. Doomed though the world is for abandoning the light, God remains committed to uphold what he made and

---

[66]Oliver Groll, *Finsternis, Tod und Blindheit als Strafe: Eine exegetische Untersuchung zu den Begriffen* κρίνειν, κρίσις *und* κρίμα *im Johannesevangelium* (EH 23/781; Frankfurt: Peter Lang, 2004).

[67]"The future judgment is only the climactic ratification of the decision already precipitated by man himself" (Schelkle, "John's Theology," p. 138). On judgment as both present and future in John, see further Ashton, *Understanding*, pp. 220-26.

has provided for its redemption. "For God so loved the world that he gave his only-begotten Son, that whoever believes in him should not perish but have eternal life" (Jn 3:16).

God's sending of the Son had in view nothing less than to reclaim the perishing cosmos. John the Baptist introduced Jesus as "the Lamb of God, who takes away the sin of the world" (Jn 1:29). God sent the Son not to condemn the world, "but that the world should be saved through him" (Jn 3:17; cf. 12:47). Samaritan believers hailed him "the Savior of the world" (Jn 4:42). Jesus claimed to be the bread that came down from heaven to give life to the world (Jn 6:33, 51) and proclaimed himself "the light of the world" (Jn 8:12; 9:5; 12:46). Jesus prayed that through the witness of his disciples the world would come to believe (Jn 17:21, 23). Jesus Christ is the propitiation for sins, not only of those in the believing community ("our sins"), but also for the whole world (1 Jn 2:2).[68] God sent his Son into the world so that we might live through him, that he might be "the Savior of the world" (1 Jn 4:9, 14). This goal will be achieved when the kingdom of the world becomes the kingdom of the Lord and of his Christ (Apoc 11:15), and heaven and earth are made new (Apoc 21:1-8).

*The question of the extent of the body of the redeemed.* Will the whole world be saved in the end, or only a part of it? Major schools of Christian thought have debated this question.

God's aspiration to save everyone is indicated by John's use of "all" (πάντες). John the Baptist was sent that "all" might believe through him (Jn 1:7). The true light enlightens "every" person (Jn 1:9), and we have "all" received of his fullness (Jn 1:16). "All" are to honor the Son as they do the Father (Jn 5:23). When Jesus is lifted up, he will draw "all people" to himself (Jn 12:32). "All people" will know Jesus' disciples by their love for one another (Jn 13:35).

Although God's intention is to save the world, not every person will be saved. Jesus came "for judgment" in the primitive sense of the Greek κρίμα: to make a "separation" in the race, to drive a wedge between the blind who gain sight and the seeing who become blind (Jn 9:39). Everywhere John reckons with these diametrical effects of Christ's advent. Some believe and escape condemnation; others do not believe and stand under the wrath, already condemned (Jn 3:18, 36). During Jesus' public career people in crowds came to opposite

---

[68]The contrast between "us" and "the whole world" makes it hard to plead that by "the world" John has in mind all kinds of people, since in the metropolitan area of Ephesus an ecclesiastical "we" is likely already to be inclusive in that sense.

conclusions about him (Jn 7:12, 25-27, 31-32, 40-52). Jesus occasioned "divisions" (σχίσματα) among the people (Jn 7:43), among the Pharisees (Jn 9:16), among "the Jews" (Jn 10:19-21).[69] Judas Iscariot, who betrayed him, turned out to be "the son of perdition" and was, according to Jesus' judgment, lost (Jn 17:12). "There is sin unto death," for which prayers do not avail (1 Jn 5:16). The Apocalypse allows glimpses of at least the beast, the false prophet and the dragon being remanded to the lake of fire forever (Apoc 19:20; 20:10). Given the warning that anyone who worships the beast will share their fate (Apoc 14:9-11), together with the prediction that all who dwell on earth whose names are not in the book of life will in fact worship the beast (Apoc 13:8), it is hard to conclude that John has in mind a merely hypothetical, null set when he writes the conditional sentence "If any one's name was not found written in the book of life, he was thrown into the lake of fire" (Apoc 20:15). Language about "the nations" in the final world order (Apoc 21:24, 26; 22:2) harks back to Old Testament prophecies of the conversion of Gentiles and serves as a backdrop for the vindication of the community of the faithful; it hardly means that the author expected the universal salvation of the race.[70]

John, then, does not look for a comprehensive salvation, including every individual human being. If the "world" and "all" statements do not encompass every individual, they must view those who are saved as representative, as "firstfruits" from humankind (Apoc 14:4). The "all" is concentrated in the token part. For God to rescue a fixed proportion is to rescue the whole in essence, even if the rest deselect themselves from participating. God's saving will is indeed universal in this sense, though it grasps but particulars.

*The problem of the scope of God's saving intent.* Otherwise, if we were to approach the problem in purely quantitative terms, were whole and part mutually exclusive concepts (rather than the quality of the whole being included in the saved part), we would face a false choice. Either God's plan to save some will have been determined by God alone subject to no external contingency, so that God intends not to save everyone (Augustinianism, Calvinism, Jansenism), or God intends potentially to save everyone but will allow the contingent decisions of his rational creatures to modify his plan (Molinism, Arminianism).

---

[69]On "division" as a characteristic of the Johannine presentation of Jesus, see Josef Blank, *Krisis: Untersuchungen zur johanneischen Christologie und Eschatologie* (Freiburg im Breisgau: Lambertus, 1964); Ashton, *Understanding*, pp. 229-32.

[70]Ronald Herms, *An Apocalypse for the Church and for the World: The Narrative Function of Universal Language in the Book of Revelation* (BZNW 143; Berlin: de Gruyter, 2006).

John lays down bodies of data that each side to this dogmatic debate champions, but he does not enter into the theoretical problem.[71]

On one hand are passages that imply a divine discrimination: the relative clause "to whom he will" in John 5:21, the verses that speak of the Father "having given" a select group out of the world to the Son (Jn 6:37, 39, 65; 10:29; 17:2, 6, 9; 18:9),[72] the quotation concerning God teaching some to come to the Son (Jn 6:45), the special relationship between Jesus and his sheep who hear his voice (Jn 10), Jesus' statement that he chose his disciples out of the world (Jn 15:16, 19),[73] the book of life containing names from the foundation of the world (Apoc 13:8; 17:8; 20:12).

On the other side are the cosmic passages just reviewed above, which, if we grant their natural force, resist all attempts to reduce them to a limited divine saving intent.[74] Nowhere does John trace human unbelief back to divine reprobation as its ultimate cause.[75] The temptation of Western readers is to let one set of data control the interpretation of the other.

It may be observed that the passages affirming divine election look at reality from the Father's eternal vantage point and lead the mind toward monism. Divine monergy (sole working of God) is the soteriological corollary. The passages that speak of a universal divine saving intent occur in contexts that pertain to God's purpose expressed in the incarnate one, who on entering into history sought all but met with reception or rejection, leading the mind toward

---

[71]"John, in a Semitic fashion, often declares truths that stand in sharp tension with each other without reconciling the two" (R. Alan Culpepper, "Inclusivism and Exclusivism in the Fourth Gospel," in Word, Theology, and Community in John [ed. John Painter, R. Alan Culpepper and Fernando F. Segovia; St. Louis: Chalice, 2002], p. 99).

[72]All of these but the first are in either the perfect or the aorist tense, pointing to a transaction in eternity past, prior to Jesus' mission, that determined its effective scope.

[73]All these passages from John's Gospel are discussed at some length in D. A. Carson, Divine Sovereignty and Human Responsibility: Biblical Perspectives in Tension (Atlanta: John Knox, 1981), pp. 181-92.

[74]André Feuillet, Le mystère de l'amour divin dans la théologie johannique (EBib; Paris: Gabalda, 1972). D. A. Carson writes, "Each of these statements not only reveals God's graciousness, but functions as an implicit invitation and a way of laying blame squarely on those who reject God's invitation. . . . The passages in John which deal with the 'cosmic' sweep of God's purposes . . . increase human responsibility in the light of God's gracious and available salvation" (Divine Sovereignty, p. 175).

[75]In the narrative structure of the Gospel both John 10:26 ("You do not believe, because you do not belong to my sheep") and John 12:38-40 ("That the word spoken by the prophet Isaiah might be fulfilled. . . . Therefore they could not believe") look back on ample opportunities that unbelievers had to respond to Jesus' signs, indicated by John 10:25 and John 12:37 respectively. To press these verses into service for a doctrine of pretemporal reprobation would be to take them out of their literary context.

a kind of dualism in which the world with a will of its own marks the boundary of the self-limited efficacy of the divine purpose. Synergy (working together) of God and those being saved is the implication in soteriology. But monism and dualism are logically incompatible, as are monergy and synergy.

The Achilles' heel of monism in Christian theology is the problem of evil. If God were the sole, ultimate cause of every event, his ordination would encompass not only the moral good but also its opposite. Then the antithesis between good and evil in the world would lose its absolute, oppositional character, for both would stem from divine decree. Augustine, reacting against Manichaeism, with its facile dualism, and setting out instead from the conviction that divine omnipotence cannot fail to achieve its ends, did not blush to conclude, on the basis of Romans 9:18 ("He has mercy upon whomever he wills, and whomever he wills he hardens") and Romans 11:22 ("Mark then the kindness and the severity of God"), that God is indeed back of both the election of some and the reprobation of the rest. Faced with the question of why God would choose only some to be saved, Augustine retreated again and again into the unsearchability of God's judgments (Rom 11:33).[76] Calvin followed suit. Though aware of the difficulties and even dangers of this view, Calvin went beyond Augustine into a voluntarism ("Whatever [God] wills, by the very fact that he wills it, must be considered righteous") and, considering God indeed the author of reprobation, confessed it a "dreadful decree" (*decretum . . . horribile*).[77] This line of thought carried the seed of its own dissolution. It happened with Jacob Arminius. A student of Calvin's protégé Theodore Beza at Geneva, Arminius later became so troubled by the problem of theodicy that he denied the irresistibility of the divine calling and opened the door to "Arminianism."

Arminianism, however, by asserting the ability of the human will to thwart God's call and by making divine election conditional upon the foreseen acquiescence of its objects, falls back into a fundamental dualism that subjects the divine will to the veto of creatures and leaves personal destiny in their hands rather than God's. What becomes impenetrable is not why God would choose only some to save, but why, in wishing to gain all, he would guarantee the salvation of none but merely lay before them the option.

---

[76]Augustine expounds Romans 9:18-21 and reflects the wording of Romans 11:22 in, for example, *Praed.* 14. He takes refuge in the inscrutability of God's judgments in *Praed.* 11, 16, 26.

[77]Calvin, *Institutes* 3.23.2; 3.23.7.

Augustinian monism thus has a God whose love succeeds in its suit but is limited in scope, whereas Arminian dualism has a God whose love is wide but in the last analysis partially ineffectual. Both systems, differing offspring of deductive logic, elaborate an old dilemma. Given the fact of evil in the world, can God be simultaneously omnipotent and good? Augustinianism champions God's omnipotence, but is he good? Arminianism has a congenial deity, but is his will done?

As we saw above, John is neither a monist nor a dualist, but believes in a genuine contest between good and evil (having this in common with dualism) in a universe under God's all-embracing sovereignty (in common with monism). Yet monism and dualism are logical alternatives. To combine them produces cognitive dissonance where they intersect and leaves mysteries dangling on the periphery.

Constructing theology from the data of Scripture is an art that involves identifying what is essential and clear and reserving the category of mystery for what has not been revealed. John is clear that God is "the Almighty." He is also clear that God is light, in him there is no darkness whatsoever; and that God is love. These are the axioms. A theological system that puts any of these truths in doubt violates its scriptural source. Moreover, nothing in John's writings contradicts either the proposition that God's efficacious moving is strictly prevenient to whatever spiritual or moral good springs from human beings, or that human malevolence, not divine, is the root of all depravity in human life. How to fit these propositions together in the same system of thought, or how sin ever originated from within God's good order—these are the mysteries that John leaves unresolved.

These fragmentary observations fall short of integrating God's ambition to reach all with his selection of some, but at least they suggest that the two perspectives need not be incompatible. In parallel statements found at John 6:39, 40, "all that he has given me" corresponds to "every one who sees the Son and believes on him." Where modern Westerners given to quantitative conceptuality see a paradox, John apparently sees congruence between a bona fide offer to everyone conditioned on faith and an eternal determination to gain a fixed group, between the vision to save a whole and the commitment to do so by saving particular ones. It is best, then, to let each set of passages bear its full witness. The generosity of God's love is seen in the breadth of an embrace that values the world without qualification (Jn 3:16), and the intensity of God's love is seen in an ardent pursuit of those whom he gives to the Son (Jn 6:44) that does not leave the last say to them in their willful straying but instead draws them and will not let go (Jn 10:28-29).[78]

## Summary

For John, the world was made by God and stands in relation to God. God was there before the world was and does not depend on the world; rather, it depends absolutely on him. At first, the relation between God and the world was a positive one, but the world turned from God and soured the relationship. God, however, loves the world, even though it has become his enemy, and intends to save it and reestablish it in a right relation to him. That is the goal of God's program of revelation and redemption in history to be consummated by Jesus Christ.

---

[78]Matthew Levering, "Predestination in John 13–17? Aquinas' *Commentary on John* and Contemporary Exegesis," *Thomist* 75 (2011): 393-414.

# GOD'S SELF-REVELATION
# IN CHRIST'S PERSON

Now that the end of this world has drawn near, into the darkness
God has sent his Son to beam forth saving light and magnify the splendor of
his love. John lived and worked in the wake of this historic event, as the nations
were just beginning to absorb its impact. It fills his purview. Christology is the
keynote of his proclamation.[1] This is true, even if the doctrines of God and of
the world as taught in prior biblical revelation give the framework within
which alone the Christ-event has meaning.

All the writings that make up the Johannine corpus deal with aspects of
Christology. As we will see, John's interest in Christ is neither theoretical nor
speculative. He does not pry into what the divine Son is in himself, but instead
sets forth his significance for us, as the Christ who came to give life (Jn 20:31).
"The Johannine Christology is essentially ordained to soteriology."[2] The
Gospel narrates the main stages in the Son's descent and reascent to heaven: his
precosmic existence with God and creative work (Jn 1:1-5); incarnation (Jn 1:6-
18); earthly ministry, consisting of an offer of salvation joined with a case
against the unbelieving world (Jn 1:19–12:50), followed by the preparation of
his disciples for his departure (Jn 13–17); his passion, death and burial (Jn 18–
19); resurrection (Jn 20); and statements looking forward to his ascension (Jn
20:17), giving of the Holy Spirit (Jn 20:22-23) and parousia (Jn 21:22-23). The
three Epistles offer pastoral assurance to a network of churches under the su-

---

[1]Rudolf Schnackenburg speaks rightly of "the basic Christological interest" (*The Gospel According to
St. John* [trans. Kevin Smyth et al.; 3 vols.; New York: Herder & Herder; Seabury; Crossroad, 1968–
1982], 1:154-56).
[2]Ibid., 1:155.

pervision of the apostle in the aftermath of a schism of proto-Gnostic heretics. Their view of the person of Christ evolved so as to be incompatible with that which John received from the Lord himself. In the Apocalypse John calls the church to live under the present and future lordship of Christ over against the claims of Rome in Anatolian culture.

John's Christology is a synthesis of many diverse elements. Research has tried to explain the medley by reference to formative factors. Early on, church fathers turned to the language of metaphysics to follow out John's compexities; the doctrines of the Trinity and of the incarnation involve holding alien truths in union.[3] Source critics posited lost fragments behind the earliest stratum of the Gospel and several editors in succession who offered disparate accents on Christ.[4] The author(s) worked in a syncretistic Hellenistic environment and drew from all quarters to set forth Jesus' universal significance.[5] According to the "Johannine community" hypothesis, an isolated branch of early Christianity found itself embroiled in controversy with several kinds of opponents over time leading up to the final form of the writings that we have and honed aspects of Christology in those conversations.[6] The author was a dialectical thinker who looked at his subject matter from multiple points of view, aware that no single perspective would be adequate.[7] While each approach highlights a possible factor in the genesis of the Johannine corpus, our task is to describe the Christology of the final product.

---

[3]The first six general councils of the patristic era followed this line. A modern critical representative of this broad approach is Stephen S. Smalley, "Diversity and Development in John," *NTS* 17 (1970–1971): 276-92.

[4]Rudolf Bultmann, *The Gospel of John: A Commentary* (ed. R. W. N. Hoare and J. K. Riches; trans. G. R. Beasley-Murray; Philadelphia: Westminster, 1971); Robert T. Fortna, *The Fourth Gospel and Its Predecessor: From Narrative Source to Present Gospel* (Philadelphia: Fortress, 1988); Albert C. Sundberg, "Christology in the Fourth Gospel," *BR* 21 (1976): 29-37.

[5]C. H. Dodd, *The Interpretation of the Fourth Gospel* (Cambridge: Cambridge University Press, 1953), pp. 1-130; E. M. Sidebottom, *The Christ of the Fourth Gospel in the Light of First-Century Thought* (London: SPCK, 1961); George MacRae, "The Fourth Gospel and *Religionsgeschichte*," *CBQ* 32 (1970): 13-24.

[6]Marinus de Jonge, *Jesus, Stranger from Heaven and Son of God: Jesus Christ and the Christians in Johannine Perspective* (SBLSBS 11; Missoula, MT: Scholars Press, 1977), pp. 193-222 ("Variety and Development in Johannine Christology"); Raymond E. Brown, *The Community of the Beloved Disciple: The Life, Loves, and Hates of an Individual Church in New Testament Times* (New York: Paulist Press, 1979); John Ashton, *Understanding the Fourth Gospel* (Oxford: Clarendon, 1991), pp. 121-377; Beate Kowalski, "Thesen zur joh Christologie," *BN* 146 (2010): 107-23.

[7]C. K. Barrett, "The Dialectical Theology of St. John," in *New Testament Essays* (London: SPCK, 1972), pp. 49-69; Paul N. Anderson, *The Christology of the Fourth Gospel: Its Unity and Disunity in the Light of John 6* (WUNT 2/78; Tübingen: Mohr Siebeck, 1996).

Christology goes into two large questions: Who was Jesus? What did he do? Since both questions and their answers come up in the Fourth Gospel ("Who?" [Jn 8:25, 53]; "What?" [Jn 18:19, 35]), the next two chapters are organized around them. The present chapter takes up the question of who Jesus was.

## THE DEITY OF CHRIST

There is no more suitable doorway into the Johannine Christology than that chosen by the Fourth Evangelist himself: a robust affirmation of Christ's deity (Jn 1:1). On this point John does not shilly-shally. The prologue lays on the table the grand conclusion to which the Gospel is designed to lead the reader.[8] A forthright Christology "from above" is a Johannine characteristic.[9]

*Explicit statements of Christ's ontological deity.* Thrice in the Gospel of John Jesus is explicitly called θεός (anarthrous in Jn 1:1, 18; articular vocative in 20:28).[10] These statements occur in the first sentence, at the end of the pro-

---

[8]Barnabas Lindars, "The Fourth Gospel: An Act of Contemplation," in *Studies in the Fourth Gospel* (ed. F. L. Cross; London: Mowbray, 1957), pp. 23-35; J. A. T. Robinson, "The Relation of the Prologue to the Gospel of St. John," *NTS* 9 (1963): 120-29; Marc Cholin, *Le prologue et la dynamique de l'Evangile de Jean* (Lyon: EMCC, 1995); Fernando F. Segovia, "John 1:1-18 as Entrée into Johannine Reality," in *Word, Theology, and Community in John* (ed. John Painter, R. Alan Culpepper and Fernando F. Segovia; St. Louis: Chalice, 2002), pp. 33-64; Stephen Voorwinde, "John's Prologue: Beyond Some Impasses of Twentieth-Century Scholarship," *WTJ* 64 (2002): 15-44; Thomas Söding, "Inkarnation und Pascha: Die Geschichte Jesus im Spiegel des Johannesevangeliums," *IKaZ* 32 (2003): 7-18; Peter M. Phillips, *The Prologue of the Fourth Gospel: A Sequential Reading* (LNTS 294; London: T & T Clark, 2006); Martin Hengel, "The Prologue of the Gospel of John as the Gateway to Christological Truth," in *The Gospel of John and Christian Theology* (ed. Richard Bauckham and Carl Mosser; Grand Rapids: Eerdmans, 2008), pp. 265-94. See also Jean Zumstein, "Der Prolog, Schwelle zum vierten Evangelium," in *Der Johannesprolog* (ed. Günter Kruck; Darmstadt: Wissenschaftliche Buchgesellschaft, 2009), pp. 49-75; Johannes Beutler, "Der Johannes-Prolog—Ouvertüre des Johannesevangeliums," in Kruck, *Johannesprolog*, pp. 77-106. Not all agree with this majority view of the role of the prologue. For example, Ashton's commitment to excavating the prehistory of the Gospel leads him to state, "It is wrong to assume that the perspective of the Prologue, which does of course have its starting-point in heaven, is shared by the rest of the Gospel" (*Understanding*, p. 353n51). Here atomization fights the text rather than illuminating it.

[9]John's Christology "from above" is not higher than the Christologies of other New Testament writers; it is presented with especial clarity. The Synoptists can hardly be said to sketch Christology "from below," given key statements in their opening chapters (Mt 1:20-23; Mk 1:1-3, 8, 11; Lk 1:32-33, 35). On the Christology of the Synoptic Gospels, see Simon J. Gathercole, *The Preexistent Son: Recovering the Christologies of Matthew, Mark, and Luke* (Grand Rapids: Eerdmans, 2006).

[10]For overviews of these passages in the context of other New Testament avowals of the deity of Christ, see Raymond E. Brown, *Jesus, God and Man: Modern Biblical Reflections* (New York: Macmillan, 1967), pp. 1-38 (Brown discusses Jn 1:18 on pp. 12-13; Jn 1:1; 20:28 on pp. 25-28); Murray J. Harris, *Jesus as God: The New Testament Use of Theos in Reference to Jesus* (Grand Rapids: Baker Books, 1992), pp. 51-129.

logue, and toward the end of the book. They frame all other christological matter and make John's point unmistakable.

John 1:1 is the most unequivocal statement of Christ's deity in the New Testament. "In the beginning" echoes the opening word of the Hebrew Scriptures (Gen 1:1).[11] The clause "was the Logos" views God's creative utterance as a reified projection from himself and thus clarifies that a second hypostasis or subject of the Godhead was there.[12] "And the Logos was with God" indicates personal communion between the two. "And the Logos was God [θεὸς ἦν]" specifies that it was the unique divine essence that existed as the Logos. The lack of a definite article with θεός makes it "qualitative, emphasizing nature."[13] There is a progression from the presence of the Logos with the creator in the first clause, implying his transcendence vis-à-vis the cosmos and his aseity, to his intercourse with God in the second, to their identity of being in the third. Hence the Logos neither came to be, as the world did (πάντα . . . ἐγένετο [Jn 1:3]), nor stands poles apart from God, as in metaphysical dualism, nor partakes of a diffuse "divinity," as do the gods of polytheism, but rather is a second eternal existent of the same monadic being.

---

[11]Günther Schwarz, "Gen 1:1; 2:2a und Joh 1:1a.3a—ein Versuch," *ZNW* 73 (1982): 136-37; E. L. Miller, "'In the Beginning': A Christological Transparency," *NTS* 45 (1999): 587-92.

[12]The relevant verses are Genesis 1:3, 6, 9, 11, 14, 20, 24, 26; cf. 1:22, 28. John's use of the phrase "In the beginning" indicates that he has God's spoken word from Genesis 1 primarily in mind when he speaks of the Logos. See Masanobu Endo, *Creation and Christology: A Study on the Johannine Prologue in the Light of Early Jewish Accounts* (WUNT 2/149; Tübingen: Mohr Siebeck, 2002). But the breadth of John's experiences, beginning in his native Palestine and including the syncretistic environment of Ephesus, may well have made him aware of connotations that the word also had in Greek philosophy, nascent Gnosticism and other streams of Hellenistic religion, Alexandrian Judaism, Jewish reflection on wisdom, and pretargumic and midrashic exegesis in Palestinian Judaism. I am not persuaded that John's prologue was influenced directly and materially by any unified, hypostatic concept of wisdom, whether Gnostic or Jewish. But for reviews and assessments of the possible religio-historical backgrounds that twentieth-century New Testament scholarship proposed for John's Logos, see Martin Scott, *Sophia and the Johannine Jesus* (JSNTSup 71; Sheffield: JSOT Press, 1992); Michael E. Willett, *Wisdom Christology in the Fourth Gospel* (San Francisco: Mellen Research University Press, 1992); Craig A. Evans, *Word and Glory: On the Exegetical and Theological Background of John's Prologue* (JSNTSup 89; Sheffield: JSOT Press, 1993); Sharon H. Ringe, *Wisdom's Friends: Community and Christology in the Fourth Gospel* (Louisville: Westminster John Knox, 1999); Nozomi Miura, "A Typology of Personified Wisdom Hymns," *BTB* 34 (2004): 138-49; Harold W. Attridge, "Philo and John: Two Riffs on One Logos," *SPhiloAnn* 17 (2005): 103-17; Martin Leuenberger, "Die personifizierte Weisheit vorweltlichen Ursprungs von Hi 28 bis Joh 1: Ein traditionsgeschichtlicher Strang zwischen den Testamenten," *ZAW* 120 (2008): 366-86.

[13]Harris, *Jesus as God*, p. 67. The last clause in John 1:1 drops the article with θεός for three reasons: (1) to clarify that it is a predicate though it stands in the emphatic position preceding the subject; (2) to underscore its quality (deity) rather than its concreteness (God); (3) to avoid any confusion between the Logos and God the Father. Harris (pp. 59-67) carefully weighs all the exegetical options to explain the lack of the article.

John is speaking, in a rare moment, of ontology. To join "the Logos" as subject with the predicate "God" using the copulative "was" (ἦν) is to state what the Logos was, not what he did.[14] Perhaps no one did more to draw attention to the predominant "functional" language of the New Testament than Oscar Cullmann. Yet he wrote candidly, "The prologue begins by referring to the *being* of the Word. . . . We do have here one of the few New Testament passages which speak in this sense of the 'being' of the pre-existent Word."[15]

John rounds off his prologue by coming back to these themes in a summary statement about divine self-revelation: "No one has ever seen God; the only-begotten God, who is in the bosom of the Father, he has made him known" (Jn 1:18). In chapter two I touched on the well-known textual problem in the second clause. My conclusion was that we should accept the conceptually difficult but weightily attested reading θεός ("God") rather than υἱός ("Son"). On the issue of punctuation (or syntactical construal), I found it most natural to take "only-begotten" as an adjective of "God," not an independent substantive. And on the lexical sense of μονογενής I opted for "only-begotten," not just "only."[16] The infinite God is unknowable to finite creatures except insofar as he makes himself known. God has done so by sending his Word to become flesh, bearing the glory of his Only-Begotten (Jn 1:14). As *God* begotten, this revealer is all that God is, God's most intimate confidant, and has an inside angle from which to explain God to others; as God *begotten*, he is not the absolute God, but exists relatively to him, and so, without compromising what God is, he can fittingly be sent to accommodate God's self-explanation to the condition of creatures. The verse turns on this differentiation of the only-begotten God from the un-begotten God, with whom he is substantially identical, the identity making the revelation valid, the difference allowing for its mediation.

Toward the end of the Gospel exacting Thomas, won over from skepticism about Jesus' resurrection by the firsthand evidence, acclaims him "My Lord and

---

[14]"Was God" is quite different from "Through him, as through no one else, God spoke and God acted. . . . In this man . . . [the apostles] had experienced God at work" (J. A. T. Robinson, *Honest to God* (Philadelphia: Westminster, 1963), p. 71.

[15]Oscar Cullmann, *The Christology of the New Testament* (trans. Shirley C. Guthrie and Charles A. M. Hall; 2nd ed.; NTL; Philadelphia: Westminster, 1963), p. 265. Most of the New Testament language about God and Christ is "functional" rather than ontological; however, doing is grounded in being. For trenchant critiques of exclusive functionalism, see Léopold Malevez, "Nouveau Testament et Théologie fonctionnelle," *RSR* 48 (1960): 258-90; Harris, *Jesus as God*, pp. 288-91.

[16]In chapter two, see the subsection "God's Unity" under the section "Impact of the Christ-Event on Our Knowledge of the Father" (esp. pp. 103-4).

my God!" (Jn 20:28). Precisely here Thomas's acclamation serves as a model, for Jesus' blessing on those who will accept testimony alone (Jn 20:29) commends the entire witness of the Gospel to its readers (Jn 20:30-31).[17] Having put the thesis of the Gospel objectively in John 1:1, John here places it on the subjective lips of a disciple, the one, for that matter, who was the hardest to convince.[18] It is a profession of unqualified personal devotion. The μου ("my") in no way makes the commitment merely relative, as though Thomas were adopting Jesus as God to him but not to others; it denotes his individual stake in a truth that is now sufficiently demonstrated for anyone else to see: the presence of God in Christ.[19]

*Jewish sensitivity to Jesus' claims.* As well as the plain statements of Christ's deity in the prologue and in Thomas's confession, the Fourth Gospel has three passages in which Jesus' Jewish antagonists take deadly action in response to his claims. These indirectly confirm the author's intent.

Accused by the Jewish authorities of violating a Sabbath regulation, Jesus once defended his healing ministry by arguing that he was imitating his Father, who sustains the world and its life on the Sabbath (Jn 5:16-17). John adds that this was why the Jews sought to kill Jesus: he "called God his own [ἴδιος] Father, making himself equal with God [ἴσον τῷ θεῷ]" (Jn 5:18). John's comment expounds not only Jesus' phrase "my [μου] Father" but also Jesus' assumption that he had a filial relationship to God unlike any other human being, one that placed him on a level with God.[20]

---

[17]The point of the pericope is neither that faith based on seeing is inadequate, as many critics have supposed, nor that Jesus is the one who enables faith. The former position is rightly rejected, and the latter proposed, in William Bonney, *Caused to Believe: The Doubting Thomas Story at the Climax of John's Christological Narrative* (BIS 62; Leiden: Brill, 2002). The point is simply that the same Jesus who proved himself to his first disciples by tokens proves himself to others by their word. See Jan G. van der Watt, "The Presence of Jesus through the Gospel of John," *Neot* 36 (2002): 89-95; Kasper Bro Larsen, *Recognizing the Stranger: Recognition Scenes in the Gospel of John* (BIS 93; Leiden: Brill, 2008), pp. 208-11.

[18]For Thomas to defer believing until he had firsthand evidence of Jesus' resurrection was appropriate in his historical context. See Margareta Gruber, "Berührendes Sehen: Zur Legitimation der Zeichenforderung des Thomas (Joh 20,24-31)," *BZ* 51 (2007): 61-83.

[19]By the time of writing, the Septuagintal collocation of "Lord" and "God" that Thomas reflected may have come to connote a direct contrast between Jesus and Domitian, who also accepted the appellation *dominus et deus noster.* See Lance Byron Richey, *Roman Imperial Ideology and the Gospel of John* (CBQMS 43; Washington, DC: Catholic Biblical Association of America, 2007), pp. xii-xiii. But this sense is not underscored in the literary structure that issues in Thomas's confession and must be secondary at most. On all aspects of the passage, see Harris, *Jesus as God*, pp. 105-41.

[20]On the binitarian Christology in John 5:18, see Albert C. Sundberg, "*Isos Tō Theō* Christology in John 5:17-30," *BR* 15 (1970): 19-31.

In the dialogue of John 8 Jesus, to substantiate Jesus' claim to be "the light of the world" and "of life" (Jn 8:12), appeals to the witness of his Father (Jn 8:18), adding that his origin is "from above" and is "not of this world" (Jn 8:23). When he warns his audience that they will die in their sins unless they believe "that I am" (Jn 8:24), they demand an explanation of who he is (Jn 8:25a). His terse adverbial reply—"originally" or "basically" (τὴν ἀρχήν [Jn 8:25b])[21]—defines the sense in which he meant "I am." Whether he is claiming pretemporal existence or self-existence makes little difference, since one implies the other. This, the first in a series of crests of the "I am" predication (Jn 8:24, 28, 58), is so cryptic that it leaves his interlocutors puzzled, or else so unexpectedly bold that they brush him off on first hearing. But as Jesus hammers on his unique relationship with God the Father (Jn 8:28-29, 38, 40, 42, 49, 50, 54-55) and throws in a promise to preserve from death anyone who keeps Jesus' word (Jn 8:51), his meaning becomes unmistakable and obnoxious. The climax comes in his claim to be before Abraham (Jn 8:56-59), using the present tense "I am" (Jn 8:58) to echo the incomparable "I am" of Yahweh (Ex 3:14; Deut 32:39; Is 41:4; 43:10, 13, 25; 46:4; 48:12; 51:12; 52:6). His import is not lost on his hearers, who immediately take up stones.

Later, in response to Jesus' statement "I and the Father are one [thing] [ἕν ἐσμεν]," some Jews made ready again to stone him, charging him with blasphemy, "because you, being a man, make yourself God [ποιεῖς σεαυτὸν θεόν]" (Jn 10:30-33). He countered on the ground that God himself can address creatures who judge in his name as "gods" (Ps 82:6).[22] How much more appropriate, then, it is to regard as "Son of God" the one whom the Father has consecrated and sent into the world to do the Father's works, in whom the Father is, and he in the Father. Again they tried to arrest him (Jn 8:34-39).[23]

That his hearers held Jesus liable of a capital offense on all three occasions indicates their sense that he had infringed the boundary between God and created beings. "R. Abbahu said: If a man say, 'I am God,' he lies; if 'the Son of

[21]Translators and commentators have been unsure how to solve this conundrum. The position of τὴν ἀρχὴν seems to make it a laconic reply in its own right, to which the following relative clause (ὅ τι) refers back. On the possible senses of the phrase that can be established from the Thesaurus linguae Graecae, see Chrys C. Caragounis, "What Did Jesus Mean by τὴν ἀρχήν in John 8:25?" NovT 49 (2007): 129-47.
[22]On the quotation, see Carl Mosser, "The Earliest Patristic Interpretation of Psalm 82, Jewish Antecedents, and the Origin of Christian Deification," JTS 56 (2005): 30-74.
[23]Thomas Söding, "'Ich und der Vater sind eins' (Joh 10,30): Die johanneische Christologie vor dem Anspruch des Hauptgebotes (Dtn 6,4f)," ZNW 93 (2002): 177-99.

Man,' he will repent; if 'I will go up to heaven,' he says but shall not perform it" (*y. Ta'an.* 2 [65b]). From the time when the Jews of Palestine came under pressure from Antiochus IV, whose coins gave the Seleucid ruler the appellative "god manifest" (θεός ἐπιφανής), many were zealous to defend that line.[24] Sentiments flared again about the time of Jesus' ministry when Pilate introduced into Jerusalem Roman military standards sporting effigies of Caesar, in contravention of the commandment prohibiting images (Josephus, *J. W.* 2.169-171; *Ant.* 18.55-59). Independently of John, the Synoptic Gospels confirm that some of Jesus' words and deeds from early in his ministry implied a self-awareness exceeding the human, sometimes raising the hackles of the Pharisees.[25] Though John chooses for his Gospel an alternative set of incidents, taken together they point to an historic seed sown by Jesus that flowered in the Johannine Christology.[26]

**Other indications of Christ's deity.** Besides the unique divine essence, the Johannine Son of God has the same constellation of attributes that God has.

Jesus was not fully known to his contemporaries (Jn 1:26-27, 31), partly because his origin is ineffable (Jn 7:28). Only he knows where he comes from and where he is going; the crowds cannot come there, for he is from above and is not of this world (Jn 7:34-36; 8:14, 21-23). He has a name inscribed "which no one knows but himself" (Apoc 19:12). Whereas "no one has ever seen God" (Jn 1:18), the sent one is likewise beyond human understanding.

He, like God, is the well of life from whom all things live. In the Logos "was life" (Jn 1:4). "To have life in himself," the property of self-existence or aseity, belongs to him as it does to the Father (Jn 5:26). He is "the eternal life which was with the Father" (1 Jn 1:2), the bread of life who came down out of heaven to give life to the world (Jn 6:33, 51), "the resurrection and the life" (Jn 11:25). The Logos was the light of humankind at creation and continues to shine on every person (Jn 1:4-5, 9). To come to him is to come to the light (Jn 3:19). He

---

[24]Martin Hengel, *Judaism and Hellenism: Studies in Their Encounter in Palestine during the Early Hellenistic Period* (trans. John Bowden; 2 vols.; Philadelphia: Fortress, 1974), 1:285-87.

[25]From the triple tradition, early in the ministry, see Matthew 9:3 // Mark 2:6-7 // Luke 5:21; Matthew 12:14 // Mark 3:6 // Luke 6:11; at the end of the ministry, Matthew 26:64-66 // Mark 14:62-64 // Luke 22:69-71. From Q there is the *Jubelruf* (Mt 11:25-27 // Lk 10:21-22).

[26]On the cleavage between Johannine claims concerning Jesus and the Jewish judgment that such claims cannot be legitimately made for a man, both of which were clarified in tension with each other, see Wayne A. Meeks, "Equal to God," in *The Conversation Continues: Studies in Paul and John* (ed. Robert T. Fortna and Beverly R. Gaventa; Nashville: Abingdon, 1990), pp. 309-21; Lori Baron, "Interpreting the *Shema*: Liturgy and Identity in the Fourth Gospel," *ASE* 27 (2010): 53-60.

is "the light of the world" (Jn 8:12; 9:5); only in him is the darkness lifted (Jn 12:35-36, 46). As we saw in chapter two, to be the dwelling place of life, and to be light itself, or its source, are qualities of God (Jn 5:26; 1 Jn 1:5).

God alone being holy (Apoc 4:8; 15:4), it is striking that the Son is "the Holy One of God" (Jn 6:69; cf. "he is pure" [1 Jn 3:3]; "the holy one" [Apoc 3:7]). His holiness is pictured by comparing his eyes to a flame of fire (Apoc 1:14b-15; 2:18; 19:12). It is implied that Jesus was a "good" (ἀγαθός) man (Jn 1:46; 7:12).[27]

Independently of all created reality, God the Son encompasses protology and eschatology as his Father does. He had glory with his Father before the foundation of the world and, after completing his work on earth, returned to take up that glory again (Jn 17:5, 24). He "was from the beginning" (1 Jn 1:1; 2:13, 14).[28] He "was before" his forerunner John the Baptist (Jn 1:15, 30). He continues forever (Jn 8:35). Even as God is the Alpha and the Omega (Apoc 1:8), the beginning and the end (Apoc 21:6), so also the Son is "the Alpha and the Omega," "the first and the last," "the beginning and end" (Apoc 1:17; 2:8; 22:13).

As God's Logos he possessed power to create, while as the Son of Man he will raise the dead and judge the world. In Jewish monotheism the acts of creation and of judgment belong to God alone. This is eloquently condensed in a rabbinic dictum from the end of the second century: "He is God, he is the Maker, he is the Creator, he is the Discerner, he is the Judge, he is the Witness, he is the Complainant, and it is he that shall judge, blessed is he, in whose presence is neither guile nor forgetfulness nor respect of persons nor taking of bribes; for all is his" (*m. 'Abot* 4:22).[29] The Johannine literature attributes all this to Jesus Christ with God. Looking back, the Logos was with God and brought all things into being (Jn 1:1-3). He is the first principle, on which the creation depends (Apoc 3:14).[30] Looking forward, he will be the agent to con-

---

[27]Jane Heath, "'Some Were Saying, "He Is Good"' (John 7.12b): 'Good' Christology in John's Gospel?" *NTS* 56 (2010): 513-35.

[28]On the cosmic sense of "from the beginning" in 1 John 1:1; 2:13, 14, see chapter 2, note 1, above. That "he who was from the beginning" is a description of Christ follows from the trinitarian cycles of 1 John 2:12-14. Forgiveness of the little children's sins (1 Jn 2:12), corresponding to their knowing the Father (Greek text 1 Jn 2:14a = English text 1 Jn 2:13c), is the Father's gift (cf. 1 Jn 1:9). Young men's overcoming of the evil one (mentioned in Greek text 1 Jn 2:13b, 14c = English text 1 Jn 2:14b) is the work of the Spirit (cf. 1 Jn 4:2, 4). Sandwiched in the middle of each cycle is their knowing of him who was from the beginning, which has point only if it refers to knowing Christ, since the Father's existence from the beginning would be a truism.

[29]Attributed to Rabbi Eleazar ha-Kappar, a contemporary of Rabbi Judah the Patriarch.

[30]For "beginning" (ἡ ἀρχή) in the sense of the first cause in reference to the creator-God, see Josephus, *Ag. Ap.* 2.190. G. K. Beale's argument that "beginning of the creation of God" in Apocalypse

summate history, exercising the divine prerogatives of calling forth the dead
(Jn 5:21, 25, 28-29; 6:39, 40, 44, 54) and of judgment (Jn 5:22, 27; 12:48; Apoc 19:11,
13). In a remarkable transfer of scriptural imagery, the white head of hair that
depicted the divine judge in Daniel 7:9 is ascribed to the one like a son of man
in Apocalypse 1:14.

Like God, the Son knows everything (Jn 1:48; 2:24-25; 4:16-19, 39; 6:64; 13:1,
3, 13; 16:19-30; Apoc 5:6). He claims to be just in judgment (Jn 5:30). He is the
righteous one, in whom there is no sin (Jn 16:10; 1 Jn 2:1; 3:7); the one who is
true, in whom there is no falsehood (Jn 7:18). In righteousness he judges and
makes war on evil (Apoc 19:11). Jesus is the good shepherd (Jn 10:11), by whom
God fulfills his promise to tend his flock Israel in person (see Is 40:11; Jer 31:10;
Ezek 34:11-31; Mic 7:14).

But above all, even as God "is love" (1 Jn 4:8, 16), so also Jesus loved his
disciples to the end (Jn 13:1), with the greatest kind of love there is, laying
down his life for them (Jn 15:13; 1 Jn 3:16), in the same way God loves him (Jn
15:9). We will have occasion in chapter five to explore further Jesus' love for
his disciples. Here we simply note that the core divine attribute of love shines
through Jesus.

Because the Son of God is all that God is, the very unicity of God is true of
the Son and of their union. Jews of the Second Temple period might speak of
an angel or of an exalted human being as sharing an isolated divine power by
delegation from God, but an outstanding feature of the use of monotheistic
formulae in Jewish literature is that they are reserved strictly, as they must be
logically, for God alone and are not predicated of any created being.[31] It is
highly significant, therefore, when the Fourth Gospel confesses Jesus to be the
"one shepherd" (Jn 10:16), who, with his Father, is "one" (Jn 10:30). The claim in
John 10:30 comes on the heels of parallel statements that no one can snatch
sheep out of the hand of Jesus (Jn 10:28) or of his Father (Jn 10:29). John 10:30
is not merely an affirmation that the Father and the Son cooperate in keeping
sheep. Jesus says, "I and the Father are one [thing, being] [ἕν ἐσμεν]," using the
neuter form of "one" and the verb "to be." The reason why they act in tandem

---

3:14 refers to the resurrection of Christ as inaugurating the new creation imports a Pauline usage
(Col 1:18) into Johannine theology (*The Book of Revelation: A Commentary on the Greek Text*
[NIGTC; Grand Rapids: Eerdmans; Carlisle: Paternoster, 1999], pp. 297-301). John nowhere else
uses ἀρχή to express that idea.
[31]Paul A. Rainbow, "Monotheism and Christology in I Corinthians 8.4-6" (D.Phil. thesis; University
of Oxford, 1987), pp. 66-100, 106.

is that they are an ontic unit. This places Jesus within the exclusive ambit of the one God.[32]

Jesus' repeated and calculated use of the absolute self-predication "I am" in the Gospel of John finds its background in monotheistic texts of the Old Testament. The relevant texts are God's special name "I am who I am" at Exodus 3:14, and the stark "I am he" (הוּא אָנֹכִי, אֲנִי הוּא) found at Deuteronomy 32:39 and in Isaiah 40–55.[33] "I am who I am" (or "I am because I am") asserts that God is self-existent, knowable only to himself, free and independent of any other being in his acts, and always consistent with his own nature. Several of the Isaiah texts contain a claim by God that he is uniquely the first and the last (Is 41:4; 43:10; 48:12). The Johannine christological accents that I have already outlined resonate with these divine self-identifications in Exodus and Isaiah. Deuteronomy 32:39, "I, even I, am he, and there is no god beside me," denies the existence of other gods. Likewise occurrences of the formula "I am he" at Isaiah 43:10, 13 flank a denial that there is any savior besides Yahweh (Is 43:11), together with a reminder that God made himself known as Israel's savior when as yet they had no strange god among them. The antipolytheistic and anti-idolatrous tenor of Isaiah 40–55 ("Is there a God besides me? There is no Rock; I know not any" [Is 44:8]; "And there is no other god besides me, a righteous God and a Savior; there is none besides me. . . . For I am God, and there is no other" [Is 45:21-22]; "My glory I will not give to another" [Is 48:11]) lends to the claim "I am he" a polemical thrust. "I am he" is an avowal of God's sole right to human devotion against any and all supposed rivals, a right that he will enforce when he vindicates himself in the sight of the nations by working

---

[32]Richard Bauckham, "Monotheism and Christology in the Gospel of John," in *Contours of Christology in the New Testament* (ed. Richard N. Longenecker; MNTS; Grand Rapids: Eerdmans, 2005), pp. 163-65.

[33]The relevant Johannine passages are John 4:26; 6:20; 8:18, 24, 28, 58; 13:19; 18:5-6, 8. The Isaiah texts are Isaiah 41:4; 43:10, 13, 25; 46:4; 48:12; 51:12; 52:6. On this complex of passages, see Raymond E. Brown, "The EGO EIMI ('I Am') Passages in the Fourth Gospel," in *A Companion to John: Readings in Johannine Theology (John's Gospel and Epistles)* (ed. Michael J. Taylor; New York: Alba House, 1970), pp. 120-24; Philip B. Harner, *The "I Am" of the Fourth Gospel: A Study in Johannine Usage and Thought* (FBBS 26; Philadelphia: Fortress, 1970); Ashton, *Understanding*, pp. 141-47; David Mark Ball, *"I Am" in John's Gospel: Literary Function, Background and Theological Implications* (JSNTSup 124; Sheffield: Sheffield Academic Press, 1996); Paul Gwynne, "YHWH and the Invisible Father," *ACR* 77 (2000): 278-91; Walther Binni and Bernado Gianluigi Boschi, *Cristologia primitiva: Dalla teofania del Sinài all'Io Sono giovanneo* (CSB 46; Bologna: EDB, 2004); Bauckham, "Monotheism and Christology," pp. 154-62; Paul N. Anderson, "The Origin and Development of the Johannine *Egō Eimi* Sayings in Cognitive-Critical Perspective," *JSHJ* 9 (2011): 139-206.

salvation at the last day.[34] Jesus' use of the formula "I am [he]" in the Fourth Gospel indicates that he is the one in whom the only God is uniquely present to do exactly that.[35]

In one remarkable passage in the Gospel the author takes over an Old Testament theophany text and makes it refer to Christ. Isaiah, says John, saw Christ's glory and spoke of him (Jn 12:41). The only passage in which the prophet claims to have seen the divine glory is Isaiah 6:1, "I saw the Lord [אֲדֹנָי] sitting upon a throne, high and lifted up; and his train filled the temple." In ensuing verses the figure on the throne is identified as Yahweh (יהוה [Is 6:3, 5]). Presumably John's reasoning is that since this figure was visible to the prophet's eye, he was not God as he is in himself, but rather a representation of his glory that fills the earth (Is 6:3). Christ is thus identical with, yet distinct from, the God of Israel; he is that very being, but manifest to the creation.[36]

The Apocalypse "presents a highly exalted view of Christ, perhaps unsurpassed in the NT."[37] Not the least of the ways John depicts Christ is as the royal plenipotentiary who alone sits directly on God's very throne (Apoc 3:21; 5:6; 7:17; 22:1).[38] From the privilege of opening the scroll of destiny in God's hand, all beings whatsoever in heaven or on earth or under the earth are excluded (Apoc 5:3). But the Lamb is worthy and, on taking the scroll, becomes, together with him who sits on the throne, the center of universal praise and obeisance (Apoc 5:6-14). In this worship scene the Lamb's position is squarely "in the midst of the throne" (ἐν μέσῳ τοῦ θρόνου [Apoc 5:6]), collocated with the creator. As noted above, the Christ of the Apocalypse is also, like God himself, the Alpha and the Omega, the First and the Last (Apoc 1:17; 22:13). His ineffable nature is indicated by a name inscribed on his diadems that no one knows but he himself (Apoc 19:12).[39]

---

[34]Catrin H. Williams, *I Am He: The Interpretation of ʾAnî Hû in Jewish and Early Christian Literature* (WUNT 2/113; Tübingen: Mohr Siebeck, 2000).

[35]Adam M. Okorie, "The Self-Revelation of Jesus in the 'I Am' Sayings of John's Gospel," *CurTM* 28 (2001): 486-90.

[36]On John 12:41, see Nils Alstrup Dahl, "The Johannine Church and History," in *Current Issues in New Testament Interpretation: Essays in Honor of Otto A. Piper* (ed. William Klassen and Graydon F. Snyder; PL; London: SCM Press, 1962), pp. 131-32; Larry W. Hurtado, *Lord Jesus Christ: Devotion to Jesus in Earliest Christianity* (Grand Rapids: Eerdmans, 2003), pp. 374-81.

[37]Larry W. Hurtado, "Christology," in *Dictionary of the Later New Testament and Its Developments* (ed. Ralph P. Martin and Peter H. Davids; Downers Grove, IL: InterVarsity Press, 1997), p. 176.

[38]Darrell D. Hannah, "Of Cherubim and the Divine Throne: Rev 5.6 in Context," *NTS* 49 (2003): 528-42.

[39]On the lofty Christology of the Apocalypse, see Traugott Holtz, *Die Christologie der Apokalypse des*

A few passages in the Apocalypse describe Christ in terms reminiscent of Old Testament accounts of angelophanies (e.g., Dan 10; see esp. Apoc 1:12-18; 14:14-16; 19:11-16).[40] There was a broad tendency in Jewish-tinged Christianity of the first four centuries to use angelomorphic elements to describe Christ.[41] Although in heterodox circles the angelic Christ was sometimes thought to be an angel subordinate to God, the use of such language need not imply that,[42] and in the Apocalypse it does not. By adapting stock Old Testament imagery for manifestations of celestial beings, John indicated Christ's appearance in the visions, not his nature. John, imbued with the monotheism of the Old Testament, was clear that angels belong to the creation and are not to be confused with the creator, either conceptually or by way of acts of worship (Apoc 19:10; 22:8-9), whereas the Lamb receives worship together with God (Apoc 4–5). What John describes in the passages under review may even be a christomorphic angel rather than an angelomorphic Christ. Just as in the Old Testament "the angel of the LORD" could speak God's words in God's own name (e.g., Ex 3:2 with Ex 3:4; Josh 5:14 with Josh 6:2) without blurring the line between God and God's agent, so the revealing angel of the Apocalypse (Apoc 1:1b) may combine visual features of angelophanies (robe, eyes of fire, body of gleaming bronze, voice like a mighty waterfall) with symbols of ultimate transcendence (hair white as wool [Apoc 1:14; cf. Dan 7:9]; claim to be the first and the last [Apoc 1:17]). The point is that God, acting through Christ as co-regent and executor of his will, is the source of the revelation mediated by the angel. This is no subordinationist Christology; it puts the Lamb on a par with the one who sits on the throne.[43]

---

*Johannes* (TUGAL 85; Berlin: Akademie-Verlag, 1962); Joseph Comblin, *Le Christ dans l'Apocalypse* (BTTB 3/6; Paris: Desclée, 1965); Richard Bauckham, *The Theology of the Book of Revelation* (NTT; Cambridge: Cambridge University Press, 1993), pp. 54-65; Martin Hengel, "Die Throngemeinschaft des Lammes mit Gott in der Johannesapokalypse," *TBei* 27 (1996): 159-75; Dan Lioy, *The Book of Revelation in Christological Focus* (SBL 58; New York: Peter Lang, 2003); John Wesley Wright, "'Blessing, Honor, Glory, and Might, Forever and Ever!' Nicea and the Christology of the Book of Revelation," *WeslTJ* 39 (2004): 7-38.

[40]Christopher Rowland, "The Vision of the Risen Christ in Rev. 1.13ff.: The Debt of an Early Christology to an Aspect of Jewish Angelology," *JTS* 31 (1980): 1-11.

[41]On the concept, see Jean Daniélou, *The Theology of Jewish Christianity*, vol. 1 of *The Development of Christian Doctrine Before the Council of Nicaea* (trans. John A. Baker; London: Darton, Longman & Todd, 1964), pp. 117-46; Richard N. Longenecker, *The Christology of Early Jewish Christianity* (SBT 17; Naperville, IL: Allenson, 1970), pp. 26-32; Charles A. Gieschen, *Angelomorphic Christology: Antecedents and Early Evidence* (AGJU 42; Leiden: Brill, 1998).

[42]Daniélou, *Theology*, pp. 118-19.

[43]Loren T. Stuckenbruck, *Angel Veneration and Christology: A Study in Early Judaism and in the Chris-

Logically, monotheism could imply either that Christ was not divine but rather an agent who spoke and acted with divine authority, or that he is of a piece with God. A. E. Harvey proposed that Jewish monotheism constrained the New Testament authors, including John, to follow the former line of reasoning.[44] But to maintain his thesis, Harvey has to remove the chief texts from the fabric of Johannine Christology and adopt tendentious interpretations of them.[45] Nor does Harvey take into account the threatened stonings of Jesus by the Jewish audiences of the first-century setting, and the vigor of the rabbinic polemic against belief in "powers in heaven" from the early second century onwards.

For John, monotheism required the opposite conclusion: the divine Christ's consubstantiality with God.[46] Ernst Käsemann was correct: "Not merely from the prologue and from the mouth of Thomas, but from the whole Gospel [the reader of faith] perceives the confession, 'My Lord and my God.'"[47]

***Personal distinction of the Son from God the Father.*** If the Johannine Son of God is strictly identified with God as to his being, we may well ask in what respects he is dissimilar to his Father.

John uses prepositional phrases to mark the distinction between the Father and the Son within the Godhead. Near the beginning of the Gospel, and again in the First Epistle, he writes, "the Logos was with [πρός] God [accusative]" (Jn 1:1), "the Eternal Life . . . was with [πρός] the Father [accusative]" (1 Jn 1:2). The use of πρός with an accusative noun has been subjected to lexical scrutiny. Used with persons, it connotes neither motion toward nor mere spatial prox-

---

tology of the Apocalypse of John (WUNT 2/70; Tübingen: Mohr Siebeck, 1995); Peter R. Carrell, *Jesus and the Angels: Angelology and the Christology of the Apocalypse of John* (SNTSMS 95; Cambridge: Cambridge University Press, 1997); Matthias Reinhard Hoffmann, *The Destroyer and the Lamb: The Relationship between Angelomorphic and Lamb Christology in the Book of Revelation* (WUNT 2/203; Tübingen: Mohr Siebeck, 2005).

[44]A. E. Harvey, *Jesus and the Constraints of History* (Philadelphia: Westminster, 1982), pp. 154-73; idem, "Christ as Agent," in *The Glory of Christ in the New Testament: Studies in Christology in Memory of George Bradford Caird* (ed. L. D. Hurst and N. T. Wright; Oxford: Clarendon, 1987), pp. 239-50.

[45]Note Harvey, *Constraints*, pp. 166, 172, and the appendix "The Divinity of Jesus in the New Testament," pp. 176-78. On the same texts, compare Harris, *Jesus as God*, pp. 51-129, and note Harris's specific comments on Harvey's "functional agent" Christology on pp. 125n95, 292.

[46]To use the technical term "consubstantial" here is hardly out of place. On the relation between the high Christology of the Apocalypse and the *homoousios* doctrine of the church, see C. Kavin Rowe, "For Future Generations: Worshipping Jesus and the Integration of the Theological Disciplines," *ProEccl* 17 (2008): 186-209.

[47]Ernst Käsemann, *The Testament of Jesus: A Study of the Gospel of John in the Light of Chapter 17* (trans. Gerhard Krodel; Philadelphia: Fortress, 1968), p. 9.

imity, but social communion.[48] Only between different persons can inter-
action take place. This sense is confirmed by the nearby word-picture of the
Son reclining in his Father's embrace: "who is in the bosom/lap [εἰς τὸν κόλπον]
of the Father" (Jn 1:18). In other groups of passages the Son is said to have been
"with" (παρά) the Father (dative) (Jn 8:38; 17:5 [2×]) and to have come "from
beside" (παρά) the Father (genitive) (Jn 1:14; 6:46; 7:29; 9:33; 16:27-28; 17:8).

The title "Son" also points to a distinction from the Father. John can use the
full phrase "Son of God,"[49] or the simple "Son," in settings that mention in the
same breath either "God" (Jn 3:16, 17) or "the Father."[50] Like Paul, John is happy
to describe Jesus as the "Son" (υἱός) of God. Unlike Paul, John designates believers never as God's "sons" (υἱοί) but rather as God's "children" (τέκνα). In
this way John highlights the uniqueness of Jesus' sonship. Since an earthly son
bears a likeness to the one who sired him, yet honors his senior, the analogy of
a filial relationship enables John to signify both the Son's community of nature
with God, and his deference to the Father.

Let us review the data for each of these senses of "Son."

(1) A narrator's comment shows that John viewed the language of sonship
as implying parity with the Father. Jesus "called God his own [ἴδιος] Father,
making himself equal [ἴσος] with God" (Jn 5:17-18). Again, when Jesus claimed
to be one with the Father (ἓν ἐσμεν [Jn 10:30]) and to be the Son of God (Jn
10:36), his Jewish interlocutors accused him of making himself out to be God
(ποιεῖς σεαυτὸν θεόν [Jn 10:33]) and were ready to stone him (Jn 10:31, 39).

Jesus' discourses in the Fourth Gospel aver that he has interactions with God
on a par with him. In a way no one else has done, the Son has seen the Father
(Jn 6:46) and knows him (Jn 7:29; 8:55; 17:25). The Father and the Son know
each other (Jn 10:15). Given that God is infinite and incomprehensible to creatures, this unqualified claim of mutual knowing is profound. Jesus also says that
the Father is in him, and he in the Father (Jn 10:38; 14:10-11, 20; 17:21, 23). As
the Father loves the Son (Jn 3:35; 5:20; 10:17; 15:9, 10; 17:23, 24, 26), so the Son
loves the Father (Jn 14:31). Besides their common essence, insofar as they are

---

[48]Murray J. Harris, "Appendix: Prepositions and Theology in the Greek New Testament," *NIDNTT*
3:1204-5; idem, *Jesus as God*, pp. 55-57.

[49]Jn 1:34, 49; 3:18; 5:25; 10:36; 11:4, 27; 19:7; 20:31; 1 Jn 3:8; 4:15; 5:5, 10, 12, 13, 20; Apoc 2:18. In
a further eight places we find "his Son," where αὐτοῦ has God as its antecedent: 1 John 1:7; 3:23; 4:9,
10; 5:9, 10, 11, 20. In 1 John 5:12 τὸν υἱόν has the same sense.

[50]Jn 3:35, 36 [2×]; 5:19 [2×], 20, 21, 22, 23 [2×], 26; 6:40; 14:13; 17:1 [2×]; 1 Jn 1:3; 2:22, 23 [2×], 24;
4:14; 2 Jn 3, 9. "Son" stands by itself (in contrast to a household slave) in John 8:35-36.

distinct personal entities, their mutual indwelling and mutual love bind them in a unity of fellowship (Jn 17:11, 22). All that the Father has—nothing less than the totality of all things that have come into being (Jn 1:3)—belongs to the Son, and all that the Son has belongs to the Father (Jn 16:15; 17:10).[51] They glorify each other: the Father glorifies the Son (Jn 8:54; 17:5), and the Son receives glory from the Father (Jn 5:41, 44; 8:50; 17:22, 24); the Son seeks the Father's glory (Jn 7:18; 11:40) and glorifies him (Jn 17:4). Father and Son act each for the other's glory (Jn 11:4; 12:23, 28; 13:31-32; 14:13; 17:1). Hence the Son in his otherness from the Father is a reciprocal counterpart, another self of the same being.

The Father and the Son participate together in operations toward the world, often side by side in the same sentence.[52] We have seen that the Logos was the divine agent who created all things (Jn 1:3). Like the Father, the Son is sovereign over all.[53] The divine act of electing a people out of the world proceeds through the Son (Jn 6:70-71; 13:18-19; 15:16, 19).[54] To the disciples the Son gives commandments (Jn 13:34; 14:15, 21, 23-24 [word]; 15:10, 12, 14, 17; 1 Jn 2:3-5), for he has disposal over them (Jn 21:22-23). On leaving to go to the Father, the Son bestows peace on his disciples, "not as the world gives" (Jn 14:27). Father and Son cooperate in preserving the eternal life of their flock (Jn 10:29-30; 17:12, 15). The Son has power to answer prayers (Jn 14:13-14). The Son, like the Father, is a co-sender of the Holy Spirit (Jn 15:26; 16:7). Father and Son cooperate in judging (Jn 8:15-16). The Son with the Father receives glory from people (Jn 1:14; 2:11; 11:4, 40; 12:41; 17:10, 24; Apoc 1:6; 5:12-13) and is recipient of the worship of all creation (Apoc 5:8-14; 7:9-10). Even if it were the case that "there is indeed evidence for a working of the Father among men independently of the Son"—all the Johannine verses that J. Ernest Davey draws from H. J. Holtzmann prove, on careful examination, the opposite[55]—the sweep of John's portrait of Christ is "that all of God's

---

[51]On "Son of God" connoting the Son's authority to dispose of the Father's property, see Jan-A. von Bühner, *Der Gesandte und sein Weg im 4. Evangelium: Die kultur- und religionsgeschichtlichen Grundlagen der johanneischen Sendungschristologie sowie ihre traditionsgeschichtliche Entwicklung* (WUNT 2/2; Tübingen: Mohr Siebeck, 1977), pp. 195-98; Ashton, *Understanding*, pp. 317-28.

[52]Jn 5:24; 14:21, 23; 17:3; 1 Jn 1:3; 2:24; 2 Jn 3; Apoc 1:2, 9; 3:12; 5:13; 6:16; 7:9-10, 17; 11:15; 12:10; 14:1, 4, 10, 12; 15:3; 20:4, 6; 21:22-23; 22:1, 3.

[53]Jn 3:31, 35; 6:6, 70-71; 13:3; 14:30; 16:15; 17:2; Apoc 5:6; 7:17; 19:12; 22:3 (many diadems), 16.

[54]The Son gives life to whom he will (Jn 5:21, 25; 14:19; 17:2). Also, the book of life is "of the Lamb" (Apoc 13:8; 21:27).

[55]John 1:33; 3:16, 35; 4:23; 5:17, 20, 32, 37; 6:40, 44; 8:18; 9:31; 10:15; 16:27; 17:4. J. Ernest Davey, *The Jesus of St. John: Historical and Christological Studies in the Fourth Gospel* (London: Lutterworth, 1958), p. 155. Only John 9:29 excludes Christ; it is in the mouth of his Pharisaic enemies.

action, whether in creation or in the redirection of that creation gone astray, is achieved by Jesus Christ."[56]

(2) On the other hand, in certain respects the relation between the Father and the Son is nonreciprocal.[57] The Logos was with God (Jn 1:1; cf. 1 Jn 1:3), not God with the Logos; the one introduced in the prologue is understood with reference to the one known from Genesis.[58] As far as the communication of the divine essence is concerned, it passes from the Father to the Son and not vice versa. It was the Father who granted to the Son to have life in himself as the Father does (Jn 5:26). Metaphorically speaking, the Son was thus "begotten of God," and therefore has God's nature in him, cannot sin, and keeps believers (1 Jn 5:18). The Son is the "only-begotten [one] from the Father" (Jn 1:14), the "only-begotten God" (Jn 1:18). In chapter two we considered the bearing of these verses on John's inchoate concept of the eternal generation of the Son. What we need to observe in the present connection is that in these sentences the Father and the Son are not interchangeable. Paternity is prime, sonship derivative.

This is plain in the host of Johannine passages—forty-four in all—that speak of the Father sending the Son. References will be given below where we explore the concept of "sending" in connection with the incarnation. For now, it is enough to note once again the irreversibility of subject and object. In every instance the Father is the sender, and the Son the one sent, without exception.

Another nonreciprocity pertains to John's peculiar grammatical use of the verb "give" (διδόναι). Where giving takes place between the Father and the Son, it is the Father who gives and the Son who receives, never the other way around. Heaven gives to the Son to increase and to John the Baptist to decrease (Jn 3:27). God has given the Spirit without measure to the one he sent into the world to speak God's words; indeed, the Father has given all things into the Son's hands (Jn 3:34, 35; 13:3; 17:7). To the Son the Father has given the following things: all

---

[56]Colin E. Gunton, "'And in One Lord Jesus Christ . . . Begotten Not Made,'" in *Father, Son and Holy Spirit: Essays Toward a Fully Trinitarian Theology* (London: T & T Clark, 2003), p. 69. On the equality of Father and Son in John, see Edith Zingg, *Das Reden von Gott als "Vater" im Johannesevangelium* (HBS 48; Freiburg: Herder, 2006), pp. 306-9. This understanding of Jesus' divine sonship is totally at odds with Margaret Davies's remarkable attempt to avoid seeing it as an attribution of divinity (*Rhetoric and Reference in the Fourth Gospel* [JSNTSup 69; Sheffield: Sheffield Academic Press, 1992], pp. 119-39).

[57]On the "hierarchical" Father-Son relationship in John, see Zingg, *Gott Als "Vater,"* pp. 304-6.

[58]Herman C. Waetjen, "Logos πρὸς τὸν θεόν and the Objectification of Truth in the Prologue of the Fourth Gospel," *CBQ* 63 (2001): 268.

judgment (Jn 5:22, 27), the having of life in himself (Jn 5:26), the works he does (Jn 5:36), those who are to be raised up at the last day (Jn 6:37, 39), the sheep that follow him (Jn 10:29), whatever he should ask (Jn 11:22), command what to say (Jn 12:49), the word or words that he has spoken (Jn 17:8, 14), authority over all flesh (Jn 17:2),[59] those people out of the world who receive eternal life (Jn 17:2, 6, 9, 24; 18:9), the work that the Son has completed (Jn 17:4), the sharing of his own name (Jn 17:11, 12), glory with God himself (Jn 17:22, 24), the cup that the Son must drink (Jn 18:11), and the content of the Apocalypse to hand on to his servants (Apoc 1:1). The Son, for his part, "received" (λαμβάνω) from his Father these: commandment to lay down his life (Jn 10:18), authority over the nations to shepherd them with an iron rod (Apoc 2:26-28), and the scroll of destiny from God's right hand (Apoc 5:7, 8, 9). Nowhere in the Johannine literature is the Son ever said to give to the Father, or the Father to receive from the Son.

Beyond this matter of giving and receiving, Jesus acknowledges the Father's priority in every dimension of his ministry. The Father has "sealed" the Son (Jn 6:27), consecrated him and sent him into the world (Jn 10:36), while the Son consecrates himself to the Father's will and purpose for the sake of his disciples (Jn 17:19). Throughout the earthly ministry the sender is "with" (μετά with genitive) the sent one (Jn 3:2; 8:29; 16:32). God communicates his deeds and words to the Son (Jn 5:20, 30; 8:26-28, 38, 40, 47 [assumed]; 12:50; 14:24; 15:15; 17:8, 14); Jesus' teaching is his sender's (Jn 7:16-17). The Son imitates his Father (Jn 5:19, 21),[60] performs God's will (Jn 4:34; 5:30; 6:38; 9:31), always does what pleases the Father (Jn 8:29), keeps his word (Jn 8:55) and his commandment (Jn 10:18; 12:49-50; 14:31; 15:10). The Son does not, indeed cannot, act "from himself" (ἀπ' ἐμαυτοῦ/ἑαυτοῦ [Jn 5:19, 30; 7:17-18, 28; 8:28, 42; 12:49; 14:10]).[61] He prays to the Father, both during his earthly sojourn (Jn 11:41-42; 12:27-28; 17; 16:26) and after his ascension (Jn 14:16) in continued advocacy for

---

[59]On "authority" (ἐξουσία) as a theme of Johannine Christology, see Rainer Metzner, "Vollmacht im Johannesevangelium," *NovT* 45 (2003): 22-44.

[60]For the cultural background to these verses, see Jan G. van der Watt, "The Father Shows the Son Everything: The Imagery of Education in John 5:19-23," *APB* 18 (2007): 263-76. Jesus' argument in John 5:19-47 refutes the assumption that he could use God's power against God's will. See Steven M. Bryan, "Power in the Pool: The Healing of the Man at Bethesda and Jesus' Violation of the Sabbath (Jn. 5:1-18)," *TynBul* 54 (2003): 7-22.

[61]On this theme, see J. Gerald Janzen, "'(Not) of My Own Accord': Listening for Scriptural Echoes in a Johannine Idiom," *Enc* 67 (2006): 137-60. Janzen suggests Numbers 16 for the Old Testament background.

them (1 Jn 2:1); and he will plead for or else accuse people to the Father on the day of judgment (Jn 5:45; 12:48).[62] Jesus as the Son looks up to his Father. He "honors" his Father (Jn 8:49) and confesses the Father to be "greater" than he (Jn 14:28). He calls God "my [μου] Father"[63] and even "my God" (Jn 20:17; Apoc 3:2, 12 [3×]).

Though it may be tempting to explain all these statements in which Jesus gives place to God on the basis of his having become incarnate so as to speak from the standpoint of human piety,[64] that route is closed to us by their contexts. He who says, "I honor my Father" (Jn 8:49) is the very one who, earlier in the same discourse, said, "You do not know whence I come or whither I am going . . . I am from above . . . I am not of this world . . . I am he" (Jn 8:14, 23, 28); and who, very shortly, will claim, "Before Abraham was, I am" (Jn 8:58). Similarly, "The Father is greater than I" (Jn 14:28) is sandwiched between "He who has seen me has seen the Father . . . I am in the Father and the Father in me" (Jn 14:9, 10, 11) and "I came from the Father and . . . [am] going to the Father" (Jn 16:28). The self-consciousness that voices such otherworldly transcendence is the very "I" who honors the Father as greater. It was before the foundation of the world—and so pertains to their eternal relationship in the Godhead—that the Father "gave" to the Son his glory (Jn 17:5, 24). In the post-Easter saying at John 20:17, "I am ascending to my Father and your Father, to my God and your God," Jesus distances his natural relation to the Father from the adoptive relation of the disciples. It is precisely as the unique Son of God, whose sonship (υἱός) is sempiternal and lies outside of the fleshly condition that he assumed to make them God's children (τέκνα) and his brethren (ἀδελφοί), that he speaks of God as his God. Likewise in the Apocalypse it is the glorified and ascended Lord speaking in the oracles to the churches, the one who calls himself "the first and the last" (Apoc 2:8), "the Son of God" (Apoc 2:18), "he who has the seven spirits of God" (Apoc 3:1), "the holy one" (Apoc

---

[62]"There is no more remarkable element in the Fourth Gospel than the consistent and universal presentation of Christ, in His life and work and words and in all aspects of His activities, as dependent upon the Father at every point" (Davey, *Jesus of St. John*, p. 90). Davey gathers the data in his chapters 4-5 (pp. 73-89, 90-157).

[63]Jn 2:16; 5:17, 43; 6:32, 40; 8:19, 49, 54; 10:18, 25, 29, 37; 14:2, 7, 20, 21, 23; 15:1, 8, 10, 15, 23, 24; 20:17; Apoc 2:28; 3:5, 21; cf. 14:1 [αὐτοῦ].

[64]On patristic writers who gave this explanation, see B. F. Westcott, *The Gospel According to St. John: The Greek Text with Introduction and Notes* (2 vols. in 1; Grand Rapids: Eerdmans, 1954), pp. 191-96. This line has been championed with passion more recently by Kevin Giles, *The Trinity and Subordinationism: The Doctrine of God and the Contemporary Gender Debate* (Downers Grove, IL: InterVarsity Press, 2002), pp. 197-99.

3:7), "the principal of God's creation" (Apoc 3:14), who in Apocalypse 3:2, 12 acknowledges God to be his God.[65]

Even if we did not have these verses and their contexts, the fact that the mission of the Son was to reveal what God is forbids us driving a wedge between God as known through the Son's mission and God as he is in himself. That the Son was subject to his Father, not only during the temporary period of the mission but also in undertaking the mission at all, is controverted by no Johannine scholar. If he was obedient in becoming incarnate and obedient as the incarnate Son, it was because he is obedient qua Son.[66]

These passages indicate the Son's veneration for his Father. Insofar as there are distinct subjects in the divine being, they are defined by an order of "begetting" and "giving," or origination, implying an order of compliance that maintains the unity of the plurality.[67]

Quite a number of Johannine specialists have been willing to speak of a "dependence" of the Son on the Father, or of a "subordination" of the Son to the Father.[68] These terms are problematic for a number of reasons. "To be subordinate" (ὑποτάσσεσθαι) features in a Pauline description of the relation of Christ to God (1 Cor 15:28; cf. the genitive construction in 1 Cor 3:23, and God as "head" in 1 Cor 11:3), but not in John. Of course, it may be legitimate to apply Paul's language if it aptly captures John's teaching as well. But the title "subordinationism" came to be associated by historians with positions taken by some

---

[65]"The subordination of Christ in *John* has been carried through into both pre-existence, 5:26; 17:24b, and post-Resurrection life, 14:16 (I will pray, etc.), 17:23, 24. . . . For *John* dependence and subordination do not merely stand for humanity but for sonship, divine sonship, i.e. they are eternal. . . . The dependence of Christ upon earth was the eternal dependence of the divine Son, not a temporary humiliation as in Paul" (Davey, *Jesus of St. John*, pp. 139, 164).

[66]On the widely accepted theological principle that the economic accords with the immanent Trinity and provides a window into God's inner life, see Henri de Lubac, *The Christian Faith: An Essay on the Structure of the Apostles' Creed* (trans. Richard Arnandez; San Francisco: Ignatius Press, 1986), pp. 90-91; John J. O'Donnell, *The Mystery of the Triune God* (New York: Paulist Press, 1989), pp. 36-38.

[67]Andreas J. Köstenberger and Scott R. Swain, *Father, Son and Spirit: The Trinity and John's Gospel* (NSBT 24; Downers Grove, IL: InterVarsity Press, 2008), pp. 114-27.

[68]Davey, *Jesus of St. John*, pp. 77-78, 90-157 ("dependence"), 165 ("subordination"); Sidebottom, *Christ of the Fourth Gospel*, p. 154 ("dependence"); Sundberg, "*Isos Tō Theō*," pp. 24, 26 ("subordination christology"); C. K. Barrett, "'The Father Is Greater Than I' (John 14.28): Subordinationist Christology in the New Testament," in *Essays on John* (Philadelphia: Westminster, 1982), pp. 19-36; John V. Dahms, "The Subordination of the Son," *JETS* 37 (1994): 351-64; Anderson, *Christology*, p. 267 ("subordinated christology"); Craig S. Keener, "Is Subordination within the Trinity Really Heresy? A Study of John 5:18 in Context," *TJ* 20 (1999): 39-51; Hurtado, *Lord Jesus Christ*, pp. 392-94 ("Subordination and Distinction"); Christopher Cowan, "The Father and the Son in the Fourth Gospel: Johannine Subordination Revisited," *JETS* 49 (2006): 115-35.

in the trinitarian debates of the third and fourth centuries that the conciliar church rightly deemed heretical: the neo-Platonic view of the Second Person of the Trinity as a divine emanation on a lower grade of being than the First Person, and the Arian denial of his co-eternity and consubstantiality with God. We might venture to distinguish between biblical "subordination" and heretical "subordinationism," were it not for the fact that the overlap in nomenclature blurs the distinction.

But most seriously, biblical scholars who have used this terminology have not always succeeded in avoiding subordinationist formulations. Although Davey clarifies that his concept of the Son's dependence does not imply "an inferiority of dignity or nature . . . but subordination in the matter of function,"[69] his assertion that Christ is "*essentially* dependent, both in time and eternity, upon the being" of the Father,[70] and his statement that "the Son is not omnipotent *per se*, for all his power is his Father's, and so with His other attributes,"[71] might be taken to negate that the Son "has life in himself" (Jn 5:26). C. K. Barrett, though wanting to hold the Logos of John 1:1 to be neither less than God nor divine in a secondary sense, says confusingly, "the Word is not indeed the whole content of deity,"[72] whereas John avers that the whole content of deity, as that phrase would normally be understood, does in fact subsist in the Word. And John V. Dahms, while stating plainly, "the essence of the Father, the essence of the Son, and the essence of the Holy Spirit is one and the same divine essence,"[73] invites grave misunderstanding when he speaks again and again of the Son's subordination as "essential and eternal" or "in his essential being."[74] If we are to describe the Johannine Son as subordinate, we must qualify it as a personal (or hypostatic) subordination, grounded to be sure in the dynamic ontology of the *communicatio essentiae*—and to that extent not merely "functional"—but certainly not essential nor touching the content of deity. The Son is everything the Father is, with but one proviso, that the Father "gave" it him to be that, from which flows the Son's invariable acquiescence even as the Father's plenipotentiary.

*Relation between the Father and the Son: Summary.* Many have observed

---

[69]Davey, *Jesus of St. John*, pp. 164-65.
[70]Ibid., p. 158 (italics added).
[71]Ibid., p. 165.
[72]Barrett, "'The Father Is Greater Than I,'" p. 23.
[73]Dahms, "Subordination of the Son," p. 363.
[74]Ibid., pp. 351, 359; see also 362.

a tension in John's portrayal of Christ "as both claiming and denying equality with the Father."[75] Albert C. Sundberg, pursuing a documentary solution in the vein of Bultmann and Fortna, found two incompatible Christologies: an older one, which is dominant, presenting Christ as God's subordinate agent, mixed with a few traces of a new, emerging binitarianism.[76] C. K. Barrett suggests that the duality may be a literary strategy by which John simplified the mystery of Christ's historic person for his readers, partly obscuring it in the process by setting up a paradox. Paul N. Anderson follows Barrett, adding that John was a dialectician who tried to integrate in his writings varied emphases that had emerged as the Johannine community found itself in dialogue with others.[77] John Ashton observes that any emissary is both less than the king in fact and the king's equal in law.[78]

It may be asked whether any of these approaches, all of which harbor insights, comes fully to grips with a Christology wherein the Son's relation to God involves perfect identity of being, equality of status and functional cooperation vis-à-vis the world, yet also reception of his very aseity from one whom he acknowledges as his own God, and subservience in carrying out his will without addition or remainder, all in continuity with a jealous monotheism. We cannot dispense with the breadth of information and precision of judgment that historical criticism makes possible, but can we penetrate John's doctrine of Christ without also coming face to face with the intricacies and conundrums of classical Christian theology? After two centuries and more of battering at the hands of Schleiermacher, Ritschl, Bultmann and many others, metaphysics is the disowned handmaiden of Christian theology. It is now fashionable and expected, and therefore sufficient in the eyes of many in the academy, for biblical scholars to belittle metaphysics with no argument and mere expressions of distaste.[79] Yet even during the ascendancy of logical positivism in the twentieth century there was a cadre of professional philosophers,

---

[75]Barrett, "'The Father Is Greater Than I,'" p. 33.
[76]Sundberg, "*Isos Tō Theō*"; idem, "Christology."
[77]Anderson (*Christology*, pp. 266-67) helpfully lays out the evidence for the two sides of the puzzle.
[78]Ashton, *Understanding*, p. 316.
[79]For example, Paul Anderson dismisses the classical approach in two pages as so many attempts "to diminish or ignore the apparent contradictions," "to harmonize the christological tensions," "to make sense of its tensions by means of metaphysical speculation or dogmatic postulation," "to overlook the tensions in John without addressing the problems they present" (*Christology*, pp. 4-6). So foreign does this description seem to my own reading of the church fathers that I am left wondering whether I have taken the author's true meaning. Is the modern historical approach the only way to reckon with tensions?

now again rapidly on the increase, who have maintained that to pursue the nature of things is to land inescapably in metaphysics. John was no metaphysician and made no use of the technical language of being and becoming, essence and existence, universal and particulars, unity and plurality, identity and difference. But can we grasp the Johannine nettle without having recourse to these perennial categories?

To judge by the sheer number of references to God and Jesus and their mutual relation in the Johannine literature, this theme would appear to be of great interest to John. God's inner nature as love, brimming over as the love of the Father for the Son and of the Son for the Father, is the transcendent basis of God's love for the world worked out in time.[80] Hence comes John's immense stress on the Son's otherness from the Father in the unity of the Godhead as the eternal object and reciprocating subject of divine love.

## THE INCARNATION OF THE LOGOS

That the Logos united himself at one moment in time to his human creatures is stated by John just as elegantly as is his deity: "The true Light . . . was coming into the world" (Jn 1:9);[81] "he was in the world" (Jn 1:10); "he came to what was his" (Jn 1:11); "the Word became flesh" (Jn 1:14);[82] "the life was made manifest . . . the eternal life which was with the Father and was made manifest to us" (1 Jn 1:2).

According to these clauses, the one who became incarnate was he who is the true light, the Word, and the eternal life. In their present literary context, the subject who bears these abstract titles was one who, himself being essentially God, had always been with God in eternal fellowship ("with God" [Jn 1:1]), the "only-begotten [one] from the Father" (Jn 1:14), the "only-begotten God, who is

---

[80]For John, the principle of love "is the law of the divine nature as well as of the human,—a universal principle or law of being. . . . The application of this principle among men is grounded in the very nature of God. . . . He [John] starts from this conception of God's nature and finds in it the divine law which ruled in the life and work of Jesus, in which men must also find the ideal for their own lives. . . . The ideal of all goodness and the law of all duty must always lie in the very being of God" (George B. Stevens, *The Johannine Theology: A Study of the Doctrinal Contents of the Gospels and Epistles of the Apostle John* [New York: Scribner, 1894], pp. 369-70). See also Angus Paddison, "Engaging Scripture: Incarnation and the Gospel of John," *SJT* 60 (2007): 144-60.

[81]Wilson Paroschi argues that John 1:9 is the point where a narrative shift takes place from referring to the precosmic existence of the Logos to his historical life (*Incarnation and Covenant in the Prologue to the Fourth Gospel (John 1:1-18)* (EH 23/820; Frankfurt: Peter Lang, 2006).

[82]Christian Grappe, "Jean 1,14(-18) dans son contexte et à la lumière de la littérature intertestamentaire," *RHPR* 80 (2000): 153-69.

in the bosom of the Father" (Jn 1:18), the Son who reminisces about having received glory as his Father's gift before the foundation of the world (Jn 17:5, 24). John conceives of him as a personal being, as surely as he knows God to be personal. John calls him "light" because he brought light to us; "eternal life," because he brought eternal life to us; and "Word," because to us he brought communication from God. These metaphors attach to a divine person. The Word, then, was not a personified Jewish Wisdom or a Greek Logos in the mind of God that first became fully personal at the incarnation (Jn 1:14), nor was "it" a divine design that became a person.[83] Quite the converse: he is, for John, an eternal person whom God sent to become God's Word, life, and light to us.

This last sentence strongly suggests that the purpose of the incarnation was to communicate or reveal the unknowable God to humankind. From the beginning to the end of the prologue of the Fourth Gospel revelation is thematic: we note "the Word" (Jn 1:1, 14), "the light shines" (Jn 1:5), John the Baptist sent to "bear witness" (Jn 1:6-8, 15), "the true light that enlightens every person" (Jn 1:9), "we have beheld his glory" (Jn 1:14), "he has explained [God]" (Jn 1:18). Moreover, this theme continues throughout the rest of the Gospel (notably at Jn 1:51; 16:25). Jesus came that people might "know" God,[84] to "manifest" God's name to his disciples (Jn 17:6, 26),[85] to "bear witness to the truth" (Jn 18:37), to give us "understanding" to know him who is true (1 Jn 5:20).[86] Surely, then, an important purpose of the incarnation was to reveal God. But is it right to elevate revelation to the controlling theme of the Gospel and of the whole Johannine theology?[87]

---

[83]Interpretations of this sort are commonly based on a hypothetical Wisdom or Logos poem that John supposedly took over from someone before him in the Johannine circle, influenced by Jewish wisdom or eastern Gnostic speculation. See James D. G. Dunn, *Christology in the Making: An Inquiry Into the Origins of the Doctrine of the Incarnation* (London: SCM Press, 1980), pp. 239-45; Ashton, *Understanding*, pp. 527-29.

[84]Jn 7:17; 8:28, 32; 10:38; 14:7 (3×), 9, 17, 20, 31; 17:3, 7, 8, 23, 25 (2×).

[85]According to Klauss Scholtissek, Jesus' farewell prayer in John 17 is a new bundling of Johannine themes presenting Jesus as God's revealer ("Das hohepriesterliche Gebet Jesu: Exegetisch-theologische Beobachtungen," *TTZ* 109 [2000]: 199-218).

[86]The same interest is seen in 1 John; Apocalypse 1:1; 6:1; 19:13; 22:16.

[87]Rudolf Bultmann, expounding the Gospel against the religio-historical background of a posited Gnostic revealer myth, took revelation to be the overarching theme (see, e.g., *Theology of the New Testament* [trans. Kendrick Grobel; 2 vols.; New York: Scribner, 1951–1955], 2:4, 6, 12-14, 33-35). For others in the same train (though less indebted to the Gnostic theory), see T. W. Manson, "The Johannine Jesus as Logos," in Taylor, *Companion to John*, pp. 33-58; John Ashton, ed., *The Interpretation of John* (IRT 9; Philadelphia: Fortress, 1986), p. 7; idem, *Understanding*, pp. 302, 381, 515-16; William R. G. Loader, *The Christology of the Fourth Gospel: Structure and Issues* (BBET 23; Frankfurt: Peter Lang, 1989).

Perhaps so—provided we include in revelation all that John includes. For he names other purposes of the incarnation too, each of which has its own web of thematic connections branching out through his literary corpus. Jesus came for this purpose: to face the hour of his death (Jn 12:27). The purpose in turn of his death was to save the world (Jn 3:16-17; 5:34; 12:47), to give life to the world (Jn 6:33; 10:9-10) as shown by all seven of the signs, to free slaves from the devil and sin (Jn 8:31-32, 36; 1 Jn 3:8), to bring about a fateful division of the race (Jn 9:39), to consecrate his disciples in the truth (Jn 17:19). And the ultimate purpose of saving his disciples was to bring glory to both the Father and the Son (Jn 12:23, 28; 13:31-32). It is as the Lamb of God who takes away sin that Jesus reveals God's glory to a world trapped in its own darkness, a darkness that is moral and spiritual and not merely cognitive. Without disputing that revelation is a prominent theme, maybe the most prominent one of all, it may be asked whether, in an existentialist reduction of Christianity that has no interest in or room for mythical things like the death of Christ to rescue people from their sins,[88] "revelation" can have anything like the significance it has for John.

*The sending of the Son of God.* In the Johannine Gospel and Epistles the pointed statements about the incarnation that we have just surveyed take their place among related motifs. One of the most pervasive is that of God having "sent" the Son. When sending is a verbal action, John uses ἀποστέλλω,[89] with God as subject[90] and for an object the "Son."[91] When John needs a substantive phrase, "the [one] having sent," he puts πέμπω into the articular aorist participle ὁ πέμψας,[92] sometimes with "the Father" as antecedent or in apposition (Jn 5:23, 37; 6:44; 8:16, 18; 12:49; 14:24), and usually "me" as object.[93] This yields in all forty-four statements that God the Father has sent the Son.

---

[88]In chapter five I will evaluate the comments by Bultmann (*Theology*, 2:52-55) on the death of Jesus.
[89]Aorist tense: Jn 3:17, 34; 5:38; 6:29, 57; 7:29; 8:42; 10:36; 11:42; 17:3, 8, 18, 21, 23, 25; 1 Jn 4:10; perfect tense: Jn 5:36; 20:21; 1 Jn 4:9, 14.
[90]Subject "God" [θεός]: Jn 3:17, 34; 6:29; 8:42; 1 Jn 4:9, 10; subject "the Father" [ὁ πατήρ]: Jn 5:36, 38 [cf. 5:37]; 6:57; 10:36; 17:3, 8, 18, 21, 23, 25 [cf. 17:1]; 20:21; 1 Jn 4:14.
[91]Jn 3:17; 1 Jn 4:9, 10, 14; "me" [με]: Jn 5:36; 6:57; 7:29; 8:42; 11:42; 17:8, 18 [ἐμέ], 21, 23, 25; 20:21; relative pronoun: Jn 3:34; 5:38; 6:29; 10:36; 17:3.
[92]Jn 4:34; 5:23, 24, 30, 37; 6:38, 39, 44; 7:16, 18, 28, 33; 8:16, 18, 26, 29; 9:4; 12:44, 45, 49; 13:20; 14:24; 15:21; 16:5.
[93]The only exceptions are John 5:23; 7:18, where we find αὐτόν. On this linguistic habit of John, see Andreas Köstenberger, *The Missions of Jesus and the Disciples According to the Fourth Gospel: With Implications for the Fourth Gospel's Purpose and the Mission of the Contemporary Church* (Grand Rapids: Eerdmans, 1998), pp. 97-106.

Other clusters of passages speak of the incarnate one as descending (καταβαίνειν: Jn 3:13; 6:33, 38, 41, 42, 50, 51, 58) and ascending (ἀναβαίνειν: Jn 3:13; 6:62; 20:17 [2×]),[94] or as coming[95] and going.[96] A related group describes him as one who originates "from" God (or the Father or heaven or the upper region), using ἀπό, ἐκ, παρά or -θεν.[97] Again and again the point is made that outsiders do not know where he is from (πόθεν εἶναι: Jn 7:27-28; 8:14; 9:29-30; 19:9),[98] giving Jesus opportunity to assert the mystery of his true home (Jn 7:28-30; 8:15-30; 9:35-38; 19:11-12a). And though he himself is "not of the world" (οὐκ ἐκ τοῦ κόσμου: Jn 8:23; 17:14, 16), he came to be in the world for a while.[99] He was "with" (μετά) his Jewish contemporaries and his disciples only for a limited time (Jn 7:33; 13:33; 14:9; 16:4; 17:12). As a king impresses a special seal on all royal correspondence, so God has stamped the Son of Man (σφραγίζω [Jn 6:27]), making him the official representative of God.

While it can be helpful to isolate these motifs for the sake of analysis—say, to inquire into possible religio-historical parallels that might bring out shades of meaning in their use by John—we must always come back to ask how they work together in their Johannine literary context. Then we see that the various expressions are inextricable from one another and from the total view of the person of Christ as the incarnate Logos that John is presenting. For example, scholars have discussed at considerable length whether the concept of the "sent"

---

[94]On Jesus' descent and ascent in the context of the Christology of the Gospel, see Godfrey C. Nicholson, *Death as Departure: The Johannine Descent-Ascent Schema* (SBLDS 63; Chico, CA: Scholars Press, 1983), pp. 10-12, 21-74.

[95]ἔρχεσθαι: Jn 1:9, 11; 3:2, 19, 31 [2×]; 5:43; 7:28; 8:14 [2×], 42; 9:39; 10:10; 11:27; 12:13 [LXX Ps 117:26]; 12:27, 46, 47; 15:22; 16:28; 18:37; 1 Jn 4:2; 5:6; 2 Jn 7; ἐξέρχεσθαι: Jn 8:42; 13:3; 16:27, 28, 30; 17:8; ἥκω: Jn 8:42; 1 Jn 5:20.

[96]ὑπάγειν: Jn 7:33; 8:21 [2×]; 13:33-34, 36 [2×]; 14:4, 5, 28; 16:5 [2×], 10, 17; πορεύεσθαι: Jn 7:35 [2×]; 14:2, 3, 12, 28; 16:7, 28; μεταβαίνειν: Jn 13:1; ἀφιέναι: Jn 14:18, 27; 16:28; ἀπέρχεσθαι: Jn 16:7; οὐκέτι εἰμὶ ἐν τῷ κόσμῳ: Jn 17:11. His coming and going can be mentioned side by side (Jn 8:14 [2×]; 13:3). On these motifs, see Adele Reinhartz, *The Word in the World: The Cosmological Tale in the Fourth Gospel* (SBLMS 45; Atlanta: Scholars Press, 1992), pp. 16-28.

[97]ἀπό (ἀπὸ θεοῦ: Jn 3:2; 13:3; 16:30; ἀπὸ τοῦ οὐρανοῦ: Jn 6:38). ἐκ (ἐκ τοῦ θεοῦ: Jn 8:42, 47; ἐκ τοῦ οὐρανοῦ: Jn 3:13, 31; 6:31-33, 38, 41-42, 50-51, 58; ἐκ τοῦ πατρός: Jn 16:28; ἐκ τῶν ἄνω: Jn 8:23). παρά (with genitive) (παρὰ τοῦ θεοῦ: Jn 6:46; 16:27; παρὰ πατρός: Jn 1:14; 16:28; 17:8; παρὰ τοῦ πέμψαντος: Jn 7:29). -θεν (ἄνωθεν: Jn 3:31).

[98]Wayne Meeks perceives the connection between the descent/ascent pattern and the enigma of Jesus' person to outsiders ("The Man from Heaven in Johannine Sectarianism," *JBL* 91 [1972]: 50-66).

[99]Entered "into the world," εἰς τὸν κόσμον: Jn 1:9; 3:17, 19; 6:14; 8:26; 10:36; 11:27; 12:46; 16:28; 17:18; 18:37; 1 Jn 4:9; was "in the world," ἐν τῷ κόσμῳ: Jn 1:10; 9:5; 17:11, 13; exited "out of the world," ἐκ τοῦ κόσμου: Jn 13:1.

one is most indebted to the language of Gnostic revealers,[100] or to the commissioning of prophets in the Old Testament,[101] particularly the prophet like Moses
(Deut 18:15-19),[102] or to the Jewish institution of the agent (*šālîaḥ*) who is to be
received "like the one who sent him" (*m. Ber.* 5:5), the law concerning which is
found in both rabbinic and Merkabah souces,[103] or to God's deputing of angels
from heaven.[104] No doubt John's word choice might have resonated, in his and
his readers' minds, with overtones from any or all of these possible settings. But
just as the etymology of a word is not its sense (which must be established
rather from its synchronous relations to other words), so too the prehistory of
a concept is not its meaning in John. The opening chapter of the Gospel is a
hermeneutical template for the whole. God's sending of the Son in the body of
the work answers to God's emitting his Word in the prologue—the Word who
was in the beginning with God and was God and has explained God. Sending
statements, to select just a few, fall in contexts indicating God's plan to save the
world (Jn 3:16-17), Jesus' power to raise the dead and judge them (Jn 5:21-23),
his giving of his life so that anyone who eats of his flesh and drinks of his blood
can live eternally (Jn 6:57), and his enemies' capital charge of blasphemy (Jn
10:36-39; cf. 10:31-33). So C. H. Dodd was on the right track to deal with the
sending as part of John's lofty concept of the Son of God.[105] The sending of the
Son bridges the gap between the infinite Logos and his having become flesh.[106]

---

[100]Rudolf Bultmann, "Die Bedeutung der neuerschlossenen mandäischen und manichäischen Quellen
für das Verständnis des Johannesevangeliums," *ZNW* 24 (1925): 104-9; Bultmann, *John*, pp. 251-52.
[101]Dodd, *Interpretation*, pp. 254-55; Ashton, *Understanding*, pp. 312-17.
[102]Juan P. Miranda, *Der Vater, der mich gesandt hat: Religionsgeschichtliche Untersuchungen zu den johanneischen Sendungsformeln, zugleich ein Beitrag zur johanneischen Christologie und Ekklesiologie*
(EH 23/7; Bern: Peter Lang, 1972); Paul N. Anderson, "The Having-Sent-Me Father: Aspects of
Agency, Encounter, and Irony in the Johannine Father-Son Relationship," *Semeia* 85 (1999): 33-57.
[103]Peder Borgen, "God's Agent in the Fourth Gospel," in Ashton, *Interpretation of John*, pp. 67-78; Juan
P. Miranda, *Die Sendung Jesu im vierten Evangelium: Religions- und theologiegeschichtliche Untersuchungen zu den Sendungsformeln* (SBS 87; Stuttgart: Katholisches Bibelwerk, 1977); Bühner, *Der
Gesandte*; Ashton, *Understanding*; James P. McIlhone, "Jesus as God's Agent in the Fourth Gospel:
Implications for Christology, Ecclesiology, and Mission," *CS* 44 (2005): 295-315.
[104]Bühner, *Der Gesandte*.
[105]Dodd, *Interpretation*, pp. 253-62. Dodd's conclusion is confirmed by Köstenberger (*Missions*, pp.
93-121).
[106]To single out one outstanding proponent of the religio-historical method: Ashton has things upside
down when he writes, "Jesus' relationship with God continues throughout to be conceived on the
analogy of the prophetic mission and the law of agency.... This aspect of John's christology, whose
ontological implications are given none of the heavy emphasis they were to receive over two centuries later in the debate against Arius, could be explained as arising from a deeply religious reflection upon the prophetic mission of Jesus within the conceptual framework of the Jewish law of
agency" (*Understanding*, pp. 316-17). Ashton's denial of ontological implications pertains to the

## JESUS' HUMAN EXISTENCE

That the Son of God became human is just as critical a part of John's proclamation as is the conviction of his deity. To the human Jesus John maintains a
consistent and emphatic witness. One reason for John's insistence on Jesus'
humanity is the fact that he speaks out of his own experience. It was socially
that John came to know Jesus; sharing daily life and ministry with him was
what drove John to conclude he was the Logos of God: "We have beheld" (Jn
1:14). Another reason is theological. Jesus' death was what he came for (Jn 12:27),
it was a key part of his "glorification," and only as a man could the Logos, intrinsically immortal, taste mortality. A tertiary reason for John's stress on the
reality of Christ's human condition was John's apostolic obligation to oppose a
novel teaching toward the end of the century that denied the fact. This was a
factor behind the Epistles (1 Jn 4:2; 2 Jn 7); many commentators suspect that it
may also explain features of the Fourth Gospel.

**Flesh.** In assembling the varied ways John bears witness to Jesus as human,
we note first his use of the word "flesh" (σάρξ) (in reference to Christ: Jn 1:14;
6:51-56; 1 Jn 4:2; 2 Jn 7). In the Old Testament the corresponding word (בָּשָׂר)
denotes "not merely the body but the whole, man as a person . . . in his transi-
toriness as one who suffers sickness, death, fright etc.," "man's creatureliness
and frailty" as "fragile, fallible, and vulnerable."[107] To say that the Logos "became"
(ἐγένετο) flesh (Jn 1:14) is to assert more than that he took up a different abode.
He underwent a change in manner of existence. Without any transmutation of
the divine essence that subsists in him (Jn 1:1c; 20:28), he who was the only-
begotten God in the bosom of the Father undertook to exist as a creature and
under creaturely conditions; he who is eternal entered into the temporal sphere;
he who is the creative source of life became mortal.[108] The following clause in

---

ordinary prophets and messengers behind the text, not to the sent one in the text of the Fourth
Gospel, who cannot be boiled down. However the truth about Jesus dawned on John, by the time
he wrote the Fourth Gospel he was no longer pressing Jesus into the mold of prophets or messengers. He saw some similarities between their functions as representatives of another, and those
of Jesus. But John is quite clear that people who saw Jesus as a mere prophet missed the truth.

[107]Horst Seebass and Anthony C. Thiselton, "Flesh," *NIDNTT* 1:672-73, 678.

[108]Against Bultmann's traditional outlook ("The theme of the whole Gospel of John is the statement:
'The word became flesh' [1:14]" [*Theology*, 2:40], Käsemann placed the emphasis on the latter half
of the verse: "The content of the Gospel" is "We beheld his glory" (*Testament*, p. 6). As both statements are juxtaposed in John, this was a false polarization. We could behold his glory only by his
becoming flesh. So Günther Bornkamm: "However justified Käsemann may have been in protesting
against taking the first half of the verse . . . in isolation . . . still it is equally mistaken, it seems to me,
to place exclusive emphasis upon the second half of the verse. . . . It is obvious that for John the thrust

1:14 explains: "And he tabernacled [ἐσκήνωσεν] among us." This rare verb, used only by John among New Testament authors (Jn 1:14; Apoc 7:15; 12:12; 13:6; 21:3), in John 1:14 and Apocalypse 21:3 evokes the Old Testament tabernacle. God instructed Moses to build it "that I may dwell in their midst" (Ex 25:8). While the people Israel were in the desert, God, without leaving his heavenly dwelling place, made himself uniquely accessible to them at a location just outside their camp. In the same way, the Second Person of the Godhead took up permanent residence in Jesus of Nazareth.[109] It has been observed that the Greek σκηνόω happens to have the same three root consonants as the Hebrew שׁכן, "the word used in the Old Testament to indicate the presence of God dwelling among his people in the tent," from which was derived the rabbinic *Shekinah*.[110]

John's word choice where Jesus invites the Jews of Capernaum to gain eternal life by eating his "flesh" and drinking his blood (Jn 6:51-56) is influenced by the common collocation of "flesh" and "blood," which has some of the same connotations as "flesh" by itself.[111] This is fitting because Jesus here alludes to his coming death, as the narrator makes unmistakable by the foreshadowing of Jesus' betrayal in John 6:70-71.[112]

---

of 1:14 is not towards affirming that Jesus was *God*, but that the Logos of God, God himself, has manifested himself, in the incarnate one, in the man *Jesus*" ("Towards the Interpretation of John's Gospel: A Discussion of *The Testament of Jesus*," in Ashton, *Interpretation of John*, pp. 91-92).

[109]Pamela E. Kinlaw, *The Christ Is Jesus: Metamorphosis, Possession, and Johannine Christology* (SBLAB 18; Atlanta: Society of Biblical Literature, 2005), pp. 93-175. Kinlaw contrasts the Johannine concept of the Logos' "permanent dwelling" in Jesus to other models of theophany that were current in the Mediterranean environment, including a god's metamorphosing into an earthly appearance, and possession of the human subject in the sense either of a temporary ecstasy or a more settled inspiration.

[110]Basil de Pinto, "John's Jesus: Biblical Wisdom and the Word Embodied," in Taylor, *Companion to John*, p. 61.

[111]Gen 2:23; 29:14; Deut 12:27; Judg 9:2; 2 Sam 5:1 [= 1 Chron 11:1]; 19:12-13; Job 2:5; 19:20; Ps 50:13; 102:5; Prov 3:8; Ezek 39:17; Mic 3:2; Mt 16:17; Lk 24:39; Jn 1:13; 1 Cor 15:50; Gal 1:16; Eph 6:12; Heb 2:14. This usage is distinct from the pair "body" and "blood" in eucharistic contexts (Mt 26:26; Mk 14:22; Lk 22:19; 1 Cor 11:24, 27).

[112]Within a few decades, Bishop Ignatius of Antioch would use the real presence of Christ's flesh in the Eucharist as an argument against the Docetists (Ign. *Smyrn* 7:1). Whether we should discern some such anti-Gnostic barb already in John 6:51-59 is doubtful. John's usual way with words is to be direct, even blunt, in making a polemical point, not to beat around the bush, even allowing for an artistic tendency to evoke. The antagonists in John 6 are Galilean Jews who reject the idea of a dying messiah; they are not Christian heretics. Against their notion that a bread-multiplying miracle worker like Jesus would make the kind of messiah who might succeed in ridding Palestine of the hated Roman occupation (Jn 6:15), Jesus drives home in graphic, even offensive language that he is headed for a violent death out of which will come life for the world. To import a concern about Gnostic Christologies into this context ignores the historical setting.

In the Johannine correspondence the apostle seeks to safeguard congregants against antichrists from out of their midst who deny that Jesus is "the Christ" (1 Jn 2:22a; cf. 5:6) and "the Son" (1 Jn 2:22b-23; cf. 5:5, 9-12), who do not affirm that Jesus Christ "has come in the flesh" (1 Jn 4:2; cf. 2 Jn 7: "coming in the flesh"), and who think he came "with the water only" and not "by water and blood" (1 Jn 5:6). These rather basic catchphrases do not enable us precisely to determine the complexion of the heresy, but the false teachers seem to want to keep things apart that John wants to unite as subject and predicate. They teach that the Logos-Son came at Jesus' water baptism but was no longer associated with the man Jesus when he shed his blood, perhaps because they assume that immortality cannot become mortal. John holds that the eternal life was manifested (1 Jn 1:3) and came "by the blood" and thus constituted the Christ. To combat the effect of the heresy, John places great emphasis in the opening paragraph of his First Epistle on his own sensory experiences of Jesus. John heard Jesus personally, saw him with his eyes, touched him with his hands, and now bears witness to those who never had that opportunity (1 Jn 1:1, 3).[113]

**Temple.** We have already touched on the Logos "tenting" among human beings. Also to the front of the Gospel, John identifies the incarnate one with the temple.[114] Jesus, standing in the temple complex (ἱερόν) in Jerusalem after driving out the merchants, challenged the Jews, "Destroy this temple [ναός], and in three days I will raise it up." They thought that he meant the building, but the narrator takes him to refer to his body (Jn 2:19, 21). John's interpretation of Jesus' saying develops the concept of the Logos "tabernacling" on earth (Jn 1:14) by superimposing the permanent temple of Solomon and the rebuilt postexilic temple. In the dominical logion, the word for "temple" (ναός) denotes the sanctum proper where the deity resides, excluding the courts out-

---

[113]Some find in the Fourth Gospel a similar emphasis on sensory experience of the incarnate one. See Dorothy Lee, "The Gospel of John and the Five Senses," *JBL* 129 (2010): 115-27.

[114]Studies of John's christological use of temple language and imagery include Stephen T. Um, *The Theme of Temple Christology in John's Gospel* (LNTS 312; London: T & T Clark, 1988); Mary L. Coloe, *God Dwells with Us: Temple Symbolism in the Fourth Gospel* (Collegeville, MN: Liturgical Press, 2001); idem, "Temple Imagery in John," *Int* 63 (2009): 368-81; Alan R. Kerr, *The Temple of Jesus' Body: The Temple Theme in the Gospel of John* (JSNTSup 220; London: Sheffield Academic Press, 2002); Paul M. Hoskins, *Jesus as the Fulfillment of the Temple in the Gospel of John* (PBM; Milton Keynes: Paternoster, 2006); Benny Thettayil, *In Spirit and Truth: An Exegetical Study of John 4:19-26 and a Theological Investigation of the Replacement Theme in the Fourth Gospel* (CBET 46; Leuven: Peeters, 2007); Harold W. Attridge, "Temple, Tabernacle, Time, and Space in John and Hebrews," *EC* 1 (2010): 261-74.

doors (cf. Mt 23:35; 27:51; Lk 1:9; Apoc 11:2, 19). According to the Old Testament view, the temple is the meeting place between God and humankind; frequently in the Pentateuch the tabernacle is called "the tent of meeting" (e.g., Ex 27:21, based on Ex 25:22: "There I will meet with you"). Such meetings are possible because Yahweh makes himself present in the temple. God dwells beyond the highest heaven and not in a house (1 Kings 8:27), yet his name (1 Kings 8:29), his glory (Ps 26:8) and he himself may be said to "dwell" (שׁכֵן) in Zion (Ps 9:11 [ישֵׁב]; 68:16, 18; 74:2; 135:21). This polytopic concept of the divine presence, unbounded in heaven yet localized on earth, is the Old Testament counterpart to John's concept of incarnation.

That Jesus is the new temple is less explicit at John 4:23-24. Here Jesus teaches the woman of Samaria that in the eschatological era people will be pilgrims neither to Mount Zion nor to Mount Gerizim but will worship God in spirit and truth. But John 4:26 identifies Jesus as the one who is already bringing about this new state of affairs.[115]

Associated with the temple in Jerusalem were the holidays of the Jewish festival calendar. The Fourth Gospel presents Jesus as absorbing several of these,[116] in particular the Passover (Jn 2:13, 23; 6:4; 11:55; and the passion account), Sukkot or the Feast of Tabernacles (Jn 7–9) and Hanukkah or the Feast of Dedication (Jn 10:22-39).

Passover commemorated God's sparing of his people in Egypt by having them sprinkle lambs' blood on their lintels, with apotropaic power to ward off the heaven-sent destroying angel of the final plague (Ex 12:23). This pointed toward Jesus' role as expiatory lamb by virtue of his death (Jn 1:29, 36; 11:50, 55; 19:36, in light of Ex 12:46).[117] Right after the exodus God provided manna for

---

[115]Um, *Temple Christology*; Thettayil, *In Spirit and Truth*, pp. 7-227.

[116]Aileen Guilding, *The Fourth Gospel and Jewish Worship: A Study of the Relation of St. John's Gospel to the Ancient Jewish Lectionary System* (Oxford: Clarendon, 1960), chaps. 5-7, 9; Gale A. Yee, *Jewish Feasts and the Gospel of John* (ZS; Wilmington, DE: Michael Glazier, 1989); Kerr, *Temple*, pp. 205-67; Michael A. Daise, *Feasts in John: Jewish Festivals and Jesus' "Hour" in the Fourth Gospel* (WUNT 2/229; Tübingen: Mohr Siebeck, 2007); Dorit Felsch, *Die Feste im Johannesevangelium:* Jüdische Tradition und christologische Deutung (WUNT 2/308; Tübingen: Mohr Siebeck, 2011).

[117]Bertil Gärtner, *John 6 and the Jewish Passover* (ConBNT 17; Lund: Gleerup, 1959); Stanley E. Porter, "Can Traditional Exegesis Enlighten Literary Analysis of the Fourth Gospel? An Examination of the Old Testament Fulfilment Motif and the Passover Theme," in *The Gospels and the Scriptures of Israel* (ed. Craig A. Evans and W. Richard Stegner; JSNTSup 104; Sheffield: Academic Press, 1994), pp. 396-428; Christine Schlund, *"Kein Knochen soll gebrochen werden": Studien zu Bedeutung und Funktion des Pesachfests in Texten des frühen Judentums und im Johannesevangelium* (WMANT 107; Neukirchen-Vluyn: Neukirchener Verlag, 2005).

Israel in the wilderness (Ex 16), which forms the backdrop to Jesus' claim to be the bread of life (Jn 6:4, 31-59).

By the first century A.D., the Feast of Booths/Tabernacles had come to include a water-drawing ceremony near the great altar that probably invoked God's blessing for rains (*m. Sukkah* 4:9).[118] Jesus takes this up when he promises rivers of living water flowing out of the believer's heart (Jn 7:37-39). His proclamation at the same feast that he is the light of the world (Jn 8:12) draws on the custom of lighting in the Court of the Women golden candlesticks that illumined the temple and all the courtyards of Jerusalem (*m. Sukkah* 5:2-3).[119]

In the time of the Maccabees (165 B.C.) was instituted the Festival of the Dedication of the temple (Hanukkah) after its desecration under Antiochus IV (1 Macc 4:59; 2 Macc 1:18; 10:6-8). John knows this feast as *Encaenia* (Jn 10:22) and sees in it a symbol of God's consecration of his Son to send him into the world (Jn 10:36).[120]

Since the temple was the place of God's "name,"[121] Jesus' repeated claim to be the one who bears God's "name" (ὄνομα [Jn 5:43; 10:25; 12:13; 17:6, 26]) sets him forth as the equivalent and therefore the replacement of the Old Testament temple.[122]

*Narrative description of Jesus' human existence.* John's Gospel gives an outline of Jesus' ministry, in the course of which Jesus shows himself to be a human being among others. His very first words, addressed to two of the Baptist's disciples, seek a point of information: "What do you want?" (Jn 1:38). He is no generic human being, but a particular individual of Jewish ethnicity (Jn

[118]George Foot Moore, *Judaism in the First Centuries of the Christian Era: The Age of the Tannaim* (3 vols.; Cambridge, MA: Harvard University Press, 1927–1930), 2:44-46.

[119]Ibid., 2:46-47; Luc Devillers, "Histoire et théologie de la fête des Tentes (Sukkot)," *RThom* 100 (2000): 469-503; Mary B. Spaulding, *Commemorative Identities: Jewish Social Memory and the Johannine Feast of Booths* (LNTS 396; London: T & T Clark, 2009). Points of contact between the Feast of Tabernacles and the vocabulary of the Apocalypse are explored in Edwin Reynolds, "The Feast of Tabernacles and the Book of Revelation," *AUSS* 38 (2000): 245-68.

[120]John C. Poirier, "Hanukkah in the Narrative Chronology of the Fourth Gospel," *NTS* 54 (2008): 465-78.

[121]E.g., Lev 20:3; 21:6; 22:2, 32; Deut 12:5, 11, 21; 14:23, 24; 16:2, 6, 11; 26:2; 2 Sam 7:13; 1 Kings 8:16.

[122]Franz Georg Untergassmair, *Im Namen Jesu—Der Namensbegriff im Johannesevangelium: Eine exegetisch-religionsgeschichtliche Studie zu den johanneischen Namensaussagen* (FB 13; Stuttgart: Katholisches Bibelwerk, 1974); Adelheid Ruck-Schröder, *Der Name Gottes und der Name Jesu: Eine neutestamentliche Studie* (WMANT 80; Neukirchen-Vluyn: Neukirchener Verlag, 1999); Jarl E. Fossum, "In the Beginning Was the Name: Onomanology as the Key to Johannine Christology," in *The Image of the Invisible God: Essays on the Influence of Jewish Mysticism on Early Christianity* (NTOA 30; Göttingen: Vandenhoeck & Ruprecht, 1995), pp. 109-34; Hurtado, *Lord Jesus Christ*, pp. 381-92; Thettayil, *In Spirit and Truth*, pp. 231-482.

4:9; cf. Apoc 12:2-5), a native of Judea (Jn 4:44)[123] hailing latterly from Nazareth (Jn 1:45-46; 18:5, 7; 19:19), son of one Joseph (Jn 1:45; 6:42), and of a living mother (Jn 2:1-5; 19:25-27),[124] with brothers (Jn 2:12) who upbraid him (Jn 7:3-10). He endures weariness, thirst and hunger (Jn 4:6, 7, 31), hides from his enemies (Jn 5:13; 8:59; 11:54; 12:36), weeps over a deceased friend (Jn 11:35), is troubled on the brink of death (Jn 12:27; 13:21).[125] Only in the Fourth Gospel does Pilate present him scourged, wearing a crown of thorns and a purple robe, with the now famous *Ecce homo*, "Behold the man" (Jn 19:5). He suffers crucifixion (Jn 19:18), entrusts his mother to the care of the Beloved Disciple as an act of filial piety (Jn 19:26-27), expires (Jn 19:30), is pierced with a lance producing a flow of blood and water (Jn 19:34), and his corpse is bound and buried (Jn 19:40-42). So normal a person was Jesus that many of his contemporaries took little notice. Some who heard his words supposed that he had a demon (Jn 7:20; 8:48, 52; 10:20). Many seeing his signs failed to see through them to his true nature as the life-giver (Jn 2:23-25; 3:2, 11-12; 6:14-15, 26, 30; 9:16; 11:47; 12:18-19, 37).

The Logos present in Jesus was anything but self-advertizing. During his

---

[123]If we accept the Gospel as it stands without rearranging its parts, John 4:43 completes a movement of Jesus from Judea (Jn 2:13, 23; 3:1, 22), where few had believed in him (Jn 2:23-25; 3:11), to Galilee (Jn 4:3-4). His "own country" (ἡ ἰδία πατρίς [Jn 4:44]), where he had found no honor, therefore, can only be Judea (so Westcott, Dodd, Hoskyns, Lindars, Fortna, Barrett, Smith). This is borne out by the concentration of the Gospel on Jesus' words and deeds there. Possibly the identification of Judea as Jesus' *patria* assumes knowledge of his actual birthplace on the part of author and readers. Not known in social circles unfamiliar with the Holy Family was the fact that Jesus' nativity in Bethlehem (Mt 2; Lk 2:1-20) occurred while Joseph and Mary were temporarily displaced from their domicile in Nazareth (Mt 2:23; Lk 1:26-27) at the time of the registration under Quirinius due to Joseph's lineage from David (Lk 2:4). According to John 7:42, some people of Jerusalem considered Jesus to be a native Galilean and concluded that he could not be the Messiah, since the Messiah must come from Bethlehem. This is the only mention of Bethlehem in the Johannine corpus. Their reasoning, based on incomplete information, is not the author's position (contra Bultmann, *Theology*, 2:41). John, writing for Christians who, like him, know the Synoptic infancy traditions, feels no need to refute the Jewish skeptics of a former day in a context where his aim is merely to illustrate popular ferment in the time of Jesus. John's knowledge of Jesus' Davidic descent comes out in the Apocalypse (Apoc 5:5; 22:16).

[124]John, being a cousin of Jesus and the guardian of Jesus' mother after his death (Jn 19:26-27), certainly knew of Jesus' virginal conception (Mt 1:18-21; Lk 1:34-38), for which fact Mary herself was the primary source in the early church (Lk 2:19). John 8:41, where the Jews say to Jesus, "We were not born of fornication," may be a backhanded slander to Jesus' face. If so, the Fourth Gospel contains indirect confirmation that Joseph was known not to have been Jesus' blood-father. That the virginal conception is not a point of Johannine emphasis is no evidence either that John was ignorant of the facts or rejected the story (contra Bultmann, *Theology*, 2:41).

[125]For a review of the emotions of Jesus, see Stephen Voorwinde, *Jesus' Emotions in the Fourth Gospel: Human or Divine?* (LNTS 284; London: T & T Clark, 2005).

lifetime he received attestation from John the Baptist (Jn 1:6-8, 15, 19-36; 3:25-30; 5:33-35; 10:41-42), from the Spirit-dove (Jn 1:32-34), from Jesus' works (Jn 5:20, 36; 10:25, 32-38; 14:10-11; 15:24), from the Scriptures (Jn 1:45; 5:37-44), of Moses in particular (Jn 5:45-46), and from God the Father (Jn 8:17-18). Since Jesus' departure, faith still rests on the testimony of the apostles (Jn 1:14; 1 Jn 1:1-4), on the converging evidence of the water, the blood and the Spirit (1 Jn 5:6-8), and on the witness of God (1 Jn 5:9-12). More human Jesus could not have been.

How significant these and similar indications of Jesus' humanity are for John's Christology was the topic of a celebrated debate in the latter twentieth century. In a series of lectures given at Yale in 1966, Ernst Käsemann, professor of New Testament at Tübingen, advanced a provocative thesis that John's Gospel, the fruit of "a conventicle with gnosticizing tendencies,"[126] presents a Christology of glory that minimizes Jesus' humanity, a naïve, unreflective kind of Docetism that fomented heretical offshoots in the second century.[127] According to Käsemann, "glory/glorification" is the key word of the whole Gospel,[128] and its Christ is "God going about on the earth."[129] John 1:14 climaxes at "we beheld his glory"; the first two clauses mean only that the Logos descended so as to come "into contact with earthly existence,"[130] changing his place but not himself.[131] The "features of the lowliness of the earthly Jesus" Käsemann does not deny, but he asserts they are "the absolute minimum of the costume" required by the Gospel genre.[132] John is "the first Christian to use the earthly life of Jesus merely as a backdrop for the Son of God proceeding through the world of man and as the scene of the inbreaking of the the heavenly glory."[133]

Critical reaction has been decisive. Among others, Günther Bornkamm insisted on the full weight of both Logos and flesh in John 1:14 and pointed out that John's very concept of glory is "anchored . . . to the paradox of the crucifixion."[134] Georg Richter strongly upheld the anti-Docetic thrust of John 1:14, though he weakened the case by judging the verse a secondary addition to

---

[126]Käsemann, *Testament*, p. 73.
[127]Ibid., chap. 2.
[128]Ibid., p. 6.
[129]Ibid., p. 9.
[130]Ibid.
[131]Ibid., p. 12.
[132]Ibid., p. 10.
[133]Ibid., p. 13.
[134]Bornkamm, "Interpretation," p. 88.

the work of the Evangelist.[135] Stephen Smalley faulted Käsemann for under-
playing the historical element in the Gospel, for preferring John 17 to the prologue as an epitome, and for giving a tendentious exegesis of John 1:14.[136] Marianne Meye Thompson's full-length monograph devotes a chapter to John 1:14
in the context of the whole book and also highlights Jesus' earthly origins, signs
and death as pointing to a genuine humanity.[137] Udo Schnelle comes to the
audaciously overdrawn opposite conclusion that the Gospel is the Johannine
community's final, comprehensive blast against Docetic tendencies, on the
basis of an especially thorough redaction-critical analysis of Jesus' signs, and
to a lesser extent of the sacraments and of the prologue.[138] And Charles Hill
shows that in the second century John's Gospel was accepted more widely
among orthodox churchmen, and was perhaps less favored in Gnostic circles,
than the reigning scholarly "orthodox Johannophobia paradigm" has held.[139]
One can only be perplexed at the virtually isolated judgment, "Käsemann has
a powerful case."[140]

***Divine qualities evident in the Son's incarnate state.*** The purpose of the
incarnation was to manifest God's glory in Jesus' flesh. "And we beheld his
glory" (Jn 1:14). Käsemann's thesis had a kernel of truth: in John's and his fellows'
eyes ("we saw") Jesus did bear divine glory, "a glory as of the only-begotten
[one] from the Father, full of grace and truth" (Jn 1:14). Key words introduced
here recycle in following verses. "Of his fullness [πλήρωμα] we all received" (Jn
1:16), "grace in place of grace [χάρις]" (Jn 1:16), "grace and truth (ἀλήθεια) came
through Jesus Christ" (Jn 1:17).[141] Glory, fullness, grace, truth—this set of terms
is associated in the rest of Scripture with deity. The Gospel narrative illustrates
the ways glory shone in the human Jesus.

[135]Georg Richter, "Die Fleischwerdung des Logos im Johannesevangelium," in *Studien zum Johannesevangelium* (ed. Josef Hainz; BU 13; Regensburg: Pustet, 1977), pp. 149-98.
[136]Stephen S. Smalley, "The Testament of Jesus: Another Look," in *Studia Evangelica VI: Papers Presented to the Fourth International Congress on New Testament Studies Held at Oxford, 1969* (ed. Elizabeth A. Livingstone; Berlin: Akademie-Verlag, 1973), pp. 495-501.
[137]Marianne Meye Thompson, *The Humanity of Jesus in the Fourth Gospel* (Philadelphia: Fortress,
1988).
[138]Udo Schnelle, *Antidocetic Christology in the Gospel of John: An Investigation of the Place of the Fourth
Gospel in the Johannine School* (trans. Linda M. Maloney; Minneapolis: Fortress, 1992).
[139]Charles E. Hill, *The Johannine Corpus in the Early Church* (Oxford: Oxford University Press, 2004).
[140]Ashton, *Understanding*, p. 490; see also p. 487.
[141]"Full" and "fullness" are unique to these verses in the Johannine literature. "Grace" figures in greetings and benedictions elsewhere (2 Jn 3; Apoc 1:4; 22:21). Besides being a quality of Jesus' words,
"truth" characterizes his person in John 14:6 (cf. Apoc. 3:7, 14; 19:11).

After the prologue, the testimony of John the Baptist prepares readers to expect a theophany: "Make straight the way of the Lord" (Jn 1:23, quoting Is 40:3). Likewise the Baptist's last word comparing Jesus to a bridegroom sees in him Yahweh's marital faithfulness to Israel.[142] When Jesus comes on the scene, the Baptist bears witness that the Spirit came down as a dove and stayed on him (Jn 1:32-33). Jesus is the one of whom John is unworthy (Jn 1:27), who will baptize others with the Holy Spirit (Jn 1:33), who is the Son of God (Jn 1:34). Only two days (and two paragraphs) later commences the theme of Jesus' supernatural insight into people as he reads Nathanael's heart (Jn 1:47-50).[143] Glory becomes visible when Jesus turns water into wine (Jn 2:11) and raises Lazarus from the dead (Jn 11:4, 40 [here the phrase is "the glory of God"]); between these bookends all the signs radiate glory. His claim that he will raise "this temple" in three days (Jn 2:19) is the first of several predictions that come true (Jn 2:22; 3:14; 12:32; 16:1-4; 17:12; 18:9, 32; 21:18-19). He enjoys immunity from arrest until his hour comes (Jn 7:30, 44; 8:59; 10:39; 11:8-10). When it does, he marches through the events of his passion with regal dignity, from the numinous "I am" that causes his captors to fall to the ground (Jn 18:4-6), through his sharp exposé of his interrogators (Jn 18:19-23), his ringing verdict on guilty Pilate (Jn 18:33–19:12),[144] and his bearing of his own cross (Jn 19:17), to the active surrender of his spirit (Jn 19:30). All along the way are his claims that to deal with the Son is tantamount to dealing with the Father, whether the issue is honoring (Jn 5:23), knowing (Jn 8:19; 14:7), believing in (Jn 12:44), seeing (Jn 12:45; 14:7-10), receiving (Jn 13:20) or hating (Jn 15:23-24) God. Jesus' resurrection reveals him as God's natural Son in a sense distinct from God's adopted children (Jn 20:17, 31).[145]

Thompson puts it well: "That Jesus reveals God is not contradicted by Jesus' humanity," in agreement with Käsemann; but against Käsemann, "that Jesus

---

[142]Summing up a theme found in many Old Testament passages (e.g., Is 50:1; 62:4-5; Jer 2:2; 3:20; Ezek 16; 23; Hos 1–3). On the messianic overtones of "bridegroom," see Jocelyn McWhirter, *The Bridegroom Messiah and the People of God: Marriage in the Fourth Gospel* (SNTSMS 138; Cambridge: Cambridge University Press, 2006). For the development of the same theme in the Apocalypse, see Ruben Zimmermann, "Nuptial Imagery in the Revelation of John," *Bib* 84 (2003): 153-83.

[143]The theme continues in John 2:24-25; 4:17-18, 31; 6:6, 64; 16:29-30; 18:4; 19:28; 21:17.

[144]On Jesus' trial before Pilate as a drama about true power and guilt, see Dirk F. Gniesmer, *In den Prozess verwickelt: Erzähltextanalytische und textpragmatische Erwägungen zur Erzählung vom Prozess vor Pilatus (Joh 18,28–19,16a,b)* (EH 23/688; Frankfurt: Peter Lang, 2000).

[145]Michel Corbin, *Résurrection et nativité: Lecture théologique de Jean 20,1-31* (Théologies; Paris: Cerf, 2002).

reveals God does not efface Jesus' humanity."[146] To bring revelation to human beings, he himself must be human; to reveal to human beings who God is, he himself must be God.

**Summary of Jesus' deity and humanity.** John, then, affirms the perfect deity of the man Jesus. He emphasizes this over against the Jewish denial that a human being can be divine, first applied to Jesus during his ministry in the late 20s. John would concur that no human being can become divine; his position rather is that God became human. His basis is Jesus' own words and deeds long gestated in his memory. John also affirms Jesus' real humanity over against Gnosticizing heretics who were causing ferment in churches around Ephesus in the closing decades of the century. John speaks out of his experience of Jesus the man. What John heard and saw while he was with Jesus, sharpened by responses of the Christian movement to others at the beginning and the end of John's involvement in it, gave rise to the marked accents of the Johannine Christology.[147]

If the foregoing is a reaffirmation of dogmas passed by the councils of Nicaea (A.D. 325) and of Chalcedon (A.D. 451), that is because the Johannine data allow of no different conclusion today from those reached by the early church after long debate. Cultural currents can tempt interpreters to overlook this or that subset of the data. Currents have changed, and the flux will continue as long as the world lasts. But the Johannine witness rises as an Everest above the swirling clouds, pointing to Jesus Christ, God and man.

## OFFICES OF CHRIST IN THE JOHANNINE LITERATURE

Thus far we have considered John's reflections on Christ's personal identity. Another part of the question of who John considered Jesus to be has to do with Jesus' roles or offices. In John's view, Christ's main role was that of God's envoy, already covered above in the section on the sending and incarnation. Around the figure of the Logos sent to become flesh John wraps other titles and motifs. Each title brings its own history and meaning to the person of

---

[146]Thompson, *Humanity of Jesus*, p. 119.
[147]Rodney A. Whitacre, *Johannine Polemic: The Role of Tradition and Theology* (SBLDS 67; Chico, CA: Scholars Press, 1982); Celestino G. Lingad, *The Problems of Jewish Christians in the Johannine Community* (TGST 73; Rome: Editrice Pontificia Università Gregoriana, 2001); James F. McGrath, *John's Apologetic Christology: Legitimation and Development in Johannine Christology* (SNTSMS 111; Cambridge: Cambridge University Press, 2001); Seán Freyne, "Christological Debates among Johannine Christians," in *The Many Voices of the Bible* (ed. Seán Freyne and Ellen van Wolde; Concilium 2002/1; London: SCM Press, 2002), pp. 59-67; Hurtado, *Lord Jesus Christ*, pp. 349-426.

Jesus. By association with the incarnate one and with one another they all gain new dimensions.[148]

***Lamb of God.*** A uniquely Johannine title for Christ is "the Lamb." John the Baptist introduces Jesus in the Fourth Gospel as in the Synoptics. A brief record of the Baptist's witness (Jn 1:19-37) leads up to a climactic double declaration: "Behold, the Lamb [ἀμνός] of God!" (Jn 1:29, 36). Described further in John 1:29 as he "who takes away the sin of the world," this designation taps a reservoir of Old Testament sacrificial connotations. In the Old Testament, "without the shedding of blood there is no forgiveness of sins" (Heb 9:22). According to the Septuagint, an ἀμνός was used for Passover (Ex 12:5; 2 Chron 35:7-8), for the daily burnt offering, the *Tamid* (Ex 29:38-41; Num 28:1-8; Ezek 46:13-15), as well as for other burnt offerings (Lev 9:3; 12:6, 8; 23:18-20; Num 15; 28:11–29:38; 2 Chron 29:32; Ezek 46:4-7, 11), and for certain sin and guilt offerings (Lev 14; Num 6:12, 14; 7; 2 Chron 29:21-22), all of which made atonement for sin and brought forgiveness (e.g., Lev 1:4 [burnt offering]; 4:20, 26, 31, 35 [sin offering]). In Isaiah 53 the suffering servant of the Lord is compared to an ἀμνός "that before its shearers is dumb" (Is 53:7). Though "Lamb," like "Logos," appears only at the head of the Gospel, its placement there is programmatic. The Evangelist wants us to read the entire book as the story of the Logos-become-flesh who laid down his life as God's Lamb.

That for John the lamb was an image of atoning sacrifice is confirmed by its use in the Apocalypse (ἀρνίον).[149] Here the Lamb, in the throne scene that defines the book's view of reality, makes a dramatic appearance as though having been slain (Apoc 5:6, 9, 12; 13:8). With his blood he has ransomed people for God (Apoc 5:9; cf. 14:4: "redeemed"), made their robes white (Apoc 7:14), and conquered the dragon-devil (Apoc 12:11). The same figure is also associated with glory: he shares God's singular throne (Apoc 5:6; 7:17; 22:1, 3), receives

---

[148]John Painter, *The Quest for the Messiah: The History, Literature and Theology of the Johannine Community* (Edinburgh: T & T Clark, 1991), pp. 108-412.

[149]In the New Testament ἀρνίον occurs only in John's writings: once in the Gospel (Jn 21:15), where it is synonymous with πρόβατον (Jn 21:16-17 [πρόβατον occurs elsewhere in the Gospel 17×]), and the rest in the Revelation (29×), which does not use ἀμνός and has but one occurrence of πρόβατον (Apoc 18:13). In the Septuagint the diminutive ἀρνίον is rare (4×), but ἀρνός is found upwards of thirty times and in sacrificial contexts (e.g., Lev 1:10; 3:7; 1 Kgdms 7:9; 2 Kgdms 6:13; 3 Kgdms 1:9, 19, 25; 1 Chron 29:21). The terms ἀμνός and ἀρνός are synonymous in different manuscripts of Exodus 12:5; Job 31:20; and in Isaiah 34:6. Probably what is significant for John is the denotation of a lamb, not any fine shade of connotation between ἀμνός and ἀρνίον. See Loren L. Johns, *The Lamb Christology of the Apocalypse of John: An Investigation Into Its Origins and Rhetorical Force* (WUNT 2/167; Tübingen: Mohr Siebeck, 2003).

worship (Apoc 5:8-13; 7:9-10), conquers the beast (Apoc 17:14), marries the bride (Apoc 19:7, 9; 21:9), and rules forever (Apoc 22:3-5).

*Teacher and prophet.* In applying the term "rabbi" to Jesus, transliterated from the Hebrew *rabbî* ("my great one, master"), John outscores all three Synoptic Gospels together by a margin of 8 to 3 (Jn 1:38, 49; 3:2, 26; 4:31; 6:25; 9:2; 11:8; also "rabboni" [ῥαββουνί] in 20:16; Synoptics: Mt 23:7-8; Mk 10:51). John also translates the word as "teacher" (διδάσκαλος) for the benefit of non-Jewish readers (Jn 1:38; 20:16). Elsewhere he can call Jesus "teacher" (Jn 3:2; 11:28; 13:13-14) and "master" (κύριος) (Jn 6:68; 11:3, 12, 21, 27, 32, 34, 39; 13:6, 9, 13-14, 16, 25) and speak of him as a father having disciples for his "children" (Jn 13:33; 21:5). Since Jesus had no formal education to match the experts in Jewish law (Jn 7:15), these were titles of respect. They point to teaching as Jesus' characteristic activity. Looking back, he tells Annas, "I have always taught in synagogues and in the temple" (Jn 18:20).[150]

Usually it is others who wonder whether Jesus is a prophet (Jn 6:14; 7:40; cf. 7:52), perhaps the eschatological prophet of Deuteronomy 18:15-19 (Jn 1:21, 25; 6:14; 7:40, 52 [P⁶⁶*]).[151] Recognition of Jesus' prophethood can be a first step toward fuller faith in him (Jn 4:19; 9:17). But in one place Jesus testifies about himself that a prophet has no honor in his own country (Jn 4:44). Often Jesus is said to speak on God's behalf;[152] that is the chief role of a prophet.[153]

Moses was regarded by Jews of the Second Temple period as the lawgiver, cultus founder and prophet par excellence because the Scripture singles him out as the greatest prophet of all (Deut 34:10-12).[154] Three passages in the Fourth Gospel set Moses and Jesus side by side, with Moses as the predecessor and

---

[150]Note also John 6:59; 7:14, 28, 35; 8:20. Unlike the Synoptists, John never has Jesus "preach" (κηρύσσω). See further Andreas J. Köstenberger, "Jesus as Rabbi in the Fourth Gospel," in *Studies on John and Gender: A Decade of Scholarship* (SBL 38; New York: Peter Lang, 2001), pp. 65-98; Michael R. Sebastian, "Le titre de Rabbi dans la Christologie de l'Évangile de Jean," *BLE* 110 (2009): 363-74.

[151]From these texts it is unclear whether the prophet of Deuteronomy 18 was expected to be a precursor of the Messiah or was a messianic figure in his own right. The conception may have been fluid.

[152]Jn 3:11, 32-34; 7:17; 8:26, 28, 38, 40, 46-47; 12:49, 50; 14:10, 24; 15:22; 17:8; 18:20.

[153]It is also emphasized that Jesus speaks truth (Jn 5:31-32; 7:18; 8:13-14, 17-18, 32, 40, 45, 46; 16:7; 18:20-23, 37-38). On the presentation of Jesus as prophet, see Sukmin Cho, *Jesus as Prophet in the Fourth Gospel* (NTM 15; Sheffield: Sheffield Phoenix Press, 2006); Stelian Tofană, "Jesus 'the Prophet' in the Witness and Belief of His Contemporaries According to the Fourth Gospel—a Johannine Theological Perspective," *SS* 7 (2009): 98-115.

[154]Stan Harstine, *Moses as a Character in the Fourth Gospel: A Study of Ancient Reading Techniques* (JSNTSup 229; London: Sheffield Academic Press, 2002), pp. 96-129; John Lierman, *The New Testament Moses: Christian Perceptions of Moses and Israel in the Setting of Jewish Religion* (WUNT 2/173; Tübingen: Mohr Siebeck, 2004).

witness pointing to the greater one who was to come. In the words of our author, "The law was given through Moses; grace and truth came through Jesus Christ" (Jn 1:17). Jesus said, "If you believed Moses, you would believe me, for he wrote of me. But if you do not believe his writings, how will you believe my words?" (Jn 5:46-47). The Jews held Moses in high regard: "We know that God has spoken to Moses, but as for this man, we do not know where he comes from" (Jn 9:29), at which statement the man marvels whose eyes Jesus has opened (Jn 9:30-33). All three passages view Moses as a mediator of divine revelation; in this respect, what God established through Moses stands in direct continuity with its fulfillment in Christ.[155] Other potential parallels John does not develop. He does not set forth Jesus as a new Moses.[156]

**Messiah = Christ.** Only John among the New Testament authors translit-erates "messiah" (מָשִׁיחַ, "anointed one") as Μεσσίας, followed by its translation (ὁ) Χριστός (Jn 1:41; 4:25). The word refers to the end-time king of Israel, the last and greatest in the anointed line from David. The title is important for John, as is clear from his inclusion of it in the summary verse at the end of the Gospel: "that you may believe that Jesus is the Christ, the Son of God" (Jn 20:31).[157] But John, like Jesus before him, distances himself from the expectation, widespread in first-century Jewish Palestine, that a national king was about to rise to lead an army against Rome and reestablish the Davidic hegemony over the nations on a grand scale.[158] John in his Gospel, no less than Mark by his purported

---

[155]T. F. Glasson, *Moses in the Fourth Gospel* (SBT 40; Naperville, IL: Allenson, 1963); Wayne A. Meeks, *The Prophet-King: Moses Traditions and the Johannine Christology* (NovTSup 14; Leiden: Brill, 1967); M.-É. Boismard, *Moses or Jesus: An Essay in Johannine Christology* (trans. Benedict T. Viviano; BETL 84A; Leuven: Leuven University Press, 1993); Anderson, "The Having-Sent-Me Father"; Stefan Schapdick, "Autorität ohne Inhalt: Zum Mosebild des Johannesevangeliums," *ZNW* 97 (2006): 177-206.

[156]For a different judgment, see John Lierman, "The Mosaic Pattern of John's Christology," in *Challenging Perspectives on the Gospel of John* (ed. John Lierman; WUNT 2/219; Tübingen: Mohr Siebeck, 2006), pp. 210-34.

[157]"The category that is used to bring together all the raw materials of his portrayal of Jesus is 'Christ' understood as the Greek equivalent of 'Messiah'" (Painter, *Quest*, p. 470).

[158]Some such concept lies behind discussions among Jews and Samaritans about whether Jesus might be the Messiah in John 1:20, 25; 3:28; 4:29; 6:14-15 ("king"); 7:26, 27, 31, 41 [2×], 42; 9:22; 10:24; 12:34. John 1:20-21 shows that the main eschatological precursors or associates of the Messiah according to the teaching of the Pharisees, priests and Levites of Jerusalem were Elijah and the prophet of Deuteronomy 18. In Samaritanism the latter figure coalesced with the Messiah. This may explain the Samaritan woman's idea at John 4:25, 29. That the Messiah would have an un-known origin (Jn 7:27) does not fit with his coming from Bethlehem (Jn 7:41-42); these different conceptions may be due to uncertainty among Jewish scholars of the time about how to reconcile Daniel 7:13 with Micah 5:2. Isaiah 9:7 and Daniel 7:14 may explain the belief that the Messiah would remain forever (Jn 12:34). On Jewish messianic expectations in Palestine in the time of Jesus,

"messianic secret" theme, portrays Jesus as abjuring messiahship in that commonly understood sense. Jesus is identified as the messiah or king of Israel by his disciples ("Christ" [Jn 1:41; 4:29; 9:22; 11:27]; "King" [Jn 1:49; 12:13, 15]),[159] tongue-in-cheek by Pilate and his forces ("King of the Jews" [Jn 18:33, 37, 39; 19:3, 14-15, 19, 21]), by the Jews who called for Jesus' crucifixion (Jn 19:12), and by the narrator (Jn 1:17; 20:31). John has Jesus apply "Christ" to himself only at John 4:26,[160] on Samaritan soil, where the concept of the Messiah was fused to that of the prophetic Restorer or Taheb,[161] and at John 17:3, in a prayer looking back over his ministry from its end. This reticence about messiahship was not the keeping of a "secret" on Jesus' part;[162] it was plain truthfulness about his immediate objective: to die on the cross, not to found a Jewish empire.

After Jesus' glorification, John no longer holds back. In the Epistles and the Apocalypse "Christ" becomes a standard title, often side by side with "Jesus" (1 Jn 1:3; 2:1, 22; 3:23; 4:2, 15; 5:1, 6, 20; 2 Jn 3, 7, 9; Apoc 1:1, 2, 5; 11:15; 12:10; 20:4, 6; 22:21).[163] At a few places in the Johannine literature the collocation of "the Christ" with "the Son of God" lends to "Christ" a connotation of deity only hinted at in Old Testament usage (Jn 1:17; 11:27; 17:3; 20:31; 1 Jn 2:22; 5:20; 2 Jn 7).[164] And the Apocalypse completes the round of Old Testament messianic texts applied to his person: Genesis 49:9-12, "the Lion of the tribe of Judah" (Apoc 5:5; 7:5); Psalm 2:6-9, "my king on Zion . . . shall break the nations with a rod of iron" (Apoc 2:26-27; 14:1; 19:15); Psalm 110:3 (LXX 109:3), "the morning

---

see William Horbury, *Jewish Messianism and the Cult of Christ* (London: SCM Press, 1998); idem, "Jewish and Christian Monotheism in the Herodian Age," in *Early Jewish and Christian Monotheism* (ed. Loren T. Stuckenbruck and Wendy E. S. North; JSNTSup 263; London: T & T Clark, 2004), pp. 16-44; Jorg Christian Salzmann, "Jüdische Messiasvorstellungen in Justins Dialog mit Trypho und im Johannesevangelium," *ZNW* 100 (2009): 247-68.

[159]Also the disciples who accompanied Jesus on his triumphal entry into Jerusalem interpreted Psalm 118:25 and Zechariah 9:9 messianically (Jn 12:12-16).

[160]Soon-Ja Park, "L'Entretien avec la Samaritaine: Jn 4,1-26," *SB* 96 (1999): 26-55.

[161]Combining Deuteronomy 18:15, 18 with Numbers 24:17: James D. Purvis, "The Fourth Gospel and the Samaritans," *NovT* 17 (1975): 161-98; John Bowman, trans. and ed., *Samaritan Documents Relating to Their History, Religion, and Life* (POTTS 2; Pittsburgh: Pickwick, 1977), pp. 263-83; Ferdinand Dexinger, "Die Taheb-Vorstellung als politische Utopie," *Numen* 37 (1990): 1-23.

[162]Nor on Mark's part, despite the proposal by William Wrede, *The Messianic Secret* (trans. J. C. G. Greig; Cambridge: James Clarke, 1971).

[163]On the Epistles, see Marinus de Jonge, "The Use of the Word ΧΡΙΣΤΟΣ in the Johannine Epistles," in *Studies in John: Presented to Professor J. N. Sevenster on the Occasion of His Seventieth Birthday* (NovTSup 24; Leiden: Brill, 1970), pp. 66-74.

[164]Only twice in the Old Testament is a royal scion of the house of David honored with a divine title: Psalm 45:6 (on which, see Murray J. Harris, "The Translation of Elohim in Psalm 45:7-8," *TynBul* 35 [1984]: 65-89); MT Isaiah 9:5 (ET Is 9:6).

star" (Apoc 22:16); Isaiah 11:1, "the Root of David" (Apoc 5:5; 22:16 [cf. Jer 23:5; 33:15; Zech 3:8; 6:12]); Isaiah 11:4, "the rod/sword of his mouth" (Apoc 1:16; 2:12; 19:15, 21); Isaiah 22:22, "the key of the house of David" (Apoc 3:7).[165] Thus the term "messiah" points to the office Jesus entered into from his ascension to his second coming and does not describe his ministry that led up to the cross. During this present age Jesus exercises his kingship by wielding truth, not a sword (Jn 18:36-37; Apoc 19:21).[166]

As we have seen, in John's writings the title "Son of God" expresses Jesus' eternal relation to his Father. In Judaism the same phrase could function, in rare texts, as a messianic title (based on 2 Sam 7:14; Ps 2:7; 89:26; 110:3),[167] and it continued sometimes to have that significance in the earliest strata of the New Testament.[168] Only vestiges of it remain in John. Nathaniel's expostulation has "Son of God" parallel to "King of Israel" (Jn 1:49). John's summary statement at John 20:31 lays "the Christ" side by side with "the Son of God," though by this advanced point in the narrative the fuller implications of Jesus' sonship are clear.

Nor is there a formal proclamation of Jesus as "Lord" (κύριος) in John parallel to Paul ("Jesus is Lord" [1 Cor 12:3; cf. Phil 2:11]) and Luke ("God has made him both Lord and Christ" [Acts 2:36]). In Luke and Paul "Lord" communicates to Hellenistic ears something of what Jewish Christians meant by "messiah." Not only does John use "Lord" less frequently,[169] but also it sometimes refers in his writings to God rather than Jesus,[170] and when it denotes Jesus in the Gospel, it is usually a conventional address expressing respect. Moreover, in the Johannine corpus there is no quotation or allusion to Psalm 110:1, the classic Old Testament prooftext for Jesus' lordship in the rest of the New Testament.[171] Nevertheless, in

---

[165]Many of these Old Testament passages (and others that come up in the Fourth Gospel: Ps 118:25 [Jn 12:13]; Is 9:6 with Dan 7:14 [Jn 12:34]; Dan 7:13 [Jn 7:27]; Mic 5:2 [Jn 7:42]; Zech 9:9 [Jn 12:12-16]) were already expounded messianically in thematic clusters in pre-Christian Judaism. See William Horbury, "Jewish Messianism and Early Christology," in *Contours of Christology in the New Testament* (ed. Richard N. Longenecker; MNTS; Grand Rapids: Eerdmans, 2005), pp. 3-24; idem, *Jewish Messianism*.

[166]Cornelis Bennema, "The Sword of the Messiah and the Concept of Liberation in the Fourth Gospel," *Bib* 86 (2005): 35-58.

[167]Dunn, *Christology*, pp. 13-22; John J. Collins, *The Scepter and the Star: The Messiahs of the Dead Sea Scrolls and Other Ancient Literature* (ABRL; New York: Doubleday, 1995), pp. 154-72.

[168]Dunn, *Christology*, pp. 33-46.

[169]Gospel, 52×; Epistles, 0×; Revelation, 21×. Compare some 210× in Luke and Acts; 275× in the Pauline Epistles.

[170]John 1:23; 12:13, 38 (2×); Apocalypse 1:8; 4:8, 11; 11:4, 15, 17; 15:3, 4; 16:7; 18:8; 19:6; 21:22; 22:5, 6.

[171]On Psalm 110:1 in early Christianity, see David M. Hay, *Glory at the Right Hand: Psalm 110 in Early Christianity* (SBLMS 18; Nashville: Abingdon, 1973); Martin Hengel, "'Sit at My Right Hand!'" in

John too "Lord" can function as an inchoate christological title: in comments by the narrator (Jn 4:1; 6:23; 11:2), in confessions by disciples (Jn 6:68; 9:38), especially after Jesus' resurrection (Jn 20:18, 20, 25, 28; 21:7, 12, 15-17), and in a few places in the Apocalypse (Apoc 11:8; 14:13; 17:14; 19:16; 22:20-21). Thus a term of the Gentile mission registered a limited impact on John, whose apostolic ministry was in Judea until the fall of Jerusalem, and in metropolitan Ephesus only late in life. This difference between John's usage and others' is a matter of authorial preference, not of theological substance. John's sparing use of the title "Lord" shows that he had no objection to it in principle, while his presentation of Jesus as Son of God, Christ and, occasionally, "Savior of the world" (Jn 4:42; 1 Jn 4:14)—in John 4 this last phrase is associated with the mission of Jesus' disciples to the non-Jewish world[172]—amounts to the same thing as "Lord."

"The Holy One of God" stands in the Johannine counterpart (Jn 6:69) to Peter's confession of Jesus as the Christ at Caesarea Philippi (Mt 16:16; Mk 8:29; Lk 9:20) and so enriches the messianic concept. Echoing the cry of a demon undergoing exorcism (Mk 1:24 = Lk 4:35), it indicates that God has set Jesus apart from other human beings for a special purpose. He is the one "whom the Father consecrated" (Jn 10:36). As the parallel Synoptic accounts move directly from Peter recognizing Jesus' messianic identity to Jesus' first prediction of his coming passion (Mt 16:21-23), so in the Fourth Gospel Jesus quickly points out that there is a devil in the midst of his faithful few, and John adds that the reference is to his betrayer (Jn 6:70-71). The holy role that Jesus must play, then, is to consecrate himself by dying for them (Jn 17:19).

An exhaustive account of ways John identifies Jesus as Messiah would have to include the royal connotations of the Logos who sits on God's lap (Jn 1:18), of the dispensing of food to crowds (Jn 6), of the metaphor of a shepherd (Jn 10),[173] of speaking a word of power (Jn 18:4-6), and of being considered divine (1:1; 20:28).[174]

---

*Studies in Early Christology* (Edinburgh: T & T Clark, 1995), pp. 119-225. Margaret Daly-Denton thinks that she can hear "echoes" of Psalm 110:1 in John 10:22-39 (taken as reminiscent of the Synoptic trial narratives), in John's use of ὑψόω, and in John 5:22-23; 19:28-30; 12:34; 20:28; 17:2; 1:1 (*David in the Fourth Gospel: The Johannine Reception of the Psalms* [AGJU 47; Leiden: Brill, 2000]). But to my ears, these echoes are extremely faint.

[172]Craig R. Koester, "'The Savior of the World' (John 4:42)," *JBL* 109 (1990): 665-80; Soon-Ja Park, "Jésus en Samarie: Jean 4,27-42," *SB* 97 (2000): 22-36. It has long been recognized that this title for Jesus directly opposes the claims of Caesar (see Richey, *Roman Imperial Ideology*, pp. 82-91).

[173]Andreas J. Köstenberger, "Jesus the Good Shepherd Who Will Also Bring Other Sheep (John 10:16): The Old Testament Background of a Familiar Metaphor," *BBR* 12 (2002): 67-96.

[174]Joachim Kügler, *Der andere König: Religionsgeschichtliche Perspektiven auf die Christologie des Johan-*

**Son of Man.** The phrase "(one like) a/the Son of Man" crops up thirteen times in John's Gospel (Jn 1:51; 3:13-14; 5:27; 6:27, 53, 62; 8:28; 9:35; 12:23, 34 [2×]; 13:31) and twice in the Apocalypse (Apoc 1:13; 14:14).[175] In John's Gospel, as in the Synoptics, this phrase is found exclusively in sayings of Jesus, with the sole exception of John 12:34, where a Jewish crowd takes up Jesus' choice of words.[176] Jesus' sayings about himself as the Son of Man, preserved in the Synoptic tradition as well as in John's own memory, supplied kernels that John developed.[177] John's usage in turn can be traced back to Daniel 7:13-14,[178] which has left its stamp on the image of one like a son of man coming on the clouds to judge (Apoc 14:14-16) and on the Gospel sayings about Jesus' role in judgment, both present (Jn 9:35) and future (Jn 5:27). In John 1:51 Jesus identifies himself as the archetype of Jacob's ladder (Gen 28:12), the channel of divine revelation, thus restating the gist of the prologue (Jn 1:1, 14, 18) in this first of the Son of Man sayings. In Daniel 7 the one like a son of man has a celestial origin yet in the

---

nesevangeliums (SBS 178; Stuttgart: Katholisches Bibelwerk, 1999). For a wider study showing how John's elusive language enables him to present Jesus as the fulfiller of Israel's messianic Scriptures in whom God has revealed himself finally, see Saeed Hamid-Khani, *Revelation and Concealment of Christ: A Theological Inquiry into the Elusive Language of the Fourth Gospel* (WUNT 2/120; Tübingen: Mohr Siebeck, 2000).

[175]Konrad Huber, *Einer gleich einem Menschensohn: Die Christusvisionen in Offb 1,9-20 und Offb 14,14-20 und die Christologie der Johannesoffenbarung* (NTAbh 51; Münster: Aschendorff, 2007).

[176]Exactly what Jesus meant by using this phrase of himself has been a matter of unresolved debate among critical New Testament scholars. For an overview, see Mogens Müller, *The Expression "Son of Man" and the Development of Christology: A History of Interpretation* (CIS; London: Equinox, 2008).

[177]Rudolf Schnackenburg, "Der Menschensohn im Johannesevangelium," *NTS* 11 (1965): 123-37; Stephen S. Smalley, "The Johannine Son of Man Sayings," *NTS* 15 (1968–1969): 278-301.

[178]Barnabas Lindars, "The Son of Man in the Johannine Christology," in *Christ and the Spirit in the New Testament: In Honour of Charles Francis Digby Moule* (ed. Barnabas Lindars and Stephen Smalley; Cambridge: Cambridge University Press, 1973), pp. 52, 57. Lindars, with the majority of commentators, is right: "[John's] use of the term keeps strictly within the categories of Jewish apocalyptic, and does not show any influence of the syncretistic mythology of the Primal Man" (p. 59). This corrects Siegfried Schulz, who, following Bultmann, posited a Gnostic background for John's Son of Man sayings (*Untersuchungen zur Menschensohn-Christologie im Johannesevangelium: Zugleich ein Beitrag zur Methodengeschichte der Auslegung des 4. Evangeliums* [Göttingen: Vandenhoeck & Ruprecht, 1957]). Robert Rhea supposes that John's concept of the Son of Man was shaped by the Jewish expectation of a prophet like Moses rather than by Daniel 7 (*The Johannine Son of Man* [ATANT 76; Zürich: Theologischer Verlag, 1990]), but Deuteronomy 18:15-19 does not use the phrase. Delbert Burkett thinks that the primary background is to be found neither in Daniel 7 nor in Gnosticism but rather in Proverbs 30:1-4 (*The Son of Man in the Gospel of John* [JSNTSup 56; Sheffield: JSOT Press, 1991]), but this obscure text seems an unlikely source, and John 5:27 shows the influence rather of Daniel 7:9-13. For a firm affirmation of the Danielic derivation of John's concept of the Son of Man, based on the full round of characteristics of this figure, see Benjamin E. Reynolds, *The Apocalyptic Son of Man in the Gospel of John* (WUNT 2/249; Tübingen: Mohr Siebeck, 2008).

end receives divine authority to rule justly on earth. Though he is not explicitly said to suffer together with the saints of the Most High before God vindicates them (Dan 7:21-22, 25, 27), that may well be implied. That the Son of Man is to suffer death is one theme in the Synoptic material (Mk 8:31; 9:9, 12, 31; 10:33, 45; 14:21, 41; Mt 12:40 = Lk 11:30); in John it becomes predominant (Jn 3:14; 6:27, 53; 8:28; 12:23, 34; 13:31).

Other Johannine accents are a broad correlation between occurrences of "Son of Man" and of the incarnational language of descent and ascent,[179] and the use of "Son of Man" in all three passages that speak of Jesus' crucifixion as his exaltation (ὑψόω, ὑψωθῆναι [Jn 3:14; 8:28; 12:32-34]). Hence John's unique contribution was to weld these logia to his particularly clear doctrine of the incarnation, making the phrase "Son of Man" a vehicle both for the enigma of Jesus' heavenly home and for his quite human death as his uplifting (Jn 12:23).[180]

While it would be too much to claim that the Son of Man cluster of sayings was the nub around which John's view of Christ formed, they are intertwined with the main lines of his Christology.[181]

## SUMMARY OF JOHN'S VIEW OF THE PERSON OF CHRIST

All the statements, themes and titles that make up John's view of Christ's person converge to present Christ as the "only-begotten God," whom God deputed from eternity to become a man, so that by dying for the world he might shine light into its darkness and bring life out of its death. Since one's being is shown by one's actions, consideration of the person of Christ will not be complete until we have reviewed his accomplishments. To that subject we now turn.

---

[179]Jn 1:51; 3:13; 6:27, 62 (enclosing occurrences of καταβαίνω in Jn 6:33, 38, 41, 42, 50, 51, 58 and ἀναβαίνω in Jn 6:62). John Ashton, "The Johannine Son of Man: A New Proposal," *NTS* 57 (2011): 508-29. The correlation is imperfect, however, for ἀναβαίνω is found twice in John 20:17 linked to Jesus' divine sonship rather than "Son of Man." This fact bears out Lindars's observation, "Descent is not part of the Johannine Son-of-Man myth" ("Son of Man," p. 48n16).

[180]Francis J. Moloney, *The Johannine Son of Man* (2nd ed.; BSR 14; Rome: Libreria Ateneo Salesiano, 1978), pp. 216, 220.

[181]William R. G. Loader, "The Central Structure of Johannine Christology," *NTS* 30 (1984): 188-216; idem, *Christology*; Benjamin E. Reynolds, "The Use of the Son of Man Idiom in the Gospel of John," in *"Who Is This Son of Man?" The Latest Scholarship on a Puzzling Expression of the Historical Jesus* (ed. Larry W. Hurtado and Paul L. Owen; LNTS 390; London: T & T Clark International, 2011), pp. 101-29; idem, *Apocalyptic Son of Man*.

# GOD'S SELF-REVELATION
# IN CHRIST'S WORK

GOD SENT HIS SON INTO THE WORLD to perform a task. His comprehensive charge to Jesus is condensed into the elegant Johannine phrase "the work" that the Father gave the Son to do.[1] In this chapter we will survey all aspects of Jesus' work as presented in John's writings: Jesus' teaching and miracles (called "signs" in the Fourth Gospel); his climactic "glorification," including his crucifixion, burial, resurrection, breathing out of the Holy Spirit and return to the Father; and the awaited events that will bring this world order to an end and usher in the age to come.

We begin with "work." "My food," says Jesus, "is to do the will of him who sent me, and to accomplish his work [αὐτοῦ τὸ ἔργον]" (Jn 4:34). Well on in the ministry he encourages his disciples, "We must work [ἐργάζεσθαι] the works [τὰ ἔργα] of him who sent me, while it is day; night comes, when no one can work [ἐργάζεσθαι]" (Jn 9:4). Mortal peril from opponents in Judea is no deterrent while Jesus' alotted time is elapsing: "If any one walks in the day, he does not stumble" (Jn 11:9). Looking back with satisfaction on his ministry and forward to its imminent completion, Jesus prays, "I glorified you on earth, having accomplished the work [τὸ ἔργον τελειώσας] that you gave me to do" (Jn 17:4).[2] As Jesus expires on the cross, he declares, "It is finished [τετέλεσται]" (Jn 19:30). His whole purpose was to complete the work that the Father gave him to do.

---

[1]Studied exhaustively in Johannes Riedl, *Das Heilswerk Jesus nach Johannes* (FreiTS 93; Freiburg: Herder, 1973), pp. 43-186.

[2]More specifically, Jesus made known his Father's name and handed on his Father's words to those people whom the Father had given him (Jn 17:6-8). Dirk G. van der Merwe, "The Exposition of John 17:6-8: An Exegetical Exercise," *HvTSt* 59 (2003): 169-90.

Jesus' "work" is identical with his function as God's Word in the prologue to the Gospel. Even before the Logos became incarnate, he was the primordial, creative light that shines in the darkness, giving life and light to human beings (Jn 1:4-5). Wherever human reason, conscience or imagination discovers truth, be it in the progress of philosophy, science, letters or art, that is made possible by the activity of the universal Logos: "In your light do we see light" (Ps 36:9). As "the true light that enlightens every person" (Jn 1:9), the Logos illumines all cultures and each individual to impart knowledge of the divine.[3] But due to sin and unbelief, the world does not benefit (Jn 1:10-11). This illumination was especially concentrated in Israel's Torah and in the history of God's covenant-keeping with them, which John regards as a special "grace" (Jn 1:16). Yet even Moses, through whom the Torah was given (Jn 1:17), though he "went up" to the top of Mount Sinai and "entered the cloud" (Ex 24:15, 18), never ascended into heaven (Jn 3:13) so as to descend with the kind of firsthand information that the Logos has brought fresh from the embrace of the Father (Jn 1:18).[4] The grace of Torah is superseded by the abounding "grace and truth" that Jesus Christ has established (χάριν ἀντὶ χάριτος, "[new] grace in place of [old] grace" [Jn 1:17]). The remainder of John's Gospel shows how the sent one revealed the sender by executing the work that the sender gave him to do.

## THE WORDS AND DEEDS OF JESUS AS GOD'S SELF-REVELATION

Jesus' work falls into two major divisions. He was born "to bear witness to the truth" (Jn 18:37); part of his work involved speaking words.[5] The other part

---

[3]R. E. O. White, "'No One Comes to the Father But by Me,'" *ExpTim* 113 (2002): 116-17.

[4]Jews of the Second Temple period speculated about the heavenly ascents of a number of Old Testament figures, including Enoch, Moses and Elijah. Since John 3:13 is part of Jesus' conversation with Nicodemus, a Pharisaic member of the Sanhedrin (Jn 3:1; 7:50), representing the same body that would later claim to be followers of Moses (Jn 9:13, 28), there is a good probability that John 3:13 has in view the widespread tendency to elevate Moses. On the traditions of Judaism about Moses, see Wayne A. Meeks, *The Prophet-King: Moses Traditions and the Johannine Christology* (NovTSup 14; Leiden: Brill, 1967), pp. 122-25, 156-59, 205-9, 232-36, 241-44, 295-96; Louis Ginzberg, *The Legends of the Jews* (trans. Henrietta Szold; 7 vols.; Philadelphia: Jewish Publication Society of America, 1909–1938), 3:107-8, 109-28; Angelo S. Rappaport, *Myth and Legend of Ancient Israel* (3 vols.; New York: Ktav, 1966), 2:308-16.

[5]John has Jesus "say" or "speak" using the verbs λέγειν, εἰπεῖν, εἰρηκέναι (total of 236×), λαλεῖν (48×), ἀποκρίνεσθαι (42×). Jesus' "words" are indicated by the nouns λόγος, λόγοι (22×) and ῥῆμα, ῥήματα (11×), as well as "truth" (ἀλήθεια) when it is the object of a verb of speaking (5×). Jesus also "bears witness" (μαρτυρέω, 11×; μαρτυρία, 6×) and "teaches" (διδάσκω, 6×; διδαχή, 3×). Less frequently, Jesus "cries aloud" (κράζω [Jn 7:28, 37; 12:44]), "calls" (φωνέω [Jn 11:28; 12:17]), "declares" (ἀπαγγέλλω [Jn 16:25]).

was his doing of all "the deeds [τὰ ἔργα] which the Father has granted me to accomplish [ἵνα τελειώσω αὐτά]" (Jn 5:36).[6] Accordingly, even though there is an interplay in the Gospel narrative between these two sides of Jesus' work, this chapter will proceed analytically for the sake of clarity by focusing first on Jesus' words and then on his deeds as highlighted in the Gospel and expounded in the Epistles and the Apocalypse.

*The words of Jesus as God's self-revelation.* Through speeches and dialogues with a variety of audiences and individuals in the Fourth Gospel Jesus imparts knowledge of himself and of God.[7] Jesus' words, John tells us, were extraordinary. A group of temple guards sent to arrest him came back to the authorities empty-handed with the excuse "No one ever spoke like this man" (Jn 7:46).[8] When he opened his mouth, what came out were not his own words but those of God (Jn 3:32, 34; 7:16-18; 8:28, 38; 12:49-50; 14:10). God sent his Son to take up a legal controversy against the world with unanswerable arguments (Jn 3:11, 32-33; 5:31-32; 7:7; 8:13-14, 17-18; 10:25; 18:37).[9] Jesus' words are completely reliable ("Amen, Amen")[10] and were destined to be fulfilled (Jn 2:22; 13:19; 14:29; 18:9, 32).[11] Corresponding to Jesus' propositions is a pervasive emphasis in the Gospel on the importance of hearers coming to "know," "re-

---

[6]Jesus "works" (ἐργάζομαι) at John 5:17; 6:30; 9:4. Plural ἔργα of Jesus are mentioned in John 5:20, 36 (2×); 7:3, 21 (ἓν ἔργον); 9:3, 4; 10:25, 32 [2×], 33, 37, 38; 14:10, 11, 12; 15:24. There are many theologically significant uses of "do, act" (ποιέω) with Jesus as subject, either with "sign(s)" as object (Jn 2:11, 23; 3:2; 4:54; 6:2, 14, 30; 7:31; 9:16; 11:47; 12:18, 37; 20:30) or without signs (Jn 2:18; 4:34, 45; 5:16, 19, 30, 36; 6:6, 38; 7:3-4, 21; 8:28-29; 9:33; 10:25, 37-38; 11:45-46; 13:7, 12, 15; 14:10, 31; 15:24; 17:4; 18:30, 35; 21:25). On these, see Riedl, *Heilswerk*, pp. 187-282.

[7]Georg Rubel, *Erkenntnis und Bekenntnis: Der Dialog als Weg der Wissensvermittlung im Johannesevangelium* (NTAbh 54; Münster: Aschendorff, 2009).

[8]C. Clifton Black, "'The Words That You Gave to Me I Have Given to Them': The Grandeur of Johannine Rhetoric," in *Exploring the Gospel of John: In Honor of D. Moody Smith* (ed. R. Alan Culpepper and C. Clifton Black; Louisville: Westminster John Knox, 1996), pp. 220-39.

[9]The theme of Jesus as "witness" continues in the Apocalypse (Apoc 1:2, 5, 9; 19:10). On Jesus "witnessing," see John Painter, *John: Witness and Theologian* (London: SPCK, 1975), pp. 8, 10-11, 90, 91; John Ashton, *Understanding the Fourth Gospel* (Oxford: Clarendon, 1991), pp. 226-29, 523-26; Andrew T. Lincoln, *Truth on Trial: The Lawsuit Motif in the Fourth Gospel* (Peabody, MA: Hendrickson, 2000); Martin Asiedu-Peprah, *Johannine Sabbath Conflicts as Juridical Controversy* (WUNT 2/132; Tübingen: Mohr Siebeck, 2001); Édouard Cothenet, *La chaîne des témoins dans l'évangile de Jean: De Jean-Baptiste au disciple bien-aimé* (LB 142; Paris: Cerf, 2005); George L. Parsenios, *Rhetoric and Drama in the Johannine Lawsuit Motif* (WUNT 258; Tübingen: Mohr Siebeck, 2010).

[10]Twenty-five times Jesus adds solemnity to what he says with the formula "Amen, Amen" (Jn 1:51; 3:3, 5, 11; 5:19, 24, 25; 6:26, 32, 47, 53; 8:34, 51, 58; 10:1, 7; 12:24; 13:16, 20, 21, 38; 14:12; 16:20, 23; 21:18). Also he repeatedly points out that he speaks the truth (Jn 5:31-32; 7:18; 8:13-14, 17-18; 32, 40, 45, 46; 16:7; 18:20-23 [καλῶς], 37).

[11]John thereby puts Jesus' words on a par with Scripture. See Carl J. Bjerkelund, *Tauta egeneto: Die Präzisierungssätze im Johannesevangelium* (WUNT 40; Tübingen: Mohr Siebeck, 1987), pp. 133-45.

ceiving" his "testimony," "hearing" and "believing"; many responded to his
words by believing in him (Jn 4:41-42; 7:31, 40; 8:30; 16:29-30; 17:8).[12] Depending on how people respond, his words have the effect either of cleansing
(Jn 15:3) and conveying eternal life or of bringing persons into judgment on the
last day (Jn 12:48; cf. 5:24; 6:63, 68; 8:31, 51-52).

What did Jesus say to make such a strong impression? Much in fact, despite
Rudolf Bultmann's claim that the Johannine Jesus "does not communicate anything, but calls men to himself." "Practically all the words of Jesus in John are
assertions about himself," yet "no definite complex of ideas can be stated as their
content and claimed to be the 'teaching' of Jesus." "Jesus as the Revealer of God
reveals nothing but that he is the Revealer. . . . John, that is, in his Gospel presents
only the fact (*das Dass*) of the Revelation without describing its content (*ihr
Was*). . . . He appears to retain in his book only the empty fact of the Revelation."[13]

Let us put Bultmann's assertions to the test. Using an edition of the New
Testament that prints the words of Christ in red ink, one can see at once that
these generalizations of Bultmann accurately describe many but not all of the
sayings ascribed to Jesus, covering 415 verses in all. The largest category consists of sayings in which Jesus talks about his relationship to God (121 verses =
29% of his words in the Gospel),[14] which we covered in the preceding chapter.
If we add those in which he claims to be the giver of life or light to people (65
verses = 16%),[15] we reach a sum of 178 verses, or 43 percent.[16] Logia in which
Jesus reproaches his naysayers for unbelief make up another 65 verses (16%).
These statements indirectly entail Jesus' claims concerning his person, for
usually it is because they reject his claims that he castigates antagonists; but
they also comprise a prophetic critique of the others.[17] Another group of asser-

---

[12]We will look at these motifs more fully in chapter seven.
[13]Rudolf Bultmann, *Theology of the New Testament* (trans. Kendrick Grobel; 2 vols.; New York: Scribner, 1951–1955), 2:41, 63, 66-67.
[14]Jn 1:51; 2:19; 3:11-13; 4:26, 32, 34; 5:17, 19-24, 26-27, 30-37, 43; 6:27, 38, 46, 62; 7:16-18, 28-29,
33-34; 8:14, 16-18, 21, 23, 25-26, 28-29, 35, 38, 40, 42, 49-50, 54-56, 58; 9:37, 39; 10:2-4, 7, 11, 15,
18, 25, 30, 31, 34-38; 12:44-45, 49-50; 14:4, 6-7, 9-11, 20; 16:28; 17:3-8, 10, 21-26; 18:4-5, 7-8, 20-21,
34, 36, 37; 19:28, 30; 20:15, 16, 27.
[15]Jn 2:7-8; 4:7, 10, 13-14, 50; 5:6, 8, 14, 21, 24-25, 28-29; 6:5, 10, 12, 20, 32-33, 35, 39-40, 48-51,
53-58, 63; 7:37-38; 8:12, 36; 9:3, 5, 7; 10:2-4, 7, 10-11, 15, 28; 11:4, 11, 14, 23, 25-26, 34, 39, 43, 44;
12:46-47; 14:4, 6; 15:1; 17:2. Here I include, besides explicit claims, the bits of conversation leading
up to each of the "signs."
[16]The sums have to be adjusted to account for the fact that I have classified eight verses (Jn 10:2-4,
7, 11, 15; 14:4, 6) in both lists.
[17]Jn 2:16; 3:10-12; 4:44, 48; 5:37-47; 6:26-27, 36, 43, 61, 64; 7:7, 19, 21-24; 8:15, 21, 23-24, 26, 34,
37-47, 55; 9:39, 41; 10:1, 5, 8, 10, 12-13, 25-26; 12:48; 15:21-25; 18:23; 19:11.

tions about himself have to do with his death (48 verses = 12%).[18] Thus far, roughly half to two-thirds of Jesus' teaching material in the Fourth Gospel has his own person and work for its subject.

The remaining third, while hardly detached from Jesus, focuses on related matters; on this material I will elaborate at the appropriate points in chapters six through eight. He points beyond his death to the dawn of a new era in salvation-history marked by his ascension, the giving of the Spirit, and the immediate foretaste of eschatological blessings to be perfected in the time of the end (41 verses = 10%).[19] He describes what it means to believe in him as the basic condition for being born of God (42 verses = 10%)[20] and lays down the nature, demands, rigors and privileges of being a disciple of his (66 verses = 16%).[21] Also there is a sizable body of teaching about the church and its mission (37 verses = 9%).[22]

All of these major categories and themes are amply paralleled in the Synoptic Gospels.[23] Bultmann's summary of the teaching of Jesus in the Fourth Gospel has a grain of truth, but it amounts to a caricature that exaggerates the differences between the Synoptic Gospels and John.[24] Bultmann minimizes those elements, such as salvation-history and ecclesiology, that do not fit into his existentialist reinterpretation.

***The deeds of Jesus as God's self-revelation.*** No less marvelous than Jesus' words were his "works." Qualitatively, Jesus did among people "the works which no one else did" (Jn 15:24). In number, "Were every one of them to be written, I suppose that the world itself could not contain the books that would

---

[18]Jn 2:4, 19; 3:14; 6:51, 53-57, 70; 7:6, 8, 19; 8:28-29, 37; 10:11, 15, 17-18; 12:7-8, 23, 27-28, 32; 13:7, 8, 11, 14, 18-19, 21, 26, 27, 31-32; 14:30-31; 15:18, 20, 23-25; 16:32; 17:1, 19; 18:11. These I will treat later in this chapter.

[19]Jn 4:21-24; 5:25; 7:37-38; 12:31; 13:33, 36; 14:1-3, 16-19, 25-29; 15:26; 16:5-16; 17:9, 11, 13; 20:17, 19, 26.

[20]Jn 3:3, 5-8; 4:14; 5:24-25; 6:29, 37, 44-45, 47; 7:37-38; 8:24, 51; 9:35; 10:2-4, 9, 14, 27; 11:15, 25-26, 40, 41-42; 12:30, 35-36, 44-45; 13:8; 14:4, 6; 17:12; 20:27, 29. These statements are concentrated in John 1–12.

[21]Jn 1:38, 39, 43; 6:67; 8:31-32; 9:4; 11:7, 9-10; 12:24-26; 13:10, 12-17, 34-35, 38; 14:12-15, 21, 23-24; 15:1-17; 16:19-27, 31-33; 21:15-18, 19, 22. A large proportion of these statements are found in John 13–16.

[22]Jn 4:35-38; 10:2-4, 16; 13:20; 15:8, 16, 18-21, 27; 16:1-4; 17:11, 14-18, 20-23; 20:21-23; 21:5-6, 10, 12. These statements come mostly from John 13–21.

[23]C. H. Dodd, *Historical Tradition in the Fourth Gospel* (Cambridge: Cambridge University Press, 1963), pp. 313-420.

[24]Simon J. Gathercole, *The Preexistent Son: Recovering the Christologies of Matthew, Mark, and Luke* (Grand Rapids: Eerdmans, 2006), p. 295.

be written" (Jn 21:25). As with his words, Jesus insisted that he did his deeds not on his own initiative but in imitation of his Father (Jn 5:17, 19-20, 30; 8:28), according to his Father's gift (Jn 5:36; 17:4) or will (Jn 4:34; 6:38; 14:31), in his Father's name (Jn 10:25), or by God acting in and through him (Jn 9:3-4; 10:32, 37-38; 14:10). He always did what pleased his Father (Jn 8:29), and he challenged opponents to dig up any taint that they could find on his record (Jn 8:46). As the "true vine" (Jn 15:1), he brought forth the kind of deeds God had looked for in vain from Israel (Is 5:1-7).[25]

Corresponding to Jesus' deeds is an emphasis throughout the Gospel on "seeing" and "believing." Some of the works of Jesus had a miraculous character that amazed onlookers (Jn 5:20; 7:21). His very works bore witness to him, prodding people to believe (Jn 5:36; 10:25, 38; 12:37; 14:11; 15:24; 20:30-31), and because of his works many did in fact believe in him (Jn 2:11, 23; 7:31; 9:16, 33; 11:45, 47-48; 12:18-19). So fundamental were Jesus' works that John can describe the whole Gospel as a collection of "signs," of "things Jesus did," selected to engender and strengthen faith (Jn 20:30-31; 21:25).[26]

***Signs as symbols of Jesus' power to give life and light.*** A special category of Jesus' works consists of miracles. John calls them "signs."[27] In themselves, the signs were displays on earth of supernatural power: Jesus turned water into wine, healed people, and so forth; and the general term "signs" is once collocated with "wonders" (τέρατα [Jn 4:48]). Beyond that, John sees the signs as symbolic pointers to the deeper meaning of the Son's work, establishing his claim to be the divine bringer of life and light to the human race in its relation to God. The signs, together with Jesus' words, were intended to awaken recognition that Jesus was the Messiah, the Son of God.[28]

---

[25]This theme of Jesus' good deeds continues in the Johannine Epistles, where Jesus is said to have been "righteous" (1 Jn 2:1, 6) and "pure" (1 Jn 3:3, 5-7), the paragon for all believers.

[26]Wolfgang J. Bittner, *Jesu Zeichen im Johannesevangelium* (WUNT 2/26; Tübingen: Mohr Siebeck, 1987); Frank Lynn Crouch, "Everyone Who Sees the Son: Signs, Faith, Peirces's Semeiotics, and the Gospel of John" (Ph.D. diss.; Duke University, 1996); Hanna Roose, "Joh 20,30f.: Ein (un)passender Schluss? John 9 und 11 als primäre Verweisstellen der Schlussnotiz des Johannesevangeliums," *Bib* 84 (2003): 326-43.

[27]σημεῖον (Jn 2:11, 18, 23; 3:2; 4:48, 54; 6:2, 14, 26, 30; 7:31; 9:16; 10:41; 11:47; 12:18, 37; 20:30).

[28]If there is a difference in connotation between the miracles John calls "works" and those he calls "signs," as Rudolf Schnackenburg holds (*The Gospel According to St. John* [trans. Kevin Smyth et al.; 3 vols.; New York: Herder & Herder; Seabury; Crossroad, 1968–1982], 1:518-25), it will be that "works" designates them intrinsically as operations of God's power through Jesus, while "signs" points to the message that they proclaim about the good things that Jesus can do for people. On Jesus' "signs," see W. D. Davies, "The Johannine 'Signs' of Jesus," in *A Companion to John: Readings in Johannine Theology (John's Gospel and Epistles)* (ed. Michael J. Taylor; New York: Alba House,

In the first half of John's Gospel, sometimes labeled the "Book of Signs," seven classic miracles are usually identified.[29]

1. Changing water into wine at the wedding feast of Cana (Jn 2:1-11)

2. Restoring a royal official's son at Capernaum from a mortal disease to life (Jn 4:46-54)

3. Restoring an invalid by the pool of Bethzatha to health (Jn 5:1-9)

4. Feeding five thousand men in the wilderness by the Sea of Galilee (Jn 6:1-14)

5. Walking on the choppy sea and bringing the disciples' boat to safe harbor (Jn 6:16-21)

6. Opening the eyes of a man born blind near the pool of Siloam, Jerusalem (Jn 9:1-7)

7. Raising Lazarus from the grave (Jn 11:1-44)

Of these the first two, the middle one, and the last two John calls "signs" (he uses the word in Jn 2:11; 4:54; 6:14; 9:16; 11:47; 12:18). Within the pages of the Gospel there are occasional references to Jesus' "signs" in the plural, indicating that John has selected a few out of many (Jn 2:23; 3:2; 6:2, 14, 26; 7:31; 9:16; 11:47; 12:37). At the end he says that Jesus did many other signs that are not written in this book (Jn 20:30). Each of the sign accounts has been carefully crafted by John to bring out the contribution it makes to his overarching theme of Jesus as the life and light of human beings (Jn 1:4).

Literary analysis shows that the event in Cana rounds off John's introduction

---

1970), pp. 91-115; William Nicol, *The Sēmeia in the Fourth Gospel: Tradition and Redaction* (NovTSup 32; Leiden: Brill, 1972); C. K. Barrett, *The Gospel According to St. John* (2nd ed.; Philadelphia: Westminster, 1978), pp. 75-78; Michael Labahn, *Jesus als Lebensspender: Untersuchungen zu einer Geschichte der johanneischen Tradition anhand ihrer Wundergeschichten* (BZNW 98; Berlin: de Gruyter, 1999); idem, "Between Tradition and Literary Art: The Miracle Tradition in the Fourth Gospel," *Bib* 80 (1999): 178-203; Willis Hedley Salier, *The Rhetorical Impact of the Sēmeia in the Gospel of John* (WUNT 2/186; Tübingen: Mohr Siebeck, 2004); R. Alan Culpepper, "Cognition in John: The Johannine Signs as Recognition Scenes," *PRSt* 35 (2008): 251-60.

[29]Jesus' cleansing of the temple in 2:13-22 is not one of the signs, despite the proposal of Andreas J. Köstenberger, "The Seventh Johannine Sign: A Study in John's Christology," *BBR* 5 (1995): 87-103. Although it is like the prophetic acts of the Old Testament, it does not share the supernatural character of the Johannine signs, John does not call it a "sign," and his specific numeration of the signs in John 2:11; 4:54 excludes it. On the seven wonder stories as Jesus' signs in the Fourth Gospel, see the massive form-critical analysis by Labahn, *Lebensspender*, especially his comments on the number "seven" and its numerological significance (pp. 493-502); Franz Zeilinger, *Die sieben Zeichenhandlungen Jesu im Johannesevangelium* (Stuttgart: Kohlhammer, 2011).

of Christ in John 1:19–2:11, since it took place "on the third day" (Jn 2:1) after an earlier series of four days ("next day" [Jn 1:29, 35, 43]), completing the initial week that began in John 1:19. Following the solemn "In the beginning" in John 1:1, this week corresponds to the first week of creation and points to Jesus as the one who ushers in the new heaven and new earth. Stone water jars for Jewish rites of purification (Jn 2:6) evoke the water of the Baptist (Jn 1:26, 33),[30] which the forerunner promised would soon give way to baptism with the Holy Spirit by the coming one (Jn 1:33). Wine was a symbol in the Old Testament prophets of the eschatological feast when death will be done away with (Is 26:6-8) and of the joy of the everlasting age to come (e.g., Joel 2:19; Amos 9:14; Mic 4:4). By changing water into wine, Jesus gave a figure of the inbreaking of those promised blessings through his presence.[31] This first of Jesus' signs continues to reverberate as Jesus explains to Nicodemus that "that which is born of the flesh is flesh, and that which is born of the Spirit is spirit" (Jn 3:6) and in Jesus' claim to the woman at the well that he can give water that will become "a spring of water welling up to eternal life" (Jn 4:13-14).

John's account of the healing of the official's son, compared to the corresponding story in Q material (Mt 8:5-13; Lk 7:1-10), underscores more strongly the fatal condition of the son (stating twice that he was about to die [Jn 4:47, 49]) and, in contrast, the life-bringing power of Jesus' word by emphasizing thrice that the son "lived" (Jn 4:50, 51, 53).

That Jesus made the invalid at Bethzatha "healthy" (ὑγιής) is stated no fewer than six times by John (Jn 5:6, 9, 11, 14, 15; 7:23), accounting for over half of all the occurrences of this rare adjective in the New Testament.[32]

Bread sustains life (Deut 8:3). The Johannine dialogue following the feeding of the five thousand explicitly makes Jesus, and especially his death, the basis of eternal life (Jn 6:22, 33, 35, 40, 47, 48, 51, 54, 58, 63, 68).[33]

---

[30]Note the same association between Jewish purity and John's baptism in John 3:23-25.

[31]Among aspects of meaning discovered in the long history of exegesis of this pericope are the manifestation of Jesus' deity and specifically of his creatorship, his ending of the period of the old covenant, and his gift of the experience of the new existence. See Adolf Smitmans, *Das Weinwunder von Kana: Die Auslegung von Jo 2,1-11 bei den Vätern und heute* (BGBE 6; Tübingen: Mohr Siebeck, 1966), pp. 37-64, 153-261.

[32]On archaeological attempts to pin down the physical setting of the healing, see Urban C. von Wahlde, "The Pool(s) of Bethesda and the Healing in John 5: A Reappraisal of Research and of the Johannine Text," *RB* 116 (2009): 111-36; on the name, see Reinhart Ceulemans, "The Name of the Pool in Joh 5,2: A Text-Critical Note Concerning 3Q15," *ZNW* 99 (2008): 112-15.

[33]Michael Labahn, "Controversial Revelation in Deed and Word: The Feeding of the Five Thousand and Jesus' Crossing of the Sea as a 'Prelude' to the Johannine Bread of Life Discourse," *IBS* 22 (2000):

Jesus walks on the sea right after the feeding miracle in John as in the Synoptic tradition, within the next few hours that same evening (Mt 14:22-33; Mk 6:45-52). John alone adds the detail "immediately the boat was at the land to which they were going" (Jn 6:21). This may recall Psalm 107:30: "and he brought them to their desired haven." Sandwiched between the feeding (Jn 6:1-14) and the discussion of its meaning (Jn 6:25-71), this miracle doubles the former and makes the same point in a different way, that Jesus is the Son of Man who came down from heaven to bring life to the world (e.g., Jn 6:33).

Jesus' opening of the eyes of a blind man shows him to be the light of the world (Jn 8:12; 9:5) so "that those who do not see may see" (Jn 9:39)—that is, may experience a reversal of the stultifying effects of sin on the heart (Jn 8:34, 43-45).[34]

From a literary perspective, John develops the story of the raising of Lazarus more fully than any other sign. It is the final one in his chosen sequence and the most dramatic. It sums up the message of all the signs.[35] Its portrayal of Jesus as the giver of life is patent: it is a narrative presentation of Jesus' power to initiate the eschatological resurrection of the dead, even now.[36]

A deeper look through the miracles to the power of Jesus to bring life and light marks John's distinctive view of them.

**Mutual reinforcement between Jesus' words and deeds.** John does not segregate Jesus' words from his deeds as I have just done. His narrative interweaves them to demonstrate that "in him was life, and the life was the light of men" (Jn 1:4).

Prominent among the many sayings of Jesus in John's Gospel are seven self-referential predications having the general form, "I am the . . .":

1. "I am the bread of life" (Jn 6:35, 48; cf. 6:41, 50, 51, 58).

2. "I am the light of the world" (Jn 8:12; 9:5).

3. "I am the door of the sheep" (Jn 10:7; cf. 10:9).

---

146-81; K. Scholtissek, "Die Brotrede Jesu in Joh 6,1-71: Exegetische Beobachtungen zu ihrem johanneischen Profil," *ZKT* 123 (2001): 35-55; Mira Stare, *Durch ihn leben: Die Lebensthematik in Joh 6* (NTAbh 49; Münster: Aschendorff, 2004); Roger David Aus, *Feeding the Five Thousand: Studies in the Judaic Background of Mark 6:30-44 par. and John 6:1-15* (SJ; Lanham, MD: University Press of America, 2010).

[34]J.-M. Maldamé, "Quand Jésus guérit: Une lecture théologique de la guérison de l'aveugle-né (Jn 9)," *EV* 112 (2002): 9-15.

[35]Stephen S. Kim, "The Significance of Jesus' Raising Lazarus from the Dead in John 11:1-44," *BSac* 168 (2011): 53-62.

[36]Otfried Hofius, "Die Auferweckung des Lazarus: Joh 11,1-44 als Zeugnis narrativer Christologie," *ZTK* 102 (2005): 17-34.

4. "I am the good shepherd" (Jn 10:11, 14).

5. "I am the resurrection and the life" (Jn 11:25).

6. "I am the way, the truth, and the life" (Jn 14:6).

7. "I am the true vine" (Jn 15:1; cf. 15:5).[37]

A glance at these statements shows that they present Jesus as one who meets the most basic of human needs: nourishment, illumination, shelter, security, direction and purpose. Each metaphor, like the signs, points beyond the earthly plane. John understands the world of physical reality to offer plentiful analogies to the verities of the world of spirit.

Although there is no simple one-to-one correspondence between these self-predications of Jesus and the seven signs, there is an evident relationship.[38] "I am the bread of life" emerges out of the dialogue (Jn 6:25-58) that follows the feeding of the five thousand (Jn 6:1-14). The opening of the blind man's eyes (Jn 9:1-7) comes just after Jesus twice declares, "I am the light of the world" (Jn 8:12; 9:5). That Jesus is both the door of a special sheepfold and the shepherd of those who hear his voice he states at a point in his ministry when people have divided over the significance of his signs and many have excluded themselves from the body of his followers (Jn 9:16, 39). Jesus claims to be the resurrection and the life as he is on the point of raising Lazarus (Jn 11:1-44). That Jesus is the universal and exclusive way to God, the very reality of God among humans, and the source of the life that God has to give them (Jn 14:6) gathers up the message of all the healings and rescues. The last "I am" statement, that Jesus is the vine, echoes the first of the signs, his making water into wine.

***Responses to Jesus' person in his words and deeds.*** A person becomes manifest by saying and doing things. To receive someone's words, to respond positively to someone's deeds, is to welcome the person. Some did not receive Jesus'

---

[37]Classic literature on this group of sayings includes Eduard Schweizer, *EGO EIMI: Die religionsgeschichtliche Herkunft und theologische Bedeutung der johanneischen Bildreden, zugleich ein Beitrag zur Quellenfrage des vierten Evangeliums* (2nd ed.; FRLANT 38; Göttingen: Vandenhoeck & Ruprecht, 1965); Raymond E. Brown, "The *EGO EIMI* ('I Am') Passages in the Fourth Gospel," in *A Companion to John: Readings in Johannine Theology (John's Gospel and Epistles)* (ed. Michael J. Taylor; New York: Alba House, 1970), pp. 118-20. More recently, increasingly sophisticated methods have made it ever more difficult to pin John's language to a particular cultural background in antiquity, suggesting that he has deliberately used polysemous, transcultural metaphors. See Silke Petersen, *Brot, Licht und Weinstock: Intertextuelle Analysen johanneischer Ich-bin-Worte* (NovTSup 127; Leiden: Brill, 2008).

[38]Leon Morris, *Jesus Is the Christ: Studies in the Theology of John* (Grand Rapids: Eerdmans, 1989), pp. 20-42.

testimony (Jn 3:11, 32). Snubbing it, they did not receive him (Jn 1:11; 5:43; 12:48). Others received Jesus' testimony (Jn 3:33), and in doing so welcomed him (Jn 1:12, 16; 17:8). Jesus made disciples of those who received his words and deeds (Jn 1:35-51). But the world at large did not know him (Jn 1:10-11, 26; 8:19; 16:3; 1 Jn 3:1). It hated him (Jn 3:20; 7:7; 15:18, 23-25).

Ostensible reasons his enemies gave for hating Jesus were that his words were those of a madman inspired by a demon (Jn 7:20; 8:48, 52; 10:20), and that he could not be a good man because among his deeds were persistent violations of the Sabbath commandment (Jn 5:9-16; 7:19-24; 9:16). Jesus met the latter charge by arguing that he was doing as his Father does, who sustains life on the Sabbath (Jn 5:17). If it is allowable to suspend Sabbath observance to circumcise a part of the body, then is a healer disallowed from bringing health to a whole person on the Sabbath (Jn 7:22-24)? Others countered the calumny that his words were demonic by asking whether a demon can open blind eyes (Jn 10:21). Jesus himself cut to the real reason why the world hated him: he testified of it that its works were evil (Jn 7:7). The unrighteous have always hated the righteous without cause (Jn 15:25).

Although it was necessary for the world to reject Jesus because the Scriptures themselves had predicted this (Jn 12:37-41), Jesus' testimony to the world in John 1–12 concludes with a little paragraph, rich in Johannine idioms, that makes one final appeal (Jn 12:44-50). The narrator observes the irony of people not having believed "although he had done so many signs [τοσαῦτα σημεῖα] in their presence" (Jn 12:37). Jesus' last word, which he "cried aloud" (ἔκραξεν καὶ εἶπεν [Jn 12:44]), states once more that he came as light into the world (Jn 12:46) and goes on to refer to his "words" (ῥήματα [Jn 12:47, 48]) and to the "word" (λόγος [Jn 12:48]) that he "spoke" (λαλέω [5× in Jn 12:48-50]; εἶπον [1×]) at the Father's behest. John thus closes the first half of his Gospel with a twin emphasis on Jesus' signs and words that showed him to be God's emissary.

## GLORIFICATION OF THE FATHER IN THE SON

John interprets the climax of Jesus' ministry through the motif of "glory" (δόξα) or "glorification" (δοξασθῆναι [lit., "to be glorified"]).[39] Jesus' glory is, as Ernst

---

[39]The most thorough and wide-ranging studies of this oft-noted theme to date are Nicole Chibici-Revneanu, *Die Herrlichkeit des Verherrlichten: Das Verständnis der* doxa *im Johannesevangelium* (WUNT 2/231; Tübingen: Mohr Siebeck, 2007); Rainer Schwindt, *Geschichte der Herrlichkeit: Eine exegetisch-traditionsgeschichtliche Studie zur paulinischen und johanneischen Christologie* (HBS 50; Freiburg: Herder, 2007). See also Johannes Beutler, "Die Ehre Gottes und die Ehre der Menschen

Käsemann correctly observed, a theme of the whole Gospel, broached already in the prologue. "We have beheld his glory, glory as of the only-begotten from the Father" (Jn 1:14).[40] John understands Jesus' glory, initially at least, in the ordinary way, as a splendor attaching to Jesus' words and deeds, indicating the divine identity of their speaker and doer.[41] The water-to-wine miracle manifested his glory (Jn 2:11); by extension, Jesus' glory shines in all the signs. Each time Jesus was glorified, he brought glory to God (Jn 11:4, 40; 12:28; 13:31-32; 14:13; 15:8; 17:1). Jesus sought and received glory from his Father, not from society (Jn 5:41, 44; 7:18; 8:50, 54). There are several references to an eternal glory that Jesus left behind when he became incarnate and in which he was reinstated on finishing his earthly work (Jn 17:5, 22, 24).[42]

Most characteristic of John is his use of the aorist tense, "was glorified" (ἐδοξάσθη), to denote the entire complex of steps that Jesus passed in returning to heaven, including his crucifixion, resurrection and ascension (Jn 7:39; 12:16, 23 [subjunctive]; 13:31).[43] It is important to see that John does not apply the motif of glory to the death of Jesus on the cross in isolation from the events that followed, but unites it with them under the rubric of Jesus' glory. For example, in the fundamental statement of John 12:24 Jesus compares himself to a seed that must die in the earth to become fruitful. Jesus' glorification consists in the bounty that results (Jn 12:23), not in the planting and dissolution of the seed per se. This is not to deny John's art of paradox where the death is concerned,[44] but to keep that in its total context.

Other vocabulary items that John uses to denote events at the end of Jesus' career are not always as carefully distinguished by commentators as they are by John. Three times in the early part of the Gospel, when talking to Jews, Jesus predicts that the Son of Man will be "lifted up" (ὑψόω [Jn 3:14; 8:28; 12:32, 34]). As is indicated by one of the narrator's comments, "He said this to show by what

---

im Johannesevangelium," *GL* 76 (2003): 83-91; Jörg Frey, "'. . . dass sie meine Herrlichkeit schauen' (Joh 17,24): Zur Hintergrund, Sinn und Funktion der johanneischen Rede von der δόξα Jesus," *NTS* 54 (2008): 375-97.

[40]Ernst Käsemann, *The Testament of Jesus: A Study of the Gospel of John in the Light of Chapter 17* (trans. Gerhard Krodel; Philadelphia: Fortress, 1968), pp. 4-26.

[41]Jesper Tang Nielsen, "The Narrative Structures of Glory and Glorification in the Fourth Gospel," *NTS* 56 (2010): 343-66.

[42]In the Apocalypse John consistently uses "glory" (17×) and "glorify" (Apoc 15:4; 18:7) in their usual doxological senses. In Apocalypse 21:23 it is said that, instead of the sun, the glory of God will illumine the new Jerusalem in the age to come.

[43]Compare the futures tenses in John 13:32 and the aorist imperatives in John 17:1, 5.

[44]The element of paradox is rightly noted in Chibici-Revneanu, *Herrlichkeit*, pp. 616, 618.

death he was to die" (Jn 12:33), John has in mind primarily the literal hoisting of Jesus on the cross. But the word ὑψόω is a curious choice. Usually it means "make high, exalt," and we probably should recognize a Johannine double entendre pointing to the crucifixion as the apex of divine love to the eye of faith.[45] Perhaps John's peculiar usage of ὑψωθῆναι was influenced by LXX Isaiah 52:13: "He will be supremely exalted [ὑψωθήσεται] and glorified [δοξασθήσεται]," followed immediately by Isaiah's description of the sufferings of the Lord's servant.[46] "Going up" (ἀναβαίνειν) and "going away" (ὑπάγειν, πορεύεσθαι, ἀπελθεῖν), however, never refer to the crucifixion; they always designate the subsequent ascension and departure, respectively, of the heavenly envoy to his celestial home.[47] The distinction in usage between "to be lifted up" (ὑψωθῆναι) on the one hand, and "to go up" or "to go away" on the other, corresponds broadly to that between the culmination of Christ's earthly work and the divine origin and destiny of his person. All these concepts are related and are components of his "being glorified" (δοξασθῆναι).

Bultmann rightly grasped Jesus' glorification as a whole, but he confounded matters by contending that for John, Jesus' crucifixion, exaltation and glorification blend into an atemporal unity, so that the resurrection has no special significance.[48] While it is true that these events form a single progression and should be viewed together, John never loses his grip on chronology. Jesus died on a Friday (the "day of preparation" for the Sabbath [Jn 19:31, 42]), rose on "the first day of the week" (i.e., Sunday [Jn 20:1]), and appeared to Mary Magdalene later that same day when he had "not yet ascended to the Father" (Jn 20:17).

*Literary movement toward the cross.* John has integrated the passion ac-

---

[45]On the device, see David W. Wead, *The Literary Devices in John's Gospel* (TD 4; Basel: Friedrich Reinhardt Kommissionsverlag, 1970), pp. 30-46; Jan G. van der Watt, "*Double Entendre* in the Gospel According to John," in *Theology and Christology in the Fourth Gospel: Essays by Members of the SNTS Johannine Writings Seminar* (ed. Gilbert van Belle, Jan G. van der Watt and P. J. Maritz; BETL 184; Leuven: Leuven University Press, 2005), pp. 463-81. For the deeper sense of the phrase in John, see John W. Romanowsky, "'When the Son of Man is Lifted Up': The Redemptive Power of the Crucifixion in the Gospel of John," *Hor* 32 (2005): 100-116; Thomas Söding, "Kreuzerhöhung: Zur Deutung des Todes Jesu nach Johannes," *ZTK* 103 (2006): 2-25; Hellen Mardaga, "The Repetitive Use of ὑψόω in the Fourth Gospel," *CBQ* 74 (2012): 101-17.
[46]Wilhelm Thüsing, *Die Erhöhung und Verherrlichung Jesu im Johannesevangelium* (3rd ed.; NTAbh 21; Münster: Aschendorff, 1979), pp. 36-37; Chibici-Revneanu, *Herrlichkeit*, p. 614. But, contra Thüsing (pp. 31-33, 289-91), none of the three sayings in question contains any hint of an "enthronement."
[47]Martinus C. de Boer, "Jesus' Departure to the Father in John: Death or Resurrection?" in van Belle, van der Watt and Maritz, *Theology and Christology*, pp. 1-19. De Boer rightly takes Käsemann to task for stating that "to depart" (ὑπάγειν) is John's characteristic description of Jesus' death.
[48]Bultmann, *Theology*, 2:48, 52-53, 56.

count into the rest of the Gospel by means of a number of literary and thematic devices.[49] Up front the Baptist introduces Jesus as "the Lamb of God, who takes away the sin of the world" (Jn 1:29; cf. 1:35). With the first of Jesus' signs the literary motif of Jesus' "hour" (ὥρα) or "time" (καιρός) begins to tick (Jn 2:4), building inexorable momentum toward his glorification: "For this purpose I have come [ἦλθον] to this hour" (Jn 12:27).[50] That Jesus should die was the divine plan, for it was determined (δεῖ [Jn 3:14]), it was the Father's specific command to Jesus (Jn 10:18; 14:31), and by doing so he fulfilled the Scriptures.[51]

Besides the sayings about his coming hour, Jesus spoke, according to John, often and from early on about his looming death. As Moses lifted up the serpent, so must the Son of Man be lifted up (Jn 3:14). The bread that Jesus would give for the life of the world was to be his flesh and blood, which people must eat to have eternal life (Jn 6:51, 53-57). One of his disciples he knew to be a devil (Jn 6:70). He was aware the authorities in Jerusalem were seeking to kill him and would lift him up in due course (Jn 7:19; 8:37, 40), but his Father had not abandoned him (Jn 8:28-29). A good shepherd lays down his life for the sheep (Jn 10:11, 15); this Jesus would do voluntarily, having received it as a charge from his

---

[49]Margaret Davies, *Rhetoric and Reference in the Fourth Gospel* (JSNTSup 69; Sheffield: Sheffield Academic Press, 1992), p. 54; Jean Zumstein, "L'interpretation johannique de la mort du Christ," in vol. 3 of *The Four Gospels 1992: Festschrift Frans Neirynck* (ed. Frans van Segbroeck et al.; BETL 100; Leuven: Leuven University Press, 1992), pp. 2119-38; Esther Straub, *Kritische Theologie ohne ein Wort vom Kreuz: Zum Verhältnis von Joh 1–12 und 13–20* (FRLANT 203; Göttingen: Vandenhoeck & Ruprecht, 2003); Ulrich Wilckens, "Christus traditus se ipsum tradens: Zum johanneischen Verständnis des Kreuzestodes Jesu," in *Der Sohn Gottes und seine Gemeinde: Studien zur Theologie der Johanneischen Schriften* (FRLANT 200; Göttingen: Vandenhoeck & Ruprecht, 2003), pp. 29-55; Jean-Marie Sevrin, "L'intrigue du quatrième évangile, ou la christologie mise en récit," *RTL* 37 (2006): 473-88; Gilbert van Belle, "The Death of Jesus and the Literary Unity of the Fourth Gospel," in *The Death of Jesus in the Fourth Gospel* (ed. Gilbert van Belle; BETL 200; Leuven: Leuven University Press, 2007), pp. 3-64; Udo Schnelle, "Cross and Resurrection in the Gospel of John," in *The Resurrection of Jesus in the Gospel of John* (ed. Craig R. Koester and Reimund Bieringer; WUNT 222; Tübingen: Mohr Siebeck, 2008), pp. 127-51.

[50]See also John 2:4; 7:6, 8, 30; 8:20; 9:4; 11:9-10; 12:1-8, 23, 27; 13:1; 17:1. See Thomas Knöppler, *Die theologia crucis des Johannesevangeliums: Das Verständnis des Todes Jesu im Rahmen der johanneischen Inkarnations- und Erhöhungschristologie* (WMANT 69; Neukirchen-Vluyn: Neukirchener Verlag, 1994), pp. 102-15; Dirk G. van der Merwe, "Ὥρα, A Possible Theological Setting for Understanding Johannine Eschatology," *APB* 13 (2002): 255-87.

[51]See John 2:17 (quoting Ps 69:9); 13:18 (quoting Ps 41:9; 17:12); 19:23-24 (citing Ps 22:18), 28 (thinking of Ps 69:21), 31-37 (quoting Ps 34:20 in v. 36, and Zech 12:10 in v. 37). The citation formula in John 1–12 is always a form of "it is written" (γεγραμμένον ἐστιν), but from the moment when Jesus announces that his hour has come (Jn 12:23), the formula becomes "that it may be fulfilled" (ἵνα πληρωθῇ). See Craig A. Evans, "On the Quotation Formulas in the Fourth Gospel," *BZ* 26 (1982): 79-83. On John's concept of fulfillment, see Nicolas Farelly, "Lire le Psaume 69 (68) en Jean 2,13-22," *ETR* 86 (2011): 195-207; Brian J. Tabb, "Johannine Fulfillment of Scripture: Continuity and Escalation," *BBR* 21 (2011): 495-505.

Father (Jn 10:17-18). In a Johannine equivalent to the Synoptic "He set his face to go to Jerusalem" (Lk 9:51), which caused fear and amazement among his disciples (Mk 10:32), Jesus resolutely proposed the final entry into Judea over their sensible objections to such a reckless course (Jn 11:7-16). Jesus defended Mary of Bethany's sacrifice of costly ointment: "Let her keep it for the day of my burial" (Jn 12:7). On being lifted up from the earth, Jesus was destined to draw all people to himself (Jn 12:32). At the Last Supper the disciples did not yet understand that Jesus' act of washing their feet prefigured his death to cleanse them, without which they would have no part in him; afterward they would know it (Jn 13:7-8, 11, 14). During the meal Jesus commissioned Judas to do his deed of treachery (Jn 13:11, 18-19, 21, 26-27). When Judas had gone out into the night, Jesus began to prepare the rest of the disciples for his passion, death, and departure (Jn 13:31-33). The ruler of the world was already on his way to do his worst; Jesus submitted only because the Father had commanded him (Jn 14:30-31). He knew full well that the world hated him and would persecute him (Jn 15:18, 20, 23-25). His disciples would be scattered, but the Father would stick with him (Jn 16:32). Jesus consecrated himself so that his disciples might be consecrated (Jn 17:19). He drank the cup that the Father was giving him (Jn 18:11).

Not only did Jesus expect death, but also the writer has structured the narrative so that the reader can follow the machinations of his enemies to bring it about. To Jesus' cleansing of the temple the authorities reacted with hostility (Jn 2:18). For his healing a man on the Sabbath they sought to kill him (Jn 5:18). He had to withdraw to Galilee, knowing that the rulers of Judea were out for his skin (Jn 7:1, 25). There were several abortive attempts to arrest him (Jn 7:30, 32, 44; 8:20; 10:39; 11:57) or to stone him (Jn 8:59; 10:31-33). About walking deliberately into jaws of malevolence his disciples had severe doubts (Jn 11:8, 16). A unique scene takes readers into the very chamber of the Sanhedrin, led by Caiaphas, where the leaders debated their course of action and settled on eliminating Jesus (Jn 11:47-53).[52] Having no specific criminal charge to pin on this "evildoer," their appeal to the Roman prefect betrays their aim to secure a capital penalty (Jn 18:31-32).

---

[52]The source of this history probably was Nicodemus, one of their number who sympathized with Jesus (Jn 7:50-51; 19:39-40), or it was someone like him (cf. Jn 12:42; Acts 6:7). On the role of the pericope in the Gospel narrative, see Tobias Nicklas, "Die Prophetie des Kajaphas: Im Netz johanneischer Ironie," *NTS* 46 (2000): 589-94; John A. Dennis, "Conflict and Resolution: John 11.47-53 as the Ironic Fulfillment of the Main Plot-Line of the Gospel (John 1.11-12)," *SNTSU* 29 (2004): 23-39.

Thus John has made several lines of his Gospel converge on Jesus' glorification, including his death, as its goal.[53] If the Synoptic Gospels are passion narratives with extended introductions,[54] the Fourth Gospel is an extended passion narrative.[55]

***Jesus' death as demonstration of Jesus' love for the Father.*** Jesus participated in the divine plan that led to his death out of free and voluntary love for his Father. That Jesus was not a victim of circumstance, but chose in obedience to his Father's will to submit to the earthly forces that pinned him to the cross, is a point of emphasis in the Synoptic tradition (Mt 26:53-54; Mk 10:32; Lk 9:51). John is even more emphatic: Jesus lays down his life and takes it up again of his own accord; no one takes it from him; he has power both to lay it down and to take it up (Jn 10:17-18). The ruler of this world has no power over him; Jesus acts only as the Father has commanded him (Jn 14:30-31). Jesus' majestic bearing throughout the passion account—knowing in advance all that was to befall him (Jn 18:4), bowling over his soon-to-be captors by declaring his identity (Jn 18:4-8), demanding the release of his disciples (Jn 18:8-9), rebuking Peter for wielding a sword in his defense (Jn 18:10-11), convicting Annas of holding an irregular interrogation (Jn 18:19-23), claiming before Pilate a kingship above this world (Jn 18:36), pronouncing divine judgment on the Roman and Jewish authorities (Jn 19:11), shouldering his own cross (Jn 19:17), providing for his mother's care (Jn 19:25-27), bowing his head and and actively giving up his spirit (Jn 19:30)—shows him to have been unconstrained all the way to the bitter end.

Only once in the Johannine literature is Jesus said to love the Father, and it is just before his death: "I do as the Father has commanded me, so that the world

---

[53]Günther Bornkamm ("Towards the Interpretation of John's Gospel: A Discussion of *The Testament of Jesus*," in *The Interpretation of John* [ed. John Ashton; IRT 9; Philadelphia: Fortress, 1986], pp. 88-89) demolished Käsemann's notion that the passion account of the Fourth Gospel is nothing more than "a mere postscript which had to be included because John could not ignore this tradition nor yet could he fit it organically into his work" (*Testament*, p. 7). Ashton (*Understanding*, pp. 485-90) acknowledges this, adding, "On the level of technical exegesis [Käsemann] is easy to fault"; yet he wants somehow to redeem Käsemann by pleading that "the essence of his argument is not so much exegetical as theological" (p. 488). If exegesis is the proper basis of theology, however, Käsemann's hearing is over.

[54]Martin Kähler described Mark in this way (*The So-Called Historical Jesus and the Historic, Biblical Christ* [trans. Carl E. Braaten; Philadelphia: Fortress, 1964], p. 80n11).

[55]Rudolf Schnackenburg can speak of "the whole way of redemption from the Incarnation to the 'lifting up' as a redemptive happening" (*St. John*, 1:158). See also Jörg Frey, "Zur johanneischen Deutung des Todes Jesu," *TBei* 32 (2002): 346-62.

may know that I love the Father" (Jn 14:31). For this reason, the Father loves him (Jn 10:17). Thus the Father's eternal love for the Son is confirmed (Jn 3:35; 5:20; 15:9-10; 17:23-24, 26), and is reciprocated by the Son, precisely at the cross.

*Jesus' death as manifestation of God's love for Jesus' disciples.* Concurrently with the glory of God and of Jesus (Jn 12:23, 27-28), Jesus' love for his disciples becomes thematic in John 13–21. "Having loved his own who were in the world, he loved them to the end" (Jn 13:1). This is the topic sentence for the remaining chapters of the Gospel; what happens hereafter is demonstration.[56] Statistics bear this out. Twelve occurrences of words for "love" precede this sentence; forty-five follow.[57] The disciple beloved of Jesus makes his appearance in the narrative (Jn 13:23; 19:26; 20:2; 21:7, 20). Jesus' love for his disciples becomes the ground of a new commandment for the community and is the model for them to emulate in loving one another (Jn 13:34-35; 15:12-13, 17). Jesus reassures the disciples of his love for them (Jn 15:9-10) and implies that he will express it concretely above all by dying for them (Jn 15:13).

Like the Gospel, John's other writings view Jesus' death or blood as the supreme act of divine love. The new commandment to love one another is "true in him" (1 Jn 2:8); he realized its content by his action. "By this we know love, that he laid down his life for us" (1 Jn 3:16). God's love for the world is manifest in this, that he sent the Son into the world, to be the propitiation for our sins (1 Jn 4:9-10). "To him who loves us and has freed us from our sins by his blood . . . to him be glory" (Apoc 1:5-6).

*A substitutionary, vicarious death.* John's writings offer perspectives on the meaning of the death of Jesus from many angles.[58] John offers no single reigning theory of atonement, but rather a body of metaphors, each a facet of a many-sided truth. This is so in the Gospel alone;[59] it is all the more so if we admit the Epistles and the Apocalypse as productions of the same mind.

For John, the death of Jesus was substitutionary, representative and vicar-

---

[56]André Feuillet, *Le mystère de l'amour divin dans la théologie johannique* (EBib; Paris: Gabalda, 1972), pp. 53-132, 181.

[57]Focusing on just ἀγάπη/ἀγαπᾶν, Michael Lattke counts six occurrences in John 1–12, and thirty-one in John 13–17 ("Einheit im Wort: Die spezifische Bedeutung von ἀγάπη, ἀγαπᾶν und φιλεῖν im Johannesevangelium" [Ph.D. diss., University of Freiburg, 1973], pp. 31-32).

[58]Martinus C. de Boer, *Johannine Perspectives on the Death of Jesus* (CBET 17; Kampen: Kok Pharos, 1996); Jintae Kim, "The Concept of Atonement in the Gospel of John," *JGRCJ* 6 (2009): 9-27.

[59]Charles A. Gieschen, "The Death of Jesus in the Gospel of John: Atonement for Sin?" *CTQ* 72 (2008): 243-61.

ious.[60] In places he speaks of Jesus dying "for" people in such a way that ὑπέρ with the genitive is equivalent to ἀντί with the genitive, "in place of, in exchange for."[61] As a shepherd might risk his life to deliver his flock from a marauding pack of wolves, so Jesus laid down his life "for [ὑπέρ] the sheep" (Jn 10:11, 15). Here the illustration requires not only that the sheep benefit from the shepherd's protective action,[62] but also that the shepherd interpose himself between them and the threat, so that the shepherd takes the brunt of it on their behalf, in their stead. This is confirmed by John's interpretation of the advice of Caiaphas to the Jewish council: "It is expedient for you that one man should die for the people [ὑπέρ τοῦ λαοῦ], and that the whole nation should not perish" (Jn 11:50 [cf. 18:14]). One man is to die instead of the many whom the Romans would otherwise punish. Caiaphas meant that it was prudent to surrender one Jew rather than involve the body politic in deeper trouble with their overlords. John holds this to be a serendipitous prophecy by the high priest that Jesus would "perish" (ἀπόληται, the same word that denotes divine judgment in Jn 3:16) in place of the nation (ὑπέρ τοῦ ἔθνους), and not "for" the nation only but also "for" other children of God (Jn 11:51-52). The proverbial statement "No one has greater love than this, to lay down one's life for one's friends [ὑπέρ τῶν φίλων αὐτοῦ]" (Jn 15:13) is most poignant when the friends are in peril, and the one forfeits life for theirs. As the disciples' representative, Jesus says he consecrates himself for their sake, "that they also may be consecrated" (Jn 17:19).[63]

*Judicial motifs.* Behind the pictures of wolves attacking a flock, Roman armies striking with brutal force, and friends whose safety is assured by the personal sacrifice of one of their number is the common element of mortal jeopardy to the group to be rescued. In the passages just reviewed John does

---

[60]Jörg Frey, "Edler Tod—wirksamer Tod—stellvertretender Tod—heilschaffender Tod: Zur narrativen und theologischen Deutung des Todes Jesu im Johannesevangelium," in van Belle, *Death of Jesus*, pp. 82-90.

[61]Murray J. Harris, "Appendix: Prepositions and Theology in the Greek New Testament," *NIDNTT* 3:1196-97.

[62]As the world benefits from Jesus' death in John 6:51, "The bread which I shall give is my flesh for the life of the world [ὑπέρ τῆς τοῦ κόσμου ζωῆς]," where ὑπέρ with the genitive of the thing connotes "for the sake of, to foster."

[63]A discussion of the ὑπέρ texts of the Gospel by J. Terence Forestell (*The Word of the Cross: Salvation as Revelation in the Fourth Gospel* [AnBib 57; Rome: Biblical Institute Press, 1974], pp. 193-94) does not come to grips with the lexically relevant facts just laid out. More penetrating is Knöppler, *Theologia crucis*, pp. 201-16. On the recent history of interpretation of these texts, see John A. Dennis, "Jesus' Death in John's Gospel: A Survey of Research from Bultmann to the Present with Special Reference to the Johannine *Hyper*-Texts," *CurBR* 4 (2006): 331-63.

not specify wherein this jeopardy consists, but in the wider fabric of his thought there is no doubt that the basic plight of the race is that of condemnation by the divine judge. That is not to neglect the very grave threats posed by the devil and sin in the Johannine scheme of things, but rather to point out that they threaten in a subordinate sense, in that they prove deadly precisely by alienating their victims from God's favor.

Judicial motifs come to the fore already in John 3:14-21. God sent the fiery serpents in the wilderness to counter Israel's complaining and told Moses to raise a brazen serpent on a pole to rescue from death those who looked to it. God is the source both of the pestilence and of the means of release from it. God so loved the world that he "gave" his only-begotten Son, that whoever believes in him "should not perish" (ἵνα μὴ ἀπόληται [Jn 3:16]). What will cause people to perish is divine judgment: although God sent the Son not "to judge [ἵνα κρίνῃ] the world" (Jn 3:17), one who does not believe "is judged [κέκριται] already" (Jn 3:18). The judgment (κρίσις) consists in the fact that people chose darkness rather than light (Jn 3:19). To skulk in the shadows and refuse to obey the Son is to dwell under the wrath (ὀργή) of God (Jn 3:36), to await dying in one's sin(s) (Jn 8:21, 23). Yet one who believes "does not come into judgment, but has passed from death to life" (Jn 5:24). Thus the nexus of diabolic deception, sin and unbelief brings judgment, and judgment under God spells death.

Jesus stepped in to deliver the race from this sentence. "Shall I not drink the cup which the Father has given me?" (Jn 18:11). Mention of a "cup" recalls the many Old Testament passages where God gives the nations a cup of wine in judgment,[64] a connotation that informs the use of "cup" in the Apocalypse (Apoc 14:10; 16:19; 18:6). Jesus drank the death warrant of the generations.[65]

Pilate's famous "Behold the man" (Jn 19:5) may be a case of Johannine double entendre. Pilate was pointing out the inconcinnity between the charge that Jesus was a revolutionary menace and the pitiful figure who had just suffered flagellation. But the author may well see Jesus as the man "in the sense that he has absorbed himself in our broken and sinful humanity"; he is "the man who fulfills a unique task of redemption in the bearing of this deep humiliation

---

[64]Ps 78:8; Is 51:17, 22-23; Jer 25:15, 17, 28; 49:12; 51:7; Lam 4:21; Ezek 23:31-34; Hab 2:15-16; Zech 2:12.

[65]Leonhard Goppelt, "ποτήριον," *TDNT* 6:149-53. That "cup" in this sense is found only in John 18:11 in the Gospel is no argument against this interpretation (contra Thüsing, *Erhöhung*, pp. 86-87).

which should, in truth, be borne by mankind; the man who in our place has thus undertaken to suffer the most grievous affliction."[66]

This legal line of thought is further developed in the First Epistle through the image of Jesus as our advocate, or counsel for the defense (παράκλητος [1 Jn 2:1]). If and when someone sins, the sinner needs a legal representative to go to the Father and plead the sinner's case. Because he is Jesus Christ "the righteous," he can ask on the ground of his own integrity that God's positive verdict on him be extended to the sinner who believes in him. The following verse explains that this sharing of sinners in God's approval of Christ is possible because he made propitiation. Here legal and sacrificial motifs blend. Addressees of the Epistle are dear children who have been forgiven "because of his name" (1 Jn 2:12)—that is, because of Christ's status and reputation as the righteous one (1 Jn 2:1; 3:7).

Courtroom procedure also informs the proclamation at Apocalypse 12:10-11 that the accuser of the saints has been thrown down and they have prevailed over him by the blood of the Lamb. The reference is to the great dragon, that ancient serpent, "who is called the Devil and Satan" (Apoc 12:9). Etymologically, a devil (διάβολος) is a legal adversary who presses charges (διαβάλλω). Śāṭān bears the same connotation in the Hebrew Bible (e.g., Job 1:6-12; 2:1-8; Zech 3:1). Now that the blood of the Lamb has been shed, the accuser has nothing to bring, no charge will stick, his leverage against the saints is removed, and he himself has been ejected from proceedings in heaven.

These judicial motifs taken together are as close as John approaches to anything like a doctrine of Christ as the penal substitute for the condemned and the source of imputed righteousness for the ungodly (cf. Is 53:4-6, 11-12). Nowhere does John come out, as Paul does, with a concise formulation to the effect that Jesus assumed the liabilities of others so that they might assume his right standing (Rom 4:25; 2 Cor 5:21), or that Jesus deflected the curse from them by becoming a cursed object himself (Gal 3:13). In comparison with Paul, the legal motifs in John are fragmentary, unsystematized and homiletical rather than theoretical. They are far from negligible, but John may have been more at home in cultic and dramatic metaphors.

*Sacrificial motifs.* From a literary standpoint, an especially pronounced

---

[66]G. Sevenster, "Remarks on the Humanity of Jesus in the Gospel and Letters of John," in *Studies in John: Presented to Professor J.N. Sevenster on the Occasion of His Seventieth Birthday* (NovTSup 24; Leiden: Brill, 1970), pp. 187.

symbol of Jesus' death in the Johannine literature is the sacrificial lamb, used in introductory scenes both in the Gospel and in the Apocalypse (ἀμνὸς τοῦ θεοῦ [Jn 1:29, 36]; ἀρνίον [28× in the Apocalypse, starting in Apoc 5:6]). Priests of Israel, by slaying lambs and pouring the collected blood at the base of the altar in the temple, made atonement for the sins of the people. That John in picturing Jesus as a lamb has cultic sacrifice in mind is unmistakable from the fact that this Lamb is said to take away sin (Jn 1:29) and to have been slain (Apoc 5:6, 12; 13:8; cf. "blood" in Apoc 7:14; 12:11).[67]

In biblical usage atonement, propitiation and expiation are closely related terms and overlap somewhat. In propitiation, emphasis falls on appeasing the offended deity; in expiation, on the removal of sin or impurity from the suppliant in the sight of the deity; and in atonement, on both these factors, in that the root idea is that of making a placative gift to God, and the effect is forgiveness for the worshiper.[68]

John certainly understood the death of Jesus as expiatory for sinners.[69] "Lamb of God" is intertwined with the Baptist's declaration that the one who comes after him will baptize—that is, cleanse people—with more than water (Jn 1:26, 33). As the Lamb of God, Jesus "takes away the sin of the world" (Jn 1:29).[70] His washing of the disciples' feet at the Last Supper was an object lesson of what his imminent death would do for them, for unless they accepted the footwashing, they would have no part in him (Jn 13:8).[71] The blood of Jesus

---

[67]Possible backgrounds to John's use of the lamb image are canvassed in Leon Morris, *The Apostolic Preaching of the Cross* (3rd ed.; Grand Rapids: Eerdmans, 1965), pp. 129-43. Helge Kjær Nielsen is overly cautious in writing, "We seem justified in saying that we find here a notion of atonement— one that does not otherwise play a particularly prominent role in John's understanding of Jesus' death" ("John's Understanding of the Death of Jesus," in *New Readings in John: Literary and Theological Perspectives; Essays from the Scandinavian Conference on the Fourth Gospel in Aarhus 1997*, ed. Johannes Nissen and Siegfried Pedersen [Sheffield: Sheffield Academic Press, 1999], p. 252). The fact is, by placing the image of the Lamb at the very front, John makes it the leading idea under which readers are to interpret the death of Jesus. See also Dietrich Rusam, "Das 'Lamm Gottes' (Joh 1,29.36) und die Deutung des Todes Jesu im Johannesevangelium," *BZ* 49 (2005): 60-80; Rainer Schwindt, "'Seht das Lamm Gottes, das hinwegnimmt die Sünde der Welt' (Joh 1,29): Zur Frage einer Sühnetheologie im Johannesevangelium," *TTZ* 119 (2010): 193-216.

[68]On the lexicography of these terms, see Morris, *Apostolic Preaching*, pp. 144-213. The connection between atonement and forgiveness is made repeatedly in the relevant Old Testament texts (e.g., Lev 4:20, 26, 31, 35; 5:10, 13, 16, 18; 6:7; 19:22; Num 15:25-26, 28).

[69]Frey, "Edler Tod," pp. 90-93.

[70]On the Lamb of God symbol as pointing to the atoning value of Jesus' death, see Knöppler, *Theologia crucis*, pp. 67-101.

[71]Georg Richter, "Die Fußwaschung Joh 13,1-20," in *Studien zum Johannesevangelium* (ed. Josef Hainz; BU 13; Regensburg: Pustet, 1977), pp. 42-48; Bruce H. Grigsby, "The Cross as an Expiatory Sacrifice in the Fourth Gospel," *JSNT* 15 (1982): 62; John Christopher Thomas, *Footwashing in John*

continually cleanses from all sin those who walk in the light (1 Jn 1:7). He appeared "to take away sins" (1 Jn 3:5). Saints are those who have made their robes clean by washing them in the blood of the Lamb (Apoc 7:14).[72]

Whether the death of Christ is rightly understood also to have satisfied or propitiated God was discussed at length by British New Testament scholars in the middle of the twentieth century, as we saw in chapter two.[73] As the careful lexical studies by Leon Morris and David Hill cited there have shown, C. H. Dodd did not succeed in proving that the ἱλασ- word group in biblical usage lost completely the sense of propitiation that it has in all ancient Greek literature outside the Bible. As far as the Johannine corpus was concerned, debate focused on the sense of the noun ἱλασμός, which occurs twice in the First Epistle (1 Jn 2:2; 4:10). We touched on the first of these in the section above on legal motifs. If a sinner requires an attorney for the defense in relation to the Father, then God's character must recoil justly against sin unless a means of pacification can be found.[74] A "propitiation for our sins" is exactly what the context demands.[75] And the latter verse, which states that God himself lovingly provided such a means by sending his Son, demolishes any uncertainty whether the utmost abomination of sin and the will to reclaim its practitioners can coexist in the divine nature. Is not that love most sublime which lays hold of offending objects at the staggering cost of satisfying its own unbending holiness on their behalf?[76] Even though the controverted vocabulary is absent

---

13 *and the Johannine Community* (JSNTSup 61; Sheffield: Sheffield Academic Press, 1991), pp. 16-17, 78, 115; Jean Zumstein, "Le lavement des pieds (Jean 13,1-20): Un exemple de la conception johannique du pouvoir," *RTP* 132 (2000): 345-60; David Gibson, "The Johannine Footwashing and the Death of Jesus: A Dialogue with Scholarship," *SJET* 25 (2007): 50-60; Otfried Hofius, "Die Erzählung von der Fusswaschung Jesu: Joh 13,1-11 als narratives Christuszeugnis," *ZTK* 106 (2009): 156-76.

[72]Paul B. Decock, "The Symbol of Blood in the Apocalypse of John," *Neot* 38 (2004): 157-82.

[73]In that chapter, see the subsection "Revelation of the Father in the Christ-Event," under the section "Impact of the Christ-Event on Our Knowledge of the Father" (pp. 110-11).

[74]"The Biblical idea is that the obstacle to forgiveness lies in his [God's] essential righteousness which so conditions his grace that without its satisfaction God cannot, in self-consistency, forgive" (George B. Stevens, *The Johannine Theology: A Study of the Doctrinal Contents of the Gospels and Epistles of the Apostle John* [New York: Scribner, 1894], p. 183).

[75]Toan Joseph Do's reopening of the lexical question in 1 John 2:2 is vitiated by a fundamental misunderstanding ("Jesus' Death as *Hilasmos* According to 1 John," in *The Death of Jesus in the Fourth Gospel* [ed. Gilbert van Belle; Leuven: Leuven University Press, 2007], pp. 537-53). The author supposes the difference between propitiation and expiation to turn on the subject who initiates the act (according to him, human in the case of propitiation, divine in the case of expiation) rather than the object (the offended deity in the case of propitiation, human sin in the case of expiation). This confusion in defining the question leads to a clouded judgment in his assessment of the evidence. Nevertheless, his bibliography on the problem is invaluable.

[76]"The meaning is that he [Christ] accomplishes for us a reconciliation with God on account of our

from the Gospel, numerous and pervasive references to people "perishing" (Jn 3:16; 10:28; 17:12; 18:9), suffering "judgment" in the sense of condemnation (Jn 3:17-18; 5:24, 29; 12:31, 48; 16:8, 11), remaining under the "wrath" of God (Jn 3:36), "dying in their sins" (Jn 6:50; 8:21, 24), or abiding in the state of death (Jn 5:24; 8:51, 52) logically require that if anyone is to be saved out of the world, it must be by God being propitiated, as becomes explicit in the First Epistle.[77]

*Redemptive motifs.* John pictures the work of Christ, and his death in particular, as a titanic conquest of the forces of evil.[78] This "Christus Victor" theme begins already in the prologue of the Gospel. Ever since the beginning of time, the light shines in the darkness, and the darkness has not "overcome" (κατέλαβεν) it (Jn 1:5). The face-off between light and its absence symbolizes the opposition between God and created beings who hold out against his good purpose. The aorist tense of καταλαμβάνω indicates a history-long assault on the light by darkness. Yet light prevails. During the era of the first creation the light shaft was the Torah; since the commencement of the eschatological era it has been the incarnate Logos, Jesus Christ (Jn 1:17).

Later in the Gospel, when Jesus' "hour" has struck (Jn 12:23), he says, "Now is the judgment of this world, now shall the ruler of this world be cast out; and I, when I am lifted up from the earth, will draw all people to myself" (Jn 12:31-32). The narrator adds that Jesus said this "to show by what death he was to die" (Jn 12:33). The subject, then, is the crucifixion of Jesus, and it is this that Jesus declares to be a realization in present, historical time (νῦν, "now") of God's final judgment on the godless world-system, especially on its ruler. That the decisive moment of judgment took place at the cross Jesus states again in his Farewell

---

sins by himself atoning for them. He is the means of rendering God favorable in so far as by his sacrificial death he has accomplished, on our behalf, the ends of punishment, and is thus in respect to our sins a means of reconciliation with God" (Stevens, *Johannine Theology*, p. 184).

[77]Perhaps the most extended attempt to argue, against the grain of the data, that John's theology of the cross emphasizes the revelation of God's love apart from any notion of atonement is Forestell, *Word of the Cross.* When all has been said, Forestell evades rather than answers objections that he anticipates to his thesis (pp. 193-202). For example, granting that the lamb image in John 1:29 is sacrificial, he tries to sideline this text on the ground that it is "isolated and disputed" (p. 194). Likewise the dual occurrence of "propitiation" in 1 John 2:2; 4:10 may well be "sacrificial," but these statements are "peripheral, secondary, and occasioned by the pastoral problem" (p. 395). If John did not see the death of Jesus atoning for sin—that is, addressing the fundamental human predicament before God—it is hard to imagine in what other way he could think that death to have been a superlative revelation of divine love.

[78]Highlighted in the history of Christian doctrine by Gustaf Aulén, *Christus Victor: An Historical Study of the Three Main Types of the Idea of the Atonement* (trans. A. G. Hebert; London: SPCK, 1931). Aulén, however, devotes only a page or so to the Johannine corpus (pp. 90-91).

Discourse: "The ruler of this world is judged [κέκριται]" (Jn 16:11), where the perfect tense points prophetically to an action soon to be completed. Similarly, the bold declaration "I have overcome [νενίκηκα] the world" (Jn 16:33), uses the vocabulary of victory achieved.

The First Epistle looks back on Jesus as a hero who went to battle and utterly undid the foe. "The reason the Son of God appeared was to destroy [ἵνα λύσῃ] the works of the devil" (1 Jn 3:8). Connotations of the verb λύω in this context are to loosen, unravel, undermine, dismantle.

In the Apocalypse John returns to his distinctive language of Jesus "overcoming" (νικᾶν) and expands it into a theme. The one who died and is alive (Apoc 1:18) states that he himself "conquered" (ἐνίκησα, historic aorist tense) and sat down with his Father on his throne (Apoc 3:21). An angelic elder informs the seer, "The Lion of the tribe of Judah, the Root of David, has conquered" (ἐνίκησεν [Apoc 5:5]). This evokes the military imagery of messianic prophecies in Genesis 49:8-12 ("Your hand shall be on the neck of your enemies . . . Judah is a lion's whelp; from the prey, my son, you have gone up . . . to him shall be the obedience of the peoples") and in Isaiah 11:1-5 ("There shall come forth a shoot from the stump of Jesse . . . with righteousness he shall judge the poor . . . he shall smite the earth with the rod of his mouth, and with the breath of his lips he shall slay the wicked"). It is by "the blood of the Lamb" that his followers conquer (Apoc 12:11). Though the dragon is already defeated, God has given him a little time to practice perfidy (Apoc 12:12-17) before the Lamb "will conquer" (νικήσει [Apoc 17:14]).[79]

Besides overthrowing the archfiend, Christ's triumph means that he has liberated his followers from the devil's thrall. John makes no use of the Synoptic terms for "ransoming" (λύτρον, λυτρόω, λύτρωσις), nor of the corresponding Pauline terms for "redemption" (ἀπολύτρωσις, ἀντίλυτρον), but has related words. Jesus has "loosed" (λύσας) us from our sins (Apoc 1:5). Angels and saints in heaven laud him for "purchasing" (ἀγοράζειν) people for God at the cost of his blood (Apoc 5:9; cf. 14:3). In this word-picture emphasis falls on the helplessness of the prisoners, the dreadful price that had to be paid, and the ensuing state of freedom for those who had once been slaves,[80] not on God

---

[79]Kamal Fahim Awad Hanna, *La passione di Cristo nell'Apocalisse* (TGST 77; Rome: Editrice Pontificia Università Gregoriana, 2001).

[80]So Morris, *Apostolic Preaching*, pp. 11-62.

doing a deal with the devil, as in some later patristic accounts drawing on the same terminology.[81]

**Jesus as Passover Lamb.** John's presentation of Jesus as the paschal lamb is a related redemptive motif. Passover, the memorial of Israel's triumphant exodus from bondage in Egypt, is known in Judaism as "the festival of freedom."

That John saw the death of Jesus as a new Passover is clear from several indications. Jesus is "the Lamb of God" (Jn 1.29, 36), a phrase that comprises the Passover lamb among other lambs used in the Levitical sacrificial system. It is at the time of Passover feasts that Jesus first alludes cryptically to the coming destruction of the temple of his body (Jn 2:13, 19), later feeds the five thousand and proclaims himself the bread of life, with reference to his flesh and blood soon to be sundered for the life of the world (Jn 6), and finally dies on the cross (Jn 11:55; 12:1; 13:1; 18:28, 39; 19:14). The Scripture allusion at the end of the Johannine passion account about not one of his bones getting broken (Jn 19:36) takes on added depth if it echoes not only an Old Testament promise for the righteous (Ps 34:20) but also the stipulation concerning the passover lamb (Ex 12:46).[82]

Two verses remain to be considered under the topic of Jesus as Passover lamb, not because they contain that idea, but because many suppose they imply it indirectly. In the Synoptic Gospels Jesus eats the lamb on Thursday evening as part of the Seder and is crucified the next day (Mt 26:17-30; Mk 14:12-26; Lk 22:7-39). Perhaps a majority of commentators on John hold that John manipulated the passion chronology to make the offering of the Passover lambs coincide with Jesus' expiration on the cross on Friday. If so, it would be a striking way for John to identify the death of Jesus with its Old Testament type. General opinion that John has done so is based on two statements. Temple officers deputed by the chief priests (Jn 18:3, 12) to accuse Jesus before Pilate would not enter the praetorium early on that Friday morning "so that they might not be defiled, but might eat the Passover" (Jn 18:28). A later statement seems to

---

[81]Discussed in Aulén, *Christus Victor*, pp. 63-71.

[82]Stanley E. Porter, "Can Traditional Exegesis Enlighten Literary Analysis of the Fourth Gospel? An Examination of the Old Testament Fulfilment Motif and the Passover Theme," in *The Gospels and the Scriptures of Israel* (ed. Craig A. Evans and W. Richard Stegner; JSNTSup 104; Sheffield: Academic Press, 1994), pp. 396-428; Christine Schlund, *"Kein Knochen soll gebrochen werden": Studien zu Bedeutung und Funktion des Pesachfests in Texten des frühen Judentums und im Johannesevangelium* (WMANT 107; Neukirchen-Vluyn: Neukirchener Verlag, 2005); Paul M. Hoskins, "Deliverance from Death by the True Passover Lamb: A Significant Aspect of the Fulfillment of the Passover in the Gospel of John," *JETS* 52 (2009): 285-99.

confirm that the lambs had not yet been slain: as Jesus awaited Pilate's decision, "it was the day of Preparation of the Passover" (Jn 19:14).

But John's narrative of the passion, while independent of and supplementary to the Synoptic accounts in its selection of material,[83] dovetails with them at many points. By no means is it clear that John means to revise the accepted chronology, or that the two verses in question were intended by him to bear the christological weight that some modern exegesis heaps on them. With the Synoptic Gospels John is in complete agreement that the final meal (Jn 13:2-38) took place after sundown (Jn 13:30) on the Thursday evening before the crucifixion, which happened on Friday (Jn 19:31, 42). Was the repast in John 13 a Passover meal? John 13:1 states that before the feast of Passover, Jesus had already determined to love his disciples to the end. When the very next sentence opens with the words "during supper" (δείπνου γινομένου), it is natural to understand this to be the Seder, especially since Jesus and his disciples are shortly seen reclining at table (Jn 13:23, 25) at night (Jn 13:30), neither of which circumstance would obtain for an ordinary meal. Some of those present thought that Jesus might be sending Judas out to get last-minute provisions for "the feast" (Jn 13:29), which haste would scarcely be necessary were the feast scheduled for the next day. Details of the meal parallel the Synoptic accounts, including Jesus' teaching on servanthood (Jn 13:4-20; cf. Lk 22:24-27), his shocking announcement of a betrayer in the midst (Jn 13:21; Mt 26:21; Mk 14:18; Lk 22:21), his sharing of dipped bread with Judas (Jn 13:26; Mt 26:23; Mk 14:20; Lk 22:21), and his prediction of Peter's denials following Peter's protestation of loyalty (Jn 13:37-38; Mt 26:33-35; Mk 14:29-31; Lk 22:33-34).

"So that . . . [the priests] might eat the passover" (Jn 18:28) is no christological statement, but rather describes the care of Jesus' accusers for their own ritual purity. Since the Passover lambs had been eaten the night before, in this context "the passover" must be the daily sin offerings consumed by the priests during the remainder of the Feast of Unleavened Bread, which blended with Passover in the popular mind.[84] We note that John's expression does not mention lambs.

---

[83]Hanjo-Christoph Kollmann, *Die Kreuzigung Jesu nach Joh 19,16-22: Ein Beitrag zur Kreuzestheologie des Johannes im Vergleich mit den Synoptikern* (EH 23/710; Frankfurt: Peter Lang, 2000).

[84]Lexicography requires exactitude. In first-century Palestine the term "Passover" had come to include the week-long Feast of Unleavened Bread that followed the day itself in the calendar (Lk 22:1; Josephus, *J.W.* 2.10; *Ant.* 14.21; 17.213; 18.29). Conversely, Passover could be called "the first day of the Feast of Unleavened Bread" (Mk 14:12; Lk 22:7; cf. Josephus, *J.W.* 2.224, 244, 280; *Ant.* 2.317). To "eat the Passover" need not refer to the roasted lamb of the Seder (Ex 12:9). It could just as well refer to the goats of the daily sin offering throughout the extended festival (Num 28:22-24). These

"The day-of-preparation of the Passover" (19:14 [my hyphens]) means the
Friday ("day-of-preparation") that fell in the week following Passover, the day
when Jewish homes made preparations for the Sabbath as they did year round
(Mt 27:62; Lk 23:54).[85] Mark says that Jesus was buried late on the "day of
preparation" and explains for the benefit of Gentile readers that the idiomatic
phrase means the "day before the sabbath" (προσάββατον, or Friday [Mk
15:42]). This sense is certain in John, for he, like all three Synoptists, uses "the
(day of) preparation" absolutely for Friday (Jn 19:31, 42) and comments, "That
sabbath was a high day" (Jn 19:31), part of the great pilgrim festival. Given this
standard first-century usage, that the words are to be grouped differently ("the
day of preparation-of-the-Passover"), implying that Jewish homes had not yet
finished their preparations for the feast, is entirely improbable.[86]

Every indication, then, is that John's chronology of Jesus' passion corresponds exactly to that of the Synoptic Gospels. Were he making a christological
point in John 18:28; 19:14, the obliqueness of these statements would diverge
from his usual directness and force ("The Word was God," "the Word became
flesh," "Behold, the Lamb of God," etc.). Therefore it is as good as certain that
John 18:28; 19:14 are not to be pressed into service to prove Jesus as the Johannine Passover lamb, even though John makes that theological identification
in other ways.[87]

---

being sin offerings, the priests would boil (Deut 16:7) and consume them (Lev 6:26). They are called
"the Passover sacrifice" both in Scripture (Deut 16:2-3) and in the Mishnah (*m. Pesaḥ.* 9:5: "At the
Passover of Egypt the lamb . . . was eaten in haste and during one night; whereas the Passover of the
generations continued throughout the seven days").

[85]These weekly duties included preparing the *Erub* (a deposit of food at the extremity of the Sabbath
limit as a temporary abode that allowed one to range beyond the normal Sabbath limit of two
thousand cubits from town) and the lighting of the Sabbath lamp (*m. Šabb.* 2:7).

[86]For the fullest and roundest discussions of the problems of John 18:28; 19:14, see Theodore Zahn,
*Introduction to the New Testament* (trans. John Moore Trout et al.; 3 vols.; New York: Scribner, 1909),
3:273-83, 293-98; Norval Geldenhuys, *Commentary on the Gospel of Luke* (NICNT; Grand Rapids:
Eerdmans, 1951), pp. 649-70; Barry D. Smith, "The Chronology of the Last Supper," *WTJ* 53 (1991):
29-45.

[87]Two factors militate against most commentators acknowledging this historical-cultural exegesis of
the phrases in question as correct. (1) The notion, traceable to the nineteenth-century Tübingen
school, persists in New Testament scholarship that John was willing to tamper with historical facts
to make theological statements. The timing of the crucifixion is taken as a notorious case, even
though John's handling of traditions has often been shown sober where we can check it against the
Synoptics. (2) It is regarded among New Testament scholars as a mark of critical objectivity and
courage to allow apparent discrepancies among the Gospels to stand and as a mark of defensiveness
to seek harmony in such cases. Yet widely accepted secular textbooks on historical method (e.g.,
Bernheim [1889], Langlois and Seignobos [1898]) demand that a historian attempt to harmonize
conflicting sources that have independent merit. John's popular expressions in John 18:28; 19:14

*Jesus' death as the food of immortality.* In the dialogue on the bread of life
(Jn 6:25-65) Jesus promises life eternal to anyone who eats his flesh and drinks
his blood. This metaphor of eating and drinking has crystallized in the course
of the dialogue. The food imagery has its starting point in the meal that Jesus
fed the five thousand (Jn 6:1-14). Jesus then offers "food" that endures to eternal
life (Jn 6:27). There are allusions to the manna that God gave Israel in the wilderness (Jn 6:31-32)[88] before Jesus identifies himself as the true bread from
heaven (Jn 6:32-33, 35, 41, 48, 50-51), with a special emphasis on his "flesh" (Jn
6:51-52), then on his "flesh" and "blood" (Jn 6:53-56). He clarifies that he is
speaking of spiritual, not fleshly, realities (Jn 6:63). Finally, he hints at his
coming betrayal by one of his disciples (Jn 6:70-71).

Side by side with this accent on Jesus—that is, on his death—as the staff of
life is an evolution in the varied terms for appropriating him. Jesus begins with
a clear call for people to "believe in" him whom God has sent (Jn 6:29-30).
Upon claiming to be the bread of life, Jesus introduces the phrase to "come to"
him (Jn 6:35). He oscillates between inviting people to "believe" (Jn 6:35, 36, 40,
47) and to "come to" him (Jn 6:37, 44, 45). Adverting once more to the manna
that the fathers ate (Jn 6:49), Jesus then launches into a section dominated by
the verb "to eat," the object being first the bread that God has sent from heaven
(Jn 6:50-52; cf. 6:57-58), then Jesus' flesh (Jn 6:53-54, 56), soon expanded by
"drinking" his blood as well (Jn 6:53-54, 56). Finally, he returns to the language
of "believing" and "coming to" him (Jn 6:64-65; cf. 6:69).

To eat Jesus' flesh and drink his blood, then, is to believe in him, specifically
as the divine sent one who will give his flesh and blood for the life of the world.
Thereby one will gain eternal life (Jn 6:27, 33, 40, 47, 50 ["not die"], 51, 53, 54, 57,
58, 63, 68), become immune from hunger and thirst (Jn 6:35), and have a share
in the resurrection at the last day (Jn 6:39, 40, 44, 54).

The question of whether the vivid language of John 6:53-58 is meant to evoke
secondary eucharistic associations will come up in chapter nine below. On the
primary level, we can note three things: (1) Jesus' audience was made up of
unbelieving Jews of the synagogue at Capernaum (Jn 6:59), most of whom rejected what he said (Jn 6:60-66), so on its face the passage does not present
itself as sacramental instruction for an existing Christian congregation; (2) all

---

have thus fallen prey to the New Testament guild's apologetic need in modern university faculties
to ward off the dread charge of letting faith influence historical judgments.
[88]Jan G. van der Watt, "I Am the Bread of Life: Imagery in John 6:32-51," *AcT* 2 (2007): 186-204.

the eucharistic texts of the New Testament speak of Jesus' "body" (σῶμα), not, as John does, of his "flesh" (σάρξ); (3) whereas in the words of institution of the Eucharist the subject is "this [bread, cup]" and the predicate is "is my body/blood/the new covenant in my blood," in John 6 the subject and predicate are reversed: the subject is Jesus ("I," "my flesh," "my blood"), and the predicate is "is true food/bread/drink." In the first place, then, John 6:51-58 is a call for saving faith in Jesus, who by his death provided the bread of immortality for the world.

**Jesus' death as exaltation.** As we saw above, a distinctive Johannine term for Jesus' death is his being "lifted up" (ὑψόω, ὑψωθῆναι [Jn 3:14; 8:28; 12:32, 34]). This usage occurs within the first twelve chapters of the Gospel, not in the passion account, while the occurrences of the synonym δοξάζω in reference to Jesus' glorification fall in John 12–17 (with the sole exception of Jn 7:39). The main reference of Jesus' lifting is to his being elevated on the cross by his enemies (Jn 8:28; 12:33), but it would be wrong to exclude the further suggestion that the figure of the crucified one portrays God's greatness to the eye of faith.[89]

In the Roman Empire crucifixion was the "extreme humiliation" (*supplicium* [Tacitus, *Ann.* 15.44]), the most dreaded form of execution, reserved for the dregs of society, the "utterly vile death of the cross" (*mors turpissima crucis*).[90] It meant not only excruciating torture but also the utmost public shame. For John to refer to it as exaltation is to employ paradox.

Isaiah 52:13 says that God's servant "will be very elevated and glorified" (LXX: ὑψωθήσεται καὶ δοξασθήσεται), in a passage that even *Targum Jonathan* interprets of the Messiah. This Old Testament text may be the source of John's remarkable lexical choices. If so, it is singular that John applies the concept of elevation to the servant's very suffering and not only to its joyous sequel.[91] The expectation that Jesus will be lifted up prepares for an accent on Jesus' kingship in the passion narrative. Jesus admitted to being a king, but one who exercises a rule of truth that finds its origin and nature beyond the world (Jn 18:36-37). Pilate, wryly entitling Jesus "King of the Jews" and refusing to withdraw the title from his flogged person, by which Pilate meant to insult his Jewish subjects

---

[89]Thüsing, *Erhöhung*.

[90]Martin Hengel, *Crucifixion in the Ancient World and the Folly of the Message of the Cross* (trans. John Bowden; London: SCM Press, 1977).

[91]There are no data whatsoever in the Fourth Gospel to warrant assertions that ὑψωθῆναι signifies Jesus' "exaltation to heaven," or that it combines with his resurrection and ascension. For such statements, see, for example, Georg Bertram, "ὕψος," *TDNT* 8:610, 611. Similar unwarranted assertions are pandemic in secondary literature.

to their faces (Jn 18:39; 19:3, 14-15, 19-22), unwittingly ratified the deep truth of the matter recognized by author and readers.[92]

Looking back on Jesus' crucifixion, John consistently sees in it the superlative act of God's love for the world (Jn 3:16; 13:1, 34; 15:9, 12; 1 Jn 3:16; 4:9-10; Apoc 1:5). It expresses God's love because in Jesus' death God bore, in the person of his Son, the divine judgment that was due to sinners, so that those who believe might become exempt; he himself undertook to make propitiation and expiation for sins against him; he shattered the devil's ascendancy and freed his captives; he brought life where there had been only death. So magnanimous a pity that unconstrainedly abased itself so far, to raise unworthy creatures so high, is not of the created order. The matchless eminence of God shines above all in his love, and his love for the world radiates from the cross. In that sense, and in that sense alone other than the literal, Jesus' crucifixion was his exaltation.

*"Extent" and efficacy of the atonement.* We saw at the end of chapter three, in considering soteriological passages that speak of the "world" and of "all," that the object of God's redeeming love in Johannine thought is nothing other than the entire world, not in the sense that impenitent infidels will be saved, but that individuals who are won over by God's prevailing love make up the significant portion of the world that represents the whole. In keeping with this, when describing the impact of the death of Christ, John can emphasize in various contexts either its generality or its efficacy for the body of concrete persons whom Christ was sent into the world to save.

To frame a question concerning the "extent" of the atonement is a mistake, for that is to press a quantitative grid foreign to John's way of thinking, and it leads to an insoluble dilemma like the one I discussed in chapter three. Either Christ will have died for all in the numerical sense, in which case the virtue of his death will be reduced to a potential sufficiency that people must actuate for themselves by believing in it (Arminianism), or else Christ died for only some, in which case his death will be efficacious for them to be sure (Calvinism), but it will be hard to show how the offer of its benefits to everyone without exception can be in good faith.

John's strong language strikes down any mirage of limits where the fruit of

---

[92]Tom Thatcher, *Greater Than Caesar: Christology and Empire in the Fourth Gospel* (Minneapolis: Fortress, 2009); Mavis M. Leung, "The Roman Empire and John's Passion Narrative in Light of Jewish Royal Messianism," *BSac* 168 (2011): 426-42.

Christ's death is concerned. Jesus gave his flesh for the life of "the world" (Jn 6:51). He died "for the nation," and not for the Jewish nation only, but "to gather into one the children of God who are scattered abroad" (Jn 11:52; cf. 18:14). As a grain drops into the earth and dies, he bears a rich harvest (Jn 12:24). Lifted up from the earth, he draws "all people" (πάντας) to himself (Jn 12:32), with reference in this context to Greeks as well as Hebrews (Jn 12:20-22). That he is the propitiation not only for "our" sins but also for the whole world (1 Jn 2:2) probably is to be understood in the same way as John 11:52 just quoted, but from the perspective of the Christian community rather than ethnic Israel: there are other children of God in the world who have yet to be gathered into the community of believers, for whom Jesus Christ made propitiation. The Lamb has taken people out of every tribe and tongue and people and nation, and he has made them a kingdom and priests to God (Apoc 5:9-10). The atonement is universal in range, in that every fair feature that constitutes the cosmos is amply represented in the microcosmos of the redeemed.

But John also proclaims boldly that God accomplished what he set out to do in making atonement for those whom he intended to save. Jesus laid down his life "for the sheep" (Jn 10:11, 15), a purpose and a category outside of which unbelievers place themselves by rejecting his signs (Jn 10:25-26). He laid down his life "for his friends" (Jn 15:13). He prayed "not for" the world but rather "for" those whom the Father gave him, and "for their sake" he consecrated himself, that they may be consecrated out of the world (Jn 17:9, 16-19). He laid down his life "for us"—the family of believers who are now to practice mutual love self-sacrificially (1 Jn 3:16). He did not just open the possibility, but actually "freed us from our sins by his blood" (Apoc 1:5). "Out of" (ἐκ) every tribe and tongue and people and nation the Lamb "ransomed people for God" (Apoc 5:9), not only paying the price for them but also taking them in hand. They have been "redeemed from mankind [ἀπὸ τῶν ἀνθρώπων] as first fruits [ἀπαρχή] for God and the Lamb" (Apoc 14:4).

We might summarize John's view of the impact of the atonement in two propositions: (1) God himself excludes no individual from an atonement that covers the world in general, "all" people; (2) God insures that particular people, whom he gave the Son before the foundation of the world, benefit from it. The latter represent the creation, being objects of a purchase and a consecration that are, in the last analysis, God's work and not theirs. Again, as with the question of the breadth of God's saving intent, how to connect these propositions in a rational system is undefined. But in themselves they are not contradictory, even if their relation remains an unsolved problem.

*The burial of Jesus.* That the body of Jesus was buried for three days was an item in the kerygma proclaimed by all the apostles, as Paul writes (1 Cor 15:4, 11), after conferring with Cephas, James the brother of the Lord, and John in Jerusalem (Gal 1:18-19; 2:1-10). John gives his own version of the event in his Gospel (Jn 19:38-42). His report of the burial, like the rest of his Gospel, both confirms and supplements facts found in the Synoptic Gospels. In harmony with the Synoptics, John has the burial take place toward evening on the Friday of the crucifixion (Jn 19:31, 42). It ends with Jesus' resurrection early on the following Sunday (Jn 20:1). Primary credit for this act of Jewish and Christian piety goes to Joseph of Arimathea, who was a disciple of Jesus. John alone points out that he had been a secret disciple due to fear of reprisal from the authorities. He adds that Nicodemus was Joseph's helper. John also supplies a note on the weight of the spices that Nicodemus contributed to the grave clothes (100 λίτρας or Roman *librae*, approximately 72 pounds [Jn 19:39]).

Unlike Paul, John does not bring out any application for believers. Paul sees the entombment of Jesus as archetypical. Christians seal the mortification of their former existence in a baptismal burial with Christ (συνθάπτεσθαι [Rom 6:4; Col 2:12]). John views the burial simply as the evidence that Jesus, having died, was stone dead.[93]

*The resurrection and postresurrection appearances of Jesus.* John proclaims, in keeping with the apostolic kerygma emanating from Jerusalem, that Jesus rose on the third day according to the Scriptures and appeared to witnesses (cf. 1 Cor 15:4-5). Early on the Sunday morning after the crucifixion, first Mary Magdalene, then Peter and the disciple whom Jesus loved, found the tomb of Jesus void of all but the collapsed graveclothes (Jn 20:1-10). Jesus had claimed that he would raise up the temple of his body three days after its destruction. This the disciples recalled after he was raised from the dead (Jn 2:19, 22). The absence of the corpse, which the Beloved Disciple connected with "the scripture, that he [Jesus] must rise from the dead," was enough to prompt him to believe (Jn 20:8-9). What Scripture, John does not say. Does John have in mind Isaiah 53:10-12, which says that God's servant will, after suffering, see his offspring, see the light of life (Qumran mss, LXX), and take satisfaction in the fruit of the

---

[93]Jerome Murphy-O'Connor, "The Descent from the Cross and the Burial of Jesus (Jn 19:31-42)," *RB* 118 (2011): 522-57.

travail of his soul? Or Jonah's three days and three nights in the belly of the fish (Jon 1:17), interpreted typologically in reference to Christ (cf. Mt 12:40)? Or perhaps Psalm 16:10, in which David expresses confidence that he will undergo no corruption in Sheol, combined with common Palestinian knowledge that corruption sets in by the fourth day (Jn 11:39; cf. Acts 2:25-31)? Or Psalm 118:22: "The stone which the builders rejected has become the head of the corner"?[94]

That Jesus would show himself living to his disciples after his death Jesus had promised in the Farewell Discourse (Jn 14:19, 21-22; 16:16-22).[95] Jesus' gentle disclosure of himself to the distraught Mary Magdalene in the garden of the tomb, calling her by name, is one of the great recognition scenes in all literature (Jn 20:11-18).[96] John also reports a further appearance to "the disciples" that evening. There was a third to the same group including Thomas a week later, and yet another to seven disciples by the Sea of Tiberias on another occasion (Jn 20:19–21:14).

Jesus' resurrection toward the end of the Fourth Gospel brings to realization the significance of all seven "signs" that precede it. His first sign, turning water into wine, was emblematic of his power to transform the present world into the world to come. A resurrection is, by its very nature, an eschatological event. His rising, then, inaugurated the turning point of the ages, commenced a resurrection-transformation that will eventually spread outwards from the individual Jesus to encompass all things. As we have seen, the other signs have as their theme the presentation of Jesus as the giver of life and light for the human race. They culminate in the resuscitation of Lazarus, the meaning of which is stated in Jesus' claim to be "the resurrection and the life" (Jn 11:25). All that the signs betokened became an actual fact from that first Easter onwards.

---

[94]This last text is the suggestion in Matthew M. Bridges, "Reunderstanding How to 'Understand the Scripture,'" *JTI* 3 (2009): 127-42.

[95]It is debated among commentators whether the promises that Jesus will "come" to the disciples (Jn 14:18), that he will "manifest" himself to them (Jn 14:21-22), and that they will "see" him (Jn 14:19; 16:16-22) refer to (1) his postresurrection appearances; (2) their deepened understanding of him through the ministry of the Spirit-Paraclete after Pentecost; or (3) his parousia at the end of the age. As Raymond E. Brown argues in his commentary, the situation demands a more permanent presence of Christ among his disciples than the post-resurrectional appearances would provide (*The Gospel According to John: Introduction, Translation, and Notes* [2 vols.; AB 29, 29A; Garden City, NY: Doubleday, 1966–1970], 2:645-46). Therefore it is simplest to understand all of John 14:16-27 to denote primarily the coming of the Spirit-Paraclete in Jesus' place, as John 14:16-17, 26 unquestionably do, without denying the possibility of a double or even a triple entendre that underscores the inner connection among all three events.

[96]On recognition scenes as a subgenre, see Kasper Bro Larsen, *Recognizing the Stranger: Recognition Scenes in the Gospel of John* (BIS 93; Leiden: Brill, 2008).

Also in the Farewell Discourse Jesus brings out the meaning of his coming resurrection for his followers. Though Jesus will soon go away to a place where the disciples cannot come (Jn 13:33, 36), the appearances will assure his immediate disciples and John's readers that he is still there.[97] "I am the way, and the truth, and the life" (Jn 14:6): because he came forth from God, he is the path by which others can arrive at God; because he is what God is, God only-begotten, people encounter the reality of God in him;[98] because "in him was life" (Jn 1:4) and he "has life in himself" (Jn 5:26), the grave could not hold him and he is able to dispense from his own fullness of life to others. "Because I live, you will live also" (Jn 14:19): his life is the foundation of his disciples' life. Had he remained dead in the tomb, what would Christianity have to offer but nihilism? "Be of good cheer, I have overcome the world" (Jn 16:33): his resurrection has reversed the inexorable lapse of the world toward oblivion.[99]

If the Gospel of John offers a narrative report of the resurrection appearances of Jesus designed to elicit and strengthen faith in his person,[100] the other parts of the Johannine corpus apply the truth of the resurrection to situations in which John found himself pastorally engaged. The Epistles presuppose the fact of Jesus' resurrection without making it a didactic theme, for the heresy in the background posed a threat on other counts. Here the eternal Son is called "the life . . . the eternal life that was with the Father and was made manifest to us" (1 Jn 1:2). He who is the fount of life could not remain subject to death. That he now lives underlies his present ministries as advocate with the Father for sinners (1 Jn 2:2), as the one in whom believers have eternal life (1 Jn 5:11-12, 20), and as the keeper of those who have been born of God so that they do not sin and the evil one does not touch them (1 Jn 5:18).

In the opening doxology of the Apocalypse Jesus is given the title "the firstborn of the dead" (Apoc 1:5). As in Colossians 1:18 (where an almost identical phrase occurs, adding a partitive ἐκ), the title points to the union between Jesus

[97]Jesper Tang Nielsen, "Resurrection, Recognition, Reassuring: The Function of Jesus' Resurrection in the Fourth Gospel," in Koester and Bieringer, *Resurrection of Jesus*, pp. 177-208.

[98]Jesus is the truth in the sense that he and the Father share a unity of life, and in love they make this life available to humankind. See Yū Ibuki, *Die Wahrheit im Johannesevangelium* (BBB 39; Bonn: Hanstein, 1972), pp. 174-75.

[99]Hans-Ulrich Weidemann, *Der Tod Jesu im Johannesevangelium: Die erste Abschiedsrede als Schlüsseltext für den Passions- und Osterbericht* (BZNW 122; Berlin: de Gruyter, 2004); Jean Zumstein, "Jesus' Resurrection in the Farewell Discourses," in Koester and Bieringer, *Resurrection of Jesus*, pp. 103-26.

[100]Larry Darnell George, *Reading the Tapestry: A Literary-Rhetorical Analysis of the Johannine Resurrection Narrative (John 20-21)* (SBL 14; New York: Peter Lang, 2000).

as pioneer and the entire body of God's people destined to be raised on the last day. This fact encourages readers who face impending tribulation (Apoc 1:9) and the possibility of imprisonment leading to martyrdom (Apoc 2:10). The glorified Lord seeks to dispel John's fears by identifying himself as "the living one" who died and is alive for evermore, having the keys of Death and Hades (Apoc 1:18). He repeats the formula of dying and coming to life in the oracle for the oppressed church at Smyrna (Apoc 2:8). Of course, all seven of the oracles to the churches (Apoc 2–3) come from one who now lives. At Apocalypse 5:6 the seer in the heavenly throne room introduces "a Lamb standing, as though it had been slain," now receiving the laudation of the universe. He continues throughout the rest of the apocalypse to reveal his present and future acts of salvation and judgment. When the souls of martyrs of the currently escalating tribulation under beastly Rome are seen to come to life, they reign with Christ for a millennial Sabbath until the end of the age (Apoc 20:4-6).

***The ascension of Jesus.*** Jesus' ascension and the giving of the Spirit at Pentecost came after the focal period covered by John's Gospel, but they happened long before needs arose for John to write his Epistles and Apocalypse. Unlike Luke, who alone records Jesus' ascension (Lk 24:51; Acts 1:6-11), but like Matthew, John ends his narrative with a few select postresurrection appearances of Jesus. All references in the Johannine corpus to what, according to Luke, happened over the next fifty days must be, therefore, either proleptic or retrospective. Yet John leaves the reader in no chronological or theological vagueness. These things had not yet come about when the resurrected Lord made himself known to Mary: "I have not yet ascended to the Father; but go to my brethren and say to them, I am ascending to my Father" (Jn 20:17). Jesus' ascension was an established fact by the time John saw the Lamb sharing his Father's throne (Apoc 3:21; 5:6; cf. 12:5). There is not the slightest textual justification for collapsing Jesus' uplifting (death), resurrection and ascension, much less Pentecost and the parousia, into a single revelatory moment, as is rife in secondary literature under the influence of the Bultmann school.[101]

John describes the ascension of Jesus to heaven using his own peculiar terminology. Luke's informal, varied vocabulary for this event—"he parted [διέστη] from them, and was carried up [ἀνεφέρετο] into heaven" (Lk 24:51); "he was lifted up [ἐπήρθη], and a cloud took him [ὑπέλαβεν] out of their sight.

---

[101]Bultmann, *Theology*, 2:53, 56, 57-58.

. . . 'This Jesus, who was taken up [ὁ ἀναλημφθείς] from you into heaven, will come in the same way as you saw him go [πορευόμενον] into heaven'" (Acts 1:9, 11)—finds scarcely a parallel in John. Paul can say that God "highly exalted" (ὑπερύψωσεν) him (Phil 2:9), but John uses "exalt" (ὑψόω) only in reference to the crucifixion, and that paradoxically. A curiosity of the Johannine literature is the lack anywhere of a statement that Christ is at God's "right hand" (δεξιᾷ) reflecting Psalm 110:1, which is so frequent in Paul. Luke, Paul and John overlap in saying Jesus "went up" (ἀναβαίνω [e.g., Jn 20:17]). A unique picture in the Apocalypse is that of Jesus being "snatched up" (ἡρπάσθη) to God and to his throne (Apoc 12:5).

In John's Gospel Jesus' ascension merges with his going to the Father in completion of his sending/return and descent/ascent. Since the Gospel story comes to an end before the return takes place and does not include an account of the ascension as such, all the references to it are anticipatory, the bulk of them falling in the Farewell Discourse (ἀναβαίνειν [Jn 3:13; 6:62; 20:17]; ἀπελθεῖν [Jn 16:7]; πορεύεσθαι [Jn 7:35; 14:2-3, 12, 28; 16:7, 28]; ὑπάγειν [Jn 7:33; 8:14, 21-22; 13:3, 33, 36; 14:4-5, 28; 16:5, 10, 17]).

Yet when Jesus stood before Pilate, he professed to have a kingship (βασιλεία) "not of this world" (Jn 18:36). Throughout the Johannine literature, where Jesus' name is linked in a confessional way with the title "Christ," his installment as God's anointed one is assumed.[102] In the Revelation we find an unveiling of the ascension in traditional messianic terms. A male child who is to "rule all the nations with a rod of iron" is caught up to God "and to his throne" (Apoc 12:5). Behind this language is the coronation-boast of Yahweh's anointed in Psalm 2:9. At the inauguration of the messianic kingdom, Michael leads his angels to expel the dragon and his angels from the regions of heaven (Apoc 12:7-9), and a voice declares, "Now the salvation and the power and the kingdom of our God and the authority of his Christ have come" (Apoc 12:10). In the remainder of the book, Christ's session in heaven defines the framework within which the forces of evil muster the world for combat with followers of the Lamb (Apoc 12:13–15:5) and are undone (Apoc 19:11–21:8).

**The giving of the Spirit by the ascended Lord.** While Jesus was still un-known, the Baptist prophesied that he would baptize people with the Holy Spirit (Jn 1:33). Jesus did nothing of the sort during his earthly ministry because,

---

[102]John 1:17; 17:3; 20:31; 1 Jn 1:3; 2:1, 22; 3:23; 4:2, 15; 5:1, 6, 20; 2 Jn 3, 7; Apoc 1:1, 2, 5; 22:21. Compare also the bare "Christ" at 2 Jn 9; Apoc 11:15; 12:10; 20:4, 6.

as the Evangelist sees from a postpentecostal vantage point, at that time Jesus "was not yet glorified" (Jn 7:39). Jesus had to reclaim the world and enter into his glory before he could give the Spirit as God's endowment for the unending age to come.

The Farewell Discourse looks forward to Jesus' imminent departure and the sending of the Spirit. Expressions for the latter event may have either the Father or the Son as the sending subject, but always the ascended Son is the executive agent. His earthly work is the content to which the Spirit's ministry points. "In my name," he says, the Father will send the Holy Spirit (Jn 14:26). Jesus will send the Paraclete from the Father (Jn 15:26); or simply will send him (Jn 16:7). Moreover, in the advent of the Spirit, the Son himself will come to be with his otherwise-orphaned followers (Jn 14:18). They will see the Son (Jn 14:19; cf. Jn 16:16-22), he will manifest himself to them (Jn 14:21), and together with the Spirit no lesser bedfellows than the Father and the Son will come and dwell with them (Jn 14:23).

Toward the end of the Gospel the risen Jesus, standing among his disciples on the evening of the first Easter, breathes on (ἐνεφύσησεν) them and says, "Receive the Holy Spirit" (Jn 20:22). Most commentators regard this transaction as the "Johannine Pentecost." True, it gathers up all earlier references in the Gospel to the giving of the Spirit and points to their fulfilment. No other event in the Johannine literature matches the Lucan Pentecost. That an interval of fifty days separates the event in John from that in Acts does not faze those who suppose John was happy to jettison chronological accuracy in the interest of driving home christological truth. But if the author of the Fourth Gospel was John the apostle, he would have been a participant on both occasions and could not have conflated them. John, well aware of the historical facts, builds his late Gospel around unrecorded incidents held in his memory that offer a supplement to Luke–Acts. On his Gospel's own terms, the Spirit could not be given until Jesus was glorified (Jn 7:39; 14:16, 26; 16:7, 13). On the day of his resurrection Jesus made it quite clear that he had not yet ascended to the Father (Jn 20:17), which event would complete his glorification (Jn 17:1, 5, 11, 13); nor had Jesus been fully glorified even some days later when he appeared again to some of his disciples by the Sea of Tiberias (Jn 21). John cannot, therefore, mean that the complete pentecostal outpouring took place already on Easter day in the evening. Jesus, before his departure from the world and while still among his disciples, granted to them by this visible exhalation a performative sign of the insufflation of the Spirit. From this moment forward, the Spirit was objectively and irretractably theirs, even if they first experienced the Spirit's full power seven weeks later. John records the dominical impulse of the grant of the Spirit; Acts its impact on the nascent church after the Ascended One commenced the exercise of his messianic office.

So close is the relationship between the glorified Lord and the Spirit that the radiant figure of Revelation 1:13-20 can be described as the one "who has the seven spirits of God" (Apoc 3:1), and the Lamb can be depicted as having seven eyes, "which are the seven spirits of God sent out into all the earth" (Apoc 5:6).

*The reign of Christ to the end of the age.* With the other New Testament authors John holds that Christ began to reign at his ascension and will continue to do so until the end of the age. In the nature of the case, the Gospel offers only foreshadowings of this fact, and the Epistles presuppose rather than proclaim it. Its literary locus is the book of Revelation.

Jesus' messianic reign was anticipated by the "Hosanna!" cry of Psalm 118:25-26 taken up by the crowd at his last, triumphal entry into Jerusalem. At the same time, he rode on a royal ass (Jn 12:13-15) according to ancient custom (1 Kings 1:33, 38, 44) as reflected in Zechariah's prophecy (Zech 9:9). His regnum began "when Jesus was glorified" (Jn 12:16). His profession to Pilate that he was in fact the king of an otherworldly realm pointed to the invisible rule that was about to commence (Jn 18:33-38). After rising from the dead, the Lord spoke of his imminent ascension (Jn 20:17) and of his will of disposal over his servants until he would come (Jn 21:22).

Christ's kingdom extends beyond those who acknowledge it. The Apocalypse unveils him as "the ruler of kings on earth" (Apoc 1:5). His "kingdom" will prevail in the sphere of international politics. This will be so even if temporary disorder now calls for patient endurance on the part of his people (Apoc 1:9). Bearer of the key of David, he "opens and no one shall shut," he "shuts and no one opens" (Apoc 3:7; cf. Is 22:22). Having conquered, he sat down with his Father on his throne and now sits (Apoc 3:21). Consistenly Christ is depicted as sharing the singular throne of God in heaven (Apoc 5:6; 7:9, 17; 12:5; 22:1), not as sitting on a second throne to its right side. From his enthronement onward (Apoc 12:5) the authority of God's Christ has come, and his foes face certain doom (Apoc 12:10-12). His majesty can be likened to that of the Ancient of Days whom Daniel saw as the judge of all earthly empires (Apoc 1:13-15; cf. Dan 7:9-10). The liturgy directed to him that will eventually encompass everything in heaven and on earth and under the earth and in the sea has already begun to cascade downward in concentric waves from heaven (Apoc 5). The scroll he takes out of the right hand of the one on the throne represents the sovereign plan of God for the destiny of the universe, of which Christ is the executor (Apoc 5:1, 7).

At present, the reigning Lord has gone away to his Father's many-roomed house "to prepare a place" for his followers (Jn 14:2), that where he is they may come to be also (Jn 17:24). The great prayer in John 17 looks not only back on Jesus' completed ministry but also forward to the interval of his absence. Central concerns are their safekeeping from evil (Jn 17:11-15), their sanctification in the truth as he sends them out into the world (Jn 17:16-19), and their unity in love, that through them the world may come to believe (Jn 17:20-26).

These same concerns, seen in other parts of the Johannine corpus, define the work of his reign. No one can snatch Christ's sheep out of his hand (Jn 10:28). After Peter denied his Lord, Jesus reinstated him as shepherd of the flock (Jn 21:15-17). Christ advocates with the Father for believers who fall into sin; as the "Righteous One" he pleads the propitiatory value of his death on their behalf with a view to securing daily forgiveness for those who confess their sins (1 Jn 1:7–2:2). As the one who has been begotten by God, Jesus keeps those born of God so that they do not sin mortally, and the evil one does not touch them (1 Jn 5:18). John sees one like a son of man walking in the midst of seven lamp-stands that, like the branches of the menorah in the temple, symbolize God's people, indicating Christ's living presence in the midst of the church (Apoc 1:13; 2:1). He holds their angel-stars firmly in his right hand (Apoc 1:20; 2:1), exhorts them to repent (Apoc 2–3), and will keep them from the hour of trial that is coming to try the whole world (Apoc 3:10).

Through the messianic community Christ is drawing the world to the salvation he has won for it. He is "the Savior of the world" (Jn 4:42). He has many sheep among the nations to unite with Israel in one fold (Jn 10:16). His intention in dying was to bear much fruit (Jn 12:24), and in being lifted up to draw all people to himself (Jn 12:32). He sent his disciples into the world to herald the word about himself (Jn 17:18; 20:21, 23). The miraculous catch of fish in the Sea of Tiberias was both a manifestation of himself to his disciples after his resurrection, and perhaps a symbol of their dependence on him and of his blessing upon them as they turn to become fishers of people (Jn 21:1-14). The results are seen in the final submission to him of individuals from every people, tongue, tribe and nation (Apoc 5:9; 7:9).

Not all are persuaded, however. Many outside the church cooperate with the leaders of Roman society in persecuting the saints and rejoicing when they fall (Apoc 11:7-10; 13:7-10). Jesus identifies and sympathizes with his people in their sufferings (Apoc 1:9; 2:8-11; 3:7-13). He stands with his redeemed and shares his own name with them (Apoc 14:1). The living souls of those who became martyrs reign with him until the dénouement of the age (Apoc 20:4, 6). Heretics who mingle with the church and do not repent feel even now the double-edged sword that Christ will wield against those who hold out against him (Apoc 1:16; 19:21); apparently the Nicolaitan false prophetess of Thyatira and some who accepted her teachings succumbed to sickness (Apoc 2:16, 22-23).

*The return of Christ at the end of the age.* John shares the early church's eager expectation of the return of Christ to wrap up the present age and issue in the everlasting order. The main events are four: the second coming of Jesus Christ, the general resurrection, the last judgment and the commencement of God's eternal kingdom. This simple scheme of events with Christ at its center, attested by the Fourth Gospel and the First Epistle of John,[103] forms the core eschatology behind the recapitulating visions of the book of Revelation.[104] It pervades all parts of the Johannine literature.

Christ's ascension inaugurated the penultimate epoch of world history, the "latter days" of Old Testament prophecy (Deut 4:30; Is 2:2; 9:1; Jer 23:20; Ezek 38:8, 16; Dan 2:28; 10:14; Hos 3:5). John sees signs that the world has already entered into its "last hour" (1 Jn 2:18).[105] Jesus' return will mark "the last day" (Jn 6:39; 11:24; 12:48).[106]

Christ's return will be his "coming" again to be reunited with his disciples

---

[103]For a massive demonstration of the eschatology of the Gospel and First Epistle of John, which Bultmann had tried to sweep under the carpet in the interest of his existentialist interpretation, see the three volumes of Jörg Frey, *Johanneische Eschatologie*.

[104]The scheme of events is given in chronological order in Apoc 20:11–21:8. J. Lambrecht, "Final Judgments and Ultimate Blessings: The Climactic Visions of Revelation 20,11–21,8," *Bib* 81 (2000): 362-85; Rainbow, *Pith*, pp. 42-44, 85-110.

[105]G. K. Beale, "The Old Testament Background of the 'Last Hour' in 1 John 2,18," *Bib* 92 (2011): 231-54; S. Mihalios, *The Danielic Eschatological Hour in the Johannine Literature* (Library of New Testament Studies 436; London: T & T Clark, 2011).

[106]Compare the references to God's "great day" in the book of Revelation: Rev 6:17; 16:14; 18:8. J. Puthussery, *Days of Man and God's Day: An Exegetico-Theological Study of ἡμέρα in the Book of Revelation* (Tesi Gregoriana, Serie Teologia 82; Rome: Editrice Pontificia Università Gregoriana, 2002).

(Jn 14:3, 28; 21:22; Apoc 2:5, 16, 25; 3:3, 11, 20; 22:7, 12, 20), his final "appearance" (1 Jn 2:28; 3:2), or his "parousia" (1 Jn 2:28). All these texts emphasize that his person will be visible. To this basic picture the book of Revelation adds color and detail through imagery derived largely from the Hebrew Bible. Jesus will come with clouds, and every eye will see him (Apoc 1:7; 14:14; cf. Dan 7:13). From his mouth will protrude a sword with which to execute judgment, symbolizing his judicial word (Apoc 2:5; 19:21; cf. Is 11:4). He will come like a thief, unexpectedly (Apoc 3:3; 16:15; cf. Mt 24:43). His appearance will be attended by cosmic dissolution portrayed as an earthquake, a shakeup of sun, moon and stars, and contortions of the earth's surface, sending people fleeing from his face in terror (Apoc 6:12-17; 16:17-21; cf. Mt 24:29-31).

A period of tribulation will precede the return of Christ, during which the world will hate his disciples and excommunicate some from the synagogues or kill them (Jn 15:18-25; 16:1-4, 20-22, 32-33). In the Epistles, John sees plural heretics who oppose the cause of Christ by teaching falsehood about him as fulfilling the apocalyptic concept of an antimessiah; John calls them "(many) antichrist(s)" (1 Jn 2:18, 22; 4:3; 2 Jn 7).[107] Applied differently, the same figure becomes in the Revelation a political "beast" representing the Roman imperial administration, and a priestly "false prophet" representing the officers of the state cultus, both inspired by the dragon from the pit of hell (Apoc 13; 17). Jesus will engage these worldly forces at the "battle" of Armageddon and take them out once and for all (Apoc 16:13-16; 17:14; 19:11-21), ridding the earth of its destroyers (Apoc 11:18) and clearing the way for the benevolent rule of God.

At Jesus' parousia he will raise the dead of all generations and assign them their lots in the age to come. Jesus claimed to be the Son of Man to whom God has given power to vivify the dead (Jn 5:21). A single, general resurrection of both the righteous and the unrighteous was an item of Jewish (Dan 12:2; Jn 11:24) and of early Christian eschatology (Acts 24:15). John has Jesus speak the words, "The hour is coming when all who are in the tombs will hear his [the Son of Man's] voice and come forth, those who have done good, to the resurrection of life, and those who have done evil, to the resurrection of judgment" (Jn 5:28-29).[108] That Jesus will raise believers on "the last day" he promises in

---

[107]On John's unique term "antichrist," see Strecker, *Letters*, pp. 236-41; S. J. Nichols, "Prophecy Makes Strange Bedfellows: On the History of Identifying the Antichrist," *JETS* 44 (2001): 75-85.

[108]Nils A. Dahl, "'Do Not Wonder!' John 5:28-29 and Johannine Eschatology Once More," in *The Conversation Continues: Studies in Paul and John*, ed. Robert T. Fortna and Beverly R. Gaventa (Nashville: Abingdon, 1990), pp. 322-36.

the discourse on the Bread of Life (Jn 6:39, 40, 44, 54). When he appears, "we shall be like him, for we shall see him as he is" (1 Jn 3:2). Resurrection is a theme to encourage hard-pressed churches in the book of Revelation (Apoc 2:7, 10-11; 3:5; 11:11; 20:4, 6). Toward the end of the latter book sits a brief but impressive description of the repositories of the dead, the sea, Death and Hades, yielding up their subjects to stand before God's great white throne and receive a final and irrevocable sentence (Apoc 20:11-15).

Jesus will act as judge on God's behalf. To him the Father has committed all judgment (Jn 5:22-23, 27, 30; Apoc 6:16-17). At issue will be people's eternal destiny, whether life or death, based on what they have done (Jn 5:29; Apoc 20:12-13). "He who rejects me . . . the word that I have spoken will be his judge on the last day" (Jn 12:48). Believers are to abide in Christ and purify themselves so that they may have confidence and not shrink from him in shame at his coming (1 Jn 2:28; 3:3). There will be a "day of judgment," and the way to have confidence for that day is to bring love to perfection by abiding in it, being like him in this world (1 Jn 4:16-17). Besides the clear outline of the Last Assize in Revelation 20:11-15, that book is filled with scenes of the ultimate destruction of evil and the exaltation of the righteous (Apoc 6:9-17; 11:18; 14:14–15:4). Typical is the sharp contrast between the fate of Lady Babylon (Apoc 17:1–19:10) and that of Lady Jerusalem (Apoc 21:9–22:9).

At the last, Jesus is shown reigning with God in a new cosmic order. The phrase "kingdom of God" occurs in the Gospel only in the account of Jesus' conversation with Nicodemus (Jn 3:3, 5) and is thereafter replaced by the concept of "eternal life" (starting in Jn 3:15). John retains "kingdom of God" as a staple term of Old Testament and Jewish eschatology and places it ahead of the other, because even in an outlook that accents the present foretaste of eschatological blessings, a proper definition of eternal life takes the future kingdom of God for its proper setting. In the Fourth Gospel there are only fleeting glimpses of a realm where the saints will live immortal (Jn 11:25-26) and the Son of God will again share his Father's glory as he did before the the world was made (Jn 17:5, 24). Where the Apocalyptist contemplates the transition from this world to that, he calls the coming one "the kingdom of our Lord and of his Christ" (Apoc 11:15). Features of the Edenic paradise (Gen 2:10-17), of Ezekiel's ideal temple-city (Ezek 47:1-12) and of Zechariah's vision of the final state (Zech 14:6-9) inform the idyllic picture of the river of the water of life flowing from "the throne of God and of the Lamb" (Apoc 22:1), a paragraph concluding with the words, "and they shall reign for ever and ever" (Apoc 22:5; cf. Apoc 11:15).

## SUMMARY

In chapters four and five we have divided John's Christology into consideration of Jesus' person and work. But these two aspects belong together. The person is manifest in his work. The nature of the divine person is such that only a work of comprehensive and epic proportions would have been suitable for him to do. The nature of the work is such that only one sent from the Father is capable of pulling it off. Jesus' words and signs alike pointed to the mystery of his person as the eternal Son whom the Father sent into the world to bring life where there was death and light where there was darkness. This he accomplished by becoming flesh, shouldering the world's sin, and dying vicariously as the Lamb of God who takes sin away; then by rising as the first, individual instance, already within the flow of history, of the general resurrection to immortality. By his ascension and heavenly session he empowers the church to rescue from the coming judgment any who will believe. As messianic king, he is guiding world affairs to the final showdown with the forces of evil that must precede the renewal of all things in the kingdom of God. The entire saga is driven by a divine love that created people to share the joy of fellowship with the Father and the Son, a love that would not take their turning away toward darkness for an answer but undertook, at inestimable cost, to fetch them back to God. In all of this the Son acts to glorify the Father and the Father to glorify the Son. The glory of the Father and of the Son shows itself to the world as the beauty, the splendor, of precisely this divine love.

Thus John's writings bear a consistent and united testimony to the centrality of Jesus' death, resurrection, ascension, messianic reign and return in the apostle's thought. These events make up the content that Christ was sent into the world to accomplish. It is by his doing of these things that Jesus was and is the Logos, the perfect self-communication of the Father. The God who wants to make himself known to human beings is the God who has done and is doing these things in his Son.[109]

Looking back over the very rich Johannine kerygma, the falsehood becomes patent of Bultmann's pronouncements that "Jesus' death as an atonement for

---

[109]W. H. Cadman, *The Open Heaven: The Revelation of God in the Johannine Sayings of Jesus* (ed. G.B. Caird; New York: Herder and Herder, 1969), pp. 3-14.

sin has no place in John," and that his resurrection "cannot be an event of special significance."[110] Bultmann rightly identified Jesus as the divine Revealer but was unable to recognize the actual content of the revelation because its core events did not jive with his secular worldview. He allowed his bent toward a naturalistic reduction of Christianity to trump exegetical and theological sense. One can only express astonishment that any other New Testament scholar, not to mention so large a cadre of them, were swayed by a treatment that missed so utterly the very marrow of the good news John proclaims.[111]

John presents us with a theology of persons divine and created and of the web of their relationships. Considering the relation between God (chapter two above) and the rebellious world that is the object of his redemptive action in Jesus Christ (chapter three), John writes simply, "We love, because he first loved us" (1 Jn 4:19). Indeed everything about God's sending of his Son into the world (chapter four) proclaims his love for us (chapter five). But there was a prior love. John might well have written that God loved us because he first loved his own Son: "As the Father has loved me, so have I loved you," said Jesus (Jn 15:9; cf. Jn 3:35; 10:17; 15:10; 17:23, 24, 26). How could God love the world were not love an eternal feature of the internal divine life? This leads us to inquire into the nature of the Holy Spirit.

---

[110]Bultmann, 2:54, 56.

[111]To take just one outstanding example: Even though existentialism became in the latter twentieth century but one of many eddies in the great stream of European intellectual culture, as late as the 1990s Ashton's continuing entrancement with Bultmann came through in his somewhat muted judgment that Jesus' death as the atonement for sin "cannot be said to be in any way central" and that a case can be made "for the superfluousness of the resurrection stories" (John Ashton, *Understanding*, pp. 491, 485).

# 6

## THE REVELATION
## OF THE FATHER IN THE SON
## BY THE SPIRIT-PARACLETE

G OD'S "SPEECH-ACT" OF SENDING HIS SON achieves its goal when the target audience grasps it and thereby enters into renewed communion with God. Just as only a divine emissary—who is everything God is—could be a fit agent to bring the content of the revelation, so also only a divine host—who can contain the whole God-idea, himself being God—could be a fit receptacle for it. Taking up residence in God's creatures, he opens them from within to welcome the message. Prayed the psalmist, "In your light do we see light" (Ps 36:9). So John's theology of revelation must include the Holy Spirit.

John's concept of the divine Spirit is vivid and profound. He focuses on just a few key aspects, in contrast to Paul, who offers a more elaborate pneumatology. The characteristically concentrated Johannine doctrine of the Spirit, added to John's maximal Christology within a strictly monotheistic outlook, gives his nascent trinitarianism an especially strong momentum toward later doctrinal formulations.[1] By reflecting on the Johannine writings in the

---

[1]"Indeed, one may speak plainly of Johannine theology having a trinitarian foundation [*Grundstruktur*]. . . . The Johannine theology itself is the first trinitarian theology [*Trinitätstheologie*] of the church. It offers not only definite beginnings for the later dogma of the Trinity, but is its biblical basis [*Grundlage*]" (Ulrich Wilckens, "Gott, der Drei-Eine: Zur Trinitätstheologie der johanneischen Schriften," in *Der Sohn Gottes und seine Gemeinde: Studien zur Theologie der Johanneischen Schriften* [FRLANT 200; Göttingen: Vandenhoeck & Ruprecht, 2003], p. 28 [my translation]). See also Michael Theobald, "Gott, Logos und Pneuma: 'Trinitarische' Rede von Gott im Johannesevangelium," in *Monotheismus und Christologie: Zur Gottesfrage im hellenistischen Judentum und im Urchristentum* (ed. Hans-Josef Klauck; QD 138; Freiburg: Herder, 1992), pp. 41-87; Udo Schnelle, "Trinitarisches Denken im Johannesevangelium," in *Israel und seine Heilstraditionen im Johannesevangelium: Festgabe für Johannes Beutler SJ zum 70. Geburtstag* (ed. Michael Labahn, Klaus Scholtissek and Angelika

context of the whole New Testament, the orthodox Fathers of the late fourth century—especially the Cappadocians: Basil the Great, Gregory of Nazianzus and Gregory of Nyssa, in dispute with heretics who denied the Spirit's divinity— concluded that God must be triune, a singular being who exists as three quite distinct but interrelated personal entities. Thus they laid the foundation for Christian theology.

As is typical of John, his understanding of the Spirit is not to be found on a page or two; rather, it is couched in varied phrases and clauses distributed in many contexts throughout his writings. The present chapter collects this ma-terial under several headings: terminology, the relation of the Spirit to the Father and the Son, the coming of the Spirit in salvation history, and the Spirit's work in believers.

## TERMINOLOGY

Already the Old Testament knew of the "Spirit of God/Yahweh" as a heaven-sent energy that came upon select judges, prophets or kings. God's Spirit gave extraordinary insights or prompted people to heroic exploits in God's service. The exact phrase "Holy Spirit" is found only twice in the Old Testament (Ps 51:13; Is 63:10-11). It became a recognized title in early Judaism, the New Tes-tament and the rabbis.[2] It points to the dynamic presence of God in human experience, a sweeping force from the transcendent otherness and moral per-fection of God. "The wind [πνεῦμα] blows where it wills, and you hear the sound of it, but you do not know whence it comes or whither it goes; so is every one who is born of the Spirit [πνεῦμα]" (Jn 3:8). John can use the full term "Holy Spirit" (τὸ πνεῦμα τὸ ἅγιον [Jn 1:33; 7:39; 14:26; 20:22]), but, like Paul, he most often refers to him simply as "the Spirit."[3]

Two uniquely Johannine descriptors are the noun "Paraclete" (παράκλητος, usually translated as "Advocate" [Lat. *advocatus*], "Comforter" or "Helper" [Jn

---

Strotmann; Paderborn: Schöningh, 2004), pp. 367-86; Evan F. Kuehn, "The Johannine Logic of Augustine's Trinity: A Dogmatic Sketch," *TS* 68 (2007): 572-94; Andreas J Köstenberger and Scott R. Swain, *Father, Son and Spirit: The Trinity and John's Gospel* (NSBT 24; Downers Grove, IL: Inter-Varsity Press, 2008). For sketches of trinitarian elements in the Apocalypse, see Friedrich Beisser, "Trinitätsaussagen in der Offenbarung des Johannes," in *Studien zur Johannesoffenbarung und ihrer Auslegung: Festschrift für Otto Böcher zum 70. Geburtstag* (ed. Friedrich Wilhelm Horn and Michael Wolter; Neukirchen-Vluyn: Neukirchener Verlag, 2005), pp. 120-35; Louis A. Brighton, "Christo-logical Trinitarian Theology in the Book of Revelation," *ConJ* 34 (2008): 292-97.
[2]References in Friedrich Wilhelm Horn, "Holy Spirit," *ABD* 3:260-65.
[3]τὸ πνεῦμα (Jn 1:32, 33; 3:5, 6, 8, 34; 4:23, 24; 6:63; 7:39; 1 Jn 3:24; 4:2, 13; 5:6, 8; Apoc 1:10; 2:7, 11, 17, 29; 3:6, 13, 22; 4:2; 14:13; 17:3; 21:10; 22:17).

14:16, 26; 15:26; 16:7]),[4] and the genitive phrase "the Spirit of truth" (Jn 14:17; 15:26; 16:13; 1 Jn 4:6; cf. Jn 4:23-24; 1 Jn 5:6). Παράκλητος has been a focus of intense study, but no consensus has emerged as to why John used this word or exactly what he meant by it.[5] In the Mediterranean cultures it had a nexus of associations: psychological (a person who offers encouragement and comfort), social (intercession and help) and legal (representation and advocacy).[6] While some studies have featured one or another of these as the clue to John's usage, it is hard to tie John down to a single connotation. Below we will take up this question more fully.

"Spirit of truth" is related to the era of "spirit and truth" (Jn 4:23, 24), the time of eschatological blessing inaugurated by Jesus' glorification. To convince the world that the reality of God, or truth of God, has come in Christ is the divine Spirit's task and concern. The Spirit has an essential part in John's theology of revelation. If the Father's sending of the Son may be represented as God putting forth his final word to communicate with the estranged creation, the sending of the Spirit has as its goal to secure a reception for that word. Ignace de la Potterie's classic studies of "truth" in John's writings are

---

[4]The same noun denotes Jesus Christ in 1 John 2:1. These five Johannine references are the sum of all occurrences in the New Testament.

[5]Every major commentary on the Fourth Gospel plus several technical monographs have delved into the question. Among the more salient are Hans Windisch, *The Spirit-Paraclete in the Fourth Gospel* (trans. James W. Cox; FBBS 20; Philadelphia: Fortress, 1968); David Earl Holwerda, *The Holy Spirit and Eschatology in the Gospel of John: A Critique of Rudolf Bultman's Present Eschatology* (Grand Rapids: Eerdmans, 1959), pp. 26-38; Raymond E. Brown, *The Gospel According to John: Introduction, Translation, and Notes* (2 vols.; AB 29, 29A; Garden City, NY: Doubleday, 1966–1970), 2:1135-44; George Johnston, *The Spirit-Paraclete in the Gospel of John* (SNTSMS 13; Cambridge: Cambridge University Press, 1970); Felix Porsch, *Pneuma und Wort: Ein exegetischer Beitrag zur Pneumatologie des Johannesevangeliums* (FrTS 16; Frankfurt am Main: J. Knecht, 1974); Eskil Franck, *Revelation Taught: The Paraclete in the Gospel of John* (ConBNT 14; Lund: Gleerup, 1985); Gary M. Burge, *The Anointed Community: The Holy Spirit in the Johannine Tradition* (Grand Rapids: Eerdmans, 1987), pp. 3-41; John Ashton, *Understanding the Fourth Gospel* (Oxford: Clarendon, 1991), pp. 420-25; Hans-Christian Kammler, "Jesus Christus und der Geistparaklet: Eine Studie zur johanneischen Verhältnisbestimmung von Pneumatologie und Christologie," in *Johannesstudien: Untersuchungen zur Theologie des vierten Evangeliums*, by Otfried Hofius and Hans-Christian Kammler (WUNT 88; Tübingen: Mohr Siebeck, 1996), pp. 87-190; Stephen S. Smalley, "'The Paraclete': Pneumatology in the Johannine Gospel and Apocalypse," in *Exploring the Gospel of John: In Honor of D. Moody Smith* (ed. R. Alan Culpepper and C. Clifton Black; Louisville: Westminster John Knox, 1996), pp. 289-300; Tricia Gates Brown, *Spirit in the Writings of John: Johannine Pneumatology in Social-Scientific Perspective* (JSNTSup 253; London: T & T Clark, 2003); David Pastorelli, *Le Paraclet dans le corpus johannique* (BZNW 142; Berlin: de Gruyter, 2006).

[6]Windisch, *Spirit-Paraclete*, p. 17. On παράκλητος as a calque for the Latin *advocatus*, with legal connotations, see Lochlan Shelfer, "The Legal Precision of the Term 'παράκλητος,'" *JSNT* 32 (2009): 131-50.

convincing, and his conclusions are widely accepted.[7] The Spirit arouses faith
in Christ

> by rendering this truth present and active in the hearts of the faithful. . . . There
> are two times of revelation . . . the time of Christ, who brings revelation objec-
> tively and historically . . . [and] the time of the Spirit, who illuminates the truth
> of Christ and renders it subjectively present in us. . . . Without the action of the
> Spirit there is no interior awareness of the truth.[8]

In 1 John, besides the typical phrases "Spirit of God" (1 Jn 4:2),[9] "Spirit" (1
Jn 3:24; 5:6, 8), and "Spirit of truth" (1 Jn 4:6), we find "the anointing which
you received from him" (1 Jn 2:27). This makes the believing community heir
to the same charismatic endowment that graced the Davidic dynasty of old
(1 Sam 16:13; Ps 89:20) and Jesus as the Messiah. In the context of the First
Epistle it stresses the knowledge with which the Holy Spirit has immunized
the apostolic community against christological falsehood spewed by a schismatic movement.[10]

The Apocalypse has an idiosyncratic vocabulary for the Spirit, but the underlying conception is, as we will see in due course, comparable to that in the
rest of the Johannine corpus. No other canonical writer portrays the plenitude
of the Spirit's potencies in terms of "seven spirits of God" (Apoc 1:4; 3:1; 4:5; 5:6),
though in John's First Epistle there is an interplay between the singular "Spirit"
and the plural "spirits" who move individual prophets (1 Jn 4:1-4).[11] Probably
the inspiration for the numerical language of the Apocalypse is Zechariah's
vision of the seven lamps of the Menorah in Zechariah 4:2 representing God's
Spirit (v. 6), interpreted as "the eyes of YHWH, which range through the whole
earth" (v. 10). A supporting passage may be Isaiah 11:2 with its list of six Hebrew
construct nouns describing "the Spirit of YHWH," expanded to seven genitives

---

[7]Ignace de la Potterie, *La vérité dans Saint Jean* (2 vols.; AnBib 73, 74; Rome: Biblical Institute Press, 1977), pp. 281-466; idem, "The Truth in Saint John," in *The Interpretation of John* (ed. John Ashton; IRT 9; Philadelphia: Fortress, 1986), pp. 58-64. See also Rudolf Schnackenburg, *The Gospel Accord-ing to St. John* (trans. Kevin Smyth et al.; 3 vols.; New York: Herder & Herder; Seabury; Crossroad, 1968-1982), 2:225-37; David J. Hawkin, "Revelation and Truth in Johannine Theology," *Chm* 116 (2002): 105-12; Nicolas Farelly, "'Je suis la vérité' dans l'évangile de Jean," *RRef* 56 (2005): 1-20. John uses "truth" and related words flexibly and with a wide semantic range, impossible to reduce to a single concept, whether Hebraic, Hellenistic or apocalyptic.
[8]De la Potterie, "Truth in Saint John," pp. 59, 63.
[9]Note also the phrase "his Spirit" (τὸ πνεῦμα αὐτοῦ [i.e., of God]) in 1 John 4:13.
[10]Georg Strecker, *The Johannine Letters: A Commentary on 1, 2, and 3 John* (ed. Harold W. Attridge; trans. Linda M. Maloney; Hermeneia; Minneapolis: Fortress, 1996), pp. 64-66.
[11]Parallel is the phrase "the God of the spirits of the prophets" in Apocalypse 22:6.

in the Septuagint. The one Spirit is manifold in his effects.[12] That these "seven spirits" are divine and should not be equated with the seven archangels (Apoc 8:2) is clear from their middle position in the trinitarian grace of Apocalypse 1:4-5, and from their function as the omniscient seven eyes of the Lamb, who shares God's throne (Apoc 5:6). Their location before God's throne, where they burn like seven torches (Apoc 4:5), is an apocalyptic representation of the element "Holy" in "Holy Spirit." The phrase "breath of life from God" (πνεῦμα ζωῆς ἐκ τοῦ θεοῦ [Apoc 11:11]) is reminiscent of a major theme of the Gospel: the Spirit is the agent of life and resurrection. And "the spirit [or Spirit] of prophecy" that testifies to Jesus (Apoc 19:10; cf. "the spirits of the prophets" [Apoc 22:6]) is similar, both in grammatical form and in significance, to the Gospel's "Spirit of truth."[13]

Here, then, are the data we must take into account when considering John's concept of the Holy Spirit.

## RELATION OF THE SPIRIT TO THE FATHER AND THE SON

God is the fount of all personality, and the increate Son exists in eternal relation to the Father; so also the divine Spirit is a personal being. Together with "him who is" and with Jesus Christ, the sevenfold Spirit is the source of grace for God's people (Apoc 1:4). If the Spirit gives birth to persons (Jn 3:5, 6, 8), he himself cannot be less than personal, for like bears like: "That which is born of the Spirit is spirit" (Jn 3:6). Nor, if the Spirit is the life-giver (τὸ ζῳοποιοῦν [Jn 6:63]), can he be other than living. During the time of Jesus' absence from the world the Spirit is the mode of Christ's coming to his own lest they be orphans (Jn 14:18), of their seeing Christ and living because of him (Jn 14:19), of their dwelling in Christ and Christ in them (Jn 14:20), of Christ's self-manifestation (Jn 14:21-22), and of the Father and the Son coming to one who keeps Jesus' word and making their home with him (Jn 14:23). Could the mode of Christ's presence be impersonal? Again and again the Spirit is the intelligent subject of

---

[12]According to one ancient Jewish conception, in God's wisdom is "a spirit that is . . . unique, manifold. . . . Though she is but one, she can do all things" (Wis 7:22, 27).

[13]See further Richard Bauckham, *The Theology of the Book of Revelation* (NTT; Cambridge: Cambridge University Press, 1993), pp. 109-25; Ferdinand Hahn, "Das Geistverständnis in der Johannesoffenbarung," in Horn and Wolter, *Studien zur Johannesoffenbarung*, pp. 3-9; Robby Waddell, *The Spirit of the Book of Revelation* (JPTSup 30; Blandford Forum: Deo, 2006). It has been observed that the function of the Spirit-Paraclete in the Gospel (Jn 14:16-20, 26; 15:26-27; 16:7-11, 13-15) corresponds to the role of prophetic preachers in the early church. See Hans Klein, "Der Paraklet als Subjekt prophetischer Rede im Johannesevangelium," SS 9 (2011): 173-88.

verbs of communication: he "teaches" and "reminds" (Jn 14:26), "bears witness" (Jn 15:26), "hears," "takes," "speaks," "declares," "guides," "glorifies" (Jn 16:13-14), "confesses" (1 Jn 4:2-3), and "says" (Apoc 2:7, 11, 17, 29; 3:6, 13, 22; 14:13; 19:10; 22:17). Being in the sphere of the Spirit is the condition for a prophet to receive God's word (Apoc 1:10; 4:2; 17:3; 21:10) and for the ears of the audience to hear and respond (Apoc 2:7, 11, 17, 29; 3:6, 13, 22). In 1 John 4:4 the Spirit is described as "he who is in you" (ὁ ἐν ὑμῖν), using the masculine (i.e., personal) form of the article.[14]

On the other hand, the Spirit's being personal need not imply that he has the same kind of relation to the Father and the Son that they have with each other. In that relationship the Son is unique as God's "only"-begotten (μονο-γενής). The Spirit, then, is not "begotten." John often speaks of Father and Son as a dyad without mentioning the Spirit. Typical statements are "This is eternal life, that they know you the only true God, and Jesus Christ whom you have sent" (Jn 17:3), and "Our fellowship is with the Father and with his Son Jesus Christ" (1 Jn 1:3). Bipartite statements of this sort abound in the Johannine literature.[15] Such formulae suggest that the relation between the Father and the Son is different from that between them and the Spirit. But the Spirit's contribution is tacit in the fact that people "know" the Father and the Son and have "fellowship" with them. In contrast to Johannine language for the Father's generation of the Son, which uses the analogy of an original person begetting another, or of a speaker projecting thought externally by a word (logos), other analogies are better suited for the spiration of the Spirit.

From a human perspective, the Spirit proceeds "from" (ἐκ, παρά + genitive) God (Jn 1:32; 15:26), but first he is "of" God (1 Jn 4:2 [τοῦ θεοῦ], 13 [αὐτοῦ]; Apoc

---

[14]John "has brought out, perhaps more consistently than any other New Testament author, the implications of the New Testament revelation that the Spirit of God is more than a personification— that he is a true person standing in relation to the Father and the Son" (Bruce Vawter, "John's Doctrine of the Spirit: A Summary View of His Eschatology," in *A Companion to John: Readings in Johannine Theology [John's Gospel and Epistles]* [ed. Michael J. Taylor; New York: Alba House, 1970], p. 177). That the Spirit is personal is shown primarily by the considerations just advanced, not solely by the grammatical fact that the masculine pronoun "he" (ἐκεῖνος) denotes the Spirit several times in the Farewell Discourse, in all of which the antecedent is perhaps the masculine ὁ παράκλητος. See Andrew David Naselli and Philip R. Gons, "Prooftexting the Personality of the Holy Spirit: An Analysis of the Masculine Demonstrative Pronouns in John 14:26, 15:26, and 16:13-14," *DBSJ* 16 (2011): 65-89.

[15]Especially in John 1–12, where the relationship between the Father and the Son is at issue. Note, for example, John 1:1-18; 3:16-17; 5:17-24; 10:30. In John 13–17, where references to the Spirit are thickest, what is stressed is his indwelling of the church, less so his relationships to the other persons of the Trinity.

3:1; 4:5, 6 [τοῦ θεοῦ]). He belongs to God, is God's own Spirit. John can picture the seven spirits of God as the seven eyes of the Lamb (Apoc 5:6)—in other words, as the Lamb's own total awareness of reality. The proper domain of the Spirit, then, is the inscape, the interior consciousness, along the same line as in Paul's statement, "The Spirit searches everything, even the depths of God. For what person knows a man's thoughts except the spirit of the man which is in him? So also no one comprehends the thoughts of God except the Spirit of God" (1 Cor 2:10-11). If it is by the Spirit that the redeemed community of human beings knows Jesus to be in them and they in Jesus (Jn 14:20), it will also be by the Spirit that the Father and the Son know themselves to indwell each other ("you in me, and I in you" [Jn 17:21, 23]).[16]

In generation the divine essence wells out from the Father to exist simultaneously in a permanent offspring distinct from him. In spiration it flows back into each of the divine persons as a perfect apprehension of the other. The Spirit is a third entity, but instead of replicating the generation of the Son from the Father and thus forming a triad or triangle with them, he takes his place between them, in each of them, and in both alike, as the immediate consequence of their differentiation, uniting them. The absolute monad cannot spawn duality without also producing relation in the dyad.[17] The Spirit is the substance of that relation. He exists in a different dimension, in his own way: back of knowledge, not as a thing known but as the transcendental ground of consciousness and perception, making knowledge of other things possible.

***Grant of the Spirit from the Father to the Son.*** Near the start of the Gospel the Baptist bears witness to the Father's gift of the Spirit to the Son at Jesus' baptism (Jn 1:32-34).[18] As in the parallel Synoptic accounts, a Spirit-dove

---

[16]"The biblical account should lead us to speak of the Spirit as the one who indwells the Father and the Son precisely as the one who brings about the mutual indwelling of Father and Son. Once again we have to emphasize that, within the biblical drama, the personhood of the Spirit is always manifest, not as an object of perception, but as an agency of intersubjectivity; the personhood of the Spirit is always manifested in the communion that he brings about between other persons—both divine and human" (Khaled Anatolios, "Divine *Disponibilité:* The Hypostatic Ethos of the Holy Spirit," *ProEccl* 12 [2003]: 299).

[17]This is why, as David Crump observes, the Johannine Spirit is never said to "be in" either the Father or the Son in precisely the same way they "are in" each other (or in the way they welcome the church into their perichoretic union) ("Re-Examining the Johannine Trinity: Perichoresis or Deification?" *SJT* 59 [2006]: 395-412). But it does not follow, as Crump infers, that John's pneumatology is limited to the Spirit's functionality in salvation-history. If the Spirit is the mode by which other persons experience perichoresis, he cannot be less eternal or essentially divine than those persons whose mutual perichoresis he facilitates.

[18]Strictly speaking, a story of Jesus' own baptism as such is lacking in the Fourth Gospel, but the

comes down out of the sky and remains on Jesus. This is the sign that Jesus is the Son of God and will baptize others not with water but with the Holy Spirit (Jn 1:33). From that moment Jesus commences his public ministry.[19] The reader is left to deduce that Jesus speaks God's words and does God's works in the rest of the Gospel by virtue of this empowerment. At the end Jesus, risen from the dead and on the point of departing to the Father, fulfills God's promise that the Son will baptize with the Spirit by breathing the Holy Spirit onto his disciples and commissioning them to forgive or retain people's sins (Jn 20:22).

Another passage declares what John 1:32-34 leaves to inference: "He whom God has sent utters the words of God, for it is not by measure that he gives the Spirit; the Father loves the Son, and has given all things into his hand" (Jn 3:34-35). The middle clause, "it is not by measure that he gives the Spirit," must have God for its giver and the Son as recipient, for (1) it explains (γάρ) how Jesus could speak on God's behalf, namely, because he possessed the Spirit in full; (2) only an infinite Person can receive the Spirit without measure (believers, on the contrary, receive partitively "of" [ἐκ] the Spirit [1 Jn 4:13]); and (3) this yields a reading that places the Father's gift of the Spirit side by side with his grant of "all things" to the Son, such that the former gift entails the latter.

Two other features of this text are noteworthy. While it undoubtedly looks back to the descent of the dove in John 1:32-33 and comments on it, God's gift was not limited to that historic event. The timeless present tense of the verb, "[God] gives [δίδωσιν] the Spirit" (Jn 3:34) points to an eternal transaction between Father and Son, the heavenly archetype of what took place at Jesus' baptism on earth. This is confirmed by the parallel clause in the following verse, "[The Father] has given [δέδωκεν] all things into his hand," where the perfect tense points to a bequest before the foundation of the world (as also in Jn 17:4, 9, 11, 12, 22, 24). Together with the having of life in himself and authority to raise the dead and execute judgment (Jn 5:25-27), the Father grants to the Son to have the Spirit without measure. As it is God's nature to impart himself, making an existence of the Father without the Son inconceivable, so he ever grants to the Son to contemplate the Father's glory, as the Father contemplates his own glory

passage forms the climax of the precursor's ministry of water baptism (Jn 1:19-34), and Jesus comes toward John in the context of John baptizing people (Jn 1:31). If Jesus Christ's coming "by/with water" (1 Jn 5:6) refers to his baptism, as many commentators suppose, this verse will be indirect evidence that John knew Jesus himself to have been baptized.

[19]Cornelis Bennema, "Spirit-Baptism in the Fourth Gospel: A Messianic Reading of John 1,33," *Bib* 84 (2003): 35-60.

in the Son—"the glory which I had with you before the world was made . . . which you have given me in your love for me before the foundation of the world" (Jn 17:5, 24). To let the glory of the divine persons be seen is the work of the Spirit (Jn 16:14). To quote the parallel "Johannine thunderbolt" from the Synoptic tradition, "All things have been delivered to me by my Father; and no one knows the Son except the Father, and no one knows the Father except the Son" (Mt 11:27).

The other point to be made is that this award of the Spirit is, together with the generation itself, the supreme expression of the Father's love. His giving of the Spirit, and his giving of all things into the Son's hand, flank the central statement, "the Father loves the Son" (Jn 3:35). Where differentiation arises from an aboriginal unity, the poles must gravitate toward each other. On the plane of earthly social relationships, the giving and receiving of presents is the basic act that unites people. As a theological metaphor, an act of exchange carries the same meaning. The donation of the Spirit immediately bridges the distinction between the Father and his Only-Begotten. Augustine, then, was on target to say,

> The Holy Spirit is a certain unutterable communion of the Father and the Son . . . through whom the two are joined, through whom the Begotten is loved by the Begetter, and loves him that begat him. . . . Therefore the Holy Spirit, whatever it is, is something common to both the Father and the Son . . . aptly called love . . . that absolute love which joins together Father and Son . . . a mutual love, wherewith the Father and the Son reciprocally love one another . . . a kind of consubstantial communion of Father and Son.[20]

***Unity of the Spirit with the Father.*** However acute Augustine's insight may be on speculative grounds, neither John nor any other New Testament author furnishes any straightforward statement of the consubstantiality of the Spirit with God comparable to John 1:1 about the Logos. We are left to infer it, partly from the analogy of the only-begotten Son, partly from the Spirit's divine attributes and functions.

For an author to oscillate between the equivalent phrases "Spirit *of God*" and "*Holy* Spirit" is to view the Spirit as all of a piece with the unique Holy One. That the dove descended onto Jesus from the sky (ἐξ οὐρανοῦ [Jn 1:32]) symbolized his heavenly provenance. His procession from the Father (παρὰ τοῦ πατρὸς

---

[20]Augustine, *Trin.* 5.11.12; 6.5.7; 7.3.6; 15.17.27, 50.

ἐκπορεύεται [Jn 15:26]), like the sending of the Son, indicates that his natural abode is with God (even if that clause in its context pertains to his mission in the world, not to his spiration within the immanent Trinity). As the wind is felt but its source and terminus are beyond human knowing, so the Spirit is ineffable (Jn 3:8). He is "without measure" (Jn 3:34). Being far more than merely living or even the life-giver, the Spirit can be equated with life itself, where Jesus offers people "living water" (ὕδωρ ζῶν [Jn 4:10, 14; 7:38]) or says that his words point to "spirit and life" (πνεῦμά ἐστιν καὶ ζωή ἐστιν [Jn 6:63]). In the same way, the Spirit is not merely true, or the Spirit "of truth," but may be said to "be truth" (τὸ πνεῦμα ἐστιν ἡ ἀλήθεια [1 Jn 5:6]). Only the divine is essential life and truth.

Besides having attributes of God, the Spirit does what only God can do. We have just touched on the Gospel's theme of the Spirit as the life-giver. This may be part of the meaning of Jesus' rescuing the wedding feast by turning water into wine (Jn 2:1-11). Jesus impresses on Nicodemus that birth from above comes by the Spirit (Jn 3:5-8). He invites the woman of Samaria to partake of his water that will become in her a well springing up to eternal life (Jn 4:10-14). Jesus offers his body and blood so that people might have "spirit and life"—that is, the life given by the Spirit (Jn 6:63). On the last day of the Feast of Tabernacles, with its pouring ritual invoking God to give rains for the harvest, Jesus promises that streams of living water will flow out of the belly of one who believes in him (Jn 7:38-39). So also in the Apocalypse it is "a breath of life from God" that enters the slain witnesses and raises them up on their feet (Apoc 11:11). At the book's close, the Spirit and the bride beckon people to help themselves from the water of life without price (Apoc 22:17). Only God can give life; the Spirit gives life.

Just as prominent as the Spirit's engendering of life is his association with God's words and God's self-revelation in the Son. The dove's descent is the sign to the Baptist of Jesus' divine sonship (Jn 1:33-34), "that he might be revealed to Israel" (Jn 1:31). It is by virtue of possessing the boundless Spirit that Jesus utters the words of God during his ministry (Jn 3:34). After Jesus' ascension there follows the period of "spirit and truth" until the end of the age, when the Spirit of truth comes to indwell the believing community and directs it to lay hold of all that Jesus is and has done (Jn 14:16-26; 16:13-15), thus offering true worship to the Father (Jn 4:23, 24). Just as the Spirit of God is the agent of prophecy in the Old Testament, so in John's writings his activity is behind the verb "to prophesy" (προφητεύειν [Jn 11:51; Apoc 10:11; 11:3]). It is explicit where

John instructs the community to test the spirits of people who claim to be prophets (1 Jn 4:1-4) and in the circle of prophets in which he takes part (Apoc 1:10; 4:2; 10:7; 11:10, 18; 16:6; 18:20, 24; 22:6, 9).

**Unity of the Spirit with the Son.** Thus far we have considered the Spirit's identity with God the Father in divine titles, attributes and functions that God cannot share with creatures. Since, as we saw in chapter 4, John conceives of the Son as consubstantial with the Father, a consideration of ways in which the Spirit is identified with the Son will underscore the Spirit's deity.

First among these is the phrase "another Paraclete" (Jn 14:16). In assigning to the Spirit the role of a Paraclete for the disciples, Jesus hands on a task that was first his own and indeed continues to devolve upon Jesus (1 Jn 2:1). Here an observation on the meaning of the word "Paraclete" is in order. A παράκλητος is, according to Walter Bauer's lexicon, "one who is called to someone's aid." "Aide" or "assistant" in English, though colorless, might represent the same potential for rich associations that the Greek word has. That Jesus was the first Paraclete, and the Spirit "another," in a passage that looks back on Jesus' ministry and forward to his glorification, indicates that the word encapsulates the entire mission of Christ. Everything that Jesus did to mediate between his Father and the world, revealing the one and redeeming the other, thus bringing desperately needed assistance to the sinful human race, is subsumed under the appellation "Paraclete" and has an echo in the ministry of the Spirit. The Spirit is our "aide" because he points to Jesus, who came to our aid.[21]

How tightly knit the Son and the Spirit are in this aiding is shown in the Farewell Discourse. Jesus promises, "I will come to you" (Jn 14:18b; cf. 14:28), a promise that God fulfills precisely by sending the Spirit (Jn 14:16-17, 26). This use of the first person in promises of the Spirit's coming is remarkable.[22] In the

---

[21]Burge, *Anointed Community*, p. 41.

[22]Commentators wrestle with whether the primary reference is to Jesus' postresurrectional appearances (the traditional "Eastern" interpretation), to the Pentecostal arrival of the Spirit (the "modern" view), or to Jesus' final advent (the "Latin" option). Among modern commentators, Rudolf Bultmann puts forth the view that John wanted to collapse Easter, Pentecost and parousia into a single existential moment of the present community (*The Gospel of John: A Commentary* [ed. R. W. N. Hoare and J. K. Riches; trans. G. R. Beasley-Murray; Philadelphia: Westminster, 1971], pp. 572-631; idem, *Theology of the New Testament* [trans. Kendrick Grobel; 2 vols.; New York: Scribner, 1951–1955], 2:56-58). In reaction, D. A. Carson champions a reference to Jesus' postresurrectional appearances (*The Gospel According to John* [Grand Rapids: Eerdmans, 1991], pp. 501-2). Holwerda (*Holy Spirit*, pp. 65-76) critiques Bultmann's view of the eschatology but defends the view that "Jesus'" coming in the Farewell Discourses is that of the Spirit. Van Hartingsveld (*Eschatologie*, pp. 110-23) thinks that "coming" in John 14:18 refers to Jesus' future literal coming, as in John 14:3; so

preceding context Jesus, envisaging an indefinite period of absence from the world between his ascension and return (Jn 14:2-3), has just spoken of the Father's gift of the Spirit-Paraclete to be with the disciples so they will not be left orphans (Jn 14:16-18a). Jesus presented himself in postresurrectional visits initially, but they were but fleeting and did not answer the need for continuing care of his orphans to the end of time. One appearance, however, brought the insufflation of the Spirit that does so (Jn 20:19-23). Again, after the first generation of disciples had "seen" (Jn 14:19b) apparitions of the living Lord "manifested" to them (Jn 14:21-22), the settling in of the Spirit resulted in a deeper, inner "seeing" of the Son's glory, who is recognized in the church but not by the world (Jn 14:17, 19a, 22). "Because I live" (Jn 14:19), as the resurrected one, "you will live also," in the life of the Spirit (Jn 14:19c). By the Spirit the disciples will perceive that Jesus is in the Father (Jn 14:20a). By the same Spirit they will be in Jesus, and Jesus in them (Jn 14:20b), so that they will love him and keep his commandments (Jn 14:21, 23, 24). Not only does the Spirit bring Jesus near, but also he makes the Father and the Son to reside in those who love Jesus (Jn 14:23). Thus the Spirit is the unspoken agent who brings about everything that Jesus promises in John 14:18-24, a paragraph that stands sandwiched between promises of the Paraclete in John 14:16-17, 26. Therefore, when Jesus says, "I will come to you," he means not only personally prior to his ascension but all the more so afterwards by his Spirit-proxy.[23] If to see the Son is to see the Father (Jn 14:9), it is also the case that to have the indwelling Spirit (Jn 14:17) is to have the Son (Jn 14:20) and the Father too (Jn 14:23).

A similar ambiguity surrounds the promise in John 16:16-22 that after an interval when the disciples will see Jesus no more, they will see him again. "You will see me" may refer in part to the first post-Easter sightings and will be fulfilled at the parousia. But the context requires a reference to the Spirit's ministry of opening their eyes in the meantime. "You will see me no more" in John 16:16 echoes an identical prediction in John 16:10. The reason for their no longer seeing him is not Jesus' burial but rather his going away to the

---

also "seeing again" in John 16:16. Ashton (*Understanding*, pp. 462-65), following Bultmann, Raymond Brown and C. K. Barrett, thinks that the postresurrectional and apocalyptic comings still echo even as the final editor reworks the passage to put emphasis on the coming of the Holy Spirit. Apart from the hypothetical editor, this interpretation rings true.

[23]The view that Jesus' coming in this passage refers to his second coming on the last day does not accord with the words of John 16:19, 22 about an immediate coming that the world will not experience. For its part, the parousia will be inescapable (e.g., Jn 5:28-29; 1 Jn 2:28; Apoc 1:7; 6:12-17).

Father and sending of the Paraclete to succeed him (Jn 16:5, 7; cf. 16:17, 28). It is after this removal that Jesus promises they will see him (Jn 16:16). When the Spirit of truth comes, he will take what belongs to Jesus and "declare it" to the disciples (Jn 16:14), so that they will ask him no more questions (Jn 16:23). In that sense too they will "see him." No doubt their sorrow will turn to joy (Jn 16:20-22) when they see Jesus again briefly after the triduum, but Jesus has in mind an indefinite period of time prior to the eschaton when "no one will take your joy from you" (Jn 16:22) in spite of their ongoing tribulation in the world (Jn 16:33), when prayers will still be necessary and will be answered (Jn 16:23-24, 26-27), when figures will drop away and Jesus will tell them plainly of the Father (Jn 16:25). These words in John 16:23-33 about the disciples' unquenchable joy, intimate prayer fellowship with Jesus and God, and full understanding of revelation build on the ministry of the Spirit promised in John 16:7-15. "You will see me" (Jn 16:16) and "I shall . . . tell you plainly of the Father" (Jn 16:25) assume concord of action between the glorified Jesus and the Spirit.

The relationship between the Son and the Spirit is like that between the Father and the Son. As the Son can do nothing of his own accord but only what he sees the Father doing, and puts into words only what he hears from the Father, so also the Spirit of truth "will not speak on his own authority, but whatever he hears he will speak" (Jn 16:13). And just as there is perfect community of goods between the Father and the Son, for all that belongs to the Father belongs to the Son and vice versa (Jn 3:35; 17:7, 10), so the Spirit of truth will take what belongs to Jesus—that which the Father has shared with Jesus (Jn 16:15)—and declare it to the disciples (Jn 16:14).

In the Apocalypse we see the same close relationship between the Christ who reveals and the prophetic Spirit. The whole book is "the revelation of Jesus Christ, which God gave him to show to his servants" (Apoc 1:1). That is, the content is from God, and Jesus Christ is the revealing agent. But only when the author is "in the Spirit" does the unveiling begin (Apoc 1:10; 4:2). Each of the oracles to the seven churches in Apocalypse 2–3 consists of the words of the one like a son of man who appears in Apocalypse 1:12-20 (Apoc 2:1, 8, 12, 18; 3:1, 7, 14), yet each invites the church to hear "what the Spirit says to the churches" (Apoc 2:7, 11, 17, 29; 3:6, 13, 22). An indissoluble unity is indicated by the fact that the seven spirits of God are the seven eyes of the Lamb (Apoc 5:6). In Apocalypse 14:13-14 a blessing pronounced by God on those who die "in the

Lord" is echoed by the Spirit. The "testimony of Jesus" is equated with the "spirit/Spirit of prophecy" (Apoc 19:10).

With the Johannine conception of the glorified Christ and the Spirit working in tandem, we might compare those remarkable statements of Paul that assert the functional equivalence of the two: "The last Adam became a life-giving spirit" (1 Cor 15:45); "This comes from the Lord who is the Spirit" (2 Cor 3:18). For both Paul and John, so close is the affinity between the ascended Son and the Spirit that to experience the Spirit is to experience the Son. And, since the Son is the very being of God existing as a personal entity distinct from the Father, it is reasonable to conclude that the Spirit is yet another existent of the same being.

**Distinction of the Spirit from the Father and the Son.** On the other hand, the Spirit is a distinct and eternal existent of the divine essence, not to be confounded with either the Father or the Son. John does not probe the inner life of the Trinity analytically. He is satisfied to record events and words in which God was manifest. But his earthly reports about Jesus point to a heavenly reality. Sooner or later the inquiring human mind passes through and beyond phenomena to the unity that explains them. How the Father, the Son and the Holy Spirit are related is an inescapable part of this question.

That they are distinct entities is suggested by the periods of revelation in history. God the Father began to reveal himself at the creation and continued through the law and the prophets (Jn 1:17a, 45; 5:37-47). At a datable moment in time the Son of God became incarnate and lived a human life. Only after Jesus was glorified was the Spirit given (Jn 7:39). These revelations build upon one another. The manifestation of the Son did not eclipse what went before but rather brought the revelation of the Father to its apex (Jn 1:16-18). In the same way, the work of the Spirit brings home to us what is revealed of the Father in the Son. Cumulative though the revelations are, they were segmented in time.

Symbols used at Jesus' revelation to Israel sharpen the impression of discrete entities in the Godhead. John the Baptist drew attention to Jesus the man. Representing God the Father was a voice (the Synoptic Gospels add "from a cloud") that, according to John, spoke about Jesus in the third person. A third element was the Spirit-dove that came down as the sign that Jesus was God's Son, also in the third person (Jn 1:29-34). This referential language distinguishes.

Jesus in turn could refer to the "Spirit" as the agent of birth "from above" (Jn 3:5); speaker, Spirit and the source of this birth make up three. Likewise the

Evangelist pictures an eternal exchange in which the Father gives, the Son receives, and the Spirit is the thing given (Jn 3:34b). Jesus promises the Spirit to anyone who will believe, before the Spirit has "been given" (a passive verb implying God as the giver [Jn 7:37]). In the Farewell Discourse Jesus says that he will "pray the Father, and he will give you another [ἄλλος] Paraclete," someone other than Jesus himself, "to be with you for ever," after Jesus has departed (Jn 14:16). Jesus continues to refer to the Paraclete or the Spirit of truth as a third party whom the Father and Jesus will send in Jesus' place (Jn 14:25-26; 15:26; 16:7-15).

Since the Spirit succeeds to Jesus' role in the community, his being sent parallels the Father's sending of the Son. In this the distinctions among the divine persons are evident. It is the Father who sends the Spirit, at Jesus' bidding (Jn 14:16), in Jesus' name (Jn 14:25). But the Son is a sender too, sending the Spirit "from the Father," for the Spirit "proceeds from the Father" (Jn 15:26). Or, simply, the Son sends him (Jn 16:7). In the same way that the Father sent the Son, the Son sends the church into the world endowed with his own life-breath (Jn 20:21-22). A sending of the Spirit from the Father is implied where the seven eyes of the Lamb, which are the seven spirits of God, are said to be "sent out into all the earth" (Apoc 5:6).

From the sending flows the fact that the Spirit is no independent authority over against the first two, even as the Son does the Father's will. The Father is God to the Spirit: he is "the God of the spirits of the prophets" (Apoc 22:6). The Spirit, for his part, worships the Father, for he is the surge by which people offer true worship "in spirit and in truth" (Jn 4:23-24). This deference to the Father the Spirit shows in common with the Son. But the Spirit is oriented toward the Son as well. The Spirit is the medium in which the Son baptizes people, in contrast to John's baptism with water (Jn 1:33). On coming, he bears witness to Christ (Jn 15:26; 1 Jn 5:7-8). Far from speaking on his own authority, the Spirit of truth glorifies Jesus by taking what belongs to Jesus and declaring it to the disciples, speaking exactly what he hears (Jn 16:13-15). Christ is the possessor "who has the seven spirits of God" (Apoc 3:1).

Above all, the Spirit's distinctness is seen in his personal interactions with the other two. "Whatever he hears he will speak" (Jn 16:13). This sentence assumes that the Spirit listens to the Father and to the Son. Jesus' words "He will take what is mine. . . . All that the Father has is mine" (Jn 16:14-15) open up a rare glimpse into a fellowship in which the Father shares everything with the

Son, and what they have in common the Spirit also has access to. When Jesus says that he and his Father will come and make their home with the believer, from the context the Spirit is the unspecified facilitator (Jn 14:23). It is not said that the Spirit dialogues with the Father and the Son, whose conversation seems to be reciprocal; nor, for that matter, is it said that the Spirit loves or is loved in the way the Father and Son love each other. These omissions in John's pneumatology probably are due not to a less clearly personal conception of the Spirit but rather to the Spirit's subliminal role. His presence is felt in the exchange, the love, between the others.

**Question of the procession of the Holy Spirit from the Son.** Jesus says that the Spirit of truth "proceeds from the Father" (Jn 15:26). In context this means that the Father sends the Spirit into the world. But based on the axiom that the sending reflects what is true of the inner life of the Trinity, Christian theologians reason that there must be an eternal procession of the Spirit.[24] Insofar as it involves a communication and sharing of the divine essence, the Spirit's procession is analogous to the eternal generation of the Son. The Spirit too proceeds from the Father. Does he also proceed from the Son?

As we saw in chapter 4, the data in the Johannine corpus for the generation of the Son are sparse but sufficiently clear. When it comes to the procession of the Spirit in the intratrinitarian sense, biblical data are all but nil. Biblical theologians may well feel justified in passing over this issue and leaving it to dogmaticians. Nevertheless the long-standing debate between the Christian East and West over the origination of the Spirit belongs to the reception history of John 15:26 and related verses (Jn 14:16; 16:7, 13-15). Sometimes the fullness of meaning latent in a rich text unveils itself only as that text becomes relevant for new questions unforeseen by the author. More and more biblical scholars today

---

[24]"The divine Trinity cannot appear in the economy of salvation as something other than it is in itself. Therefore one cannot posit temporal trinitarian relations within the economy of salvation which are not grounded in the primal trinitarian relations. This means that the relation between the Son and the Holy Spirit cannot be restricted to the temporal sending of the Holy Spirit through Christ. Rather there must be an inner-trinitarian basis for the temporal sending of the Spirit through Christ, the Son of God. Otherwise we would have to suppose some kind of contradiction in God himself. Even with all the necessary apophatic preservation of the mystery and the unsearchable freedom of God, we must for God's sake hold fast to this, that God cannot contradict himself" (Jürgen Moltmann, "Theological Proposals towards the Resolution of the *Filioque* Controversy," in *Spirit of God, Spirit of Christ: Ecumenical Reflections on the Filioque Controversy* [ed. Lukas Vischer; FOP 103; London: SPCK; Geneva: World Council of Churches, 1981], pp. 165-66). See also the philological study by Albert Patfoort, "Emplois bibliques et patristiques du verbe ἐκπορεύομαι: Une enquête," *RThom* 102 (2002): 63-72.

are coming to recognize that reception history (*Wirkungsgeschichte*) can bring out integral facets of a text's potential meaning.[25] Therefore a review of the historic debate in which these pregnant Johannine verses have figured so prominently is in order.[26]

First let us fix in mind what is at issue. The Niceno-Constantinopolitan Creed (A.D. 381, 451) confesses the Son to be "God from God, Light from Light, true God from true God, begotten, not made, of one being with the Father." In its oldest and universally accepted form the parallel statement about the Holy Spirit read, " . . . who proceeds from the Father." The Third Council of Toledo (589), drawing upon a long tradition of theological opinion in the West, added the single word *filioque* ("and from the Son"), which Western Christianity has retained there ever since over strident objections of the Eastern churches.[27] Does the Spirit proceed "from the Father" alone, as the East holds, or from the Father "and the Son," as affirmed by the West?

The East observes that the procession of the Spirit from the Father (Jn 15:26) is matched by no explicit biblical statement of a procession from the Son. In the Godhead there can be but one principle of unity. Yet to say that the Spirit proceeds from the Son, as the West does, seems to imply a second principle beside the Father. What, then, is the unity from which plurality descends? Jealous to guard the *monarchia* (μοναρχία) of the Father as the "fount" (πηγή), "root" (ῥίζα), "principle" (ἀρχή) and "cause" (αἰτία) of divinity, the Orthodox suspect that the Western doctrine drifts toward locating the origin of the procession in an abstract divine essence common to the Father and the Son rather

---

[25]"Wrestling with *Wirkungsgeschichte* . . . permits us to see dimensions of meaning that successive contexts of reading bring into sharper focus for our attention" (Anthony C. Thiselton, *Thiselton on Hermeneutics: The Collected Works and New Essays of Anthony Thiselton* [ACTR; Aldershot: Ashgate, 2006], p. 304). On the hermeneutical theory, see ibid., pp. 40-45, 290-94; Mark Knight, "Wirkungsgeschichte, Reception History, Reception Theory," *JSNT* 33 (2010): 137-46; David Paul Parris, *Reception Theory and Biblical Hermeneutics* (Eugene, OR: Pickwick, 2009); Anthony C. Thiselton, "Reception Theory, H. R. Jauss and the Formative Power of Scripture," *SJT* 65 (2012): 289-308. Outstanding examples of the discipline are Ulrich Luz's three-volume commentary on Matthew in the Hermeneia series (Minneapolis: Fortress, 2001–2007), and Judith Kovacs and Christopher Rowland, *Revelation: The Apocalypse of Jesus Christ* (BBC; Oxford: Blackwell, 2003).

[26]The collaboration between Andreas Köstenberger (a New Testament specialist) and Scott Swain (a systematic theologian) is commendable in this respect. On the present point, see Köstenberger and Swain, *Father, Son and Spirit*, pp. 179-85.

[27]For much fuller reviews of the historical and dogmatic issues involved in the addition of the *filioque*, see J. N. D. Kelly, *Early Christian Creeds* (3rd ed.; London: Longman, 1972), pp. 358-67; Hans Küng and Jürgen Moltmann, eds., *Conflicts about the Holy Spirit* (Concilium 128; New York: Seabury, 1979); Vischer, *Spirit of God*; Yves M. J. Congar, *I Believe in the Holy Spirit* (trans. David Smith; 3 vols.; New York: Seabury, 1983), 3:xiii-xxi, 1-214.

than in the person of the Father. This would tend toward the heresy of modalism, which underplays the hypostatic distinctions.[28]

On the Western side, it may be asked whether the Father would take what he has bequeathed to the Son by generation and make a further bequest of it to the Spirit, without securing the cooperation of the Son as co-possessor. After all, Jesus clarifies that the Father will send the Spirit "in my name" (Jn 14:26), and adds, "All that the Father has is mine" (Jn 16:15). It may also be urged that by denying that the Son is a spirator in his own right, the East (1) raises the question of whether it views the Son as being indeed equal to the Father in all respects save paternity, and (2) puts itself in the position of having to assert that there is a profound difference between the Father's lone acts of generation and of spiration, without being able to specify wherein that difference consists. Where the difference is obscure, there lurks a heresy of dual Sons (or two Spirits).

If, argues the West, both the Father (Jn 14:26) and the Son "sent" the Spirit into the world (Jn 15:26; 16:7), and if, moreover, it is the Son who breathes out the Spirit onto the church (Jn 20:22), then the Son must be involved with the Father in spirating him eternally. Moreover, if the Father and the Son have all things in common (Jn 16:15) except paternity versus filiation, they must join in the act of spiration, for this lies outside of that relation.[29] To this the East re-

---

[28]Augustine, admitting his lack of familiarity with the great trinitarian fathers of the East because he read Greek with difficulty, declared that "the Father and the Son are a Beginning [*principium*, singular] of the Holy Spirit, not two beginnings," and "The Holy Spirit, according to the Holy Scriptures, is neither of the Father alone, nor of the Son alone, but of both" (*Trin* 5.14.15; 25.17.27). These statements seemed to make the Spirit proceed from the abstract divine essence common to the Father and the Son. For a concise exposition of Augustine's view, see J. N. D. Kelly, *Early Christian Doctrines* (5th ed.; London: Adam & Charles Black, 1977), pp. 271-79. For defenses of the Orthodox view and criticisms of Augustine and the West, see Markos A. Orphanos, "The Procession of the Holy Spirit According to Certain Later Greek Fathers," in Vischer, *Spirit of God*, pp. 21-45; Theodore Stylianopoulos, "The Orthodox Position," in Küng and Moltmann, *Conflicts*, pp. 23-30; Vladimir Lossky, "The Procession of the Holy Spirit in Orthodox Trinitarian Theology," in *Eastern Orthodox Theology: A Contemporary Reader* (ed. Daniel B. Clendenin; Grand Rapids: Baker Books, 1995), pp. 163-82; Timothy Ware, *The Orthodox Church* (rev. ed.; London: Penguin, 1997), pp. 210-18.

[29]Augustine put it this way: "But from Him [the Father], of whom the Son has it that He is God (for He is God of God), He certainly has it that from Him [the Son] also the Holy Spirit proceeds: and in this way the Holy Spirit has it of the Father Himself, that He should also proceed from the Son, even as he proceeds from the Father. . . . [The Spirit] proceeds at the same time from both: although this the Father has given to the Son, that He [the Spirit] should proceed from Him [the Son] also, even as He proceeds from Himself. . . . In the same way as the Father, who has life in Himself, has given to the Son also to have life in Himself; so has he given that life should proceed from Him [the Son], even as it also proceeds from Himself" (*Tract. Ev. Jo.* 99.8 = *Trin.* 15.27.48). These clauses by Augustine safeguard the Father's fountainhead and set the dogmatic context within which the wor-

plies that the Father, in communicating the divine essence to the Son, does not share with the Son his own hypostatic property of being the cause of the other two hypostases. That would introduce confusion between the hypostasis of the Father and that of the Son. Says the West in rejoinder, even as to beget and to be begotten are opposites and so distinguish the Father and the Son from each other, so to originate a further act of self-communication and to collaborate in that impulse are clearly distinct acts and entail no confusion whatsoever. And so, for over a thousand years, the West and the East have been in stalemate.

John's careful phraseology hints at a solution. John holds that the Spirit is sent from the Father ultimately (*"whom the Father will send* in my name" [Jn 14:26]; "whom I shall send to you *from the Father"* [Jn 15:26]) and from the Son proximately ("whom the Father will send *in my name"* [Jn 14:26]; *"whom I shall send to you* from the Father" [Jn 15:26]; "I will send him to you" [Jn 16:7]). The Son is the Father's agent in the sending. Applied to the speculative realm of intratrinitarian relations of origin, this suggests that the Son is the Father's agent in the eternal spiration. The ingenerate Father initiates, and the Son completes, the act of spiration; the impetus comes from the Father and involves the Son. We must bear in mind that "proceeding," like "being begotten," is a theological metaphor. To say that the Spirit "proceeds" is not to say that he comes to be or gains existence, for he exists eternally, but rather that the essence proper to the Father (and belonging to the Son by grant) is communicated to him to be his essence too. God's essence, infinite and eternal, can subsist only in hypostatic existents who are equally infinite and eternal. In the Trinity neither the unitary essence considered abstractly nor the three hypostases in which it subsists are derived or derivable. Each is an irreducible datum; each "has life in himself" (Jn 5:26). The question of relations of "origin" has to do not with the becoming of two nonpaternal divine persons qua persons, for they do not become, but rather with the dynamic motion of the divine essence within the Godhead, namely, the order in which each nonpaternal person is granted to have life in himself, to be *a se* and *autotheos* as the Father is. The divine essence in itself is neither generated nor spirated but rather is communicated

---

risome quotations in the preceding note are to be interpreted rightly. The Johannine influence on Augustine's language is patent. For fine statements of the Western perspective on the matter, see Michael Fahey, "Son and Spirit: Divergent Theologies Between Constantinople and the West," in Küng and Moltmann *Conflicts*, pp. 15-22; Gerald Bray, "The Double Procession of the Holy Spirit in Evangelical Theology Today: Do We Still Need It?" *JETS* 41 (1998): 415-26; Marc A. Pugliese, "How Important Is the *Filioque* for Reformed Orthodoxy?" *WJT* 66 (2004): 159-77.

whole, indivisible and immutable, from the Father to the Son, then by the Father together with the Son, to the Third Person. To put this in strictly Johannine terms: All that the Father has becomes the Son's, without ceasing to be properly the Father's; what the Spirit then receives, says Jesus, is not only "the Father's" but also "mine" (Jn 16:14-15). Just as it is the Father who sends the Son, not vice versa, because it is the Father who has granted to the Son to have life in himself, so it is the Father and the Son who send the Spirit because, it must be, the Father's grant to the Spirit to have life in himself is conjoint with the Son's consent and execution as prior grantee.

The peculiar property of the Father is, then, to be the native possessor of the divine essence (what the East calls the "fount of divinity"), the sole donor to the Son, the prime donor to the Spirit, and in no way a recipient of the essence. The peculiar property of the Son is to be the first recipient of deity from the Father and the cooperator in communicating it to the Spirit. The peculiar property of the Spirit is to be a recipient of the Father's essence by a joint act of the Father and of the Son and not a communicator of it to either of the others.[30] Thus the primacy of the Father is upheld, and two principles denied, while allowing the Son a role in the procession of the Spirit corresponding to and providing the basis for his role in the sending of the Spirit.

How does procession differ from generation? In generation the Father gives an individual gift of love, granting to another eternally existing hypostasis, the Son, to be what the Father is in all his perfections and attributes save fatherhood. In spiration a similar loving act, granting to yet another hypostasis, the Holy Spirit, to be all that God is (save fatherhood or sonship) is born out of the loving fellowship of the Father and the Son. Generation flows from a self-imparting person, procession flows from the united working of two self-imparting persons, while what is given remains proper to the Father. That procession entails love between the givers themselves, as the foundation of love between each giver and the recipient constitutes its characteristic. This suggests that the Spirit is a unifying force, not only in that the Father gives him to the Son (Jn 3:34) but also in his very "origin." If generation differentiates the Father and the Son, spiration reunites them; if the one movement is centrifugal, the other is centripetal. In this way, instead of opening the Trinity to the possibility of an endless genealogy, the Spirit closes and seals the trinitarian relations.

---

[30]The unique property of each trinitarian hypostasis has to be discerned in relation to both of the other two.

Whether the addition of *filioque* to the creed adequately expresses these intricacies is questionable. Whether to retain or drop it must be left to the churches in ecumenical dialogue with one another.

**Monotheism and the Holy Spirit.** Consideration of the unity of the persons in the Godhead, now seen to be three, leads us back to the matter of monotheism, broached in chapter two above. John absorbed from his Jewish heritage the tenet that God is one. Influenced by Jesus, whom John took to be God's Only-Begotten living a human life, and whom John heard speak of the Spirit-Paraclete as his surrogate, John came to think of God as a Father, a Son and a Holy Spirit. Yet John went on using the language of Jewish monotheism: the Father remained the "only" God (Jn 5:44; 17:3); the "true" God (Jn 17:3; 1 Jn 5:20); God "alone" (Apoc 15:4). How did John reconcile the conception of three eternal, concrete entities in the Godhead with the fact of the divine unity?

(1) The three persons are consubstantial. John held the Father to "have life in himself" (Jn 5:26)—that is, to possess, or rather be, a substance that is *a se*, absolute, infinite, intrinsically incapable of multiplication or of distribution, utterly other than and incommunicable to any created thing. Insofar as the Son is said to "be God" (Jn 1:1) or the Spirit to be the "Holy Spirit," their divinity consists in an identity of essence with the Father. This essence is numerically and qualitatively singular. Father, Son and Holy Spirit are not, for John, three individuals belonging to the general class of "god," nor are they three particular instances of the universal, "god," as would be the case in polytheism. They are the three and only three eternal persons, in each of whom subsists whole a sole essential deity that is in a class by itself and without peer.

(2) The three persons have one point of origin, the Father. Deity is the intrinsic property of the Father (Jn 17:3; 1 Jn 5:20; Apoc 15:4), who stands alone as the "begetter" of the Son (Jn 1:14, 18; 1 Jn 5:18) and as the one from whom ultimately the Spirit proceeds (Jn 15:26). The Father imparts his deity to constitute a divine society of love. Insofar as the Son is really distinct from the Father, and the Spirit from both together and from either severally, neither the Son nor the Spirit has divinity in his own right (neither being in this respect the *fons deitatis*), but each has been granted by the Father to have life in himself as the Father does, to be *autotheos* (Jn 5:26). Son and Spirit, being eternal, come into possession of that which in itself does not become. To be divine is to have aseity, but to have aseity is communicated from Father to Son, and from the Father with the Son to the Spirit. This dynamic concept of divine self-"giving"

enables John to affirm both that each person is what the others are, and that there is but one prime giver. Thus the plurality of persons in the Godhead is founded on a unit who is logically, not temporally, first among them.

(3) The Father is the exemplar in all divine work. Neither the Son nor the Spirit claims to speak or to act on his own authority apart from the Father. The Son speaks what he hears and always does the will of his Father. So too the Spirit will speak only what he hears and will take what belongs to the Son (which the Son has received from the Father) and make it known to the disciples (Jn 16:13-15). Out of a valid concern lest God be falsely thought to have a rival, the rabbis of the second and third centuries conducted a strenuous polemic against Jewish groups that speculated about plural "powers" or "two powers" in heaven. John makes it plain that he does not conceive of the Son or the Spirit as independent heavenly authorities. In any divine decision or action there is perfect and total concurrence among the three persons, in which the Father is determinative.

(4) The three exist in a harmonious union of love facilitated by the Holy Spirit. Insofar as the Son is differentiated from the Father, their difference is bridged by the Spirit, who is the agent of intersubjectivity. Since Father and Son must cooperate in granting to the Spirit to have life in himself, the very donation of self-existence to the Spirit establishes a bond between the first two. Since it is from the Father that the divine essence is given to the Son, and the Father initiates their common giving to the Spirit, the Spirit is the "Spirit of God" in a sense ontologically prior to his being the eyes of the Lamb (Apoc 5:6). But he does pertain to both. In giving the Spirit to the Son without measure, the Father expresses his supreme love for the Son, and in receiving the Spirit, the Son expresses his love for the Father, cementing the relationship (Jn 3:34-35).

(5) It is the Father's program begun in the Old Testament saga that the Son culminates, to which accomplishment the Spirit draws attention. Monotheism consists not in an abstruse, mathematical idea of unity but rather in the integrity and continuity of the historic plan driven forward by the sole creator, governor and judge of the universe. Everything done by the Johannine Son of God is geared to this purpose. Of the creation of Genesis 1–2 the only-begotten Son was the efficient agent (Jn 1:1-3; Apoc 3:14). In taking on the role of the Lamb of God (Jn 1:29, 36), he provided the effective atonement of which the sacrifice of animals under the Levitical order could be only an object lesson. Corresponding to the rescue of Israel from bondage in Egypt, the Son liberates

people from profound slavery to sin (Jn 8:34, 36). He gives the divine Spirit that the prophets foresaw enlivening Israel in the eschatological age. Thus Christ constitutes one people for the one God, one flock under one shepherd (Jn 10:16), according to God's promise that through Abraham's seed would come blessing for the nations. God's covenant established through Jesus does not lack commandments (Jn 14:15), and their moral content is the same as under the Mosaic covenant. To the Son of Man God has committed power to bring about the final resurrection and judgment (Jn 5:21-23). At the end of all things we see God dwelling with his people in his perfected kingdom, fulfilled by Jesus' return (Jn 14:3; 17:24); of this there is a foretaste in the Spirit's indwelling of the community (Jn 14:16-17, 20-21, 23). At no point does the incarnation of the Son of God, or the outpouring of the Spirit that followed, undermine the program of the one God, but instead brings it step by step to completion.

(6) Worship is directed to God (Apoc 19:10; 22:9), together with the Lamb on the Father's throne, for God's sake (Apoc 4:8, 11; 5:13), in the power of the Holy Spirit (Jn 4:23-24). John's triadic conception of the supreme being does not divide the act of human worship into three diverging paths leading to multiple objects, but instead concentrates it along a line terminating on the Father.

(7) Nor does devotion to Jesus fostered by the Spirit in any way adulterate the purity of love for God demanded by the Shema: "with all your heart, and with all your soul, and with all your might" (Deut 6:4). Possession of the Holy Spirit alone makes possible that robust commandment-keeping which demonstrates love for the divine Son, and, he says, "He who loves me will be loved by my Father" (Jn 14:21).

From the point of view of what God is, the three share a substantial identity. From the point of view of how God exists, the three form a system of inseparable entities who interpenetrate and mutually reinforce the Father and one another. Unlike modern rabbinic Judaism and Islam, Christianity does not stop at affirming the divine monad. It holds firmly to the monad at the ontological level, but this simple essential unity gives birth to a rich unity where the divine existents are concerned. How can God be truly personal unless he loves? How can there be eternal love except among eternal persons? How can God be self-existent and self-sufficient in love unless there was already an exchange of love within the divine being independently of the world, before the world was made? Therefore John's inchoate trinitarianism is a development of Jewish monotheism in the light of Christmas and Pentecost. In the history of religions

John represents the the furthest point reached in the New Testament canon along a path leading to a dynamic concept of oneness against which Judaism and, under the impact of Judaism, Islam would react. But the split was not between monotheism, represented by these other religions, and a Christian dilution; it was between the trinitarian and the unitarian forms of monotheism.

## COMING OF THE SPIRIT IN SALVATION HISTORY

Now that we have looked into who the Spirit is and how he relates to the Father and to the Son, let us turn to the subject of his mission.[31] Since the Fourth Gospel records no event after Jesus' earthly ministry, an account of the first Christian Pentecost is lacking in the Johannine corpus. We have to piece together John's understanding of it from things that he reports Jesus saying about it prospectively and from his own comments looking back.

The Spirit came shortly after Jesus' ascension. Jesus' words to the woman of Samaria, "The hour is coming, and now is, when the true worshipers will worship the Father in Spirit and truth" (Jn 4:23) pertain to the time of the end, which is already under way. Jesus' cry at the Feast of Tabernacles, "He who believes in me, as the scripture has said, 'Out of his belly shall flow rivers of living water'" (Jn 7:38), conflates a group of Old Testament prophecies that picture streams flowing out from the midst of the temple in the eschatological era and applies them to the believer by way of fulfillment.[32] John's gloss adds that Jesus was speaking of the Spirit, which his disciples were about to "receive," for as yet he "was not," because Jesus was not yet glorified (Jn 7:39). Jesus' glorification marked the commencement of the time of the Spirit. "Was not" is hardly a denial that the Spirit moved in Israel. John was well aware of the Old Testament history. He avers that the Spirit's ministry of drawing faithful Israelites to the Torah in the period of the first creation has given way to opening human hearts to the arrival of grace and truth that has come about through Jesus Christ (Jn 1:17).

The timing of the Spirit's advent is further defined in the Farewell Discourse.

---

[31]On the sending of the Spirit, see the middle section of Josef Kuhl, *Die Sendung Jesu und der Kirche nach dem Johannes-Evangelium* (SIMSVD 11; St. Augustin: Steyler, 1967).

[32]Background passages sometimes listed by commentators include Proverbs 18:4; Isaiah 44:3; 55:1; 58:11. See, for example, Michael A. Daise, "'If Anyone Thirsts, Let That One Come to Me and Drink': The Literary Texture of John 7:37b-38a," *JBL* 122 (2003): 687-99. Daise puts in a plug for Isaiah 55:1, but surely Ezekiel 47:1-12; Joel 3:18; Zechariah 14:8 are at least as apt. The latter passages also inform Apocalypse 22:1-2.

Jesus' imminent departure to the Father forms the backdrop for his promise to his disciples of the Spirit, who will replace him as their Paraclete (Jn 13:33, 36; 14:2-5, 12, 18, 28; 16:5-7, 16-19, 28). Not until Jesus has departed and is with the Father will the Spirit be sent: "whom I shall send to you from the Father. . . . I am going to him who sent me. . . . It is to your advantage that I go away, for if I do not go away, the Paraclete will not come to you; but if I go, I will send him to you" (Jn 15:26; 16:5, 7). Unless John's Gospel is self-contradictory, it was after the ascension of Jesus, and not on the evening of Easter day when Jesus breathed on the disciples, that they entered into the full experience of what Jesus gave by exhaling (Jn 20:22). On this point the Fourth Gospel agrees with Acts, which likewise sets Pentecost in the light of Jesus' exaltation (Acts 1:8-9; 2:33). As urged by interpreters who see in John 20:22 the "Johannine Pentecost," the inbreathing here is indeed the fulfillment of promises earlier in the Gospel of the sending of the Spirit.[33] But John highlights this Easter incident, over against Luke's report of what happened to the gathered church in Jerusalem fifty days later on Pentecost, because it so visibly grounds the giving of the Spirit in Christology. John recalls an act Christ performed on earth while he was still with his disciples that set in motion the downpour from heaven that they enjoyed seven weeks afterwards. Jesus' objective conferral of the Spirit by a sacramental sign and their subjective experience of receiving him were separated in time, but these events together formed a single baptism in the Spirit.[34] John's eye is on Christ the sender.[35]

John uses various phrases to denote the Spirit's coming. God's Son was to be

---

[33]One out of many defenders of this view is Burge, *Anointed Community*, pp. 116-31.

[34]Jesus' act in John 20:22 was no mere anticipatory sign pointing to the real giving of the Spirit at a later time (D. A. Carson; Andreas Köstenberger). That was the view of Theodore of Mopsuestia, condemned by the Second Council of Constantinople, Canon 12 (553). "For it was not possible that Christ deceived them when he said this, nor could he say 'Receive,' without giving" (Cyril of Alexandria, *Comm. Jo.* 12 [PG 717A]). Other proposals for reconciling John's and Luke's accounts with each other are too numerous to review here. There is merit in the idea that Christ's giving of the Spirit was a process begun on Easter and completed at Pentecost (Joost van Rossum, "The 'Johannine Pentecost': John 20:22 in Modern Exegesis and in Orthodox Theology," *SVTQ* 35 [1991]: 149-67). His entrance into the messianic role—the basis for his sending of the Spirit—itself came in steps. We can pinpoint two phases. From the day of his resurrection Christ already had full authority in principle over all things in heaven and in earth (Mt 28:18; Rom 1:4). After forty days he would have commenced the official exercise of that authority at his enthronement. Correspondingly, he granted the whole gift of the Spirit to the nuclear church on Easter (Jn 20:22); the impact was delayed until the Jewish feast of Pentecost.

[35]From John 20:22-23 to the end of the Gospel John's narrative lacks any accounts of Jesus' disciples engaging in glossolalia, bold proclamation to outsiders, or miracle-working, unlike what we might expect if John were presenting this event as an equivalent to the Pentecost experience of the disciples.

the one to baptize people with the Holy Spirit (ὁ βαπτίζων [Jn 1:33]). While his ministry was in progress, Jesus' disciples were about to "receive" the Spirit (λαμβάνειν [Jn 7:39; cf. 14:17; 20:22]); the Spirit "was" not yet (ἦν [Jn 7:39]). The Father will "give" him to them (δώσει [Jn 14:16; 1 Jn 3:24; 4:13]), will "send" him (πέμψει [Jn 14:26; 15:26; 16:7; Apoc 5:6]); he "proceeds" from the Father (ἐκπορεύεται [Jn 15:26]), he will "come" (ἐλεύσεται [Jn 16:7, 8, 13]). Again, John's intention is not to devalue what the Old Testament teaches about the Spirit's work, whether at creation (Gen 1:2; 6:3; Ps 104:30) or through Moses (Num 11:17, 25), the judges of Israel (e.g., Judg 3:10), the kings of Judah (1 Sam 10:10; 16:13; Ps 51:11), the prophets (Zech 7:12) and the whole Hebrew people of God (Is 63:11, 14; Hag 2:5; Zech 4:6). Rather, John's teaching is in keeping with Old Testament prophecies to the effect that the messianic age will witness an unprecendented inundation of all flesh with God's Spirit (Is 32:15; 44:3; 59:21; Ezek 11:19; 36:26-27; 37:14; 39:29; Joel 2:28-29; Zech 12:10).[36] In the Old Testament the Spirit awakened people to divine revelation consisting of promises and Torah. Far greater is his role as awakener to God's final and supreme revelation in the Logos, a revelation containing in itself all the blessings of the new creation, already coming to be because of what Christ accomplished. This cosmic contrast is indicated in Jesus' first sign, turning water (representing the first creation) into wine (Jn 2:1-11), followed by his words to Nicodemus, "That which is born of the flesh is flesh, and that which is born of the Spirit is spirit" (Jn 3:6).

The First Epistle is addressed to an anointed community that knows the truth in contrast to what many antichrists are saying, whose denials point to its being the last hour (1 Jn 2:18-27). God's giving of the Spirit provides experiential evidence of his abiding in the community that has remained in the apostolic tradition (1 Jn 3:24; 4:13; 5:8). Members encounter the Spirit in prophecies that accord with orthodox Christology (1 Jn 4:1-6) and in acts of mutual love (1 Jn 4:11-13). This epistle assumes that the Holy Spirit is the sum of God's eschatological blessings (cf. Joel 2:28-29; Lk 11:13; Gal 3:14).[37]

---

[36]On the fulfillment of Old Testament covenant theology in the Farewell Discourses, see Johannes Beutler, *Habt keine Angst: Die erste johanneische Abschiedsrede (Joh 14)* (SBS 116; Stuttgart: Katholisches Bibelwerk, 1984), pp. 15-24.

[37]It is unclear why Judith Lieu downplays the theme of the Spirit in the Johannine Epistles (*The Theology of the Johannine Epistles* [NTT; Cambridge: University Press, 1991], pp. 45-49): "not a key theme, and little is said about it" (p. 45); "does not stand at its [1 John's] centre and is only cautiously articulated" (p. 49). Especially impenetrable, in view of 1 John 4:1-6, is her judgment that "we cannot assume from this language that the spirit was experienced in a prophetic or 'charismatic' way in the community of I John" (p. 46). Sound biblical scholarship should not step beyond the text, but

Several of John's nontechnical terms for the coming of the Spirit are also used elsewhere of the coming of Christ. In this way the author underlines his belief that the mission of the Spirit parallels that of Christ and succeeds to it. John says this plainly. Jesus calls the Spirit "another Paraclete," implying that Jesus himself was the first (Jn 14:16). Jesus speaks of the Spirit's coming as Jesus' own (Jn 14:18), says the Father will send the Spirit in Jesus' name (Jn 14:26), and insists that he must go away so as to send the Spirit, which will be to the disciples' advantage (Jn 16:7). Tertullian captured John's concept nicely in giving the Spirit the title "the Vicar of Christ" (*vicarius Christi*) (*Praescr.* 28.6).[38]

This virtual duplication of Paracletes is theologically significant. The Holy Spirit points to Jesus Christ, as Jesus pointed to the Father. "He will glorify me," says Jesus (Jn 16:14). Far from attracting attention to himself, the orientation of the Spirit is to Christ, thereby participating in the Son's which is to God.

## Work of the Holy Spirit

Now that Jesus has ascended to the Father and has sent the Spirit from the Father, in what ways is the Spirit at work?

In general, the Spirit is the agent between the absent Lord and the world over which he rules. This is the thrust of the Farewell Discourse: Jesus' departure "must be succeeded by some kind of presence-in-absence. This of course is what we do find: indeed it may be said to be *the* subject of the discourse."[39] To the believing community the indwelling of the Spirit (Jn 14:17) is the mediated presence of Jesus (Jn 14:18); to a hostile world the Spirit brings conviction of sin, righteousness and judgment (Jn 16:8-10). A single verse in the Apocalypse paints the big scene with a broad stroke, showing a Lamb with seven eyes sitting in the midst of his Father's throne. The eyes, explains the author, symbolize the spirits of God sent out into all the earth (Apoc 5:6). By virtue of the omnipresent Spirit, every created thing is subject to the gaze of Christ, who reigns on his Father's behalf.

---

neither should it stop short. Rudolf Schnackenburg concludes that the doctrine of the Spirit in 1 John is in agreement with that in John's Gospel, albeit applied to a situation involving heresy in which the believers need confirmation that they have the truth (*The Johannine Epistles: Introduction and Commentary* [trans. Reginald Fuller and Ilse Fuller; New York: Crossroad, 1992], pp. 191-95).

[38]See also D. Bruce Woll, *Johannine Christianity in Conflict: Authority, Rank, and Succession in the First Farewell Discourse* (SBLDS 60; Chico, CA: Scholars Press, 1981); Ashton, *Understanding*, pp. 456, 467, 470. "In John, the Spirit is presented less as the divine power that has directed Jesus' ministry than as the divine power that continues and completes it; the Spirit is, as it were, the perpetuation of Jesus' presence among his disciples" (Vawter, "Doctrine of the Spirit," p. 178).

[39]Ashton, *Understanding*, p. 456. See also George L. Parsenios, *Departure and Consolation: The Johannine Farewell Discourses in Light of Greco-Roman Literature* (NovTSup 117; Leiden: Brill, 2005).

With the coming of the Spirit comes the first phase in the fulfillment of God's grand plan to bring about a new and final order: "Behold, the dwelling of God is with humankind" (Apoc 21:3). God has given the Spirit "to be with you [ἵνα μεθ' ὑμῶν ᾖ] for ever . . . for he dwells with you [παρ' ὑμῖν μένει]" (Jn 14:16-17). These words of Jesus about the Spirit-Paraclete take up the frequently repeated Old Testament promise that God will dwell among Israel in the new creation: "My dwelling shall be with them; and I will be their God, and they shall be my people" (Ezek 37:27).[40] Jesus makes it plain to his disciples that he is referring to a bestowal of the Spirit on them in the near future, not to the universal manifestation of God's kingdom at the end of time (Jn 14:17, 19). Judas, looking for the apocalyptic scenario, is confused (Jn 14:22). Jesus clarifies: in the light of what he has just been saying, it is in the person of the Spirit (Jn 14:16-17) that the Father and the Son will come to them and make their home (μονή) with them for now (Jn 14:23).

The Spirit arrives as an interior presence in the disciples, invisible to the world. He will be "in [ἐν] you" (Jn 14:17). By this the disciples will know that Jesus is in the Father, they in Jesus, and Jesus "in" (ἐν) them (Jn 14:20). Major English versions of the Bible without exception translate John 20:22, "[Jesus] breathed [ἐνεφύσησεν] *on* them," but the same verb is used of the animation of Adam in LXX Genesis 2:7, "[God] breathed *into* [ἐνεφύσησεν εἰς] his face the breath of life." Jesus exhaled the Spirit, that the disciples might inhale him. In 1 John 4:4 the Spirit of God is "he who is in [ἐν] you." And, to raise Christian martyrs in the Apocalypse, the Spirit of life from God enters into (εἰσῆλθεν ἐν) them (Apoc 11:11). All other ministries of the Spirit flow from this inhabitation.

**The Spirit and baptism.** John the Baptist contrasted his baptism "with water" (ἐν ὕδατι [Jn 1:26, 33]) to the baptism of the one who was to come after him, which would be "with (the) Holy Spirit" (ἐν πνεύματι ἁγίῳ [Jn 1:33]). In these expressions an instrumental "in" denotes the fluid in which the subject is plunged for washing. John's baptism was a preparatory bath in the wilderness for the great theophany of the final day (Is 40:3-5, quoted in Jn 1:23). Even though the Jews had been circumcised and were practicing priestly lustrations according to Pharisaic halakot (Mk 7:3-4), John the Baptist, like the prophets of old, required them to undergo a purification of heart in view of the imminent arrival of God. He offered the sprinkling "with clean water" that God

[40]See also Exodus 15:17; 25:8; 29:45-46; Leviticus 26:11-12; Psalm 68:16; 76:2; Isaiah 65:17-19; 66:22-23; Ezekiel 37:26-28; 43:7.

promised through Ezekiel (Ezek 36:25), which was to accompany, symbolize and convey forgiveness of sins (Mk 1:4). He left it to his successor to give Israel a new heart of flesh instead of stone, and to give them God's Spirit to cause them to walk in God's ordinances (Ezek 36:26-27).

Not all contemporaries responded positively to the Baptist's demand. Jesus castigated Nicodemus, a "ruler of the Jews" (Jn 3:1; 7:47-52), for his incomprehension of such a fundamental theme of Old Testament prophecy (Jn 3:9-12). Another anonymous Jew disputed with John's disciples about purifying (Jn 3:25), perhaps contesting his need to go through John's baptism. On this point the Fourth Gospel finds a parallel in Luke, who relates that "the Pharisees and the laywers rejected God's purpose for themselves, not having been baptized by [John]" (Lk 7:30).

Jesus admonished Nicodemus that one cannot enter the kingdom of God without being born "of water and Spirit" (ἐξ ὕδατος καὶ πνεύματος [Jn 3:5]). Associated under the single preposition "of," water and spirit form the dual means, the sign and the reality, by which God had promised to cleanse Israel according to Ezekiel's prophecy.[41] Since John's baptism had lately invited Israel to this very cleansing, Nicodemus had no plea of ignorance.

At the end of the Gospel the resurrected Christ, after breathing the Spirit onto the disciples, gives them authority to forgive or retain sins (Jn 20:22-23). We probably should envisage them doing this in the setting of baptizing converts. Baptism was the rite in which sins were ordinarily forgiven, even though John's wording characteristically focuses on the essential event rather than the outward form.

*The Spirit and life.* God's Spirit is the life force that vivifies all living things, especially those people who gain eternal life. In the Genesis creation account the Spirit is pictured as a wind stirring the face of the primordial sea (Gen 1:2). In a psalmist's meditation on God's blessings in nature the Spirit gives breath to living creatures (Ps 104:30). Since water is a necessity of life, it can symbolize the Spirit in Johannine contexts where eschatological life is in view. One must

---

[41]Another exegetical possibility is to take "water and Spirit" as a hendiadys for the spiritual cleansing effected by the Spirit. But since John's water baptism is mentioned both before (Jn 1:25-34) and after Jesus' conversation with Nicodemus (Jn 3:25–4:3), there seems no good reason to debar this historical setting from informing the natural sense of "water" in Jesus' words. "Water" in John 3:5 cannot refer to physical birth, for in the next verse physical birth is contrasted to spiritual (Jn 3:6), not aligned with it as are water and Spirit in John 3:5; and in any case, physical birth is not a requirement for eternal life, but may be assumed.

be born of water and Spirit to enter God's kingdom (Jn 3:5). Jesus dispenses living water that will become in people a fountain leaping up to eternal life (Jn 4:10, 14),[42] streams of running water flowing out of the believer's belly (Jn 7:37-39), and, in paradisiacal imagery, the river of the water of life in the new Jerusalem, nourishing the fruit trees of life and bringing healing to the nations (Apoc 22:1-2). Of this water people are invited to drink their fill (Jn 4:10, 13-14; 7:37; Apoc 22:17).

In particular, the Spirit is the agent of birth from above. John distinguishes between natural and spiritual birth, between being born into this present aeon and being born into the world to come: "who were born, not of bloods nor of the will of the flesh nor of the will of man, but of God" (Jn 1:13 [cf. Jn 3:3-8; 1 Jn 2:29; 3:9; 4:7; 5:4, 18]). The first birth is a matter of the "flesh," with its Old Testament connotations of weakness, corruptibility, temporal limitation and death; the last birth is "from above" (ἄνωθεν), eternal, from the Spirit: "That which is born of the flesh is flesh, and that which is born of the Spirit is spirit" (Jn 3:6). Like wind, this latter birth makes a decisive impact on human experience but comes from beyond human knowledge or control (Jn 3:8).

Jesus, after offending many of his Jewish followers by telling them they must eat his flesh and drink his blood to gain eternal life, explained that he was referring not to a physical meal but rather to the work of the Spirit: "It is the spirit that gives life, the flesh is of no avail; the words that I have spoken to you are spirit and life" (Jn 6:63). In the preceding dialogue consuming Jesus' flesh, the bread of the world, and imbibing his blood function as metaphors for believing in his crucified person. In such a believer the life-giving power of the Spirit becomes effective.

To be born of God includes sharing his character. Those born of God do not sin, for God's "seed" (σπέρμα) abides in them, making sin just as impossible for the offspring as it is for the Father (1 Jn 3:9). It is of little consequence whether by "seed" John means the Holy Spirit himself indwelling the believer or a new principle of anthropological life planted there by the Holy Spirit. Seeds manifest what they are by a gradual process of growth. So also God's "seed" in the believer brings about a progressive purification that begins during the time of hope leading up to the parousia of Christ (1 Jn 3:3) and will reach

---

[42]The living water of John 4:10, 14 is shown to be the Holy Spirit later in Jesus' conversation with the Samaritan woman, when he speaks of an eschatological time characterized by "[S]pirit and truth" (Jn 4:23-24).

its term when Christ appears and makes his children "as he is" by raising them immortal (1 Jn 3:2).

*The Spirit and knowledge of Christ.* Now that the Son of God by words and deeds has made the Father known, it falls to the Spirit to open the human heart to the revelation. The Holy Spirit is the great teacher who interprets the Son, and thereby the Father, to the church and to the world.[43]

Before his departure, Jesus said that the Holy Spirit would teach his disciples all things, and bring to their remembrance all he had said to them (Jn 14:26). Within the next few days they were to learn a great deal, and looking back after Jesus' glorification, they came to a deepened appreciation of who he was. Narrator's comments illustrate this work of the Spirit. They came to understand how Jesus' zeal for the temple fulfilled the pattern of God's righteous sufferer (Jn 2:17). What Jesus meant by the destruction and raising up again of the temple of his body dawned on them (Jn 2:22). They were struck by how much more the crowd's messianic acclamation at his triumphal entry meant than the crowd realized (Jn 12:16). The deeper truth of the footwashing, pointing to his mortal service to the race on the cross, came home to them (Jn 13:7). They realized that his rising from the dead had been predicted in Scripture (Jn 20:8-9).

At the very end of his career Jesus still had many more things to say to the disciples, which they were as yet unable to bear. He told them that the Spirit would "guide" them into "all the truth" and "declare" to them the things that were "to come" (Jn 16:12-13). These coming things, in the literary context (Jn 13–17), are the events about which he was making a point of teaching his disciples before they happened (Jn 13:19; 14:29; 16:1, 4): his betrayal (Jn 13:18-30), death (Jn 14:30-31), resurrection (Jn 14:19), departure (Jn 14:28), resumption of glory with the Father (Jn 17:5), absence to prepare a place for them (Jn 14:2), sending of the Spirit as his substitute (Jn 16:7), fellowship with them in their trials (Jn 15:18–16:4) and return to take them to himself (Jn 14:3; 17:24). How little the disciples understood of any of these things at the time is evident from their questions. To where was Jesus going away, and by what path (Jn 14:5)?

---

[43]Ashton (*Understanding*, pp. 420-24) brings out the association between God's word and the Spirit, which he judges to have been neglected in much secondary literature on John. He cites as exceptions to this neglect Porsch, *Pneuma und Wort*; Burge, *Anointed Community*. One may also consult Cornelis Bennema, *The Power of Saving Wisdom: An Investigation of Spirit and Wisdom in Relation to the Soteriology of the Fourth Gospel* (WUNT 2/148; Tübingen: Mohr Siebeck, 2002), which accentuates the Spirit's role as the agent of the believer's cognitive and affective relationship to the saving God—Father and Son.

Might they be allowed to see the Father—not knowing, despite all the time they had been with Jesus, that to see him is to see the Father (Jn 14:9)? How is it that the expected apocalyptic theophany will affect the church and not yet the world at large (Jn 14:22)? What is the "little while" after which they will not see Jesus and then will see him again (Jn 16:17-18)?

From the Fourth Gospel it is clear that the incarnation, from Jesus' baptism to his ascension, was the cap of divine revelation in salvation history, leaving nothing further but the eschatological events of resurrection and judgment that will close the present age and issue in the coming one. The Holy Spirit's way, far from adding to what is objectively revealed, is to take God's historic revelation and impress it subjectively on people's consciousness (Jn 16:13-15). Therefore the Johannine standpoint is inimical to doctrinal innovation. Sayings such as "he will guide you into all the truth" and "he will declare to you the things that are to come" (Jn 16:13) mean that the Spirit will bring out all the hidden depths of what God said and did in Christ,[44] not that there will be any further, independent truth, moving away from the Christ-event in new directions (however organically) or contrary to the apostolic presentation of it.

Faced with proto-Gnostics at the end of the first century, John declared that "any one who goes ahead and does not abide in the doctrine of Christ does not have God" (2 Jn 9). Those anointed by the Holy One have knowledge, a communal *sensus fidei*, that enables them to cleave to the truth as given and hold firm against others who would deceive them (1 Jn 2:20-21, 27). According to an oddly phrased passage in 1 John 5:6-8, the Spirit is the one who presently bears witness to the past reality of Jesus as God's Son incarnate. Speaking through Christian prophets (cf. 1 Jn 4:2), the Spirit reproduces in the church's mind a true image of Christ's person. He convinces believers that the Son came in the man Jesus, not only "with water," probably meaning his baptism (Jn 1:29-34), but also—what the false prophets denied (1 Jn 4:3; 2 Jn 7)—"with blood," referring to his death.

***The Spirit and prophecy.*** John's concept of the Holy Spirit as the force behind prophecy underscores the Spirit's role as the servant of historic revelation.

---

[44]"Things to come," in its historical and literary context, points to Jesus' ensuing death, burial, resurrection and departure, about to be related in John's passion account and sequel. This is not to deny that the Spirit continued to offer guidance to the Christian community through prophecies about present (1 Jn 3:24–4:3) and future circumstances (the Apocalypse), as argued by Crinisor Stefan, "The Paraclete and Prophecy in the Johannine Community," *Pneuma* 27 (2005): 273-96. But that is not the main point of the saying in John 16:13.

John stands in the line of the prophets of Israel who attributed their prophecies to God's Spirit.[45] A major part of the Hebrew prophets' task was to recall the nation to the terms of the Mosaic covenant when backsliding.[46] "To the Torah and to the testimony!" (Is 8:20). "Remember the Torah of my servant Moses, the statutes and the ordinances that I commanded him at Horeb for all Israel" (Mal 4:4). Late contributors to the Hebrew canon were in agreement that God rose above blame for the ignominious end of the monarchy by sending, over the course of centuries, a row of prophets one after another whom the people consistently refused to heed before he finally brought on them the covenant curses outlined in Leviticus 26 and Deuteronomy 28 (2 Kings 17:13-14; Dan 9:5-6, 10; Zech 1:3-6; 7:7, 12). Of course, biblical prophecy looks forward as well as back. But even the eschatological events of theophany, judgment, national restoration and divine rule to which the prophets pointed are already indicated in outline in the five books of Moses. The Pentateuch, with its narrative of God's promises to the patriarchs, Israel's deliverance from slavery in Egypt, and its body of covenantal stipulations, is foundational for subsequent revelation.[47] Speaking through the prophets, God's Spirit adapted the word of God to the changing circumstances of the people, not giving fresh revelational content but rather urging them to respond to what had been given.

In the same way, according to John, the prophetic Spirit of the last days points to God's definitive revelation in Jesus Christ. In the Apocalypse, where John's own prophetic gift is more conspicuous than in any other part of his output,[48] we find the maxim "The testimony of Jesus is the spirit of prophecy" (Apoc 19:10). The revealing angel has just rebuked John for falling at his feet to worship him, explaining that he is a fellow servant of God with John and his brothers and sisters "who hold the testimony of Jesus." "The testimony of Jesus" functions elsewhere in the book as an almost technical term for holding publicly to the truth that Jesus is Lord, in contrast to pagan society, which professes

---

[45]E.g., Gen 41:38; Num 11:25; 24:2; 1 Sam 10:10; 19:20, 23; 2 Sam 23:2; 2 Kings 2:9, 15; 2 Chron 15:1; 20:14; 24:20; Is 61:1; Ezek 2:2; Zech 7:12.

[46]This statement is based on a canonical reading of the Hebrew Bible. It will be rejected by critics in the mold of Julius Wellhausen, whose historical judgments invert the parts of the Hebrew canon and make the prophets the predecessors of the authors of the Pentateuch.

[47]The Tannaim recognized this by regarding the Torah as having a higher degree of sanctity than the Prophets and the Writings. See Sid Z. Leiman, *The Canonization of Hebrew Scripture: The Talmudic and Midrashic Evidence* (TCAAS 47; Hamden, CT: Archon, 1976), pp. 15, 60-66.

[48]John's personal claim to prophetic inspiration is found in Apocalypse 1:1, 10; 4:2; 17:3; 21:10; his claim to belong to the class of prophets, in Apocalypse 19:10; 22:6, 9.

loyalty to the beastly emperor (note esp. Apoc 12:11, 17; 20:4). Jesus testified to
the truth about himself before Pilate (Jn 18:33-38), and Christian prophets urge
the church to do the same. For John and other Christians in Asia to testify to
Jesus in their situation is to bear the same sort of prophetic witness to God's
will that all prophets in all ages have borne—and suffered for it (Apoc 6:9; 11:7;
20:4). God's Spirit, who spoke through the old prophets against Canaanite
idolatry infiltrating Israel, continues to speak through John and his "brethren
the prophets" (Apoc 22:9) against worldliness infecting the churches (cf. Apoc
2–3). Not only does the Spirit direct God's people to Christ by words that
summon them to be faithful, but also he opens ears that they might hear and
take the message to heart (Apoc 2:7, 11, 17, 29; 3:6, 13, 22).

John's epistolary instructions about testing spirits are similarly christocentric. When John was obliged to write letters to reassure a group of churches
troubled by a recent schism, it was still customary for traveling prophets to
circulate from town to town, receiving hospitality from fellow Christians for a
few days in return for bringing them words of God.[49] Such prophets did not
merely expound Scripture as local teaching pastors did, but served as mouth-
pieces for living messages from God for each congregation (e.g., Acts 11:27-30;
13:1; 20:23; 21:9-11).[50] It had always been necessary for churches to put ostensible prophecies to the test, since impostors could easily win a following (Mt
24:4-5, 11; 1 Cor 14:29; 1 Thess 5:19-22). Knowing that proto-Gnostic teachers,
whom John branded "antichrists" (1 Jn 2:22; 4:3), were teaching a nonincarna-
tional Christology, he laid down a christological criterion for judging prophetic
claims: "Every spirit which confesses that Jesus Christ has come in the flesh is
of God, and every spirit which does not confess Jesus is not of God" (1 Jn 4:2-3).
Since the same Spirit who prompts utterance also guarantees its reception, a
second test pertaining to the audience is like the first: "Whoever knows God
listens to us, and he who is not of God does not listen to us" (1 Jn 4:6). The
community that confesses orthodoxy—the Father sent his Son into the world,
and Jesus is that Son—is the community that has received God's Spirit (1 Jn
4:13-15).

Toward the end of the first century the church in Asia faced a threat of heresy
within fomented by false prophets, and the peril of persecution from without

---

[49]There is evidence for the same practice in *Didache* 11–13.
[50]On New Testament prophecy generally, see David E. Aune, *Prophecy in Early Christianity and the Ancient Mediterranean World* (Grand Rapids: Eerdmans, 1983).

by society in the name of the state. John's Epistles and the Apocalypse illustrate ways in which the Spirit of truth continued to guide the church into all the truth about Jesus (Jn 16:13).

*The Spirit and Christian community.* As the Holy Spirit is the power of unity between the Father and the Son, so is he the bond of love that forms Christian community (Jn 6:56; 15:4-10).[51]

How can Jesus' disciples "abide in" (μένειν ἐν) him when Jesus is going away and will be absent from them?[52] Suffusing the context of the similitude of the vine and the branches (Jn 15:1-10) is the promise of the Spirit, both before (Jn 14:16, 26) and after (Jn 15:26; 16:7-15). Jesus' presence-in-absence in the person of this "other Paraclete" (Jn 14:16) is the sphere in which they are to abide. The Spirit who will "be in you" (Jn 14:17 [cf. 1 Jn 2:27; 3:9, 24; 4:12, 15, 16]) is the unmentioned agent by whom persons indwell one another, whether it is a matter of the Father and the Son being in each another (Jn 14:10, 11, 20; 17:21, 23) or of the disciples being in Jesus, he in them, and all in God (Jn 14:20; 17:21, 23, 26). Jesus' command to his disciples to love one another (Jn 15:12-17) assumes that they abide in him and he in them (Jn 15:1-11) by the Spirit.

If the work of the Spirit in sustaining the "abiding" relationship among the members of the Trinity and the people of God must be inferred from the drift of the context in John 14–17, it becomes explicit in 1 John. "By this we know that he abides in us, by the Spirit which he has given us" (1 Jn 3:24). Concrete manifestations of the Spirit's abiding presence come in the form of prophetic pronouncements in gatherings of the community (1 Jn 4:1-6). Just as abiding in the vine is juxtaposed with loving one another in John 15, so in 1 John the gift of the Spirit to the community (1 Jn 3:24–4:6) flows directly into love (1 Jn 4:7–5:5). "If we love one another, God abides in us" (1 Jn 4:12). How does God abide? By his Spirit. "By this we know that we abide in him and he in us, because he has given us of his own Spirit" (1 Jn 4:13). Loving and abiding are intertwined. "God is love, and he who abides in love abides in God, and God abides in him" (1 Jn 4:16).

Putting together John 15:1-17 and 1 John 3:24–5:5, we see that for persons, divine and human, to abide in one another reciprocally is to know and love one another, and this love is fostered by the Holy Spirit.

---

[51]Heribert Mühlen, "'Wir als wir selbst sind mit euch': Grundverheissung des Neuen Bundes," *TGl* 95 (2005): 48-79.

[52]Compare 8:31: μένητε ἐν τῷ λόγῳ τῷ ἐμῷ. This distinctive phraseology reappears in 1 John 2:6, 24, 27, 28; 3:6, 24; 4:13, 15.

*The Spirit's outreach to the world.* Although the Holy Spirit dwells especially in the church and not in the world (Jn 14:17, 19, 22), his work is by no
means limited to the elect. Into a world that hates and persecutes Jesus and
his followers without excuse (Jn 15:18-25) the Spirit of truth is sent to bear
witness to Jesus (Jn 15:26). This he does by prompting Jesus' disciples to bear
witness (Jn 15:27). The Christian fellowship is not a closed group; it looks out
toward the world and speaks a word through which others may come to believe (Jn 17:20). Even the new commandment to love one another, which in
itself says nothing about loving human beings generally, has as its larger
purpose to demonstrate God's unifying presence among believers before the
eyes of a watching world, so as to attract the world into the Christian community (Jn 13:35; 17:21, 23). To this end the Spirit is breathed onto and into the
church, to give the disciples divine authority either to forgive sins, in the case
of those who respond to the word about Jesus, or to retain the sins of those
who reject it (Jn 20:22-23).

The pairing of Spirit and church that we see in John 15:26-27; 20:22-23 for
the purpose of evangelization is also found in the Apocalypse. "The Spirit and
the Bride say, 'Come'" (Apoc 22:17). Whether or how the eschatological gift of
the Spirit might operate in the world apart from the organ of the church are
questions that John does not take up. The church is the ordinary agency
through which the Spirit is present in the world in his fullness.

Not all will believe. "If they persecuted me, they will persecute you; if they
kept my word, they will keep yours also," said Jesus (Jn 15:20). Against human
unbelief the Spirit presses a court case. "When he comes, he will convict
[ἐλέγξει] the world concerning sin and righteousness and judgment" (Jn
16:8). Sin is rooted in the fact that the world does not believe in Jesus; from
this denial of reality stem all other sins (Jn 16:9). The world did not see Jesus'
mysterious departure to the Father. Looking back on the end of his life, it sees
only his condemnation by the Sanhedrin on a charge of blasphemy and his
crucifixion under a Roman charge of treason; only in the word of the gospel
are these negative judgments turned on their head and Jesus' righteousness
vindicated (Jn 16:10). Without the world's knowing it, God has instead already passed judgment on the devil and on the world that he holds in thrall
(Jn 16:11).[53]

---

[53]John Aloisi, "The Paraclete's Ministry of Conviction: Another Look at John 16:8-11," *JETS* 47
(2004): 55-69.

To convince the world of these points, the Spirit works through the church, both in prophetic denunciation and in evangelistic invitation. His "witness" and the church's pick up where God's legal suit through Jesus left off (Jn 5:31-32; 7:7; 8:13-14). For the present the church has tribulation; by the Spirit Jesus has bequeathed to his disciples enduring peace and has overcome the world (Jn 14:27; 16:33). But the struggle requires fortitude and stamina. In 1 John, where the world shows up in the shape of antichristian teachers, John can represent the church as a group of young men engaged in strife and strengthened by the Holy Spirit (1 Jn 2:13, 14).[54] Victory is assured; in fact, it is in the pocket. "You are of God, and have overcome [νενικήκατε, perfect tense] them; for greater is he who is in you than he who is in the world" (1 Jn 4:4). In the Apocalypse, where the combat is with the draconian devil, the pseudomessianic beast and the false prophet (Apoc 13:11-18; 16:13-14; 19:20), John and the other prophets of God are most directly opposed to the last (Apoc 19:10; 22:6, 9). The 144,000 who signify the church (Apoc 14:1-5) stand in antithesis to the hordes of earth-dwellers who follow the beast (Apoc 13:7-8, 12-17). But the whole church can be symbolized as two witnesses (a sufficient number to establish a capital charge [Deut 19:15]) having an appointment to prophesy in the spirit and power of Jeremiah, Elijah and Moses (Apoc 11:3-7). At the end of the book the Spirit and the bride together call the world to "come" and take the water of life without price (Apoc 22:17).

*The Spirit and resurrection.* Since the Holy Spirit is the ground of both natural and eternal life, his is also the energy that will bring about the final resurrection. To raise up the martyr church, decimated in the earthly arena by the beast for testifying faithfully to the truth, a breath of life from God enters into the two witnesses and they stand up on their feet (Apoc 11:11). In the Pauline literature too the Holy Spirit is resurrection power (Rom 1:4; 8:11; 1 Tim 3:16).

*The Holy Spirit in the Johannine corpus: Summary.* The foregoing survey of the concept of the Holy Spirit in the Johannine corpus is restricted to passages that speak of the Spirit overtly. As we have seen, however, the Spirit is not often an object of contemplation in his own right. His contribution to the work of the Trinity is indispensable but is subliminal and oriented to the Father and

---

[54]The poem in 1 John 2:12-14 depicts the church from three perspectives within a trinitarian scheme. In relation to God the Father, Christians are little children who have been forgiven and given a secure place in the Father's family; in relation to the Son, they have been given wisdom ("fathers") to know the Son who is from the beginning; in relation to the Holy Spirit, they are strong young men seeking to overcome the evil one.

the Son. In keeping with his nature, his influence is pervasive but usually out of view. Wherever life is generated, the light of knowledge shines, God's word finds a welcome, faith is awakened, deeds of heroism are done, or persons dwell in one another through love, there the divine Spirit has accompanied the Logos of God in hidden and transcendental effect.

# THE BELIEVER AND
# THE TRUE GOD

*Coming to Christ*

GOD IN HIS LOVE FOR THE PERISHING WORLD gave, toward the end of days, his own Son, and then his Spirit to beckon the world into the eternal fellowship of the Father and the Son. To know the God who has revealed himself in this way is to know the true God, and this is eternal life (1 Jn 5:20). So teaches John. How does one gain access to this salvation, this eternal life? In this chapter and the next we will explore the saving relationship between Christ as God's agent and the believer.

Following John's manner of speech, the main accent here will fall on God's relationship with the individual Christian, leaving consideration of the church to the last two chapters. Corporate and individual aspects of existence are inseparable, even if they can be distinguished for the sake of clarity. Often John uses grammatically singular forms to make generalizations that are true of anyone in relation to Christ. Examples: Christ is "the true light that enlightens every man [πάντα ἄνθρωπον]" (Jn 1:9). "Unless one [τις] is born anew, he cannot see [οὐ δύναται ἰδεῖν] the kingdom of God" (Jn 3:3). "He who says [ὁ λέγων] he abides in him ought to walk in the same way in which he walked" (1 Jn 1:6).[1] An individual perspective goes hand in hand with John's emphasis

---

[1] These quotations from the RSV Bible (New Testament, 1946) antedate the use of gender-inclusive language in academe since the 1980s. The RSV has the virtue of translating singular forms in the Greek directly as singulars: "man," "he," and so forth. My choice of the RSV for the present chapter and the next is grammatically motivated, and it no more implies an aim to hide women from view than did in some places the use of generic forms in standard English style.

on the presence of eschatological reality in Christ.[2]

John's way of speaking in terms of the representative individual is not to be misconstrued as individualism. Nowhere does he privilege the concrete individual over the covenantal community. His language does, however, recognize the value of individual existence and underscores the relation of each person to the Lord.[3]

## THE LIVING CHRIST AS THE SPHERE OF SALVATION

Union with Christ, the Savior who died and now lives, is the relation in which all other gifts and graces of God are now available to human beings. John describes this relationship as an "abiding" of the disciple in God/Christ (Jn 6:56; 15:4, 5, 6, 7; 1 Jn 2:6, 24, 27, 28; 3:6, 24; 4:13, 15, 16)[4] and, conversely, of the divine persons in the human person (Jn 6:56; 15:4, 5; 1 Jn 3:24; 4:12, 13, 15, 16).[5] Or, as an equivalent, John can speak simply of a reciprocal being "in" him (Jn 4:23, 24; 14:20; 15:2; 16:33; 17:21; 1 Jn 2:5; 5:20; Apoc 1:6, 9; 4:2; 14:13; 17:3; 21:10)[6] and of him "in" the believer (Jn 14:17, 20; 17:23, 26; 1 Jn 4:4).[7] On this point John overlaps with Paul's much discussed concept of being "in Christ." To abide and to be "in" God/Christ mean the same thing. The expressions are parallel in John

---

[2]In "The Individualism of the Fourth Gospel," *NovT* 5 (1962): 171-90, C. F. D. Moule observes that John's realized eschatology is found in passages having to do with the individual in relation to God. In passages about the cosmos, Moule notes, John's eschatology looks to the future, as does Luke's. Moule carries the same argument into the First Epistle in "A Neglected Factor in the Interpretation of Johannine Eschatology," in *Studies in John: Presented to Professor J. N. Sevenster on the Occasion of His Seventieth Birthday* (NovTSup 24; Leiden: Brill, 1970), pp. 155-60. Here he urges that the reason why futuristic eschatology is more prominent in the Epistle than in the Gospel is that the address is to a community. These observations help us, in Moule's judgment, to maintain common authorship and to see the author's eschatology as of a piece with the rest of the New Testament.

[3]Eduard Schweizer, *Church Order in the New Testament* (trans. Frank Clarke; London: SCM Press, 1961), pp. 122-24; John F. O'Grady, *Individual and Community in John* (Rome: Pontifical Biblical Institute, 1978).

[4]Disciples are said to abide in Christ's word in John 8:31, and in Christ's love in John 15:9, 10.

[5]God's word is said to abide in people in John 5:38 (not); 8:37 (not); 15:7; 1 John 2:14, 24. God's love abides in people in 1 John 3:17; 4:12. The passages listed here and above are the focus of Jürgen Heise, *Bleiben: Menein in den Johanneischen Schriften* (HUT 8; Tübingen: Mohr Siebeck, 1967); Judith Lieu, *The Theology of the Johannine Epistles* (NTT; Cambridge: University Press, 1991), pp. 41-45; Georg Strecker, *The Johannine Letters: A Commentary on 1, 2, and 3 John* (ed. Harold W. Attridge; trans. Linda M. Maloney; Hermeneia; Minneapolis: Fortress, 1996), pp. 44-45; Peter Rhea Jones, "A Presiding Metaphor of First John: μένειν ἐν," *PRSt* 17 (2010): 179-93; Andrew Brower Latz, "A Short Note Toward a Theology of Abiding in John's Gospel," *JTI* 4 (2010): 161-68.

[6]Human good works are said to have been wrought in God in John 3:21.

[7]God's word is said to be in people in 1 John 1:10 (not), his seed in people in 1 John 3:9, and his love in people in John 5:42 (not); 17:26. A further expression, found only in the Epistles, is "to have" (ἔχειν) God (or the Son): 1 John 2:23; 5:12; 2 John 9.

15:2, 5: "Every branch *in* me . . . He who *abides in* me. . . ." Mutual inbeing is effected by the Spirit (Jn 14:17, 20). It is not radically a matter of mystical or ecstatic experience, but rather of communication (implied by mention of Christ's "word" [Jn 15:3, 7; 1 Jn 1:10][8] and of prayer [Jn 15:7]). One person indwells another when they share the same thoughts, values (1 Jn 4:4-6), dreams, purposes, choices (1 Jn 2:5-6) and affections (Jn 17:26). Abiding and inbeing are Johannine ways of describing an interpersonal relationship between the believer and Christ/God.[9]

## BENEFITS OF UNION WITH CHRIST

What benefits does union with Christ bring? In him one has confidence for the day of judgment, cleansing from sin, resurrection both in this life and in the age to come, fullness of life, freedom from sin's domination, and an open relationship with God.

*No condemnation.* Rescue from the state of condemnation plays a less prominent role in John's writings than does justification in Paul's, but it is a theme also for John. He states it twice in his Gospel. With divine judgment in view, by which evil-working human beings will perish for their deeds (Jn 3:16, 19-21), John declares that God sent his Son to salvage the race from that outcome (Jn 3:17) and adds, "He who believes in him is not judged [οὐ κρίνεται]," whereas the one who does not believe has been "judged already [ἤδη κέκριται]" (Jn 3:18). The Greek present and perfect tenses point to a verdict in the here and now, be it positive or negative. Similarly, Jesus claims that the person who receives his word "has eternal life; he does not come into judgment [εἰς κρίσιν ἔρχεται], but has passed [μεταβέβηκεν] from death to life" (Jn 5:24). A person whom God has raised to life enjoys God's positive verdict; such a person need fear neither condemnation nor death.[10] Such is the case with Jesus, the sole human being who lives in eschatological glory, and, by extension, with those who by believing in him share in his vicarious, penal death and resurrection-vindication.

---

[8]Compare "my commandments" (Jn 15:10); "these things I have spoken to you" (Jn 15:11).

[9]Klaus Scholtissek, *In ihm sein und bleiben: Die Sprache der Immanenz in den johanneischen Schriften* (HBS 21; Freiburg: Herder, 2000).

[10]In the two verses quoted "to be judged" (κρίνεσθαι) and "judgment" (κρίσις) refer to condemnation. A believer need not fear being damned in the final judgment. John is not saying that the believer will be exempt from appearing before God to give an account. Even believers will undergo a scrutiny of their earthly lives and receive a final verdict (Jn 5:29; 1 Jn 2:28–3:3; 4:17-18; Apoc 11:18; 20:11-15).

John's First Epistle brings out the significance of this amnesty for Christians in their ongoing exposure to temptation. If anyone sins, Jesus Christ the righteous one steps in as advocate and sees that the Father is propitiated on the sinner's behalf (1 Jn 2:1-2). In this context παράκλητος takes on its legal sense of counsel for the defense and implies that Christ satisfies the judge. Later in the same letter John wants his readers to have "confidence for the day of judgment" that casts out fear of punishment (1 Jn 4:17-18). Such boldness finds its ultimate ground in an abiding relationship with God (1 Jn 4:12-13, 15-16).

The Apocalypse represents the same truth by the powerful image of Michael and his angels casting out of heaven the draconian prosecutor of saints. "The accuser of our brethren has been thrown down, who accuses them day and night before our God. And they have conquered him by the blood of the Lamb" (Apoc 12:10-11). Christ's blood invalidates any charge that the devil might try to bring against God's people in the heavenly court. They have been cleared, and the suit against them is closed.

Closely related to the suspension of judgment is the forgiveness of sins. The phrase is found once in the Fourth Gospel, where Jesus authorizes his followers to pronounce people forgiven (Jn 20:23). In the First Epistle God is said to be faithful to forgive the sins of those who confess them (1 Jn 1:9). Those whom God forgives for his name's sake become his children (1 Jn 2:12).

Other metaphors in the Apocalypse fill out the theocentric picture of a restored relationship between former sinners and God. When the opening doxology speaks of Christ as having loosed (λύσας) people from their sins, the mention of his blood puts emphasis on cultic removal of guilt in the presence of the holy deity (Apoc 1:5). Likewise, it was by being slaughtered (σφάζω) and shedding his blood that the Lamb ransomed (ἀγοράζω) people of all nations from certain destruction and claimed them for God (Apoc 5:9). The rest of humankind will worship the beast (Apoc 13:4, 8, 12) and, for doing so, will drink the wine of God's wrath (Apoc 14:9-11); but God has kept a perfect number whom he has redeemed (ἀγοράζω) for himself and for the Lamb (Apoc 14:3, 4).

*Cleansing from sin.* Not quite synonymous with forgiveness is the expiatory concept of cleansing, for which John uses a varied vocabulary. In the Gospel this theme surfaces in the footwashing scene (Jn 13). During supper Jesus removed his garments, wrapped himself with a towel, and began to "wash" (νίπτειν) the disciples' feet (Jn 13:5-8, 12, 14). They were already "bathed" (λελουμένος) and "clean" (καθαρός) (Jn 13:10), making Peter's request for a full bath (Jn 13:9) redundant. How they had come to be clean is indicated only later in the narrative. They had been made clean (καθαροί) by receiving the word that Jesus spoke to them (Jn 15:3).

Jesus' blood cleanses (καθαρίζειν) from sin those who walk in the light (1 Jn 1:7). God, in forgiving those who confess their sins, also cleanses them from all unrighteousness (1 Jn 1:9).

The Apocalypse speaks of a laundering of people's linen robes to make them white (πλύνειν [Apoc 7:14; 22:14]). Echoing in the background is Zechariah's image of Joshua the high priest exchanging soiled garments for clean ones (Zech 3:1-5). A theme of the Apocalypse is how "clean" (καθαρός [Apoc 15:6; 19:8, 14; 21:18]), "bright" (λαμπρός [Apoc 15:6; 19:8]) and "white" (λευκός [Apoc 3:4, 5, 18; 6:11; 7:9, 13; 19:14]) the garments of the saints are.[11]

***Life in the full sense.*** Life is a theme that permeates all parts of John's corpus.[12] John may be called "the Evangelist of life." Of the verb "live" (ζάω), the Fourth Gospel has roughly as many occurrences (17×) as do Matthew, Mark and Luke together (19×); of the noun "life," more than double the number (36× in John, 16× in the Synoptics). John's epistolary occurrences of "life" (13× in 1 Jn, 17× in the Apocalypse; 30× in all) balance Paul's (36× in all thirteen letters) even though the Johannine material is but a third as voluminous. John and Paul are more nearly proportional in their use of "live" (14× in 1 Jn and the Apocalypse together, versus Paul's 54×).

To set forth Jesus as the Son of God who brings life to human beings is John's aim in the Gospel, as he says plainly in his declaration of purpose: "These [signs] are written . . . that believing you may have life in his name" (Jn 20:31). Jesus makes thematic proclamations. "I came that they may have life, and have it abundantly" (Jn 10:10). "I am the way, the truth, and the life" (Jn 14:6). "Because I live, you will live also" (Jn 14:19). In chapter 5 above we saw that Jesus' offer of life (of which the motif of light is ancillary) (Jn 1:4-5, 7-8, 9; 3:19; 8:12; 9:5; 12:35-36, 46) is the pervasive message that John finds in the signs that Jesus wrought and in his "I am" sayings.[13] In fact, life and light in the Johannine

---

[11]"Fine linen" (βύσσινος [Apoc 19:8, 14]) is naturally white.

[12]David Asonye Ihenacho, *The Community of Eternal Life: The Study of the Meaning of Life for the Johannine Community* (Lanham, MD: University Press of America, 2001).

[13]Andre Feuillet, "Man's Participation in God's Life: A Key Concept in John," in *A Companion to John: Readings in Johannine Theology (John's Gospel and Epistles)* (ed. Michael J. Taylor; New York: Alba House, 1970), pp. 141-51; Ashton, *Understanding*, p. 217.

Gospel virtually replace the Synoptic theme of the kingdom of God (apart from vestiges of the latter in Jn 3:3, 5).[14]

About a third of the occurrences of "life" in the Johannine literature form part of the special phrase "eternal life" (ζωὴ αἰώνιος: 17× in the Gospel, 5× in 1 John), which John shares with others of his time and culture.[15] "Eternal" describes a life that belongs qualitatively to the aeon (ὁ αἰών) to come; note the contrast of two aeons in John 12:25: "He who hates his life in *this world* will keep it for *eternal life*." It is coterminous with that age, which is, in Jewish and Christian reckoning, without end.[16] Doing what must be done now to gain eternal life, always with a view to the coming world, was a concern of at least some Jews in the time of Jesus (Dan 12:2; *T. Ash.* 5:2; *Pss. Sol.* 3:12; *1 En.* 37:4; 40:9; *m. ʾAbot* 2:7; Mt 19:16, 29; Mk 10:17, 30; Lk 10:25; 18:18, 30). John, however, thinks of eternal life as a property of believers in Jesus in the present.[17] Apart from the statement in the Gospel prologue about the Logos at creation, "The life was the light of men" (Jn 1:4), where a pregnant "life" comprises both the worldly and the otherworldly, John uses the unqualified noun "life"[18] and the phrase "eternal life" synonymously to denote the latter.[19]

It is in this theological setting that the Johannine phrases "children of God" (Jn 1:12; 11:52; 1 Jn 3:1, 2, 10; 5:2) and "sons of light" (Jn 12:36) are seen to be metaphors pointing to an infusion of supernatural, eschatological life. The

---

[14]See André Feuillet, "Participation in the Life of God According to the Fourth Gospel," in *Johannine Studies* (trans. Thomas E. Crane; Staten Island, NY: Alba House, 1964), pp. 169-80; Ashton, *Understanding*, p. 214.

[15]In the Synoptics: Matthew 19:16, 29; Mark 10:17, 30; Luke 10:25; 18:18, 30. In Paul: Romans 2:7; 5:21; 6:22-23; Galatians 6:8. In the Pastoral Epistles: 1 Timothy 1:16; 6:12; Titus 1:2; 3:7. See also Acts 13:40, 48. For a wider collection of Old Testament and other Jewish references, see David Hill, *Greek Words and Hebrew Meanings: Studies in the Semantics of Soteriological Terms* (SNTSMS 5; Cambridge: Cambridge University Press, 1967), pp. 163-201.

[16]Oscar Cullmann, *Christ and Time: The Primitive Christian Conception of Time and History* (trans. Floyd V. Filson; Philadelphia: Westminster, 1964); Eric C. Rust, "Time and Eternity in Biblical Thought," *ThTo* 10 (1953): 327-56; Henri Blocher, "Yesterday, Today, Forever: Time, Times, Eternity in Biblical Perspective," *TynBul* 52 (2001): 183-202.

[17]Jn 3:15, 16, 36; 4:14, 36; 5:24-25; 6:27, 40, 47, 54, 68; 10:28; 12:50; 17:2, 3; 1 Jn 3:15; 5:11, 13, 20. Only in John 5:39; 12:25; 1 John 2:25 does "eternal life" pertain exclusively to the age to come.

[18]Jn 3:36; 5:24, 29, 40; 6:33, 35, 48, 51, 53, 63; 8:12; 10:10; 11:25; 14:6; 20:31; 1 Jn 3:14; 5:11, 12, 16.

[19]This synonymity is evident in John 3:36; 5:24; 1 John 5:11-12. The seventeen uses of "life" in the Apocalypse have the peculiarity that all are genitive modifiers, in the phrases "tree of life" (Apoc 2:7; 22:2, 14), "wreath of life" (Apoc 2:10), "book of life" (Apoc 3:5; 13:8; 17:8; 20:12, 15; 21:27; 22:19), "water(s) of life" (Apoc 7:17; 21:6; 22:1, 17) and "spirit/breath of life" (Apoc 11:11), all of which signify life eternal. The only exception is "soul of life" (ψυχὴ ζωῆς), meaning an animal. On "eternal life" and simple "life" as synonymous, see Jan G. van der Watt, "The Use of αἰώνιος in the Concept ζωὴ αἰώνιος in John's Gospel," *Neot* 33 (1989): 217-28.

same is true of the related phrases "born of God," versus being born of blood, flesh, or man (Jn 1:13; 3:5, 6, 8; 1 Jn 2:29; 3:9; 4:7; 5:1, 4, 18);[20] "born from above," rather than from below (Jn 3:3, 7);[21] instilled with God's "seed" (σπέρμα [1 Jn 3:9]); and being "of God" (εἶναι ἐκ τοῦ θεοῦ [Jn 1:13; 3:3-8; 1 Jn 2:29; 3:9; 4:7; 5:1, 4, 18]) rather than "of the world" (οὐκ ἐκ τοῦ κόσμου [Jn 15:19; 17:6, 14, 16]). This birth from above, like Paul's concept of adoption into God's family, means a new and positive objective relationship between God as Father and the believer as child, but John's concept goes further. The "seed" that God plants (1 Jn 3:9) is a new vital principle in the depth of the believer's being, an affinity to God's moral nature, prompting spontaneous delight in God and in all that God values—truth, goodness, love—that transforms behavior from the heart outwards.[22] There is no way around it. For John, Christians exist in the present world order as unbelievers do, but they belong to the celestial and coming world order in a way unbelievers do not. Life on this higher plane is not due to any quality that was inherent in them prior to their birth from God; rather, it is an act of the Father, the "gift of God" (Jn 4:10, 14), and is offered to everyone without price (δωρεάν [Apoc 21:6; 22:17]).

As being born to human parents introduces a child into a family, so spiritual birth carries rights and privileges. Paramount among these are boldness of approach to God and answered prayer as an eschatological privilege of the redeemed (Jn 14:13-14; 15:7, 16; 16:23-24, 26-27; 1 Jn 3:21-22; 5:14-15; Apoc 5:8; 6:10; 8:3-4).[23]

For sentient beings, life consists in relationships with others and, above all, in knowing God. Jesus, communing with his Father, confessed, "This is eternal

---

[20]Juan Miguel Díaz Rodelas, "La generación divina de los creyentes en los escritos joánicos," *EstBib* 66 (2008): 369-86; M. J. J. Menken, "'Born of God' or 'Begotten by God'? A Translation Problem in the Johannine Writings," *NovT* 51 (2009): 352-68.

[21]On "from above," rather than "again," as the correct understanding of ἄνωθεν in these verses, see Karl Olav Sandnes, "Whence and Whither: A Narrative Perspective on Birth ἄνωθεν (John 3,3-8)," *Bib* 86 (2005): 153-73; Pierre-Marin Boucher, "Γεννηθῆναι ἄνωθεν: La valeur de l'adverb ἄνωθεν en Jn 3,3 et 7. Iʳᵉ partie. La réception chrétienne," *RB* 115 (2008): 191-215; idem, "Γεννηθῆναι ἄνωθεν: La valeur de l'adverb ἄνωθεν en Jn 3,3 et 7. IIᵉ parie. Les acceptions du terme ἄνωθεν en grec classique et koinè non sémitisé," *RB* 115 (2008): 568-95.

[22]Rudolf Schnackenburg, *The Johannine Epistles: Introduction and Commentary* (trans. Reginald Fuller and Ilse Fuller; New York: Crossroad, 1992), pp. 162-69; Lieu, *Theology*, pp. 33-41; Strecker, *Johannine Letters*, pp. 83-85; Dirk G. van der Merwe, "Salvation in the Johannine Epistles," *HvTSt* 60 (2004): 544.

[23]See the chapter "The Doctrine of Prayer," in George B. Stevens, *The Johannine Theology: A Study of the Doctrinal Contents of the Gospels and Epistles of the Apostle John* (New York: Scribner, 1894), pp. 290-311.

life, that they know you the only true God, and Jesus Christ whom you have sent" (Jn 17:3).

John's constant reversion to the theme of life in Christ makes the vivification (or, in the language of systematic theology, regeneration) of human beings the keystone of his message. Within the canon of the New Testament John thus provides a counterpoise to Paul's special interest in justification. To be sure, Paul no more ignores the vital aspect of salvation than John wholly neglects the forensic, but each apostle shows a definite leaning in emphasis.

*Resurrection now.* At the end of the age God will raise the dead to immortality in the world to come. A notable feature of the Gospel of John is its stress on resurrection life as a present reality. To abide in Christ is to be joined to one who has undergone death and risen into glory. Humanity's end, realized in him, begins to take shape in his disciples. "Johannine eschatology is a function of christology";[24] "in John, Christ is really the 'eschatological present.'"[25] One who hears Jesus' word and believes in God "has passed [μεταβέβκεν, perfect tense] from death to life"; the hour now is, when the dead will hear, and will live (Jn 5:24-25). "If anyone keeps my word," cries Jesus, "he will never see death" (Jn 8:51). "I am the resurrection and the life; he who believes in me, though he die, yet shall he live, and whoever lives and believes in me shall never die" (Jn 11:25-26). The same emphasis is found in the Johannine correspondence. "We have passed out of death into life" (1 Jn 3:14). In the Apocalypse a pastoral application is made to those who suffer for their witness to Christ. John sees the souls of martyrs come to life and reign with Christ in what he calls their "first resurrection" (Apoc 20:4-6).

Such Johannine statements build on a common Jewish and Christian expectation and bring a vision of the end of the world to bear on the present. John has a scheme of eschatology much like that given in the Olivet Discourse of the Synoptic Gospels (Mt 24; Mk 13; Lk 21) without making it a conspicuous part of his proclamation. As we saw in chapter 5 when considering the future work of Christ, John looks for the rise of antichrist (1 Jn 2:18, 22; 4:3; 2 Jn 7; Apoc 13; 16:13-16; 17:9-14; 19:15-21; 20:7-9),[26] a time of tribulation for the saints (Jn

---

[24]Josef Blank, *Krisis: Untersuchungen zur johanneischen Christologie und Eschatologie* (Freiburg im Breisgau: Lambertus, 1964), p. 38.

[25]Rudolf Schnackenburg, *The Gospel According to St. John* (trans. Kevin Smyth et al.; 3 vols.; New York: Herder & Herder; Seabury; Crossroad, 1968–1982), 1:160.

[26]The clause "You have heard that antichrist is coming" in 1 John 2:18 makes it clear that this belief was part of the pattern of teaching presupposed by the Epistle.

16:1-4), the parousia of Jesus (Jn 14:2-3; 1 Jn 2:28; Apoc 1:7; 20:11), a general resurrection and judgment (Jn 5:28-29; 1 Jn 2:28–3:3; Apoc 20:12-15) on the "last day" (Jn 6:39, 40, 44; 12:48), and the establishment of God's everlasting kingdom (Jn 3:3, 5; Apoc 21–22) in which the saints will be conformed to Christ in glory and will enjoy the *visio Dei* (1 Jn 3:2; Apoc 22:4). As is apparent from the fragmentary nature of the references just given, however, John's Farewell Discourse (Jn 13–17), the literary counterpart to the synoptic Olivet Discourse, barely touches on select points from this scheme. We have to cobble it together from verses scattered throughout John's writings.

What is most striking about John's eschatology is an emphasis on the coming about of these elements in the present. Antichrist is coming, but already it is the last hour and many antichrists have come (1 Jn 2:18; 2 Jn 7). Even now the church is undergoing tribulation (Jn 16:1-4, 20-22, 32-33; Apoc 1:9; 2:10). Jesus' presence (the basic sense of *parousia*) is currently mediated by the Spirit-Paraclete (Jn 14:16-27). Wherever God engenders birth from above, a raising from the dead takes place (Jn 5:24-25). The judgment of the world began at the time of the crucifixion of Jesus (Jn 12:31-33; Apoc 12:10), and it rests over any who take up a stance of unbelief toward him (Jn 3:18, 36). Now the darkness of the world-system is passing away (1 Jn 2:8, 17).

How to integrate the present and future aspects in John's eschatology has been a subject for debate among New Testament scholars.[27] Patristic, medieval and post-Reformation interpreters took the futuristic scenario quite literally but for the most part failed to appreciate how radical was John's assertion that its elements are being actualized. For Christian rationalists and liberals of the eighteenth and nineteenth centuries, the apocalyptic language was a husk to strip away while retaining the moral and spiritual truths of the superior religion of Jesus. Around the turn of the twentieth century this outlook was shattered by a pair of celebrated German studies that restored Jewish apocalypticism to its rightful place in the fabric of Jesus' preaching and teaching.[28] In reaction, the British scholar C. H. Dodd proposed the concept of "realized eschatology" to bring attention back to the inbreaking of God's kingdom in the ministry of Jesus, though in later publications he

---

[27]For an overview of the discussion up to about 1970, see George Eldon Ladd, *A Theology of the New Testament* (Grand Rapids: Eerdmans, 1974), pp. 57-60.

[28]Johannes Weiss, *Die Predigt Jesu vom Reiche Gottes* (Göttingen: Vandenhoeck & Ruprecht, 1892); Albert Schweitzer, *Von Reimarus zu Wrede: Eine Geschichte der Leben-Jesu-Forschung* (Tübingen: Mohr Siebeck, 1906).

moderated his view and made more allowance for the future even in John.[29] Rudolf Bultmann aggressively uprooted all futurist eschatology from the Fourth Gospel by his hypothesis of a redactor who interpolated the passages that contain it. Positing that in its original form the Gospel had a present "eschatology" of divine transcendence in place of the chronological eschatology of earlier Christian tradition, Bultmann fancied that he had found a biblical model to support his program of reinterpreting New Testament "myth" in terms of existentialism.[30] Bultmann's proposal, which faced formidable objections from the outset,[31] was demolished at the exegetical level by Jörg Frey's massive three-volume review of the Johannine eschatology. Frey concluded that John embraces both present and future.[32] Although pockets of criticism in continental Europe cling to a fond demythologization, the view that John, with the other authors of the New Testament, holds an eschatology in two phases has won over the majority of Johannists.[33]

---

[29]C. H. Dodd, *The Parables of the Kingdom* (London: Nisbet, 1935), pp. 34-110. For a trenchant critique of Dodd's concept of realized eschatology, see Clayton Sullivan, *Rethinking Realized Eschatology* (Macon, GA: Mercer University Press, 1988). Dodd still refers to his early study of the Synoptic parables in his late work on John: *The Interpretation of the Fourth Gospel* (Cambridge: Cambridge University Press, 1953), p. 447.

[30]Rudolf Bultmann, *The Gospel of John: A Commentary* (ed. R. W. N. Hoare and J. K. Riches; trans. G. R. Beasley-Murray; Philadelphia: Westminster, 1971); idem, *Theology of the New Testament* (trans. Kendrick Grobel; 2 vols.; New York: Scribner, 1951–1955), 2:3-92. Bultmann is followed in this one-sidedness, though not in all aspects of his program of demythologization, by Schnackenburg, *St. John*, 2:426-37; Jürgen Becker, "Die Hoffnung auf ewiges Leben im Johannesevangelium," *ZNW* 91 (2000): 192-211.

[31]Bultmann's literary partition theory was criticized in Eugen Ruckstuhl, *Die literarische Einheit des Johannesevangeliums: Der gegenwärtige Stand der einschlägigen Forschungen* (2nd ed.; NTOA 5; Freiburg: Universitätsverlag; Göttingen: Vandenhoeck & Ruprecht, 1987); Bent Noack, *Zur johanneischen Tradition: Beiträge zur Kritik an der literarkritischen Analyse des vierten Evangeliums* (LSSTS 3; Copenhagen: Rosenkilde & Bagger, 1954). Bultmann's denial of futurist eschatology was found wanting by, among others, Ruckstuhl, *Literarische Einheit*; Alf Corell, *Consummatum Est: Eschatology and Church in the Gospel of St John* (trans. The Order of the Holy Paraclete; London: SPCK, 1958); Lodewijk van Hartingsveld, *Die Eschatologie des Johannesevangeliums: Eine Auseinandersetzung mit R. Bultmann* (VGTB 36; Assen: Van Gorcum, 1962). On both problems, see also Raymond E. Brown, *The Gospel According to John: Introduction, Translation, and Notes* (2 vols.; AB 29, 29A; Garden City, NY: Doubleday, 1966–1970), 1:cxv-cxxi.

[32]Jörg Frey, *Die johanneische Eschatologie* (3 vols.; WUNT 96, 110, 117; Tübingen: Mohr Siebeck, 1997). It is also instructive to compare critical studies of John's eschatology that preceded the debate of the twentieth century. That by George B. Stevens, for example (*Johannine Theology*, pp. 328-54), frankly acknowledges both the realized (present) and the unrealized (future) elements.

[33]See, for example, R. Alan Culpepper, "Realized Eschatology in the Experience of the Johannine Community," in *The Resurrection of Jesus in the Gospel of John* (ed. Craig R. Koester and Reimund Bieringer; WUNT 222; Tübingen: Mohr Siebeck, 2008), pp. 253-76. That the Apocalypse has a theology of history leading to a goal appointed by God need not be argued at length. See, for a starter, Michael Gilbertson, *God and History in the Book of Revelation: New Testament Studies in*

In light of this debate, some of the passages gathered above require further comment. John 5:24-25 in its immediate context (Jn 5:24-29) affirms a present resurrection of those who hear Jesus' word, while keeping clearly in view their bodily rising from the dead at the end of days. An hour is coming, "and now is"—has already struck—when the dead who hear the voice of the Son of God will live (Jn 5:25). But another hour "is coming"—in connection with which the text has no "now"—when all who are in the tombs, whether they have heard in the sense of believing or not, will come forth to his summons, either to a resurrection of life or to one of judgment, depending on their deeds (Jn 5:29). Here present and future eschatology are indissoluble. The passage is a decisive refutation of any theory to the effect that the realized element in John's eschatology has displaced the end of the world. John's bold avowal that things that in their nature belong to the end have begun to happen gains its power from his unswerving hope that there will be a grand fulfillment in due course.

John 8:51 and John 11:26 are parallel denials that one who believes in Jesus will ever die. Such a person partakes of indestructible life, implying a future without limit.

Jesus' remarkable asseverations in John 11:25-26 have been taken in different ways by interpreters. The most straightforward view is as follows. With the statement "I am the resurrection and the life," Jesus tells Martha that she need not wait for a remote "last day" for Lazarus to rise again, according to the prevailing Pharisaic expectation (Jn 11:24). Immortality is centered in Jesus' person even now. The two ensuing sentences elucidate this truth by reiterating it in chiasmus (AB/BA).

| Natural Life/Death | Eternal Life/Death |
| --- | --- |
| "He who believes in me, though he die (A), | yet shall he live (B), |
| and whoever lives (B) and believes in me | shall never die (A)." |

Figure 7.1

On this view, "yet shall he live" (Jn 11:25) and "shall never die" (Jn 11:26) both refer to a life that does not cease with the death of the body.[34] The resuscitation

*Dialogue with Pannenberg and Moltmann* (SNTSMS 124; Cambridge: Cambridge University Press, 2003).
[34]"The two parallel verses are synonymous, and in each case the statement about the true life comes

of Lazarus was a visible sign of this eternal life dispensed by the Lord from the time of his own resurrection onwards.

The millennial co-regency of martyrs with Christ in Apocalypse 20 is another exegetical crux.[35] Without going into many of its related problems,[36] suffice it to say that on the subject of resurrection John offers guidance. "This is the first resurrection" (Apoc 20:5) is an interpretive gloss on the vision just described of persons rising to reign with Christ. "First resurrection" (Apoc 20:5-6) implies a second, even as "second death" (Apoc 20:6, 14) implies a first. Since where death is concerned, first and "second" refer to two phases through which an individual passes, one pertaining to this world ("the first heaven and the first earth" [Apoc 21:1]) and one to eternity, the same will hold true of the "first" and second resurrections. In the case of the faithful who resist the beast and become martyrs, John arrestingly labels death their "first resurrection" in

---

at the end" (Schnackenburg, *St. John*, 3:331). This is the usual interpretation, upheld by Westcott, Bultmann, Morris, Schnackenburg, Ridderbos and many others. Were it the case that "yet shall he live" (Jn 11:25) referred to the resurrection of the age to come rather than to life unbroken by death in the present (e.g., Dodd, *Interpretation*, p. 147), Jesus would be saying precisely nothing beyond Martha. If "whoever lives and believes in me" in the second statement (Jn 11:26) referred to possession of eternal life rather than of natural life (Calvin, Bernard, Brown, Carson) or to the life of the final resurrection (Murray J. Harris, *Raised Immortal: Resurrection and Immortality in the New Testament* [Grand Rapids: Eerdmans, 1985], pp. 211-14), then the following "shall never die" would be a truism. There is nothing "trite" (Carson, *The Gospel According to John* [Grand Rapids: Eerdmans, 1991], p. 413) about the statement, taken as a whole, that one who believes in Jesus in the setting of natural life will never die in the deeper sense. Jesus, in conversation with a grieving Martha, may be applying the truth that he is the resurrection and the life, first to people in Lazarus's position as having already died (Jn 11:25b), then to those in Martha's, who still lives (Jn 11:26) (so Westcott).

[35]For overviews of options for interpretation, both traditional and critical, see Arthur W. Wainwright, *Mysterious Apocalypse: Interpreting the Book of Revelation* (Nashville: Abingdon, 1993), pp. 21-103; J. Webb Mealy, *After the Thousand Years: Resurrection and Judgment in Revelation 20* (JSNTSup; Sheffield: JSOT Press, 1992), pp. 13-58; Paul A. Rainbow, *The Pith of the Apocalypse: Essential Message and Principles for Interpretation* (Eugene, OR: Wipf & Stock, 2008), pp. 99-110.

[36]The interpretation of the millennium in Apocalypse 20 depends on how we understand the setting, structure and symbolism of the entire book. For an outline of the problems, see Rainbow, *Pith*, pp. 13-66. A strong case can be made that in the "little scroll" signaled by Apocalypse 10:2, 8-11, previewed in Apocalypse 11:1-13, and laid out at length in Apocalypse 12:1–15:4 together with a mirror narrative in Apocalypse 19:11–21:8, John sees elements of eschatology coming to initial fulfillment in events and personages of his own day. Dragon, beast and false prophet, like the antichrists in 1 John 2:18, are already at work mobilizing the world against the church. Christ's intervention at Armageddon (Apoc 19:11-21) uses futuristic imagery drawn from Old Testament messianic prophecies to depict the present clash between the gospel of Christ and the pro-Roman and Nicolaitan propaganda that is infecting the seven churches of Asia (compare Apoc 19:21 with Apoc 2:16). The millennium, then, will transpire between the Asian crisis that John and his churches face at the time of writing and the replay of the eschatological schema at the temporal end of the age (Apoc 20:7-15). Its backbone is the reign of the ascended Christ until he returns as judge (Apoc 1:9, 18; 3:21; 5:6-7; 7:15-17; 12:5, 10; 14:1-5; 20:4, 6).

order to drive home that it is their entrance into incontrovertible life, a life that precludes the "second death," to which the "first resurrection" is directly opposed. If this exegetical reasoning is sound, then the Apocalypse, like John 11:25-26, applies the resurrection concept to the intermediate state of departed believers between death and the end of the age rather than to regeneration as most of the relevant passages in the Gospel and First Epistle do. But it testifies to the same strong tendency to see the eschaton thrusting into the present.[37]

***Other immediate effects of union with Christ.*** Unlike Paul, who explores the effects of sin on humankind in terms of bondage (e.g., Rom 7), John has but a single short paragraph bringing out the fact that sin makes slaves of those who commit it (Jn 8:31-36). And only two statements in that paragraph speak of freedom, whereas freedom in Christ is thematic for Paul.[38] In the setting of a Feast of Tabernacles at Jerusalem, when Jews commemorate their social and political liberation from slavery in Egypt (Jn 7:2), Jesus promised liberty from sin: "If you abide in my word, you are truly my disciples, and you will know the truth, and the truth will make you free" (Jn 8:31-32). Soon he reiterated: "If the Son makes you free, you will be free indeed" (Jn 8:36). Like John's more typical contrast between blindness and sight (Jn 9; 12:40; 1 Jn 2:11), the lone mention of Christian freedom in John probably is to be viewed as part of his all-embracing theme of life.

A salvation-historical perspective informs Jesus' statement, unique in the Gospels, that his disciples are "no longer" slaves but friends, "for the slave does not know what his master is doing; but . . . all that I have heard from my Father I have made known to you" (Jn 15:15). In Mediterranean antiquity slaves were regarded as living property, living tools, articulate instruments,[39] and a master was under no obligation to explain orders. Friends, however, met as equals and spoke their minds to one another.[40] Jesus' language picks up on the contrast between these social models as found in Jeremiah's prophecy of the new covenant. God proved himself "lord" (בָּעַלְתִּי) to disobedient Israel (Jer 31:32),[41] but in the last days will put his Torah within his people and write his statutes

---

[37]On realized participation in salvation according to the Apocalypse, see Ferdinand Hahn, "Die Offenbarung des Johannes als Geschichtsdeutung und Trostbuch," *KD* 51 (2005): 55-70.

[38]In Paul's writings, in reference to salvation: ἐλευθερία, "freedom" (6×); ἐλεύθερος, "free" (9×); ἐλευθερόω, "set free" (5×).

[39]Aristotle, *Pol.* 1.2.4-5, 1253b; *Eth. nic.* 8.2; Varro, *Rust.* 1.17.1.

[40]Gail R. O'Day, "Jesus as Friend in the Gospel of John," *Int* 58 (2004): 144-57.

[41]The last clause in Jeremiah 31:32 is often translated concessively, "although I was a husband to them," but the NAB's "and I had to show myself their master" suits the context at least as well.

on their heart, so that they will not have to teach one another, for all will know him (Jer 31:31-34). An imposed obedience gives way to responsiveness that springs from shared understanding. After Jesus' death and resurrection the indwelling Spirit-Paraclete would bring about the latter on the part of God's covenanters (Jn 14:26; 16:13).

All the blessings of acquittal, forgiveness, cleansing, life, adoption, freedom and friendship with God can be summed up in the word "peace" (εἰρήνη), which rings with the overtones of the Hebrew שָׁלוֹם, "well being." Jesus promised to bequeath *shalom* to his disciples before his departure (Jn 14:1, 27; 16:33) and granted it on the evening of that first Easter (Jn 20:19, 21). It remained the standard element in early Christian formulae of greeting, whether by itself (3 Jn 15) or enriched by the addition of "grace" (Apoc 1:4) and "mercy" (2 Jn 3).

## COMING TO CHRIST

How, then, does one enter into this union with Christ that brings wellness in every facet of life? John wrote his Gospel to strengthen the faith of those who already believe and to invite others to believe savingly ("that you may believe" [Jn 20:31]).[42]

*Divine initiative, human response.* In John's thought world salvation begins with God's purpose, not with people seeking God. Birth from above is an act "of God," and human genesis is ruled out forcefully: it is "not of bloods nor of the will of the flesh nor of the will of man" (Jn 1:13).[43]

Though predestination belongs to the Pauline vocabulary and not to the Johannine, John certainly affirms God's sovereignty in saving people, which he expresses in other words.[44] All the concepts that make up the doctrine are

---

[42]Sandra M. Schneiders, *Written That You May Believe: Encountering Jesus in the Fourth Gospel* (New York: Crossroad, 1999). Jean Zumstein summarizes John's intention as "to awaken the faith of the faithful" (*Kreative Erinnerung: Relecture und Auslegung im Johannesevangelium* [ATANT 84; Zürich: Theologischer Verlag Zürich, 2004], p. 36).

[43]Admittedly the contrast here is between supernatural and natural birth, not between the Augustinian-Calvinian and the Pelagian-Arminian construals of soteriology. But in the context of John's theology a denial of human initiative in soteriology cannot be excluded. The plural "bloods" betrays a prescientific view of sexual reproduction wherein male semen was thought to contain the whole individual to be *in nuce*, including its blood, which, incubating in the mother's womb, mingled with her blood until birth. So we have the ancient comment, "Men are born of the blood of male and female" (Augustine, *Tract. Ev. Jo.* 2.14, on Jn 1:13). "Will [θέλημα] of the flesh" refers to sexual urge (as in 1 Cor 7:37), and "will of man [ἀνδρός]" to the husband's desire for his wife.

[44]Jeffrey A. Trumbower, *Born from Above: The Anthropology of the Gospel of John* (HUT 39; Tübingen: Mohr Siebeck, 1992). Trumbower, however, forces John into the religio-historical category of a Gnosticizing determinism.

there. (1) Invincible depravity: The human will in its blindness and bondage to sin is helpless of itself either to recognize God's objective revelation in Christ or to respond to it positively (Jn 5:42-44; 6:65; 8:43, 47; 10:26; 12:39-40). (2) Prevenient election: God "gave" or "has given" a select group of people to the Son to be saved (Jn 6:37, 39, 64-65; 10:29; 17:2, 6, 9; 18:9);[45] the Son gives eternal life to whom he will (Jn 5:21) and chose his own out of the world before they chose him (Jn 6:70-71; 13:18; 15:16, 19); the names of those to be redeemed have been written in the Lamb's book of life from the foundation of the world (Apoc 13:8; 17:8; 20:12; 21:27). (3) Intentional atonement: To rescue these, the good shepherd laid down his life for the sheep (Jn 10:10, 15). (4) Effectual calling: No one can come to the Son unless drawn and taught by the Father (Jn 6:44-45); when Jesus calls, his sheep hear his voice and follow; he knows them and they him (Jn 10:3-5, 14, 27; 12:32; 18:37). (5) Preservation by God: All who come to the Son he will raise up on the last day without losing one (Jn 6:37, 39); no one can snatch them out of his hand or his Father's (Jn 10:28-29); God keeps them from the evil one so long as they are in the world (Jn 17:11-12, 15; 1 Jn 5:18); none will perish (Jn 6:39; 17:12; 18:9). These truths add up to a robust belief that God is the prime mover in the salvation of human beings.

On what ground did God earmark some and not others for salvation? Over this question rages a historic and unresolved debate among Christian theologians. Augustine held that the reason must be perfectly just, being internal to God, but is known to him alone and inscrutable to human beings.[46] Already in Augustine's lifetime objectors, following his opponent Pelagius, maintained that faith originates in the human person and so is not granted by God, but God recognizes and increases it; God's choice to save fell on those whose response of faith and obedience God foresaw in advance.[47] Augustine countered in terms of causality. People are elected, he said, not "because they have believed" but "that they may believe." "They did not choose Him that He should choose them, but He chose them that they might choose Him" (*Praed.* 34.17). Vincent of Lérins replied that Augustine's interpretation

---

[45]John's concept of election is scarcely conveyed by his few uses of ἐκλέγεσθαι (Jn 6:70; 13:18; 15:16, 19), which are covered by Daniel Kerber, *"No me eligieron ustedes a mí, sino que yo los elegí a ustedes": Estudio exegético teológico sobre al verbo ἐκλέγομαι en el cuarto evangelio* (Montevideo: Facultad de Teología del Uruguay, 2002). The adjective ἐκλεκτός occurs in 2 John 1, 13; Apocalypse 17:14, without enough context to develop a doctrine.

[46]See, for example, Augustine, *Grat.* 41.20; 43.21; 45.23; *Praed.* 11.6; 16.8; 26.14.

[47]Augustine describes their view in, for example, *Praed.* 3.2; 38.19.

of Scripture was novel and could not be shown to meet the triple test of catholicity, antiquity and general consent. It has remained a minority position in the greater church ever since.

Theologians face an alternative. Either God's decision whom to save is located wholly in God's hidden will and is taken without human input (Augustine's answer influenced a number of luminaries, including Aquinas, Luther, Calvin and Jansen), or else God takes into account people's reactions, which makes salvation dependent on a synergy between divine grace offered and its reception (Pelagius's perspective was developed by Cassian, Vincent of Lérins, Molina, Arminius and their heirs). The former highlights the pure gratuity of salvation; the latter, the significance and responsibility of creatures.

John, for his part, assumes the fact of the predestination of the elect but leaves its basis unexplained. His writings present stark truths without connecting them. That God's love strictly precedes the love of the redeemed is a point of emphasis: "We love, because he first loved us" (1 Jn 4:19). Only by God's drawing can anyone come to Christ (Jn 6:44-45). But to infer from those propositions that in choosing a limited number to be saved God willfully passed over the rest of humankind, withholding from them an efficacious grace that would have turned them too from eternal ruin, is to violate the contours of the Johannine data. For were the divine decree of reprobation, like predestination, temporally and logically prior not only to any deeds, but even to any religious attitude, any response to God's offered grace—anything whatsoever—in the person, it would become formidably hard, if not a lost cause, to sustain the equally plain declaration that "God is light and in him is no darkness at all" (1 Jn 1:5). Everywhere in the Johannine corpus the damned bear the blame for their intransigence; nowhere is their end ascribed to a unilateral fiat of God. Even in the conclusive denunciation of Jesus' opponents in John 12:36b-40 the flow of John's thought runs thus: Jesus did many signs; they, having no excuse, refused to be persuaded; this fulfilled Scripture; therefore God blinded their eyes and hardened their heart to prevent them from believing (as in Scripture he had said he would do). The divine will to save is antecedent to saving faith, but divine hardening follows human rejection of God's bona fide call to repentance.[48]

---

[48]To be sure, Augustine based his view of "double predestination" more squarely on his reading of Paul than on John. On its face, Romans 9:18, "[God] has mercy upon whomever he wills, and whomever he wills he hardens," appears to trace both predestination and reprobation to God's free

How to unite the asymmetrical truths that God gets all credit for persuading the elect to believe, but that human stubbornness explains the nonelection of the remainder, is a conundrum. These two statements, which encapsulate the Johannine perspective, comprise the nonnegotiable raw material from which systematic theology must set out on its quest for coherence.[49]

***Believing, knowing and loving God.*** Three prominent verbs John uses to describe a Christian's response to God through Christ are "believe," "know" and "love." All were in the common parlance of the day and occur frequently in other New Testament books. Often, as in John, they refer to matters other than the divine-human relationship. To gain a rough picture of John's preference for these words we can compare the statistics of his usage with others. Although the Johannine corpus makes up but a fifth of the volume of the New Testament (19%), it presents almost half of the occurrences of "believe" (107 of 228 = 47%), over a third of "know" (190 of 508 = 37%) and over half of the verb "love" (85 of 154 = 55%). Comparing John's Gospel alone to the Synoptic Gospels as a group, we that find it has nearly triple the number of occurrences of "believe" (98 in John, 35 in the Synoptics), a fourth again as many of "know" (133

---

will (Augustine cites the verse in *Praed.* 14.8). But Augustine did not consider other factors in the same literary context that might have qualified or at least nuanced his conclusion. For example, when Paul says four verses further down that God "has endured [ἤνεγκεν] with much patience the vessels of wrath" (Rom 9:22), he hardly presents God as the active, ultimate party in barring hearts from coming to faith in himself. According to Romans 10:21, God spreads his hands all day long to a disobedient and contrary people. And branches were cut off from the olive tree "because of unbelief" (τῇ ἀπιστίᾳ, dative of cause), while those who have been grafted in stand "because of faith" (τῇ πίστει) (Rom 11:20). Both states are reversible, depending not on God's "kindness and severity" alone, but also on people's persistence in or abandonment of faith or unbelief (Rom 11:21-23). When Romans 9:18 is correctly read in its historical setting against the backdrop of Paul's running argument with Jewish nomism (e.g., Rom 9:30–10:13), "whomever he wills" must be saying that God is not bound to elect for himself either progeny in the lineage of Abraham (Rom 9:8) or those who do good works (Rom 9:11), but rather is free to show mercy according to any criterion he might choose. God's liberty to operate apart from the law in his dealings with human subjects need not mean, however, that he asserts an absolute and untrammeled determination over them that pays no regard to their passive reception or otherwise of his grace. The charge of "injustice" that Paul anticipates (Rom 9:14) arises from a quite specific Judaic perplexity at the thought that God, having given Torah, should ignore people's performance of it in assigning his blessing, not from a doctrine of divine partiality in the matter of election. Likewise, the imaginary objector in Romans 9:19 is troubled that Pharaoh was condemned even though his recalcitrance served as a foil for God's power and reputation, not that God disposes human beings to salvation or damnation out of the mystery of his own will. Augustine, in his tussle with the Pelagians over the freedom of the human will, brought to this passage a philosophical problematic that the passage was not designed to address, and he found in it a view of divine omnipotence and sovereignty that conflicts with the tenor of Scripture, carrying serious consequences for theodicy.

[49]Schnackenburg, *St. John*, 2:259-74.

in John, 106 in the Synoptics), and not far from twice as many of "love" (50 in John, 30 in the Synoptics).

For John, believing, knowing and loving God color one another.[50] Believing and knowing run parallel: "We have believed, and have come to know, that you are the Holy One of God" (Jn 6:69). Earlier in the same chapter those who learn from the Father (and so know) are said to come to believe (Jn 6:45-47). That believing involves knowing is clear in any case from the expression "to believe that . . ." (πιστεύειν ὅτι . . . ). To believe also involves loving: God's single command is that we believe in Jesus and love one another (1 Jn 3:23); and one who believes in Jesus loves God (1 Jn 5:1). Knowing and loving are also related. It is by loving in deed and truth that we know we are of the truth (1 Jn 3:18-19). "He who loves . . . knows God" (1 Jn 4:7). All three acts occur together: "So we know and believe the love God has for us" (implying our love for him) (1 Jn 4:16).

**Believing in God.** Let us examine the Johannine concepts of believing, knowing and loving God one by one, then put them back together.

Characteristically, to name the act of faith John uses a variety of terms and phrases: "believing," "seeing,"[51] "coming to" Jesus or to the light, "receiving" Jesus or his word, eating his body and drinking his blood, and entering into his sheepfold through him as the door.

It is customary and correct in studies of Johannine theology to observe that John uses the verb "believe" (πιστεύω) frequently but hardly ever uses the noun "faith" (πίστις). That he knew and had no objection to the noun is evident from its sole occurrence at 1 John 5:4, "This is the victory that overcomes the world, our faith," as well as from four instances in the Apocalypse, where it shades over into the virtue of "fidelity" or "faithfulness" (Apoc 2:13, 19; 13:10; 14:12). But his habit was to denote believing as an action.

From the varied linguistic patterns in which John uses "to believe" we see its main elements. Believing involves affirming certain truths about God and Jesus, as indicated by the construction "to believe that . . ." (πιστεύειν ὅτι . . . [Jn 6:69; 8:24; 9:18; 11:27, 42; 13:19; 14:10, 11; 16:27, 30; 17:8, 21; 20:31; 1 Jn 5:1, 5]) and the absolute "believe," where the context implies a proposition (Jn 1:7, 50; 3:12; 6:64; 10:25; 19:35). Truths believed include (representatively): that Jesus is

---

[50]Pascal-Marie Jerumanis, *Réaliser la communion avec Dieu: Croire, vivre et demeurer dans l'évangile selon S. Jean* (EBib 32; Paris: Gabalda, 1996).

[51]On the relationship between believing and seeing, see Jean Galot, "Vedere e Credere," *CivCat* 151 (2000): 242-53.

the Holy One of God (Jn 6:69), the Christ, the Son of God (Jn 11:27; 20:31); that he came from God (Jn 16:27, 30); that the Son is in the Father and the Father in him (Jn 14:10, 11). An equivalent expression is "to receive testimony" (λαμβάνειν μαρτυρίαν) about him (Jn 3:11, 32, 33; 12:48 [τὰ ῥήματά μου]; 1 Jn 5:9; cf. Apoc 3:3.).

Believing also means entrusting oneself personally to God in Jesus for salvation. This is indicated by the constructions "to believe in" him (πιστεύειν εἰς αὐτόν[52] or ἐν αὐτῷ Jn 3:15) and "to believe in the name of" a divine person (εἰς τὸ ὄνομα [αὐτοῦ] [Jn 1:12; 2:23; 3:18; 1 Jn 5:13]). "To come to" the light (ἔρχεσθαι πρός τὸ φῶς [Jn 3:20, 21]) and "to come to" Jesus (Jn 5:40; 6:35, 37, 44, 45, 65; 7:37; cf. Apoc 22:17) means the same thing. So does eating Jesus' flesh and drinking his blood (Jn 6:52-59). How these terms interrelate is perhaps clearest in John 6:29-69.[53] A variant of "to come to" (ἐλθεῖν εἰς) Jesus is "to enter into" (εἰσελθεῖν) his sheepfold (Jn 10:9). One may also trust him by "receiving" (λαμβάνειν) him (Jn 1:12, 16; 5:43; 13:20; Apoc 22:17 [receive "water"]).

John's usage thus suggests a distinction between the propositional and interpersonal aspects of faith, yet they belong together. Some constructions John may use either way. "To believe" may have an object that is propositional ("Do you believe this [τοῦτο]?" referring to a statement Jesus has just made [Jn 11:26]) or personal (we "believe the love [ἀγάπην] God has for us" [1 Jn 4:16]). Likewise, when "believe" takes a direct object dative, it may be words (Jn 2:22 [γραφῇ, λόγῳ]; 4:50 [λόγῳ]; 5:47 [γράμμασιν, ῥήμασι]; 12:38 [ἀκοῇ]) or a person (Jn 4:21 [μοι]; 5:24 [τῷ πέμψαντί με], 38 [ὃν ἀπέστειλεν . . . τούτῳ], 46 [Μωϋσεῖ, ἐμοί]; 6:30 [σοι]; 8:31 [αὐτῷ], 45, 46 [both μοι]; 10:37, 38 [both μοι, also ἔργοις in the latter]; 14:11 [μοι]; 1 Jn 3:23 [ὀνόματι]; 4:1 [πνεύματι]; 5:10 [θεῷ]). Absolute "believe" may tip either way, depending on its context.[54] Though "believing in [εἰς]" almost always has a personal object, its object is God's "testimony" (μαρτυρίαν) in 1 John 5:10. Both aspects can be juxtaposed,

---

[52]Jn 2:11; 3:16, 18, 36; 4:39; 6:29, 35, 40; 7:5, 31, 38, 39, 48; 8:30; 9:35, 36; 10:42; 11:25, 26, 45, 48; 12:11, 36, 37, 42, 44, 46; 14:1, 12; 16:9; 17:20; 1 Jn 5:10.

[53]John 6 has, in linear order, "believe in" him (Jn 6:29), "believe" him (Jn 6:30), "come to" him parallel to "believe in" him (Jn 6:35), "believe" (Jn 6:36), "come to" him (Jn 6:37 [2×]), "believe in" him (Jn 6:40), "come to" him (Jn 6:44, 45), "believe" (Jn 6:47), "eat of" the bread from heaven (Jn 6:50, 51), "eat [Jesus'] flesh and drink [his] blood" (Jn 6:53, 54, 56), "eat" him (Jn 6:57), "eat" this bread (Jn 6:58), "believe" (Jn 6:64 [2×]), "come to" him (Jn 6:65), "believe" (Jn 6:69).

[54]Propositional: John 12:39 (following the "report" in the preceding verse); 16:31 (assuming the confession in 16:30); 20:31 (assuming the confession in the same verse). Personal: John 3:18 (following εἰς αὐτόν in 3:16, 18); 4:41 (following εἰς αὐτόν in 4:39); 5:44 (following τούτῳ in 5:38); 6:36 (following εἰς αὐτόν in 6:35); 9:38 (following εἰς αὐτόν in 9:35, 36); 14:11 (parallel to "believe me").

as where hearing Jesus' word passes over into believing in the one who sent him (Jn 5:24), or even, in the same clause: "Believe me [personal] that [propositional] I am in the Father and the Father in me" (Jn 14:11). Believing a proposition and believing in the person coalesce in those few contexts where the simple "to believe" is truly absolute (Jn 1:48, 53; 11:15, 40; 14:29; 20:8, 25, 29).

We may conclude that Johannine faith is a compound of trust in the living God (including Jesus Christ) and of assent to the content that he reveals about himself.

*The personal object of faith.* In keeping with John's christocentric monotheism, faith directed to God centers on Christ.

In the Old Testament the proper object of faith is God. Abraham "believed in [הֶאֱמִן בְּ־] the LORD" (Gen 15:6), and Daniel "trusted in [הֵימִן בְּ־] his God" (Dan 6:23 [MT 6:24]).[55] Because God works in history through chosen human agents, faith in God includes faith in his agents, whom God accredits with signs. At the Red Sea Israel "believed in the LORD and in his servant Moses" (Ex 14:31; cf. 4:1-9). King Jehoshaphat exhorted Judah to believe in the Lord and in his prophets (2 Chron 20:20).

In the Johannine corpus the greater number by far of passages that mention a divine person as the object of human faith have Jesus,[56] the Son (of God/of man) (Jn 3:15, 16, 18, 36; 6:40; 9:35, 36; 1 Jn 5:10), his name (Jn 1:12; 2:23; 3:18; 1 Jn 3:23; 5:13) or his word(s) (Jn 5:47). This is what we would expect, given John's christological focus. But a few passages call for faith in Jesus as the one sent by the Father (Jn 5:38; 6:29; 11:42; 16:27, 30; 17:8, 21). These show that John's devotion to Jesus by no means upstages his Judaic faith in God.

Though passages that speak of faith in God are few in number, in the structure of John's thought they are fundamental. Jesus pointed beyond himself. To hear Jesus' word is to believe the one who sent him, who is the source of eternal life (Jn 5:24). "He who believes in me," cries Jesus at a climactic moment, "believes not in me but in him who sent me" (Jn 12:44).

Therefore, when Jesus before his passion encouraged his disciples to "believe in God, believe also in me" (Jn 14:1), he was not dividing their faith between two independent and potentially rival objects. Since God's identical being sub-

---

[55]For God alone as object of faith, see also Numbers 14:11; 20:12; Deuteronomy 1:32; 9:23; 2 Kings 17:14; Psalm 106:12; 119:66; Isaiah 7:9; 43:10; Jonah 3:5.

[56]Jn 2:11; 4:39; 5:46; 6:30, 35, 36, 69; 7:5, 31, 38, 39, 48; 8:24, 30, 31, 45, 46; 10:37, 38, 42; 11:25-26, 27, 45, 48; 12:11, 36 [the light], 37, 42, 44, 46; 13:19; 14:1, 12; 16:9; 17:20; 1 Jn 5:1, 5.

sists in God's Son and accomplishes all that God does through that Son, human faith that adheres to the Son adheres thereby to the Father. The disciples must believe that the Son is in the Father and the Father in him, that Jesus' words and works are the words and works of his Father (Jn 14:10-11).

Because it was God who sent his Son into the world to be the propitiation for sins, as faith contemplates the cross, it believes the love of God (1 Jn 4:9-10, 16). Ultimately, God is the one who has borne witness to his Son. A person who believes in the Son has received the testimony of God about him; a person who does not believe that testimony does not believe God (1 Jn 5:9-10).

In John's view, one can no more believe in the true God without believing in Jesus than one can believe in Jesus without believing in God. One believes in God precisely by believing in Jesus, and by believing in Jesus, it is God in whom one believes.

**Grounds for believing.** Because knowing is part of believing, faith has a secure basis. John does not neglect the epistemology of faith.

Faith rests ultimately on the firm truth of God's word. Merely to hear what Jesus said was enough to persuade many (Jn 4:41-42; 8:30). Jesus expected his disciples, perceiving his divinity, to accept his claims: "Believe me that I am in the Father and the Father in me" (Jn 14:11a). But despite the indubitability of statements that come from the eternal verity, sinful people in an environment of untruth can remain unmoved. Some heard Jesus but did not believe because they did not belong to his sheep (Jn 10:25-26). Nor did all who initially believed continue to do so (compare Jn 8:30 with Jn 8:31, 45-47).

Knowing that human beings, unable to trust each other, would hesitate to trust what is absolutely trustworthy, God multiplied witnesses to Jesus. Jesus' authoritative self-testimony is inherently credible (Jn 8:14). However, he condescends to the lawcourt rule requiring two or three independent lines of testimony (Jn 5:31-32; 8:16-18). Pointing to Jesus as the paragon of divine revelation are (1) the prophetic witness of John the Baptist (Jn 5:33-35; cf. 1:6-8, 19-34); (2) the works that the Father granted Jesus to do (Jn 5:36); and (3) the tenor of the Hebrew Scriptures (Jn 5:37-47). Additionally, over against deniers of the incarnation the Father himself bore a trifold witness to Jesus as his Son through "the water," "the blood" and "the Spirit" (1 Jn 5:6-10). Jesus "came" in the past by the water of baptism and by the blood of his death on the cross; since then, the present voice of the Spirit through approved prophets has confirmed that he came in the flesh (cf. Jn 4:2).

*Jesus' signs as grounds for faith.* A special role in evoking and confirming faith belongs to Jesus' "works" or "signs." Critical New Testament scholarship of the twentieth century, heir to the antisupernaturalism of the European Enlightenment, largely denied the causal link from miracles to faith. Though Bultmann was but typical of many, he was perhaps the most influential spokesman for a dominant school of thought. Unable to reconcile miracles with a naturalistic worldview, he portrayed believing as a stark decision needing no evidence for support. To find even the author of the Fourth Gospel to disparage the kind of faith that depends on signs was a tour de force. Jesus' words to the royal official whose son was dying, "Unless you see signs and wonders you will not believe" (Jn 4:48), and again what he said to Thomas, "Have you believed because you have seen me? Blessed are those who have not seen and yet believe" (Jn 20:29), Bultmann took to be rebukes of sign-based faith. For him, these sayings meant that miraculous occurrences "do not furnish Jesus with legitimating credentials."[57]

This was seriously to misrepresent John. John consistently and forcefully presents Jesus' miracles as constitutive of faith. His whole Gospel is built around a selection of signs he wrote down "that you may believe" (Jn 20:30-31). Nathanael confesses Jesus to be the Christ "because" (ὅτι) Jesus knew him from a distance; although Jesus promises a deeper revelation to follow, in no way does he denigrate this way of coming to faith (Jn 1:50-51). Jesus' turning water into wine stirred his disciples' faith (Jn 2:11). Again his healing of the official's son in absentia moved that household to believe (Jn 4:53). Without first becoming acquainted with the woman of Samaria, Jesus could tell her all that she ever did; on account of this (διὰ τὸν λόγον) many others from her town believed (Jn 4:39). Some Jews believed in him when they saw how many signs he did (Jn 7:31). Others were unsure; Jesus challenged them to consider his works (Jn 10:37-38). In particular his raising of Lazarus was meant to occasion faith. Jesus did it "so that you may believe" (Jn 11:15; cf. 11:42), "therefore" (οὖν) many Jews did in fact believe (Jn 11:45), and for some time afterwards people continued to go away believing "on account" of seeing Lazarus (δι᾽ αὐτόν [Jn 12:9-11]). Jesus' reputation for performing signs was a major factor in the rapid growth of his movement, a fact not lost on the chief priests and Pharisees (Jn 11:47-48). His contemporaries were inexcusable for remaining unconvinced

---

[57]Bultmann, *Theology*, 2:44-45.

"though he had done so many signs before them" (Jn 12:37). Even if Jesus' disciples could not accept his claim to coinhere in the Father, he invited them to believe "for the sake of the works themselves" (Jn 14:11). When they were afraid to ask him the meaning of an enigma, he penetrated their whisperings and explained it; "by this" (ἐν τούτῳ) they believed that he came from God (Jn 16:30). Doubt gave way to confession when Thomas met the living Lord (Jn 20:24-29). John views faith as rightly founded on the signs.[58]

That is not to say that marvels were guaranteed to bring about saving faith. People could witness Jesus doing wonders and still not perceive him as the Father's envoy to take away the sin of the world (Jn 2:23-25; 3:2; 4:45, 48; 6:30 [cf. 6:26], 36; 12:37; 16:31). The ninth chapter of the Fourth Gospel is a study in how people either came to faith or refused to do so in response to an unmistakable sign wrought by Jesus. Others besides God's messenger can work prodigies, in their case to deceive dwellers on earth (Apoc 13:13-15). Miracles from God should stimulate and consolidate faith, and in themselves they are a sufficient ground for believing, but sin and unbelief can put up effective resistance.

Bultmann's interpretation of John 4:48 and John 20:29 twisted the sense of these sayings. The isolated dominical saying "Unless you [plural] see signs and wonders you [plural] will not believe" (Jn 4:48) can hardly be a disavowal of the connection between Christ and his authenticating miracles that John so clearly affirms everywhere else. Jesus was prodding the royal official to "believe"—that is, to move beyond normal human fascination with a healing thaumaturge (Jn 2:23-25; 4:45) toward a deeper faith in Jesus' total message flowing out of the mystery of his person. In this case he succeeded. The official went away believing Jesus' mere promise of life for the son (Jn 4:50). The man's incipient faith was solidified when the promise came true (Jn 4:53).

After Jesus' death an encounter with the risen Christ blew away Thomas's skepticism (Jn 20:24-29). Thomas insisted on having firsthand evidence, and when it came, he was convinced to worship. Jesus, knowing that many others

---

[58]Wilhelm Wilkens, *Zeichen und Werke: Ein Beitrag zur Theologie des 4. Evangeliums in Erzählungs-sund Redestoff* (ATANT 55; Zürich: Zwingli, 1969); W. D. Davies, "The Johannine 'Signs' of Jesus," in Taylor, *Companion to John*, pp. 91-115; D. Bruce Woll, *Johannine Christianity in Conflict: Authority, Rank, and Succession in the First Farewell Discourse* (SBLDS 60; Chico, CA: Scholars Press, 1981), pp. 518-22; Frank Lynn Crouch, "Everyone Who Sees the Son: Signs, Faith, Peirces's Semeiotics, and the Gospel of John" (Ph.D. diss.; Duke University, 1996); Willis Hedley Salier, *The Rhetorical Impact of the Sēmeia in the Gospel of John* (WUNT 2/186; Tübingen: Mohr Siebeck, 2004); Craig R. Koester, "Jesus' Resurrection, the Signs, and the Dynamics of Faith in the Gospel of John," in Koester and Bieringer, *Resurrection of Jesus*, pp. 47-74.

who were yet to hear of him through the word of his apostles (Jn 15:17; 17:20) would never have an opportunity to be eyewitnesses for themselves, pronounced a blessing on those who would believe without seeing (Jn 20:29). Here Jesus commends faith based on credible testimony, not faith based on unauthenticated claims.[59]

*Coming to faith: Kinds and degrees of faith.* John is attentive to the psychology of faith. No biblical writer offers a more sophisticated portrayal of the process of coming to believe or a more acute analysis of kinds and levels of human faith.

The nuances, however, are not reflected in John's vocabulary as such. He typically uses the verb "to believe" categorically, often in simple opposition to not believing.[60] There is no clear example in his corpus of a present tense to denote coming to believe as a progressive action.[61] In this respect, John's linguistic usage contrasts with Paul's, who can accent continuance or growth in faith. But John makes artful use of real people, some named and some anonymous, to illustrate faith in various stages and degrees of development.[62]

---

[59]Rightly, William Bonney, *Caused to Believe: The Doubting Thomas Story at the Climax of John's Christological Narrative* (BIS 62; Leiden: Brill, 2002), pp. 17-19, 169-71.

[60]The verb πιστεύειν ("to believe") occurs in the narrative aorist tense in John 2:11, 22, 23; 4:39, 41, 50, 53; 7:31, 48; 8:30; 9:18; 10:42; 11:45; 12:42; 17:8; 20:8 (total of 16×). Nonnarrative aorists occur in John 1:7; 4:48; 5:44; 6:30; 7:39; 8:24; 9:36; 11:15, 40, 42; 12:38, 39; 14:29; 20:29; 1 John 3:23 (total of 15×). The perfect tense is less common: John 3:18; 6:69; 8:31; 11:27; 16:27; 20:29; 1 John 4:16; 5:10 (total of 8×). Virtually all occurrences of the present tense may be classified as aoristic (without progressive aspect): John 1:50; 3:12; 4:21, 42; 5:38, 47; 6:29, 36, 64; 8:45, 46; 9:35, 38; 10:25, 26, 37, 38 (2×); 11:26; 12:36, 44; 13:19; 14:1 (2×), 10, 11 (2×); 16:9, 30, 31; 17:21; 19:35; 20:31 (2×); 1 John 4:1 (so far, total of 35×); especially those in the frequent participial construction ὁ πιστεύων and its case variants: John 1:12; 3:15, 16, 18 (2×), 36; 5:24; 6:35, 40, 47, 64; 7:38; 11:25, 26; 12:44, 46; 14:12; 17:20; 1 John 5:1, 5, 10 (2×), 13 (total of 23×; all the presents total 58×).

[61]Thomas Barrosse suggests, with hesitation, 1 John 5:13, maybe 1 John 5:10 ("The Johannine Relationship of Love to Faith," in Taylor, *Companion to John*, pp. 157-58nn7-8).

[62]Elizabeth Liebert, "That You May Believe: The Fourth Gospel and Structural Development Theory," *BTB* 14 (1984): 67-73; David R. Beck, *The Discipleship Paradigm: Readers and Anonymous Characters in the Fourth Gospel* (BIS 27; Leiden: Brill, 1997); John P. Bowen, "Coming to Faith in the Gospel of John," *Anvil* 19 (2002): 277-83; Margaret M. Beirne, *Women and Men in the Fourth Gospel: A Genuine Discipleship of Equals* (JSNTSup 242; London: Sheffield Academic Press, 2003); Alain Marchadour, *Les personnages dans l'évangile de Jean: miroir pour une christologie narrative* (LB 139; Paris: Cerf, 2004); Annegret Meyer, *Kommt und seht: Mystagogie im Johannesevangelium ausgehend von Joh 1,35-51* (FB 103; Würzburg: Echter, 2005); Kelli S. O'Brien, "Written That You May Believe: John 20 and Narrative Rhetoric," *CBQ* 67 (2005): 284-302; Gary M. Burge, "Revelation and Discipleship in St. John's Gospel," in *Challenging Perspectives on the Gospel of John* (ed. John Lierman; WUNT 2/219; Tübingen: Mohr Siebeck, 2006), pp. 235-54; Judith Hartenstein, *Charakterisierung im Dialog: Die Darstellung von Maria Magdalena, Petrus, Thomas und der Mutter Jesu im Johannesevangelium im Kontext anderer frühchristlicher Traditionen* (NTOA 64; Göttingen:

He and fellow disciples in the narrative of the Gospel are examples of faith's gradual awakening. After spending a day in Jesus' company, Andrew announced to Peter the discovery of the Messiah (Jn 1:41). Soon afterwards, Nathanael hailed Jesus as Son of God and King of Israel (Jn 1:49). Yet both confessions fell short of recognizing Jesus to be the supreme channel of divine revelation between heaven and earth (Jn 1:51). None of the disciples really began to believe until Jesus turned water into wine (Jn 2:11). By the time of the mass defection of Galilean disciples in Capernaum, Simon Peter and the other close disciples were sure that Jesus was the Holy One of God (Jn 6:69). Still, they had a grasp of neither the facts nor the significance of his death, resurrection, ascension and breathing out of the Spirit to come, until after these things took place. At the Last Supper, when Jesus told them that he was going away, they were bewildered and demoralized (Jn 13:36; 14:1; 16:6). When he spoke of his return in the person of the Spirit-Paraclete, they could not fit what he was saying into their cosmic eschatology (Jn 14:23). All these events, which were to be the core elements of the kerygma, they were unable to bear only hours before they transpired (Jn 16:12). At least they took his point that he had come from God (Jn 16:30). Not until Peter and John found Jesus' tomb empty on the third day does John say that he "believed" and began to be struck by how the Scripture was coming to fulfillment (Jn 20:8-9). And only from the perspective of Jesus' postresurrection appearances did his early dictum about the destruction and rebuilding of the temple of his body start to make sense (Jn 2:19-22).

If the experience of the Twelve may serve as a typical pattern, John also has an eye for individual responses to Jesus that diverged from it.[63] Some Jews saw Jesus as a worker of signs but never trusted him as their savior from sin. These included nameless crowds in Jerusalem (Jn 2:23-25) and Galilee (Jn 4:45). A man healed of his illness ungratefully informed against Jesus to the authorities (Jn 5:1-15). Some of the five thousand were ready to make Jesus king, but only

---

Vandenhoeck & Ruprecht, 2007); Cornelis Bennema, "A Theory of Character in the Fourth Gospel with Reference to Ancient and Modern Literature," *BibInt* 17 (2009): 375-421; Susan Hylen, *Imperfect Believers: Ambiguous Characters in the Gospel of John* (Louisville: Westminster John Knox, 2009); Simon Vibert, "Lives Jesus Changed: Character Studies in John's Gospel," *Anvil* 26 (2009): 7-19.

[63]One of the first to categorize these was Marinus de Jonge, *Jesus, Stranger from Heaven and Son of God: Jesus Christ and the Christians in Johannine Perspective* (SBLSBS 11; Missoula, MT: Scholars Press, 1977). See also Nicolas Farelly, *The Disciples in the Fourth Gospel: A Narrative Analysis of Their Faith and Understanding* (WUNT 2/290; Tübingen: Mohr Siebeck, 2010).

because they had eaten their fill of loaves (Jn 6:15, 26). Quite a few seeing his signs concluded that he was a prophet (Jn 7:40).

Some followed Jesus for a while but later abandoned him. Many in the synagogue at Capernaum lost interest when he proclaimed his flesh and blood (i.e., his coming death) to be the true manna that gives life to others (Jn 6:60, 66). Another group that believed initially (Jn 8:31) could not stomach his insistence that they were slaves to sin and sons of the devil, and they took mortal umbrage at his bold claim to predate Abraham (Jn 8:59).

One man's faith developed rapidly through several stages under pressure from the Pharisees. The congenitally blind man at first testified simply to the fact that Jesus had opened his eyes (Jn 9:8-12). Under interrogation, he realized that Jesus was a prophet (Jn 9:13-17) and a righteous man (Jn 9:24-25). As they persisted, it became clear that Jesus must be from God (Jn 9:26-33). At last he believed in Jesus as the Son of Man and worshiped him (Jn 9:34-38).

For fear of the Pharisees' threat to expel confessors of the Christ from the synagogue, some people adhered to Jesus secretly. The blind man's parents positively identified their son but would not be drawn out on how he came to see (Jn 9:20-23). Many of the priestly and Sadducean authorities likewise "believed in him, but . . . did not confess it" (Jn 12:42). John censures this sort (Jn 12:43), having admiration for the few who dared to profess faith in Jesus at cost to themselves (Jn 9:34-38; 11:16). Joseph of Arimathea was among the clandestine until, after Jesus' death, he plucked up courage to request the corpse for burial (Jn 19:38).

Martha represents a devout Jew who subscribed to Pharisaic orthodoxy about the future resurrection. She had only to hear Jesus in order to acknowledge him as God's agent to bring it about (Jn 11:24-27).

Nicodemus appears to have been a late bloomer. A member of the Sanhedrin in Jerusalem, he was intrigued enough by reports of Jesus' signs to seek him out for a private audience. He started the conversation by acknowledging the work of God in those signs (Jn 3:1-2). This ruler had not submitted to John's baptism, and Jesus castigated him that night for his lack of spiritual understanding (Jn 3:3-12; cf. Lk 7:28-29). Some time later, when the council had made up its mind against Jesus and began to seek his death (Jn 5:18; 7:25, 30, 32, 45), Nicodemus placed himself in a minority of one by asking whether the law did not require Jesus to be given a fair hearing, resulting in the council aspersing him as being from Galilee (Jn 7:50-52). In this circumstance, for Nicodemus to join Joseph of Arimathea in the pious deed of interring Jesus (Jn 19:39-40) was in effect to distance himself from the negative vote of the Sanhedrin and declare himself a follower indeed.[64]

From John we learn nothing of Mary Magdalene's coming to faith (cf. Lk 8:2). She appears among four women who kept vigil near Jesus' cross (Jn 19:25). At Jesus' empty tomb she remained behind when the rest of the "we" who had approached the tomb (Jn 20:2) had left. The ensuing scene implies that she was the first person to meet the risen Lord. Emphasis falls on her inconsolable grief hindering her recognition of Jesus (Jn 20:11-15), giving way to a rush of joy grounded in the mistaken belief that Jesus had returned from death to resume his social presence among the disciples ("Do not hold me" [Jn 20:17]). She was also the first to report to others that he was alive (Jn 20:18).[65]

Faith can falter temporarily, even in God's elect. The Evangelist traces Peter's course. He was spokesman for the Twelve in confessing Jesus (Jn 6:68-69). On the eve of the Passion he professed his willingness to die for Jesus (Jn 13:37). His actually denying Jesus three times was the nadir (Jn 18:17, 25-27). But after the crisis he sorrowfully reaffirmed his love for his Lord, and Jesus reinstated him as shepherd of the flock (Jn 21:15-17). Peter crowned his career with martyrdom (Jn 21:18-19).

John leaves the impression there may be as many unique faith stories as there are individual believers in Jesus.

**Window of opportunity to believe.** Like the Hebrew prophets, John holds that God gives each nation, generation and individual more than sufficient time to repent and believe but will eventually close the window of opportunity for those who do not respond. "Seek the LORD while he may be found, call upon him while he is near" (Is 55:6).[66] In the Fourth Gospel this grim moment comes for the Judean leaders in the middle of John 12. Jesus warns the crowd they will have the light with them for a little longer; they must walk and believe in the light while they have it, before darkness falls. Shortly thereafter he hides

---

[64]Mary T. Brien, "Latecomers to the Light: A Reflection on the 'Emergence' of Joseph of Arimathea and Nicodemus: John 19:38-42," *NTR* 17 (2004): 48-56; Christine Renouard, "Le personnage de Nicodème comme figure de nouvelle naissance," *ETR* 126 (2004): 577-86.

[65]Susanne Ruschmann, *Maria von Magdala im Johannesevangelium: Jüngerin—Zeugin—Lebensbotin* (NTAbh 40; Münster: Aschendorff, 2002).

[66]This theme is especially prominent in Jeremiah, who prophesied when Israel's long season for repentance had come to a disappointing end. Jeremiah was told to stop praying for the nation because God would not hear; the Babylonian captivity had become a certainty. See Gerhard von Rad, *Old Testament Theology* (trans. D. M. G. Stalker; 2 vols.; New York: Harper & Row, 1962–1965), 2:197-99.

himself and does not address a crowd again in the remainder of the Gospel, but only his disciples. Then follow the author's reflections on the fulfillment of Isaiah's prophecies about people's unbelief and hardening by God, plus a summary of Jesus' essential message from the first twelve chapters (Jn 12:35-50).

In the Apocalypse Christ urgently calls his churches to repent (Apoc 2:5, 16, 21, 22; 3:3, 19) before judgment falls once and for all on the impenitent world (Apoc 9:20, 21; 16:9, 11).

*Believing and eternal life/light.* With the act of believing John regularly associates its immediate result: birth from above into eternal life and light. A person without faith in Jesus stands in a state of condemnation, "is condemned already" (Jn 3:18), and unless such people turn and believe, they will die in their sins (Jn 8:24). But to all who received Christ, who believed in his name, God gave power to "become children of God" (Jn 1:12). Whoever believes in him gains eternal life (Jn 3:15-16; 11:25-26; 20:31), "has passed from death to life" (Jn 5:24), "out of his belly shall flow rivers of living water" (Jn 7:39), for God's command is eternal life (Jn 12:50). Those who believe in the light "become sons of light" and do not remain in darkness (Jn 12:36, 46). "Every one who believes that Jesus is the Christ is a child of God" (1 Jn 5:1).

Moreover, one who believes will do the works that Jesus did and will do works even greater than those of Jesus (Jn 14:12). Since Jesus' "work" consisted in gathering fruit for God through his word (Jn 4:34-38) and his death (Jn 12:24), "greater works" refers to the evangelistic harvest of the world after Jesus' death and resurrection. Reproduction is one of the signs of life. Vital faith breeds faith in others.

*Persevering faith as victory over the world.* Saving faith is persevering faith. It involves more than a momentary decision to trust Jesus. It follows through and endures trials all the way to the end. To those who had believed in him (πρὸς τοὺς πεπιστευκότες, perfect tense) Jesus said, "If you continue [μείνητε] in my word, you are truly my disciples" (Jn 8:31). Some did not continue. To them Jesus said that they had the devil for their father, they were not "of God," they had never known him (Jn 8:44, 47, 55). Perseverance is not an optional extra. It marks a difference between those who are "truly disciples" and those who are no disciples at all.

Believing in Jesus entails not only professing the truth about his person but also loving God's other offspring. Having believed and become a child of God, everyone who loves the begetter loves what he has begotten, and we know that we love God's children when we love God and do his commandments (1 Jn 5:2). Those who abide in Jesus—that is, ingest Jesus' word(s) in this practical way (Jn 15:3, 7)—will be fruitful and so will "prove to be" (lit., "become," γένεσθαι) his disciples (Jn 15:8). Any branch in the vine that does not bear fruit the Father removes (Jn 15:2),[67] casts aside to wither, and commits to burning (Jn 15:6). Loving, commandment-keeping, and fruit-bearing are not discretionary; they constitute believers genuine followers of Jesus and separate them from those whose end is destruction.

Jesus knew that his disciples would face opposition from the world and prepared them for it, lest they stumble (Jn 16:1, 4; 16:20-22, 32). "In the world you have tribulation; but be of good cheer, I have overcome [νενίκηκα] the world" (Jn 16:33). If the victor in the Gospel is Jesus, those who maintain faith in him emerge as victors in the First Epistle. Believers may be pictured as strong young men who have overcome the evil one because the word of God "abides" in them (1 Jn 2:13-14). Imbued with the Spirit of God (1 Jn 3:24), who is greater than the spirits of false prophets, the church has overcome them and does not hear them (1 Jn 4:5). Everything born of God overcomes the world, and this victory is the church's faith (1 Jn 5:4).

**Knowing God.** Another group of words of thematic importance in John's soteriology has to do with knowing God and being known by him. John uses "know" (either γινώσκω[68] or οἶδα),[69] "see" (βλέπω, ὁράω, θεάομαι, θεωρέω) and "hear" (ἀκούω);[70] to know the "truth" or what is "true" (ἀλήθεια, ἀληθής,

---

[67]The proposal of a small school of dispensationalist interpreters that αἴρω here means not "remove" but "lift up," with reference to the viticultural practice of elevating a rotting branch to make it fruitful, is unconvincing. True, in John's Gospel the verb αἴρω can mean either "lift up" (Jn 5:8-12; 8:59; 10:24) or "take away" (Jn 1:29; 2:16; 10:18; 11:39, 41, 48; 16:22; 17:15; 19:15, 31, 38; 20:1, 2, 13, 15), but the two sentences in John 15 ("Every branch in me that bears no fruit, he *airei*" and "Every branch that does bear fruit he prunes, that it may bear more fruit") are antithetical, not parallel. This requires the sense "take away" for αἴρω, which is confirmed by John 15:6.

[68]Of all the New Testament occurrences of γινώσκω (222×), over a third (87× = 39%) are in the Johannine corpus (Gospel, 57×; Epistles, 26×; Apocalypse, 4×). This compares to 76× (34%) in the Synoptic Gospels and Acts together (Matthew, 20×; Mark, 12×; Luke and Acts, 44×) and to 50× (23%) in Paul, even though Luke's corpus is 36% and Paul's 16% longer than John's. These counts omit most of the General Epistles. But John uses γνωρίζω ("to make known") only thrice versus Paul's 18×, and the noun γνῶσις ("knowledge") not at all versus Paul's 23×.

[69]John appears to use γινώσκω and οἶδα synonymously. Of all the New Testament occurrences of οἶδα (318×), over a third (112× = 35%) are in the Johannine corpus (Gospel, 84×; Epistles, 16×; Apocalypse, 12×). This compares to 89× (28%) in the Synoptic Gospels and Acts (Matthew, 24×; Mark, 21×; Luke and Acts, 44×) and to 102× (32%) in Paul.

[70]Verbs for seeing and hearing are common and distributed throughout all parts of the New Testament. Theologically significant statements about hearing are found in John 4:42; 5:24-25; 6:45; 8:43, 47; 10:3, 8, 16, 27; 12:47; 18:37; 1 John 4:5-6.

ἀληθινός)[71] as opposed to "falsehood" ("false" [Apoc 2:2; 21:8]; "to lie" [1 Jn 1:6; Apoc 3:9]; "false prophet" [1 Jn 4:1; Apoc 16:13; 19:20; 20:10]; "falsehood" [Jn 8:44; 1 Jn 2:21, 27; Apoc 14:5; 21:27; 22:15]; "liar" [Jn 8:44, 55; 1 Jn 1:10; 2:4, 22; 4:20; 5:10]); to "confess" (ὁμολογέω [Jn 9:22; 12:42; 1 Jn 2:23; 4:2, 3; 15; 2 Jn 7]) as opposed to "deny" (Jn 1:20; 1 Jn 2:22-23); to "remember" (Jn 15:20; 16:4, 21; Apoc 2:5; 3:3)[72] and to have "understanding" (διανοία [1 Jn 5:20]).[73] Equivalent expressions include having God's word abide in one (Jn 5:38) or find room in one (Jn 8:37); the truth being in one (1 Jn 1:8; 2:4; 2 Jn 2); a person being "of the truth" (Jn 18:37; 1 Jn 3:19), or having the testimony in oneself (1 Jn 5:10). Also relevant is the fact that John, like the Synoptists, regularly designates Jesus' most loyal followers "disciples" (μαθηταί), meaning those who attached themselves to a master to learn from him. In the Johannine corpus believing, knowing, seeing, hearing and confessing form a nexus.[74] Knowing by gospel recipients corresponds to Jesus' revelatory activities of speaking and "showing" (φανερόω).[75]

As with believing, so with knowing, John's usage covers knowing facts and knowing persons. On the cognitive side, one can know "this" (τοῦτο, ταῦτα [Jn 3:10; 12:16; 13:17, 28]) or "that which" (ὅ [Jn 3:11; 4:22]), or "that" (ὅτι) something is the case,[76] or the answers to questions, direct or indirect: "where from/to" (πόθεν/ποῦ [Jn 2:9; 3:8; 7:27-28; 8:14; 9:29-30; 12:35; 14:5; 1 Jn 2:11; Apoc 7:14]); "who" (τίς [Jn 5:13; 6:64; 9:21; Apoc 7:14]); "whether" (εἰ, πότερον [Jn 7:17; 9:25]);

---

[71]The number of occurrences of the noun ἀλήθεια in the Johannine corpus (total of 45×: Gospel, 25×; Epistles, 20×) is comparable to those in Paul (47×). This word is less frequent in the Synoptic writers (Matthew, 1×; Mark, 3×; Luke and Acts, 6×; New Testament total, 109×). But John greatly outdistances the others in his use of the adjectives ἀληθής (John, 18×; Paul: 4×; New Testament total, 26×) and especially ἀληθινός (John, 23×; Paul, 1×; New Testament total, 28×).

[72]Related is the Spirit's work of "reminding" (Jn 14:26).

[73]Only here in the Johannine corpus; 12× in the New Testament.

[74]On John's "gnoseological" terminology, see Franz Mussner, *Die johanneische Sehweise und die Frage nach dem historischen Jesus* (QD 28; Freiburg: Herder, 1965). On believing, knowing and seeing as related, see W. K. Grossouw, "Christian Spirituality in John," in *A Companion to John: Readings in Johannine Theology (John's Gospel and Epistles)* (ed. Michael J. Taylor; New York: Alba House, 1970), pp. 217-20. For a narrative approach to "knowing" in John's Gospel, see Andreas Leinhäupl-Wilke, *Rettendes Wissen im Johannesevangelium: Ein Zugang über die narrativen Rahmenteile (John 1,19-2,12-20,1-21,25)* (NTAbh 45; Münster: Aschendorff, 2003). On knowing God according to the Epistles, see Lieu, *Theology*, pp. 27-33.

[75]The number of occurrences of φανερόω in the Johannine corpus (20×) is comparable to those in Paul (22×). This word is rare in the Synoptic writers (Matthew, 0×; Mark, 3×; Luke and Acts, 0×). The New Testament total is 49×.

[76]Jn 3:2; 4:1, 25, 42, 53; 5:6, 32, 42; 6:15, 61, 69; 7:26; 8:27, 28, 37, 52; 9:20, 24, 25, 29, 31; 10:38; 11:22, 24, 42; 12:9, 50; 13:1, 3, 35; 14:31; 15:18; 16:19, 30; 17:7, 8, 23, 25; 19:4, 10, 28, 35; 20:14; 21:4, 12, 15, 16, 17; 21:24; 1 Jn 2:3, 5, 18, 29; 3:2, 5, 14, 15, 19, 24; 4:13; 5:2, 13, 15, 18, 19, 20; 3 Jn 12; Apoc 2:23; 3:9, 17; 12:12.

"what" (τί [Jn 6:6; 7:51; 10:6; 15:15; 16:18]); "where" (ποῦ [Jn 9:12; 11:57; 20:2, 13; Apoc 2:13]); "how" (πῶς [Jn 9:21]). Most often the object of knowing is a thing, a fact or an idea.[77] Jesus came to speak and testify to the truth, thus undoing the lies of the devil (Jn 5:33; 8:40, 44-46; 16:7; 18:37-38); this usage is identical to people testifying in court to what they have seen (cf. Jn 5:31-32; 8:13, 14, 17). On the basis of Jesus' testimony, brought to remembrance by the "Spirit of truth" (Jn 14:17; 15:26; 16:13), his disciples can know the truth about him and find freedom in it (Jn 8:32; 1 Jn 2:21; 3:19–4:6; 2 Jn 1-2). "To know" can be used intransitively in the sense "to have knowledge" in a context having to do with the correct confession about God's Son (1 Jn 2:20).

Jesus' calling of Andrew, Peter, and Nathanael in John 1:35-51 is a paradigm of discipleship.[78] These individuals met Jesus and almost immediately began to articulate perceptions of him as "messiah" (Jn 1:41), "Son of God" and "king of Israel" (Jn 1:49). Among other things to be known or confessed about Jesus are the truths that, as he put it, "I am he" (Jn 8:28), that he bears glory as the Only-Begotten of the Father (Jn 1:14), is the Son of the Father (Jn 6:40; 1 Jn 2:22-23), is in his Father (Jn 14:20); that he knows all things (Jn 16:30) and received all things from his Father (Jn 17:7); that the Father sent him (Jn 17:23, 25), he came from the Father (Jn 17:8; 1 Jn 5:20) in the flesh (1 Jn 4:2; 2 Jn 7) and ascended to where he was before (Jn 6:62); that he is the track of divine revelation (Jn 1:51), the Savior of the world (Jn 4:42), the Holy One of God (Jn 6:69), the Son of Man (Jn 9:35-37), the Christ (1 Jn 2:22); that his teaching is from God (Jn 7:17); that he is righteous (1 Jn 2:29); that he appeared to take away sins (1 Jn 3:5); that his followers have passed out of death into life (1 Jn 3:14) and will be like him when he appears finally (1 Jn 3:2). If interpersonal knowing be more, it is never less than knowing about the person. To know the good shepherd and his care, his sheep must know at least that he and the Father are one (Jn 10:30), that the Father consecrated him and sent him into the world (Jn 10:36), and that he laid down his life for them (Jn 10:11). Thus religious knowledge has for

---

[77]Objects include "the gift of God" (Jn 4:10), "food" (Jn 4:32), "letters" (Jn 7:15), "the law" (Jn 7:49), "the truth" (Jn 8:32; 1 Jn 2:21; 2 Jn 1), "the speech" (τὴν λαλιὰν [Jn 8:43]), "nothing" (Jn 11:49), "what" someone does or says (Jn 13:7, cf. 13:12; 18:21), "the way" (Jn 14:4-5), "the place" (Jn 18:2), "all things" (Jn 18:4; 21:17; 1 Jn 3:20), "the scripture" (Jn 20:9), people's "works" and "labor" or "love" (Apoc 2:2, 19; 3:1, 8, 15), people's "distress" and "poverty" (Apoc 2:9), a "name" (Apoc 2:17; 19:12), "the deep things of Satan" (Apoc 2:24). Even if the object is a person, knowledge may be about rather than of the person (Jn 1:26, 31, 33; 2:25; 6:42; 13:11).
[78]Mary Margaret Pazdan, "Discipleship as the Appropriation of Eschatological Salvation in the Fourth Gospel" (Ph.D. diss., University of Toronto, 1982).

John a definite doctrinal content that can be put into propositions.[79]

Knowing goes beyond mere cognition. Its object may be a person who loves, or a way of life involving practical steps. Nathanael was taken aback when Jesus read his inmost character as though having been familiar with him for a long time (Jn 1:47-48). If sheep know the shepherd's voice, they follow (Jn 10:27). As the good shepherd, Jesus knows his sheep and they know him (Jn 10:14). Such knowing involves covenantal commitment (cf. Ezek 34:23-25). Reciprocal knowledge is perfect between the Father and the Son (Jn 10:15). The intended readers of John's First Epistle were members of the Father's family (1 Jn 2:13). For the world not to know the children of God, or not to know God himself, means having no commonality with God or with his people (1 Jn 3:1). Knowing, then, can be an "I-Thou" relationship with another person in his or her totality.[80]

*The personal object of knowing.* In the Old Testament the proper object of religious knowledge is the God of Israel. God led Abraham's descendants out of Egypt and made a covenant with them at Mount Sinai so that they themselves and surrounding nations would know him to be the Lord their God (Ex 6:7; 7:5; 2 Kings 19:19), and that there is no other besides him (Deut 4:35). Thus God came to be known in Judah, his name became great in Israel (Ps 76:1), and Israel became conscious of having in the Torah a unique revelation, ordinances that no other nation knew (Ps 147:20). Looking beyond Israel's unfaithfulness to a coming era, the writing prophets envisaged a time when "the earth shall be full of the knowledge of the LORD as the waters cover the sea" (Is 11:9). In that day Israel's sons will all be "taught by the LORD" (Is 54:13, quoted at Jn 6:45) and will no longer need to teach one another, for "they shall all know me" (Jer 31:34). "Then you will know that I am the LORD" (Ezek 36:11 [cf. 36:23, 38]).

John locates this eschatological knowledge of God squarely in the incarnate Son. Knowledge of the Hebrew Scriptures leads straight to recognition of God's sent one. Said Jesus, "If you believed Moses, you would believe me, for he wrote

---

[79]"The study of the vocabulary in the Fourth Gospel would put the presuppositions on the side of a rational or reflective content in the term 'knowledge'. . . . The author of the Fourth Gospel has moved in the direction of intellectualizing the mystical experience which constitutes the redemptive process. . . . 'Knowledge' was contingent upon the reflective evaluation of the life of Jesus, a process which rested upon testimony susceptible of proof in the intellectual realm" (Mary Redington Ely, *Knowledge of God in Johannine Thought* [New York: Macmillan, 1925], pp. 40, 138, 147.

[80]"Even when the concept of knowledge of God is most fully intellectualized, it remains true that it involves a personal union with Christ, which goes beyond mere intellectual apprehension" (Dodd, *Interpretation*, p. 178). Strecker (*Johannine Letters*, pp. 222-26) points out that this is as true of the Greek use of γινώσκειν as it is in the Hebrew Bible.

of me" (Jn 5:46). Conversely, God's self-revelation in the Son unveils God himself: "If you knew me, you would know my Father also" (Jn 8:19). In Jesus' works is seen the glory of God (Jn 11:40). To see God's agent is to see God the sender (Jn 12:45).

Many of Jesus' contemporaries did not know him. In rejecting God's Son, they turned away from the sending Father (Jn 5:38; 8:19, 55; 15:21; 16:3; 17:25; 1 Jn 3:1). True ignorance mitigates guilt, but ignorance deliberately chosen deepens guilt (Jn 9:39-41; 15:24). After Jesus' departure the world sees him no more (Jn 14:19).

At the outset of the Farewell Discourse Jesus piled claim upon claim. He was going to the Father (Jn 14:2-4). He is the unique way for others to get to the Father and is the "truth," or very reality of the divine, among human beings (Jn 14:5-6). Embodiment of the divine in him is the mode by which the Father lets himself be known (Jn 14:7). An uncomprehending Philip followed up with a request for Jesus to show them the Father. Jesus, incredulous that one of his own disciples could miss the very point of his incarnation, countered, "He who has seen me has seen the Father" (Jn 14:8-9).

As with believing, John does not propound two separate objects of religious knowledge. Disciples do not know the Son in addition to the Father, much less instead of the Father. In knowing the Son, it is the essence of the Father that they encounter. For this reason, John in his Epistles defends the doctrine of the incarnation against proto-Gnostic schismatics. Denying the Son cuts off the denier from the Father; confessing the Son unites to the Father (1 Jn 2:23; 2 Jn 9).

John's christocentric epistemology does not compromise his ontological monotheism, but makes knowledge of the one God accessible by locating the revelation in that agent who is eminently suited to disclose the heart of the personal God.

***Possibility of the knowledge of God.*** Given the fact that no mortal has ever seen God, which John reiterates as a refrain (Jn 1:18; 5:37; 6:46; 1 Jn 4:12), how is it possible to know God? Only God can speak for God. He has sent one derived from and sharing his own being to be the authentic divine word. "The only-begotten God, who is in the embrace of the Father, he has explained him [ἐξηγήσατο]" (Jn 1:18). He spoke of what he knew (Jn 3:11; 8:26, 55). God sent the Spirit of truth to the disciples to dwell with them and be in them, that knowing the Spirit (Jn 14:17) they might see their absent Lord (Jn 14:19), experience the presence of the coinherent Father and Son (Jn 14:20-21, 23), and grasp all that Jesus revealed (Jn 14:26).

Not only must God take the initiative to disclose himself, but also God knew his creatures before they could know him. "I know my own [sheep] and my own know me," said Jesus (Jn 10:14). The priority is all on his side. He knows whom he has chosen (Jn 13:18); he chose them, they did not choose him (Jn 15:16). Brought into the sphere of his care, they seek to know him in return.

Back of this reciprocal knowledge of shepherd and sheep is the mutual knowledge of the Father and the Son in heaven. "The Father knows me and I know the Father" (Jn 10:15); "I know him" (Jn 7:29; 8:55; cf. 17:25). Human beings can know God because there is interpersonal knowing within the Godhead, a fellowship that God himself has opened to creatures.

*Three dimensions of knowing God.* According to John's First Epistle, God is truth, goodness and love. Knowing God means seeing what God is, admiring, and becoming like him. So one who knows God, according to John, hears the truth, does God's will, and loves those whom God loves.

Whoever knows God is stable in God's unchanging truth. John lived to a time when some who supposed that they were Christians departed from the truth by denying the doctrine of the incarnation. Them he called liars and antichrists (1 Jn 2:22-23), moved by a spirit not of God but of the world (1 Jn 4:1-5). Those who are of God have an anointing from the Holy One. They "have knowledge," know "the truth," have no need for anyone to teach them, and abide in what they heard from the beginning (1 Jn 2:20, 24, 26-27). Such persons agree with Christ's apostles that Jesus Christ came in the flesh. They distance themselves from heretics (1 Jn 4:2, 6; 2 Jn 7).

Knowing God and performing his will go hand in hand. Jesus' own claim to know God passed directly into keeping his word (Jn 8:55). So must it be also among his disciples. A shepherd goes before his sheep; they follow because they know his voice (Jn 10:4-5). "If you know these things, blessed are you if you do them" (Jn 13:17). Whether a person knows Christ is indicated by whether that person keeps his commandments. Someone who claims to know him but disregards his commandments is a liar (1 Jn 2:3-4). Anyone who sins is shown thereby to have neither seen God nor known him (1 Jn 3:6).

Since God is love and has demonstrated love by sending his Son, anyone who knows God loves God's children as God loves them. "He who loves is born of God and knows God. He who does not love does not know God" (1 Jn 4:7-8).

Such love will not be in word or speech only but in deed and truth (1 Jn 3:18). Knowledge of God results in loving God's family.

Right belief, right action and love harmonize in such a way as to define one another. A profession of faith is a saving one only if it results in the keeping of God's commandments and love for his offspring. Performance of the commandments is without value unless it recognizes God in his Son and has fellowship with God's church. True love stems from a relationship with God through his Son and takes the form of fulfilling his commandments. These ideals are intertwined in 1 John 5:1-5.

Knowing God is so bound up with holding to the truth, doing his will and showing love, that these are criteria by which to determine whether professed knowledge of God is genuine. The phrase "by this we know," a refrain throughout John's First Epistle, lays down tests that fall neatly into these three categories: orthodoxy (1 Jn 4:2, 13-16; cf. 2:22-23; 4:6; 5:10-13), righteous action (1 Jn 2:3-4, 5-6; 3:10, 24; 5:2; 3 Jn 11; cf. 1 Jn 3:7-8) and love (1 Jn 3:10, 16-17, 19; 4:16-17; 5:1-2; cf. 2:9-11; 3:14; 4:7-8, 20). The direction of John's logic is noteworthy. He does not say that if we know God, we will confess his Son, do what he says and love his family—true though that may be. He says rather that if we confess, if we do, if we love, then we truly know God. "By this we may be sure we know him: if we keep his commandments" (1 Jn 2:3). "He who confesses the Son has the Father also" (1 Jn 2:23). "He who loves is born of God and knows God" (1 Jn 4:7). Dogmatic truth, moral truth and love are not merely consequences; they are the very stuff of which knowledge of God consists. They constitute and consolidate such knowledge.

***Knowing God and eternal life.*** With the profundity of simplicity, John has Jesus define eternal life as knowing God and Jesus Christ, whom he sent (Jn 17:3). To receive God's self-disclosure is to be raised out of the realm of flux into the permanent realm of the revealer. Eternal life is not some fountain of youth that can be had for itself apart from a relationship with the living God. The eternal God who is very life communicates life by communicating himself in relationship, and he communicates himself by sending his Son. The destiny of Jesus' followers is to be with him to behold his glory, which the Father gave him (Jn 17:24), to see him as he is (1 Jn 3:2), to see God's face (Apoc 22:4).

When John describes church members metaphorically as "fathers," part of the point of the comparison is longevity, an aspect of eternal life. They are fathers because they know the Second Person of the Trinity, "him who is from

the beginning" (1 Jn 2:13, 14). Knowledge of "that which was from the beginning" (1 Jn 1:1), of "the eternal life that was with the Father and was made
manifest to us" (1 Jn 1:2), has generated in them a life of the same quality and
duration as his.

Knowledge of God is identical with eternal life again at the finale of John's
First Epistle (1 Jn 5:20). The coming of the Son brought understanding to
human beings "to know him who is true." This refers to "the true God" of
Jewish monotheism, God the Father. But because God is unknown apart from
what he says about himself, and his self-revelation reached its apex in the incarnation of his Son, the statement that "we are in him who is true" requires a
qualification: we are "in his Son Jesus Christ." "This"—the one God who has
divulged himself by the sending of him who was born of God (1 Jn 5:18)—"is
the true God and eternal life." Any other divine construct is an idol (1 Jn 5:21).
Eternal life belongs to him and is gained by knowing him.

Knowing God and being known by him, then, is the goal and content of life.

*Loving God.* Union with Christ involves, besides believing and coming to
know God, entering with God into a relationship of love.

That God loves his people is a motif of all parts of the Johannine corpus.
Here we are thinking not of the sole statement in which John says God loved
the world at large (Jn 3:16), but of that special love God has for Jesus' disciples,
who have become beneficiaries of God's covenant love. Before the foundation
of the world the Father gave to the Son out of the world those whom he loved,
even as he loved his Son (Jn 17:2, 23; Apoc 13:8; 17:8). This love was primal and
self-motivated from within God. People in the covenant community love God
because he loved them first (1 Jn 4:19), not because they loved him (1 Jn 4:10).
Love is the core of who God is. "God is love" (1 Jn 4:8, 16). He demonstrated it
by sending his Son to be the propitiation for sins (1 Jn 4:9-11a, 16). The love by
which God has made people his children, not in name only but in reality, is
prodigious (1 Jn 3:1). A person who loves Jesus will be loved by the Father (Jn
14:21, 23). "The Father himself loves you, because you have loved me," said Jesus
(Jn 16:27).

God the Son loves God's people as his Father does, and the Father's love is
revealed in the way the Son loved them. "He loved them to the end" (Jn 13:1).
This brief topic sentence introduces the Johannine Last Supper and passion
account, wherein most of Jesus' declarations of love for his disciples are concentrated. It means that Jesus went on loving his disciples until the end of his

sojourn on earth, and that he did so to the uttermost degree. His washing of the disciples' feet, which follows, points forward to his humbling on the cross, by which he cleansed them of sin (Jn 13:4-11). Again and again he reassures the disciples of his love for them. "I have loved you; abide in my love" (Jn 15:9-10). The greatest love of all is to lay down one's life for one's friends—a reference to Jesus' own looming death (Jn 15:13). After he departs, they are to love one another as he has loved them (Jn 13.34, cf. 15:12). He will love the one who keeps his commandments (Jn 14:21). The author of the Gospel, in referring to himself as an anonymous disciple whom Jesus loved, probably does not mean to claim a special status for himself among the disciples, but instead is directing attention away from himself. The most significant thing about him is his being an object of Christ's love (Jn 13:23; 19:26; 20:2; 21:7, 20).[81] John's First Epistle and the Apocalypse pick up the theme of Jesus' love for his disciples (1 Jn 3:16-17; Apoc 1:5; 3:9, 19).

Naturally, those who are so loved learn thereby to love in return. The main requirement for being a Christian is to love Jesus. He described his disciples as those who loved him and believed that he came from the Father (Jn 16:27). Here loving precedes believing. Nominally religious people had no love for God, therefore they did not believe in Jesus (Jn 5:42; 8:42). No disciple loves perfectly at first. As late as the night before Jesus' crucifixion his disciples' love for him was still shot through with self-regard (Jn 14:28). To restore Peter after Peter had denied him three times, Jesus gave him the opportunity thrice to affirm his love for his Lord (Jn 21:15-17). This shows that love for Jesus, more even than orthodox confession or moral behavior, is the distinguishing mark of a Christian.

***The personal object of love for God.*** As was the case with believing and knowing, the object of religious love in John's thought is ultimately God even if Jesus is its proximate focal point. The Shema enjoins undivided love for the one God enlisting the whole of every human faculty without remainder: "You shall love the LORD your God with all your heart, and with all your soul, and with all your might" (Deut 6:5). In criticizing some of his contemporaries for having no love of God in themselves, the Johannine Jesus assumes that love toward God is the norm (Jn 5:42). Likewise it is a presupposition of John's First Epistle that love is to be directed to God (1 Jn 2:5, 15; 4:20–5:3).

How, then, does John reconcile devotion to Jesus with the exclusive love of

---

[81] After all, Lazarus too was one whom Jesus loved (Jn 11:3, 5, 36).

God demanded by his Bible and his background in Judaism? God the Father, John holds, loves his Son supremely, infinitely, eternally (Jn 3:35; 5:20; 10:17; 15:9, 10; 17:23, 24, 26). How can one claim to love God without loving him whom the Father loves above all? Far from being jealous of people's love for Jesus, God loves those who love Jesus, precisely because they do so. "He who loves me," says Jesus, "will be loved by my Father" (Jn 14:21). "If a man loves me . . . my Father will love him" (Jn 14:23). "The Father himself loves you, because you have loved me" (Jn 16:27). These statements about love are grounded in the Johannine Christology. As God's Only-Begotten, the Son is not an independent heavenly being but rather a distinct existent of God's identical being. To love him who is all that God is, him whom God loves as his unique alter ego, is by that very act to love the indivisible God with an unshared devotion.

God the Father, God the Son, and the body of disciples are the chief parties in this fellowship of love. In places the current of love flows down from one to another in an ordered chain. Jesus told his disciples, "As the Father has loved me, so I have loved you" (Jn 15:9); and he prayed to the Father "that the love with which you have loved me may be in them, and I in them" (Jn 17:26). In other places the characters form a triangle of mutual love. Anyone who loves Jesus and keeps his word the Father will love, "and we will come to him and make our home with him" (Jn 14:21, 23). The Father has loved them, even as he has loved the Son (Jn 17:23).[82]

***Loving God and keeping his commandments.*** A remarkable feature of the Johannine passages about loving God is the way many of them pass directly from loving to its outworking in obedience. "If you love me, you will keep my commandments," says Jesus, over and over again (Jn 14:15; cf. 14:21, 23-24; 1 Jn 2:5; 4:20–5:3). "We love God and keep his commandments. For this is the love of God, that we keep his commandments" (1 Jn 5:2-3). "This is love, that we follow his commandments" (2 Jn 6). "You have abandoned the love you had at first. . . . Repent and do the works you did at first" (Apoc 2:4-5). To "keep" (τηρεῖν) or "do" (ποιεῖν) God's commandments are phrases characteristic of the piety of the Old Testament and Judaism. The idea that love for God expresses itself in the performance of particular statutes given by him comes from the book of Deuteronomy (Deut 7:9; 10:12-13; 11:1, 13, 22; 13:3-4; 19:9; 30:16, 20) and

---

[82]Dirk G. van der Merwe, "The Character of Unity Expected among the Disciples of Jesus, According to John 17:20-23," *APB* 13 (2002): 224-54.

is contained by the Shema itself (Deut 6:4-9).

Love for God is incompatible with love for the world. Whoever loves the world will pass away along with it, but whoever does the will of God will remain forever (1 Jn 2:15-17). Love for God drives away dread of divine judgment, for it conforms the disciple in the world to Jesus (1 Jn 4:17-18).

John brings out the reciprocal nature of the divine-human love relationship that God initiates. He emphasizes that God showed his love by giving his Son, and disciples show theirs by doing his will.

**An "order of salvation" (ordo salutis)?** Thus far, we have considered believing in, knowing and loving God as the means by which, according to John, a person enters into the divinely given life and light that are available in Christ. Which of these actions is the starting point? Is one of them the radix of the others?

From word order the answer is by no means clear. Where two of our three verbs are found in strings of text, no pattern of priority emerges. Believing can precede knowing (Jn 6:69) or loving (1 Jn 3:23; 5:1). Learning and knowing can precede believing (Jn 6:45-47; 1 Jn 4:16). Loving can precede knowing (1 Jn 3:18-19; 4:7-8). It would appear that John was not a very linear thinker. He expressed himself flexibly and was more interested in how believing, knowing and loving work together than in which comes first, whether in logic or in time.

Nevertheless, we can get some clues to our question by surveying his literary output more broadly. While words for knowing and believing are distributed more or less evenly throughout the Gospel and Epistles, words for love are noticeably densest in John 13–21, where Jesus addresses his disciples, and in the First Epistle (especially the meditation on love in 1 Jn 4:7–5:3), which was written to Christian churches already established. Moreover, only in those portions are recipients of divine revelation the grammatical subject(s) who love, with God or Christ as the object(s)—except where Jesus denies that his opponents love God (Jn 5:42; 8:42). From where these data lie it seems reasonable to conclude that only people who know and believe in God can love him. This is underscored by statements that the world loves darkness and hates the light (Jn 3:19; 7:7; 15:18, 23-25; 1 Jn 2:15).

Whether knowing or believing precedes the other we can determine only by logical analysis. Above we saw that believing has a cognitive as well as a volitional component, and that knowing can involve a personal relationship. These two verbs cover the same semantic range but with a different accent. It is hard to imagine how people could commit themselves to trust someone about whom they have no knowledge. Seeing God for the love that he is must be the root of conscious trust, and trusting knowledge comes to perfection in reciprocal love. Of that process Christ is the agent and the locus, and the relationship thus formed is salvation.

A saving relationship with God through Jesus Christ commences, then, with believing based on knowledge. Since "we love, because he first loved us" (1 Jn 4:19), loving God cannot be a precondition for coming to him, for one must come to him first before loving in return becomes possible. Once a union is established by faith, however, God's love engenders love, and this in turn qualifies faith. Faith that saves is faith that comes to love God and other people. "Every one who believes that Jesus is the Christ is a child of God, and every one who loves the parent loves the child" (1 Jn 5:1). Otherwise, if faith does not learn to love, it is shown not to be saving faith. "He who does not love does not know God" (1 Jn 4:8). Knowing faith is the radix, but is conditioned by love as its consequent product.

To the question how the process unfolds during the journey from meeting Jesus until his coming, let us now turn.

# THE BELIEVER AND
# THE TRUE GOD

*Abiding in Christ*

COMING TO CHRIST INTRODUCES A PERSON to the Father, which is to have life eternal, already in the here and now. But eternal life also has a future aspect belonging to the world to come, which the believer will taste only on completing an earthly journey as Christ's disciple. This journey John describes as "walking." Along the path, God sees to it that the disciple fulfills all prerequisites for entrance into God's eschatological kingdom. Believing in, knowing and loving God remain fundamental. The further condition for gaining the fullness of eternal life is to abide in Christ and walk with him, following, imitating and obeying him.

Believing becomes obedience. A person who believes (ὁ πιστεύων) has already passed out of death into life (Jn 5:24), yet there remains a condition for immortality: if someone keeps his word (ἐάν τις τὸν ἐμὸν λόγον τηρήσῃ), that person will never die (Jn 8:51-52). To believe in an ongoing way takes the form of keeping his word. The Johannine opposite to believing is disobeying (ἀπειθεῖν [Jn 3:36]).[1]

---

[1] "'Faith' signifies submission to all that Jesus teaches and prescribes as his commandments" (Rudolf Schnackenburg, "Christian Morality According to John," in *A Companion to John: Readings in Johannine Theology [John's Gospel and Epistles]* [ed. Michael J. Taylor; New York: Alba House, 1970], p. 191). In this respect, John shares the view of other New Testament authors. According to Paul, what will prevail with God at the last judgment is faith working through love (Gal 5:6)—that is, faith expressed in works, which he describes in other places using the elegant phrase "work of faith" (1 Thess 1:3; 2 Thess 1:11). James likewise writes that saving faith is active along with works and is completed by works (Jas 2:22), and that this total complex brings final justification (Jas 2:24). For a fuller exploration of the soteriology of Paul and of James, see Paul A. Rainbow, *The Way of Salvation: The Role of Christian Obedience in Justification* (Milton Keynes: Paternoster, 2005).

Knowing and obeying also go together. For Jesus, knowing God entails keeping his word (Jn 8:55). Sheep hear the shepherd's voice and follow him (Jn 10:4). "If you know these things, happy are you if you do them" (Jn 13:17). Anyone who knows God will make good on the claim by keeping his commandments (1 Jn 2:3-4).

Loving is also fertile with obedience. "If you love me," says Jesus, "you will keep my commandments" (Jn 14:15 [cf. Jn 14:21, 23-24; 15:10, 14; 1 Jn 2:5; 5:2-3; 2 Jn 6]).

This chapter will highlight the nature of this walk, from one's first coming to know God until one beholds him.

## SALVATION: INAUGURATED AND TO BE CONSUMMATED

Several epigrammatic statements lay out the twofold structure of John's scheme of soteriology. Faith lays hold of salvation; continuation in Jesus' word completes it.

"If you continue [μένειν] in my word," said Jesus to a group of people who had "believed" (ἐπίστευσαν, aorist) in him (Jn 8:30), "you are truly [ἀληθῶς] my disciples" (Jn 8:31-32). Jesus distinguishes between entry into faith and genuine discipleship. Not ephemeral profession, but rather steadfast abiding in his word, is the condition ("If . . .") for authenticity. Jesus' word includes not only his claims about his unique relation to the Father (cf. Jn 7:28-30; 8:23-24) but also his commandments;[2] so perseverance involves both profession and conduct. A disciple acknowledges the truth about Jesus, a true disciple does what he says. Lacking these things, people show themselves to be children of the devil (Jn 8:44) and "not of God" (Jn 8:47).

A similar statement in John 15:8 to Jesus' inner circle makes the same point: "By this my Father is glorified, that you bear much fruit, and so prove to be [γένησθε, lit., 'become') my disciples." The disciples whom Jesus was addressing were "already made clean" by his word (Jn 15:3) and had stuck with him when others apostatized (Jn 6:66-71). Yet it remained for them to become his disciples indeed. This they would do by bearing fruit.

A warning passage in John's Second Epistle reinforces the point: "Look to yourselves, that you may not lose what we[3] have worked for, but may win a

---

[2]Compare the equivalent statements in John 14:23, "If a man loves me, he will keep my word," and John 14:15, "If you love me, you will keep my commandments."

[3]"We" includes the readers as well as the apostolic author. Manuscripts differ as to whether the text

full reward" (2 Jn 8). The Christian life is a course of labor. By ceasing to walk in truth and love (a walk commended in 2 Jn 4-6) through error (2 Jn 7-11), the readers could forfeit their reward. Loss of reward would amount to not having God (2 Jn 9). The reward in store is not something extra tacked onto salvation; it is the very relationship with God in which eternal life consists. At stake is nothing less than that.

A passage in the Apocalypse comprises the beginning and the end of sal vation (Apoc 21:6b-8). "To the thirsty I will give from the fountain of the water of life without payment. He who conquers shall have this heritage." God invites people to drink "without price" (cf. Apoc 22:17). Salvation is gratuitous. Yet the one who will inherit the blessings of the new creation is "he who conquers." Conquering involves keeping Christ's works to the end (cf. Apoc 2:26). Those who fail to conquer are the cowardly, the faithless, the polluted, murderers, fornicators, sorcerers, idolaters and all liars, whose lot will be in the lake that burns with fire and brimstone, the second death. Whether one pursues conduct befitting a disciple, or does not do so, is just as critical for individual destiny as is faith in Christ, for action is not separate from faith but rather is the very way that saving faith exists.

As a condition for reaching final salvation, obedience is secondary and subordinate because it depends on the main requirements of believing, knowing and loving God and flows from the new birth. Yet Christian obedience is a further condition, because where regeneration is present, obedience is bound to follow. For someone whose salvation is under way, this conditionality does not put the outcome in doubt; final salvation is not an eventuality that hangs in the balance for being conditional. As a living branch produces fruit, as a healthy newborn moves its limbs, so a person whose faith in Christ is vital delights in doing what pleases him. Fulfillment of the subcondition is a natural consequence of the basic condition. The fact that attainment of the eternal state

---

reads "you have worked" (εἰργάσασθε [א A Ψ *al.*]) or "we have worked" (εἰργασάμεθα [B *al.*]). Even though, as the editors of UBS⁴ argue, the latter reading is to be preferred (the paucity of its manuscript support being overridden by the consideration that the more difficult first-person form is more likely to be due to the author than to copyists), the second-person form probably expresses an implication of the original text (see Bruce M. Metzger, *A Textual Commentary on the Greek New Testament* [2nd ed.; Stuttgart: Deutsche Bibelgesellschaft; United Bible Societies, 1994], pp. 652-53). David Smith suggested that the first-person form includes the readers: "we [apostles, your fellowworkers]" (*The Expositor's Greek Testament* [ed. W. Robertson Nicoll; 5 vols.; London: Hodder & Stoughton, 1897–1910]), 5:202). Logically a wage/reward is due to workers. If the readers are encouraged not to lose their reward, they can hardly be excluded from having worked.

depends upon meeting this further condition merely reflects the biblical ontology. Truth lies not in what people say but in what they do (Jn 3:21; 1 Jn 1:6).
It is a fact with which the disciple of Christ must reckon.

*Law and grace.* In having outstanding stipulations that the people of God
must meet in order to apprehend God's eschatological blessings, the new covenant has the same structure as the covenant that God made with Israel of old.

John uses the word "covenant" (διαθήκη) but once (Apoc 11:19), yet the
concept of the divine-human covenant is a presupposition of his theology and
informs his writings at many points.[4] That John symbolizes the consummation of God's kingdom (Apoc 11:15-18) as the unveiling of the ark of God's
covenant (Apoc 11:19) shows that John sees the new order of Christ as con-
tinuous with the commonwealth of Israel.

According to the Pentateuch, God redeemed Israel from Egypt because he
loved them in spite of their want of merits in his eyes (Deut 4:37; 7:7-8). They
had nothing to do but to stand still, watch God work for them, and believe in
him (Ex 14:13-14, 31). He showed himself to be their savior and took them to be
his people before he gave them the law (Ex 19:4). These retrospective facts form
the preface to the Ten Commandments: "I am the LORD your God, who
brought you out of the land of Egypt, out of the house of bondage" (Ex 20:2).
The basic condition for Israel to be God's people, therefore, was God's own
undertaking on their behalf without their input, except to receive his saving
benefits by faith.

Yet God configured the covenant in such a way that each generation's enjoyment of its blessings—land, progeny, prosperity, God's presence and favor—
would depend on their walking in his statutes and ordinances. If they kept his
covenant, being holy as God is holy, they would be his royal priests among the
nations, and his promised blessings would remain theirs (Ex 19:5; Lev 26:3-13;
Deut 28:1-14; 30:15-16; Josh 23:1-14). If they disobeyed, covenant curses would
come upon them (Lev 26:14-39; Deut 28:15-68; 30:17-18; Josh 23:15-16). Faith in
God manifests itself in obedience to his will. Even though God bound himself
unilaterally to bless Abraham and his descendants, an individual Israelite's
share was contingent, not only upon the basic requirement of faith, but also

[4]Argued convincingly by John W. Pryor, *John, Evangelist of the Covenant People: The Narrative and Themes of the Fourth Gospel* (Downers Grove, IL: InterVarsity Press, 1992); H. A. A. Kennedy, "The Covenant-Conception in the First Epistle of John," *ExpTim* 28 (1916): 23-26; Edward Malatesta, *Interiority and Covenant: A Study of εἶναι ἐν and μένειν ἐν in the First Letter of Saint John* (AnBib 69; Rome: Biblical Institute Press, 1978).

upon obedience, which became the subcondition for continued blessing. So had it been in God's original promise to Abraham (Gen 12:1; 17:1-2, 9-14; 18:19; 22:15-18; 26:1-5). So was it again when God gave a charter to the house of David (2 Sam 7:14; Ps 89:30-32; 132:12).

As the rest of Israel's saga shows, from the book of Judges to 2 Kings, the nation proved unfaithful and broke the covenant. Israel lost its unity, its monarchy, and found itself in captivity in Babylon. Major writing prophets began to look forward to a new covenant to be established in the last days. God would undertake for Israel again, at last to provide a thoroughgoing purification from the guilt of sin, together with inner motivation to perform God's will (Is 59:20-21; Jer 31:31-34; Ezek 36:24-31).[5] But even under the new covenant, God's blessing would be linked to repentance, faith, and obedience: "if then their uncircumcised heart is humbled and they make amends for their iniquity" (Lev 26:41 [cf. 26:43]); "if you obey the voice of the LORD your God . . . if you turn to the LORD your God with all your heart and with all your soul" (Deut 30:10); "to those in Jacob who turn from transgression" (Is 59:20); "then you will remember your evil ways, and your deeds that were not good; and you will loathe yourselves for your iniquities and your abominable deeds" (Ezek 36:31).

What distinguishes the new covenant from the old is not a repeal of stipulations, but rather God's commitment to renovate his subjects so that they will fulfill them. "The LORD your God will circumcise your heart" (Deut 30:6). "My spirit which is upon you, and my words which I have put in your mouth, shall not depart" (Is 59:21). "I will put my law within them, and I will write it upon their hearts" (Jer 31:33). "A new heart I will give you, and a new spirit I will put within you . . . and cause you to walk in my statutes and be careful to observe my ordinances" (Ezek 36:26-27).[6]

---

[5]These passages are anticipated in the Pentateuch at Leviticus 26:40-45; Deuteronomy 30:1-10.

[6]It is an oversimplification to think of God's covenant with Israel at Mount Sinai as conditional, and of his covenants with Abraham and David and the new covenant as unconditional. Biblical critics and dispensationalists are both guilty on this count, for different reasons. When faced with conditional elements of so-called unconditional or promissory covenants, rationalist critics have explained the superimposition by positing multiple literary sources behind the various passages. Dispensationalists create similar categories and distinctions but within their theological system. But in fact, "all covenants, all contracts, have their conditions" (Dennis J. McCarthy, *Old Testament Covenant: A Survey of Current Opinions* [Richmond: John Knox, 1972], p. 3). In this respect, "there are no differences in the formulations of the covenant formula, whether these relate to the patriarchs, to the deliverance from Egypt, to the encounter with God at Sinai/Horeb, or to a 'new' covenant still impending" (Rolf Rendtorff, *The Covenant Formula: An Exegetical and Theological Investigation* [trans. Margaret Kohl; Edinburgh: T & T Clark, 1998], p. 83). See further Bruce K. Waltke, "The Phenom-

In the light of Old Testament covenantal history, the full meaning of John 1:17 shines out: "For the law was given through Moses; grace and truth came through Jesus Christ." John describes the new order as the time when grace and truth have arrived. We should be careful not to force John into a Pauline mold. This verse does not set up an antithesis between law and grace in the manner of Paul.[7] By no means is John denying that grace and truth were revealed in Torah. The grace that has come with Christ replaces a grace that was in existence before ("grace instead of grace" [Jn 1:16]). But neither does the verse teach continuity without a difference. It asserts a qualitative advance in the way God shows grace in the messianic era, with the advent of eschatological reality ("truth").[8] What Isaiah, Jeremiah and Ezekiel intimated in their prophecies of a new covenant is now being realized. The Lamb of God has taken away the sin of the world and has sent the Spirit-Paraclete from the Father.

Two statements in John's Gospel about human "work" outline its relation to divine grace. Asked by fellow Jews what they must do to meet their religious obligation, Jesus answered, "This is the work of God, that you believe in him whom he has sent" (Jn 6:29). Here the covenantal duty of human beings to God, previously defined by the commandments of Torah, is distilled into one basic requirement: to believe in Christ. From faith in Christ flow forgiveness, spiritual birth and all the virtues. Apart from union with Christ, there is only guilt and bondage to sin, and all attempts to please the God of the covenant will fail

---

enon of Conditionality within Unconditional Covenants," in *Israel's Apostasy and Restoration: Essays in Honor of Roland K. Harrison* (ed. Avraham Gileadi; Grand Rapids: Baker Books, 1988), pp. 123-39; Ronald W. Pierce, "Covenant Conditionality and a Future for Israel," *JETS* 37 (1994): 27-38; Scott Hahn, "Covenant in the Old and New Testaments: Some Current Research (1994–2004)," *CurBR* 3 (2005): 263-92.

[7]Paul's negative view of the law is a corollary of his associating it with the history of an unbelieving nation still in solidarity with Adam. On Paul's meaning, see Rainbow, *Way of Salvation*, pp. 70-96.

[8]If John is to be compared with Paul, John 1:17 finds its nearest parallel in 2 Corinthians 3:9-11, which contrasts the spendor of the old covenant with the surpassing splendor of the new. The remaining difference lies in this, that Paul views the old covenant from the vantage point of the mass of Israelites who broke it, as "the dispensation of death" and "of condemnation" (2 Cor 3:7, 9). John views the old covenant from the standpoint of the faithful remnant in Israel, who found in it the grace of God that led to life (e.g., Ps 119:92-93). This difference in perspective becomes especially clear if we compare Romans 8:7-8, "The mind that is set on the flesh is hostile to God; it does not submit to God's law, indeed it cannot; and those who are in the flesh cannot please God," with 1 John 5:3, "His commandments are not burdensome" (cf. Deut 30:11-14). This disparity may be attributed to different psychodevelopmental paths. Once Paul became an apostle of Christ, he, looking back, saw his former zeal for Torah, which moved him to persecute the church, as having been rooted in a fundamental unbelief toward God that had undermined even his accomplishments in Judaism (1 Tim 1:13). John, as far as we know, had a faith in the God of Israel that progressed in step with God's self-revelation in Christ, without a wrenching change of attitude vis-à-vis God.

(Jn 8:24, 34). So faith in Christ is the basic requirement for salvation.

An earlier paragraph of the Gospel envisages the final judgment (Jn 3:16-21). There too, to be sure, "whoever believes" will not perish (Jn 3:16), "he who believes" is not condemned (Jn 3:18). But these phrases pass directly over into "he who does [ὁ ποιῶν] what is true" (Jn 3:21). Such a person "comes to the light, that it may be clearly seen that his deeds [τὰ ἔργα] have been wrought in God" (Jn 3:21). In contrast to John 6:29, with its focus on believing, the accent here falls on doing. The believer who does what is true is the one who will stand in the day of judgment. This one's deeds will count as worthy because they will have been "worked in God" (ἐν θεῷ ἐστιν εἰργασμένα [Jn 3:21]).

Under the new covenant, God does not place the burden of performing his stipulations on his human partner unaided. A redeemed human being is no independent subject capable of acting without God's moving. God performs God's works in and through the human agent. God provided in Christ for the removal of sins without human aid; in Christ God enlists human participation as he brings it about that the agent should accomplish his will. So the new covenant breathes grace from start to finish.

***Rewards in store for the faithful.*** What is in store for believers who persevere in Christ's word that they do not possess in this present age? Above all, there are promises of God's immediate presence. Jesus will gather his disciples to be with him where he is, in the glory of his Father (Jn 14:3; 17:24). God will shelter them, banish pain and tears from them, and refresh them with living water (Apoc 7:15-17; 21:3-4). They will see his face (Apoc 22:4).

To bring this life-giving relationship to the full, the Son of Man will raise them from the dead on the last day (Jn 5:29; 6:39, 40, 44, 54; Apoc 11:11-12). Unlike Paul's, John's writings offer no details about the nature of the glorified body. Paul's reflections on that subject in 1 Corinthians 15 are spare enough. John says bluntly, "It does not yet appear what we shall be" (1 Jn 3:2).[9] But resurrection will mean life in the presence of God together with his people (Apoc 21:3, 7, 22) in the environment of a new creation (Apoc 21–22), cleared of the curse (Apoc 22:3).

The Apocalypse taps into a number of biblical images pointing to aspects of the life to come. Reversing the divine ban of Eden (Gen 3:22-24), the ransomed

---

[9]That believers will have a new identity whose nature is undisclosed during the present life is also the point of the enigmatic saying about their receiving a white stone with a new name written on it (Apoc 2:17).

will be allowed to partake of the tree of life in paradise (Apoc 2:7; 22:2, 14, 19). Christ will hand them the crown of life, and the second death will not touch them (Apoc 2:10-11). Manna that is now hidden will sustain them, and the gift of a white stone will bestow on them a new name (Apoc 2:17). They will share in Christ's power to rule the nations with a rod of iron, and he will give them the morning star (Apoc 2:26-28). They will wear white garments; their names will be in the book of life; Christ will confess their names before his Father and the angels (Apoc 3:5). A victory wreath awaits them (Apoc 3:11). Each will become a pillar in God's everlasting temple, inscribed with the name of God and of his Son (Apoc 3:12). They will sit with Christ on his throne (Apoc 3:21).

None of these amenities is available at present to those who have eternal life. How, then, are they to be gained? They are the "reward" (μισθός) for labor (Jn 4:36; 2 Jn 8) and for serving God with proper fear (Apoc 11:18). The blessings of Apocalypse 2–3 are promised by the living Lord, who knows people's works (Apoc 2:2, 19; 3:1, 8, 15), "to him who conquers" (Apoc 2:7, 11, 17, 26; 3:5, 12, 21).

*The last judgment.* Between the present age and that which is to come stands a judgment based on deeds. That there will be a last assize is an expectation of Old Testament and Jewish apocalypticism[10] that figures prominently in all sectors of John's literary output (esp. Jn 3:16-21; 5:22-29; 12:47-48; 1 Jn 2:28–3:3; 4:17; Apoc 11:18; 20:11-15), as it does in the teaching of Jesus[11] and in Paul's preaching (Acts 17:31; 24:15) and letters.[12] According to the Johannine passages, which present a prospect no different from the others, on the last day the living and the dead of all times and places without exception will come forth to stand before God for a review of the way they lived.[13] The upshot of this event will

---

[10]Kent L. Yinger, *Paul, Judaism, and Judgment According to Deeds* (SNTSMS 105; Cambridge: Cambridge University Press, 1999).

[11]E.g., in Matthew alone, Mt 7:21-27; 11:21-24; 12:33-37; 13:40-43, 47-50; 18:23-35; 20:1-16; 25:14-30, 31-46. See Blaine Charette, *The Theme of Recompense in Matthew's Gospel* (JSNTSup 79; Sheffield: Sheffield Academic Press, 1992); David C. Sim, *Apocalyptic Eschatology in the Gospel of Matthew* (SNTSMS 88; Cambridge: Cambridge University Press, 1996).

[12]E.g., Rom 2:5-11; 8:31-34; 14:10-18; 1 Cor 3:12–4:5; 2 Cor 5:10; Gal 5:4-6; 6:7-9; 2 Thess 1:6-12. See Geerhardus Vos, *The Pauline Eschatology* (Princeton, NJ: Princeton University Press, 1930), pp. 261-87.

[13]One theory of eschatology muddies the doctrine of the general resurrection and judgment by proposing, against the tenor of all the New Testament passages that have to do with this subject, that there will be more than one resurrection involving more than one human group. Chiliasm, or premillennialism, finds in the unique vision of Apocalypse 20:4-6 a prediction of a future period of a thousand years between Christ's second coming and the end of the age, during which Christ will reign on earth. Supposedly, a "first" bodily resurrection of some people will precede, and a second resurrection of others will follow, this regnum. But although premillennialists champion a literal

be a judgment that God will pronounce upon the total life of each individual. His verdict will result in a division of the race between two ultimate and opposite destinies: either salvation or condemnation (Jn 3:17; 12:47), eternal life or everlasting wrath (Jn 3:36), life or judgment (Jn 5:29), shame or the vision of God (1 Jn 2:28; 3:2), rewards or personal destruction (Apoc 11:18), the new heaven and new earth or the lake of fire (Apoc 20:14-15; 21:1-8). A correct understanding of the pivotal significance of the judgment is critical for Johannine (and New Testament) soteriology.[14]

---

approach to the interpretation of this notoriously obscure passage, they ignore those crystalline verses in John's Gospel that place both the resurrection of the saints and the judgment firmly "on the last day" (resurrection: Jn 6:39, 40, 44, 54; judgment: Jn 12:48), excluding the possibility of a subsequent millennium. If the rejoinder is to argue for an extension of "the last day" to comprise the millennium, this is to insist on a forced and unnatural sense for a simple phrase in plain prose, to maintain a literalistic reading of an apocalyptic vision in violation of its genre. A very different reading of Apocalypse 20:4-6 takes its language just as soberly and does not conflict with the amillennial eschatology of the Gospel. Given the fact that the first and "second" death (Apoc 20:6, 14) refer to two phases of death according to the scheme of two ages—temporal death in the "first" world and eternal death in the new creation (Apoc 21:1, 8)—then the same will hold true of the two resurrections. As the second death is "second" from the point of view of the damned, whose sentence in the final order will make their penalty of death for sin permanent and irreversible, so the "first resurrection" is first from the point of view of those who experience it, namely, believers, whose second resurrection is thereby guaranteed. During the time of the present age all human beings suffer the first death, which means, for God's saints, in an arresting but deeply true turn of phrase, "resurrection"—life with God (Jn 11:25-26)—from which unbelievers are excluded; at the commencement of the age to come all human beings will participate in the resurrection, which will mean, for unbelievers, in truth "death"—banishment from God's presence—from which the saved are exempt. This reading of the passage about the millennium makes its graphic vision of martyrs' souls coming to life immediately relevant for John's first readers, some of whom were facing persecution and possible martyrdom (Apoc 1:9; 2:10, 13). It also accords with the amillennial eschatology of the bulk of the Apocalypse (e.g., Apoc 11:15-18; or Apoc 19:6-8 compared with Apoc 21:2, 9) as well as of the rest of the New Testament (e.g., Mt 13:40-43; 25:31-46; 2 Thess 1:6-10). On the problems of interpreting the millennium, see Paul A. Rainbow, *The Path of the Apocalypse: Essential Message and Principles for Interpretation* (Eugene, OR: Wipf & Stock, 2008), pp. 99-110.

[14]A tenacious streak in Protestant exegesis since the Reformation holds that for believers, the last judgment will have a limited purpose. God will award prizes for service, believers' personal salvation having been settled and secured at their first coming to faith in Christ. This is another oversimplification. Paul, to be sure, can distinguish between the person who will be saved and rewards for work, which the person will either gain or lose on the day of testing by fire (1 Cor 3:11-15); or, again, between the flesh of a Christian who flaunts a particular sin, which flesh is destroyed now, and his spirit, which will be saved (1 Cor 5:5). But shall we rip these verses from the fabric of Paul's thought and make them controls that neutralize the great principles of judgment that he states elsewhere in his epistles? For Paul, as for the other New Testament authors, God "will render to every man according to his works" (Rom 2:6), and certain behaviors, if pursued without repentance, will exclude their doer from the kingdom of God (1 Cor 6:9-10; Eph 5:5). Insofar as deeds are the index of character and disposition, they serve as a criterion of judgment against which there is no plea. Paul's hope of salvation for those who build with "wood, hay, straw" (1 Cor 3:12), as well as for the man who was living in incest with his stepmother (1 Cor 5:1), must have been based on a realization that such admixtures of carnality (1 Cor 3:3) can stand out as anomalies in lives whose tendency is to

Even though there is a very real sense in which people's responses to Christ place them already in the proleptic categories of the justified or the condemned in anticipation of God's final verdict (Jn 3:18, 36; 5:24), the last assize remains the moment when God's assessment will be definitive. For present time allows for flux, when professors of faith can cease to believe (Jn 6:66; 8:31, 48), and unbelievers have opportunity to repent (Jn 8:24), changing from one category to the other (Apoc 22:10-17; cf. Ezek 18:21-32).[15] The last judgment will bring this period of probation to an end and bring out each person's fundamental attitude toward God as demonstrated by deeds, on which God will pass sentence. At the present time, the sole human being who can look back on the judgment as a fait accompli is he who has passed through resurrection into glory, Jesus Christ. As Paul argues more clearly than John does from the analogy of Adam and the universality of death, those who are in Christ, the other corporate head of the race, have a share even now in Christ's own state of justification (Rom 4:25; 5:18; 1 Tim 3:16). John puts it in terms of being members of God's family now (1 Jn 3:1). But in the end each believer must also undergo a scrutiny to find the correlation between what Christ did on behalf of, and what the Spirit has been doing in, that individual.

It is the consistent teaching of all major contributors to the New Testament, who took it from the Old Testament and Judaism, that the last assize will proceed on the basis of people's works (Jesus: Mt 16:27; 25:31-46; Paul: Rom 14:10-12; 1 Cor 3:10-15; 4:2-5; 2 Cor 5:10; Gal 5:6). John concurs. According to the Jesus of the Gospel, the judgment will bring to light whether a person's deeds were "evil" or "true" (Jn 3:19-21). Those destined for a resurrection to life are those who will have "done good" (οἱ τὰ ἀγαθὰ ποιήσαντες); those slated for judgment are those who will have "done evil" (οἱ τὰ φαῦλα πράξαντες) (Jn 5:29). Already before the age ends, in the oracles to the seven churches of Asia, the

---

produce fruits testifying to vitality in Christ. The more checkered are the empirical data of a person's life, the more will it depend on the infinite wisdom of God to discern the thoughts and intents of the heart—and the less certain now is that person's standing in Christ with a view to final salvation. But as a rule, fruit indicates the tree (Mt 7:16-20) and points to the destiny, whether justification or condemnation, death or eternal life (Mt 12:33-37; Rom 6:21-22). If Paul, the apostle of grace and faith, calls upon believers to work out their (unfinished) salvation with fear and trembling (Phil 2:12) and can say that the judgment will result in either glory, honor, immortality and peace for those who "do good" or else in wrath, fury, tribulation and distress for those who "do evil" (Rom 2:7-10), and if, moreover, "the doers of the law will be justified" (Rom 2:13), does it not contradict him to deny that salvation itself is sealed at the last judgment?

[15]This statement applies to the empirical realm. From the eternal perspective of the electing God, "The Lord knows those who are his" (1 Tim 2:19).

living Christ evaluates each church by its actual "works" and presses charges accordingly, to bring them to repentance in time (Apoc 2:2, 5, 6, 19, 23, 26; 3:1, 2, 8, 15).[16] In the great judgment scenes of the Apocalypse the principle is unequivocal: God will reward (δοῦναι τὸν μισθόν) those who fear his name and will destroy those who destroy the earth (Apoc 11:18). Lady Babylon will receive double "according to her deeds" (Apoc 18:6). "The dead were judged by what was written in the books, according to their works [κατὰ τὰ ἔργα αὐτῶν]" (Apoc 20:12-13). Says the glorified Lord to his church, "I will give to each of you as your works deserve" (Apoc 2:23); "I am coming soon, bringing my recompense [μισθόν], to repay every one as his work is [ὡς τὸ ἔργον ἐστὶν αὐτοῦ]" (Apoc 22:12).

So between regeneration and the bliss of the new creation lies the judgment, and leading up to the judgment is the path of Christian authenticity. Let us look at the Johannine concepts that define it.

## THE PATH OF LIFE

Jesus describes the Christian life as a walk through the world, illumined by the light of his presence. "He who follows me will not walk in darkness, but will have the light of life" (Jn 8:12 [see also Jn 11:9, 10; 12:35]).[17] A number of important Johannine terms fill out the picture of this journey, including "abiding in" and "following" Jesus, "working," "keeping" God's "commandments" and "conquering" the world.

**Abiding.** To abide in Christ is the basic mode of Christian existence and discipleship.[18] Jesus is the true vine, every believer a branch in him (Jn 15:1-11). "To abide" (μένειν) means both to dwell in Christ, drawing life and sustenance from him,[19] and to stay, continue and persevere in him to the end.[20] The vine metaphor (Jn 15) follows the promise of the Spirit (Jn 14) and pictures the new reality in Christ; abiding in Christ is a function of the Spirit-Paraclete, who

---

[16]On the seven oracles as covenant lawsuit speeches, see Alan S. Bandy, "Patterns of Prophetic Lawsuits in the Oracles to the Seven Churches," *Neot* 45 (2011): 178-205.

[17]This dominical metaphor has influenced 1 John 1:6-7; 2:6, 11; 2 John 4, 6; 3 John 3-4; Apocalypse 16:15.

[18]C. H. Talbert, "The Fourth Gospel's Soteriology between New Birth and Resurrection," *PRSt* 37 (2010): 133-45.

[19]The same verb indicates spending a day at the house where Jesus was living, where he made his home, in John 1:38-39.

[20]The sense of continuance or permanence comes through in texts such as John 1:32-33; 8:35; 12:34. See Christopher D. Bass, "A Johannine Perspective of the Human Responsibility to Persevere in the Faith through the Use of MENΩ and Other Related Motifs," *WTJ* 69 (2007): 305-25.

indwells the church and makes it share in the life of its invisible Lord. Like the sap that courses through a vine, the Spirit energizes Jesus' disciples, making them fruitful. Fruit in this context (Jn 15:2, 4, 5, 8, 16) is both ethical in nature and missional. It consists of love for one another in the circle of disciples (Jn 15:12-17) and of bearing witness to the world (Jn 15:18-27). These are not two kinds of fruit, but one: it is by loving one another that Jesus' disciples bear their most cogent witness to others (Jn 13:35; 17:23). Abiding also brings about fellowship with Christ in his suffering, his being rejected by a hostile world (Jn 15:18–16:4), and leads to effective mission (Jn 15:27–16:15), peace (Jn 14:27; 16:33) and joy (Jn 15:11; 16:16-33).

Abiding in Christ cannot be reduced to mystical experience, if by mystical we mean an intuitive consciousness of union with Christ cut loose from correct doctrine or discipline. The passage about abiding in the vine speaks of concrete instruments for doing so: Christ's words and commandments brought to remembrance (Jn 14:26; 15:7, 10) and the disciple's prayers (Jn 15:7, 16). Words in both directions mediate the abiding relationship. This shows that abiding has to do with personal communion.

The "grace" of which John 1:17 speaks is latent in the passage about the vine and the branches. To be in the vine, branches must first undergo a thorough cleansing by Christ's word (Jn 15:3). Afterwards, the Father as vinedresser cleanses them again and again that they may be increasingly fruitful (Jn 15:2). Their vitality comes from him, not from their own resources. They cannot bear fruit unless they abide in the vine (Jn 15:4). "Apart from me," says Christ, "you can do nothing" (Jn 15:5). But as his words abide in the branches, and their words appeal to the Father in prayer, they bear much fruit, their discipleship is confirmed, and the Father is glorified (Jn 15:7-8).

*Following Jesus.* Where John employs the motif of following (ἀκολουθεῖν) Jesus (in a figurative, spiritual sense: Jn 1:43; 8:12; 10:4, 5, 27; 12:25-26; 21:19, 22; Apoc 14:4), he has in view specifically Jesus' way to the cross, with an emphasis on the disciple's renunciation of the present world in order to gain that which is to come. Jesus' invitation to Philip, "Follow me" (Jn 1:43), is a paradigmatic call to discipleship, with the promise of eternal life implicitly attached (Jn 8:12; 10:27-28). As Jesus had to die before entering into glory, so the disciple must let go of life (ψυχή) in this world in order to keep it for life eternal (Jn 12:25). A servant who follows the master to the point of death has the promise of honor from the Father (Jn 12:26). For Peter, following Jesus meant loving Jesus, feeding Jesus' sheep as the good shepherd had done (Jn 21:15-17), and, in the end, suffering the martyrdom of crucifixion under Nero (Jn 21:18-19). In the Apocalypse, following the Lamb wherever he goes (Apoc 14:4) means resisting the beast and not receiving its mark—the vignette in Apocalypse 14:1-5 gives a contrasting image to Apocalypse 13:16-18. Following also involves preserving virginity by abstaining from "women" (Apoc 14:4a), a reference to the symbol of the harlot who represents the Roman social and commercial system (Apoc 18).

A related body of passages calls upon Christ's disciples to imitate Christ.[21] As he abased himself to wash their feet, they must wash one another's feet (Jn 13:12-16). As he loved them, they must love one another (Jn 15:12). By keeping the Son's commandments, they will abide in his love, even as the Son kept his Father's commandments and abides in his Father's love (Jn 15:10). As a result, the world will persecute them as it persecuted him (Jn 15:20-21). In the First Epistle points of imitation include walking in the light (1 Jn 1:7; cf. 2:6), laying down one's life for one's brothers and sisters (1 Jn 3:16), and loving one another (1 Jn 4:11). These passages are summed up in an admonition to imitate (μιμεῖσθαι) not the evil but the good (3 Jn 11) and in a crisp summary of the christological pattern: "as he is so are we in this world" (1 Jn 4:17).

*Walking in the light.* For sinners who are accustomed to walk in darkness and cannot find the path, Jesus' promise of light on the way is both a gift and a demand (Jn 8:12; 12:35). Those who walk in the light, in the center of God's will, enjoy divine protection even in the midst of earthly perils, as Jesus made clear to his disciples when they hesitated to follow him back into Judea, where the authorities had just sought to stone him (Jn 11:9-10). People who walk in the daylight while they have it are on the way to becoming (γενηθῆναι) "sons of light," taking on its nature as their characteristic (Jn 12:36).

In the Johannine Epistles the expression "walk in the light" (1 Jn 1:7) refers to performing the moral will of God, as can be seen from its equivalents, "do the truth" (1 Jn 1:6),[22] "be in the light" (1 Jn 2:9), "abide in the light" (1 Jn 2:10),

---

[21] Dirk G. van der Merwe, "*Imitatio Christi* in the Fourth Gospel," *VerbEccl* 22 (2001): 131-48.

[22] On the moral connotation of "truth" in John, which he took over from a background in Jewish apocalyptic and wisdom texts, see Ignace de la Potterie, "The Truth in Saint John," in *The Interpretation of John* (ed. John Ashton; IRT 9; Philadelphia: Fortress, 1986), pp. 54-56. Moral truth is not only a theoretical body of standards to which behavior must conform; it is also (and all the more) a quality of concrete acts. The union of truth and act, or the actuality of moral truth, is built into John's very language. He speaks of "doing the truth" (Jn 3:21; 1 Jn 1:8), of loving "in deed and truth" (1 Jn 3:18), of "walking in truth" (2 Jn 4; 3 Jn 3-4), of being "fellow workers with the truth" (3 Jn 8). In Christ's act of self-sacrifice for others the commandment to love became "true" in the sense that he

"walk in the truth" (2 Jn 4; 3 Jn 3, 4), have "truth" of being (3 Jn 3) and "walk according his commandments," which are comprised in the command to love (2 Jn 5-6). The opposites are "walk in darkness" (1 Jn 1:6; 2:11), "sin" (1 Jn 1:7) and "hate one's brother" (1 Jn 2:11).

Significantly, daily cleansing from sin is contingent upon walking in the light (1 Jn 1:7), as it is upon confessing sins (1 Jn 1:9). Confession must be backed up with repentance.[23] That the author does not have an idealistic doctrine of Christian perfection is evident from the fact that he knows that his little children will need cleansing and points to God's provision for it. But anyone whose tenor of life is not to walk in the light, who has no intention of repenting of a sin and making a change of ways, should not dwell in the self-deception of being cleansed by God of that sin, or any other, even if it be confessed. The grammar of 1 John 1:7 bears peculiar testimony to John's scheme of soteriology. John does not write that if the blood of Jesus has cleansed a person, that person will walk in the light, true though that may be; rather, he writes that if a person walks in the light, the blood of Jesus will cleanse that person. Only in union with Christ and by virtue of the bath that his cross provides (Jn 13:10) can a sinner, hitherto plunged in darkness, begin to walk in the light. On the other hand, only for one who pursues the journey in the light is the blood of Christ efficacious to cleanse.[24]

Again the model of Christian behavior is Christ: "He who says he abides in him is obligated [ὀφείλει] to walk in the same way in which he walked" (1 Jn 2:6).

In the Apocalypse the metaphor of walking reappears with new and fresh meanings. At a time when demonic deception is mobilizing the kings of the world against God's people, John reminds them to keep their garments lest they walk naked and suffer shame (Apoc 16:15). Walking with Christ in white garments (Apoc 3:4) and walking in the light of the new Jerusalem (Apoc 21:24) are rewards for those who do not soil their garments.

---

carried it out (1 Jn 2:8). In the Third Epistle those who testify to Gaius's "truth" are testifying of what he has done in providing hospitality for traveling missionaries (3 Jn 3). Another aspect of the relation between truth and act is the fact that the truth makes people free (Jn 8:32). Truth thus both illumines the mind and quickens the will.

[23]Unlike the Synoptic Gospels, in which Jesus conjoins repentance and faith in his invitation to enter the kingdom of God (e.g., Mk 1:15), John's Gospel speaks only of believing in Jesus. "Repent" is found in the Johannine writings only in the Apocalypse, where the summons to repent is addressed to people who are already believers but are not fully faithful (Apoc 2:5, 16, 22; 3:3, 19). Unbelievers have the same opportunity to repent but do not avail themselves of it (Apoc 2:21; 9:20, 21; 16:9, 11).

[24]John's teaching on this point is comparable to the dominical teaching, according to Matthew, about being forgiven and offering forgiveness (Mt 6:14-15; 18:23-35).

***Working, doing.*** Works done by human beings may be either "good" (καλά
[Jn 10:32-33]) or "evil" (πονηρά [Jn 3:19-20; 7:7; 1 Jn 3:12; 2 Jn 11; cf. 3 Jn 9-10]).
The former stem ultimately from God (Jn 3:21; 9:4) through the power of Christ
(Jn 14:12). As in Judaism, Abraham is the exemplar of good works (Jn 8:39-
40).²⁵ Works belonging to the latter category spring from the devil (Jn 8:41; 1
Jn 3:8) and include works of the Nicolaitans (Apoc 2:6) and of Jezebel (Apoc
2:22), idols made by people's hands (Apoc 9:20) and deeds of the citizens of the
beast's kingdom (Apoc 16:11).

Because John sets the labor of God's people within the framework of
grace, as something done by God's power in and through a believing agent
(whose "deeds [ἔργα] have been wrought [εἰργασμένα] in God" [Jn 3:21]),
John's view of Christian "works" and "working" is positive. On this point
John stands in contrast to a view of Paul that has become widespread, whose
name is often associated—at least in Protestant exegesis since the sixteenth
century—with an antithesis found in certain Pauline texts between "works
of the law," which cannot lead to salvation, and divine grace correlated with
human faith, which does.²⁶

When John has Jesus surprise his nomistic Jewish hearers by telling them
that the singular "work" that God requires of them is to believe on the one God
sent (Jn 6:27-29)—in the sole Johannine passage in which we find an emphasis
on simple faith in contrast to an expectation that God demands works—we
should note that the audience consists of people who do not believe in Jesus (cf.
Jn 6:60-61, 66-67). In answer to their question "What must we do, to be doing
the work of God?" Jesus urges that apart from the life that he makes possible
by the Spirit (Jn 6:63), there is nothing at all they can do to please God. They
must start by coming to him.

Everywhere else in his writings John enjoins upon believers that they
perform good works. To the disciples Jesus says, "We must [δεῖ ἡμᾶς] work the
works of him who sent me while it is day" (Jn 9:4). They will duplicate his own
works on a greater scale (Jn 14:12). Church members are to love not in word or
speech but rather in deed (ἐν ἔργῳ) and truth (1 Jn 3:18). A Christian community exposed to heretical teaching is to watch out lest they lose the reward
for which they have worked (2 Jn 8). Whatever Gaius works for the community

²⁵On Abraham in Second Temple Judaism, see Joachim Jeremias, "Ἀβραάμ,"*TDNT* 1:8.
²⁶In truth, Paul too speaks positively of works when he is thinking of the good works of believers.
  See passages and discussion in Rainbow, *Way of Salvation*, pp. 79-96.

is faithful (3 Jn 5). So Christians ought to be fellow workers (συνεργοί) with the truth (3 Jn 8). In commending the churches of the Apocalypse, Christ recognizes their works and labor (Apoc 2:2, 19; 3:8). He looks for growth in works over time (Apoc 2:19) and rebukes churches whose works have lost the warmth of their first love (Apoc 2:4-5) or are seriously defective (Apoc 2:22; 3:1-2, 15). Christ threatens them with removal of their lampstands from their places among the churches (Apoc 2:5) and with judgments of the sort that will come upon the world (Apoc 2:16, 22-23; 3:3). The one who keeps Christ's works to the end will receive authority to reign with him (Apoc 2:26). As for those who die in the Lord, their labor has ended, and their works follow them (Apoc 14:13).

Synonymous with working are the verbs "do" (ποιεῖν) and "practice" (πράσσειν), when their content is moral.[27] A person may do good (τὰ ἀγαθά [Jn 5:29]), the truth (τὴν ἀλήθειαν [Jn 3:21; 1 Jn 1:6]), the works of God (Jn 6:28), the will of God (Jn 7:17; 9:31; 1 Jn 2:17), what pleases God (Jn 8:29; 1 Jn 3:22), righteousness (1 Jn 2:29; 3:7, 10; Apoc 22:11; cf. 19:8), the works of Abraham (Jn 8:39), the law (Jn 7:19), God's commandments (1 Jn 5:2), just as Jesus did to his disciples (Jn 13:15), the works Jesus did (Jn 14:10), what Jesus commands (Jn 15:14), a faithful thing (3 Jn 5) or well (καλῶς [3 Jn 6]). Such doing is possible only in the order of grace and truth in Christ. Concerning these deeds Jesus says, "Apart from me you can do nothing" (Jn 15:5).

Alternatively, one may do evil (κακόν [Jn 18:30; cf. 3 Jn 10-11]; φαῦλα [Jn 3:20; 5:29]), what is false (Apoc 22:15), deeds or desires of the devil (Jn 8:38, 40, 41, 44), sin (ἁμαρτίαν [Jn 8:34; 1 Jn 3:4, 8, 9]), lawlessness (ἀνομίαν [1 Jn 3:4]), or abomination (Apoc 21:27). Closely related exhortations are to imitate good rather than evil (μιμεῖσθαι τὸ ἀγαθόν/κακόν [3 Jn 11]), to do good rather than evil (ἀγαθοποιεῖν/κακοποιεῖν [3 Jn 11]), to demonstrate faithfulness (πίστις [Apoc 2:19; 13:10]), to serve (διακονεῖν [Jn 12:26; cf. Apoc 2:19]), to hate evil (Apoc 2:6) and to come out of Babylon (Apoc 18:4).

At the end of a stint of earthly labor a worker gets a wage. John's vocabulary rounds off the metaphor applied to the religious life. There will be a complete tally of a person's work, of all that one has done, at the last judgment, and then God will repay (ἀποδίδωμι [Apoc 18:6; 22:12]), and each laborer will receive in recompense (ἀπολαμβάνω [2 Jn 8]) the deserved wage (μισθός [Jn 4:36; 2 Jn 8; Apoc 11:18; 22:12]). Obviously, this language is figurative and is not meant to

---

[27]Noël Lazure, *Les valeurs morales de la théologie johannique* (EBib; Paris: Gabalda, 1965), pp. 65-118.

suggest that creatures could ever place God in their debt, or that the wage will be limited to what is strictly commensurate with the value of the work.

Evaluation of deeds by God is ongoing in the present. Jesus was able to tell the Samaritan woman everything that she had done (Jn 4:29, 39). The Christ of the Apocalypse identifies what to commend and what to reprove in the life of each of the seven churches even now, before it is too late for them to repent (Apoc 2–3).[28]

*Keeping God's commandments.* Abiding in Jesus, following him, walking in the light and laboring to do God's will become concrete in the phrases "keep [God's/Christ's] commandment(s)" (τηρεῖν . . . ἐντολήν/ἐντολάς)[29] and "keep [his] word(s)" (τηρεῖν . . . λόγον/λόγους) (Jn 8:51, 52, 55; 14:23, 24; 15:20; 17:6; 1 Jn 2:5; Apoc 3:3 [implied], 8, 10; 22:7, 9).[30] John makes commandment-keeping a key element of abiding: "All who keep his commandments abide in him, and he in them" (1 Jn 3:24). Phrases of this type are especially concentrated in the Johannine corpus, occurring there with greater frequency than in the rest of the New Testament books put together.[31] The vocabulary is characteristic of Judaism of the same period, being sprinkled from the Septuagint to Josephus, and is endemic in rabbinic Hebrew.[32] John, immersed in Torah, continued all

---

[28]David Graves, *The Seven Messages of Revelation and Vassal Treaties: Literary Genre, Structure, and Function* (GD 41; Piscataway, NJ: Gorgias, 2009).

[29]As usual in the Johannine literature, we find this concept denoted by a set of related but always varied expressions. God or Christ can "give" (δίδωμι) a command (Jn 12:49; 13:34; 1 Jn 3:23), and people "receive" (λαμβάνω) it (Jn 10:18; 2 Jn 4). Synonymous with the former is the simple verb "command" (ἐντέλλεσθαι [Jn 15:14, 17]). Synonymous with the latter is the phrase "have [a commandment] from him" (1 Jn 4:21). For the collocation "to keep" the commandments, John prefers the verb τηρεῖν (Jn 14:15, 21; 15:10; 1 Jn 2:3, 4; 3:22, 24; 5:3; Apoc 12:17; 14:12), though in one place he uses the typically Septuagintal φυλάσσειν (Jn 12:47 [with ῥήματα as object]), in another "do, perform [commandments]" (ποιεῖν [1 Jn 5:2]), and in yet another "walk according to [commandments]" (2 Jn 6).

[30]A particular commandment is to "keep the sabbath" (Jn 9:16). One is blessed for keeping the things written in the Apocalypse (Apoc 1:3) and will receive a prize for keeping Christ's works to the end (Apoc 2:26). On the use of τηρεῖν in the Apocalypse, see Marcello Marino, *Custodire la Parola: Il verbo* τηρεῖν *nell'Apocalisse alla luce della tradizione giovannea* (SRB 40; Bologna: Dehoniane, 2003).

[31]In the New Testament we find the phrases "keep" (τηρεῖν) the law or the commandment(s) or the tradition (Mt 19:17; 23:3; 28:20; Mk 7:9; Acts 15:5; 1 Tim 6:14; Jas 2:10; cf. 1 Cor 7:19), "do" (ποιεῖν) them (Mt 5:19; 23:3), "walk" (πορεύεσθαι) in them (Lk 1:6), "transgress" (παραβαίνειν) them (Mt 15:3), "set" them "aside" (ἀθετεῖν) (Mk 7:9), "go past" (παρελθεῖν) them (Lk 15:29). Also there are a few instances of "keeping" (φυλάσσειν) in this sense (Mt 19:20 // Mk 10:20 // Lk 18:21; Lk 11:28; Acts 7:53; 16:4; 21:24; Rom 2:26; Gal 6:13; 1 Tim 5:21).

[32]In the Septuagint φυλάσσειν is the usual word choice for שָׁמַר ("keep") with reference to the law in hundreds of places. This translation naturally influenced Jewish literature depending on the Septuagint. In LXX Proverbs τηρεῖν renders נָצַר six times and שָׁמַר five times, the object usually being the words or ways of the instructor. The verb τηρεῖν occurs with a legal object in 1 Samuel (LXX 1

his life to find this phraseology apt to denote people's duty to God, alongside other words. Jesus says, "We must [ἡμᾶς δεῖ] work the works of him who sent me" (Jn 9:4), and "You should [ὀφείλετε] do as I have done to you" (Jn 13:15 [cf. 1 Jn 3:16]). The elder of the Epistles adds, "He who claims to abide in him is bound [ὀφείλει] to walk in the same way in which he walked" (1 Jn 2:6), and "We ought [ὀφείλομεν] to love one another" (1 Jn 4:11) and "ought to support such men" (3 Jn 8). For John, Christians have no option to disobey. Divine requirements remain a feature of the new covenant, as of the old.

"[God's] commandment is eternal life," said Jesus (Jn 12:50). The position of this statement at the close of the first half of John's Gospel gives it special prominence. Having the copula ("is") with "eternal life," it is like John 17:3: "This is eternal life, that they know you the only true God." Conflating the two verses, we see that to know God is to know what is his will, what he commands, and in the doing thereof consists eternal life. In the context of John 12:50a God's command refers, in the first instance, to what he enjoined upon Jesus to say and speak to the world (Jn 12:49, 50b). While Jesus' word includes his claim of unity with the Father (Jn 12:44-45), it also includes his sayings for people to "keep" (Jn 12:47). So God told Jesus what to command his disciples, that they might have life. This could be taken in either of two ways. It could mean, in keeping with a topos of the Old Testament and of Judaism, that God's commandment promises eternal life, that doing his will now is the way to insure life in the age to come;[33] or it could mean that God's commandments describe human life as God intends it to be, so that eternal life itself consists of performing them (perhaps the sense of Lev 18:5; Deut 32:46-47; Ps 119:93; Ezek 20:11; Sir 45:5; Jn 5:39). Between these alternatives we need not choose. John's diction may well comprise both.

Love for Jesus takes the form of keeping his commandments (Jn 14:15). What someone values and stands for shows who that person is. To love the person is to share that person's passions (and hatreds). One who is drawn to things that Jesus hates and is repelled by things that he loves can hardly claim to love Jesus. In his commandments Jesus has told his disciples what he values and what he abominates. By doing what Jesus commands, a disciple demonstrates esteem

---

Kingdoms) 15:11 (for הֲקִים); Tob 14:9; Sir 6:26; 29:1; T. Dan 5:1; Josephus, Ant. 8.120, 395; 9.222; Ag. Ap. 2.273. In rabbinic usage שָׁמַר and עָשָׂה ("do") alternate. See Georg Bertram, "φυλάσσω," TDNT 9:236-39; Harald Riesenfeld, "τηρέω," TDNT 8:140-44.

[33]Deut 30:15-20; Neh 9:29; Ezek 33:15; Sir 51:30; Pss. Sol. 9:5; 14:2-3; Mt 19:17; Lk 10:26-28; Rom 7:10; Gal 3:21; m. ʾAbot 2:7, 16; 4:10; 6:11.

for the Savior. There is no tension in John's thought between love and law.[34]

Conversely, "If you keep my commandments, you will abide in my love, just as I have kept my Father's commandments, and abide in his love" (Jn 15:10). Here it is a matter not of the disciple loving Jesus, but of Jesus loving the disciple. The condition for the disciple to abide in Jesus' love is to keep Jesus' commandments. This conditionality does not mean that the disciple must strive to retain Jesus' favor by conforming to his will for fear that Jesus would withdraw his love, any more than Jesus has to hold on to the Father's love by obeying him. In that case, Jesus would have said, "If you keep my commandments, my love will abide in you." Rather, "you will abide in my love" means that Jesus has expressed love for his disciples by laying down guidelines for their welfare, and it is by heeding his ways that they will relish the life and wellness that he lovingly intends for them.

Far from setting faith and keeping of the commandments in mutual opposition, John fully integrates them. Twice he defines saints as those who "keep the commandments of God" and either "bear testimony to Jesus" (Apoc 12:17) or "keep the faith of Jesus" (Apoc 14:12). On its face, this designation starts from a typically Jewish commitment to walk according to the divine law and adds to it fidelity to Jesus. Bearing testimony to the unique lordship of Jesus required great courage toward the end of the first century in an Asian environment that pressured people to confess Caesar as lord and god. A macarism in Apocalypse 14:13 contrasts the rest and refreshment in store for Christians who pay the ultimate price with the unceasing torment experienced by those who capitulate to the beast (cf. Apoc 14:10-11).

In a related passage in John's First Epistle (1 Jn 3:23-24) God's singular "commandment" (ἐντολή) is "that we should believe in the name of his Son and," the writer adds, "love one another, just as he has commanded us." Immediately this adjoined command to love passes over into keeping God's plural "commandments" (ἐντολάς). So while human duty under the new covenant may be summed up in the elegant phrase "to believe in Jesus," believing implies loving people, which requires specific duties known to writer and readers alike, presumably from the Hebrew Scriptures.

***Summaries of the commandments.*** Already among the leading teachers of

---

[34]G. Charles A. Fernando, *The Relationship between Law and Love in the Gospel of John: A Detailed Scientific Research on the Concepts of Law and Love in the Fourth Gospel and Their Relationship to Each Other* (EH 23/772; Frankfurt: Peter Lang, 2004).

Judaism before and around the time of John there were efforts to distill the many precepts of the Torah down into short lists that could be easily memorized.[35] The most widespread solution was to take the Ten Commandments as a digest of the law.[36] It has often been observed that the Johannine writings, although they speak of "commandments" in the plural, have a dearth of specific injunctions.[37] But that statement reflects the judgment, pervasive in New Testament criticism, that the Apocalypse at least, and possibily the Epistles, were written by authors other than the one who wrote the Gospel. In fact, most of the Ten Commandments are echoed or presupposed in the corpus as a whole. The supreme duty is to worship the one God (προσκυνεῖν [Jn 4:23-24; 9:38; Apoc 5:13; 7:9-10; 11:1; 14:7; 15:2-4; 19:10; 22:9]; λατρεύειν [Apoc 7:15; 22:3]).[38] Christians are to keep themselves from idolatry (1 Jn 5:21; Apoc 2:14, 20). It goes without saying that blasphemy is wrong (Jn 10:33, 36; Apoc 13:1; 17:3). Jesus on the cross gave an example of filial piety (Jn 19:25-27). Murder is opposed to the Johannine value of life (1 Jn 3:15). Strongly censured are fornication (Apoc 2:14, 20, 21; 9:21; 14:8; 17:1, 2, 4, 5, 15, 16; 18:3, 9; 19:2) and luxury (Apoc 18:3, 7, 9). It counts against Judas that he used to steal from the common purse of Jesus and

---

[35]In a famous homily recorded in the Talmud (b. Mak. 23b-24a) Rabbi Simlai (early third century A.D.) compressed the commandments into eleven principles from David (Ps 15), six from Isaiah (Is 33:15-16), three from Micah (Mic 6:8), two from Isaiah (Is 56:1) and one from Habakkuk (Hab 2:4).

[36]In the biblical narrative the giving of the Decalogue at the head of the Mosaic legislation (Ex 20), inscribed on two tables of stone (Ex 24:12), makes the Ten Commandments foundational. From time immemorial, recitation of the Ten Commandments accompanied sacrifices in the temple, as Psalm 50 (esp. Ps 50:16-20) seems to attest and as becomes explicit in m. Tamid 5:1. In the Nash Papyrus (Egypt, between 165 and 37 B.C.), the Decalogue and the Shema stand together on a single sheet that may have been used for catechesis or liturgy, indicating the credal character of the material. Jesus and Paul instinctively quoted from the Decalogue (Mt 19:17-19; Rom 13:9). Josephus boasts that Jews on being questioned about their laws are able to repeat them more readily than their own names (Ag. Ap. 2.178). Philo frequently states that the Ten Commandments are general principles containing all the more detailed rules (Her. 167, 173; Cong. 120; Dec. 19-20, 154; Spec. 2.189). The rabbis agreed, saying that between each commandment and the next were written "all of Torah's letters" (y. Šeqal. 6:1, 49d; Num. Rab. 13:15-16). "The rabbis regard the [Decalogue] as the quintessence of the Law and hold that all 613 precepts were somehow contained or alluded to therein" (R. J. Zwi Werblowsky and Geoffrey Wigoder, eds., The Encyclopedia of the Jewish Religion [New York: Adama, 1986], p. 111).

[37]Georg Strecker goes further and denies outright that the plural "commandments" in the Johannine writings refers to the Old Testament at all. Instead, he asserts, they are "emanations of the one ἐντολή" (The Johannine Letters: A Commentary on 1, 2, and 3 John [ed. Harold W. Attridge; trans. Linda M. Maloney; Hermeneia; Minneapolis: Fortress, 1996], p. 48). No doubt they are particular aspects of the love-command, but what these particulars would be, in the mind of a Jewish-Christian author like John, if not Old Testament precepts, he does not venture to explain.

[38]The several worship scenes of the Apocalypse express a poignant monotheism over against the cult of the Roman imperial family that was sweeping through Asia in the 90s.

his disciples (Jn 12:6). There is to be no speaking of falsehood (1 Jn 1:6; 2:21; Apoc 14:5). The vice lists of the Apocalypse incorporate the prohibitions of the second, sixth, seventh and eighth commandments several times over (Apoc 9:20-21; 21:8, 27; 22:15).

If these points are distributed sparsely in the Gospel and more densely in the Apocalypse, that is due to different aims. The Gospel presents Jesus as the Christ of God and has no reason to go into practicalities of godly living except in general terms.[39] The schismatics against whom the Epistles seek to reassure John's catholic community questioned the validity of ethics in principle, not piecemeal. Only in the Apocalypse did John have to take up a prophetic stance against serious encroachments of Asian culture into the very life of the churches. There he concentrated on the points of pressure.

Another way to categorize the precepts, common among Jewish experts, was to divide them into two broad groups: those concerned with duty to God, and those with duty to fellow human beings. This outlook drove speculations to the effect that the two tables of the law in the time of Moses each had five commandments, with the fifth, to honor parents, forming a bridge in that it required honor toward God and toward the social order (Philo, *Her.* 168, 172; *Dec.* 50, 106, 121; *Spec.* 2.242; 3.7; Josephus, *Ant.* 3.101, 138 [cf. 4.262]; *Mek. Exod.* to 20:13 [*Baḥodesh* 8:69-95]). When Jesus, challenged by a scribe to name the great commandment, pointed to two, quoting the Shema on love for God (Deut 6:4-6) and Leviticus 19:18 on love for neighbor, he was not innovating but ratified the deepest insights of the Jewish legal establishment (Mt 22:34-40; Mk 12:28-34).[40] John does not relate Jesus' dual love-command as such, but he remembered it, for it informs passages in the First Epistle without his citing it (1 Jn 2:3-5; 4:20–5:2).

*"Love one another."* What is distinctive in the Johannine literature is a unique formulation of Jesus' love rule in terms of a single demand that his disciples love one another as Jesus loved them. "A new commandment I give to you," says Jesus, "that you love one another" (Jn 13:34-35 [cf. Jn 15:12-17; 1 Jn 2:7-10; 3:11, 14,

---

[39]But the Fourth Gospel assumes the Ten Commandments. See Jey J. Kanagaraj, "The Implied Ethics of the Fourth Gospel: A Reinterpretation of the Decalogue," *TynBul* 52 (2001): 33-60.

[40]It had long been a custom for every Jewish male to recite the Shema twice daily. Rabbi Akiba (early second cent. A.D.) declared Leviticus 19:18 "the great *kelal* in Torah" (*Sipra Lev.* to 19:18 = 89b; *Gen. Rab.* 24:7). The latter verse of Scripture is identical in import to the Golden Rule (Mt 7:12 // Lk 6:31), which likewise had precedents in Judaism (Tob 4:15; *b. Šabb.* 31a [Rabbi Hillel]; Lk 10:27; Palestinian Targum on Lev 19:18).

23; 4:7-21).[41] This exhortation to fraternal charity falls in the part of the Gospel where Jesus is alone with his disciples. They are to love, not the darkness (Jn 3:19), nor their lives in this world (Jn 12:25), nor the praise of other people rather than the praise of God (Jn 12:43), but God (Jn 5:42), Jesus (Jn 8:42; 21:15-17; 16:27) and other members of the community around Jesus (Jn 15:12-17).

In the First Epistle the "old" commandment is the familiar injunction of the Old Testament to love one's neighbor, meaning one's fellow Israelite (1 Jn 2:7, alluding to Lev 19:18). What is "new" in the eschatological age is not the content of the requirement but the fact that Jesus carried it out to the ultimate extent by laying down his life for others, providing an inspirational model for his followers. In the time of grace and truth the command to love has come to be "true in him and in you" (1 Jn 2:8).[42] The fledgling realization of the ideal of love among Christians is the dawn that portends the end of the world's night with its hatreds (1 Jn 2:8-11). Jesus' followers are to show love not "in word or speech but in deed and truth" (1 Jn 3:18). Here John shares the ontology of the Hebrew Bible, wherein reality is constituted by thoughts carried out in action.

The greatest meditation on love in John's writings, and one of the greatest in the Bible, is found in the First Epistle (1 Jn 4:7–5:3). In this respect, at least, the Epistle gives evidence of reflective depth beyond what is found in the Gospel.[43] At the head of the passage is an exhortation to practice love in the Christian community in the spirit of Jesus' single love-command (1 Jn 4:7). What makes this possible is God's own nature as love: "God is love" (1 Jn 4:8, 16). God demonstrated his love, above all, by sending his Son to make propitiation for those who did not love him. The initiative was with God. He showed love toward the unlovely, evoking a response of love toward himself and showing them how to love one another. The dual love-command of Judaism, refracted through Jesus, informs the mandate "This commandment we have from him, that he who loves God should love his brother also" (1 Jn 4:21). Christians who thus love God and love one another are born of God, know God, abide in God, and make visible on earth the presence of the invisible God (1 Jn 4:12).

In the Apocalypse the love-command does not recur in the imperative, but it is assumed where the risen Christ castigates the church at Ephesus for having

---

[41]Lazure, *Valeurs morales*, pp. 207-51. "The exhortation to love of the brethren is the characteristic feature of Johannine moral teaching" (Schnackenburg, "Christian Morality," p. 199).

[42]Schnackenburg, "Christian Morality," pp. 199-201.

[43]Thomas Barrosse, "The Johannine Relationship of Love to Faith," in Taylor, *Companion to John*, pp. 153-54n2.

abandoned its "first love" (Apoc 2:4) and commends the church at Thyatira for its ongoing love (Apoc 2:19). Both contexts associate "love" with "works" (Apoc 2:5, 19). Otherwise the Apocalypse has parallels to two peculiar uses of the verb "love" in the Gospel: loving and practicing falsehood (Apoc 22:15) is like loving darkness (Jn 3:19), and not loving one's life even unto death (Apoc 12:11) recalls what Jesus said about hating one's life in this world (Jn 12:25).

Some readers of John are troubled by his apparent narrowing of Jesus' command of neighbor love to a concentration on fraternal love in the community of faith.[44] John's focus on the brotherhood can be taken as contrasting unfavorably to Jesus' unqualified teaching about loving enemies (Mt 6:43-48). In John's stress on love among Christians some have even found evidence that the so-called Johannine community was a sectarian enclave at odds with its social environment and perhaps in tension with other branches of the first-century church.[45]

But this is to distort John's intent by taking one small part of his teaching out of the tissue of his thought. The very first occurrence of "love" in the Fourth Gospel falls in the statement that God "loved the world" (Jn 3:16). Jesus repeatedly invites his disciples to imitate him, as he imitates the Father. So they too must love the world. Moreover, one important purpose for loving one another is to attract from the world any who are persuadable (Jn 13:35; cf. 17:23). This is hardly the language of a closed sect. In sharp contrast to the Qumran covenanters, whose community rule required that they love the sons of light and hate the sons of darkness (e.g., 1QS I, 9-10; IX, 21-22), nowhere does John call on Christians to hate others. God, Jesus and the community around John do love the world and continue to hold out to it an evangelistic invitation to repent and join the fellowship.[46]

But as any lover knows, love is amplified when it resonates with a corresponding love; it cannot come to full measure where it is not received and re-

---

[44]Herbert Preisker, *Die urchristliche Botschaft von der Liebe Gottes im Lichte der vergleichenden Religionsgeschichte* (AWRBR 5; Giessen: Töpelmann, 1930), pp. 47, 58-59; Clayton R. Bowen, "Love in the Fourth Gospel," *JR* 13 (1933): 39-49; Ernst Käsemann, *The Testament of Jesus: A Study of the Gospel of John in the Light of Chapter 17* (trans. Gerhard Krodel; Philadelphia: Fortress, 1968), pp. 59-61.

[45]See, for example, Judith Lieu, *The Theology of the Johannine Epistles* (NTT; Cambridge: University Press, 1991), pp. 68-70. Lieu cites a selection of earlier publications from a large bibliography.

[46]"The *agapē* commandment, although it has its original location in the ecclesiology of the Johannine circle, contains a positive and universalist tendency, and thus points beyond the boundaries of the ἐκκλησία" (Strecker, *Johannine Letters*, p. 231).

turned. Insofar as the world at large rejects God's self-revelation in Christ, it deselects itself from the white-hot core of the divine love. Within God's being and among his people love comes into its own, and John is not waiting for recalcitrant unbelievers.[47]

That the divine-human love relationship is conditional upon obedience from the human side is illustrated by John's teaching about prayer. "If you abide in me, and my words abide in you, ask whatever you will, and it shall be done for you" (Jn 15:7). "We receive from him whatever we ask, because we keep his commandments and do what pleases him" (1 Jn 3:22). God hears and answers the prayers of those who are disposed to obey him as their covenant Lord (Ps 66:17-20; 91:14-16) but refuses the prayers of those who cherish wickedness (Job 27:8-10; 35:12-13; Prov 1:28; 28:9; Is 1:15-17; Mic 3:4; Jas 4:3). Therefore the intercession of a faithful believer for an offending brother or sister has strategic efficacy (1 Jn 5:16-17).

**Perfection.** God's children will be manifest when God raises and glorifies them on the last day. Looking ahead to this end, throughout their lives in this world they purify themselves as he is pure (1 Jn 3:1-3).[48] The outcome will be final conformity to Christ in all physical, moral and spiritual respects. "We shall be like him [ὅμοιοι αὐτῷ]" (1 Jn 3:2).

Even as John, with a mind that always goes to the nub, fastens on love as the motive behind Christ's mission and as the heart of Christian ethics, so he views Christian perfection as maturity in love. Love comes up in all five uses of the τελειο- word group in the First Epistle. To keep Christ's word is to love God perfectly (1 Jn 2:5). Since Christ's word was that his disciples should love one another, their showing of love brings to completion their love of God, which only flourishes in his love for them (1 Jn 4:12). Such perfect love casts out fear of the coming judgment (1 Jn 4:17-18).

**Conquering.** Conquering (vanquishing, overcoming) evil is one of John's most distinctive themes.[49] Of the twenty-eight New Testament occurrences of the verb νικάω, twenty-four are in the Johannine corpus.[50] John's First Epistle has the sole instance of the noun νίκη ("victory" [1 Jn 5:4]). Outside the New

---

[47]W. K. Grossouw, "Christian Spirituality in John," in Taylor, *Companion to John,* pp. 222-23.

[48]Lazure, *Valeurs morales,* pp. 253-83.

[49]Jens-Wilhelm Taeger, "'Gesiegt! O himmlische Musik des Wortes!' Zur Entfaltung des Siegesmotivs in den johanneischen Schriften," *ZNW* 85 (1994): 23-46.

[50]Gospel, 1× (Jn 16:33); Epistles, 6× (1 Jn 2:13, 14; 4:4; 5:4 [2×], 5); Apocalypse, 17× (Apoc 2:7, 11, 17, 26; 3:5, 12, 21 [2×]; 5:5; 6:2 [2×]; 11:7; 12:11; 13:7; 15:2; 17:14; 21:7).

Testament, these words are found in the military, legal and athletic domains.

For John, the victory of Christians over temptation and sin is rooted in Christ's conquest of the forces of evil at the cross. On the eve of his crucifixion Jesus told his disciples that he had "overcome" the world; the Greek perfect tense (νενίκηκα) points to prophetic certainty (Jn 16:33). Looking back from glory, the risen Christ announces that he has conquered (Apoc 3:21). Christians participate in Christ's great victory by imitation. "He who conquers" corresponds to "as I myself conquered" (Apoc 3:21). "They have conquered [the dragon] by the blood of the Lamb" (Apoc 12:11).

Victory comes in stages. Conversion involves siding with the victorious Christ and becoming an alien to the world. John in his First Epistle puts this choice in either the perfect tense (νενικήκατε [1 Jn 2:13-14; 4:4]) or an aorist participle (1 Jn 5:4). Essentially it involves entrusting the self to Christ: "This is the victory that overcomes the world, our faith" (1 Jn 5:4); and receiving the Spirit-Paraclete as an indwelling power: "greater is he who is in you than he who is in the world" (1 Jn 4:4). John emphasizes this initial phase of victory where his pastoral concern is to reassure the churches of their state of salvation over against the rival claims of secessionists who have unsettled them.

Thereafter begins the long challenge (and good cheer) of repeated confrontations with the enemy. Conquering becomes thematic in the Apocalypse. The Lion of the tribe of Judah has already conquered (Apoc 5:5) and will finally conquer the powers of the world (Apoc 17:14). In the meantime, even though the imperial beast will conquer the saints on earth, making martyrs of them (Apoc 6:2; 11:7; 13:7), they are the true victors (Apoc 12:11; 15:2). They conquer not with worldly weapons but "by the blood of the Lamb and by the word of their testimony" (Apoc 12:11). They confess the crucified Christ to be Lord over against Caesar, even under pressure to recant. A key verse sets "he who conquers" (ὁ νικῶν) and "he who keeps my works until the end" in apposition; conquering involves persistence in doing righteousness (Apoc 2:26). Those who resist the attractions of Rome in Asia and keep themselves to the voice of their Lord are the overcomers who will eat of the tree of life (Apoc 2:7), never be harmed by the second death (Apoc 2:11), receive the hidden manna (Apoc 2:17), rule the nations with Christ (Apoc 2:26-27), be clothed in white garments (Apoc 3:5), be pillars in the temple (Apoc 3:12), and sit with Christ on his Father's throne (Apoc 3:21).

**Joy.** Joy suffuses the Christian who thus walks with Christ and overcomes.

After a hard day's work in the field, employer and wage earners rejoice together (Jn 4:36). Fruitful branches fill up the joy of Christ and have joy themselves (Jn 15:11). As the pangs of childbirth give way to euphoria, so the sorrows of discipleship in this world are more than compensated for by the rapture that disciples will have when they see their Lord, which no one can take away from them (Jn 16:20-23). Jesus invited his disciples to pray, so that in receiving their requests their joy may be full (Jn 16:24). Jesus himself went to God so that they might have his joy fulfilled in themselves (Jn 14:28; 17:13).

The elder wrote the Johannine Epistles to increase his apostolic joy and that of his hearers (1 Jn 1:4; 2 Jn 12). He rejoices whenever he hears reports that the members of his churches are walking in truth and love (2 Jn 4, 12; 3 Jn 3-4).

When the Almighty establishes his reign, the seer of the Apocalypse hears voices erupt like the thunder of many waters: "Let us rejoice and exult and give him glory" (Apoc 19:7).

## HAZARDS TO THE LIFE OF THE BELIEVER

As long as believers live and walk in the world, surrounded by "the lust of the flesh and the lust of the eyes and the pride of life" (1 Jn 2:16), they can commit sins and incur guilt. Guilt for sin poses a threat to eternal life. The new covenant, like the old, makes provision for atonement through the blood of Christ. He is the propitiation for those who walk in the light and confess.

John offers a more rounded pastoral theology than does Paul. The latter is content to teach that in Christ a person has a new orientation and bent toward righteousness. Paul hardly considers, at least in his extant epistles, the challenge of entrenched and uneradicated patterns of behavior from the Adamic past, in spite of the catalogue of actual problems with which he had to deal.[51] Sin, for Paul, is a feature of the fallen creation; it stands opposed to the new reality in Christ and must give way before it.[52] John agrees that regeneration instils a tendency to the good. Indeed, he puts it in the most forceful of terms. "No one

---

[51]In, say, his Corinthian correspondence. I assume that Romans 7:7-25 describes life under the law outside of Christ, being an elaboration of Romans 7:5, even as Romans 8:1-17 expands Romans 7:6 and describes life in the Spirit. Pivotal occurrences of νῦν and νυνί ("now") in Romans 7:6 and Romans 8:1 make this clear. Romans 7:24 is the cry of frustration of a man who is not merely in a tussle with sin (as in Gal 5:17), but rather faces the utter sabotage of his best efforts, inevitable defeat. In view of Romans 6:14; 7:6, 25a; 8:3-4, this cry cannot come from a Christian.

[52]This point was made with some exaggeration in a monograph on Paul's doctrine of the Christian and sin: Paul Wernle, *Der Christ und die Sünde bei Paulus* (Leipzig: Mohr Siebeck, 1897). For a critique, see Vos, *Pauline Eschatology*, p. 56.

who abides in [Christ] sins. . . . No one born of God commits sin; for God's seed [σπέρμα] abides in him, and he cannot sin [οὐ δύναται ἁμαρτάνειν], because he is born of God" (1 Jn 3:6, 9). "Any one born of God does not sin, but He who was born of God keeps him, and the evil one does not touch him" (1 Jn 5:18). Yet there are passages, especially in his Epistles, in which John grapples with the anomaly of sin in the Christian life.

John acknowledges frankly that believers can sin. In the Gospel he includes Peter's denials of the Lord (Jn 13:37-38; 18:15-17, 25-27) followed by Peter's reinstatement (Jn 21:15-17). Peter seems to be a representative figure, for Jesus' prediction that all his disciples will scatter at his arrest (Jn 16:32) finds fulfillment only in the narrative about Peter. In the First Epistle John not only assumes that believers sin, but also says that they deceive themselves and align themselves with falsehood if they deny it (1 Jn 1:8, 10). The labored tone of these statements suggests that John may have been countering the claims of heretics who considered themselves beyond sinning, even though their conduct did not match Jesus' example and teaching (cf. 1 Jn 1:5-6; 2:3-6).

Sin is no natural or necessary phenomenon of Christian life. Quite to the contrary, when John says, "I am writing this to you so that you may not sin [ἵνα μὴ ἁμάρτητε, categorical aorist]" (1 Jn 2:1), he holds that Christians have all the spiritual resources they need to avoid it. Yet the if-clause that follows, "If any one does sin . . .," is no remote, theoretical possibility, but surely takes into account what every believer has to own, as experience teaches. In terms of the famous breakdown of Latin theology, the Christian is neither, like Adam before the fall, in a state of innocence though "able to sin" (the *posse peccare*), nor, like the race after the fall, vitiated and "unable not to sin" (the *non posse non peccare*), but rather is in a process of restoration and "able not to sin" (the *posse non peccare*) while not yet in the blessed state of being "unable to sin" (the *non posse peccare*).[53]

How to reconcile the realism of 1 John 1:8, 10 with the disavowals that one born of God can sin in 1 John 3:6, 9 is a puzzle. 1 John 3 can hardly mean to deny what the author so markedly stresses only a few dozen words earlier in 1 John 1:7–2:2, the need for an honest self-inventory of offenses. John's Semitic literary style can allow a saying in one place to qualify another elsewhere, without uniting them in a compound sentence. Context also provides a key.

---

[53] Augustine (*Corrept.* 33) gave impetus to this terminology.

The paragraph in 1 John 3:4-10 expands on the third verse: hope stimulates progressive purification. Here John inveighs against inertia, even as 1 John 1 strikes out against a perfectionism blind to its faults. In 1 John 3 he uses present tenses to denote elegantly what are in reality dynamic tendencies toward eschatological outcomes. No one who abides in Christ, who has God's seed abiding within, can sink ever deeper into sin as the characteristic of one's existence, but rather, freed from its bondage, must grow toward that righteousness which expresses one's true being—though there be inexcusable slips along the way.[54]

With John, it is certainly not the case that because the sins of believers have been forgiven (ἀφέωνται, perfect tense [1 Jn 2:12]), disobedience to the Lord is a matter of no concern. If and when sin happens, it is deadly, whether committed by an unbeliever or by a person of faith. Because the wicked ignore the Son, the wrath of God abides on them (Jn 3:36). Believers too, if they sin, need propitiation, and they depend on Christ's advocacy (1 Jn 2:1-2). A believer who sees a fellow believer committing sin is to pray for that person's very life (1 Jn 5:16). "All wrongdoing [ἀδικία, lit., 'unrighteousness'] is sin," John writes (1 Jn 5:17), and, he might have added, all sin is worthy of death and tends to death apart from divine intervention. That fact, plain in Scripture (e.g., Gen 2:17; cf. Rom 6:16; 8:13), lies behind John's exhortation for the community of believers to plead for errant members.[55]

If wayward professors of Christianity fail to repent, the risen Lord warns that they too will be caught in the judgment that is coming upon the world. To have their lampstand removed from its place signifies loss of status among the people of God (Apoc 2:5). For Christ to war against such with the sword of his mouth is to meet them as foe and not savior (Apoc 2:16; cf. 19:21). It is to the unsaved world, including unrepentant members of the church, that Christ will come as a thief (Apoc 3:3; cf. 1 Thess 5:2-4), to deal out death (Apoc 2:21-23) and blot out their names from the book of life (Apoc 3:5). Therefore his summons to those he loves and chastens is "Be zealous and repent" (Apoc 3:19).

To be sure, the historic atonement that Jesus made suffices for sins past,

---

[54]John Bogart, *Orthodox and Heretical Perfectionism in the Johannine Community as Evident in the First Epistle of John* (SBLDS 33; Missoula, MT: Scholars Press, 1977). Colin Kruse suggests that when believers sin (1 Jn 1:6–2:10), they do not commit ἀνομία ("rebellion"), the sin of the devil ("Sin and Perfection in 1 John," *ABR* 51 [2003]: 60-70). However, ἀνομία simply means violating God's Torah, and it is hard to deny the applicability of that concept to the sins of believers.

[55]Strecker, *Johannine Letters*, pp. 206-8.

present and future. Jesus can plead the perennial value of his sacrifice before his Father for whomever needs it and whenever it is needed. But it is not automatically efficacious in isolation from people's response, as though Christians could wallow in sinful practices without forsaking and confessing them and still presume God to have forgiven them once and for all. For recovery from the mortal peril of sins after conversion, God has appointed repentance and confession, sustained by the intercession of fellow believers and of Christ. To confess is to acknowledge the vile nature of the sin as God sees it, with abhorrence and disgust. Repentance means actual turning from sin to God to act in a new and different way.

A person who, like Peter at the Last Supper, has already bathed does not require a full bath every time his or her feet get soiled, but only a footwash (Jn 13:8-10).[56] Being cleansed has two aspects: a comprehensive plunge that is not repeated (indicated by the perfect tense ὁ λελουμένος), and the washing of a part, such as the feet, that suffers defilement subsequently (νίψασθαι) (Jn 13:10). Both sorts of washing flow from Jesus' death, as his nod toward the narrative sequel shows (Jn 13:7). The former cleansing can hardly signify anything other than baptism;[57] the latter, the daily forgiveness for which Jesus taught his disciples to pray (Mt 6:12; Lk 11:4).[58] Both are critical for salvation, comprised in Jesus' saying, "If I do not wash you, you have no part in me" (Jn 13:8).

Those who walk in the light, repenting of sins of which they are aware, enjoy ongoing, plenary cleansing of all sins (1 Jn 1:7). God is faithful to forgive the offenses of those who confess (1 Jn 1:9), for the sake of his Son, who ever re-

---

[56]The textual evidence for John 13:10 is muddled and has occasioned much discussion among commentators. But the words εἰ μὴ τοὺς τόδας ("except for his feet") are a constant feature of almost all the variants in the best manuscripts (attested, in effect, by P⁶⁶.⁷⁵ A B C D *f*¹ *f*¹³, to select only the outstanding witnesses). This longer reading is far better supported than the shorter one that omits the bit about the feet (ℵ, some Latin MSS, a few patristic quotations) and should form the basis for exegesis. See John Christopher Thomas, "A Note on the Text of John 13:10," *NovT* 29 (1987): 46-52; idem, *Footwashing in John 13 and the Johannine Community* (JSNTSup 61; Sheffield: Sheffield Academic Press, 1991), pp. 19-25.

[57]Peter and the other eleven disciples had been baptized in water by John the Baptist (Acts 1:21-22; suggested in the Fourth Gospel by the association of Andrew and Peter with the Baptist in Jn 1:40). Jesus took over this rite (Jn 3:5, 22; 4:1). There is no evidence that his disciples were ever baptized again, not even after the rite assumed the full significance of the Christian sacrament following Jesus' death, resurrection and pouring out of the Holy Spirit. Jesus' sayings that they "are clean" (Jn 13:10) and "are already made clean by the word which I have spoken to you" (Jn 15:3) presuppose the forgiveness of their sins in John's baptism (Mk 1:4), confirmed by Jesus' person and teaching during the course of his ministry.

[58]Thomas, *Footwashing*, pp. 155-72.

mains the propitiation for them (1 Jn 2:2). If and when believers do sin, their
hearts rightly condemn them, for sin is subject to divine condemnation. But
God is greater than their hearts; he knows everything, he has his eye not only
on the sin, but also, more fundamentally, on the propitiation that he himself
has provided. So to cleave to Jesus Christ while exerting oneself to love the
believing community is to be not only a *peccator* ("sinner"), but also *simul
justus* ("simultaneously righteous"), and "we shall know that we are of the truth,
and reassure our hearts before him" (1 Jn 3:18-24).[59]

*Apostasy.* John warns against apostasy and tells believers how to steer clear
of it. He also comforts believers with the knowledge that their salvation is in
God's hands. These two classes of passages coexist in the Johannine corpus.
Each must receive a full hearing.

Apostasy is the total renunciation or abandonment of God and all for which
he stands. "Many of his disciples" committed this act when Jesus invited them
to eat his flesh and drink his blood (Jn 6:60). Jesus called this "stumbling"
(σκανδαλισθῆναι [Jn 6:61]), and John says that they "drew back" (ἀπῆλθον εἰς
τὰ ὀπίσω) from following Jesus (Jn 6:66). As is proved by this actual instance,
the possibility of defection is real. When Jesus alerts his disciples that his Father
will discard every fruitless branch to wither and burn in the fire, he is referring
to branches "in me" (ἐν ἐμοί [Jn 15:2; cf. 15:6]).[60] Jesus, to keep them from
"falling away" (ἵνα μὴ σκανδαλισθῆτε [Jn 16:1]), told them ahead of time how
the world would hate them. John directs his "elect" readers (2 Jn 1) away from
eternal disaster by cautioning them not to be deceived by the antichrist lest they
lose what they with the apostle(s) have worked for (2 Jn 8).[61] Christ exhorts
churches in Thyatira and Philadelphia to "hold fast" (κρατέω) what they have

---

[59]Angelo Scarano, *Storia dell'interpretazione ed esegesi di 1 Gv 3,18-22* (AnBib 157; Rome: Pontificio Istituto Biblico, 2005).

[60]As we noted in chapter 7, the proposal that αἴρω here means not "remove" but "lift up," with reference to the viticultural practice of elevating a rotting branch to make it fruitful, is unconvincing. Although in John's Gospel the verb αἴρω can mean either "lift up" (Jn 5:8-12; 8:59; 10:24) or "take away" (Jn 1:29; 2:16; 10:18; 11:39, 41, 48; 16:22; 17:15; 19:15, 31, 38; 20:1, 2, 13, 15), the two sentences in John 15:2 ("Every branch in me that bears no fruit, he *airei*" and "Every branch that does bear fruit he prunes, that it may bear more fruit") are antithetical, not parallel. This requires the sense "take away" for αἴρω, which is confirmed by John 15:6.

[61]John wants his readers to "win a full reward," but this neither places the emphasis on getting rewards as distinct from salvation itself nor justifies any supposition that they themselves could be saved without getting a reward. In the immediate context John is warning them not to abandon the truth about the incarnation of Jesus Christ in favor of a heresy, which would result in their not having God (2 Jn 7, 9). The reward that stands in jeopardy, then, is nothing less than God himself.

until he comes, so that no one may snatch their crown (Apoc 2:25; 3:11), "the crown of life" (Apoc 2:10). Hearers of the Apocalypse are to come out of Babylon lest they take part in her sins and share in (λάβητε, "receive") her plagues (Apoc 18:4).

There is no single cause that leads some disciples to apostatize. External tribulation in the world can be a factor (Jn 16:1-4, 21, 33; Apoc 1:9; 2:9, 10; 7:14; 11:2; 12:17; 13:7, 10, 15, 17), including social ostracization resulting in poverty, slander or imprisonment (Apoc 2:9-10). Internally, some are led off course by doctrinal novelties (1 Jn 2:19; 2 Jn 8), while others are seduced by practices opposed to Judeo-Christian morals, such as idolatry or sexual immorality (Apoc 2:14-15, 20-21). Yet others may simply lose the fervency of their love for one another and for God (Apoc 2:4-5).

Deliberate persistence in known sin can harden the heart irreversibly. John knows of a kind of sin that leads to death, for which intercessory prayer is useless (1 Jn 5:16). Death in this passage is the negation of life in God; nothing in the context limits it to the physical plane.[62] What distinguishes nonmortal sin is that recovery is possible through the means that God has appointed. Nonmortal sin crops up in the life of a person who walks in the light (1 Jn 1:7) and looks constantly to God for forgiveness (1 Jn 1:9; 2:1-2). It is the uncharacteristic lapse of a believer due to the fragility of the flesh. Though flesh is the seat where God plants divine seed, it has to make its way in the world, exposed to temptation on all sides (1 Jn 2:1). Mortal sin is that of a person who, though professing to be born again, chooses to walk in darkness, perhaps denying being sinful (1 Jn 1:6, 8, 10); who has no regard for God's commandments (1 Jn 2:4); whose love is for the world and all that is in it (1 Jn 2:15-16); who denies that Jesus is the Christ (1 Jn 2:22); for whom deepening sin is a way of life (1 Jn 3:6, 8, 10). Subjectively considered, mortal sin has a reflexive impact on the person who does it, disposing the will not to seek life by repentance or confession.[63] Sins of members of God's family do not lead to death; sin done by those

---

[62]Elsewhere in the same Epistle (1 Jn 3:14) death can only be spiritual.

[63]John's distinction between nonmortal and mortal sin is more rudimentary than that in Catholic moral theology between venial and mortal sins based on the relative gravity of various offenses' objective matter and the degree of their destructive effect on charity in the heart (*Catechism of the Catholic Church* [trans. United States Catholic Conference; Vatican City: Libreria Editrice Vaticana; San Francisco: Ignatius Press, 1994], §§1854-55). Given John's rhetorical situation, he probably had in mind the heretics who had left the church claiming a higher revelation than that of apostolic Christianity, having no inclination to return (1 Jn 2:19). After being immersed in the life of the church and then rejecting the light of the gospel of Jesus Christ for a religious system of their own

outside of God's family or of persons falsely claiming membership is fatal, for it has not Christ to atone for it.[64] The difference between nonmortal and mortal sin is illustrated in John's Gospel by the contrast between Peter and Judas. Peter denied his Lord but soon reaffirmed his love, with grief over his fall (Jn 21:17), and went on to a lifetime of Christian service ending in martyrdom for Christ's cause. Judas after betraying Jesus entered into perdition.[65]

*Loss of salvation?* Does the fact that sin leads to ruin, or that apostasy is possible, mean that Christians can lose their salvation?

Salvation in John's view is, as we have seen, a love relationship with God in which God graces one's personal existence with his covenantal blessings. To suppose salvation to be a state of blessed existence in itself to which a relationship with God is tangential, whether optionally superadded or subtracted, is to think anthropocentrically. Only in the age to come, the age of permanence, will God's blessings themselves be permanent. Eternal life is a reality now, but what is "eternal" about it is the fact that it involves an ongoing relationship with the living God, who dwells in eternity. Immortality is native to God alone; creatures participate in it by constant communication of life from him. If the question is, at bottom, whether Christian believers have entered into a state of personal safety that God has bound himself never to undo even if they fail to fulfill the outstanding conditions that God has set for its everlasting enjoyment—that is, whether the branches possess a vitality of their own, independent of their abiding in the vine and producing fruit—the answer must be no. That is why the Johannine Scriptures, like other Scriptures, contain dire warnings about sin and apostasy.

Those whom God vivifies in Christ live in God and act in God (Jn 3:21). With God's seed abiding in them, their nature is to do righteousness (1 Jn 3:9). God's voice prompts them with positive injunctions to do his will and checks them with admonitions to avoid unbelief and disobedience. His Spirit dwells in them and stirs them to love. It is by acceding to God's impulse, heeding and doing

---

concoction, their apostasy set them beyond the pale. At the back of his mind John may have compared them to the Pharisees who saw Jesus' signs yet refused to take their obvious import, whom Jesus warned about committing sin against the Holy Spirit, an eternal sin because it cut them off from precisely the means given by God to bring them to faith in Jesus (Mk 3:28-30).

[64]George B. Stevens, *The Johannine Theology: A Study of the Doctrinal Contents of the Gospels and Epistles of the Apostle John* (New York: Scribner, 1894), pp. 149-55; Dirk G. van der Merwe, "Salvation in the Johannine Epistles," *HvTSt* 60 (2004): 540-43.

[65]Dongsu Kim, *An Exegesis of Apostasy Embedded in John's Narratives of Peter and Judas against the Synoptic Parallels* (SBEC 61; Lewiston, NY: Mellen, 2004).

what he says, not by ignoring his conditions, that the regenerate will reach that state wherein God's blessings belong to them incontrovertibly forever. If the question is whether God insures that those whom he gave to the Son will keep his word so that they may be saved finally (Jn 17:6), the answer must be yes.

Salvation is not the irremovable possession of an indestructible commodity. It is God who makes sure that none of his elect, in love relation with him, will lose it.

**Preservation and perseverance.** In the previous chapter we considered how John's doctrine of pretemporal election traces faith back to the will of God. In the present context it is appropriate to consider John's doctrine of the divine preservation of the elect. Briefly put, God preserves his saints by means of their perseverance, not apart from it.

John's writings are rich in statements of God's intention to watch over those whom he loves, yielding several of the strongest affirmations in the Bible. "This is the will of him who sent me," said Jesus, "that I should lose nothing of all that he has given me, but raise it up at the last day" (Jn 6:39). A token of this comes in the passion narrative, where the disciples are freed from harm and only Jesus is arrested (Jn 18:9; cf. 17:12). The good shepherd gives eternal life to his sheep, they never will perish, no one can snatch them out of his hand or out of the hand of his Father, who gave them, who is greater than all (Jn 10:28-29). Jesus' farewell prayer in John 17 includes a supplication for their safekeeping as Jesus leaves them behind in the world. While Jesus was with them he guarded them; now his request is that the Father keep them from evil in Jesus' absence (Jn 17:11-13, 15).

God preserves his beloved ones from their own inner weakness as well as from pressures from without. Those who are born of God do not sin, but God's Son keeps them, and the evil one does not touch them (1 Jn 5:18). Here it is a matter of the devil reaching for people by tempting them. Again, the verse does not negate that believers commit daily sins for which they must seek forgiveness. The devil is allowed to harass to a limited extent. But following the verses about sin unto death (1 Jn 5:16-17), 1 John 5:18 indicates that Christ will prevent regenerate persons from being overcome by sin to the point of perdition. He will always recall them to penitence and the expression of their true nature.

The Apocalypse uses figurative language to drive home the same point. Christ holds the lampstands, which represent the churches, in his right hand (Apoc 1:16, 20; 2:1). He will shield them, as God protected Israel at the time of the plagues on Egypt, from the eschatological plagues with which he will test dwellers on earth (Apoc 3:10; 7:1-3; 9:4). Addressing their wills, he reproves and chastens those whom he loves, to stimulate them to repent (Apoc 3:19).

On the human end, perseverance is the correlate of God's gracious preservation. Several of the passages just gathered mention human work together with God's work. The Father's will that the Son lose nothing is not fulfilled apart from loyalty to Jesus when a mass of other disciples withdraws (Jn 6:66-69). If the Father and the Son hold the sheep firmly in their grip, it is not without the sheep hearing the shepherd's voice and following him (Jn 10:27). Those for whom Jesus prayed at the end of his ministry, whom the Father gave to the Son, had in fact kept God's word (Jn 17:6), and Jesus prayed that God henceforth sanctify them in his truth (Jn 17:17, 19). He who was eternally born of God keeps those from sin who respond to the imperatives to abide in him (Jn 15:4, 9; 1 Jn 2:24, 27, 28). Side by side with the dramatic image in the Apocalypse of the risen one clutching his lampstands are paraenetic passages encouraging the churches to have endurance (ὑπομονή [Apoc 1:9; 2:2, 3, 19; 3:10; 13:10; 14:12]), to bear up (βαστάζειν [Apoc 2:3]), to be faithful (γίνεσθαι πιστός [Apoc 2:10; cf. 2:13; 17:14]), to hold fast what they have (κρατεῖν [Apoc 2:13, 25; 3:11]), not to deny the faith or the name of Christ (Apoc 2:13; 3:8), and, if necessary, to suffer martyrdom (Apoc 2:10, 13; 6:9-11; 11:7; 12:11; 16:6; 17:6; 18:24; 19:2).

In soteriology, what God does is always anterior to what human beings do. The saints will persevere because God preserves them, but divine preservation operates precisely through the agency of their faithful perseverance. Both are necessary. A concurrence of the divine and the human factors is an inescapable condition for a saved person to enter into final salvation.

***Assurance of salvation.*** If salvation is already had by the believer in certain respects and not yet realized in others, and if its future realization is conditional upon faith, obedience and perseverance therein, can one be sure of one's salvation?

In John's Gospel the issue of personal assurance does not arise. Despite the attention that John gives to epistemology, the focus is on knowing that Jesus is the Christ, the Son of God. Nevertheless, this objective outlook is arguably the only sound basis for healthy self-reflection. It is in knowing that Jesus is the Christ who died to make propitiation for the sins of the world and then rose to open a new mode of human existence that one comes to believe in him and so gains life in his name (Jn 20:31).

However strung out in time the full complement of requirements for salvation may be, John can distill them in terms of believing in Jesus. Whoever believes in him will not perish, but have eternal life (Jn 3:16). The work that God demands is to believe in him whom God has sent (Jn 6:29). Out of faith unfold renunciation of the world, Christian obedience, persistence in the face of ridicule, suffering for Christ's sake, and endurance to the end, as faith wends its way toward the dawning age. These are not supplemental acts in addition to faith; they are the very practical forms that faith itself takes as it meets various situations. Precisely because faith exists only in these concrete forms, on them the judgment according to deeds will base its findings. As conditions, they point to developmental stages of the animate spirit; they are subconditions that will certainly be met provided the main condition is met. Faith is never squeezed out by them but rather comes to full manifestation in them. And the Savior to whom faith clings is the one who gives life to whom he will (Jn 5:21; 17:2). The God who grants people to come to Christ (Jn 6:65), who draws them to him (Jn 6:44), and who clenches them in his almighty fist is greater than all (Jn 10:29). That is the foundation on which a troubled soul can rest.

But how can one know that one is indeed a recipient of God's favor now and will be on the last day? To this question about whether individuals are included in God's saving purpose John devotes a large share of his First Epistle. The church had been shaken by some of its own members who boasted of a more sophisticated revelation from God and a better method of attaining salvation. John wrote to reassure his little children that they knew the true God in Jesus Christ (1 Jn 5:20). Of course, he reminds them in his letter of the great objective truths that form the bedrock of their confidence. Jesus, the eternal life who was with the Father, was made manifest as the incarnate one (1 Jn 1:1-2; 2:22-23; 4:2-3), made propitiation for sins by his blood (1 Jn 2:2; 4:10; 5:6-8), rose again "so that we might live through him" (1 Jn 4:9), and will appear again to conform believers to himself (1 Jn 2:28–3:2). Building on those truths, the elder adds more particular, experiential grounds for assurance. As a community they have been anointed by the Holy Spirit (1 Jn 2:20, 27), and his presence and work in their midst is evidence that God abides in them (1 Jn 3:24; 4:13). Specifically, the Spirit gives messages to the community through prophets (1 Jn 4:1-6) and fosters the love of God and of one another (1 Jn 4:7–5:5).

Running through the First Epistle is the refrain, with minor variations, "By this we/you know" (1 Jn 2:3; 3:16, 19, 24; 4:2, 6, 13, 16; 5:2). What the community is to know is that they know him, that they are of the truth, that they abide in him and he in them, and so forth. The climactic statement is "I write this . . . that you may know that you have eternal life" (1 Jn 5:13). Classifying the criteria, we find empirical grounds for knowing that one is in a state of salvation. They fall into three categories: (1) confession of the truth about Jesus (1 Jn 4:14-15; 5:10-13); (2) walking in his commandments (1 Jn 2:3-6; 3:10); (3) loving one another (1 Jn 3:14, 19-20). John does not base assurance of salvation solely on what Christ did for the believer, but also finds confirmation in what the Spirit is doing in the believer. Because doubts, transgressions and breaches of love occur, begging for forgiveness (1 Jn 1:8, 10; 2:1), the empirical criteria can be neither the sole nor the primary ground, otherwise the conflicting facts of the case may undermine rather than strengthen assurance. But if God's seed is planted in regenerate people (1 Jn 3:9), it will produce a measurable difference in their speech and conduct. God has imparted his own being to his Son, God is righteous, God is love; so any human person who has the gift of divine life will recognize the Son, will be righteous, will love.[66] To the extent that, in the case of an individual church member, such a differential is not in evidence, confidence of that individual's salvation diminishes.[67]

A further question arises. Can one know at present, with indubitable certainty, that one will still be in a state of salvation come the day of judgment? The First Epistle looks to the future and exhorts believers to do what is requisite now to have confidence versus shame before Christ at his coming (1 Jn 2:28) and to cast off fear of judgment (1 Jn 4:17-18). Remarkably, John has nothing to say on this point beyond what he said about present assurance. With a view to standing before Christ at his parousia, believers are told to abide in him (1 Jn 2:28), do right (1 Jn 2:29), and press on with purifying themselves as he is pure

---

[66]Robert Law, *The Tests of Life: A Study of the First Epistle of St. John* (3rd ed.; Edinburgh: T & T Clark, 1914), pp. 208-78; Lieu, *Theology*, pp. 49-71. Note especially Lieu's formulations: the themes "born of God" and "children of God" are "never independent of lives lived. When contradicted by clear 'tests of life' all such claims to religious experience are but self-deception" (pp. 49-50). "The invisible reality of relationship with God and the visible realities of behaviour are interdependent" (p. 58). "The approach taken by I John does not need to face the polarity between 'faith and works' as means to salvation; he sees only the inner and outer expressions of a relationship with God as a single whole, as present in their completeness or not present at all" (p. 109).

[67]For a fuller defense of the thesis that assurance of salvation is "grounded" on Christ's work and "supported" by the lifestyle of the Christian, see Christopher D. Bass, *That You May Know: Assurance of Salvation in 1 John* (NACSBT 5; Nashville: B & H Academic, 2008). The drift of the formulae "that you may know" is better captured by saying that assurance is grounded on Christ's work insofar as the Christian's individual lifestyle manifests its effects.

(1 Jn 3:3). If their hearts condemn them and need reassurance, they are to find it in loving one another in deed and truth (1 Jn 3:14-20).[68] Perfect love—of God and of one another—casts out fear of judgment (1 Jn 4:18). Confidence for the day of judgment consists in the fact that "as he is so are we in this world" (1 Jn 4:17). The criteria by which the believer may be sure of a happy future are identical with those that will come into play on the day of judgment by deeds.

In other words, precisely where the heart seeks certainty about the future it faces the uncompromisingly conditional structure of God's soteriological plan. God does not hand out salvation all at once, on a plate, to be grabbed as though the giver did not matter, as though there were no ongoing responsibility to maintain the covenantal relationship with him and his will. The way to ensure the outcome of judgment day is to refrain from persuading oneself that one's salvation is already in the bag, that truth, righteousness and love have nothing to do with it. What binds the present state of salvation to a positive final verdict is continuity in practicing those values. And what calms the believer's trembling heart is God's promise that as he acted in the first Paraclete to make the believer his child, so he will continue to act through the second Paraclete to bring his seed to fruition. Personal salvation is the believer's project for the believer's good, but ultimately it is God's project for God's glory. God will have his glory. Therefore God will bring it about that the believer will fulfill God's conditions.

## Conclusion: Jesus as the Way to the Father

Putting together the present chapter with the previous one, we are in a position to determine in what senses Jesus is "the way" (Jn 14:6). Being human, he himself traversed a path from this world to his Father (Jn 13:33, 36; 14:28; 16:5). The believer is following Jesus on the same journey. Jesus is the way, first, in that he lovingly laid down his life for his friends, making an atonement that they could not have made for themselves. This act awakens their love for God and establishes them in the relationship with him that is eternal life.

He is the way, second, in that he gave them an example of truth, righteousness and love to imitate. Born of the Father and enlivened by God's Spirit, the mutual love between God and Jesus' disciples becomes fruitful in the disciples' loving one another. This communal love fulfills God's commandments

---

[68]"John is not saying here that loving good works on our part can outweigh previous guilt; his purpose is rather to give us a criterion for our participation in the life of God" (Schnackenburg, "Christian Morality," p. 202).

and meets the outstanding condition to cement the triangular love relationship as everlasting.

People undertake the journey by believing in Jesus. At the start, faith means receiving what Jesus did for them. Along the way, it means abiding in him, walking as he walked, and coming to be more and more like him in love. Salvation is inaugurated when one gets on the path; it is completed in the vision of God (1 Jn 3:2; Apoc 22:4).

9

# DISCIPLES OF CHRIST
# IN COMMUNITY

People who come to Jesus find that they are not alone. God has drawn others too. In this penultimate chapter the topic is the Johannine view of believers in relation to one another. For, as is already evident in Jesus' command to love, God's purpose to save individuals does not come to rest until he has set them in an earthly community that reflects the divine society. This brings up John's doctrine of the church.

Johannine ecclesiology reflects what the church had become by the end of the first century. As witnesses to the state of the church, patristic memoirs can supplement the New Testament record. The sources offer a completely different portrait of John from the construct, still prevalent in academic circles, of a sectarian Johannine Christianity. Many critics, agnostic about the authorship and historicity of the documents in the New Testament canon and skeptical of the reliability of the church fathers, replaced the apostle John with an anonymous tradition. That there are several editorial stages behind the Fourth Gospel, with shifting emphases or even contradictory points of view among the layers, is a widely accepted postulate. Some try to apply sociological theory to the origins of the Christian movement despite the lack of statistical data. On this hypothetical canvas recent scholarship has drawn its picture of an embattled Jewish-Christian community justifying a recent break from the synagogue, rocked by dissension within, and becoming more and more isolated from the church at large, under the influence of a Gnosticizing leader or leaders having no direct relation to the apostles of Jesus. Such a portrayal diverges widely from the conclusions that we will reach if we approach the same documents not uncritically, but as bona fide accounts yielding knowledge.

## JOHN AS CHURCHMAN

We begin with a concise survey of the church's development in the first century, highlighting John's place in it. From the ancient sources John emerges as one who took a strong interest in the catholic church and contributed to its development.

*John as a leading participant in the Jesus movement.* According to the Synoptic Gospels, John and his (probably elder) brother James, two sons of Zebedee the fisherman, were among the first whom Jesus called in Galilee, together with Peter and Andrew, to form the nucleus of his followers (Mt 4:21-22). In New Testament lists of the twelve apostles John's name always stands in the top four (Mt 10:2; Mk 3:17; Lk 6:14; Acts 1:13). John was one of the trio (with Peter and James) who accompanied Jesus on special tasks by invitation (Mk 1:29; 5:37; 9:2; 13:3; 14:33) and who received from the Lord special appellations (Mk 3:16-17). Toward the end of the ministry, when Jesus went to Jerusalem with his staunchest disciples, he chose Peter and John to prepare his last Passover in the upper room (Lk 22:8). In the Fourth Gospel the partnership between Peter and the disciple Jesus loved (Jn 13:23-24; 18:10, 15-16, 26; 20:2-10; 21:7, 20-22) parallels that between Peter and John in Luke's writings.

After Jesus' ascension, John's name appears among the leaders of the 120 who remained in the city awaiting the gift of the Spirit (Acts 1:13). With John, Peter proclaimed the gospel in the temple and defended it before the Sanhedrin (Acts 3:1, 3, 4, 11; 4:13, 19). The apostles (including John) stayed in Jerusalem through the persecution led by Saul (Acts 8:1). When they heard later that Philip had evangelized Samaria, they dispatched Peter and John to mediate the gift of the Holy Spirit and thus unify the Samaritan converts with the mother church (Acts 8:14).

In about the year A.D. 46, when Paul, now a preacher of Christ in his own right, paid a return visit to Judea from Antioch of Syria (Acts 11:30; Gal 2:1), John was in Jerusalem (Gal 2:9).[1] Barnabas, deputy of the Jerusalem church to the fertile mission field of Antioch, had fetched Paul from Tarsus to help direct the rapidly multiplying mixed Jewish/Gentile congregations in that Hellenistic metropolis (Acts 11:22-26). Facing criticism from Judean Christians for not having Titus circumcised, Paul sought out and spread his gospel before

---

[1]This reconstruction with its early date for Galatians 2:1-10 is based on two reasonable assumptions: (1) the two visits to Jerusalem in Paul's autobiographical travelogue (Gal 1:18; 2:1) correspond to the same sequence in Acts (Acts 9:26-30; 11:30; 12:25); (2) Paul counts the fourteen years to the second visit (Gal 2:1) from the time of his call to preach Christ (Gal 1:16), approximately A.D. 32-46.

three "pillars" of the Jerusalem hierarchy, one of whom was John (together with James the Lord's brother and Cephas). They ratified Paul's and Barnabas's policies among the Gentiles and committed themselves to continue their own work among the Jews. They asked only to have the poor in Judea remembered (Gal 2:2-10). Paul's collection occupied him for the next eleven years. It had not only charitable but also ecumenical significance in that it cemented the Gentile congregations to their spiritual forebears in Palestine (Rom 15:27).

If John, entrusted by Jesus with the care of his mother (Jn 19:26-27), had the Jerusalem area for his base until the fall of the Holy City to Rome, that might explain how Luke, on visiting Jerusalem in A.D. 57 (Acts 21:17), became aware of Mary's unique memories of Jesus' infancy (Lk 1–2, esp. Lk 2:19). John's long association with the Lord's mother and his brother James (Gal 2:9) will only have enhanced his standing in the Christian community.

The testimonies of Matthew, Mark, Luke and Paul thus converge to place John at the very hub of the church from its fledgling days and, after Jesus' departure, in the highest echelon of apostolic leadership. Moreover, they make John a key member of that central body during the foundational decades, when the apostles at Jerusalem were exercising close oversight of the church's advance northward through Samaria, Syria and beyond to the west, with a view to securing the cohesiveness of the church worldwide as it blossomed in an ever expanding medley of Mediterranean cultures. In chapter 1 we reviewed reasons for identifying this apostle John as the author of the Johannine corpus.

***John as ecclesiastical superintendent at Ephesus: New Testament evidence.*** What role did John play in the church during the period when he would have written the literature attributed to him, after the destruction of Jerusalem and during the Ephesian phase of his ministry? There are a number of clues that he acted as a sort of metropolitan bishop (minus the title) in Ephesus and its suburbs.

The Fourth Gospel yields a minimum of information about its author at the time of writing. He was revered and famous, for a rumor among believers that Jesus had predicted that he was not to die had to be checked (Jn 21:23). He was surrounded by devotees persuaded of his veracity as an eyewitness to Jesus (Jn 21:24).

Assuming that the Johannine Epistles form a trilogy addressed to the church at three levels—to the host of a house-church (3 John), to the association of house-congregations of an urban locality (2 John), and to those of a wider region (1 John)—we learn a good deal more. The very fact that "the elder" who wrote these Epistles (2 Jn 1; 3 Jn 1) took Paul for his literary model in the same geographical area (Philemon, Colossians, Ephesians) indicates that he, like Paul before him, was a supervisor of these churches.[2] His having had direct dealings with the incarnate one (Jn 1:14; 1 Jn 1:1-3) made him a paternal figure to those whose faith depended on his and others' testimony, whom he called "(my) little children" (τεκνία [μου] [1 Jn 2:1, 12, 28; 3:7, 18; 4:4; 5:21]) or "my children" (τὰ ἐμὰ τέκνα [3 Jn 4]). In writing to them, he expects them, learning from the Spirit as their main instructor (1 Jn 2:20-21, 27), to heed him.

The Third Epistle affords an especially clear glimpse of the elder's ecclesiastical position. He resides in a town other than that of the recipient, Gaius, probably host of a house-church, for the writer has gotten news about Gaius's activities from itinerant missionaries or prophets who had enjoyed hospitality at his home (3 Jn 3, 5-8). Gaius's warmth toward them stands in stark contrast to Diotrephes, pastoral overseer of perhaps yet another house-church. Diotrephes asserts control (ὁ φιλοπρωτεύων [3 Jn 9]) by refusing to welcome the travelers, and he excommunicates any members of his church who do so (3 Jn 10). Diotrephes "does not receive us as guests" (οὐκ ἐπιδέχεται ἡμᾶς [3 Jn 9]), referring to the elder's own delegates.[3] Moreover, he is undermining the reputation of the elder (3 Jn 10). The elder, then, maintains contact with a number of churches through a body of co-workers, even as Paul had leaned on the services of Timothy and Titus. Concerned that Diotrephes' power play jeopar-

---

[2]If Christians at Ephesus began to collect Paul's letters shortly after his martyrdom at Rome in around A.D. 65—this date for the collection being required by the reference to such a corpus already in 2 Peter 3:16 (assuming that Peter commissioned this second letter during his lifetime by the hand of an amanuensis whose style differed markedly from that of Silvanus, who wrote 1 Peter [1 Pet 5:12])—this may explain how the letter that we now identify as Paul's letter to the Ephesians, lacking a designated recipient in Ephesians 1:1 (according to P[46] ℵ B*) and therefore probably intended as a circular letter, came to be identified with Ephesus. It also sheds light on how John, living there several decades later, might have been aware of Paul's triple missive to churches of Asia. Evidence that Paul sent Philemon, Colossians and Ephesians on the same occasion is laid out in J. B. Lightfoot, *St. Paul's Epistles to the Colossians and to Philemon* (London: Macmillan, 1879), pp. 32-37; Theodore Zahn, *Introduction to the New Testament* (trans. John Moore Trout et al.; 3 vols.; New York: Scribner, 1909), 1:439-91. That these three epistles correspond to levels of church organization is observed by Zahn (p. 486) and in Kirsopp Lake, *The Earlier Epistles of St. Paul: Their Motive and Origin* (2nd ed.; London: Rivingtons, 1914), p. 363. J. Ramsey Michaels suggests that 1 John may have been a circular letter addressed to all of Asia Minor ("Reflections on the Three Epistles of John," in *A Companion to John: Readings in Johannine Theology [John's Gospel and Epistles]* [ed. Michael J. Taylor; New York: Alba House, 1970], pp. 257, 269-70), while 2 John went to "one particular church" (p. 269), and 3 John not to a church but rather "to a certain Gaius" (p. 270).

[3]Margaret M. Mitchell, "'Diotrephes Does Not Receive Us': The Lexicographical and Social Context of 3 John 9-10," *JBL* 117 (1998): 299-320.

dize church unity, this superelder affirms Gaius and plans to pay a visit to take public action against the troublemaker.[4]

John sent his Apocalypse as an encyclical to all the churches of the Roman province of Asia, represented by the seven cities that he names (Apoc 1:4, 11). First in the list is Ephesus, where the author may have taken up residence on his return from the island of Patmos to the mainland. The other cities trace a semicircle clockwise along trade routes northwards, then around to the southeast. The author is known to all these churches simply as "John" (Apoc 1:1, 4, 9; 22:8). He classes himself among Christian prophets (Apoc 1:3; 10:11; 19:10; 22:6-7, 9-10, 18-19) and adopts the apocalyptic genre, but by enclosing the prophecy in an epistolary frame (Apoc 1:4-5; 22:21) he makes it an apostolic intervention in the life and discipline of the Asian churches.

From the New Testament writings themselves, then, we get a picture of an undisputed leader among the leaders of the churches of proconsular Asia, Diotrephes' attitude toward him being the sole exception.

***John as ecclesiastical superintendent at Ephesus: Patristic evidence.*** To fill out the circumstantial evidence of the New Testament, we have a number of independent but converging patristic testimonies from Asia Minor dating back to the earliest decades of the second century, within but a few years of John's

---

[4]Nothing in 3 John suggests that Diotrephes foreshadows the monarchic episcopate, against which development the elder would be striving to conserve a more primitive, charismatic order. For the proposal, see Adolf von Harnack, "Über den dritten Johannesbrief" (TUGAL 15/3; Leipzig: Hinrichs, 1897), pp. 3-27; Ernst Käsemann, "Ketzer und Zeuge," ZTK 48 (1951): 292-311; Hans von Campenhausen, *Ecclesiastical Authority and Spiritual Power in the Church of the First Three Centuries* (trans. J. A. Baker; Stanford, CA: Stanford University Press, 1969), pp. 121-23; Eduard Schweizer, *Church Order in the New Testament* (trans. Frank Clarke; London: SCM Press, 1961), pp. 137-38. It rests on the doubtful inference that the silence of 3 John about polity means that its author had no official position. Its fatal weaknesses are the fact that John (if he was the author) was regarded as a bishop of bishops by all ecclesiastical writers of the second to the fourth centuries, and the total lack of evidence that Diotrephes had any real influence beyond the house-church that he oversaw. Diotrephes has expelled members of his own church who refused to toe his line (3 Jn 10), but from the way the elder informs Gaius of Diotrephes' program (3 Jn 9-10), it would appear that Gaius belonged to a different congregational cell in the same city that owed no obedience to Diotrephes. Truth be told, it is easier to interpret Diotrephes' actions as an assertion of independent congregationalism against the strengthening fabric of the church catholic, represented by the elder and the traveling Christian workers. For surveys of possible reconstructions, see Raymond E. Brown, *The Epistles of John: Translated, with Introduction, Commentary, and Notes* (AB 30; Garden City, NY: Doubleday, 1982), pp. 728-39; Judith Lieu, *The Theology of the Johannine Epistles* (NTT; Cambridge: University Press, 1991), pp. 150-54; Barth L. Campbell, "Honor, Hospitality and Haughtiness: The Contention for Leadership in 3 John," *EvQ* 77 (2005): 323-25. Through the author's rhetorical strategy Campbell descries a tussle over honor as expressed by the giving of hospitality. This may well overlap with implications for church polity.

death. One "tradition of the primitive elders" says that John, "urged on by his disciples, and, divinely moved by the Spirit, composed a spiritual Gospel" (Clement of Alexandria, *Hypotyposes*, paraphrased by Eusebius, *Hist. eccl.* 6.14.7). From about the same date, the Muratorian Canon of Rome reports that John wrote his memoirs down "when his fellow-disciples and bishops urged him" (line 10), anachronistically making John out to have been a "bishop."[5]

Of the numerous patristic sources that bear testimony to John's having lived at Ephesus in Asia until the reign of Trajan, several are specific about the nature of his activites. Irenaeus (A.D. 180s) says that many presbyters of Asia associated with John (*Haer.* 2.22.5; 5.33.3). Among the elders who knew John in Asia was Papias, bishop of Hierapolis to around A.D. 130, whom Irenaeus calls a "hearer" of John (*Haer.* 5.33.4). Also the illustrious Polycarp, who lived to around A.D. 155/161, bishop of Smyrna and honored among all the Asian bishops, was a protégé of John and perhaps his successor. Tertullian (ca. A.D. 200), citing the register of the episcopal succession at Smyrna, tells us that Polycarp "was placed therein by John" (*Praescr.* 32).[6] Clement of Alexandria (ca. A.D. 200) says that John used to "go, when he was asked, to the neighbouring districts of the heathen, in some places to appoint bishops [ἐπισκόπους ἐπιστήσων], in others to reconcile whole churches, and in others to ordain [κλῆρον κληρώσων] some one of those pointed out by the Spirit" (*Quis div.* 42, preserved in Eusebius, *Hist. eccl.* 3.23.6). According to Tertullian, "the sequence of bishops" of Asia, "traced back to its origin will be found to rest on the authority of John" (*Marc.* 4.5). Jerome adds that John "founded and built churches throughout all Asia" (*Vir. ill.* 9).[7]

---

[5]It may have been in the generation after John's lifetime that the terms *episkopos* and *presbyteros* came to designate stratified orders of ministry as they do in the letters of Ignatius. In the New Testament, and as late as 1 *Clement* and the *Didache*, the same church officials may be called either a local council of "elders" or each the "overseer" of a house-church. Ignatius, only two or three decades later, knows of the episcopate and the presbyterate, together with the diaconate, as three tiers of authority. Ignatius uses the terminology as though it is established and generally understood in his day.

[6]Irenaeus speaks more generally when he says that all the churches of Asia in his day, and the present successors of Polycarp, bear witness that Polycarp was appointed bishop "by apostles" (*Haer.* 3.3.4). Elsewhere Irenaeus confirms that Polycarp had dealings with John in Asia (*Letter to Florinus*, quoted by Eusebius, *Hist. eccl.* 5.20.6; *Letter to Victor*, quoted by Eusebius, *Hist. eccl.* 5.24.16). Jerome's phrase "Polycarp, disciple of the apostle John and by him ordained bishop of Smyrna" may be dependent on these earlier reports (*Vir. ill.* 17).

[7]On the emergence of the episcopate in Asia through John's influence following the pattern of James' presidency of the Jerusalem elders, J. B. Lightfoot's book-length essay "The Christian Ministry" remains a classic of painstaking critical scholarship (in *St. Paul's Epistle to the Philippians* [1881; repr., Lynn, MA: Hendrickson, 1981], pp. 181-269, esp. pp. 195-214).

It is unclear what we should make of the claim of Polycrates, bishop of Ephesus around A.D. 190, that John at one time "became a priest wearing the leaf [πέταλον]" (*Letter to Victor,* quoted by Eusebius, *Hist. eccl.* 3.31.3). Polycrates was a younger contemporary of Polycarp and should have had sound facts at hand in the traditions of Ephesus, where John had died and was buried. "The leaf" was the unique plate worn by the high priest in Jerusalem on the crown of his turban when performing ceremonial duties in the temple (Ex 28:32-34; Lev 8:9).[8] Surely Polycrates would have been aware that John had been unqualified to be a Jewish high priest in any literal sense. Therefore we should interpret the phrase metaphorically.[9] His curious statement finds a parallel in Epiphanius, who says of James the Lord's brother that he wore the *petalon* (*Pan.* 29.4; 78.13-14).[10] In the case of James, we may hazard a guess as to the meaning. The high-priestly leaf had the function of bearing before God national guilt, to atone for it (Ex 28:38; *m. Pesah.* 7:7; *m. Zebah.* 8:12; *m. Menah.* 3:3; cf. *Prot. Jas.* 5:1). James was known for going into the temple to pray and seek forgiveness for the Jewish people (Hegesippus, according to Eusebius, *Hist. eccl.* 2.23.6). Could "to wear the leaf" have been an expression for doing such intercessory penitence in the temple? Might John have become such a leader among Jewish Christians, taking on himself James's mantle after the latter's death in approximately A.D. 62, until the revolt of A.D. 66-70? If John was still in Jerusalem at that time, the responsibility would have devolved upon him by default, as the last resident "pillar," and as one who may have been at least as closely related to the Lord's family (being a cousin of Jesus), as was Simeon son of Clopas, who was elected after the war (Hegesippus, according to Eusebius, *Hist. eccl.* 3.11; 4.22.4).[11] If this line

---

[8]Descriptions of the plate from the Second Temple period include Sirach 45:12; *Let. Arist.* 98; Philo, *Mos.* 2.114, 131-132; Josephus, *J.W.* 5.235; *Ant.* 3.178.

[9]F. F. Bruce, "St. John at Ephesus," *BJRL* 60 (1978): 342-43. For a contrary argument, see Richard Bauckham, "Papias and Polycrates on the Origin of the Fourth Gospel," *JTS* 44 (1993): 24-69. Bauckham urges that the phrase, taken literally, identifies John of Ephesus (whom he takes to be someone other than the son of Zebedee and apostle of Jesus) as John the chief priest of Acts 4:6. But to read Papias (Eusebius, *Hist. eccl.* 3.39.4) as suggesting the existence of a second, Asian John is, as we noted in chapter 1, precarious at best. And to try to prove that Polycrates, a bishop of the church, would want to identify one of the Christian luminaries of Asia with a member of the priestly aristocracy in Jerusalem, whom Luke designates as "*their* rulers" (Acts 4:5), a group opposed to the spread of Christianity, who interrogated Peter and John and prohibited them from speaking in the name of Jesus, is a remarkable tour de force.

[10]Probably depending on Hegesippus in both contexts.

[11]Hegesippus gives the impression that the succession passed directly from James to Simeon. But Eusebius, following Hegesippus at this point, places the election of Simeon after the capture of Jerusalem (*Hist eccl.* 3.11), leaving an interim of about eight years unaccounted for after James's death.

of inquiry is anywhere near the truth, John, on moving to Asia, will have carried with him the aura not only of being the longest living of the three chosen out of the Twelve by Jesus, but also of having served briefly as functioning patriarch of the church that was mother of all the churches.

The portrait of John built up by these sources taken together is of a churchman and ecumenist of the first rank. After the Roman campaign of A.D. 66-70, which decimated Palestinian Jewry including the churches of Judea, the populous urban centers of the northeastern Mediterranean basin from Antioch of Syria to Ephesus emerged as the cradle of Christianity going forward into the second century. Laboring in precisely that theater, John, perhaps more than any other, insured the continuity of the faith, order and discipline of the catholic church of the early second century with the dominical church of Jerusalem. He was anything but the sectarian demagogue created by postmodern historiography.

## JOHANNINE TERMS FOR THE CHURCH

In John's thought the church singled out from the world is the object of the saving activity of the Father and the Son, and then, imbued with the Spirit, it is taken up into a working partnership and sent into the world to continue the sent one's work with joy and love. A study of John's terminology for the church will lead into his ecclesiology.[12]

*Varied terms.* That John never uses the word "church" (ἐκκλησία) and shows "no specifically ecclesiological interest"[13] are notions of radical biblical criticism that stand or fall with the assumptions of that style of scholarship.[14] For

---

In those tumultuous days John, as former vice-president of the Jerusalem elders under James (Peter having left Jerusalem), may have filled the post de facto though never elected to it formally.

[12]For a survey of scholarship on this topic, see R. Alan Culpepper, "The Quest for the Church in the Gospel of John," *Int* 63 (2009): 341-54.

[13]Rudolf Bultmann, *Theology of the New Testament* (trans. Kendrick Grobel; 2 vols.; New York: Scribner, 1951–1955), 2:91. Ernst Käsemann pushes the caricature to the limits in *The Testament of Jesus: A Study of the Gospel of John in the Light of Chapter 17* (trans. Gerhard Krodel; Philadelphia: Fortress, 1968), pp. 27-55. Less provocative in tone but not much more restrained in tendency is Eduard Schweizer, "The Concept of the Church in the Gospel and Epistles of St. John," in *New Testament Essays: Studies in Memory of Thomas Walter Manson, 1893–1958* (ed. A. J. B. Higgins; Manchester: Manchester University Press, 1959), pp. 230-45. These works emanate from a fashion in New Testament scholarship in continental Europe that accentuated what is distinctive in each sector of the New Testament at the expense of the common theology.

[14]Robert Kysar, in his survey of scholarship on John's Gospel 1963–1973, states that Bultmann's judgment "has not been widely accepted on this matter" (*The Fourth Evangelist and His Gospel: An Examination of Contemporary Scholarship* [Minneapolis: Augsburg, 1975], p. 241).

while it is true that the Fourth Gospel has no occurrence of the noun ἐκκλησία, the word occurs three times in 3 John and no fewer than twenty times in the Apocalypse. As for the fact that our author says next to nothing about the institutional, liturgical, sacramental and disciplinary aspects of church life,[15] is this not a case of interpreters pressing their own interests? The Gospel, highlighting Jesus as he was during his ministry when he and his disciples constituted the embryonic church, arguably sticks to historical reality.[16] Even if the Epistles were written to mature churches in the wake of a secessionist schism, and the Apocalypse calls churches to renounce the world, the author saw fit to address these issues in terms of principles rather than practices. John's whole theology is a theology of persons, and what he says about the church bears that stamp.

In fact, John uses a wide array of terms to denote the church.[17] He speaks of the "children of God" (τέκνα θεοῦ [Jn 1:12; 11:52; 1 Jn 3:1-2, 10; 5:2]),[18] the "disciples" (μαθηταί) of Jesus (74× in the Gospel),[19] and Jesus' "sheep" (15× in Jn 10) or "flock" (ποίμνη [Jn 10:16]) whom Jesus gathers in a "sheepfold" (αὐλὴ τῶν προβάτων [Jn 10:1, 16]). The church is the "much fruit" of the grain of wheat that dies to multiply (Jn 12:24). Jesus refers to "my own who are in the world" (οἱ ἴδιοι οἱ ἐν τῷ κόσμῳ [Jn 13:1; cf. 10:3-4, 12]), those whom the Father has given the Son out of the world (Jn 6:37-39; 17:2, 6, 9; cf. 17:11),[20] and "my brethren" (Jn 20:17).[21] Jesus used plural pronouns as spokesman for an emergent com-

---

[15]"I cannot conceive that Christian proclamation . . . could be without ecclesiology. . . . Even the basic elements of congregational life, worship, the sacraments and ministry, play such insignificant roles that time and again John's interest in them has been doubted" (Käsemann, *Testament*, p. 27).

[16]Käsemann's rebuttal is unconvincing. If John could change "the Galilean teacher into the God who goes about on earth," argues Käsemann (ibid.), could he not also have superimposed the later church organization on his sources? The corollary falls with its premise. Raymond Brown's cautions about the argument from silence are telling (*The Gospel According to John: Introduction, Translation, and Notes* [2 vols.; AB 29, 29A; Garden City, NY: Doubleday, 1966–1970], 1:cv-cxi).

[17]Klaus Haacker, "Jesus und die Kirche nach Johannes," *TZ* 29 (1973): 179-201.

[18]The phrase is thus distributed between the Gospel and the First Epistle. Haacker ("Jesus und die Kirche," pp. 180-82) points out that by appropriating this Old Testament term (Deut 14:1; Hos 2:1), John claims a legitimacy for the new community of faith in Jesus that Jews who reject Jesus lack.

[19]"Disciples" does not occur in the Epistles or in the Apocalypse, written at a time when Jesus' circle of disciples had become the church. But already in the Gospel "disciples" can refer to Jesus' closest companions, or to a wider circle of serious adherents, or to all believers of later generations. Context usually makes the scope clear. See Rudolf Schnackenburg, *The Gospel According to St. John* (trans. Kevin Smyth et al.; 3 vols.; New York: Herder & Herder; Seabury; Crossroad, 1968–1982), 3:205-9.

[20]On these expressions, see Leander E. Keck, "Derivation as Destiny: 'Of-Ness' in Johannine Christology, Anthropology, and Soteriology," in *Exploring the Gospel of John: In Honor of D. Moody Smith* (ed. R. Alan Culpepper and C. Clifton Black; Louisville: Westminster John Knox, 1996), pp. 274-88.

[21]This dominical usage was taken up by the church (Jn 21:23; 1 Jn 3:13-14; 5:16; 3 Jn 3, 5, 10; Apoc

munity in strained dialogue with the Sanhedrin: "we," "you" (ἡμεῖς, ὑμεῖς [Jn 3:9-11; cf. 4:22]).[22] Corresponding to the Pauline concept of many church members united in Christ's body is the Johannine image of the vine with many branches (Jn 15:1-11).[23]

Later in the Epistles John musters family images to help people in Christian communities see how to relate to one another.[24] He reminds the churches that they are the bearers of orthodoxy and the doers of righteousness (1 Jn 2:19-20, 27-28; 5:1-2; 2 Jn 2, 7-11).[25]

In the Apocalypse the church (ἐκκλησία, 20×) consists of "the saints" (οἱ ἅγιοι [14×]), God's "servants" (δοῦλοι [9×]) and God's "prophets" (8×). The Apocalypse starts with oracles addressed to churches (Apoc 2–3). Symbols for the church include the seven golden lampstands (Apoc 1:12, 20), the 144,000 (Apoc 7:2-8; 14:1-5), the temple and the two witnesses who are also olive trees and lampstands and who testify in the spirit and power of Elijah and of Moses (Apoc 11:1-12), and the woman in the sky clothed with the sun (Apoc 12). Over against the squalid whoredom of Lady Babylon (Apoc 14:8; 16:19; 17:1–19:10) is the glory of Lady Jerusalem (Apoc 12; 19:7; 21:2; 21:9–22:9, 17).[26]

***Origin of the church in the time of the historical Jesus.*** The Fourth Gospel yields information not found in other places about the origins of the church in the ministry of Jesus. It shows more vividly than the Synoptic Gospels do how

---

1:9; 6:11; 12:10; 19:10; 22:9). The family metaphor for the church is less developed in the Gospel than in the Epistles, in spite of the focused readings by Joan Cecelia Campbell, *Kinship Relations in the Gospel of John* (CBQMS 42; Washington, DC: Catholic Biblical Association of America, 2007); Mary L. Coloe, *Dwelling in the Household of God: Johannine Ecclesiology and Spirituality* (Collegeville, MN: Liturgical Press, 2007).

[22]Echoes occur in Peter's speech at John 6:69 and in the use of "we" throughout the First Epistle (e.g., 1 Jn 2:19).

[23]Schweizer, *Church Order*, p. 118. On the communal overtones of the parables of the flock (Jn 10) and of the vine, see John F. O'Grady, "The Good Shepherd and the Vine and the Branches," *BTB* 8 (1977): 86-89; idem, *Individual and Community in John* (Rome: Pontifical Biblical Institute, 1978); Schnackenburg, *St. John*, 3:209-11.

[24]Paul Trebilco, "What Shall We Call Each Other? Part Two: The Issue of Self-Designation in the Johannine Letters and Revelation," *TynBul* 54 (2003): 51-73; Dirk G. van der Merwe, "Eschatology in the First Epistle of John: κοινωνία in the *Familia Dei*," *VerbEccl* 27 (2006): 1045-76; idem, "Family Metaphorics: A Rhetorical Tool in the Epistle of 1 John," *APB* 20 (2009): 89-108. Aspects of this metaphor have been traced back to the Gospel: Mary L. Coloe, "Households of Faith (Jn 4:46-54; 11:1-44): A Metaphor for the Johannine Community," *Pacifica* 13 (2000): 326-35.

[25]John's church has a "profoundly rooted community-consciousness" (Rudolf Schnackenburg, "Is There a Johannine Ecclesiology?" in Taylor, *Companion to John*, p. 248).

[26]Felise Tavo, "The Ecclesial Notions of the Apocalypse in Recent Studies," *CurBR* 1 (2002): 112-36; idem, *Woman, Mother and Bride: An Exegetical Investigation Into the "Ecclesial" Notions of the Apocalypse* (BibTS 3; Leuven: Peeters, 2007).

Jesus' circle began with Galilean followers of John the Baptist. Andrew and another disciple (Jn 1:35-36, 40), Simon Peter (Jn 1:40-42) and Philip (Jn 1:43-44) hailed from the village of Bethsaida, Nathanael from Cana of Galilee (Jn 1:45-51; 21:2). When the Baptist pointed to Jesus as the Lamb of God, the first two of these went with Jesus and stayed with him for the rest of the day. The encounter persuaded them, and soon others, that Jesus was the Messiah (Jn 1:41, 49). In the context of this Johannine call narrative Jesus speaks and people respond by believing in him (Jn 1:38, 39, 42-43, 47, 48, 50-51). Thereby is established a pattern of discipleship for the whole Gospel. The church is constituted by Jesus' word. It is the body of those who receive Jesus' word as the word of God. Jesus prays, "They have kept your word [λόγον]. . . . I have given them the words [ῥήματα] which you gave me, and they have received them, and know in truth that I came from you" (Jn 17:6, 8). In this empirical respect the disciples of Jesus stand out from the world.[27]

For a while the two baptizing movements operated side by side in what some took to be competition (Jn 3:22-23). The Baptist's group bled adherents to that of Jesus (Jn 3:26) until its leader was obliged to counter the envy of some of his votaries: "He must increase, but I must decrease" (Jn 3:30).[28]

A group's self-definition crystallizes out of its inner sense of identity and its recognition by outsiders. At Nicodemus's interview with Jesus the narrator has both men use the plural "we." Each was aware of increasing distance between the subcommunity that he represented and the other, a Pharisee versus Jesus with his followers (Jn 3:2, 11). From John the Baptist, Jesus had taken over the message of the imminent kingdom of God and the rite of baptism (Jn 3:3, 5) that marked out both the Baptist's movement and his own from the more Torah-centered concerns of the scribes and Pharisees (Jn 4:2).[29] Eventually the Pharisees took note that Jesus' group had outgrown the Baptist's, prompting Jesus to withdraw from Judea to Galilee (Jn 4:1). At a sobering moment when many of Jesus' disciples deserted, Peter articulated the common belief of those who stuck with him: "To whom shall we go? . . . We [ἡμεῖς] have believed, and

---

[27]Paul S. Minear, "Logos Ecclesiology in John's Gospel," in *Christological Perspectives: Essays in Honor of Harvey K. McArthur* (ed. Robert F. Berkey and Sarah A. Edwards; New York: Pilgrim, 1982), pp. 95-111.

[28]Jerome H. Neyrey and Richard L. Rohrbaugh, "'He Must Increase, I Must Decrease' (John 3:30): A Cultural and Social Interpretation," *CBQ* 63 (2001): 464-83.

[29]The Synoptic Gospels indicate that the scribes and Pharisees by and large refused John's baptism (Mt 21:23-27 pars.; Mt 21:28-32; Lk 7:30).

have come to know, that you are the Holy One of God" (Jn 6:68-69). When Nicodemus's fellows in the Sanhedrin turned on him for defending Jesus' right to a fair hearing, they isolated Nicodemus with a stinging query about whether he too were from Galilee (Jn 7:52).

Nothing consolidates an emerging group's identity more effectively than ostracization by the established body. John remembers the Pharisees agreeing that anyone who confessed Jesus to be the Christ should be put out of the synagogues (Jn 9:22; 12:42). This policy he attests only for the Judean heartland around Jerusalem, where the influence of the Pharisees was most concentrated. It was a temporary measure; the pluperfect tense in John 9:22 (συνετέθειντο) indicates that it obtains no longer at the time of writing.

By the end of Jesus' ministry there was a line of cleavage between his disciples and "the Jews"—even though his disciples were Jewish (Jn 13:33)—between his disciples and "all men" (Jn 13:35), between his disciples and "the world" (14:17; cf. 14:22). Questioned by Annas the honorary high priest "about his disciples and his teaching" (Jn 18:19), Jesus denied that they were a secret sect. He had always taught in synagogues and in the temple, public places "where all Jews come together," he had said nothing seditious in conclave (Jn 18:20). A chasm had opened between those who saw him as God's agent and those who did not.

## CHURCH IN SALVATION HISTORY

John is aware that the church is heir to God's covenant with Israel[30] and will become the city of God in the age to come. He sums up this truth in the figure of a celestial woman (Apoc 12; 21). She is clothed with the sun, stands on the moon, and has twelve stars in her crown (Apoc 12:1), images that reach back to the patriarchs (Gen 37:9-10). In the great chiasmus of the Apocalypse she becomes the bride of the Lamb.[31] The woman represents the corporate reality of the church that perdures through history, for she is a perfect idea in the mind of God, unassailable and impregnable (Apoc 12:6, 13-16), even as her children—

---

[30]Nils Alstrup Dahl, "The Johannine Church and History," in *Current Issues in New Testament Interpretation: Essays in Honor of Otto A. Piper* (ed. William Klassen and Graydon F. Snyder; PL; London: SCM Press, 1962).

[31]The chiasmus runs as follows. ABCD: Lady Jerusalem (Apoc 12) is attacked by the dragon (Apoc 12), who works through the beast and the false prophet (Apoc 13) and through Lady Babylon (Apoc 14:8; 16:19; 17:6; 18:24); D'C'B'A': Christ overthrows Lady Babylon (Apoc 17:1–19:10), the beast and the false prophet (Apoc 19:11-21) and the dragon (Apoc 20:1-10), then marries Lady Jerusalem (Apoc 21:9).

individual believers—go through the crucible of persecution (Apoc 12:17).[32]

***Covenant-historical framework.*** John being a Palestinian Jew, his view of the church grows out of Israel's consciousness of being the recipient of God's covenantal love. The Old Testament people of God are defined by the twin poles of monotheism and of Israel's special relation to the creator. "Hear, O Israel: The LORD our God, the LORD is one" (Deut 6:4). The Shema declares the nation's bond with God as well as God's unity. An early rabbinic prayer condenses the elements of the covenant: "We are all a people of the Name; we, who received one Torah from the One" (*2 Bar.* 48:23b-24a).

These twin themes are intertwined in Israel's saga. God called Abraham from serving other gods (Josh 24:2-3) and required him to be circumcised as the sign of God's covenant with him and his descendants (Gen 17:2, 4, 7). The plagues against Egypt demonstrated spectacularly that there is no god like Yahweh (Ex 7:5, 17; 8:10; 9:14, 29; 10:2), and that Yahweh makes a distinction between Israel and other nations (Ex 6:7; 7:5; 8:22). At Sinai God formalized his taking of Israel from among the peoples of the earth to be his own possession, a "kingdom of priests and a holy nation" (Ex 19:5-6). Israel learned that there is no other besides him (Deut 4:32-40) and became aware of their privilege in receiving God's statutes: "He has not dealt thus with any other nation; they do not know his ordinances" (Ps 147:20). Throughout the story of Israel's conquest of Canaan and their settlement there until the exile, each regent in succession is evaluated by the prophetic authors according to whether he held the populace to the first two commandments of the Decalogue (e.g., 1 Kings 15:3, 11-14). Stretches of poetry in the Hebrew Bible that contain the strongest asseverations of the unicity of God affirm his jealous commitment to Israel his people (e.g., Deut 32:8-9, 39, 43; Is 43:10-13; 44:6-8).

John takes over this history and makes it that of the church. When the Logos came into the world, he came to "his own people" (τὰ ἴδια, οἱ ἴδιοι [Jn 1:11]). First-century Judea rejected the one sent by God ("his own people received him not" [Jn 1:11]), just as, according to the prophets, many in past generations had opted out of God's favor. God showed himself true nevertheless by sending the Logos to them first. God gave the law through Moses; "grace and truth" came through Jesus Christ (Jn 1:17). This is a salvation-historical sequence, not an opposition in substance, for both dispensations embody grace according to the

---

[32]For a full review of various interpretations of the heavenly woman in Apocalypse 12, see Bertrand Buby, "The Fascinating Woman of Revelation 12," *MS* 50 (1999): 107-26.

preceding verse, "one grace in place of another" (χάριν ἀντὶ χάριτος [Jn 1:16]). In direct continuity with the grace of Torah, through Jesus Christ the world gains the fuller grace of "truth," eschatological reality.

"Israel" remains in the Gospel and the Apocalypse a title of honor, a denomination of the body that enjoys God's promises.[33] Jerusalem is the geographical center of John's ecumene. Over against the Samaritans' rival claim for Mount Gerizim, Jesus points to Mount Zion: "Salvation is from the Jews" (Jn 4:20, 22). In the Apocalypse the multicultural city of God of the new creation still bears the name of Jerusalem (Apoc 21:2, 10).

But in John's outlook God's self-revelation as Father, Son and Holy Spirit puts his unique people in a new light. The Father remains Lord of the covenant as he brings it to fulfillment. Reception of God's final agent, through whom God has confirmed the covenant, marks out the covenant people. And the Spirit makes the will of God expressed in God's commandments spring from the interiority of their hearts.

***People of God the Father: New covenant.*** To denote the relationship between God and human beings mediated by Jesus Christ, several New Testament authors use the term "new covenant," taken from Jeremiah 31:31.[34] These authors include Luke (Lk 22:20), Paul (1 Cor 11:25; 2 Cor 3:6) and the writer to the Hebrews (Heb 8:8, 13; 9:15; 12:24), but not John. The only occurrence of the noun "covenant" (διαθήκη) in the Johannine corpus is in the Apocalypse. At the end of the series of seven trumpets, after the establishment of the everlasting kingdom of God (Apoc 11:15-17), "God's temple in heaven was opened, and the ark of his covenant was seen within his temple" (Apoc 11:19). Here, as in the Old Testament, the ark represents God residing among his people. The projection of this symbol from the deep past onto the blended earthly and heavenly plane of the final order shows that John views the covenants of the sacred history as variations of a single, overarching covenant, "his [God's] covenant." Whatever

---

[33]John uses "Israel" and "Israelite" to denote that portion of Jewry that recognizes Jesus as the Messiah (Jn 1:31, 47, 49; 3:10; 12:13; Apoc 2:14; 7:4; 21:12). Those who reject Jesus are "the Jews." See Severino Pancaro, "The Relationship of the Church to Israel in the Gospel of St. John," *NTS* 21 (1975): 396-405.

[34]The concept of an eschatological covenant is based widely in the Old Testament. Certain passages in the Pentateuch peer forward in time beyond Israel's exilic chastening for persistent violations of the Sinaitic covenant to a brighter day when Israel will repent, return to God with circumcised heart, and keep his statutes (Lev 26:40-45; Deut 30). All three major prophets know of a covenant that will last forever (Is 42:6; 49:8; 54:10; 55:3; 59:20-21; 61:8; Jer 31:31-34; 32:40; 33:19-26; Ezek 16:60-63; 34:25-31; 36:24-31; 37:24-28); note also Hosea 2:19-23; Malachi 3:1.

new elements come to the fore in connection with Christ amount not to a departure from the way God has acted in the past but rather to a fulfillment of his long-term plan. That view accords with John's emphasis on the continuity between Moses and Jesus Christ (Jn 1:16-17; 2:9), and with a conservative mindset that was content to minister among nomistic Jews in Judea.

Although John speaks but once of the "covenant," several elements that together make up the covenant concept appear in his writings. These include at least God's presence, protection, instruction, statutes and peace.[35]

*God's presence.* Often in the Old Testament God's exclusive bond with Israel is compared to a marriage (e.g., Is 50:1; 61:10; 62:5; Jer 2:2, 32; 3:1; Ezek 16; Hos 1–3). This metaphor informs Johannine language about the church as the bride of Christ (Jn 3:29; Apoc 19:7; 21:2, 9; 22:17). The marrow of the Old Testament covenant relation was God's dwelling among his people. God promised to live among Abraham's offspring and be God to them (Gen 17:7-8), a promise that he kept by making his glory reside in the tabernacle/temple.[36] Corresponding to this, Jesus' incarnation marked the coming of the divine Logos to pitch tent among human beings (Jn 1:14; 2:18-22). A further installment of God's presence is the gift of the Paraclete (Jn 14:3, 16-18, 20, 23, 28; 16:7, 16). The descriptions of God's everlasting abode in the final order echo Old Testament phraseology.[37]

---

[35]That the Old Testament covenant concept informs John's writings has been a strengthening conviction of scholars. Edward Malatesta traced covenantal themes in 1 John (*Interiority and Covenant: A Study of εἶναι ἐν and μένειν ἐν in the First Letter of Saint John* [AnBib 69; Rome: Biblical Institute Press, 1978]). John's concept of love has the structure of nuptial, social and religious covenants (Yves Simoens, *La gloire d'aimer: structures stylistiques et interprétatives dans le Discours de la Cène [Jn 13–17]* [AnBib 90; Rome: Biblical Institute Press, 1981], pp. 200-250; Johns Varghese, *The Imagery of Love in the Gospel of John* [AnBib 177; Rome: Gregorian and Biblical Press, 2009]). John Pryor found more covenantal elements in the Fourth Gospel (*John, Evangelist of the Covenant People: The Narrative and Themes of the Fourth Gospel* [Downers Grove, IL: InterVarsity Press, 1992], pp. 148-50, 157-80). Birger Olsson finds a "covenantal background" in 1 John 1:9; 2:3, 7-8, 12-14, 20, 27; 3:9, 23-24; 5:20 ("*Deus Semper Maior?* On God in the Johannine Writings," in *New Readings in John: Literary and Theological Perspectives; Essays from the Scandinavian Conference on the Fourth Gospel in Aarhus 1997* [ed. Johannes Nissen and Siegfried Pedersen; Sheffield: Sheffield Academic Press, 1999], p. 148n11). Several elements of the biblical covenants are listed in Rekha M. Chennattu, *Johannine Discipleship as a Covenant Relationship* (Peabody, MA: Hendrickson, 2006), pp. 58-66. She finds covenant language, themes and patterns in John 1:35-51; 13–17; 20–21. For yet another approach, see Alexander Tsutserov, *Glory, Grace, and Truth: Ratification of the Sinaitic Covenant According to the Gospel of John* (Eugene, OR: Pickwick, 2009).

[36]Ex 25:8; 29:45-46; 40:34-38; Lev 9:24; 11:45; 22:33; 25:38; 26:12; Num 5:3; 35:34; Deut 12:11; 1 Kings 8:10-11; Ps 46:7, 11; Ezek 14:11. Moses predicted that God would forsake Israel in a future generation (Deut 31:16-18). Ezekiel had a vision of God's glory departing from the temple in his day (Ezek 10–11) and not coming back until the eschatological commonwealth (Ezek 43:2-5; 44:4).

[37]Apoc 21:3, 7, 22; 22:1, 3-4; cf. Lev 26:45; Ezek 11:20; 34:30; 36:28; 37:23, 26-28; 43:7; Zech 2:5, 10; 8:3.

*God's protection.* The God of the covenant kept the patriarchs and their progeny from all harm so that he could fulfill his promises to their descendants (Gen 28:15, 20; Num 6:24; Deut 32:10; Ps 105:8-15). John believes that God acts similarly through Jesus to protect his flock (Jn 6:37-40; 10:27-30; 17:11-19), keep them from sin (1 Jn 5:18), preserve them to the end in a hostile world (Apoc 12:6, 13-16), and shield them from the plagues with which he will test the inhabitants of the earth (Apoc 3:10; 7:2-3).

*God's instruction.* Having God's words is one of the boons that he gives to his people. As God made himself known in the Old Testament (Ps 147:19-20; Is 59:21), so also he does through Jesus according to John (Jn 1:1, 18; 6:68; 17:8, 17, 19; 2 Jn 2). Heeding God's words leads to knowledge of God. In the time of the new covenant, Jeremiah predicted, all members of the community would know God (Jer 31:34). The eternal life that Jesus offers is to know God (Jn 17:3), and such knowledge distinguishes his disciples from the world (Jn 6:45; 17:25-26; 1 Jn 2:20-21, 27; 5:20).

*God's statutes.* All the biblical covenants stipulate things that the human partner must do in order to continue enjoying God's favor,[38] and in John's thought the divine-human relationship has the same structure. As we saw in chapter 8, those who love Jesus will keep his commandments, especially to love one another, for God's commandments are not burdensome (1 Jn 5:3). Jesus' words are not imposed upon his followers but rather abide within them (Jn 14:26; 15:7, 15; 16:13), as the prophets said would be the case in the new covenant (Deut 30:6; Ps 40:6-8; Is 59:21; Jer 31:33; Ezek 11:19-20; 36:26-27).[39]

*God's peace.* God made covenants to bestow well-being on his human subjects (Num 25:12; Is 54:10; Ezek 34:25; 37:26; Mal 2:5). Likewise, Jesus left peace (*shalom*) with his followers (Jn 14:27; 16:33; 20:19, 21, 26).

Though John makes use of covenantal motifs, he gives no quotations or unmistakable allusions to any of the chief "new covenant" passages of the Old Testament. Yet he speaks of a "new" commandment, one that is old in content, in that it requires love, but new in that Jesus has, by the pattern of his life and death, spearheaded its full implementation in the community that he founded (Jn 13:34; 1 Jn 2:7-8). And even as Isaiah placed God's "everlasting covenant"

---

[38]Even before the promulgation of the law of Moses the patriarchs had commandments to keep (Gen 18:19; 26:5).

[39]For a fuller exploration of this theme in John's Gospel, see Hanna Stettler, "Die Gebote Jesu im Johannesevangelium (14,15.21; 15,10)," *Bib* 92 (2011): 554-79; in 1 John, Malatesta, *Interiority and Covenant.*

with Israel (Is 61:8) in the setting of "new heavens and a new earth" (Is 65:17; 66:22), so the eternal (αἰώνιος) life that Jesus brings is of a piece with the life of the coming age (αἰών) in the new heaven and earth (Apoc 21:1, 5) with its new Jerusalem (Apoc 3:12; 21:2).

John, then, does not feature the phrase "new covenant," but instead holds that God's one covenant with Israel has attained a wholly new depth in the light of the eschatological coming of God's Son.

**People of God the Son: Christocentricity of the church.** Faith in God through God's incarnate Son distinguishes the church. Jesus declared his body to be the earthly tabernacle of God (Jn 1:14; 2:19, 21). Peter said to Jesus, "We have believed, and have come to know, that you are the Holy One of God" (Jn 6:69), and Jesus to his disciples, "Believe in God, believe also in me" (Jn 14:1).

In this respect, Christianity stands out from its Jewish matrix. After all, most Jews of the first century believed in God the creator, many awaited the Messiah, and Jewish Christians were not the only Palestinians who supposed that the last days were imminent. At least the Qumran sect also pledged themselves to uphold the covenant of God in the belief that the end of the world was near.[40] But for them, as for their rivals the Pharisees, God's self-revelation in Torah was the grid for interpreting the Messiah, not vice versa. Based on the tenet that God gave the Torah once and for all, immutable for all ages to come, their concept of the new covenant, and of themselves as God's eschatological planting, remained within the ambit of Judaism.[41]

The Johannine Christ sums up in his person the covenantal functions and provisions of Torah. In the covenant of Sinai God bound his chosen people to himself under specific terms. Led by Moses, the ancient tribes of Israel vowed to keep God's commandments as the condition on which God would bless

---

[40]They called it the "everlasting covenant," "covenant of repentance," "covenant of steadfast love" or "new covenant." The chief new covenant references are CD-A VI, 19; VIII, 21; CD-B XX, 12; 1QpHab II, 3-4. For further references, see the secondary literature in the next note.

[41]What defined the new covenant for the men of Qumran was an exposition of the Mosaic law given by an inspired interpreter, the priestly Teacher of Righteousness. As far as we know, he never claimed to be God's comprehensive agent of creation, redemption and consummation. On the concept of the covenant at Qumran, see David Noel Freedman and David Miano, "People of the New Covenant," in *The Concept of the Covenant in the Second Temple Period* (ed. Stanley E. Porter and Jaqueline C. R. de Roo; JSJSup 71; Leiden: Brill, 2003), pp. 7-26; Craig A. Evans, "Covenant in the Qumran Literature," in Porter and de Roo, *Concept of the Covenant*, pp. 55-80; Lawrence H. Schiffmann, "The Concept of Covenant in the Qumran Scrolls and Rabbinic Literature," in *The Idea of Biblical Interpretation: Essays in Honor of James L. Kugel* (ed. Hindy Najman and Judith H. Newman; JSJSup 83; Leiden: Brill, 2004), pp. 257-78.

them as his vassals (Ex 19:5, 7-8; 21:1; 24:3-4, 7; 34:27-28). The covenant was concluded with burnt offerings and peace offerings, the sprinkling of the people with some of the blood, and a fellowship meal at which God hosted Moses, the chief priests and seventy elders on the summit (Ex 24:5-6, 8, 9-11). Thereafter God sanctified Israel by giving them statutes and ordinances (Lev 18:1-5). To observe God's directives and to keep his covenant were one and the same thing (e.g., Deut 33:9; 1 Kings 11:11; 2 Kings 17:15; 23:3).

For John, Jesus' was the Lamb's death that took away sin and purchased people for God (Jn 1:29, 36; 19:31-33, 36; Apoc 1:5-6; 5:9-10; 14:4). The only occurrence in the Fourth Gospel of λαός, the common Septuagintal word for God's covenant people, is where the high priest says that one man must die for the people (Jn 11:50; cf. 18:14). Jesus calls his death a self-consecration undertaken that his followers might be consecrated to God (Jn 17:19). This death to benefit others is the norm of the new love mandate, which is at once old (Lev 19:18) and, inspired by Jesus' act, new (Jn 13:34; 15:12, 17; 1 Jn 2:7-8; 3:16). By abiding in the vine, his disciples become fruitful in love and in the keeping of his commandments (Jn 15:1-17). Fidelity to him sets them apart from the world (Jn 15:18–16:4; 17:14, 16, 25; 1 Jn 3:1; 5:19; Apoc 14:4; 18:4).[42] Around Jesus a family of disciples formed whose response to the word of God united them more closely than blood ties.[43] That the risen Christ is the center of the church is signified in the Apocalypse by his appearing in the midst of the seven golden lampstands (Apoc 1:13).

For John, then, Jesus Christ absorbs and fulfills Torah's role as the contract of union God imposed on his covenant people.

***People of God's Spirit: Pneumatic endowment of the church.*** Besides the shift from bare Torah to its actualization in Christ as the basis for God's covenant with humanity, a further factor in John's perspective on the people of God was the coming of God's Spirit. During the final segment of world history, while Jesus' hidden messiahship remains a matter of faith and hope, his community enjoys messianic blessing in the form of endowment with the Spirit-

---

[42]For a study of the ecclesiological themes of John's Gospel with special reference to John 17, see Johan Ferreira, *Johannine Ecclesiology* (JSNTSup 160; Sheffield: Sheffield Academic Press, 1998).

[43]Arguably, Jesus entrusted his widowed mother to the Beloved Disciple rather than to one of his own unbelieving siblings (Jn 19:26-27; cf. 7:5) for the same reason that he declared those who hear the word of God and do it to be his mother and his brothers (Mk 3:34-35). See Johannes Nissen, "Community and Ethics in the Gospel of John," in Nissen and Pedersen, *New Readings in John*, p. 211.

Paraclete. John's pneumatology and ecclesiology interpenetrate each other.[44]

The Old Testament prophets expected God to pour out his Spirit on Israel in the last days. Moses had wished that the Lord would put his spirit on all the people and make them prophets (Num 11:29). But it would have to wait until the days of the Messiah, who himself would be graced with God's Spirit (Is 11:2; 42:1; 62:1). Then there would be an unprecedented distribution of charismata to the rank and file of the faithful (Is 32:15; 34:16; 44:3; Ezek 36:26-27; 37:14; 39:29; Joel 2:28-29; Zech 12:10). John the Baptist predicted that Jesus would be the one to bring this promise to realization (Jn 1:33); John the Evangelist has recorded the event. By the Lord's insufflation, his disciples carry on the mission of the Sent One until he returns (Jn 20:22).

John expresses the vital union of the Spirit and the church in striking ways. What the temple stood for—God's dwelling on earth—came to fulfillment first when the Logos pitched his tabernacle among human beings (Jn 1:14; 2:19, 21), then, secondarily, in the grant of the Spirit to flow like life-giving water out of believers (Jn 7:37-39).[45] As the Father equipped Jesus with the Spirit (Jn 1:32), so Jesus equipped his disciples (Jn 1:33; 20:22). Jesus' sending of the Spirit (Jn 15:26a; 16:7) parallels his sending of the church (Jn 13:20; 17:18; 20:21-23). John's language, inching toward trinitarianism, already generates tripartite formulae naming the figures of the Father, the Son and the Holy Spirit in a single breath (Jn 1:33; 3:34-35; 14:16-17; Rev 1:4-5; 4:5 [in the context of the heavenly throne and the Lamb]). Remarkably often the church appears in the third place.[46]

In John's Gospel teaching about the Spirit-Paraclete and many aspects of ecclesiology are concentrated in the Farewell Discourse.[47] Jesus' love for his own disciples (Jn 13:1) is an image of his Father's love for him (Jn 3:35; 5:20; 10:17), and their reciprocal love for Jesus reflects his love for the Father (Jn 14:31). Divine love flows, then, from Father, to Son, to church (Jn 15:9-10; 17:26). In this way the church becomes a third partner in the mutual love of the Father and the Son (Jn 14:21, 23; 16:27; 17:23; 1 Jn 1:3b). Jesus' promise that his disciples will do "greater works" than he did (Jn 14:12-15) comes about through the power of the Spirit, who indwells them in place of the Son (ἄλλον παράκλητον [Jn

[44]Pierre Le Fort, *Les structures de l'Église militante selon Saint Jean: Étude d'ecclésiologie concrète appliquée au IV évangile et aux épîtres johanniques* (NST 25; Geneva: Labor et Fides, 1970), pp. 169-74.
[45]Taking the "rivers of living water" exuding from the belly of the believer (Jn 7:38) as an allusion to the river of life flowing from under the threshold of the temple in Ezekiel 47:1-12.
[46]Jn 13:20; 14:10, 12, 20-21, 23; 15:9-10; 17:18, 21, 22, 23a, 26; 20:2; 1 Jn 1:3b; 2:24, 27; 5:20; 3 Jn 3.
[47]S. T. Potgieter, "'n Johannese Ekklesiologie?" *VerbEccl* 23 (2002): 502-15.

14:16-17; see also 14:26; 15:26-27; 16:7-13; 20:22]). The Spirit enacts his role as Jesus' witness in the world (Jn 15:26b) through the disciples' witness (Jn 15:27).

By the time John wrote his First Epistle, he could remind his loyal churches of their anointing in order to reassure them over against the claims of heretical secessionists (1 Jn 2:20-21, 27). The Spirit indwells the church as a force greater than any force in the world (1 Jn 4:4).

Throughout the Apocalypse the church has above all a Spirit-driven prophetic function in calling the world to repentance and admonishing it for its its rejection of God. The prophets Moses, Elijah and Jeremiah (Jer 5:14) serve as Old Testament types of the church's prophesying in the last days (Apoc 11:3, 5-7). The unholy trio of the dragon (the devil), the beast (Roman imperial might) and the false prophet (the imperial cult) counterfeit the trinity of God, the Lamb and the prophetic church. Foul and demonic spirits (πνεύματα [Apoc 16:13-14]) stand in direct contrast to the spirits of the prophets (Apoc 22:6). A dual invitation to readers from the Spirit and the bride, "Come," typifies the relation between the two (Apoc 22:17).[48]

Suffused with God's Spirit, the church is Jesus' partner in mission (Jn 17:18), in works (Jn 14:10, 12), in persecution by the world (Jn 13:20), in glory (Jn 17:22) and in a fellowship of love (Jn 14:20-21, 23; 17:26; 1 Jn 1:3b; 5:20).

## THE CONSTITUENCY OF THE ONE PEOPLE OF GOD

The church, then, is for John the people of God's one covenant, bound to God by the Christ who is their Savior and Lord, vivified by the outpouring of the divine Spirit in the last days. Even as John's divine Christology did not dislodge his tenacious Jewish commitment to monotheism, so his conviction that God has chosen Israel did not give way before his recognition that the eschatological ingathering of Gentiles is taking place. God proves faithful to ethnic Israel by performing his promises for the elect from among them, who believe in Jesus Christ.[49] Believing Gentiles too are beneficiaries of God's faithfulness. Criteria for membership consist, on God's side, of election, and, on the human side, of faith in God's agent. Election and faith transcend ethnic and cultural bound-

---

[48]On the relation between God's word and human words in the Apocalypse, see Tobias Nicklas, "Der Ewige spricht in die Zeit—Gotteswort und Menschenwort in der Offenbarung des Johannes," *SS* 9 (2011): 113-22.

[49]On the concept of eschatological Israel in John's Gospel, see Jörn-Michael Schröder, *Das eschatologische Israel im Johannesevangelium: Eine Untersuchung der johanneischen Israel-Konzeption in Joh 2–4 und Joh 6* (NET 3; Tübingen: Francke, 2003).

aries. God's special people, defined by reference to Christ and the Spirit-Paraclete, remains for John a body set apart from the world.

**Inclusion of Gentiles.** That God always intended to have Gentiles together with Jews in his covenant is a consistent teaching of the Old Testament. From the beginning, according to the Hebrew Scriptures, God's covenant with Abraham and his offspring was to spread God's blessing to all peoples. "By you all the families of the earth shall be blessed" (Gen 12:3). Israel's uniqueness is instrumental; it is the organ through which God works to bring salvation to the human race. "May God be gracious to us and bless us . . . that your way may be known upon earth, your saving power among all nations" (Ps 67:1-2). In the end, not only Israel, but also Egypt and Babylon, Philistia and Tyre, and Ethiopia will know God and receive citizenship of Zion (Ps 87:4-6). Assyria and Egypt will be at peace, and Israel will be the third with them, "a blessing in the midst of the earth," for God will declare Egypt to be "my people," Assyria "the work of my hands," and Israel "my heritage" (Is 19:23-25). "Clap your hands, all peoples! Shout to God with loud songs of joy! . . . God reigns over the nations; God sits on his holy throne. The princes of the peoples gather as the people of the God of Abraham" (Ps 47:1, 8-9a).

Inclusion of obedient Gentiles in the people of God in the last days compensates for the cutting off of Jews who prove intractable. The prophets spared no infidel on the basis of an Israelite pedigree. To a society that broke God's covenant Hosea declared in God's name, "You are not my people and I am not your God" (Hos 1:9). Through most of the writing prophets runs the theme of the "remnant" of Israel that will be saved: "For though your people Israel be as the sand of the sea, only a remnant of them will return" (Is 10:22). By means of this remnant God will bring his Abrahamic promises to fruition (Mic 5:7-9; Zech 8:11-13).

In the Gospel of John the true Israelite in whom is no guile is Nathanael, who, on meeting Jesus, immediately hails him as God's Son and King of Israel (Jn 1:47-49). Not birth to a Jewish mother, but rather the birth that God brings about through his Spirit, qualifies a person to enter God's kingdom (Jn 3:3, 5). The blind man, one of the common people (*ʿam hāʾāreṣ*) scorned by the Pharisees, comes to see Jesus as the Son of Man and worships him, while the Pharisees with their expertise in Torah remain blind (Jn 9:35-41). These examples point to reception of God's agent as the criterion of the remnant of Israel.

This criterion admits believing Gentiles to the newly delimited people of God.

Jesus' discourse on mission (Jn 4:34-38) falls in the setting of a visit to Samaria, where a people of mixed ethnicity had a syncretistic religion that had been at loggerheads with the Judaism of Judea since postexilic times. Speaking with the woman at the well, Jesus explained that an era was dawning in which worship in Spirit and truth would replace locality and ritual (Jn 4:21-24). Now, as Samaritans stream to him from the town of Sychar, Jesus observes that the time of harvest has "already" begun (Jn 4:35). Many other Samaritans, John tells us, came to believe that Jesus is "the Savior of the world" (Jn 4:42). John sees the evangelization of a Samaritan village as harbinger of an ecumenical enterprise.

In the parable of the sheepfold Jesus reworks Ezekiel 34 to picture the faithful in Israel as his flock (Jn 10:1-6). Jesus has other sheep, not of this fold, who also will heed his voice (Jn 10:16). His saying, "There shall be one flock, one shepherd" (Jn 10:16b), adapts a prophecy of Ezekiel about the reunification of Israel and Judah under an eschatological David (Ezek 37:17, 19, 22, 24). Now Jews and Gentiles are to be joined in the final community. Those who belong to this flock are sheep who "hear his voice" and "follow him" (Jn 10:3-5, 27), his "own" who know him (Jn 10:14). Gentiles who believe will be full members of the flock. People who do not believe, even if their blood is Jewish, are not his sheep (Jn 10:26).

Commenting on the *sensus plenior* of Caiaphas's statement that it was expedient that one man should die for the people lest the whole nation perish (Jn 11:50), John applies it to the Jewish people and beyond. Jesus died not for the nation only, "but to gather into one the children of God who are scattered abroad" (Jn 11:52).[50] The fact that some Greeks approached Jesus' disciples shortly before his last Passover (Jn 12:20-22) gave Jesus occasion to declare that when he was lifted up in crucifixion, he would draw "all men to myself" (Jn 12:32).

Unlike Matthew's Gospel, which ends with Jesus commanding his apostles to go and make disciples of all nations (Mt 28:18-20), or the book of Acts, which illustrates the spread of the gospel after A.D. 30 from Jerusalem to Samaria and to the ends of the earth (cf. Lk 24:47; Acts 1:8), the writings of John contain no programmatic announcement of a mission to Gentiles. From what was said

---

[50]John A. Dennis, *Jesus' Death and the Gathering of True Israel: The Johannine Appropriation of Restoration Theology in the Light of John 11:47-52* (WUNT 2/217; Tübingen: Mohr Siebeck, 2006). For an attempt to trace the actual history of the Johannine community's reception of Gentiles, see Xavier Levieils, "Juifs et Grecs dans la communauté johannique," *Bib* 82 (2001): 51-78.

above about John's activities in the first-century church, it is clear that John watched with interest and approval as others conducted the worldwide mission. His own calling was, for most of his career, to the more patient task of evangelizing among the Jewish people in and around Jerusalem (Gal 2:9).

Israel's privilege as God's royal priests among the nations (Ex 19:6) remains for the author of the Apocalypse the charter of the new holy people. By the time John wrote that book, the catholic church in Asia had more Gentiles than Jewish Christians. To a largely Gentile readership John can write that Jesus Christ by his blood made "us" a "kingdom, priests to his God and Father" (Apoc 1:6). Anyone who conquers will become a pillar in the temple of Jesus' God (Apoc 3:12). The hymn to the Lamb is even more explicit: the Lamb ransomed people for God "from every tribe and tongue and people and nation," and precisely these he has made "a kingdom and priests to our God" (Apoc 5:9-10). Those who come out of the great tribulation, "from every nation, from all tribes and peoples and tongues" (Apoc 7:9), are "before the throne of God" as royal attendants and "serve him day and night in his temple" as priests (Apoc 7:15). For a thousand years "they shall be priests of God and of Christ, and they shall reign with him" (Apoc 20:6). The description of the eschatological glory of Jerusalem has elements both hieratic and regal (Apoc 21:9–22:5).[51] John's bold application to believing Gentiles of Exodus 19:6, the verse that defines Israel's unique prerogatives, is thematic and elaborately spun.[52]

***Israel remains the nucleus of the covenant people.*** Yet Israel's privilege as the primary object of God's covenantal fidelity persists. Everywhere that Jews and Gentiles appear side by side in the one people of God, the Jewish element takes precedence. Those God keeps through the great tribulation are symbolized first as 144,000 Israelites (twelve thousand from each of the twelve tribes) (Apoc 7:4-8), then in juxtaposition as a multinational throng (Apoc 7:9-12). The celestial woman who represents the people of God stands amidst the sun, the

---

[51]The hieratic elements fall in Apocalypse 21:11-22: the glory of God that replaces the temple (Apoc 21:11, 22; cf. Ex 40:34), the cubical inner sanctum (Apoc 21:16; cf. 1 Kings 6:20) and the adornment with twelve precious stones (Apoc 21:19-20; cf. Ex 28:17-21). Royal elements come in Apocalypse 21:23–22:5: the tribute brought by the kings of the earth (Apoc 21:24-26), the throne of God and of the Lamb (Apoc 22:1, 3) and a court of servants who will reign with him forever (Apoc 21:3-5).

[52]Thereby is obliterated the alleged distinction between Israel and the church on which the entire hermeneutical edifice of dispensationalism rests. See Martin Hasitschka, "Die Priestermetaphorik der Apokalypse als Ausdruck der Verbundenheit der auf Erden lebenden mit den zur Auferstehung gelangten Christen," *SNTSU* 29 (2004): 179-92; Philip L. Mayo, *"Those Who Call Themselves Jews": The Church and Judaism in the Apocalypse of John* (PTMS 60; Eugene, OR: Pickwick, 2006).

moon and twelve stars (Apoc 12:1), figures lifted from Joseph's dream of Jacob, Rachel and the patriarchs (Gen 37:9-10). Her offspring are "those who keep the commandments of God and bear testimony to Jesus" (Apoc 12:17; cf. 14:12). Together they sing "the song of Moses, the servant of God, and the song of the Lamb" (Apoc 15:3). Redeemed society is centered in "the holy city Jerusalem" (Apoc 21:10), even if the gates stay open permanently for the nations to enter (Apoc 21:25). In two septipartite chiasms that depict the city (Apoc 21:9-22; 21:23–22:5), the former has the names of the sons of Israel on the gates and the names of the (Jewish) apostles of the Lamb on the foundations of the wall (Apoc 21:12, 14), commingled with numerology focusing on the integer twelve and its multiples (Apoc 21:12-14, 16-17, 19-21), while the latter shows how the city brings light and healing to "the nations" (Apoc 21:24, 26; 22:2).[53]

But status as God's chosen people does not give Jews immunity from divine judgment for downright impiety. Those who could not bear to hear the word of God's accredited agent Jesus declared to be of their father the devil (Jn 8:43-44). "The reason why you do not hear them is that you are not of God" (Jn 8:47). "You do not belong to my sheep" (Jn 10:26). And when Jews of Asia took it upon themselves to inform against Christians to the Roman authorities ("slander"), resulting in imprisonments and martyrdoms, the prophet of the Apocalypse disowned them as Jews, calling them "a synagogue of Satan" who say that they are Jews but are not (Apoc 2:9-10; 3:9). Just as Isaiah had promised that those who oppressed Israel would come bending low and bowing at the feet of Jerusalem in its eschatological glory (Is 60:14), so the Christ of John's Apocalypse will make these Jews come and bow down before the feet of his faithful ones "and learn that I have loved you" (Apoc 3:9).

## Divine Qualities of the Church

In the Johannine thought world the church is, to be sure, a congeries of unworthy sinners whom the Lamb ransomed for God, whose sins are forgiven. But more than that, God invites them into the fellowship of the trinitarian life, takes them up into cooperation with him, and has sent them into the world to carry on the work of the sent one in the power of the other Paraclete.[54] The

---

[53]One of two concentric ABCDC'B'A' patterns consists of the elements holy temple-city (Apoc 21:10-11, 22), gates of the wall (Apoc 21:12-13, 21), foundations of the wall (Apoc 21:14, 19-20) and city square (Apoc 21:15-17). The other has God as the city's light (Apoc 21:23; 22:5), the nations serving God (Apoc 21:24-26; 22:3b-4), no more curse (Apoc 21:27; 22:3a) and river of life (Apoc 22:1-2).

[54]"The Church in fact is assigned a quite definite position in the work of salvation" (Schnackenburg,

church, which is of the creation and, unlike the Father and the Son, has no life in itself, participates in moral and spiritual qualities of God. This elevated view of the church, of which we see glimmers throughout the Johannine corpus, appears with special clarity in the last prayer of Jesus (Jn 17:6-26).

In general terms, the people whom God gave the Son out of the world exist "in" God's "name" (Jn 17:11-12), even as Jesus came in his Father's name (Jn 5:43; 12:13; cf. 17:6, 26) and did works in his Father's name (Jn 10:25). In the Apocalypse the name of the Lamb and of his Father is inscribed on the foreheads of the 144,000 (Apoc 14:1; 22:4), and the risen Christ promises to write these names forever on anyone who conquers (Apoc 3:12). Besides a share in God's name, Christ gives the church a share in God's glory (Jn 17:22), in Christ's other-worldly origin and character ("they are not of the world" [Jn 17:14, 16]) and final destiny ("that they also . . . may be with me where I am" [Jn 17:24]).[55] To this end God keeps them as they traverse their earthly path (Jn 17:11-12, 15; 1 Jn 5:18; Apoc 1:10). The church is more than a merely human society; it represents God to other human beings.

To be specific, the church as John understands it embodies the divine virtues of truth, love, unity and universality. Of these, truth and love are prominent in John's Epistles, love and unity in the Gospel, and universality in all John's writings.

***Truth in doctrine.*** Jesus prayed that his followers might be consecrated in the truth, which is God's word (Jn 17:17, 19). The word of the one who spoke the world into being is not judged according to reality, for it configures and judges reality. Christians, distinct from the world in which they they live, are set apart to address the world in God's name and with his authority. Even as prophets spoke to Israel on God's behalf, so Christ's church is the mouthpiece by which God addresses the world until by his fiat he makes it new. The Spirit-Paraclete "will bear witness to me; and you also are witnesses" (Jn 15:26b-27).

That the church has a prophetic role in the world is developed in John's Epistle and in the Apocalypse. The Epistles are set against a social background in which people purporting to be apostles, prophets or teachers would travel from town to town offering messages from God for the edification of Christian

"Johannine Ecclesiology?" p. 248). On the earthly community as the means to fellowship with God, see Dirk G. van der Merwe, "'Having Fellowship with God' According to 1 John: Dealing with the Intermediation and Environment through Which and in Which It is Constituted," *AcTS* 8 (2006): 165-92.
[55]Keck, "Derivation as Destiny."

assemblies and receiving hospitality from them in return (Eph 4:11; 3 Jn 5-6; *Did.* 11–13). Some mavericks were propagating a Christology at odds with the teaching of the apostles.[56] At the very outset of the First Epistle the author reminds readers that the apostolic proclamation, founded on direct sensory experience of the word of life, is what conveys to them the life that was with the Father and was manifested once for all in history (1 Jn 1:1-3).[57] In a paragraph about testing prophetic messages to see whether the spirits are from God, John points out that the world hears false prophets and will not listen to "us" who have the unconquerable Spirit (1 Jn 4:1-6). In the Apocalypse an equal danger is posed by "Nicolaitans." All that we know reliably about the Nicolaitans is what the Apocalypse itself tells us: they did works that Christ hated (Apoc 2:6). In particular, they encouraged church people to eat food sacrificed to idols and to practice sexual immorality (Apoc 2:14-15; cf. 2:20). The church at Ephesus is commended for testing and exposing false apostles (Apoc 2:2). In contrast to the counterfeit prophets, the church is symbolized by the lampstands of the Levitical menorah beaming God's light on earth (Apoc 1:12, 20; 11:4). It is also represented by two prophetic witnesses modeled after Moses, Elijah and Jeremiah of old (Apoc 11:3, 5-6).[58] Behind this conception of the church probably is Joel's prediction that in the last days all the people of God would prophesy (Joel 2:28-29). John's view is not that the church contains some prophets, but rather that since the moment when the risen Christ breathed upon it the Holy Spirit (Jn 20:22), the entire church from greatest to least has inherited the mantle of the prophets of old (Apoc 11:3-10, 18; 16:6; 18:20, 24; 22:6, 9).[59]

Against teachings of pseudoapostles and false prophets Christ's church enjoys the bulwark of an anointing from God that gives them knowledge of the things of God (1 Jn 2:20-21, 27). God's Spirit abiding in believers engenders

---

[56]They denied "the Father and the Son" (1 Jn 2:22-23) and that Jesus Christ had come in flesh (1 Jn 4:2-3; 2 Jn 7). This sounds like a denial that the human Jesus was the Son of God incarnate. They could have been crude Docetists like those opposed by Ignatius (Ign. *Trall.* 10:1; Ign. *Smyrn.* 2:1; 4:2; 5:2; 7:1) or followers of teachers such as Basilides or Cerinthus, who agreed that the Spirit-Christ descended on Jesus at his baptism and departed before his crucifixion (Irenaeus, *Haer.* 1.24.4; 1.26.1).

[57]Georg Strecker, *The Johannine Letters: A Commentary on 1, 2, and 3 John* (ed. Harold W. Attridge; trans. Linda M. Maloney; Hermeneia; Minneapolis: Fortress, 1996), pp. 16-19.

[58]The number "two," like all numbers in the Apocalypse, is not to be taken literally; rather, it underscores the church's function of testifying against the world before the divine tribunal, for in capital cases there must be at least two witnesses (Num 35:30; Deut 17:6; 19:15).

[59]Schweizer, *Church Order*, pp. 134-36.

in them an intuitive understanding, a nose that recoils from the stink of doctrinal falsehood. This inner sense belongs to the laity, is a *sensus fidei* ("sense of the faith") residing in the body politic, hence a *sensus fidelium* ("sense of the faithful"). Even the authority of one who knew Jesus adds nothing essential to what the Spirit has taught: "you have no need that any one should teach you" (1 Jn 2:27).[60] Yet it does not render apostolic ministry superfluous. The elder wrote the letter in which he says this very thing. The magisterium of the church upholds, clarifies and defends truth inculcated by the Spirit in the first instance.[61]

John's view of catechetical tradition was conservative, negative toward novel ideas about Christ.[62] "Let what you heard from the beginning abide in you" (1 Jn 2:24). The starting point (ἀρχή) of the Christian movement is normative (1 Jn 2:7, 24; 3:11; 2 Jn 5-6). Jesus is the model for disciples (Jn 13:34-35; 15:10, 12; 1 Jn 2:8), and their duty is to "keep" (τηρεῖν) his word[63] and "abide" (μένειν) in it (Jn 8:31; 15:7; 1 Jn 2:14, 24, 27; 2 Jn 2, 9).[64] What God's anointing teaches will always be consistent with what it taught in the past (1 Jn 2:27). Some people "go ahead" and "do not abide in the doctrine [διδαχή] of Christ" (2 Jn 9). These progressives are deceivers and antichrists. The ravings that they foment have the potential to rob believers of their reward. Such teachers have neither the Father nor the Son. They are not to be offered hospitality or even greeted (2 Jn 7-10). Truth is defined by God's word (Jn 17:17), and God does not change or evolve. The witness of the apostles remains the firm foundation of the church even into the permanent era to come (Apoc 21:14).[65]

In Asia the Christians to whom John circulated the Apocalypse lived in a society that saw advantages in meeting every demand of Rome, and they

---

[60]Garrett C. Kenney, *Leadership in John: An Analysis of the Situation and Strategy of the Gospel and the Epistles of John* (Lanham, MD: University Press of America, 2000), pp. 121-22.

[61]Le Fort, *Structures de l'Église*, pp. 161-62.

[62]Hans Conzelmann, "Was von Anfang war," in *Neutestamentliche Studien für Rudolf Bultmann: Zu seinem 70. Geburtstag am 20. August 1954* (ed. Walther Eltester; BZNW 21; Berlin: Töpelmann, 1957), pp. 194-201; Schweizer, *Church Order*, pp. 125-26; Rodney A. Whitacre, *Johannine Polemic: The Role of Tradition and Theology* (SBLDS 67; Chico, CA: Scholars Press, 1982); Lieu, *Theology*, pp. 94-97; Strecker, *Johannine Letters*, pp. 244-49; Horst Hahn, *Tradition und Neuinterpretation im ersten Johannesbrief* (Zürich: Theologischer Verlag, 2009).

[63]Jn 8:51-52; 14:15, 21-24; 15:10; 17:6; 1 Jn 2:3-5; 3:22, 24; 5:3; Apoc 1:3; 2:26; 3:3, 8, 10; 12:17; 14:12; 16:15; 22:7, 9.

[64]Klaus Haacker, *Die Stiftung des Heils: Untersuchungen zur Struktur der johanneischen Theologie* (AzTh 1/47; Stuttgart: Calwer, 1972), pp. 69-90.

[65]David Mathewson, "A Note on the Foundation Stones in Revelation 21.14, 19-20," *JSNT* 25 (2003): 487-98.

sometimes had to choose between confessing the lordship of Christ or of Caesar. John envisages some being called upon to bear witness in Roman courts with their necks slated for the executioner's chopping block (Apoc 20:4; cf. 6:9). To tell the truth and not a lie in such a setting is a prime virtue (Apoc 14:5; 21:8, 27; 22:15).

In answer to Jesus' forward-looking prayer, the church as truth-bearer enjoys divine preservation. Jesus had entrusted God's word, which is truth, to them (Jn 17:14, 17). Jesus' request was that God sanctify them in the truth in the midst of the world (Jn 17:17, 19b). For this reason, John had complete confidence toward the close of the first century in the church's infallibility. The truth not only "abides in us" but also "will be with us for ever" (2 Jn 2). This is not a claim that an individual Christian, church leader or even sector of the church would never lapse into error. An influential heretical movement arose out of a number of churches before John's eyes, throwing those whom he cared for into doubt and requiring his pastoral intervention. But they "were not of us," as they demonstrated by leaving (1 Jn 2:19). They were a branch that rotted and, in the providence of God, was lopped from the stock (Jn 15:2, 6). Among those who abide in the vine, the truth of the gospel will endure to the end of time and so will never be lost in the world of darkness.

*Truth of walk: Righteousness, goodness, holiness.* Another mark of the church is truth of life. "One who does the will of God abides for ever" (1 Jn 2:17). Truth is not only cognitive and doctrinal, but also volitional and moral (Jn 3:21; 8:32; 1 Jn 1:8; 2:8; 3:18; 2 Jn 4; 3 Jn 3, 4, 8), and so comprises good deeds. Goodness, like truth, will become apparent at the last judgment (Jn 5:29) and is to be imitated (3 Jn 11). One who does righteousness (ὁ ποιῶν τὴν δικαιοσύνην) or does good (ὁ ἀγαθοποιῶν) is born of God (1 Jn 2:29; 3 Jn 11), as opposed to one who practices sin or lawlessness, who is of the devil (1 Jn 3:4-10).

In the Johannine Epistles this mark operates, together with orthodoxy, to distinguish between the people of God and schismatics. The church is made up of people who walk in the light as God is in the light (1 Jn 1:6-7), who keep God's commandments and walk as Jesus walked (1 Jn 2:3-6), who do not love the world or the things in the world (1 Jn 2:15-17), who do righteousness (1 Jn 2:29; 3:7, 10, 12), who purify themselves as he is pure (1 Jn 3:3), who demonstrate love for God by keeping his commandments and conquering the world (1 Jn 5:2-4).

In John's varied vocabulary the church is also "holy" (ἅγιος). Jesus is the Holy One of God par excellence (Jn 6:69; 10:36). He consecrated (ἁγιάζειν) himself so that his disciples may be consecrated (Jn 17:17, 19), and he baptized them in the Holy Spirit (Jn 1:33; 7:39; 14:26; 20:22). Therefore throughout the Apocalypse they are "the saints" (οἱ ἅγιοι, "holy ones" [Apoc 5:8; 8:3, 4; 11:18; 13:7, 10; 14:12; 16:6; 17:6; 18:20, 24; 19:8; 20:9; 22:21]). This designation was apropos for churches in Asia, where they were under pressure to conform to Roman values at the cost of commitment to Christ, illustrated especially by the severely compromised churches at Sardis and Laodicea (Apoc 3:1-6, 14-22). The saints are those who rise above their environment and do righteous deeds (δικαιώματα [Apoc 19:8]). John pictures them wearing fine white linen (Apoc 3:4-5, 18; 6:11; 7:9, 13; 19:8, 14), taking their place in his sacred temple (Apoc 3:12; 7:15; 11:1-2), and comprising God's holy city (Apoc 11:2; 21:2, 10; 22:19). They are, metaphorically, male celibates who have kept themselves from women, echoing the Old Testament prophetic representation of idolatry as spiritual fornication (Apoc 14:4). A voice from heaven summons God's people to come out of Babylon lest they take part in her sins and share in her plagues (Apoc 18:4). Those who resist the beast to the bitter end are declared blessed and holy (Apoc 20:6). A dichotomy between the world and the church is seen in the opposite destinies of Lady Babylon (Apoc 17:1–19:10) and of Lady Jerusalem (Apoc 21:9–22:9). "Let the evildoer still do evil, and the filthy still be filthy, and the righteous still do right, and the holy still be holy" (Apoc 22:11).

So the church in the world, like Israel in the ancient Near East, is a people separate from others, holy to God.

*Love.* Another note of the church is love for God and for one another. Jesus provided the supreme example of self-abnegating service to others and commanded his disciples to do the same (Jn 13:12-17).[66] The new commandment to love one another (Jn 13:34-35) demands a quality of mutual love that becomes possible only in a community that recognizes the love of God in Jesus and imitates it in practice.[67] Given that one purpose of the intracommunal love command is to draw the world to know God, this kind of love is anything but sectarian (Jn 13:35; 17:21, 23).[68]

---

[66]A "cardinal tenet of Johannine theology" is that "Jesus' love for his disciples is recapitulated in their love for one another" (D. Moody Smith, "Theology and Ministry in John," in *Johannine Christianity: Essays on Its Setting, Sources, and Theology* [Columbia: University of South Carolina Press, 1984], p. 216).

[67]The command is developed further in John 15:12-17; 1 John 2:7-11; 3:11-18; 4:7–5:5; 2 John 4-6; 3 John. On these passages, see Jörg Augenstein, *Das Liebesgebot im Johannesevangelium und in den Johannesbriefen* (BWANT 7/14; Stuttgart: Kohlhammer, 1993); Nissen, "Community and Ethics"; Jan G. van der Watt, "Ethics and Ethos in the Gospel According to John," *ZNW* 97 (2006): 147-76.

[68]Enno Edzard Popkes, *Die Theologie der Liebe Gottes in den johanneischen Schriften: Zur Semantik der*

Closely related to love is "fellowship" (κοινωνία). Jesus invited his first disciples to join the eternal fellowship that he shares with the Father, and they in turn welcomed others into this joy (1 Jn 1:3).[69] In John's First Epistle the fellowship of love provides another test, besides orthodox Christology and moral truth, that distinguishes the church from those who seceded (1 Jn 2:10; 3:10-18, 23; 4:7–5:3). Willful breaking of fellowship by the latter group was in itself a breach of love. Also they may not have been as charitable to their own needy as John and his brother James encouraged the church to be (Jas 1:27; 2:15-16; 1 Jn 3:11-18). Charity to orphans and widows became a hallmark of the Christian community.[70]

Truth is primary, definitive and foundational for the Christian concept of love. The elder loves a sister church "in the truth" (2 Jn 1). Fellowship with one another is conditioned upon all walking in the light (1 Jn 1:7). If people professing to be brothers and sisters in Christ depart into doctrinal heresy, showing contempt for the word of God, those who maintain the apostolic teaching are neither to greet them nor to offer them hospitality, for to do so would be to participate in their wicked work (2 Jn 10-11). Should some, such as the Nicolaitans, choose to walk in the way of the world rather than of Christ, Christ commends hatred of their works and says that he too hates those works (Apoc 2:6). Since there is no middle term between light and darkness, there can be no love for evil as such. Love can only proclaim the truth to those in darkness in the hope that they will come to the light (Apoc 22:11, 17).

*Unity.* Loving relationships among those who agree in the truth manifest unity. God's church is but one.

In the Fourth Gospel Jesus states God's intent to unite his followers: "There shall be one flock, one shepherd" (Jn 10:16). Jesus died, says John, to gather into one the scattered children of God, consisting of believing Gentiles together with the elect from the Jewish nation (Jn 11:51-52). Toward the end of his ministry as he peered into the future, Jesus prayed for his Father to keep his followers who would remain in the world, that concord might prevail among them (Jn 17:11, 20-23).

---

*Liebe und zum Motivkreis des Dualismus* (WUNT 2/197; Tübingen: Mohr Siebeck, 2005), pp. 264-68, 316-54.

[69]"The 'intra-divine' love mentioned so frequently in the Gospel finds expression in the relationship between the Son and the disciples, which in its turn shapes the fellowship of the disciples" (Olsson, "*Deus Semper Maior?*" p. 160).

[70]Christian apologists of the second century explained to outsiders that alms collected at the weekly Eucharist were used to relieve those in the community who were in want (Justin, *Apol. 1* 67; Tertullian, *Apol.* 39).

Unity among Christians is founded on that of the Father and the Son.[71] The Son claimed to be identical in being with the Father (neuter ἕν, "one thing"); precisely he is the sole shepherd of the flock (Jn 10:16). What will keep the sheep is the Father's singular name granted to the Son, in which the church too is safeguarded (Jn 17:11), and the Father's incomparable glory, given to the Son and passed on to his disciples (Jn 17:22).[72] This divine name, this divine glory, unites human elements without homogenizing their native diversity. Even as the Father and the Son are distinct personal entities whose deeper unity consists partly in the fact that they indwell each other ("even as you, Father, are in me, and I in you" [Jn 17:21, cf. 17:23]), perfectly sharing each other's thoughts, intentions, resolutions, desires and delights, so the unity of the church is a matter of mutual love and common purpose among individuals and local communities. Such oneness does not necessarily mean sharing a monolithic institutional life, desirable though institutional structures are as visible symbols of unity. More profoundly, it means affirming the divine life in one another, fostering its welfare, and cooperating in mission. Jesus' goal in praying for his disciples to reflect the unity of divine love was that the world may believe and know the Father has sent him (Jn 17:21, 23).

Christian unity is impaired neither by defection nor by secession from the church of those not chosen. For a time, Judas Iscariot associated with the other disciples whom Jesus invited to follow him. But Jesus knew in advance that he was a devil (Jn 6:70-71; 13:18-19). Judas's financial graft as treasurer (Jn 12:6) already showed that he was not born of God, and in the end he fell away and became the agent of Satan who betrayed his Lord (Jn 13:2, 27). Because he proved to be the "son of perdition" (Jn 17:12), he was no exception to the rule that Jesus "lost not one" of those whom the Father had given him (Jn 18:9).

In much the same way, a body of people had split off from the believers to whom John directed his First Epistle. The Johannine Epistles have the distinction that they are the only writings in the canon of the New Testament that look back on a division of the visible church as a fait accompli.[73] John makes

---

[71] John F. Randall, "The Theme of Unity in John 17:20-23," *ETL* 41 (1965): 373-94; Le Fort, *Structures de l'Église*, p. 108.

[72] "God's love, which is wholly directed to the Son, also comprises all who are in communion with the Son (16:27) and is, therefore, also to flow as a unifying force to all who are united with Christ (17:26)" (Schnackenburg, "Johannine Ecclesiology?" p. 254).

[73] The Tübingen school in the mid-nineteenth century adopted F. C. Baur's notion of a prolonged conflict between Jewish (Petrine) and Gentile (Pauline) Christianities, based on his reading of Acts 6; 1 Corinthians 1:10-17; Galatians 2:11-14; and the *Clementine Homilies*. But Baur's construct

it plain that the departure of the secessionists was no division among believers, for their denial of the Father and the Son showed them to be antichrists. They had associated with the church for a while and "went out from us," but "they were not of us" (1 Jn 2:19). Their hatred of the believing community amounted in effect to fratricide according to the model of Cain (1 Jn 3:12-13).[74] Not every parting of professing Christians, then, is a tear in the fabric of Christ's church. The unity of those who refuse to compromise truth or goodness stands out all the more solidly when a putrid branch falls to wither and die.

For the formal severance of bodies of authentic believers from communion with one another, as happened between Eastern Orthodoxy and the Western papacy (climaxing in 1054) and later between the Western hierarchy and the Protestant Reformers (1517 onwards), neither the Johannine writings nor anything else from the period of the New Testament furnishes a precedent.

*Catholicity.* The church, thus manifesting unity in truth, goodness and love, is extensive and inclusive in both time and space. Catholicity is therefore yet another mark of the church of God.

Jesus prayed not only for his immediate disciples but also for future ones who would believe in him through their word (Jn 17:20). Not all would have the opportunity that Thomas had to touch the risen Lord, and Jesus pro-

---

tendentiously served a passing intellectual fad—the Hegelian dialectic of history—and rode rough-shod over its supporting texts rather than exegeting them. Acts 6 points to cultural diversity and different theological emphases within subcommunities of the earliest Palestinian Jewish church, not to strife between Jewish and Gentile Christianities (Martin Hengel, "Between Jesus and Paul," in *Between Jesus and Paul: Studies in the Earliest History of Christianity* [trans. John Bowden; London: SCM Press, 1983], pp. 1-29). Paul himself testified that he submitted his gospel to Peter, among others, for review and received the right hand of fellowship (Gal 2:1-9; 1 Cor 15:5-11), and that the two operated independently in mission with mutual respect (Gal 2:9-10). There was no "dispute" between them at Antioch according to Galatians 2:11-14, as is so often alleged. Paul publicly called Peter on the carpet for weakening in the presence of "the circumcision faction" from Judea so as to violate the understanding of the gospel and its consequences for table fellowship with Gentile con-verts that Peter and Paul shared (Gal 2:14). Immature factions in the church at Corinth flocked around outstanding personalities, but there is no evidence from the time of Paul that they broke fellowship with one another and went separate ways. Corinth participated, as far as we know, in Paul's collection (1 Cor 16:1-4; 2 Cor 8–9), which had as one of its objectives the consolidation of Paul's Gentile converts with the sending church of Jerusalem into a catholic whole (Rom 15:27; 2 Cor 8:14). The *Clementine Homilies* show Peter opposing Simon Magus, not Paul; contra Baur, the former is no cipher for the latter. The ostensible century-long squabble between Jewish and Gentile Christianities is a chimera that passed from an influential scholar's imagination into lecture notes and secondary literature and, though easily refuted from the sources themselves, lives on cheerfully in the consensus of generations of like-minded scholars.

[74]John Byron, "Slaughter, Fratricide and Sacrilege: Cain and Abel Traditions in 1 John 3," *Bib* 88 (2007): 526-35.

nounced a blessing on those whose faith would rest on hearing rather than sight (Jn 20:29). His prospective prayer and blessing comprehended all the generations of believers that succeed one another until his return. As the conjunction of "believe" with "through their word" in John 17:20 shows, what defines the identity of this ever more diverse body as it permeates all cultures is a common response of faith to the word about Jesus.

God builds his church by gathering his children from among peoples scattered over the globe (Jn 10:16; 11:52; 12:20-22, 32).[75] By the time John wrote, the gospel had spread westward round the northern Mediterranean basin from Jerusalem probably as far as Spain. Of its progress in fits and starts southward through Egypt to North Africa, and eastward toward Mesopotamia, documentation is spottier. In the end, says the seer of the Apocalypse, every tribe, tongue, people and nation will have contributed representatives to the church (Apoc 5:9; 7:9; 14:6).

As the church expanded geographically, Christians quickly came to think of it as an international whole. Already at mid-century Paul could speak of "(all) the churches" of a region (Judea [Gal 1:22; 1 Thess 2:14], Galatia [1 Cor 16:1; Gal 1:2], Asia [1 Cor 16:19], Macedonia [2 Cor 8:1], Achaea [2 Cor 1:1]), or of "all the churches of the Gentiles" (Rom 16:4), or more universally of "(all) the church(es) of God/Christ/the saints" (Rom 16:16; 1 Cor 10:32; 11:16; 14:33; 15:9; Gal 1:13; 2 Thess 1:4; 1 Tim 3:15), or of "every church/all the churches" (1 Cor 4:17; 7:17; 2 Cor 8:18, 19, 23, 24; 11:28; 12:13), or simply of "the church" (1 Cor 12:28; Eph 1:22; 3:10, 21; 5:23, 24, 25, 27, 29, 32; Col 1:18, 24). Likewise John, a member of the apostolic college that presided from Jerusalem over the first missions and who later followed in Paul's footsteps at Ephesus, could symbolize the churches of Asia by choosing seven (e.g., Apoc 1:4, 11, 20). He also wrote several times the phrase "the churches" (Apoc 2:7, 11, 17, 29; 3:6, 13, 22; 22:16) and once even "all the churches" (Apoc 2:23).

With a worldwide presence came a need to organize and communicate. In each region there emerged a metropolitan hub: Jerusalem in Judea, Antioch in Syria, Ephesus in Asia (Acts 19:8-10; Apoc 1:4, 11), Corinth in Achaea (2 Cor 1:1), Rome in Italy, and, in the second century, Alexandria in Egypt. An apostle could, by sending a circular letter to the hub for distribution, reach churches at the local and house-church levels (2 Corinthians, Ephesians, 1 John). Suba-

---

[75]On the implications of these gathering texts for the concept of a universal church, see Schnackenburg, *St. John*, 3:213-17.

postolic delegates or occasional travelers carried instructions, epistles and greetings from place to place.[76] Paul intended his famous collection to cement ties between his Gentile converts in the West and the churches of Judea (Rom 15:27; 2 Cor 8:13-15). References in the Johannine Epistles and the Apocalypse testify to John's full participation in these crystallizing patterns (2 Jn 4, 13; 3 Jn 3-4, 6-7, 10, 12, 15; Apoc 2:2).

Just as the prophets of the Old Testament sometimes portrayed the city of Jerusalem as a mother and its individual citizens as her offspring (e.g., Ps 87:5-6; Is 50:1; 60:4; Ezek 19:2, 10; Hos 2:2), so John thought of each local church as a lady having for her children its congregants (2 Jn 1, 13). The same metaphor can also apply to the ideal church universal and her members on earth (Apoc 12).

## CHURCH IN PRACTICE

John was a churchman in a spreading movement that had become, by the end of the first century, an interterritorial network sharing the same faith, ethical way of life, personnel and resources. His writings afford few glimpses of practicalities in the churches that he served, perhaps owing to his bent for fundamental concepts. We know that believers worshiped together, had ministers of word and sacrament, and engaged in evangelization, but John offers virtually no reflective practical theology.

**Worship.** As far as communal worship is concerned, the Johannine literature, like the earlier books of the New Testament, gives few if any clues to the orders or customs that were in use.[77] We have brief descriptions of Christian meetings and daily prayers from the second and third centuries (*Did.* 7–14; Justin, *Apol. 1* 61-67; Hippolytus, *Apostolic Tradition*).[78] In light of these, liturgiologists agree that the earliest Christians freely adapted worship practices from the synagogue.[79] To these adaptations John may have contributed, but they left no imprint on anything that he wrote. Even the hymns of the Apocalypse do not

---

[76]Acts 17:14-15; 18:5; 19:22; 20:3-6; 21:16; Rom 16:1-2; 1 Cor 1:11; 16:3, 10-12; Eph 6:21-22; Phil 2:25-30; Col 4:7-9; 1 Thess 3:1-2, 6; 1 Tim 1:3; 2 Tim 4:9, 11-13; Tit 1:5; 3:12-13.

[77]On the difficulties of method involved in prying into early Christian worship, see Ferdinand Hahn, *The Worship of the Early Church* (trans. David E. Green; Philadelphia: Fortress, 1973), pp. 1-5.

[78]See further Hans Lietzmann, *Die Entstehung der christlichen Liturgie nach den ältesten Quellen* (Darmstadt: Wissenschaftliche Buchgesellschaft, 1963).

[79]C. W. Dugmore, *The Influence of the Synagogue upon the Divine Office* (London: Oxford University Press, 1944); William D. Maxwell, *An Outline of Christian Worship: Its Developments and Forms* (London: Oxford University Press, 1945), p. 5.

reflect songs used in first-century Christian meetings;[80] rather, they take inspiration from biblical models (e.g., compare Apoc 4:8 with Is 6:3; Apoc 15:3-4 with Ex 15:1-18) and are geared to counter pagan acclamations of the emperor.[81]

About all we can find on worship in John's corpus are broad principles. Since the time of Christ, worship is done "in Spirit and truth" (Jn 4:23-24). To the Samaritan woman this would have meant that in contrast to the former age, when access to God's glory on earth was had through the temple in Jerusalem with its priestly rituals (Jn 4:20-22), in the messianic era (Jn 4:25-26) experience of God is mediated by the Paraclete now dwelling in the hearts of God's people wherever they are (cf. Jn 14:17).[82]

Inspired by that Spirit, Christian worship is directed to God alone through the Lamb alone (Apoc 4–5; 15:3-4; 19:1-8). To acclaim any created thing as divine, in particular the Roman emperor whose cult was surging through Asia, is a travesty (Apoc 13).[83]

In no way does the fact that John speaks of worship only in general terms mean that he was uninterested in how to conduct services. The opening vision of the Apocalypse came to John on a Sunday ("the Lord's day" [Apoc 1:10]). Incidentally, this underscores the fact that the early Christians had shifted their meetings from the Sabbath to the first day of the week to commemorate Jesus' resurrection (cf. Acts 20:7; 1 Cor 16:2).[84] When a question arose in the mid-

---

[80]For proposals that the liturgy shaped material in the Apocalypse, see Otto A. Piper, "The Apocalypse of John and the Liturgy of the Ancient Church," *CH* 20 (1951): 10-22; Lucetta Mowry, "Revelation 4–5 and Early Christian Liturgical Usage," *JBL* 71 (1952): 75-84; Massey H. Shepherd, *The Paschal Liturgy and the Apocalypse* (ESW 6; Richmond: John Knox, 1960); Pierre Prigent, *Apocalypse et liturgie* (CahT 52; Neuchâtel: Delachaux et Niestlé, 1964). G. K. Beale rightly points out that John intended his Apocalypse to be read the other way, as an unveiling of heavenly worship that should inform earthly (*The Book of Revelation: A Commentary on the Greek Text* [NIGTC; Grand Rapids: Eerdmans; Carlisle: Paternoster, 1999], pp. 312-13). For further criticisms of this type of theory, see John J. O'Rourke, "Hymns of the Apocalypse," *CBQ* 30 (1968): 402; David R. Carnegie, "Worthy Is the Lamb: The Hymns in Revelation," in *Christ the Lord: Studies in Christology Presented to Donald Guthrie* (ed. Harold H. Rowdon; Downers Grove, IL: InterVarsity Press, 1982), p. 246.

[81]David E. Aune, "The Influence of Roman Imperial Court Ceremonial on the Apocalypse of John," *BR* 28 (1983): 5-26; Russell Morton, "Glory to God and to the Lamb: John's Use of Jewish and Hellenistic/Roman Themes in Formatting His Theology in Revelation 4–5," *JSNT* 83 (2001): 89-109; David Seal, "Shouting in the Apocalypse: The Influence of First-Century Acclamations on the Praise Utterances in Revelation 4:8 and 11," *JETS* 51 (2008): 339-52.

[82]Schnackenburg, "Johannine Ecclesiology?" pp. 254-55.

[83]J. Nelson Kraybill, *Imperial Cult and Commerce in John's Apocalypse* (JSNTSup 132; Sheffield: Sheffield Academic Press, 1996); idem, *Apocalypse and Allegiance: Worship, Politics, and Devotion in the Book of Revelation* (Grand Rapids: Brazos, 2010).

[84]Stephen R. Llewelyn, "The Use of Sunday for Meetings of Believers in the New Testament," *NovT* 43 (2001): 205-23.

second century about how to reckon the date of Easter,[85] several bishops of Asian cities cited John to support their quartodeciman position.[86] This fact, attested by church fathers but not in the New Testament, should caution us against assuming that John's writings contain his thoughts about everything that he considered important. What John said about topics he addressed we know. Where his writings are silent, we have no warrant for drawing negative inferences.

*Offices.* No organization can be efficient without structure and leadership. John, however, says little about offices in the church. From his silence some have concluded too hastily that John favored a liquid, charismatic style of leadership that had to compete against the gradual rise of local monarchic bishops toward the end of the first century.[87] John demonstrates, even by his missives, more than he says. Scattered fragments in his corpus shed indirect light on the early development of two of the three offices that came to be distinguished in the second century, the presbyterate and the episcopate.[88]

Relevant to any church office is the general rule Jesus made after washing his disciples' feet. If he, whom they righly regarded as their teacher and master, humbled himself to wash their feet, they too ought to wash one another's feet (Jn 13:12-17). This is the Johannine counterpart to the Synoptic teaching that the heart of Christian leadership is service (Mt 20:25-28 pars.).[89]

---

[85]In most parts of the Roman world the churches adjusted the date of Easter each year to make it fall always on a Sunday. When Victor, bishop of Rome, tried to force the churches of Asia Minor to conform to this rule rather than follow their own custom, for which they claimed apostolic precedent, of observing Easter according to the Jewish calendar on Nisan 14 (on whatever day of the week it fell), controversy ensued. Eusebius (*Hist. eccl.* 5.24) chronicles the matter. The term *quartodeciman*, by which church historians have named the controversy, is based on the Latin for "fourteenth."

[86]Polycrates, bishop of Ephesus (Eusebius, *Hist. eccl.* 5.24.3, 6); Polycarp, bishop of Smyrna (Eusebius, *Hist. eccl.* 5.24.16).

[87]Adolf von Harnack set forth this view largely on the basis of the *Didache.* See, for example, *The Mission and Expansion of Christianity in the First Three Centuries* (trans. James Moffatt; New York: Harper, 1962 [1906]), pp. 319-80, 439, 445-82. Hans von Campenhausen, building on Harnack, spoke of "the free spirituality of the Johannine world, with its horror of all hierarchical organization and its intense confidence in the power of the 'truth'" (*Ecclesiastical Authority*, p. 136). Ernst Käsemann accepted the same picture, saying that the author of the Fourth Gospel "is not at all interested in a differentiation of the gifts of the Spirit as the basis of a church order" (*Testament*, p. 32). The legacy lives on in, for example, Ferreira, *Johannine Ecclesiology*, p. 44. For an answer to Harnack, defending Lightfoot's view that the triple order of ministry (deacon, presbyter, bishop) stemmed from Jerusalem in the first generation, see Joseph Armitage Robinson, "The Christian Ministry in the Apostolic and Sub-Apostolic Periods," in *Essays on the Early History of the Church and the Ministry by Various Writers* (ed. H. B. Swete; London: Macmillan, 1918), pp. 57-92.

[88]John's writings contain no instance of the diaconate (Acts 6:1-6; Rom 16:1; 1 Tim 3:8-13; cf. Phil 1:1).

[89]Jey J. Kanagaraj, "Johannine Jesus, the Supreme Example of Leadership: An Inquiry into John 13:1-20," *Them* 29 (2004): 15-26.

According to the Gospel, Jesus as founder of the church created its first leaders. He himself chose "the Twelve" out of all his followers (Jn 6:13, 67, 70-71; 20:24) and appointed them "apostles" (Apoc 21:14) to go and bear fruit (Jn 15:16).[90] They baptized disciples on his behalf (Jn 4:2), made food purchases for the community (Jn 4:8; 6:5; 13:29), screened Jesus from throngs who sought his attention (Jn 12:20-22), and distributed alms (Jn 13:29). John alone among the Evangelists recalls the detail that the burgeoning movement had a treasurer (Jn 12:6; 13:29).[91] After Jesus' departure they served as eyewitnesses to what he had said and done. The qualification for this was to have been with Jesus from the beginning (Jn 15:27; 17:20). In this respect, their witness to the rest of the church remains fundamental and unrepeatable. John himself testifies of having seen the incarnate glory of God's Word (Jn 1:14).[92] To undermine what may be incipient Docetism, he belabors how he experienced Jesus by the senses of hearing, sight and touch (1 Jn 1:1-4). Disciples to come, who will never have met Jesus, will depend on the word of those who did (Jn 17:20; 20:29).

While apostles like Peter and Paul traveled far to make Jesus known, John appears to have stayed put for whole periods of years or even decades, first at Jerusalem, then at Ephesus. The residential nature of his apostolic ministry anticipated the episcopate.[93] John with Peter represented the Christian cause before the Sanhedrin (Acts 4–5). Also with Peter he laid hands on new believers of Samaria for their reception of the Holy Spirit (Acts 8:14-17). He was

---

[90]After Jesus' time the word "apostle" (ἀπόστολος) came to be applied to a wider circle of persons who saw the risen Christ and received from him a commission to evangelize and supervise churches, including Barnabas and Paul (Acts 14:14), James the Lord's brother (Gal 1:19), Andronicus and Junia (Rom 16:7). John does not concern himself with this extension of the term.

[91]Luke names donors (Lk 8:2-3).

[92]The "obvious reading" of John 1:14 ("we beheld his glory") is that "the evangelist is associating himself with those who saw the glory of the Incarnate Logos while he was actually dwelling 'among us'" (John Ashton, *Understanding the Fourth Gospel* [Oxford: Clarendon, 1991], p. 438), contra Bultmann, who tried to explain the "we" as believers of every generation.

[93]John thus offers a counter instance to J. B. Lightfoot's theory that "the episcopate was formed not out of the apostolic order by localisation but out of the presbyteral by elevation" ("Christian Ministry," p. 196). In the decade or two before John's arrival at Ephesus, Paul's stationing of Timothy there ("remain at Ephesus" [1 Tim 1:3]) marked a transitional phase between an apostle's roving oversight and a permanent local presence. On the other hand, the rise of James the Lord's brother to the head of the Jerusalem presbytery within the first twelve years after Jesus, which served as a precedent for all later bishoprics, lends support to the theory (Acts 12:17; 15:19; 21:18; Eusebius, *Hist. eccl.* 2.1.3; 7.19). In fact, bishops emerged from place to place in different ways depending on local circumstances and individual personalities, some sooner, some later.

among the three "pillars" who evaluated Paul's gospel and ratified his mission
(Gal 2:1-10). Probably he participated in the Jerusalem presbytery that
oversaw and normalized Christianity at Antioch by deputy (Acts 11:22) and
council (Acts 15). After the war John superintended churches in the urban
area of Ephesus (Clement of Alexandria, according to Eusebius, *Hist. eccl.*
3.23.6). During this final period of his ministry he called himself an "elder,"
and church members his "children." He enforced his ways by visits face to
face (2 Jn 12; 3 Jn 13-14). John wore his apostolic authority lightly, confident
that the communities he served were anointed by God and able to distinguish
truth from error, good from evil, so that they needed no heavy hand to direct
them (1 Jn 2:20, 27). Still, he used his office when necessary. Just as Paul had
authority to appoint local elders (Acts 14:23), later acting through delegates
to ordain (1 Tim 5:22; Tit 1:5) and to discipline them on evidence of griev-
ances (1 Tim 5:19-21), so John meant to intervene personally in the case of
Diotrephes (3 Jn 9-10).[94]

In the first generation primacy among the apostles devolved upon Peter. The
unique account in the Fourth Gospel of Jesus' early dubbing of Simon with the
title "Cephas" (כֵּיפָא, πέτρος, "rock") at Bethany beyond the Jordan (Jn 1:28, 42)
confirms this point in the better-known Synoptic record of a similar event at
Caesarea Philippi further on in Jesus' ministry (Mt 16:17-18; Mk 3:16; Lk 6:14).[95]
Jesus saw from the beginning the role that this motivator and model among
fishing comrades would play among his disciples (Mk 1:36; Jn 21:3). In John's
Gospel Peter is spokesman for the others (Jn 6:68-69; 13:8-9, 36-37), taker of
initiatives (Jn 13:24; 18:10-11; 21:3), one of only two who followed Jesus to his
trial before Caiaphas (Jn 18:15-16, 24-25), the first to enter Jesus' empty tomb
(Jn 20:6), and a celebrated martyr (Jn 21:18-19). His reinstatement after denying
his Lord is a paradigm of Christian discipleship.[96] Thrice he had abjured his
association with Jesus (Jn 18:17, 25, 26); thrice Jesus probed his love (Jn 21:15-

---

[94]Judith Lieu (*Theology*, pp. 23-27) accurately describes the modesty of the figure who wrote the
Epistles as his egalitarian "witness" to the readership (1 Jn 1:2), but she underestimates the strength
of a self-consciousness that can simply announce that he is coming soon and expect to be welcomed,
provided for, and heeded (2 Jn 12; 3 Jn 13-14).

[95]Neither John's account of Jesus' assigning Peter an appellation nor Peter's confession that Jesus was
the Holy One of God, the latter of which took place in Capernaum (Jn 6:59, 68-69), matches up
geographically with the confession of Peter at Caesarea Philippi recorded in the Synoptic Gospels
(Mt 16:13-20 pars.). These units illustrate John's penchant for recalling minor incidents that complement the better-known events of the Synoptic tradition.

[96]R. Alan Culpepper, "Peter as Exemplary Disciple in John 21:15-19," *PRSt* 37 (2010): 165-78.

17).[97] Thus love for Jesus is the sine qua non; John typically puts his finger on the pith of the matter. That Jesus reappointed Simon son of John to feed his flock[98] is congruent with the fact that Peter had the leading place among the other disciples (cf., e.g., Lk 22:31-32; Acts 1:15; 2:14). In view of these considerations, the notion current in some secondary literature that the Fourth Gospel holds up the figure of the Beloved Disciple as the exemplar of discipleship over against Peter (and the other eleven)[99] distorts the facts. The few and self-effacing references to the disciple whom Jesus loved (Jn 13:23; 19:26; 20:2; 21:7, 20) in no way detract from Peter's seniority among the Twelve or from his exemplary role as a leading disciple.[100]

By the end of the century most apostles of the first generation had died. Others took their place, traveling from city to city to solidify the network among the churches. These included missionaries (3 Jn 5-8; *Did.* 11:1-2) and prophets (1 Jn 4:1-6; *Did.* 11:3, 5, 7-12; 13), whose activities are attested from mid-century onwards (Acts 11:27-28; 13:1; 21:10; 1 Cor 12:28-29; Eph 2:20; 3:5; 4:11; 2 Pet 3:2).[101] Some of them took the title of "apostle" (Apoc 2:2; *Did.* 11.3-6; 12). Among them were charlatans who could be identified by the unorthodoxy of their teachings (2 Jn 7, 10-11; Apoc 2:2) or their greedy demands for money and goods (*Did.* 11:9, 12; 12:5). John was in contact with some of the faithful among these itinerants (3 Jn 3, 6) and praised their service (3 Jn 6-8).

---

[97]Given John's habit of varying his vocabulary, attempts to squeeze significance out of the change from ἀγαπᾶν (Jn 21:15-16) to φιλεῖν (Jn 21:17) must be doubtful. See Leon Morris, *Jesus Is the Christ: Studies in the Theology of John* (Grand Rapids: Eerdmans, 1989), pp. 293-319. But such attempts likely will never cease. For different takes on the difference, compare Ernest Evans, "The Verb ἀγαπᾶν in the Fourth Gospel," in *Studies in the Fourth Gospel* (ed. F. L. Cross; London: Mowbray, 1957), pp. 64-71, and David Shepherd, "'Do You Love Me?' A Narrative-Critical Reappraisal of ἀγαπάω and φιλέω in John 21:15-17," *JBL* 129 (2010): 777-92.

[98]Ulrich Heckel, *Hirtenamt und Herrschaftskritik: Die urchristlichen Ämter aus johanneischer Sicht* (BTS 65; Neukirchen-Vluyn: Neukirchener Verlag, 2004).

[99]For example, Alv Kragerud, *Der Lieblingsjünger im Johannesevangelium: Ein exegetischer Versuch* (Oslo: Osloer Universitätsverlag, 1959); Graydon F. Snyder, "John 13:16 and the Anti-Petrinism of the Johannine Tradition," *BR* 16 (1971): 5-15; Raymond F. Collins, *These Things Have Been Written: Studies on the Fourth Gospel* (LTPM 2; Louvain: Peeters, 1990), pp. 38-45, 68-86; R. Alan Culpepper, *John, the Son of Zebedee: The Life of a Legend* (SPNT; Columbia: University of South Carolina Press, 1994), pp. 56-88; Melvyn R. Hillmer, "They Believed in Him: Discipleship in the Johannine Tradition," in *Patterns of Discipleship in the New Testament* (ed. Richard N. Longenecker; Grand Rapids: Eerdmans, 1996), pp. 87-89.

[100]Bradford B. Blaine, *Peter in the Gospel of John: The Making of an Authentic Disciple* (SBLAB 27; Atlanta: Society of Biblical Literature, 2007).

[101]On itinerant missionaries, teachers and prophets in the time of the "Johannine community," see Hans-Josef Klauck, "Gemeinde ohne Amt? Erfahrungen mit der Kirche in den johanneischen Schriften," *BZ* 29 (1985): 193-220.

Diotrephes (3 Jn 9) is the sole representative in the Johannine corpus of a class of church leaders said elsewhere to have been appointed by apostles to offer ongoing pastoral care to believers in a given municipality (Acts 14:23; 1 Tim 5:22; Tit 1:5). Individually each was known as a "shepherd" in relation to his flock (ποιμήν, Lat. *pastor* [Eph 4:11; cf. 1 Pet 5:2]) or, alternatively, as an "overseer" (ἐπίσκοπος [1 Tim 3:2; Tit 1:7]). Collectively in local council they formed a body of "elders" (πρεσβύτεροι).[102] Their chief tasks were to govern and teach (Eph 4:11; 1 Tim 3:2, 4-5).[103] The origins of the office are obscure.[104] It probably developed on the analogy of synagogal councils (Lk 7:3),[105] when there was a numerical explosion of converts in Jerusalem in the weeks following Pentecost (Acts 2:41; 4:4). Having no public buildings, congregational cells met in private homes and were small, amounting to only a few dozen members.[106] This created an urgent need for multiple leaders throughout Jerusalem.[107] When evangelists planted churches in other cities, they reproduced

---

[102]Thus "overseer" and "elder," which the New Testament uses synonymously for the same persons, overlap but are not strictly interchangeable, in passages such as Acts 20:17, 28; Titus 1:5, 7; 1 Peter 5:2 (textually questionable); *1 Clement* 44:1, 4, 5.

[103]Lightfoot, "Christian Ministry," pp. 194-95.

[104]A body of elders at Jerusalem, fully intact and operational, pops abruptly into the narrative of Acts at 11:30 and remains a feature thereafter.

[105]Note also the occurrence of the term πρεσβύτεροι in the Theodotus inscription from predestruction Jerusalem (Adolf Deissmann, *Light from the Ancient East: The New Testament Illustrated by Recently Discovered Texts of the Graeco-Roman World* [trans. Lionel R. M. Strachan; Grand Rapids: Baker Books, 1978], pp. 439-41). For further instances of synagogue "elders," see Günther Bornkamm, "πρέσβυς," *TDNT* 6:660-61. On the synagogue as model, see Lightfoot, "Christian Ministry," pp. 192-93.

[106]Archaeologists of Christian antiquity estimate the size of house-churches by measuring the remaining foundations of Greco-Roman villas and calculating how many people they could hold. Typically, the largest inner room, the *atrium*, could accommodate a maximum of fifty guests for a Eucharist, more likely two or three dozen, allowing floor space for furniture (Willy Rordorf, "Die Hausgemeinde der vorkonstantinischen Zeit," in *Kirche: Tendenzen und Ausblicke* [ed. C. W. Williams; Berlin: Burckhardthaus-Verlag, 1971], p. 191; Jerome Murphy-O'Connor, *St. Paul's Corinth: Texts and Archaeology* [GNS 6; Wilmington, DE: Michael Glazier, 1983], pp. 153-61). Larger occasional gatherings of one hundred to two hundred people would have had to spill into the outdoor peristyle court (E. Earle Ellis, *Pauline Theology: Ministry and Society* [Grand Rapids: Eerdmans; Exeter: Paternoster, 1989], pp. 143-44).

[107]House-congregations at Jerusalem are mentioned or implied in Acts 1:13; 2:2, 46; 12:12. If the figure of five thousand men in Acts 4:4 implies somewhere in the neighborhood of fifteen thousand followers of Jesus, including women and children, and if only a tenth of these (1,500) stayed as permement residents of the city when festival pilgrims returned home, there would have been nearly forty cells of forty members within just a short time after Pentecost, a number that would continue to grow (Acts 6:7). As the number of house churches approached seventy, the body of their leaders would have approximated the size of the Sanhedrin (seventy-one). Jewish Christians took over the term "elder" from the Old Testament (e.g., Ex 3:16; 24:1) and the Sanhedrin (e.g., Mt 16:21; Acts 4:5), with perhaps the Roman *senatus* ("senate," from *senex*, "old man") in remote view.

the same ecclesiastical pattern.[108] The "elders" of a town are almost always plural in the New Testament.[109]

The measures that Diotrephes took unilaterally to advance his own agenda overrode the local leadership team of which he was a part and were insubordinate toward the author of 3 John, his apostolic overseer. Here a particular church cell fell under the tyranny of one self-important personality who wanted to act independently of the higher level of authority, embodied in the Johannine elder and the itinerant teachers. Their charge was to maintain the communion of churches in a region wide enough to require journeys, visits and hospitality for the travelers. It is plain that the elder holds that communion to have priority over Diotrephes' local situation and is ready to intervene to insure a happy outcome for all.[110]

When we combine the few references to Christian leadership in John's writings with the New Testament and patristic testimonies to John's activities reviewed above, we see that John, though he does not theorize on the subject, was an energetic bearer and exponent of the ministry structures of the early catholic church that were rapidly taking shape in his day.

**Sacraments.** Concerning the sacraments of the gospel—baptism and the Lord's Supper—John likewise says little. Yet we would be remiss to conclude from his paucity of statements that they were unimportant to him. To what extent John's thought is sacramental has been debated long, widely and warmly. On one extreme lies the view that he was anti- or nonsacramental; on the other, that he was an ultrasacramentalist, many of whose symbols carry oblique refer-

---

[108]Acts 11:30; 14:23; 15:2, 4, 6, 22, 23; 16:4; 20:17; 21:18; 1 Tim 5:17, 19; Tit 1:5; Jas 5:14; 1 Pet 5:1, 5. House-churches are documented in Acts 20:8 (Troas); 20:20 (Ephesus); 1 Corinthians 16:19 (Corinth); Romans 16:5 (Rome); Colossians 4:15 (Colossae); Philemon 1:2 (Colossae); 2 John 10 (Ephesus). Christians apparently did not build meeting halls until much later. Whether sparse literary references to places of Christian meeting from the end of the second century refer to independent buildings designed for worship is unclear (Tertullian, *Cor.* 13; Minucius Felix, *Oct.* 9). Archaeological evidence for church buildings dates from the early to mid-third century, at Tel Megiddo in Israel and Dura-Europus in Syria (Clark Hopkins, *Christian Church at Dura-Europus. 1. The Christian Church* [New Haven: Yale University Press, 1934]; Vassilios Tzaferis, "Inscribed 'To God Jesus Christ,'" *BAR* 33, no. 2 [2007]: 38-49). Not until the closing decades of the third century does Eusebius mention church buildings (*Hist. eccl.* 7.13.2; 15.4 [A.D. 261]; 30.19 [A.D. 270s]; 30.22; 32.32; 8.1.5 [all about A.D. 297]).

[109]Only as authors of epistles do Peter and John refer to themselves in the singular (1 Pet 5:1 [συμπρεσβύτερος]; 2 Jn 1; 3 Jn 1).

[110]Paul too put the claims of the catholic church above those of a local church. This comes out especially in his letters to Corinth (1 Cor 1:2; 4:17; 11:16; 14:33b, 36; 15:11; 2 Cor 1:1) and to Colossae (Col 1:6, 23; 2:19).

ences to baptism or the Eucharist.[111] Neither interpretive tendency is war-
ranted. It seems reasonable to assume, barring contrary evidence, that John was
at one with his fellow apostles in holding both sacraments to be ordinary instruments of God's saving power applied to individuals.[112] Yet the fact of the
matter is that John was more taken up with the realities that they signify than
with how divine grace operates in and through them.

   *Baptism.* The Fourth Gospel presents John the Baptist mainly as a witness
to him who was to come. There are only a few brief notices of John baptizing
Jews with water (Jn 1:25-26, 31, 33; 3:23). These verses do not explain the meaning
of the rite as the Synoptic Gospels do. Nor does the Evangelist put much emphasis on the bare fact that Jesus took it over (Jn 3:22, 26; 4:1-2). Some scholars
have surmised that the Evangelist's community at the time of writing was still
in competition with lingering adherents of the Baptist's sect. The laconic
treatment of John's baptism could be part of a strategy to divert readers' attention from the rival movement. Were the Fourth Gospel written somewhere
in Palestine or Syria, this hypothesis might be plausible. But the only twelve
such disciples of the Baptist we know of in the vicinity of Ephesus were baptized as Christians by Paul in A.D. 52 (Acts 19:1-7). If we accept the apostolic
authorship, postwar date and Ephesian provenance of the Johannine corpus,
the probable reason for the author's tangential treatment of John's water baptism
is that the Synoptic tradition addresses it adequately, and it forms no part of
his christological focus.

   Four verses in John's writings have a bearing on the doctrine of Baptism.
None is direct.

   *John 3:5.* Jesus told Nicodemus that one must be "born of water and Spirit"
(γεννηθῇ ἐξ ὕδατος καὶ πνεύματος) in order to see the kingdom of God. Commentators have proposed a number of interpretations of "water."[113] Since Jesus

---

[111]For surveys of the options, see Raymond E. Brown, "The Johannine Sacramentary," in Taylor,
   *Companion to John,* pp. 225-46; Herbert Klos, *Die Sakramente im Johannesevangelium* (SBS 46;
   Stuttgart: Katholisches Bibelwerk, 1970); C. K. Barrett, "Sacraments," in *Essays on John* (Philadelphia: Westminster, 1982), pp. 80-97; G. R. Beasley-Murray, *Gospel of Life: Theology in the Fourth
   Gospel* (Peabody, MA: Hendrickson, 1991), pp. 85-101; Frederick W. Guyette, "Sacramentality in
   the Fourth Gospel: Conflicting Interpretations," *Eccl* 3 (2007): 235-50.
[112]For a review of the New Testament teaching on baptism and the Eucharist, see Ralph P. Martin,
   *Worship in the Early Church* (rev. ed.; Grand Rapids: Eerdmans, 1974), pp. 87-129.
[113]Among the more common are the following. (1) The amniotic sack, representing physical birth (cf.
   "that which is born of the flesh is flesh" [Jn 3:6a]). But Jesus' requirement in John 3:5 pertains to a
   subject (τις, "one") who, as is self-evident, already exists; to make natural birth part of the condition
   for entering God's kingdom would be redundant and trivial. (2) "Water and Spirit" could be a

expects this teacher of Israel to understand him at the time of speaking (cf. Jn 3:10), almost certainly he is alluding to the Scripture in which Ezekiel associates water of sprinkling with God's gift of the Spirit in the eschatological era (Ezek 36:25-27). The fulfillment of this Scripture began with John's water baptism, which was soon taken up into the full Spirit baptism of Jesus (Jn 1:33). Being a Pharisee (Jn 3:1), Nicodemus has thus far spurned John's baptism (Lk 7:30). Ezekiel's (and Jesus') figure of speech points to a cleansing and enlivening of the heart by God the Spirit. What is indispensable for salvation is this interior reality, even if the phrase names the external element that signifies it in baptism.

*John 13:10.* While washing the disciples' feet, Jesus told Peter, "He who has bathed [ὁ λελουμένος] does not need to wash [νίψασθαι], except for his feet, but he is clean all over." This is the only occurrence in the Johannine corpus of the verb λούειν ("to bathe"). In the perfect tense it points back to the accomplished event of their reception of Jesus' word by which they were cleansed (cf. Jn 15:3). But Christian readers could hardly escape hearing an echo of baptism (Heb 10:22; cf. λουτρόν in Eph 5:26; Tit 3:5). For the author and for them, the saying became a dictum about postbaptismal sin. Baptism is once for all. A baptized believer who commits sin through weakness does not thereby lapse from salvation and need to undergo Christian initiation all over again, but rather receives forgiveness on confession and repentance (1 Jn 1:9).

*John 20:23.* Jesus, in giving the Holy Spirit to his disciples, authorized them to forgive or retain people's sins. The initial basis for applying divine forgiveness to individuals is their response to the proclamation of the gospel. Those who came to faith in Jesus in the apostolic age submitted to baptism immediately as a matter of course (Acts 2:37-41; 8:12, 35-38; 9:17-18; 10:44-48; 16:14-15, 30-33; 18:8; 19:4-5; 22:16). Baptism signifies and conveys forgiveness (Mk 1:4; Acts 2:38; Col 2:12-13), and commentators who propose baptism as a natural setting for John 20:23 are certainly right. But the same power to pronounce someone forgiven might come into play in other settings too, such as prayer for the life of

---

compound expression for "spiritual semen" (cf. "that which is born of the Spirit is spirit" [Jn 3:6b]). But this euphemistic sense of "water," though demonstrable from rabbinic, Mandaean and Hermetic sources, would be unique in John, who does not shrink from calling semen by the usual word "seed" (σπέρμα [1 Jn 3:9]). And to superimpose a figurative use of water on a hendiadys would create a rare density of speech. (3) Water could denote Christian baptism. But on that view, the ceremony of initiation would be necessary for salvation. While the New Testament nowhere contemplates a convert remaining unbaptized voluntarily, Jesus is talking here about the work of the Spirit, not about a rite of the church, which had not yet come into being when the conversation with Nicodemus took place.

a fellow believer entangled in nonmortal sin (1 Jn 5:16-17) or prayer for physical healing (Jas 5:14-16).

*Apocalypse 7:2-3; 9:4; 14:1; 22:4.* Behind the apocalyptic imagery of an angel putting a seal (σφραγίζειν) on the foreheads of God's elect for their protection from God's plagues may be the custom of tracing the sign of the cross on baptizands. There is no explicit evidence in the New Testament or the Apostolic Fathers that the first generations of Christians used this symbolic gesture. But around the end of the second century at least three patristic writers attest its general use by Christians: Tertullian in North Africa (*Cor.* 3),[114] Clement in Alexandria (*Strom.* 2.3; 6.11; 7.12) and Hippolytus in Rome (*Trad. ap.* 37). The wide geographical distribution of these authors at roughly the same time bears witness to the great antiquity of the custom, and indeed Tertullian (A.D. 211) calls it an "ancient practice" with origins shrouded in tradition. Baptism itself is a "seal" (σφραγίς) according to a good many fathers of the second century (e.g., 2 *Clem.* 7.6; 8.6; Herm. *Sim.* 8.6.3; 9.16.3-5; Clement of Alexandria, *Quis div.* 42.4; Eusebius, *Hist. eccl.* 3.23.8). "Sealing" the forehead means making the sign of the cross on it, and Hippolytus (*Trad. ap.* 22.3) includes this as part of the traditional Roman ceremony of baptism. Apocalypse 7:3 reworks Ezekiel 9:4, where the God of Israel, on the point of executing judgment on Jerusalem, instructs an angel to place a mark of exclusion on the foreheads of the faithful. The mark is specifically a *tau* (וָת), which, in the Palaeo-Hebrew scripts of Ezekiel's time, took the form of a cross (+ or ×). John may also allude to Israel's apotropaic splashing of blood on doorposts and lintels at Passover (Ex 12:7, 22-23), which reminded Roman Christians of the cross shape (Hippolytus, *Trad. ap.* 37). These factors taken together suggest, even though they do not establish beyond doubt, that John may have known of the baptismal use of the sign of the cross.

Whether John held a robustly sacramental view of Christian baptism—God's saving grace operates through the physical rite—depends on whether he is to be read in union with other New Testament authors. Adherents of the Johannine sectarianism hypothesis can readily see John as a nonconformist who scorned the gelling sacramental tradition. If John was indeed a churchman as

---

[114]"We have an ancient practice. . . . If no passage of scripture has prescribed it, assuredly custom, which without doubt flowed from tradition, has confirmed it. . . . At every forward step and movement, at every going in and out, when we put on our clothes and shoes, when we bathe, when we sit at table, when we light the lamps, on couch, on seat, in all the ordinary actions of daily life, we trace upon the forehead the sign" (Tertullian, *Cor.* 3).

the early church held, and not the idiosyncratic quasi-Gnostic of some critical reconstructions, then the verses reviewed here taken together are sufficient to suggest that he shared the common apostolic view of baptism[115] as the rite of initiation into Christ, administered on profession of faith, wherein the convert receives the washing away of sins (Acts 22:16; 1 Cor 6:11; Eph 5:26; Col 2:13c-14; Tit 3:7; Heb 10:22; 1 Pet 3:21), the Holy Spirit (Mk 1:8; Acts 2:38; 1 Cor 6:11; 12:13; Tit 3:5-6), birth to new life (Rom 6:4-5; Col 2:12-13; Tit 3:5), and sealing with God's Spirit (Eph 1:13; 4:30).

*Lord's Supper.* A peculiarity of the Fourth Gospel is its lack of an account of the institution of Holy Communion (cf. Mt 26:26-29; Mk 14:22-25; Lk 22:14-20).[116] The Last Supper is present in John's Gospel, to be sure, the night before Jesus' passion and, as I argued earlier (chap. 5), was a Passover meal (Jn 13:1-2, 21-30). But John barely mentions the meal ("during supper" [Jn 13:2]) and tells instead of Jesus washing the disciples' feet and instructing them to serve one another (Jn 13:3-20). In this way John elaborates on material found in this setting in Luke alone of the Synoptists (Lk 22:24-27).

A single passage in the Gospel has eucharistic overtones, but it is far removed from John's account of the Last Supper. Speaking in the synagogue at Capernaum on the day after he fed the crowd of five thousand, Jesus warned that they could not have eternal life without eating his flesh and drinking his blood (Jn 6:53-59). His language here, graphic though it is, is metaphorical.[117] The motif of eating came from the feeding miracle (ἐσθίειν, φαγεῖν [Jn 6:23, 26, 31, 49, 50, 51, 52, 53, 58]; τρώγειν [Jn 6:54, 56, 57, 58]). Jesus offered to give people "bread" (ἄρτος [Jn 6:23, 31, 32, 33, 34, 35, 41, 48, 50, 51, 58]) and "food" (βρῶσις [Jn 6:27, 55]) that would truly satisfy, over against mere "manna" (Jn 6:31, 49), which would let them "hunger/thirst" again (Jn 6:35) and eventually "die" (Jn 6:49, 50, 58). Interspersed thematically in the dialogue with "eating" are other figures ("coming to" Jesus [Jn 6:35, 37, 44, 45, 65]; "believing in" Jesus [Jn 6:29, 30, 35, 36, 40, 47, 64, 69]; "seeing" the Son [Jn 6:40]; "being taught" by God [Jn 6:45]) for obtaining eternal "life/living" (Jn 6:27, 33, 35, 40, 47, 48, 51, 53, 54, 57, 58, 63, 68) and final resurrection in Christ (Jn 6:39, 40, 44, 54). The narrative culminates in Peter's confession, "You have the words of eternal life; and we have believed, and have come to know, that you are the Holy One of God" (Jn

---

[115]G. R. Beasley-Murray, *Baptism in the New Testament* (Grand Rapids: Eerdmans, 1973).

[116]Paul's review in 1 Corinthians 11:23-25 is most like Luke's.

[117]Pierre Berthoud, "Le pain de vie," *RRef* 55 (2004): 67-78.

6:68-69). To eat Jesus, then, is to put faith in his person, specifically in his coming act of dying.[118] Eating Jesus' flesh and drinking his blood means renouncing the immediate hope of an earthly king, a thaumaturge who could fill people's stomachs free of charge (Jn 6:15, 26), to embrace as God's appointee a messiah who would save in another way by giving himself up in death (Jn 6:51, 71). It was this idea that gave offense to many of Jesus' own disciples (Jn 6:60-61, 66). The Jews in the synagogue on that occasion could not possibly have taken Jesus to be referring to a sacramental meal that lay in the future, though in the context of the Passover season (Jn 6:4) they might have understood Jesus to be offering himself in place of the Passover sacrifice.[119]

Nevertheless, Christian readers familiar with the words of institution inevitably hear echoes of them in John 6:53-58.[120] True, Jesus speaks in John of eating his "flesh" (σάρξ), rather than his "body" (σῶμα), and uses a less common verb for eating (τρώγειν). These vocabulary choices set apart the account in John. Moreover, John's paragraph has Jesus talk about his death in terms of a meal ("My flesh is food indeed" [Jn 6:55]), which is the grammatical converse of his words in the other Gospels, where Jesus interprets elements of the meal with reference to his coming death ("This [bread] is my body"). Still, the separation of flesh from blood, the appropriation of the one to eating and the other to drinking, and the very order remind Christians of the Eucharist.

John does in John 6:53-58 what he did in John 3:5. He orients readers' thoughts to the spiritual essence rather than the outer mode of each sacrament. In John 3 Jesus points to the regenerating work of the Holy Spirit, and in John 6 to the life-giving value of his atoning death, as requisite for salvation. John clothes each statement in words that evoke the ordinary sacramental means by which God grants the gift to the believer: a water bath and a repast of bread and, by implication, of wine. So naturally does John employ the sign for the mystery signified, that he must view them as a unity. Only if the reality is given in the symbol does it work for John to put the symbol for the reality in a statement about the latter.[121] But that the reality subsists in the symbol is an

---

[118]David Gibson, "Eating Is Believing? On Midrash and the Mixing of Metaphors in John 6," *Them* 27 (2002): 5-15; Stephen W. Need, "Jesus the Bread of God: The Eucharist as Metaphor in John 6," *Theology* 105 (2002): 194-200.

[119]Godfrey W. Ashby, "Body and Blood in John 6:41-65," *Neot* 36 (2002): 57-61.

[120]Jane S. Webster, *Ingesting Jesus: Eating and Drinking in the Gospel of John* (SBLAB 6; Atlanta: Society of Biblical Literature, 2003), pp. 151-53.

[121]An underlying doctrine of the real presence of Christ explains several turns of phrase elsewhere in the New Testament. At the Last Supper Jesus said, "This [bread] is my body" (Mt 26:26; Mk 14:22).

unstated assumption, not the main point of the passage. Could we corner John with our dogmatic question whether there is a real presence of Christ in the sacrament, almost certainly he would say yes. But our concern was not his, and he does not set out to answer it. He directs us to the immolated victim whose death brings us life.

Of the many other verses in the Johannine literature that pansacramentalists have milked for further references to baptism and the Lord's Supper, the only one worthy of special mention is John 19:34. The author, present at the crucifixion of Jesus, testifies that when the soldiers pierced his side, "at once there came out blood and water." Scores of commentators have seen here a cryptic statement that the saving virtue of Jesus' death comes to the believer through both sacraments. Given John's propensity for symbolism, it would be a mistake to bar allegory entirely from the field of Johannine exegesis. But this perhaps pardonable flight of imagination misses the explicit point of the verse. John relates the incident as yet another of those fulfillments of Scripture that dot his passion account (Jn 19:36-37). We do well to accept his own explanation as the sufficient one.

Why John offers but one short paragraph, and that an oblique one, touching on a matter so important to Christian worship and life as Holy Communion belongs to the larger puzzle of why the New Testament canon as a whole says so little on this topic.[122] Part of the answer is that what was said and done in the liturgy belonged to tradition, in the same way that the bulk of sacrificial procedure in Israel escaped the book of Leviticus, although the Mishnah tractate *Tamid* preserves some of it. Acts and 1 Corinthians between them attest that the Lord's Supper was a regular feature of the Christian meeting every Sunday.[123] Beyond that, apparently the apostolic age saw no doctrinal contro-

---

This is best taken as a statement neither of strict identity (as in theories of transubstantiation or consubstantiation) nor of mere representation, but rather of definition: within the frame of the memorial rite the rule is that to partake of the elements is indeed to partake of Christ. Paul says that the cup and the bread are a "participation in" Christ's blood and body (κοινωνία τοῦ αἵματος/ τοῦ σώματος τοῦ Χριστοῦ), even as Israel's consumption of offerings made them "participants in" the altar (κοινωνοὶ τοῦ θυσιαστηρίου) (1 Cor 10:16, 18). Therefore anyone who partakes of the bread or the cup in an unworthy manner desecrates not just a symbol, but "the body and blood of the Lord" (1 Cor 11:27).

[122]The parallel accounts of the Last Supper from the Gospels cited above in this section, a few passages in Acts about the "breaking of bread" (Acts 2:42, 46; 20:7, 11), two places in 1 Corinthians on abuses (1 Cor 10:3-4, 16-22; 11:17-34), and the mention of "love feasts" in Jude 12 make up the sum total of New Testament references to Holy Communion.

[123]Acts 20:7: "On the first day of the week, when we were gathered together to break bread. . . ." Paul

versy over the Lord's Supper. The Gospels record its founding, while the Epistles deal with other issues that boiled up among the churches. As for John, had he been a "school" sequestered from the great church, as radical criticism makes "him" out to be, the absence of teaching could plausibly be taken as evidence of antisacramentalism, or at least of scant interest in the sacraments. But if he was the son of Zebedee, he may have felt no need to repeat in his Gospel what was already known from the Synoptic tradition and had become a practice and a doctrine universal among the churches.

## Conclusion

Taking the extant writings of John together, then, we see that he presents key perspectives on the church. This stands to reason. Christology implies ecclesiology. As André Feuillet observed, the Son of God "cannot be the Messiah without a messianic community, a Shepherd without a flock." Even though his person is the central focus of God's final revelation that came in Jesus of Nazareth, "in so far as it is Christological, it is also ecclesial, since it is principally in the Church that these riches are offered."[124]

Our account neither of the Johannine concept of the church nor of the world is complete until we see how they relate to each other. To that question we now turn.

---

simply assumes this: "When you come together . . . When you assemble as a church . . . When you meet together . . . When you come together to eat . . . lest you come together to be condemned" (1 Cor 11:17, 18, 20, 33-34).

[124]André Feuillet, "The Time of the Church in St. John," in *Johannine Studies* (trans. Thomas E. Crane; Staten Island, NY: Alba House, 1964), p. 149.

# THE COMMUNITY
# OF CHRIST'S DISCIPLES
# IN THE WORLD

OUR SURVEY OF RELATIONSHIPS among the main persons, divine and human, that populate the Johannine universe is almost complete. God the Father (chap. 2) loves God the Son eternally (chap. 4) and is united to him by God the Spirit (chap. 6). He also loves the world that he made, despite its rebellion toward him (chap. 3). He sent his Son to show his love supremely by making propitiation for the world's sin on the cross (chap. 5). The Son, on returning to glory, sent the Spirit to indwell his disciples (chap. 6) so that they might abide in the Son, both individually (chaps. 7-8) and corporately (chap. 9), until he comes again for them.

This last chapter brings together two corporate characters that we have already considered separately: the community of Jesus' disciples (chap. 9) and the world (chap. 3). Following Christ's departure, his disciples remained to carry on his witness in the power of the Spirit of truth. They, like the incarnate Son before them, are on mission "in the world" but are "not of this world." Permutations of those twin themes in the various evangelistic and pastoral situations to which John directed his writings constitute John's understanding of the church in relation to the world. Under this rubric two main headings come up for consideration: the mission of evangelization on which Jesus sent his disciples, and the world's hatred through which God will keep them until Jesus' parousia.

## CHURCH "IN" THE WORLD BUT NOT "OF" IT
For John, the church is a group of people whom God has taken out of the world

to be his own. Church and world are as different as light and darkness. "We are of God, and the whole world lies in the evil one" (1 Jn 5:19).

*According to the Fourth Gospel.* John wrote his Gospel to present Jesus as the life-giving Christ to a broad cultural spectrum of readers both in the church and beyond it. In this work, with its evangelistic tenor, the church's presence in the world after Jesus' departure is associated with the motifs of witness and of persecution until the end of the age.

Concerning God's Logos John says that "he was in the world" (ἐκ τῷ κόσμῳ ἦν) during the brief time of Jesus' earthly life (Jn 1:10). The prologue to John's Gospel presents the Son's incarnation as a ray of eternal light penetrating the darkness in the same way God's creative word dispelled the primordial chaos (Jn 1:5, 9). While he was in the world, he was its light (Jn 9:5), and he spoke from God until the time came when he was no longer in the world (Jn 17:11, 13). But his origin and eternal home were from above. In contrast to those who rejected him, he was not "of" the world (Jn 8:23, 26).

As a whole, the world did not know or receive the true light (Jn 1:10-11). But some did receive him; to them God gave the right to be his children (Jn 1:12). The world, made by the Logos, refused to acknowledge the Logos; only those born of God proved receptive (Jn 1:13). The decisive factor separating the God-born from the rest of the human race is God's will, though they also, quickened by God's life-giving power, distinguish themselves by their free response to him as their Father. A line of demarcation divides those who belong to God from those who are of the world. Yet it is not a case of "dualism," of two essentially different races of human beings. God's children were once part of the world. God, not their intrinsic nature, set them apart.

Either light or darkness characterizes people's reactions to God's love (Jn 3:19-21). God loved the world and sent his Son to save it (Jn 3:16-17). But the saving event created two choices, and before them the race parts ways. Those who believe escape judgment already during the course of this age; those who do not believe remain in the state of damnation that hangs over the world-system (Jn 3:18). People generally hate the light and will not come to the light, lest their deeds be exposed (Jn 3:19-20). But there are some who do what is true. As they come to the light, God receives glory as the source of their deeds (Jn 3:21). Again, both groups belonged to the world and were destined to perish. Out of that single, doomed world come, by God's birthing, those who believe and are divinely energized to do deeds pleasing to God.

As it gradually becomes plain in the Gospel narrative that the religious establishment is set against Jesus and will murder him (Jn 7:19), he takes up the language of "above" and "below." "You are from below [ἐκ τῶν κάτω ἐστέ], I am from above [ἐκ τῶν ἄνω εἰμί]; you are of this world [ἐκ τούτου τοῦ κόσμου], I am not of this world" (Jn 8:23). In the formulations "from below" and "of this world" the preposition ἐκ indicates participation and shared characteristic, not ultimate origination, for all things were made by God through his Logos (Jn 1:3). To be "from below" and "of this world" means to have had a glimpse of the true light (Jn 8:12) and yet to have made the fateful choice to remain in the dark rather than to heed Jesus. He came "for judgment" (εἰς κρίμα)—that is, to drive a wedge, "that those who do not see may see, and that those who see may become blind" (Jn 9:39). In order to gain eternal life, a disciple must hate his or her life in this world (Jn 12:25). In Jesus' parting shot to those who have repudiated him, he warns them one last time to believe in the light while they still have a bit of daylight, "that you may become sons of light" (Jn 12:36).

In John 13–17 Jesus' aura as the one who does not belong to the world extends to the circle of his disciples. They are "his own" who are "in the world" (ἐν τῷ κόσμῳ [Jn 13:1]). Especially in the Farewell Discourse the distinction between his own and the world is drawn sharply.[1] To his disciples Jesus promises the Spirit-Paraclete; the world can receive neither the Spirit nor Jesus' peace (Jn 14:17, 19, 22, 27). Because Jesus' disciples are chosen "out of the world" (ἐκ τοῦ κόσμου) and it loves only its own, the world hates them (Jn 15:19). They are to carry on Jesus' word and witness in the midst of the world's hostility already demonstrated toward Jesus and soon to be turned against them as well (Jn 15:20-21; 15:26–16:4). In the world the disciples have tribulation, but Jesus has overcome it. Like a woman in childbirth, their anguish will soon be turned to joy (Jn 16:20-22, 31-33). In Jesus' final prayer the disciples are those the Father has given him out of the world, though they continue to live in it (Jn 17:6, 9, 11).[2] "They are not of the world" (οὐκ εἰσιν ἐκ τοῦ κόσμου), even as Jesus is not of the world (Jn 17:14, 16). Jesus asks the Father to consecrate them in the truth as Jesus is about to consecrate himself (Jn 17:17-19). The world has not known the Father, but these have known that the Father sent the Son (Jn 17:24).

---

[1]Takashi Onuki, *Gemeinde und Welt im Johannesevangelium: Ein Beitrag zur Frage nach der theologischen und pragmatischen Funktion des johanneischen "Dualismus"* (WMANT 56; Neukirchen-Vluyn: Neukirchener Verlag, 1984).

[2]Pierre Le Fort, *Les structures de l'Église militante selon Saint Jean: Étude d'ecclésiologie concrète appliquée au IV évangile et aux épîtres johanniques* (NST 25; Geneva: Labor et Fides, 1970), pp. 102, 180.

To Pilate, a man of the world if ever there was one, Jesus states that his kingdom is not of this world (Jn 18:36). With that, he becomes king exalted on the cross (Jn 19). On rising from the dead, after commissioning his disciples and breathing the promised Spirit into them (Jn 20:21-23), he ascends to his Father, leaving them behind in the world.

*According to the Johannine Epistles.* For the recipients of the Johannine correspondence, a community of churches from which some high-sounding antichrists and their followers have departed, the world turns out to have been in their midst incognito until that group showed its colors and made its exit. Those who have remained faithful from the beginning stand out from those who withdrew as day from night. In this rhetorical situation the motifs of witness and of persecution that are so prominent in the Gospel drop away. Emphasis falls on affirming the unique identity of God's beloved ones and on encouraging them to remain true over against those who have gone out.

God is light without any shadow, and he brooks no darkness in his people. If they incur sin as they keep walking in the light, and turn to God with confession, God cleanses and forgives them (1 Jn 1:5–2:6; 5:16-17). The world with its lusts "is not of the Father," and is passing away, and has nothing for God's people (1 Jn 2:15-17). There is a "we" from whom the secessionists have removed themselves, and a "they" who went out, showing that they were never really "of us" (οὐκ ἦσαν/εἰσίν ἐξ ἡμῶν [1 Jn 2:19]). The readers are children of God not just in name but in reality. Owing to the fact that the world did not know the Son, neither does it know them (1 Jn 3:1). The schismatics are "children of the devil," as seen by their practice of sin and by their hatred of the faithful community (1 Jn 3:10). The one group is "of God" (ἐκ τοῦ θεοῦ [1 Jn 4:4, 6]) and speaks prophecies from the spirit of truth. Their faith overcomes the world (1 Jn 2:13, 14; 5:4-5). The others are "of the world" (ἐκ τοῦ κόσμου) and are governed by the spirit of error, speaking falsehoods that originate from the world; to them the world listens gladly (1 Jn 4:5). John's readers are to have love for one another (1 Jn 2:10; 3:10b-18, 23; 4:7–5:5), and they assure themselves of a happy judgment from God by being like Jesus "in this world," who laid down his life for us (1 Jn 3:16; 4:17). The alternative is to practice hatred and murder (1 Jn 2:9, 11; 3:12-15, 17). Believers can be rescued from sin by prayer, but the sin of pseudo-believers tends to death (1 Jn 5:16-17). "We" are "of God," having been snatched from the realm of the evil one (1 Jn 5:19).

The rift between the church and societies of the deceived is seen in John's commending those who offer hospitality to missionaries who bring the truth (3 Jn 5-8) while prohibiting the same to doctrinal innovators (2 Jn 10-11).

***According to the Apocalypse.*** In the Apocalypse the world comes in the form of a pagan environment agog over the Roman values of power, wealth and pleasure. In this case, the world threatens both to corrupt the church from within and to molest it from without. This is clear in the opening oracles to the seven churches (Apoc 2–3). Christ calls on five of the churches to repent, tempted as they are to accommodate themselves to society in varying degrees. Two local churches come in for no moral criticism (Smyrna, Philadelphia); they are under intense social pressure to conform, involving slander (Apoc 2:9), imprisonment and the possibility of execution (Apoc 2:10). The book as a whole is a summons to keep the faith both in word and in deed (Apoc 1:3). It exhorts its hearers to behave consistently as the Lamb's followers (Apoc 14:9-11; 16:15; 18:4, 20) and promises rewards to those who pay the extreme penalty (Apoc 6:9-11; 11:4-13; 13:10; 14:12; 20:4-6).

This Christian prophecy uses antithetical imagery to accentuate the contrast between church and world. In heaven the souls of those slaughtered for the word of God cry for vindication (Apoc 6:9-11); in the background are their worldly executioners. Directly opposed to the 144,000 who have the name of the Lamb and of his Father imprinted on their foreheads (Apoc 7:1-8; 9:3-6; 14:1-4) are the hordes of the nations who receive the mark of the beast on their foreheads (Apoc 13:7-8, 15-17). Two witnesses symbolize the church's indictment against the nations; they prophesy until the beast slays them (Apoc 11:3-13). The final generation sums up societies of all times and places. There are two municipal communities: heavenly Jerusalem (Apoc 12; 19:6-8; 21:9–22:9) and earthly Babylon (Apoc 14:8; 16:19; 17:1–19:10). Each city is personified as a woman, one of virtue, one of vice. God's voice summons his people to come out of Babylon the great, lest they take part in her sins and share in her plagues (Apoc 18:4). Only the faithful enjoy the new Jerusalem; nothing unclean, nor any who practice abomination or falsehood, will enter it (Apoc 21:27). Gates separate people inside, whose robes are washed, from the vices outside and those given to them (Apoc 22:14-15).[3]

Opposed though these eschatological communities are, they consist of human beings made by God, plunged in their own sin and in the world's, and

---

[3]Gordon Campbell, "Antithetical Feminine-Urban Imagery and a Tale of Two Women-Cities in the Book of Revelation," *TynBul* 55 (2004): 81-108.

offered salvation by him who illumines every person (Jn 1:9). We have already considered John's rudimentary doctrine of election above (chaps. 3, 7) and found it to be no rigid determinism. True, the Apocalypse knows of a book in heaven that has contained the names of the followers of the Lamb since the foundation of the world (Apoc 13:8; 17:8; 20:12, 15), but it also issues an open invitation to anyone to come and take the waters of life (Apoc 22:17). Even in an Epistle that holds the world and those who are not of the world as far apart categorically as can be done, John can still say that Jesus Christ is the propitiation not only for "our" sins, but also "for [those of] the whole world" (περὶ ὅλου τοῦ κόσμου [1 Jn 2:2]). Believers benefit, but the sacrifice that God provided has no boundaries. Jesus, having been lifted up, "draws all" to himself (Jn 12:32). God gives to the Son those who are to be saved out of the world and draws them so that they come. But God loves the world and is never said to deselect people unless they deselect themselves from his good purpose by refusing him.

**Sectarianism?** John understands himself, then, to belong to a group of people in the light over against the human race in darkness. This is the ecclesiological corollary of the so-called Johannine dualism, his tendency to split reality between stark spiritual and moral antitheses. To postmodern readers who regard any human perspective as inescapably limited and relative, and all truth claims as being on equal ground, John's absolute clarity with no shades of gray can come across as dogmatic, simple, exclusive, intolerant, cranky, arrogant, bigoted, repulsive. One social-scientific approach explains his rigidity by recourse to group dynamics. He could be seen as spokesman for a fledgling sect struggling for self-definition over against its established parent group.

From about 1970 Johannine specialists in North America combined sociological and anthropological theory with a long post-Enlightenment tradition of exegesis to posit a "Johannine community." On this scenario, some Jewish believers in Jesus, originally members of synagogues beyond the control of the Judean Pharisees and sages (in northern Palestine? Syria? Alexandria? Asia?), alienated themselves from their Jewish fellows by entertaining ever higher concepts of the Messiah. Eventually they went beyond the pale, and the others judged their Christology to compromise monotheism. Shunned by or thrust out of synagogues, they disputed with local Jewish authorities. The two sides flung blasphemy charges at each other of the sort reflected in John 5–12. A deepening conviction on the part of the Christian group that they were the unique bearers of truth in a world of falsehood, of goodness in a world of sin and evil, of love in a world of hatred and murder, can then be interpreted as a strategy on their part to reinforce their wobbly sense of identity against the odds, even to turn their increasing isolation into a virtue.

Features of sectarian religious movements[4] that have been thought pertinent to early Christianity,[5] and to the Johannine community in particular,[6] include rejection of the world and of the dominant party's worldview; a claim to special truth, associated with an alternative worldview unique to the new group; construal of reality in terms of binary oppositions; voluntary membership; intimate acceptance, love and fellowship among insiders; and a demand of unreserved commitment to the new way. Attitudes expressed in the Johannine literature toward the Roman Empire and the Jews fit this pattern. But Raymond Brown cautions against assuming that the Johannine churches segregated themselves from other Christians, seeing that radical interpretations of Johannine theology and ecclesiology (antisacramentalism, anti-Petrinism, anticlericalism, naïve Docetism) have not won the day among scholars.[7]

Those scholars who subscribe to the "Johannine community" hypothesis posit a sectarian eddy within multifarious streams of early Christianity having its own idiosyncratic traditions about Jesus and about common life.

---

[4]For general definitions of a religious sect, see Max Weber, *Wirtschaft und Gesellschaft*, vol. 3 of *Grundriss der Sozialökonomik* (Tübingen: Mohr, 1922), p. 812; idem, *The Methodology of the Social Sciences* (trans. and ed. Edward A. Shils and Henry A. Finch; Glencoe, IL: Free Press, 1949), pp. 93-94; Joachim Wach, *Sociology of Religion* (Chicago: University of Chicago Press, 1944), pp. 196-205; J. Milton Yinger, *Religion in the Struggle for Power: A Study in the Sociology of Religion* (Durham, NC: Duke University Press, 1946); Werner Stark, *Sectarian Religion*, vol. 2 of *The Sociology of Religion: A Study of Christendom* (MR 2; London: Routledge & Kegan Paul, 1967); Bryan R. Wilson, ed., *Patterns of Sectarianism: Organization and Ideology in Social and Religious Movements* (London: Heinemann, 1967), pp. 1-21; idem, *Religious Sects: A Sociological Study* (WUL; London: Weidenfeld & Nicolson, 1970), pp. 14-35.

[5]For the application of sect theory to the early church, see Robin Scroggs, "The Earliest Christian Communities as Sectarian Movement," in *Early Christianity*, vol. 2 of Christianity, *Judaism and Other Greco-Roman Cults: Studies for Morton Smith at Sixty* (ed. Jacob Neusner; SJLA 12; Leiden: Brill, 1975), pp. 1-23. John Gager uses the terms "millenarian movement" or "cult" (*Kingdom and Community: The Social World of Early Christianity* (PHSR; Englewood Cliffs, NJ: Prentice-Hall, 1975), pp. 20-65.

[6]Wayne A. Meeks, "The Man from Heaven in Johannine Sectarianism," *JBL* 91 (1972): 44-72; Raymond E. Brown, *The Community of the Beloved Disciple: The Life, Loves, and Hates of an Individual Church in New Testament Times* (New York: Paulist Press, 1979), pp. 14-17; D. Moody Smith, "Johannine Christianity," in *Johannine Christianity: Essays on Its Setting, Sources, and Theology* (Columbia: University of South Carolina Press, 1984), pp. 1-36; David Rensberger, *Johannine Faith and Liberating Community* (Philadelphia: Westminster, 1988), pp. 25-29.

[7]Brown, *Community*, pp. 16-17.

The Achilles' heel of the construct has always been a dearth of documentation. Already in a seminal 1972 essay one of its architects summed up the situation with candor: "Unfortunately we have no independent information about the organization of the Johannine group, and even the Johannine literature gives little description of the community and hardly any statements that are directly 'ecclesiological.'"[8] What the putative sect's own corpus leaves unattested is even less discernible in patristic sources, which situate John in the catholic church. Some forty years after Wayne Meeks's article, the data set supporting the sectarian theory remains null. Yet that fact has hardly slowed the alacrity with which the academy has embraced the theory following a cadre of leading New Testament scholars and snowballing collegial opinion. Such is the reflexive aversion of the New Testament guild to the other viable explanation of this literary corpus: the authorship of John the son of Zebedee and apostle of Jesus.

At the phenomenal level, early Christianity did have a number of traits in common with religious sects of other times and places. Causes may well be sought among social forces known to produce such a phenotype in the modern world where analogous cases are accessible to study, subject to the proviso that causes so uncovered not be taken reductionistically as the complete explanation of the phenomena.[9] Other causes must also be taken into account. From a biblical-theological standpoint, it is telling that the most important influences on John—the Old Testament and Jesus—rarely observe the righteous having the upper hand in worldly affairs. In the Old Testament Cain slew innocent Abel; a stiffnecked and mutinous people drove Moses to desperation again and again; Israel rejected Samuel and the judges; Saul pursued David, God's anointed; Judah's king remanded Jeremiah the prophet to a cistern; in the Psalter the righteous poor cry to God for deliverance from the powerful wicked; Isaiah depicts the future servant of the Lord suffering for the nation. Jesus got crucified. According to the Synoptics as well as John's Gospel, Jesus before his death steeled his followers for persecutions that he knew they were certain to face (Mt 10:16-39 pars.; Mt 24:9-14 pars.; Jn 15:18–16:4). John sees the first fratricide as paradigmatic of relations between the righteous and the wicked for all time (1 Jn 3:12-13). He has the sweep of Scripture and of history on his side.

---

[8]Meeks, "Man from Heaven," p. 69.
[9]As is done, for example, in the work of the Marxist Karl Kautsky, *Foundations of Christianity* (London: Allen & Unwin, 1925 [1908]).

In assessing the extent to which the Johannine outlook might be considered sectarian, we do well to bear in mind the large tracts of John's thought that cannot be characterized that way. An instructive exercise is to inquire which of H. Richard Niebuhr's five types of relation between church and culture are represented in the Johannine corpus. A careful analysis will conclude that "Christ Against Culture" is neither the only, nor even the primary, model that fits John. Arguably, "Christ Above/Completing Culture" is a better starting point. John has a robust doctrine of God as creator; he views Christ as fulfilling, not abolishing, all that is noble and beautiful in Judaism (save only its vendetta against Jesus); and he is happy to take over from Ephesian culture terms and concepts that aid in his presentation of Christ—not only "Logos," "Savior of the world," "Lord and God," and so forth, but also wine, health, bread, immortality, and many others. In all these respects, John's Christ shows himself to be the Lord of Jewish, Greco-Roman, and indeed all human cultures, who formed them and can take from them symbols worthy to be attached to his own person. Insofar as the world has been defaced by sin, "Christ and Culture in Paradox" describes John's hope for a world redeemed, combined with his suspicion toward any institution governed by unredeemed humanity. Even in the Apocalypse, where "Christ Against Culture" captures the hardening ideological antagonism between a pro-Roman Asia and a marginalized church, angelic hosts fall down before the creator God and look for every living being in heaven, on earth, and under the earth finally to worship him.[10] John's attitude toward the world is finely textured. To label him as a sectarian is a faddish oversimplification.

Finally, we ought not to lose sight of John's individual genius. That each of the Gospels represents more the interests of a regional church than of an individual author is nothing more than a working postulate of form criticism, and an improbable one at that.[11] If John authored the corpus ascribed to him, it may fairly be asked whether a "Johannine Christianity," considered as a discrete

---

[10]Because John has a strong doctrine of sin, it would be impossible for him to espouse the type "Christ Of Culture," the optimistic view that culture is evolving upwards toward a divinely appointed goal. Nor does he provide much grist for "Christ Transforming Culture," the view that the kingdom of God can be realized on earth through missionary endeavor and social reconstruction going hand in hand. For the five types, see H. Richard Niebuhr, *Christ and Culture* (New York: Harper, 1951).

[11]Martin Hengel, *The Johannine Question* (Philadelphia: Trinity Press International, 1990); Richard Bauckham, *Jesus and the Eyewitnesses: The Gospels as Eyewitness Testimony* (Grand Rapids: Eerdmans, 2006); idem, *The Testimony of the Beloved Disciple: Narrative, History, and Theology in the Gospel of John* (Grand Rapids: Baker Academic, 2007).

subcommunity within the church, ever existed at all. John became a guru in
the churches of Judea and of Asia, to be sure, but he was not the founder of
those churches, nor was he ever the sole Christian leader in either place. It is
doubtful whether his writings or his apostolic presence could have stamped his
image on those churches to the degree that it shows in what he wrote. And, as
we have seen throughout this study, John was an idealist, a born theologian
whose mind went straight to the quiddity of whatever issue he took up. Without
denying the legitimacy of inquiries into second-generation Christianity along
social lines, we must insist that John's personal, incisive style of thought and
expression sheds a great deal more light on the contrasts in the Johannine literature than does the thesis of Johannine sectarianism.

## "IN THE WORLD" FOR THE WORLD: THE CHURCH'S MISSION

According to John, Jesus commissioned his disciples to make known God's love
(Jn 3:16; 13:35) and forgiveness (Jn 20:21-23). The love of God reaching out to a
world in peril is the driving force behind Jesus' preaching, and it also drives the
mission of the church.[12] Matthew chronicles the change from a focus on Israel
exclusively during Jesus' ministry (Mt 10:5-6; 15:24) to an aggressive propa-
gation of the gospel to all nations after his rising from the dead (Mt 28:19-20).
Luke charts the gospel's progress from Jerusalem to Rome (Acts 1:8). In comparison, John's concept of evangelization is more centripetal, putting stress on
attracting people into the united community of love (Jn 13:35; 17:21, 23).[13] In
this respect, John's language is typical of the Jewish approach to proselytization,
while embracing Gentiles no less generously than the Synoptists do.

*Church as sent.* The transcendent, theological basis for the church's mission
lies in the divine sendings that originate in the inner life of the triune God.[14] God
loves the world and intends it not to perish (Jn 3:16). Having created it through
the Logos, God sent his Logos-Son into the world to save it and thus glorify the
Father (3:16-17). This the Son did by dying, as a grain of wheat must disintegrate

---

[12]Miguel Rodriguez Ruiz, *Der Missionsgedanke des Johannesevangeliums* (FB 55; Würzburg: Echter Verlag, 1987).

[13]The chief language complexes are "gathering" a harvest (Jn 4:35-38; 11:52) and "bringing" or "drawing" people to Jesus (Jn 6:44, 65; 10:16; 12:32). See Johannes Nissen, "Mission in the Fourth Gospel: Historical and Hermeneutical Perspectives," in *New Readings in John: Literary and Theological Perspectives; Essays from the Scandinavian Conference on the Fourth Gospel in Aarhus 1997* (ed. Johannes Nissen and Siegfried Pedersen; Sheffield: Sheffield Academic Press, 1999), p. 219.

[14]Josef Kuhl, *Die Sendung Jesu und der Kirche nach dem Johannes-Evangelium* (SIMSVD 11; St. Augustin: Steyler, 1967).

in order to multiply (Jn 12:24). From this we see that the mission of the church is rooted in the historic death and resurrection of Jesus. Before his return to heaven Jesus, the first Paraclete, sent the other Paraclete to indwell his disciples (Jn 14:16), empowering them to repeat Jesus' works on a greater scale (Jn 14:12) and to testify to the Son (Jn 15:26; 16:14-15). Out of the belly of believers streams the Spirit (Jn 7:38), bringing health to the nations (Apoc 22:2).[15]

Apart from these divine sendings the church has no independent missionary mandate. The Father's sending of the Son, and the Son's sending of his disciples, are analogous in that the giver imposes a task on the receiver in a sort of chain (Jn 13:20; 17:18; 20:21). But there the analogy ends. In no way is the church a continuing incarnation of Jesus. The person of the Logos become flesh was absolutely sui generis, and his work as the Lamb of God who takes away the sin of the world was foundational and unrepeatable.[16] Rather, the church is the human organ of the Spirit's mission.[17] The witness of the Spirit to the Son fuses with the witness of Jesus' disciples (Jn 15:26-27). Jesus has sent his disciples endued with the Spirit (Jn 20:22). It is the Spirit and the bride who invite anyone and everyone to come to the water of life (Apoc 22:17).

From an anthropological standpoint, the possibility and productivity of missionary work rest on the fact that all people have received the light of life from the creative Logos (Jn 1:4), who illumines every person (Jn 1:9). To be human is to have the intellectual, moral and spiritual capability for fellowship with God, together with full responsibility for how one responds to God's self-revelation in Christ.

***Eschatological window for gathering disciples.*** Now that the old world has entered its final period and the blessings of the coming age are already breaking in upon it, the church's mission has become urgent. Various Old Testament texts looked for an ingathering of Gentiles who would turn to the God of Abraham in the last days.[18] Embedded in John's narrative of Jesus' trek through Samaria, at precisely the point where the topic shifts from Christology (Jn 4:1-26) to the Samaritans' response, is a paragraph about the mission of Jesus'

---

[15]Both John 7:38 and Apocalypse 22:2 hark back to Ezekiel's vision of the water of life flowing from the threshold of the temple (Ezek 47:1-12).

[16]Andreas Köstenberger, *The Missions of Jesus and the Disciples According to the Fourth Gospel: With Implications for the Fourth Gospel's Purpose and the Mission of the Contemporary Church* (Grand Rapids: Eerdmans, 1998).

[17]Le Fort, *Structures de l'Église*, pp. 169-74.

[18]E.g., Ps 47:9; 72:11; 87:5-6; 102:22; Is 2:2-4; 11:9; 19:24-25; 45:14, 24; 49:7; 66:18-21; Zech 8:23; Mal 1:11.

disciples. According to Jesus, no longer is the harvest four months away; the fields are already white for harvesting (Jn 4:35).[19] Jesus as the land's master and primary sower is mobilizing all hands to bring in the crop, so that he and his reapers may share the joy (Jn 4:36-38).[20] The task is huge and will require teamwork with division of labor (Jn 4:37-38).[21] These principles apply to all subsequent missionary activity.

What happened at Sychar of Samaria was the first instance of the eschatological harvest of non-Israelites. For the most part, the Fourth Gospel portrays Jesus as pressing his claims on his own compatriots in Galilee and Judea. But the encounter between Jesus and the Samaritans is a paradigm of crosscultural communication, wherein he makes himself understood by using their language and concepts to address their concerns.[22] Other isolated sayings about Gentile believers refer to them as "other sheep" to be integrated into Jesus' fold (Jn 10:16), scattered children to be gathered (Jn 11:52), or inquisitive Greeks representing the whole human race whom Jesus will draw to himself on the cross (Jn 12:20, 24, 32). These statements look to the future, as the worldwide mission did not get under way until after Jesus was glorified. Its outcome will be countless masses of believers from all nations praising God for their ransom (Apoc 1:5-6; 5:9-10; 7:9-12).

Jesus was aware that he had only a limited time to make his message known,

---

[19]The punctuation of John 4:35-36 is disputed. In my view, the last word in the Greek of John 4:35 (ἤδη, "already") belongs with what precedes in that verse, not with the statement that follows in John 4:36. It makes a suitable contrast to the earlier ἔτι τετράμηνός ἐστιν ("there are yet four months"). It would contribute nothing to the chiasmus in John 4:36, where reaper and sower rejoice together, the latter because his barns are full and the former because he gets his wage. This "already" in John 4:35 answers to the hour that is coming and "now is" in John 4:23.

[20]That Jesus is the master and his disciples are the reapers is plain in John 4:38. Jesus sowed the word of God in his conversation with the woman at the well. She sowed it in the village (Jn 4:28-29, 39, 42). Jesus is the main sower, and she, and perhaps the first people she told who talked with their acquaintances, are the plural "others" into whose labor Jesus' disciples enter (Jn 4:38). The aorist "I sent" (ἀπέστειλα) and the perfect "you have entered" (εἰσεληλύθατε) correspond to the use of the Semitic perfect tense to express instantaneous action, "an act in the present by which that very act is completed" (Ronald J. Williams, *Hebrew Syntax: An Outline* [2nd ed.; Toronto: University of Toronto Press, 1976], §164). So the saying in John 4:35 uses harvest imagery to denote eschatological urgency, as does Matthew 9:37-38, and the christic interpretation of the sower in John 4:36-37 is like that at Matthew 13:24, 37.

[21]A concrete example of this division of labor is the offering of hospitality to traveling teachers or missionaries by those who cannot travel themselves (3 Jn 5-8).

[22]Eric J. Wyckoff, "Jesus in Samaria (John 4:4-42): A Model for Cross-Cultural Ministry," *BTB* 35 (2005): 89-98. On the establishment of Christianity in Samaria, see Jürgen K. Zangenberg, *Frühes Christentum in Samarien: Topographische und traditionsgeschichtliche Studien zu den Samarientexten im Johannesevangelium* (TANZ 27; Tübingen: Francke, 1998).

after which darkness would fall (Jn 9:4-5). While it was "day," he was willing to go straight into personal danger, confident that no harm would come to him as long as he was walking in his Father's will (Jn 11:8-10). He prepared his disciples to bear witness in the face of the world's ongoing hatred and persecution (Jn 15:18-27). He knew that for some it would mean expulsion from synagogues or even capital punishment (Jn 16:1-4). He prayed for God to keep them from the evil one so that they, consecrated in the truth, could carry God's word to others (Jn 17:11, 15, 19-20).

**Greater works than Jesus did.** During Jesus' absence his disciples do the same works that Jesus did, and his going to the Father enables them to do yet greater works (Jn 14:12). In this dominical saying emphasis falls not on the miracles that the apostles undoubtedly did, for the healings (e.g., Acts 3:7) and resuscitations from the dead wrought by their hands (Acts 9:36-43) scarcely top the seven Johannine signs of the Christ. Nor is Jesus thinking merely of the impressive statistics of the global mission that would outstrip his meager results in Palestine. "Greater" is qualitative. If the climactic miracle of Jesus in the Fourth Gospel is his raising of Lazarus from the grave, the exalted Lord acting through the word of his Spirit-empowered disciples is even now bestowing eternal life on all who hear his voice (Jn 5:25). Fruits of evangelization are greater, to the extent that the life of the age to come is of a higher order than that of the present age.

God is glorified when Jesus' disciples "bear much fruit" as Jesus has appointed them to do (Jn 15:8, 16). "Fruit" in this context denotes first of all love as the sum of God's commandments. This we see from the juxtaposition of "bearing much fruit" in John 15:8 with abiding in Jesus' love by keeping his commandments in John 15:9-10, and from the framing of "I appointed you that you should go and bear fruit" in John 15:16 between statements of the love command (Jn 15:12, 17). But the effect of practicing love in the community of disciples will be that the world will know and some will believe (Jn 13:35; 17:21, 23). The moral fruit that is love, itself becomes fruitful in the form of more and more converts (cf. "fruit" in Jn 4:36; 12:24).

Whether the bountiful catch of fish in the epilogue to the Fourth Gospel (Jn 21:1-14) has implications for ecclesiology and mission is debatable.[23] Some commentators read the story allegorically in the light of the Synoptic saying

---

[23]J. D. M. Derrett thinks that fishing symbolizes evangelization ("The Mission Originates in Captivation: ἁλιεύω, πιάζω, σύρω, ἕλκω [Jn 21:6-11]," *FilNeot* 15 [2002]: 95-109).

of Jesus that he would make his disciples "fishers of people" (Mt 4:19 pars.). The number 153 (Jn 21:11) can then symbolize the elect from the nations,[24] all the more so if subjected to numerological analysis.[25] That the church can fulfill its mission only through the presence and blessing of Jesus would be the point. But the author does not give his readers strong encouragement to take this route.[26] He interprets the untorn net full of fish christologically as yet a third appearance of the risen Lord (Jn 21:7, 14), in addition to John 20:19, 26. That is the primary significance of the prodigious catch. Any further significance is secondary.

**Outcome.** How effective in quantitative results does John expect the church's mission to be? He is no triumphalist, but neither is he so pessimistic as to put the worth of the enterprise in question.

The Gospel speaks only in a general way of a time of "harvest" (Jn 4:35), of a gathering into one of God's children who are scattered beyond the nation (Jn 11:51-52), of Jesus' death bearing "much fruit" through his disciples' abiding in him (Jn 12:24; 15:5, 8), of his being lifted up drawing "all people" to him (Jn 12:32), of the disciples doing "greater works" than his (Jn 14:12), of sins being either forgiven or retained by Jesus' deputies (Jn 20:23), perhaps, symbolically, of a miraculous catch of fish under Jesus' direction (Jn 21:4-11). But the disciples are to expect to meet with hatred, misunderstanding, persecution and death in Jesus' cause (Jn 15:18–16:4) until the end of the age (Jn 16:16-33).

The Epistles know that apostolic mission work can be undone by rival ideologues (2 Jn 8). Those who retain the apostolic faith are to aid and abet accredited itinerant prophets and missionaries so that all may be "fellow workers in the truth" (3 Jn 8). This many-tiered activity of persuading people to believe goes on in a world that lies in thrall to the evil one (1 Jn 5:19), that largely does not hear the truth (1 Jn 4:5-6).

At the time of the Apocalypse the church was in "the tribulation and the kingdom and the patient endurance" (Apoc 1:9). In this tripartite phrase "the kingdom" occupies the central place and is flanked by words describing

---

[24]Joseph A. Romeo, "Gematria and John 21:11—the Children of God," *JBL* 97 (1978): 263-64. Romeo adds up the numerical values of the Hebrew letters in the phrase בני האלהים ("the sons of God").

[25]Augustine observed that 153 is the triangular number of 17 (1 + 2 + 3 + . . . . + 17) (*Tract. Ev. Jo.* 122.8). Ancient zoologists apparently knew of 153 kinds of fish (Jerome, *Commentary on Ezekiel*, on 47:9-12). See further Richard Bauckham, "The 153 Fish and the Unity of the Fourth Gospel," *Neot* 36 (2002): 77-88; Marc Rastoin, "Encore une fois les 153 poissions (Jn 21,11)," *Bib* 90 (2009): 84-92.

[26]Much less is the fish fry for breakfast meant to evoke the Lord's Supper (Jn 21:9-14).

the church's current difficulties. This captures the situation of the missional church in a nutshell.

On the one hand, John looks for massive numbers of converts in the end. The picture of "every creature in heaven and on earth and under the earth and in the sea, and all therein" falling down to offer adoration before the throne in heaven can only be eschatological, since it is not the case during this present age (Apoc 5:13). Destined to praise God and the Lamb are "a great multitude which no one could number, from every nation, from all tribes and peoples and tongues" (Apoc 7:9). Singing, they make a noise like a thunderous waterfall (Apoc 14:2). In the new heaven and new earth the nations will walk by the light of the Holy City, Jerusalem, and the kings of the earth will bring their treasures inside its gates (Apoc 21:24-25). The leaves of the tree of life, flourishing on both sides of the river of the water of life, will be for the healing of the nations (Apoc 22:2). These pictures of a multicultural community enjoying God's blessing upon Jerusalem come straight from the Old Testament prophets (Is 60:6-7; 66:10-12; Ezek 47:12). They point to the fulfillment of God's promise to Abraham that in him all the families of the earth will be blessed (Gen 12:3; 18:18; 22:18). While no nation is excluded, however, these verses do not mean that salvation will be universal in the sense that it will encompass every person without remainder.[27]

For, on the other hand, the idyllic utopia is achieved at the cost of staggering destruction. Sun, moon, stars and sky must go dark, every mountain and island must be moved out of its place, all strata of society must flee before the wrath of the enthroned judge (Apoc 6:12-17). As horrific plagues come upon the world (Apoc 8:6–9:21), "the rest of mankind" (Apoc 9:20-21), those not sealed against the plagues (Apoc 7:1-3; 9:4), harden themselves against the commands of God. In a judgment that Joel envisaged (Joel 3:13), the divine sickle must reap the fields, the clusters of the vine of the earth be trodden in the winepress of the wrath of God (Apoc 14:14-20).[28] On those who raise fists to heaven hailstones heavy as a hundredweight will crash down (Apoc 16:21). The entire global community, symbolized by Babylon the harlot, will devour itself and sink in a suicidal drunken stupor (Apoc 16:19c; 17:16-17; 18:1–19:10). Beast, false

---

[27]David Mathewson, "The Destiny of the Nations in Revelation 21:1–22:5: A Reconsideration," *TynBul* 53 (2002): 121-42.

[28]G. K. Beale, *The Book of Revelation: A Commentary on the Greek Text* (NIGTC; Grand Rapids: Eerdmans; Carlisle: Paternoster, 1999), pp. 773-79; Eckhard J. Schnabel, "John and the Future of the Nations," *BBR* 12 (2002): 243-71.

prophet and dragon will be remanded to the lake of fire that burns with sulfur (Apoc 19:20; 20:10). At the last assize, anyone whose name is not found inscribed in the book of life will be thrown into the lake of fire (Apoc 20:14).

Nowhere does John speculate on the proportion of the human race that will yield to evangelization. The most we can say is that many will be saved and, apparently, many lost.

## "NOT OF THIS WORLD": WORLD VERSUS CHURCH UNTIL THE END OF TIME

According to John, the circle of Jesus' disciples is open and welcomes any from the surrounding society who will believe, but it remains a divinely stamped body that belongs to a realm other than the world and therefore finds itself embroiled in spiritual conflict until the end of the age.

*Hatred of the church's truth telling by the world.* Hatred (John uses the verb μισεῖν) is the world's attitude toward God and toward those who belong to God (Jn 15:18, 19; 17:14; 1 Jn 3:13).[29] The world's hatred centers primarily on God's Son, for he exposed sin (Jn 7:7; 15:22) and proved that he was speaking from God by doing irrefutable works (Jn 15:24). Jesus gave the world no cause to hate him except that he made it face itself for what it is (Jn 15:25). Hatred of Jesus carries over into hatred of his followers (Jn 15:18-21; 16:1-4). Like Cain, the world hates the believers because their good deeds show the deeds of the world to be evil by contrast (1 Jn 3:12-13).

In the Roman province of Asia in the 90s some Jews made themselves a "synagogue of Satan" by defaming the Christians to officials who had authority to imprison them; however, Christ will make the informers come and bow down and learn that he has loved them (Apoc 2:9; 3:9). Throughout the "little apocalypse" within the visions of the Apocalypse[30] runs a combat motif (πολεμεῖν, πόλεμος). Nations will attack the saints;[31] Christ will step in to vindicate them (Apoc 19:11). Threats to the church in the seer's contemporary situation he depicts as eschatological antagonists to the divine cause. Civic

---

[29]In the single instance where God's people are the subject of this verb, its object is the "works of" the Nicolaitans (Apoc 2:6).

[30]The little apocalypse is introduced into the sequences of seals, trumpets and bowls in the form of a "little scroll" (Apoc 10:2) that the prophet must eat, becoming a second prophecy within the main one (Apoc 10:9-11). After a preview of its plot (Apoc 11:1-13), the full contents follow in Apocalypse 12:1–15:4; 19:11–21:8.

[31]Apoc 11:7; 12:7, 17; 13:4, 7; 16:14; 17:14; 19:19; 20:8; cf., using a wider vocabulary, Apoc 11:2; 13:7-10, 15-17.

priests serving the cult of the emperor in Asia (Apoc 13:11-18) become the "false prophet" of the last days (cf. Mt 24:11, 24). Behind them, the imperial court with its global, quasi-messianic pretensions is the beastly antichrist, doing nothing to hinder local persecutions of God's people.[32] Inflaming them all is demonic incitement by the ancient chaos monster recently freed from the abyss.[33]

What stirs the world's hatred above all is the church's prophetic testimony concerning human godlessness. Jesus said, "The world . . . hates me because I testify of it that its works are evil" (Jn 7:7). Jesus' disciples, bearing witness through the Spirit of truth (Jn 15:26-27), continue to press charges concerning sin, righteousness and judgment (Jn 16:7-11). Unbelief toward Jesus constitutes the world's fundamental sin (Jn 16:9). He, whom the religious and political leaders of Palestine handed over to pay the extreme criminal penalty, is with his Father in highest honor, fully vindicated as righteous in God's eyes (Jn 16:10). Already the ruler of the world is judged, while all who with the devil seek the world's good apart from its creator await the same damnation (Jn 16:11). The faithful point out that false prophets speak from the devil, and the world turns a deaf ear to the word from God that the faithful offer instead (1 Jn 4:5-6). John the seer considers that civic representatives of the imperial cult speak "like a dragon" (Apoc 13:11), yet their words and signs prevail, and all classes of people receive the mark of the beast (Apoc 13:12-17). Therefore the church wears sackcloth in anticipation of the world's inevitable demise (Apoc 11:3). From society in these last days the church is utterly alienated. God's word in their mouth burns like fire (Apoc 11:5; cf. Jer 5:14). In the spirit and power of Moses and of Elijah the church announces doom (Apoc 11:6), and its word of divine judgment torments earth dwellers (Apoc 11:10).[34] The task to which

---

[32]On the impact of the cult of the living emperor in Roman Asia, see S. R. F. Price, *Rituals and Power: The Roman Imperial Cult in Asia Minor* (Cambridge: Cambridge University Press, 1984); Steven J. Friesen, *Imperial Cults and the Apocalypse of John: Reading Revelation in the Ruins* (Oxford: Oxford University Press, 2001); Hamilton Moore and Philip McCormick, "Domitian," *IBS* 25 (2003): 74-101; Paul Barnett, "Revelation in Its Roman Setting," *VR* 74 (2009): 26-34; Michael Naylor, "The Roman Imperial Cult and Revelation," *CurBR* 8 (2010): 207-39; Martin Ebner and Elisabeth Esch-Wermeling, eds., *Kaiserkult, Wirtschaft und* spectacula: *Zum politischen und gesellschaftlichen Umfeld der Offenbarung* (NTOA 72; Göttingen: Vandenhoeck & Ruprecht, 2011).

[33]After symbolizing the people of God as a heavenly woman (Apoc 12:1-2), the narrative of the conflict brings in the enemies one by one (dragon [Apoc 12:3-17], beast [Apoc 13:1-10], false prophet [Apoc 13:11-18]). Their overthrow takes place in reverse order, creating a chiasm within the little apocalypse (prophet and beast [Apoc 19:11-21], dragon [Apoc 20:1-10], glorification of the new Jerusalem as bride of the Lamb [Apoc 21:1-8]).

[34]Antoninus King Wai Siew, *The War between the Two Beasts and the Two Witnesses: A Chiastic Reading of Revelation 11:1–14:5* (LNTS 283; London: T & T Clark, 2005).

God calls his church is to bear faithful witness to him in the midst of a warped world, to worship him rightly and him alone in the Lamb.[35]

John himself in the Apocalypse acts as prophet to the whole church. Here his critique of the world and of its institutions is at its most trenchant. But this critique comes in a tract addressed to the churches, not to the world that it denounces. It is designed to make clear to the eye of faith God's damning judgment on the pomp and blandishments of humanistic society, lest God's people too be carried away by popular enthusiasm for Roman values.[36] God enthroned with his Lamb, though invisible as long as this present age lasts, holds the destiny of all things in a divinely written scroll (Apoc 4–5). God is the sole authority worthy to receive worship.[37] Heavenly temple scenes (Apoc 4–5; 7:9-17; 11:15-19; 15:2-4; 19:1-8) impress on John's congregations what is real, far above earthly propaganda, as an antidote to the skewed construal of reality in Roman hubris.[38] At a time of unprecedented secular peace and affluence in Asia, John reminds readers that civilization is in fact moving inexorably toward catastophe (seals [Apoc 6; 8:1-5]; trumpets [Apoc 8:6–9:21; 11:14-19]). Behind the stage of current events the devil, the ancient conniving chaos monster who has failed to stop God's Messiah, is having a last fling at mobilizing worldly forces against the saints (Apoc 12).[39] Roman military and political might may be supreme over the nations, unconquerable and irrepressible (Apoc 13:2-4), but God has limited the term of the beast (Apoc 19:20-21). Reli-

---

[35]Brian K. Blount, "Reading Revelation Today: Witness as Active Resistance," *Int* 54 (2000): 398-412; Gordon Campbell, "True and False Proclamation in the Book of Revelation," *IBS* 25 (2003): 60-73; Olutola K. Peters, *The Mandate of the Church in the Apocalypse of John* (SBL 77; New York: Peter Lang, 2005).

[36]Harry O. Maier, *Apocalypse Recalled: The Book of Revelation after Christendom* (Minneapolis: Fortress, 2002); Ian Smith, "A Rational Choice Model of the Book of Revelation," *JSNT* 85 (2002): 97-116; Stephen Pattemore, *The People of God in the Apocalypse: Discourse, Structure and Exegesis* (SNTSMS 128; Cambridge: University Press, 2004); David A. deSilva, "The Strategic Arousal of Emotion in John's Visions of Roman Imperialism: A Rhetorical-Critical Investigation of Revelation 4–22," *Neot* 42 (2008): 1-34.

[37]Russell Morton, "Glory to God and to the Lamb: John's Use of Jewish and Hellenistic/Roman Themes in Formatting His Theology in Revelation 4–5," *JSNT* 83 (2001): 89-109; idem, *One upon the Throne and the Lamb: A Tradition Historical/Theological Analysis of Revelation 4–5* (SBL 110; New York: Peter Lang, 2007); Gottfried Schimanowski, *Die himmlische Liturgie in der Apokalypse des Johannes: Die frühjüdischen Traditionen in Offenbarung 4–5 unter Einschluss der Hekhalotliteratur* (WUNT 2/154; Tübingen: Mohr Siebeck, 2002).

[38]Russell Morton, "Revelation 7:9-17: The Innumerable Crowd before the One upon the Throne and the Lamb," *ATJ* 32 (2000): 1-11; Franz Tóth, *Der Himmlische Kult: Wirklichkeitskonstruktion und Sinnbildung in der Johannesoffenbarung* (ABG 22; Leipzig: Evangelische Verlagsanhalt, 2006).

[39]Jürgen H. Kalms, *Der Sturz des Gottesfeindes: Traditionsgeschichtliche Studien zu Apokalypse 12* (WMANT 93; Neukirchen Vluyn: Neukirchener Verlag, 2001).

gious acclamation of the living emperor (Apoc 13:8, 12-15) will lead to punishment in fire and sulfur forever (Apoc 14:9-11). Rome's economic engine, the envy of the kings of the earth (Apoc 17:1-2, 15; 18:9-19), is personified as a besotted whore appointed to drink to her own downfall (Apoc 16:19).[40] Three angels streak across midheaven announcing that the hour of God's judgment, and of his compensating faithful saints, has come (Apoc 14:6-13). Then in serial fashion we see the powers fall: the world-system (bowls [Apoc 15:5–16:21]), Babylon the harlot (Apoc 17:1–19:10),[41] beast and false prophet with the kings and their armies (Apoc 19:11-21), the dragon (Apoc 20:1-10). After the general resurrection and the last assize based on deeds (Apoc 20:11-15), the new creation comes into view (Apoc 21:1-9), in which Lady Jerusalem will be radiant in God's light forever (Apoc 21:9–22:9).

This stout Johannine no pronounced over a world that will not repent (Apoc 9:20-21; 16:11), but instead only hardens in its blasphemies (Apoc 13:1, 6; 17:3) and curses the very God who gave it existence (Apoc 16:9, 11), refreshes a theme of the Old Testament prophets (e.g., Is 13–27; 34–35; Jer 46–51; Ezek 25–32). God Almighty will counteract and conquer the evil that has permeated his world. God will resoundingly show himself blameless over against the intractability in wickedness that is the root of human suffering.[42]

Abundant images of divine vengeance in the Apocalypse remind some modern readers of vindictiveness in human relations. Therefore these readers judge the book sub-Christian.[43] This is to misunderstand gravely John's noble concept of the biblical deity and of his government of the universe.[44] The

---

[40]Richard Bauckham, "The Economic Critique of Rome in Revelation 18," in *The Climax of Prophecy: Studies on the Book of Revelation* (Edinburgh: T & T Clark, 1993), pp. 338-83; Peter S. Perry, "Critiquing the Excess of Empire: A *Synkrisis* of John of Patmos and Dio of Prusa," *JSNT* 29 (2007): 473-96; Craig R. Koester, "Roman Slave Trade and the Critique of Babylon in Revelation 18," *CBQ* 70 (2008): 766-86.

[41]Ulrike Sals, *Die Biographie der "Hure Babylon": Studien Zur Intertextualität der Babylon-Texte in der Bibel* (FAT 2/6; Tübingen: Mohr Siebeck, 2004); Peter F. Gregory, "Its End Is Destruction: Babylon the Great in the Book of Revelation," *CTQ* 73 (2009): 137-53.

[42]Beate Kowalski, "'Lichtfrau, Drache, Zornesschalen . . .': Zur Bedeutung eschatologischer Zeichen in der Offenbarung des Johannes," *ETL* 78 (2002): 358-84.

[43]For example, John E. Phelan, "Revelation, Empire, and the Violence of God," *ExAud* 20 (2004): 65-84; Susan Hylen, "Metaphor Matters: Violence and Ethics in Revelation," *CBQ* 73 (2011): 777-96. Phelan is concerned that God's violence might be used to underwrite our own, even though the Apocalypse inculcates not Zealotism, but passive resistance to the point of martyrdom like that of Jesus. Hylen proceeds on the unexamined assumption that violence is wrong per se, without asking by what authority, toward what human dispositions, or for what end.

[44]William Klassen, "Vengeance in the Apocalypse of John," *CBQ* 28 (1966): 300-311; Richard A. Spencer, "Violence and Vengeance in Revelation," *RevExp* 98 (2001): 11-33.

proper background to John's visions is the constant Old Testament affirmation
that God is a faithful covenant keeper and just avenger who will rise in the end
to redress the sufferings of his innocent people at the hands of the malicious
(e.g., Deut 32:34-43; Ps 9:12; 72:12-14; Joel 3:19-21).[45] Throughout the Bible
believers refrain from avenging themselves precisely because they hope in God,
who alone is righteous, to undertake on their behalf (1 Sam 24:1-15; 25:32-39;
Apoc 6:9-11). God esteems what he has created and requires a reckoning for it.
Any who shed human blood deserve to have their own blood shed (Gen 9:5-6).
Retributive justice has always been the law undergirding moral exchange.
"Render to her as she herself has rendered" (Apoc 18:6). "People have shed the
blood of saints and prophets, and you have given them blood to drink. It is their
due. . . . True and just are your judgments!" (Apoc 16:6-7; cf. 19:2). Nothing in
the teaching of Jesus or of his apostles shook this pillar of the cosmic fabric;
rather, they reaffirmed it (Lk 18:7-8; Rom 12:19; 2 Thess 1:8). That God will move
at the appointed time to destroy the destroyers of the earth is axiomatic (Apoc
11:18). John neither vents hatred toward his enemies nor gloats over their
downfall. The purpose of the prophecies is to give timely warning, to bring
about repentance (Apoc 9:21; 16:11). With all the terrifying pictures vivid in the
reader's mind, the Apocalypse closes with an open invitation from the Spirit
and the bride, addressed no less to the evildoer and the filthy than to the
righteous and the holy (Apoc 22:11), to "Come" and imbibe the water of life
without price (Apoc 22:17).

How should Christians view the authority of the state? John offers no reflective, well-rounded political theology, but his scathing satire on imperial
power in Apocalypse 13; 17; 19 serves as a counterpoise to the basically positive
attitude toward government in the teaching of Jesus (Mt 22:21 pars.), of Paul
(Rom 13:1-7) and of Peter (1 Pet 2:13-17). If and when the state requires idolatry
of its citizens, the saints are called to civil disobedience and the bearing of bold
testimony against it, even to the point of martyrdom.[46]

***Divine presence with and preservation of the church.*** As the beast raises its

---

[45]R. V. G. Tasker, "The Biblical Doctrine of the Wrath of God," *Them* 26 (2001): 4-17; Leon Morris,
*The Biblical Doctrine of Judgment* (London: Tyndale, 1960); H. G. L. Peels, *The Vengeance of God: The
Meaning of the Root NQM and the Function of the NQM-Texts in the Context of Divine Revelation in
the Old Testament* (OtSt 31; Leiden: Brill, 1995).

[46]Craig R. Koester, "The Church and Its Witness in the Apocalypse of John," *TTKi* 78 (2007): 266-82;
Thomas B. Slater, "Context, Christology and Civil Disobedience in John's Apocalypse," *RevExp* 106
(2009): 51-65.

ugly heads again and again throughout history to silence the church (Apoc 17:8-11), God preserves his beloved people. Jesus guards his flock, which knows his voice (Jn 10:1-9). None can take them from him or from his Father (Jn 10:28-29). He prays earnestly for the truth, unity and safekeeping of those whom the Father has given him (Jn 17:11, 12, 15).[47] None is lost except the son of perdition, that the Scripture may be fulfilled (Jn 18:8-9). God's Son keeps those born of God, and the evil one does not touch them (1 Jn 5:18). God's people are shielded from the plagues that he will send on the earth in the last days (Apoc 3:10; 7:1-8; 9:4), as his people Israel in the land of Goshen were separated from Egypt. God shelters them from the harm wrought by the devil. The church, as a corporate whole, is the inner sanctum of God's temple that suffers no damage (Apoc 11:1), though externally its court is trampled by the nations (Apoc 11:2). The church is a woman of the sky (Apoc 12:1), kept hidden on earth by God's protective power as the dragon in desperation throws his worst at her (Apoc 12:6, 14, 16). This does not mean that there will be no individual confessors and martyrs (Jn 16:2; Apoc 2:13; 6:9-11; 11:2; 12:17; 13:10; 17:6; 18:24; 20:4); however, Jesus said, "No one shall snatch them out of my hand" or "out of the Father's hand" (Jn 10:28-29). They resist the beast passively and without violence, following the example of their Lord, who was crucified (Apoc 12:11).[48] God promises to reverse their fortunes, set them on thrones, and commit judgment to them (Apoc 20:4-6).

For Jesus promised peace to his disciples while he was still with them (Jn 14:27; 16:33). After his resurrection from the dead he dispensed this peace by a triple grant (Jn 20:19, 21, 26). He takes joy in his friends (Jn 15:11) and gives them a fullness of joy that no one can take from them (Jn 15:11; 16:20-22, 24; 17:13; 2 Jn 12; 3 Jn 4). Already since Jesus' enthronement the victory paeon has begun to sound in heaven above (Apoc 12:10-12). As God's plan for the universe unfolds and his justice clears it of refractory elements, the swell of rejoicing will become richer (Apoc 18:20; 19:1-8 [fourfold "Hallelujah"]) until it engulfs every creature in heaven and earth and under the earth and in the sea (Apoc 5:8-14).

**Telos.** John knew very well the biblical view of the shape of history. The Hebrew Scriptures open with an account of God's creation of the world (Gen 1–2), continue with its human stewards choosing sin and death (Gen 3), lay out

---

[47]Dirk J. van der Merwe, "The Protection Believers Can Expect from God in the Fulfilment of Their Mission," *SK* 21 (2000): 135-55.

[48]Mark Bredin, *Jesus, Revolutionary of Peace: A Nonviolent Christology in the Book of Revelation* (PBM; Milton Keynes: Paternoster, 2003).

God's gracious provision for the atonement of sin (Lev 1–7; 16; Is 53), and look for a eucatastophe in which all things will be restored with a glory surpassing that at the beginning (e.g., Is 65–66; Ezek 40–48; Dan 7:13-14, 27; Zech 14). Critically important though the history of redemption is, including God's promises throughout the period of the Old Testament culminating in Jesus' incarnation, death, resurrection, messianic reign, mission of the church driven by the Spirit, and return, that subnarrative takes place within the framing narrative of God's purpose for his creation. Put simply, God did not create the world in order to redeem it; he is redeeming it to achieve his creational goal for it. In Johannine terms, at the Alpha-point of the story, out of the eternal love between the Father and the Only-Begotten of his bosom (Jn 1:1-2, 18) came the making of the world (Jn 1:3-5; Apoc 4:11); at the Omega-point will be the everlasting kingdom of God (Jn 3:3, 5; Apoc 11:15; 22:5).

To depict the end of all things, John uses again the primordial image of light (Gen 1:3; Jn 1:4-5). God, who is light and in whom is no darkness at all (1 Jn 1:5), will shine on the city of his people, the new Jerusalem. "The city has no need of sun or moon to shine upon it, for the glory of God is its light, and its lamp is the Lamb" (Apoc 21:23). "Night shall be no more . . . for the Lord God will be their light" (Apoc 22:5). Then once and for all human blindness will give way to the *visio Dei*: "We shall see him as he is" (1 Jn 3:2); "They shall see his face" (Apoc 22:4). God's design for his creation will have reached its end, the great end for which Jesus prayed: those whom the Father gave to the Son will be with the Son finally, to behold the Son's glory which the Father gave him in his love for him before the foundation of the world (Jn 17:24). Into the everlasting splendor of that divine love the creation, represented by its firstfruits the church, will have entered once and for all.[49] "And they shall reign for ever and ever" (Apoc 22:5).

"Amen. Come, Lord Jesus!"

"The grace of the Lord Jesus be with all the saints. Amen." (Apoc 22:20-21)

---

[49]Hans Boersma, "A New Age Love Story: Worldview and Ethics in the Gospel of John," *CTJ* 38 (2003): 103-19.

# BIBLIOGRAPHY

Albright, W. F. "Recent Discoveries in Palestine and the Gospel of John." In *The Background of the New Testament and Its Eschatology: In Honour of Charles Harold Dodd*, edited by W. D. Davies and David Daube, pp. 153-71. Cambridge: Cambridge University Press, 1954.

Alexander, Philip S. "The 'Parting of the Ways' from the Perspective of Rabbinic Judaism." In *Jews and Christians: The Parting of the Ways, A.D. 70 to 135*, edited by James D. G. Dunn, pp. 1-25. WUNT 66. Tübingen: Mohr Siebeck, 1992.

Aloisi, John. "The Paraclete's Ministry of Conviction: Another Look at John 16:8-11." *JETS* 47 (2004): 55-69.

Anatolios, Khaled. "Divine *Disponibilité*: The Hypostatic Ethos of the Holy Spirit." *ProEccl* 12 (2003): 287-308.

Anderson, Bernhard W., ed. *The Old Testament and Christian Faith*. New York: Harper & Row, 1963.

Anderson, Paul N. "Beyond the Shade of the Oak Tree: The Recent Growth of Johannine Studies." *ExpTim* 119 (2008): 365-73.

———. *The Christology of the Fourth Gospel: Its Unity and Disunity in the Light of John 6*. WUNT 2/78. Tübingen: Mohr Siebeck, 1996.

———. *The Fourth Gospel and the Quest for Jesus: Modern Foundations Reconsidered*. LNTS 321. London: T & T Clark, 2006.

———. "The Having-Sent-Me Father: Aspects of Agency, Encounter, and Irony in the Johannine Father-Son Relationship." *Semeia* 85 (1999): 33-57.

———. "The Origin and Development of the Johannine *Egō Eimi* Sayings in Cognitive-Critical Perspective." *JSHJ* 9 (2011): 139-206.

Anderson, Paul N., Felix Just, and Tom Thatcher, eds. *Aspects of Historicity in the Fourth Gospel*. Vol. 2 of *John, Jesus, and History*. SBLECL 2. Atlanta: Society of Biblical Literature, 2009.

———, eds. *Critical Appraisals of Critical Views*. Vol. 1 of *John, Jesus, and History*. SBLSymS 44. Atlanta: Society of Biblical Literature, 2007.

Appold, Mark L. *The Oneness Motif in the Fourth Gospel: Motif Analysis and Exegetical Probe into the Theology of John*. WUNT 2/1. Tübingen: Mohr Siebeck, 1976.

Ashby, Godfrey W. "Body and Blood in John 6:41-65." *Neot* 36 (2002): 57-61.

Ashton, John, ed. *The Interpretation of John*. IRT 9. Philadelphia: Fortress, 1986.

———. "The Johannine Son of Man: A New Proposal." *NTS* 57 (2011): 508-29.

———. *Understanding the Fourth Gospel*. Oxford: Clarendon, 1991.

Asiedu-Peprah, Martin. *Johannine Sabbath Conflicts as Juridical Controversy*. WUNT 2/132. Tübingen: Mohr Siebeck, 2001.

Attridge, Harold W. "Philo and John: Two Riffs on One Logos." *SPhiloAnn* 17 (2005): 103-17.

———. "Temple, Tabernacle, Time, and Space in John and Hebrews." *EC* 1 (2010): 261-74.

Augenstein, Jörg. *Das Liebesgebot im Johannesevangelium und in den Johannesbriefen*. BWANT 7/14. Stuttgart: Kohlhammer, 1993.

Aulén, Gustaf. *Christus Victor: An Historical Study of the Three Main Types of the Idea of the Atonement*. Translated by A. G. Hebert. London: SPCK, 1931.

Aune, David E. "The Influence of Roman Imperial Court Ceremonial on the Apocalypse of John." *BR* 28 (1983): 5-26.

———. *The New Testament in Its Literary Environment*. LEC. Philadelphia: Westminster, 1987.

———. *Prophecy in Early Christianity and the Ancient Mediterranean World*. Grand Rapids: Eerdmans, 1983.

———. *Revelation*. 3 vols. WBC 52A, 52B, 52C. Dallas: Word, 1997–1998.

Aus, Roger David. *Feeding the Five Thousand: Studies in the Judaic Background of Mark 6:30-44 par. and John 6:1-15*. SJ. Lanham, MD: University Press of America, 2010.

Baldensperger, Wilhelm. *Der Prolog des vierten Evangeliums: Sein polemisch-apologetischer Zweck*. Freiburg: Mohr, 1898.

Ball, David Mark. *"I Am" in John's Gospel: Literary Function, Background and Theological Implications*. JSNTSup 124. Sheffield: Sheffield Academic Press, 1996.

Bandy, Alan S. "The Layers of the Apocalypse: An Integrative Approach to Revelation's Macrostructure." *JSNT* 31 (2009): 469-99.

———. "Patterns of Prophetic Lawsuits in the Oracles to the Seven Churches." *Neot* 45 (2011): 178-205.

Barnett, Paul. "Revelation in Its Roman Setting." *VR* 74 (2009): 26-34.

Baron, Lori. "Interpreting the *Shema*: Liturgy and Identity in the Fourth Gospel." *ASE* 27 (2010): 53-60.

Barr, James. *The Semantics of Biblical Language*. Glasgow: Oxford University Press, 1961.

Barrett, C. K. "Christocentric or Theocentric? Observations on the Theological Method of the Fourth Gospel." In *Essays on John*, pp. 1-18. Philadelphia: Westminster, 1982.

———. "The Dialectical Theology of St. John." In *New Testament Essays*, pp. 49-69. London: SPCK, 1972.

———. "'The Father Is Greater Than I' (John 14.28): Subordinationist Christology in the New Testament." In *Essays on John*, pp. 19-36. Philadelphia: Westminster, 1982.

———. *The Gospel According to St. John*. 2nd ed. Philadelphia: Westminster, 1978.

———. "John and the Synoptic Gospels." *ExpTim* 85 (1974): 228-33.

———. "Sacraments." In *Essays on John*, pp. 80-97. Philadelphia: Westminster, 1982.

Barrosse, Thomas. "The Johannine Relationship of Love to Faith." In *A Companion to John: Readings in Johannine Theology (John's Gospel and Epistles)*, edited by Michael J. Taylor, pp. 153-76. New York: Alba House, 1970.

Bartholomä, Philipp F. "John 5,31-47 and the Teaching of Jesus in the Synoptics: A Comparative Approach." *Bib* 92 (2011): 368-91.

Barton, Stephen C. "Johannine Dualism and Contemporary Pluralism." In *The Gospel of John and Christian Theology*, edited by Richard Bauckham and Carl Mosser, pp. 3-18. Grand Rapids: Eerdmans, 2008.

Bass, Christopher D. "A Johannine Perspective of the Human Responsibility to Persevere in the Faith through the Use of MENΩ and Other Related Motifs." *WTJ* 69 (2007): 305-25.

———. *That You May Know: Assurance of Salvation in 1 John*. NACSBT 5. Nashville: B & H Academic, 2008.

Bauckham, Richard. "The Economic Critique of Rome in Revelation 18." In *The Climax of Prophecy: Studies on the Book of Revelation*, pp. 338-83. Edinburgh: T & T Clark, 1993.

———. *God Crucified: Monotheism and Christology in the New Testament*. Grand Rapids: Eerdmans, 1998.

———, ed. *The Gospels for All Christians: Rethinking the Gospel Audiences*. Grand Rapids: Eerdmans, 1998.

———. "Historiographical Characteristics of the Gospel of John." *NTS* 53 (2007): 17-36.

———. *Jesus and the Eyewitnesses: The Gospels as Eyewitness Testimony*. Grand Rapids: Eerdmans, 2006.

———. "John for Readers of Mark." In *The Gospels for All Christians: Rethinking the Gospel Audiences*, edited by Richard Bauckham, pp. 147-71. Grand Rapids: Eerdmans, 1998.

———. "Messianism According to the Gospel of John." In *Challenging Perspectives on the Gospel of John*, edited by John Lierman, pp. 34-68. WUNT 2/219. Tübingen: Mohr Siebeck, 2006.

———. "Monotheism and Christology in the Gospel of John." In *Contours of Christology in the New Testament*, edited by Richard N. Longenecker, pp. 148-66. MNTS. Grand Rapids: Eerdmans, 2005.

———. "The 153 Fish and the Unity of the Fourth Gospel." *Neot* 36 (2002): 77-88.

———. "Papias and Polycrates on the Origin of the Fourth Gospel." *JTS* 44 (1993): 24-69.

———. *The Testimony of the Beloved Disciple: Narrative, History, and Theology in the Gospel of John*. Grand Rapids: Baker Academic, 2007.

———. *The Theology of the Book of Revelation*. NTT. Cambridge: Cambridge University Press, 1993.

———. "The Throne of God and the Worship of Jesus." In *The Jewish Roots of Christological Monotheism: Papers from the St. Andrews Conference on the Historical Origins of the Worship of Jesus*, edited by Carey C. Newman, James R. Davila and Gladys S. Lewis, pp. 43-69. JSJSup 63. Leiden: Brill, 1999.

Bauckham, Richard, and Carl Mosser, eds. *The Gospel of John and Christian Theology.* Grand Rapids: Eerdmans, 2008.

Bauer, Walter. *Orthodoxy and Heresy in Earliest Christianity.* Edited by Robert A. Kraft and Gerhard Krodel. Translated by the Philadelphia Seminar on Christian Origins. Philadelphia: Fortress, 1971 [1934].

Baum, A. D. "Hat die Perikope von der Ehebrecherin (Joh 7,53–8,11) kanonische Autorität? Ein interkonfessioneller Zugang." *TBei* 43 (2012): 7-20.

Baur, Ferdinand Christian. *Kritische Untersuchungen über die kanonischen Evangelien, ihr Verhältniss zu einander, ihren Charakter und Ursprung.* Tübingen: Verlag Fues, 1847.

Beale, G. K. *The Book of Revelation: A Commentary on the Greek Text.* NIGTC. Grand Rapids: Eerdmans; Carlisle: Paternoster, 1999.

———. "Can the Bible Be Completely Inspired by God and Yet Still Contain Errors? A Response to Some Recent 'Evangelical' Proposals." *WTJ* 73 (2011): 1-22.

———. *John's Use of the Old Testament in Revelation.* JSNTSup 166. Sheffield: Sheffield Academic Press, 1998.

———. "The Old Testament Background of the 'Last Hour' in 1 John 2,18." *Bib* 92 (2011): 231-54.

———. *The Use of Daniel in Jewish Apocalyptic Literature and in the Revelation of St. John.* Lanham, MD: University Press of America, 1984.

Beasley-Murray, G. R. *Baptism in the New Testament.* Grand Rapids: Eerdmans, 1973.

———. *Gospel of Life: Theology in the Fourth Gospel.* Peabody, MA: Hendrickson, 1991.

———. *John.* WBC 36. Waco, TX: Word, 1987.

Beck, David R. *The Discipleship Paradigm: Readers and Anonymous Characters in the Fourth Gospel.* BIS 27. Leiden: Brill, 1997.

Becker, Jürgen. "Die Hoffnung auf ewiges Leben im Johannesevangelium." *ZNW* 91 (2000): 192-211.

———. *Johanneisches Christentum: Seine Geschichte und Theologie im Überblick.* Tübingen: Mohr Siebeck, 2004.

Beirne, Margaret M. *Women and Men in the Fourth Gospel: A Genuine Discipleship of Equals.* JSNTSup 242. London: Sheffield Academic Press, 2003.

Beisser, Friedrich. "Trinitätsaussagen in der Offenbarung des Johannes." In *Studien zur Johannesoffenbarung und ihrer Auslegung: Festschrift für Otto Böcher zum 70. Geburtstag*, edited by Friedrich Wilhelm Horn and Michael Wolter, pp. 120-35. Neukirchen-Vluyn: Neukirchener Verlag, 2005.

Belano, Alessandro. "Il significato della preposizione ἀντί con particolare riferimento a Gv 1,16." *RevistB* 57 (2009): 223-29.

Ben-Daniel, John, and Gloria Ben-Daniel. *The Apocalypse in the Light of the Temple: A New Approach to the Book of Revelation.* Jerusalem: Beit Yochanan, 2003.

Bennema, Cornelis. "The Identity and Composition of οἱ Ἰουδαῖοι in the Gospel of John." *TynBul* 60 (2009): 239-63.

———. *The Power of Saving Wisdom: An Investigation of Spirit and Wisdom in Relation to the Soteriology of the Fourth Gospel.* WUNT 2/148. Tübingen: Mohr Siebeck, 2002.

———. "Spirit-Baptism in the Fourth Gospel: A Messianic Reading of John 1,33." *Bib* 84 (2003): 35-60.

———. "The Sword of the Messiah and the Concept of Liberation in the Fourth Gospel." *Bib* 86 (2005): 35-58.

———. "A Theory of Character in the Fourth Gospel with Reference to Ancient and Modern Literature." *BibInt* 17 (2009): 375-421.

Berger, Klaus. *Im Anfang war Johannes: Datierung und Theologie des vierten Evangeliums.* 2nd ed. Stuttgart: Gütersloher, 2003.

Bergmeier, Roland. "Die Bedeutung der Synoptiker für das johanneische Zeugnisthema: Mit einem Anhang zum Perfekt-Gebrauch im vierten Evangelium." *NTS* 52 (2006): 458-83.

Berthoud, Pierre. "Le pain de vie." *RRef* 55 (2004): 67-78.

Beutler, Johannes. "Der Johannes-Prolog—Ouvertüre des Johannesevangeliums." In *Der Johannesprolog*, edited by Günter Kruck, pp. 77-106. Darmstadt: Wissenschaftliche Buchgesellschaft, 2009.

———. "Die Ehre Gottes und die Ehre der Menschen im Johannesevangelium." *GL* 76 (2003): 83-91.

———. *Habt keine Angst: Die erste johanneische Abschiedsrede (Joh 14).* SBS 116. Stuttgart: Katholisches Bibelwerk, 1984.

———. *Judaism and the Jews in the Gospel of John.* SubBi 30. Rome: Pontifical Biblical Institute, 2006.

Bieringer, Reimund, Didier Pollefeyt, and Frederique Vandecasteele-Vanneuville, eds. *Anti-Judaism and the Fourth Gospel: Papers of the Leuven Colloquium, 2000.* JCH 1. Assen: Van Gorcum, 2001.

———. "Wrestling with Johannine Anti-Judaism: A Hermeneutical Framework for the Analysis of the Current Debate." In *Anti-Judaism and the Fourth Gospel: Papers of the Leuven Colloquium, 2000*, edited by Reimund Bieringer, Didier Pollefeyt and Frederique Vandecasteele-Vanneuville, pp. 3-37. JCH 1. Assen: Van Gorcum, 2001.

Binni, Walther, and Bernado Gianluigi Boschi. *Cristologia primitiva: Dalla teofania del Sinài all'Io sono giovanneo.* CSB 46. Bologna: EDB, 2004.

Bittner, Wolfgang J. *Jesu Zeichen im Johannesevangelium.* WUNT 2/26. Tübingen: Mohr Siebeck, 1987.

Bjerkelund, Carl J. *Tauta egeneto: Die Präzisierungssätze im Johannesevangelium.* WUNT 40. Tübingen: Mohr Siebeck, 1987.

Black, C. Clifton. "Short Shrift Made Once More." *ThTo* 57 (2000): 386-94.

———. "'The Words That You Gave to Me I Have Given to Them': The Grandeur of Johannine Rhetoric." In *Exploring the Gospel of John: In Honor of D. Moody Smith*, edited by R. Alan Culpepper and C. Clifton Black, pp. 220-39. Louisville: Westminster John Knox, 1996.

Blaine, Bradford B. *Peter in the Gospel of John: The Making of an Authentic Disciple.* SBLAB 27. Atlanta: Society of Biblical Literature, 2007.

Blanchard, Yves-Marie. "Lumière et ténèbres dans la tradition johannique." *Transversalités* 85 (2003): 103-17.

Blank, Josef. *Krisis: Untersuchungen zur johanneischen Christologie und Eschatologie.* Freiburg im Breisgau: Lambertus, 1964.

Blinzler, Jozef. *Johannes und die Synoptiker: Ein Forschungsbericht.* SBS 5. Stuttgart: Katholisches Bibelwerk, 1965.

Blocher, Henri. "Yesterday, Today, Forever: Time, Times, Eternity in Biblical Perspective." *TynBul* 52 (2001): 183-202.

Blomberg, Craig L. *The Historical Reliability of John's Gospel: Issues and Commentary.* Downers Grove, IL: InterVarsity Press, 2002.

Blount, Brian K. "Reading Revelation Today: Witness as Active Resistance." *Int* 54 (2000): 398-412.

Blumenthal, Christian. "Χάρις ἀντι χάριτος (Joh 1,16)." *ZNW* 92 (2001): 290-94.

Böcher, Otto. *Der johanneische Dualismus im Zusammenhang des nachbiblischen Judentums.* Gütersloh: Mohn, 1965.

———. "Johanneisches in der Apokalypse des Johannes." *NTS* 27 (1981): 310-21.

Boersma, Hans. "A New Age Love Story: Worldview and Ethics in the Gospel of John." *CTJ* 38 (2003): 103-19.

Bogart, John. *Orthodox and Heretical Perfectionism in the Johannine Community as Evident in the First Epistle of John.* SBLDS 33. Missoula, MT: Scholars Press, 1977.

Boismard, M.-É. *Moses or Jesus: An Essay in Johannine Christology.* Translated by Benedict T. Viviano. BETL 84A. Leuven: Leuven University Press, 1993.

Boman, Thorleif. *Hebrew Thought Compared with Greek.* Translated by Jules L. Moreau. LHD. Philadelphia: Westminster, 1960.

Bond, Helen K. *Caiaphas: Friend of Rome and Judge of Jesus?* Louisville: Westminster John Knox, 2004.

Bonney, William. *Caused to Believe: The Doubting Thomas Story at the Climax of John's Christological Narrative.* BIS 62. Leiden: Brill, 2002.

Borgen, Peder. *Bread from Heaven: An Exegetical Study of the Concept of Manna in the Gospel of John and the Writings of Philo.* NovTSup 10. Leiden: Brill, 1965.

———. "God's Agent in the Fourth Gospel." In *The Interpretation of John*, edited by John Ashton, pp. 67-78. IRT 9. Philadelphia: Fortress, 1986.

———. "John's Use of the Old Testament, and the Problem of Sources and Traditions." In *Philo, John, and Paul: New Perspectives on Judaism and Early Christianity*, pp. 145-57. BJS 131. Atlanta: Scholars Press, 1987.

——. "The Old Testament in the Formation of New Testament Theology." In *Philo, John, and Paul: New Perspectives on Judaism and Early Christianity*, pp. 159-70. BJS 131. Atlanta: Scholars Press, 1987.

——. *Philo, John, and Paul: New Perspectives on Judaism and Early Christianity*. BJS 131. Atlanta: Scholars Press, 1987.

——. "The Prologue of John—as Exposition of the Old Testament." In *Philo, John, and Paul: New Perspectives on Judaism and Early Christianity*, pp. 75-101. BJS 131. Atlanta: Scholars Press, 1987.

Bornkamm, Günther. "πρέσβυς." *TDNT* 6:651-83.

——. "Towards the Interpretation of John's Gospel: A Discussion of *The Testament of Jesus*." In *The Interpretation of John*, edited by John Ashton, pp. 79-98. IRT 9. Philadelphia: Fortress, 1986.

Boucher, Pierre-Marin. "Γεννηθῆναι ἄνωθεν: La valeur de l'adverb ἄνωθεν en Jn 3,3 et 7. I$^{re}$ partie. La réception chrétienne." *RB* 115 (2008): 191-215.

——. "Γεννηθῆναι ἄνωθεν: La valeur de l'adverb ἄνωθεν en Jn 3,3 et 7. II$^e$ parie. Les acceptions du terme ἄνωθεν en grec classique et koinè non sémitisé." *RB* 115 (2008): 568-95.

Boughton, Lynne Courter. "The Priestly Perspective of the Johannine Trial Narratives." *RB* 110 (2003): 517-51.

Bousset, Wilhelm. *Die Religion des Judentums im späthellenistischen Zeitalter*. Edited by Hugo Gressmann. 3rd ed. HNT 21. Tübingen: Mohr Siebeck, 1926.

——. *Kyrios Christos: A History of the Belief in Christ from the Beginnings of Christianity to Irenaeus*. Translated by John E. Steely. Nashville: Abingdon, 1970.

Bowen, Clayton R. "Love in the Fourth Gospel." *JR* 13 (1933): 39-49.

Bowen, John P. "Coming to Faith in the Gospel of John." *Anvil* 19 (2002): 277-83.

Bowman, John, trans. and ed. *Samaritan Documents Relating to Their History, Religion, and Life*. POTTS 2. Pittsburgh: Pickwick, 1977.

Boyarin, Daniel. "The Gospel of the *Memra*: Jewish Binitarianism and the Prologue to John." *HTR* 94 (2001): 243-84.

——. "A Tale of Two Synods: Nicaea, Yavneh and the Making of Orthodox Judaism." *Exemplaria* 12 (2000): 21-62.

——. "Two Powers in Heaven; or, the Making of a Heresy." In *The Idea of Biblical Interpretation: Essays in Honor of James L. Kugel*, edited by Hindy Najman and Judith H. Newman, pp. 331-70. JSJSup 83. Leiden: Brill, 2004.

Braun, F.-M. *Jean le théologien*. 4 vols. EB. Paris: Gabalda, 1959–1972.

Braun, Herbert. *Qumran und das Neue Testament*. 2 vols. Tübingen: Mohr Siebeck, 1966.

Bray, Gerald. "The Double Procession of the Holy Spirit in Evangelical Theology Today: Do We Still Need It?" *JETS* 41 (1998): 415-26.

Bredin, Mark. *Jesus, Revolutionary of Peace: A Nonviolent Christology in the Book of Revelation*. PBM. Milton Keynes: Paternoster, 2003.

Bretschneider, Karl Gottlieb. *Probabilia de evangelii et epistolarum Joannis, Apostoli, indole et origine*. Leipzig: Sumtibus Jo. Ambros. Barthii, 1820.

Bridges, Linda M. "Aphorisms of Jesus in John: An Illustrative Look at John 4.35." *JSHJ* 9 (2011): 207-29.

Bridges, Matthew M. "Reunderstanding How to 'Understand the Scripture.'" *JTI* 3 (2009): 127-42.

Brien, Mary T. "Latecomers to the Light: A Reflection on the 'Emergence' of Joseph of Arimathea and Nicodemus: John 19:38-42." *NTR* 17 (2004): 48-56.

Briggs, Robert A. *Jewish Temple Imagery in the Book of Revelation*. SBL 10. New York: Peter Lang, 1999.

Brighton, Louis A. "Christological Trinitarian Theology in the Book of Revelation." *ConJ* 34 (2008): 292-97.

Brodie, Thomas L. *The Quest for the Origin of John's Gospel: A Source-Oriented Approach*. New York: Oxford University Press, 1993.

Brooke, A. E. *A Critical and Exegetical Commentary on the Johannine Epistles*. ICC. New York: Scribner, 1912.

Brouwer, Wayne. *The Literary Development of John 13–17: A Chiastic Reading*. SBLDS 182. Atlanta: Society of Biblical Literature, 2000.

Brown, Jeannine K. "Creation's Renewal in the Gospel of John." *CBQ* 72 (2010): 275-90.

Brown, Raymond E. *The Community of the Beloved Disciple: The Life, Loves, and Hates of an Individual Church in New Testament Times*. New York: Paulist Press, 1979.

———. "The *EGO EIMI* ('I Am') Passages in the Fourth Gospel." In *A Companion to John: Readings in Johannine Theology (John's Gospel and Epistles)*, edited by Michael J. Taylor, pp. 117-26. New York: Alba House, 1970.

———. *The Epistles of John: Translated, with Introduction, Notes, and Commentary*. AB 30. Garden City, NY: Doubleday, 1982.

———. *The Gospel According to John: Introduction, Translation, and Notes*. 2 vols. AB 29, 29A. Garden City, NY: Doubleday, 1966–1970.

———. *An Introduction to the Gospel of John*. Edited by Francis J. Moloney. ABRL. New York: Doubleday, 2003.

———. *An Introduction to the New Testament*. ABRL. New York: Doubleday, 1997.

———. *Jesus, God and Man: Modern Biblical Reflections*. New York: Macmillan, 1967.

———. "The Johannine Sacramentary." In *A Companion to John: Readings in Johannine Theology (John's Gospel and Epistles)*, edited by Michael J. Taylor, pp. 225-46. New York: Alba House, 1970.

———. "The Qumran Scrolls and the Johannine Gospel and Epistles." *CBQ* 17 (1955): 403-19, 559-74.

Brown, Tricia Gates. *Spirit in the Writings of John: Johannine Pneumatology in Social-Scientific Perspective*. JSNTSup 253. London: T & T Clark, 2003.

Bruce, F. F. "St. John at Ephesus." *BJRL* 60 (1978): 339-61.

Brunson, Andrew C. *Psalm 118 in the Gospel of John: An Intertextual Study on the New Exodus Pattern in the Theology of John*. WUNT 2/158. Tübingen: Mohr Siebeck, 2003.

Bryan, David J. "A Comparative Literary Study of Daniel and Revelation: Shaping the End." *JSOT* 79 (1998): 134-35.

Bryan, Steven M. "Power in the Pool: The Healing of the Man at Bethesda and Jesus' Violation of the Sabbath (Jn. 5:1-18)." *TynBul* 54 (2003): 7-22.

Buby, Bertrand. "The Fascinating Woman of Revelation 12." *MS* 50 (1999): 107-26.

Büchsel, Friedrich. "μονογενής." *TDNT* 4:737-41.

Bühner, Jan-A. von. *Der Gesandte und sein Weg im 4. Evangelium: die kultur- und religionsgeschichtlichen Grundlagen der johanneischen Sendungschristologie sowie ihre traditionsgeschichtliche Entwicklung*. WUNT 2/2. Tübingen: Mohr Siebeck, 1977.

Bultmann, Rudolf. "Die Bedeutung der neuerschlossenen mandäischen und manichäischen Quellen für das Verständnis des Johannesevangeliums." *ZNW* 24 (1925): 100-146.

———. "The Eschatology of the Gospel of John." In *Faith and Understanding*, edited by Robert W. Funk, translated by Louise Pettibone Smith, pp. 165-83. New York: Harper & Row, 1969.

———. *The Gospel of John: A Commentary*. Edited by R. W. N. Hoare and J. K. Riches. Translated by G. R. Beasley-Murray. Philadelphia: Westminster, 1971.

———. "The History of Religions Background of the Prologue to the Gospel of John." In *The Interpretation of John*, edited by John Ashton, pp. 18-35. IRT 9. Philadelphia: Fortress, 1986.

———. *The Johannine Epistles: A Commentary on the Johannine Epistles*. Edited by Robert W. Funk. Translated by R. Philip O'Hara, Lane C. McGaughy and Robert W. Funk. Hermeneia. Philadelphia: Fortress, 1973.

———. *Theology of the New Testament*. 2 vols. Translated by Kendrick Grobel. New York: Scribner, 1951–1955.

———. "What Does It Mean to Speak of God?" In *Faith and Understanding*, edited by Robert W. Funk, translated by Louise Pettibone Smith, pp. 53-65. New York: Harper & Row, 1969.

Burge, Gary M. *The Anointed Community: The Holy Spirit in the Johannine Tradition*. Grand Rapids: Eerdmans, 1987.

———. "Revelation and Discipleship in St. John's Gospel." In *Challenging Perspectives on the Gospel of John*, edited by John Lierman, pp. 235-54. WUNT 2/219. Tübingen: Mohr Siebeck, 2006.

Burkett, Delbert. *The Son of Man in the Gospel of John*. JSNTSup 56. Sheffield: JSOT Press, 1991.

Burkholder, Benjamin J. "Considering the Possibility of a Theological Corruption in Joh 1,18 in Light of Its Early Reception." *ZNW* 103 (2012): 64-83.

Burridge, R. A. *What Are the Gospels? A Comparison with Greco-Roman Biography*. SNTSMS 70. Cambridge: Cambridge University Press, 1992.

Busse, Ulrich. *Das Johannesevangelium: Bildlichkeit, Diskurs und Ritual; Mit einer Bibliographie über den Zeitraum 1986–1998.* BETL 162. Leuven: Leuven University Press, 2002.

Byron, Brian. "Non-Explicit Allusions to the Pentateuch in the Gospel of John: Catch-Words for Catechesis on Jewish Basics?" *ABR* 82 (2005): 335-45.

Byron, John. "Slaughter, Fratricide and Sacrilege: Cain and Abel Traditions in 1 John 3." *Bib* 88 (2007): 526-35.

Byrskog, Samuel. *Story as History—History as Story: The Gospel Tradition in the Context of Ancient Oral History.* WUNT 123. Tübingen: Mohr Siebeck, 2000.

Caba, José. "La iniciativa del Padre en la historia de la salvación según la teología joanea." *Greg* 87 (2006): 239-61.

Cadman, W. H. *The Open Heaven: The Revelation of God in the Johannine Sayings of Jesus.* Edited by G. B. Caird. New York: Herder & Herder, 1969.

Callahan, Allen Dwight. *A Love Supreme: A History of the Johannine Tradition.* Minneapolis: Fortress, 2005.

Calloud, Jean. "Je suis l'alpha et l'oméga: L'Apocalypse à la lettre." *SB* 128 (2007): 23-38.

Campbell, Barth L. "Honor, Hospitality and Haughtiness: The Contention for Leadership in 3 John." *EvQ* 77 (2005): 321-41.

Campbell, Gordon. "Antithetical Feminine-Urban Imagery and a Tale of Two Women-Cities in the Book of Revelation." *TynBul* 55 (2004): 81-108.

———. "True and False Proclamation in the Book of Revelation." *IBS* 25 (2003): 60-73.

Campbell, Joan Cecelia. *Kinship Relations in the Gospel of John.* CBQMS 42. Washington, DC: Catholic Biblical Association of America, 2007.

Campenhausen, Hans von. *Ecclesiastical Authority and Spiritual Power in the Church of the First Three Centuries.* Translated by J. A. Baker. Stanford, CA: Stanford University Press, 1969.

Caragounis, Chrys C. "What Did Jesus Mean by τὴν ἀρχήν in John 8:25?" *NovT* 49 (2007): 129-47.

Carnegie, David R. "Worthy Is the Lamb: The Hymns in Revelation." In *Christ the Lord: Studies in Christology Presented to Donald Guthrie,* edited by Harold H. Rowdon, pp. 243-56. Downers Grove, IL: InterVarsity Press, 1982.

Carrell, Peter R. *Jesus and the Angels: Angelology and the Christology of the Apocalypse of John.* SNTSMS 95. Cambridge: Cambridge University Press, 1997.

Carson, D. A. *Divine Sovereignty and Human Responsibility: Biblical Perspectives in Tension.* Atlanta: John Knox, 1981.

———. *The Gospel According to John.* Grand Rapids: Eerdmans, 1991.

———. "John and the Johannine Epistles." In *It Is Written: Scripture Citing Scripture; Essays in Honour of Barnabas Lindars,* edited by D. A. Carson and H. G. M. Williamson, pp. 245-64. Cambridge: Cambridge University Press, 1988.

———. "Syntactical and Text-Critical Observations on John 20:30-31: One More Round on the Purpose of the Fourth Gospel." *JBL* 124 (2005): 693-714.

Carson, D. A., and Douglas J. Moo. *An Introduction to the New Testament*. 2nd ed. Grand Rapids: Zondervan, 2005.

Carter, Warren. *John and Empire: Initial Explorations*. London: T & T Clark, 2008.

Casey, Maurice. *Is John's Gospel True?* London: Routledge, 1996.

*Catechism of the Catholic Church*. Translated by United States Catholic Conference. Vatican City: Libreria Editrice Vaticana; San Francisco: Ignatius Press, 1994.

Cazelles, Henri J. "Johannes: Ein Sohn des Zebedäus, 'Priester' und Apostel." *IKaZ* 31 (2002): 479-84.

Cebulj, Christian. *Ich bin es: Studien zur Identitätsbildung im Johannesevangelium*. SBB 44. Stuttgart: Katholisches Bibelwerk, 2000.

Ceulemans, Reinhart. "The Name of the Pool in Joh 5,2: A Text-Critical Note Concerning 3Q15." *ZNW* 99 (2008): 112-15.

Charette, Blaine. *The Theme of Recompense in Matthew's Gospel*. JSNTSup 79. Sheffield: Sheffield Academic Press, 1992.

Charles, R. H. *A Critical and Exegetical Commentary on the Revelation of St. John*. 2 vols. ICC. New York: Scribner, 1920.

Charlesworth, James H. *The Beloved Disciple: Whose Witness Validates the Gospel of John?* Valley Forge, PA: Trinity Press International, 1995.

———. "A Critical Comparison of the Dualism in 1QS III,13–IV,26 and the 'Dualism' Contained in the Fourth Gospel." *NTS* 15 (1968–1969): 389-418.

———. "The Historical Jesus in the Fourth Gospel: A Paradigm Shift?" *JSHJ* 8 (2010): 3-46.

———, ed. *John and the Dead Sea Scrolls*. COL. New York: Crossroad, 1972.

Chennattu, Rekha M. *Johannine Discipleship as a Covenant Relationship*. Peabody, MA: Hendrickson, 2006.

Chibici-Revneanu, Nicole. *Die Herrlichkeit des Verherrlichten: Das Verständnis der doxa im Johannesevangelium*. WUNT 2/231. Tübingen: Mohr Siebeck, 2007.

Cho, Sukmin. *Jesus as Prophet in the Fourth Gospel*. NTM 15. Sheffield: Sheffield Phoenix Press, 2006.

Cholin, Marc. *Le prologue et la dynamique de l'Evangile de Jean*. Lyon: EMCC, 1995.

Clark, David J. "The Word *Kosmos* 'World' in John 17." *BT* 50 (1999): 401-6.

Cohen, Shaye J. D. *From the Maccabees to the Mishnah*. LEC 7. Philadelphia: Westminster, 1987.

Collins, John J. *The Scepter and the Star: The Messiahs of the Dead Sea Scrolls and Other Ancient Literature*. ABRL. New York: Doubleday, 1995.

Collins, Raymond F. *These Things Have Been Written: Studies on the Fourth Gospel*. LTPM 2. Louvain: Peeters, 1990.

Coloe, Mary L. *Dwelling in the Household of God: Johannine Ecclesiology and Spirituality*. Collegeville, MN: Liturgical Press, 2007.

———. *God Dwells with Us: Temple Symbolism in the Fourth Gospel*. Collegeville, MN: Liturgical Press, 2001.

———. "Households of Faith (Jn 4:46-54; 11:1-44): A Metaphor for the Johannine Community." *Pacifica* 13 (2000): 326-35.

———. "Temple Imagery in John." *Int* 63 (2009): 368-81.

Coloe, Mary L., and Tom Thatcher, eds. *John, Qumran, and the Dead Sea Scrolls: Sixty Years of Discovery and Debate.* SBLEJL 32. Atlanta: Society of Biblical Literature, 2011.

Colpe, Carsten. *Die religionsgeschichtliche Schule: Darstellung und Kritik ihres Bildes vom gnostischen Erlösermythus.* FRLANT 60. Göttingen: Vandenhoeck & Ruprecht, 1961.

Colwell, E. C. *The Greek of the Fourth Gospel: A Study of Its Aramaisms in the Light of Hellenistic Greek.* Chicago: University of Chicago Press, 1931.

Comblin, Joseph. *Le Christ dans l'Apocalypse.* BTTB 3/6. Paris: Desclée, 1965.

Congar, Yves M. J. *I Believe in the Holy Spirit.* Translated by David Smith. 3 vols. New York: Seabury, 1983.

Conway, Colleen M. "Speaking through Ambiguity: Minor Characters in the Fourth Gospel." *BibInt* 10 (2002): 324-41.

Conzelmann, Hans. "Was von Anfang war." In *Neutestamentliche Studien für Rudolf Bultmann: Zu seinem 70. Geburtstag am 20. August 1954*, edited by Walther Eltester, pp. 194-201. BZNW 21. Berlin: Töpelmann, 1957.

Cook, W. Robert. *The Theology of John.* Chicago: Moody, 1979.

Copan, Paul, and William Lane Craig. *Creation Out of Nothing: A Biblical, Philosophical, and Scientific Exploration.* Grand Rapids: Baker Academic; Leicester: Apollos, 2004.

Corbin, Michel. *Résurrection et nativité: Lecture théologique de Jean 20,1-31.* Théologies. Paris: Cerf, 2002.

Corell, Alf. *Consummatum Est: Eschatology and Church in the Gospel of St John.* Translated by The Order of the Holy Paraclete. London: SPCK, 1958.

Cothenet, Édouard. *La chaîne des témoins dans l'évangile de Jean: De Jean-Baptiste au disciple bien-aimé.* LB 142. Paris: Cerf, 2005.

Cowan, Christopher. "The Father and the Son in the Fourth Gospel: Johannine Subordination Revisited." *JETS* 49 (2006): 115-35.

Crehan, Joseph. *The Theology of St. John.* New York: Sheed & Ward, 1965.

Crouch, Frank Lynn. "Everyone Who Sees the Son: Signs, Faith, Peirces's Semeiotics, and the Gospel of John." Ph.D. diss. Duke University, 1996.

Crump, David. "Re-Examining the Johannine Trinity: Perichoresis or Deification?" *SJT* 59 (2006): 395-412.

Cullmann, Oscar. *Christ and Time: The Primitive Christian Conception of Time and History.* Translated by Floyd V. Filson. Philadelphia: Westminster, 1964.

———. *The Christology of the New Testament.* Translated by Shirley C. Guthrie and Charles A. M. Hall. 2nd ed. NTL. Philadelphia: Westminster, 1963.

———. *The Johannine Circle.* Translated by John Bowden. Philadelphia: Westminster, 1976.

————. "L'Évangile johannique et l'histoire du salut." *NTS* 11 (1965): 111-22.

Culpepper, R. Alan. *Anatomy of the Fourth Gospel: A Study in Literary Design.* Philadelphia: Fortress, 1983.

————. "Cognition in John: The Johannine Signs as Recognition Scenes." *PRSt* 35 (2008): 251-60.

————. "Inclusivism and Exclusivism in the Fourth Gospel." In *Word, Theology, and Community in John*, edited by John Painter, R. Alan Culpepper, and Fernando F. Segovia, pp. 85-108. St. Louis: Chalice, 2002.

————. *The Johannine School: An Evaluation of the Johannine-School Hypothesis Based on an Investigation of the Nature of Ancient Schools.* SBLDS 26. Missoula, MT: Scholars Press, 1975.

————. *John, the Son of Zebedee: The Life of a Legend.* SPNT. Columbia: University of South Carolina Press, 1994.

————. "Peter as Exemplary Disciple in John 21:15-19." *PRSt* 37 (2010): 165-78.

————. "The Quest for the Church in the Gospel of John." *Int* 63 (2009): 341-54.

————. "Realized Eschatology in the Experience of the Johannine Community." In *The Resurrection of Jesus in the Gospel of John*, edited by Craig R. Koester and Reimund Bieringer, pp. 253-76. WUNT 222. Tübingen: Mohr Siebeck, 2008.

Dahl, Nils Alstrup. "'Do Not Wonder!' John 5:28-29 and Johannine Eschatology Once More." In *The Conversation Continues: Studies in Paul and John*, edited by Robert T. Fortna and Beverly R. Gaventa, pp. 322-36. Nashville: Abingdon, 1990.

————. "The Johannine Church and History." In *Current Issues in New Testament Interpretation: Essays in Honor of Otto A. Piper*, edited by William Klassen and Graydon F. Snyder, pp. 124-42. PL. London: SCM Press, 1962.

————. "The Neglected Factor in New Testament Theology." *Reflection* 73 (1975): 5-8.

Dahms, John V. "The Generation of the Son." *JETS* 32 (1989): 493-501.

————. "Isaiah 55:11 and the Gospel of John." *EvQ* 53 (1981): 78-88.

————. "The Johannine Use of *Monogenēs* Reconsidered." *NTS* 29 (1983): 222-32.

————. "The Subordination of the Son." *JETS* 37 (1994): 351-64.

Daise, Michael A. *Feasts in John: Jewish Festivals and Jesus' "Hour" in the Fourth Gospel.* WUNT 2/229. Tübingen: Mohr Siebeck, 2007.

————. "'If Anyone Thirsts, Let That One Come to Me and Drink': The Literary Texture of John 7:37b-38a." *JBL* 122 (2003): 687-99.

Daly-Denton, Margaret. *David in the Fourth Gospel: The Johannine Reception of the Psalms.* AGJU 47. Leiden: Brill, 2000.

Daniélou, Jean. *The Theology of Jewish Christianity.* Vol. 1 of *The Development of Christian Doctrine Before the Council of Nicaea*. Translated by John A. Baker. London: Darton, Longman & Todd, 1964.

Davey, J. Ernest. *The Jesus of St. John: Historical and Christological Studies in the Fourth Gospel.* London: Lutterworth, 1958.

Davies, Margaret. *Rhetoric and Reference in the Fourth Gospel.* JSNTSup 69. Sheffield: Sheffield Academic Press, 1992.

Davies, W. D. "The Johannine 'Signs' of Jesus." In *A Companion to John: Readings in Johannine Theology (John's Gospel and Epistles),* edited by Michael J. Taylor, pp. 91-115. New York: Alba House, 1970.

de Boer, Martinus C. "Jesus' Departure to the Father in John: Death or Resurrection?" In *Theology and Christology in the Fourth Gospel: Essays by Members of the SNTS Johannine Writings Seminar,* edited by Gilbert van Belle, Jan G. van der Watt and P. J. Maritz, pp. 1-19. BETL 184. Leuven: Leuven University Press, 2005.

———. *Johannine Perspectives on the Death of Jesus.* CBET 17. Kampen: Kok Pharos, 1996.

Decock, Paul B. "The Scriptures in the Book of Revelation." *Neot* 33 (1999): 373-410.

———. "The Symbol of Blood in the Apocalypse of John." *Neot* 38 (2004): 157-82.

DeConick, April D. *Voices of the Mystics: Early Christian Discourse in the Gospels of John and Thomas and Other Ancient Christian Literature.* JSNTSup 157. Sheffield: Sheffield Academic Press, 2001.

Deissmann, Adolf. *Light from the Ancient East: The New Testament Illustrated by Recently Discovered Texts of the Graeco-Roman World.* Translated by Lionel R. M. Strachan. Grand Rapids: Baker Books, 1978.

de Jonge, Marinus. *Jesus, Stranger from Heaven and Son of God: Jesus Christ and the Christians in Johannine Perspective.* SBLSBS 11. Missoula, MT: Scholars Press, 1977.

———, ed. *L'Évangile de Jean: Sources, rédaction, théologie.* BETL 44. Gembloux: Duculot, 1977.

———. "The Use of the Word ΧΡΙΣΤΟΣ in the Johannine Epistles." In *Studies in John: Presented to Professor J. N. Sevenster on the Occasion of His Seventieth Birthday,* pp. 66-74. NovTSup 24. Leiden: Brill, 1970.

de la Potterie, Ignace. *La vérité dans Saint Jean.* 2 vols. AnBib 73, 74. Rome: Biblical Institute Press, 1977.

———. "The Truth in Saint John." In *The Interpretation of John,* edited by John Ashton, pp. 58-64. IRT 9. Philadelphia: Fortress, 1986.

de Lubac, Henri. *The Christian Faith: An Essay on the Structure of the Apostles' Creed.* Translated by Richard Arnandez. San Francisco: Ignatius Press, 1986.

Demke, Christoph. "Das Evangelium der Dialoge: Hermeneutische und methodologische Beobachtungen zur Interpretation des Johannesevangeliums." *ZTK* 97 (2000): 164-82.

Denaux, Adelbert, ed. *John and the Synoptics.* BETL 101. Leuven: Leuven University Press, 1992.

Dennis, John A. "Conflict and Resolution: John 11.47-53 as the Ironic Fulfillment of the Main Plot-Line of the Gospel (John 1.11-12)." *SNTSU* 29 (2004): 23-39.

———. *Jesus' Death and the Gathering of True Israel: The Johannine Appropriation of Restoration Theology in the Light of John 11:47-52.* WUNT 2/217. Tübingen: Mohr Siebeck, 2006.

————. "Jesus' Death in John's Gospel: A Survey of Research from Bultmann to the Present with Special Reference to the Johannine *Hyper*-Texts." *CurBR* 4 (2006): 331-63.

de Pinto, Basil. "John's Jesus: Biblical Wisdom and the Word Embodied." In *A Companion to John: Readings in Johannine Theology (John's Gospel and Epistles)*, edited by Michael J. Taylor, pp. 59-67. New York: Alba House, 1970.

Derrett, J. D. M. "The Mission Originates in Captivation: ἁλιεύω, πιάζω, σύρω, ἕλκω (Jn 21:6-11)." *FilNeot* 15 (2002): 95-109.

deSilva, David A. "The Strategic Arousal of Emotion in John's Visions of Roman Imperialism: A Rhetorical-Critical Investigation of Revelation 4-22." *Neot* 42 (2008): 1-34.

de Smidt, Kobus. "A Meta-Theology of ὁ θεός in Revelation 1:1-2." *Neot* 38 (2004): 183-208.

Dettwiler, Andreas. *Die Gegenwart des Erhöhten: eine exegetische Studie zu den johanneischen Abschiedsreden (Joh 13,31–16,33) unter besonderer Berücksichtigung ihres Relecture-Charakters*. FRLANT 169. Göttingen: Vandenhoeck & Ruprecht, 1995.

Devillers, Luc. "Histoire et théologie de la fête des Tentes (Sukkot)." *RThom* 100 (2000): 469-503.

de Villiers, Pieter G. R. "Divine and Human Love in the Revelation of John." *APB* 18 (2008): 43-59.

————. "Prime Evil and Its Many Faces in the Book of Revelation." *Neot* 34 (2000): 57-85.

Dexinger, Ferdinand. "Die Taheb-Vorstellung als politische Utopie." *Numen* 37 (1990): 1-23.

Díaz Rodelas, Juan Miguel. "La generación divina de los creyentes en los escritos joánicos." *EstBib* 66 (2008): 369-86.

Diefenbach, Manfred. *Der Konflikt Jesu mit den "Juden": Ein Versuch zur Lösung der johanneischen Antijudaismus-Diskussion mit Hilfe des antikes Handlungsverständnisses*. NTAbh 41. Münster: Aschendorff, 2002.

Dilley, Frank B. *Metaphysics and Religious Language*. New York: Columbia University Press, 1964.

Do, Toan Joseph. "Jesus' Death as *Hilasmos* According to 1 John." In *The Death of Jesus in the Fourth Gospel*, edited by Gilbert van Belle, pp. 537-53. BETL 200. Leuven: Leuven University Press, 2007.

Dodd, C. H. *The Bible and the Greeks*. London: Hodder & Stoughton, 1935.

————. "The First Epistle of John and the Fourth Gospel." *BJRL* 21 (1937): 129-56.

————. *Historical Tradition in the Fourth Gospel*. Cambridge: Cambridge University Press, 1963.

————. *The Interpretation of the Fourth Gospel*. Cambridge: Cambridge University Press, 1953.

————. *The Johannine Epistles*. MNTC. New York: Harper, 1946.

————. *The Parables of the Kingdom*. London: Nisbet, 1935.

Dudrey, Russ. "1 John and the Public Reading of Scripture." *SCJ* 6 (2003): 235-55.

Dugmore, C. W. *The Influence of the Synagogue upon the Divine Office*. London: Oxford University Press, 1944.

Dunderberg, Ismo. "Johannine Anomalies and the Synoptics." In *New Readings in John: Literary and Theological Perspectives; Essays from the Scandinavian Conference on the Fourth Gospel in Aarhus 1997*, edited by Johannes Nissen and Siegfried Pedersen, pp. 108-25. Sheffield: Sheffield Academic Press, 1999.

Dunn, James D. G. *Christology in the Making: An Inquiry Into the Origins of the Doctrine of the Incarnation.* London: SCM Press, 1980.

———. "Was Christianity a Monotheistic Faith from the Beginning?" *SJT* 35 (1982): 303-36.

du Plessis, Isak J. "Christ as the Only Begotten." In *The Christ of John: Essays on the Christology of the Fourth Gospel; Proceedings of the Fourth Meeting of Die Nuwe-Testamentiese Werkgennskap van Suid-Afrika*, pp. 22-31. Neotestamentica 2. Potchefstroom, South Africa: Pro Rege, 1971.

Durand, Emmanuel. "Λόγος, Μονογενής et Υἱός: Quelques implications trinitaires de la christologie johannique." *RSPT* 88 (2004): 93-103.

Ebner, Martin, and Elisabeth Esch-Wermeling, eds. *Kaiserkult, Wirtschaft und* spectacula: *Zum politischen und gesellschaftlichen Umfeld der Offenbarung.* NTOA 72. Göttingen: Vandenhoeck & Ruprecht, 2011.

Ekenberg, Anders. "The Fourth Gospel and the History of Jesus." *CV* 44 (2002): 182-91.

Ellis, E. Earle. *Pauline Theology: Ministry and Society.* Grand Rapids; Eerdmans; Exeter: Paternoster, 1989.

Ely, Mary Redington. *Knowledge of God in Johannine Thought.* New York: Macmillan, 1925.

Endo, Masanobu. *Creation and Christology: A Study on the Johannine Prologue in the Light of Early Jewish Accounts.* WUNT 2/149. Tübingen: Mohr Siebeck, 2002.

Ensor, Peter W. *Jesus and His "Works": The Johannine Sayings in Historical Perspective.* WUNT 2/85. Tübingen: Mohr Siebeck, 1996.

———. "The Johannine Sayings of Jesus and the Question of Authenticity." In *Challenging Perspectives on the Gospel of John*, edited by John Lierman, pp. 14-33. WUNT 2/219. Tübingen: Mohr Siebeck, 2006.

Eslinger, Lyle M. "The Enigmatic Plurals Like 'One of Us' (Genesis i 26, iii 22, and xi 7) in Hyperchronic Perspective." *VT* 56 (2006): 171-84.

Evans, Craig A. "Covenant in the Qumran Literature." In *The Concept of the Covenant in the Second Temple Period*, edited by Stanley E. Porter and Jaqueline C. R. de Roo, pp. 55-80. JSJSup 71. Leiden: Brill, 2003.

———. "On the Quotation Formulas in the Fourth Gospel." *BZ* 26 (1982): 79-83.

———. *Word and Glory: On the Exegetical and Theological Background of John's Prologue.* JSNTSup 89. Sheffield: JSOT Press, 1993.

Evans, Ernest. "The Verb ἀγαπᾶν in the Fourth Gospel." In *Studies in the Fourth Gospel*, edited by F. L. Cross, pp. 64-71. London: Mowbray, 1957.

Fahey, Michael. "Son and Spirit: Divergent Theologies Between Constantinople and the West." In *Conflicts about the Holy Spirit*, edited by Hans Küng and Jürgen Moltmann, pp. 15-22. Concilium 128. New York: Seabury, 1979.

Farelly, Nicolas. *The Disciples in the Fourth Gospel: A Narrative Analysis of Their Faith and Understanding.* WUNT 2/290. Tübingen: Mohr Siebeck, 2010.

———. "'Je suis la vérité' dans l'évangile de Jean." *RRef* 56 (2005): 1-20.

———. "Lire le Psaume 69 (68) en Jean 2,13-22." *ETR* 86 (2011): 195-207.

Fekkes, Jan. *Isaiah and Prophetic Traditions in the Book of Revelation: Visionary Antecedents and Their Development.* JSNTSup 93. Sheffield: JSOT Press, 1994.

Felsch, Dorit. *Die Feste im Johannesevangelium:* Jüdische Tradition und christologische Deutung. WUNT 2/308. Tübingen: Mohr Siebeck, 2011.

Fenske, W. *Der Lieblingsjünger: Das Geheimnis um Johannes.* BG 16. Leipzig: Evangelische Verlagsanstalt, 2007.

Fernando, G. Charles A. *The Relationship between Law and Love in the Gospel of John: A Detailed Scientific Research on the Concepts of Law and Love in the Fourth Gospel and Their Relationship to Each Other.* EH 23/772. Frankfurt: Peter Lang, 2004.

Ferreira, Johan. *Johannine Ecclesiology.* JSNTSup 160. Sheffield: Sheffield Academic Press, 1998.

Feuillet, André. *Le mystère de l'amour divin dans la théologie johannique.* EBib. Paris: Gabalda, 1972.

———. "Man's Participation in God's Life: A Key Concept in John." In *A Companion to John: Readings in Johannine Theology (John's Gospel and Epistles),* edited by Michael J. Taylor, pp. 141-51. New York: Alba House, 1970.

———. "Participation in the Life of God According to the Fourth Gospel." In *Johannine Studies,* translated by Thomas E. Crane, pp. 169-80. Staten Island, NY: Alba House, 1964.

———. "The Time of the Church in St. John." In *Johannine Studies,* translated by Thomas E. Crane, pp. 149-68. Staten Island, NY: Alba House, 1964.

Fitzmyer, Joseph A. "The Semitic Background of the New Testament *Kyrios*-Title." In *A Wandering Aramaean: Collected Aramaic Essays,* pp. 115-42. SBLMS 25. Missoula, MT: Scholars Press, 1979.

Forestell, J. Terence. *The Word of the Cross: Salvation as Revelation in the Fourth Gospel.* AnBib 57. Rome: Biblical Institute Press, 1974.

Fortna, Robert T. *The Fourth Gospel and Its Predecessor: From Narrative Source to Present Gospel.* Philadelphia: Fortress, 1988.

———. *The Gospel of Signs: A Reconstruction of the Narrative Source Underlying the Fourth Gospel.* SNTSMS 11. London: Cambridge University Press, 1970.

Fossum, Jarl E. "In the Beginning Was the Name: Onomanology as the Key to Johannine Christology." In *The Image of the Invisible God: Essays on the Influence of Jewish Mysticism on Early Christology,* pp. 109-34. NTOA 30. Göttingen: Vandenhoeck & Ruprecht, 1995.

Franck, Eskil. *Revelation Taught: The Paraclete in the Gospel of John.* ConBNT 14. Lund: Gleerup, 1985.

Frankfurter, David. "Jews or Not? Reconstructing the 'Other' in Rev 2:9 and 3:9." *HTR* 94 (2001): 403-25.

Freed, Edwin D. *Old Testament Quotations in the Gospel of John*. NovTSup 11. Leiden: Brill, 1965.

———. "Variations in the Language and Thought of John." *ZNW* 55 (1964): 167-97.

Freedman, David Noel, and David Miano. "People of the New Covenant." In *The Concept of the Covenant in the Second Temple Period*, edited by Stanley E. Porter and Jaqueline C. R. de Roo, pp. 7-26. JSJSup 71. Leiden: Brill, 2003.

Frey, Jörg. "'. . . dass sie meine Herrlichkeit schauen' (Joh 17,24): Zur Hintergrund, Sinn und Funktion der johanneischen Rede von der δόξα Jesus." *NTS* 54 (2008): 375-97.

———. "Die Bildersprache der Johannesapokalypse." *ZTK* 98 (2001): 161-85.

———. *Die johanneische Eschatologie*. 3 vols. WUNT 96, 110, 117. Tübingen: Mohr Siebeck, 1997.

———. "Die johanneische Theologie als Klimax der neutestamentlichen Theologie." *ZTK* 107 (2010): 448-78.

———. "Edler Tod—wirksamer Tod—stellvertretender Tod—heilschaffender Tod: Zur narrativen und theologischen Deutung des Todes Jesu im Johannesevangelium." In *The Death of Jesus in the Fourth Gospel*, edited by Gilbert van Belle, pp. 65-94. BETL 200. Leuven: Leuven University Press, 2007.

———. "Erwägungen zum Verhältnis der Johannesapokalypse zu den übrigen Schriften im Corpus Johanneum." In *Die johanneische Frage: Ein Lösungsversuch*, by Martin Hengel, pp. 326-429. WUNT 67. Tübingen: Mohr Siebeck, 1993.

———. "Licht aus den Höhlen? Der 'johanneische Dualismus' und die Texte von Qumran." In *Kontexte des Johannesevangeliums: Das vierte Evangelium in religions- und traditionsgeschichtlicher Perspektive*, edited by Jörg Frey and Udo Schnelle, pp. 117-203. WUNT 175. Tübingen: Mohr Siebeck, 2004.

———. "Zur johanneischen Deutung des Todes Jesu." *TBei* 32 (2002): 346-62.

Frey, Jörg, Jan G. van der Watt, and Ruben Zimmermann, eds. *Imagery in the Gospel of John: Terms, Forms, Themes, and Theology of Johannine Figurative Language*. WUNT 200. Tübingen: Mohr Siebeck, 2006.

Freyne, Seán. "Christological Debates among Johannine Christians." In *The Many Voices of the Bible*, edited by Seán Freyne and Ellen van Wolde, pp. 59-67. Concilium 2002/1. London: SCM Press, 2002.

Friesen, Steven J. *Imperial Cults and the Apocalypse of John: Reading Revelation in the Ruins*. Oxford: Oxford University Press, 2001.

Gager, John G. *Kingdom and Community: The Social World of Early Christianity*. PHSR. Englewood Cliffs, NJ: Prentice-Hall, 1975.

———. *The Origins of Anti-Semitism: Attitudes toward Judaism in Pagan and Christian Antiquity*. New York: Oxford University Press, 1983.

Gagné, André. "Caractérisation des figures de Satan et de Judas dans le IV^e évangile: Stratégie narrative et déploiement des intrigues de conflit." *ScEs* 55 (2003): 263-84.

Gallus, Laslo. "The Exodus Motif in Revelation 15–16: Its Background and Nature." *AUSS* 46 (2008): 21-43.

Galot, Jean. "Vedere e Credere." *CivCat* 151 (2000): 242-53.

Gardner-Smith, Percival. *Saint John and the Synoptic Gospels.* Cambridge: Cambridge University Press, 1938.

Gärtner, Bertil. *John 6 and the Jewish Passover.* ConBNT 17. Lund: Gleerup, 1959.

Gathercole, Simon J. *The Preexistent Son: Recovering the Christologies of Matthew, Mark, and Luke.* Grand Rapids: Eerdmans, 2006.

Geldenhuys, Norval. *Commentary on the Gospel of Luke.* NICNT. Grand Rapids: Eerdmans, 1951.

George, Larry Darnell. *Reading the Tapestry: A Literary-Rhetorical Analysis of the Johannine Resurrection Narrative (John 20–21).* SBL 14. New York: Peter Lang, 2000.

Gibson, David. "Eating Is Believing? On Midrash and the Mixing of Metaphors in John 6." *Them* 27 (2002): 5-15.

———. "The Johannine Footwashing and the Death of Jesus: A Dialogue with Scholarship." *SJET* 25 (2007): 50-60.

Gieschen, Charles A. *Angelomorphic Christology: Antecedents and Early Evidence.* AGJU 42. Leiden: Brill, 1998.

———. "The Death of Jesus in the Gospel of John: Atonement for Sin?" *CTQ* 72 (2008): 243-61.

Gilbertson, Michael. *God and History in the Book of Revelation: New Testament Studies in Dialogue with Pannenberg and Moltmann.* SNTSMS 124. Cambridge: Cambridge University Press, 2003.

Giles, Kevin. *The Trinity and Subordinationism: The Doctrine of God and the Contemporary Gender Debate.* Downers Grove, IL: InterVarsity Press, 2002.

Ginzberg, Louis. *The Legends of the Jews.* Translated by Henrietta Szold. 7 vols. Philadelphia: Jewish Publication Society of America, 1909–1938.

Glasson, T. F. *Moses in the Fourth Gospel.* SBT 40. Naperville, IL: Allenson, 1963.

Gniesmer, Dirk F. *In den Prozess verwickelt: Erzähltextanalytische und textpragmatische Erwägungen zur Erzählung vom Prozess vor Pilatus (Joh 18,28–19,16a,b).* EH 23/688. Frankfurt: Peter Lang, 2000.

González Faus, José Ignacio. "Sin of the World, Light of the World." In *2000: Reality and Hope*, edited by Virgil Elizondo and Jon Sobrino, pp. 39-49. Concilium 1999/5. London: SCM Press, 1999.

Grant, Robert M. *Gnosticism: A Source Book of Heretical Writings from the Early Christian Period.* New York: Harper, 1961.

Grappe, Christian. "Jean 1,14(-18) dans son contexte et à la lumière de la littérature intertestamentaire." *RHPR* 80 (2000): 153-69.

Graves, David. *The Seven Messages of Revelation and Vassal Treaties: Literary Genre, Structure, and Function.* Gorgias Dissertations 41. Piscataway, NJ: Gorgias, 2009.

Gregory, Peter F. "Its End Is Destruction: Babylon the Great in the Book of Revelation." *CTQ* 73 (2009): 137-53.

Grelot, Pierre. *Les Juifs dans l'evangile selon Jean.* CahRB 34. Paris: Gabalda, 1995.

Griffith, Terry. *Keep Yourselves from Idols: A New Look at 1 John.* JSNTSup 233. London: Sheffield Academic Press, 2002.

Grigsby, Bruce H. "The Cross as an Expiatory Sacrifice in the Fourth Gospel." *JSNT* 15 (1982): 51-80.

Groll, Oliver. *Finsternis, Tod und Blindheit als Strafe: Eine exegetische Untersuchung zu den Begriffen κρίνειν, κρίσις und κρίμα im Johannesevangelium.* EH 23/781. Frankfurt: Peter Lang, 2004.

Grossouw, W. K. "Christian Spirituality in John." In *A Companion to John: Readings in Johannine Theology (John's Gospel and Epistles)*, edited by Michael J. Taylor, pp. 205-24. New York: Alba House, 1970.

Gruber, Margareta. "Berührendes Sehen: Zur Legitimation der Zeichenforderung des Thomas (Joh 20,24-31)." *BZ* 51 (2007): 61-83.

Gruenler, Royce Gordon. *The Trinity in the Gospel of John: A Thematic Commentary on the Fourth Gospel.* Grand Rapids: Baker, 1986.

Guilding, Aileen. *The Fourth Gospel and Jewish Worship: A Study of the Relation of St. John's Gospel to the Ancient Jewish Lectionary System.* Oxford: Clarendon, 1960.

Gunton, Colin E. "'And in One Lord Jesus Christ . . . Begotten Not Made.'" In *Father, Son and Holy Spirit: Essays Toward a Fully Trinitarian Theology*, pp. 58-74. London: T & T Clark, 2003.

Guthrie, Donald. *New Testament Introduction.* 3rd ed. Downers Grove, IL: InterVarsity Press, 1970.

Guttesen, Paul F. *Leaning into the Future: The Kingdom of God in the Theology of Jürgen Moltmann and in the Book of Revelation.* PTMS 117. Eugene, OR: Pickwick, 2009.

Guyette, Frederick W. "Sacramentality in the Fourth Gospel: Conflicting Interpretations." *Eccl* 3 (2007): 235-50.

Gwynne, Paul. "YHWH and the Invisible Father." *ACR* 77 (2000): 278-91.

Haacker, Klaus. *Die Stiftung des Heils: Untersuchungen zur Struktur der johanneischen Theologie.* AzTh 1/47. Stuttgart: Calwer, 1972.

———. "Jesus und die Kirche nach Johannes." *TZ* 29 (1973): 179-201.

Hägerland, Tobias. "John's Gospel: A Two-Level Drama?" *JSNT* 25 (2003): 309-22.

Hahn, Ferdinand. "Das Geistverständnis in der Johannesoffenbarung." In *Studien zur Johannesoffenbarung und ihrer Auslegung: Festschrift für Otto Böcher zum 70. Geburtstag*, edited by Friedrich Wilhelm Horn and Michael Wolter, pp. 3-9. Neukirchen-Vluyn: Neukirchener Verlag, 2005.

———. "Die Offenbarung des Johannes als Geschichtsdeutung und Trostbuch." *KD* 51 (2005): 55-70.

———. *The Worship of the Early Church*. Translated by David E. Green. Philadelphia: Fortress, 1973.

Hahn, Horst. *Tradition und Neuinterpretation im ersten Johannesbrief*. Zürich: Theologischer Verlag, 2009.

Hahn, Scott. "Covenant in the Old and New Testaments: Some Current Research (1994–2004)." *CurBR* 3 (2005): 263-92.

Hakola, Raimo. "The Burden of Ambiguity: Nicodemus and the Social Identity of the Johannine Christians." *NTS* 55 (2009): 438-55.

———. *Identity Matters: John, the Jews and Jewishness*. NovTSup 118. Leiden: Brill, 2005.

Haldimann, Konrad. *Rekonstruktion und Entfaltung: Exegetische Untersuchungen zu Joh 15 und 16*. BZNW 104. Berlin: de Gruyter, 2000.

Hamid-Khani, Saeed. *Revelation and Concealment of Christ: A Theological Inquiry into the Elusive Language of the Fourth Gospel*. WUNT 2/120. Tübingen: Mohr Siebeck, 2000.

Hanna, Kamal Fahim Awad. *La passione di Cristo nell'Apocalisse*. TGST 77. Rome: Editrice Pontificia Università Gregoriana, 2001.

Hannah, Darrell D. "Of Cherubim and the Divine Throne: Rev 5.6 in Context." *NTS* 49 (2003): 528-42.

Hanson, Anthony Tyrrell. *The Prophetic Gospel: A Study of John and the Old Testament*. SEBS. Edinburgh: T & T Clark, 1991.

Harnack, Adolf von. *The Mission and Expansion of Christianity in the First Three Centuries*. Translated by James Moffatt. New York: Harper, 1962 [1906].

———. *Über den dritten Johannesbrief*. TUGAL 15/3. Leipzig: Hinrichs, 1897.

Harner, Philip B. *The "I Am" of the Fourth Gospel: A Study in Johannine Usage and Thought*. FBBS 26. Philadelphia: Fortress, 1970.

———. *Relation Analysis of the Fourth Gospel: A Study in Reader-Response Criticism*. Lewiston, NY: Mellen, 1993.

Harris, Murray J. "Appendix: Prepositions and Theology in the Greek New Testament." *NIDNTT* 3:1171-1215.

———. *Jesus as God: The New Testament Use of Theos in Reference to Jesus*. Grand Rapids: Baker Books, 1992.

———. *Raised Immortal: Resurrection and Immortality in the New Testament*. Grand Rapids: Eerdmans, 1985.

———. "The Translation of Elohim in Psalm 45:7-8." *TynBul* 35 (1984): 65-89.

Harstine, Stan. *Moses as a Character in the Fourth Gospel: A Study of Ancient Reading Techniques*. JSNTSup 229. London: Sheffield Academic Press, 2002.

Hartenstein, Judith. *Charakterisierung im Dialog: Die Darstellung von Maria Magdalena, Petrus, Thomas und der Mutter Jesu im Johannesevangelium im Kontext anderer frühchristlicher Traditionen*. NTOA 64. Göttingen: Vandenhoeck & Ruprecht, 2007.

Hartman, Lars. "Johannine Jesus-Belief and Monotheism." In *Aspects on the Johannine*

*Literature: Papers Presented at a Conference of Scandanavian New Testament Exegetes at Uppsala, June 16-19, 1986*, edited by Lars Hartman and Birger Olsson, pp. 85-99. ConBNT 18. Uppsala: Almqvist & Wiksell, 1987.

Harvey, A. E. "Christ as Agent." In *The Glory of Christ in the New Testament: Studies in Christology in Memory of George Bradford Caird*, edited by L. D. Hurst and N. T. Wright, pp. 239-50. Oxford: Clarendon, 1987.

———. *Jesus and the Constraints of History*. Philadelphia: Westminster, 1982.

Hasel, Gerhard F. "The Meaning of 'Let Us' in Gn 1:26." *AUSS* 13 (1975): 58-66.

———. *New Testament Theology: Basic Issues in the Current Debate*. Grand Rapids: Eerdmans, 1978.

Hasitschka, Martin. "Die Priestermetaphorik der Apokalypse als Ausdruck der Verbundenheit der auf Erden lebenden mit den zur Auferstehung gelangten Christen." *SNTSU* 29 (2004): 179-92.

Hawkin, David J. "Revelation and Truth in Johannine Theology." *Chm* 116 (2002): 105-12.

Hay, David M. *Glory at the Right Hand: Psalm 110 in Early Christianity*. SBLMS 18. Nashville: Abingdon, 1973.

Hayward, Robert. *Divine Name and Presence: The Memra*. Totowa, NJ: Allanheld, Osmun, 1981.

Headlam, Arthur C. *The Fourth Gospel as History*. Oxford: Blackwell, 1948.

Heath, Jane. "'Some Were Saying, "He is Good"' (John 7.12b): 'Good' Christology in John's Gospel?" *NTS* 56 (2010): 513-35.

Heckel, Ulrich. *Hirtenamt und Herrschaftskritik: Die urchristlichen Ämter aus johanneischer Sicht*. BTS 65. Neukirchen-Vluyn: Neukirchener Verlag, 2004.

Heinze, André. *Johannesapokalypse und johanneische Schriften: Forschungs- und traditionsgeschichtliche Untersuchungen*. BWANT 142. Stuttgart: Kohlhammer, 1998.

Heise, Jürgen. *Bleiben: Menein in den Johanneischen Schriften*. HUT 8. Tübingen: Mohr Siebeck, 1967.

Heiser, Michael S. "Monotheism, Polytheism, Monolatry, or Henotheism? Toward an Assessment of Divine Plurality in the Hebrew Bible." *BBR* 18 (2008): 1-30.

Hengel, Martin. "Between Jesus and Paul." In *Between Jesus and Paul: Studies in the Earliest History of Christianity*, translated by John Bowden, pp. 1-29. London: SCM Press, 1983.

———. *Crucifixion in the Ancient World and the Folly of the Message of the Cross*. Translated by John Bowden. London: SCM Press, 1977.

———. *Die johanneische Frage: Ein Lösungsversuch*. WUNT 67. Tübingen: Mohr Siebeck, 1993.

———. "Die Schriftauslegung des 4. Evangeliums auf dem Hintergrund der urchristlichen Exegese." *JBTh* 4 (1989): 249-88.

———. "Die Throngemeinschaft des Lammes mit Gott in der Johannesapokalypse." *TBei* 27 (1996): 159-75.

———. *The Johannine Question*. Philadelphia: Trinity Press International, 1990.

———. *Judaism and Hellenism: Studies in Their Encounter in Palestine during the Early Hellenistic Period*. Translated by John Bowden. 2 vols. Philadelphia: Fortress, 1974.

———. "The Old Testament in the Fourth Gospel." In *The Gospels and the Scriptures of Israel*, edited by Craig A. Evans and W. Richard Stegner, pp. 380-97. JSNTSup 104. Sheffield: Sheffield Academic Press, 1994.

———. "The Prologue of the Gospel of John as the Gateway to Christological Truth." In *The Gospel of John and Christian Theology*, edited by Richard Bauckham and Carl Mosser, pp. 265-94. Grand Rapids: Eerdmans, 2008.

———. "'Sit at My Right Hand!'" In *Studies in Early Christology*, pp. 119-225. Edinburgh: T & T Clark, 1995.

Hengel, Martin, and Roland Deines. "E. P. Sanders' 'Common Judaism,' Jesus, and the Pharisees." *JTS* 46 (1995): 1-70.

Hennecke, Edgar. *New Testament Apocrypha*. Edited by Wilhelm Schneemelcher. Translated and edited by R. McL. Wilson. 2 vols. Philadelphia: Westminster, 1963.

Herms, Ronald. *An Apocalypse for the Church and for the World: The Narrative Function of Universal Language in the Book of Revelation*. BZNW 143. Berlin: de Gruyter, 2006.

Hill, Charles E. *The Johannine Corpus in the Early Church*. Oxford: Oxford University Press, 2004.

Hill, David. *Greek Words and Hebrew Meanings: Studies in the Semantics of Soteriological Terms*. SNTSMS 5. Cambridge: Cambridge University Press, 1967.

Hillmer, Melvyn R. "They Believed in Him: Discipleship in the Johannine Tradition." In *Patterns of Discipleship in the New Testament*, edited by Richard N. Longenecker, pp. 77-97. Grand Rapids: Eerdmans, 1996.

Hoffmann, Matthias Reinhard. *The Destroyer and the Lamb: The Relationship between Angelomorphic and Lamb Christology in the Book of Revelation*. WUNT 2/203. Tübingen: Mohr Siebeck, 2005.

Hofius, Otfried. "'Der in des Vaters Schoß ist' Joh 1,18." *ZNW* 80 (1989): 163-71.

———. "Die Auferweckung des Lazarus: Joh 11,1-44 als Zeugnis narrativer Christologie." *ZTK* 102 (2005): 17-34.

———. "Die Erzählung von der Fusswaschung Jesu: Joh 13,1-11 als narratives Christuszeugnis." *ZTK* 106 (2009): 156-76.

Hofrichter, Peter Leander, ed. *Für und wider die Priorität des Johannesevangeliums: Symposion in Salzburg am 10. März 2000*. TTS 9. Hildesheim: Olms, 2002.

Holtz, Traugott. *Die Christologie der Apokalypse des Johannes*. TUGAL 85. Berlin: Akademie-Verlag, 1962.

Holwerda, David Earl. *The Holy Spirit and Eschatology in the Gospel of John: A Critique of Rudolf Bultman's Present Eschatology*. Grand Rapids: Eerdmans, 1959.

Hopkins, Clark. *Christian Church at Dura-Europus. 1. The Christian Church*. New Haven: Yale University Press, 1934.

Horbury, William. "The Benediction of the Minim and the Early Jewish-Christian Controversy." *JTS* 33 (1982): 19-61.

———. "Jewish and Christian Monotheism in the Herodian Age." In *Early Jewish and Christian Monotheism*, edited by Loren T. Stuckenbruck and Wendy E. S. North, pp. 16-44. JSNTSup 263. London: T & T Clark, 2004.

———. "Jewish Messianism and Early Christology." In *Contours of Christology in the New Testament*, edited by Richard N. Longenecker, pp. 3-24. MNTS. Grand Rapids: Eerdmans, 2005.

———. *Jewish Messianism and the Cult of Christ*. London: SCM Press, 1998.

Horn, Friedrich Wilhelm. "Holy Spirit." *ABD* 3:260-80.

Hort, F. J. A. "On ΜΟΝΟΓΕΝΗΣ ΘΕΟΣ. Note D: Unicus *And* Unigenitus *Among the Latins*." In *Two Dissertations*, pp. 48-53. Cambridge: Macmillan, 1876.

Hoskins, Paul M. "Deliverance from Death by the True Passover Lamb: A Significant Aspect of the Fulfillment of the Passover in the Gospel of John." *JETS* 52 (2009): 285-99.

———. *Jesus as the Fulfillment of the Temple in the Gospel of John*. PBM. Milton Keynes: Paternoster, 2006.

Howard, W. F. *Christianity According to St. John*. London: Duckworth, 1943.

———. "The Common Authorship of the Johannine Gospel and Epistles." *JTS* 48 (1947): 12-25.

——— *The Fourth Gospel in Recent Criticism and Interpretation*. Edited by C. K. Barrett. 4th ed. London: Epworth, 1955.

Huber, Konrad. *Einer gleich einem Menschensohn: die Christusvisionen in Offb 1,9-20 und Offb 14,14-20 und die Christologie der Johannesoffenbarung*. NTAbh 51. Münster: Aschendorff, 2007.

Huber, Lynn R. *Like a Bride Adorned: Reading Metaphor in John's Apocalypse*. ESEC 10. London: T & T Clark, 2007.

Hübner, Hans. *Evangelium secundum Iohannem*. Vol. 1.2 of *Vetus Testamentum in Novo*. Göttingen: Vandenhoeck & Ruprecht, 2003.

Hultgren, Arland J. *The Rise of Normative Christianity*. Minneapolis: Fortress, 1994.

Hurtado, Larry W. "Christology." In *Dictionary of the Later New Testament and Its Developments*, edited by Ralph P. Martin and Peter H. Davids, pp. 170-84. Downers Grove, IL: InterVarsity Press, 1997.

———. "Early Jewish Opposition to Jesus-Devotion." In *How on Earth Did Jesus Become a God? Historical Questions about Earliest Devotion to Jesus*, pp. 152-78. Grand Rapids: Eerdmans, 2005.

———. "First-Century Jewish Monotheism." In *How on Earth Did Jesus Become a God? Historical Questions about Earliest Devotion to Jesus*, pp. 111-33. Grand Rapids: Eerdmans, 2005.

———. *God in New Testament Theology*. LBT. Nashville: Abingdon, 2010.

———. *How on Earth Did Jesus Become a God? Historical Questions about Earliest Devotion to Jesus*. Grand Rapids: Eerdmans, 2005.

————. *Lord Jesus Christ: Devotion to Jesus in Earliest Christianity*. Grand Rapids: Eerdmans, 2003.

————. *One God, One Lord: Early Christian Devotion and Ancient Jewish Monotheism*. Philadelphia: Fortress, 1988.

Hylen, Susan. *Allusion and Meaning in John 6*. BZNW 137. Berlin: de Gruyter, 2005.

————. *Imperfect Believers: Ambiguous Characters in the Gospel of John*. Louisville: Westminster John Knox, 2009.

————. "Metaphor Matters: Violence and Ethics in Revelation." *CBQ* 73 (2011): 777-96.

Ibuki, Yū. *Die Wahrheit im Johannesevangelium*. BBB 39. Bonn: Hanstein, 1972.

Ihenacho, David Asonye. *The Community of Eternal Life: The Study of the Meaning of Life for the Johannine Community*. Lanham, MD: University Press of America, 2001.

Jackson, Howard M. "Ancient Self-Referential Conventions and Their Implications for the Authorship and Integrity of the Gospel of John." *JTS* 50 (1999): 1-34.

Jackson, John. Introduction to *Tactitus: Histories, Books IV-V; Annals, Books I-III*, pp. 225-42. LCL 249. Cambridge, MA: Harvard University Press, 1931.

Janssens, Aloysius. *The Mystery of the Trinity*. Fresno, CA: Academy Library Guild, 1954.

Janzen, J. Gerald. "'(Not) of My Own Accord': Listening for Scriptural Echoes in a Johannine Idiom." *Enc* 67 (2006): 137-60.

Jauhiainen, Marko. "Recapitulation and Chronological Progression in John's Apocalypse: Towards a New Perspective." *NTS* 49 (2003): 543-59.

————. *The Use of Zechariah in Revelation*. WUNT 2/199. Tübingen: Mohr Siebeck, 2005.

Jensen, Alexander S. *John's Gospel as Witness: The Development of the Early Christian Language of Faith*. ANCT. Aldershot: Ashgate, 2004.

Jerumanis, Pascal-Marie. *Réaliser la communion avec Dieu: Croire, vivre et demeurer dans l'évangile selon S. Jean*. EBib 32. Paris: Gabalda, 1996.

Johns, Loren L. *The Lamb Christology of the Apocalypse of John: An Investigation into Its Origins and Rhetorical Force*. WUNT 2/167. Tübingen: Mohr Siebeck, 2003.

Johnston, George. *The Spirit-Paraclete in the Gospel of John*. SNTSMS 13. Cambridge: Cambridge University Press, 1970.

Jonas, Hans. *The Gnostic Religion: The Message of the Alien God and the Beginnings of Christianity*. 2nd ed. Boston: Beacon, 1963.

Jones, Peter Rhea. "A Presiding Metaphor of First John: μένειν ἐν." *PRSt* 17 (2010): 179-93.

Kähler, Martin. *The So-Called Historical Jesus and the Historic, Biblical Christ*. Translated by Carl E. Braaten. Philadelphia: Fortress, 1964.

Kalms, Jürgen H. *Der Sturz des Gottesfeindes: Traditionsgeschichtliche Studien zu Apokalypse 12*. WMANT 93. Neukirchen-Vluyn: Neukirchener Verlag, 2001.

Kammler, Hans-Christian. *Christologie und Eschatologie: Joh 5,17-30 als Schlüsseltext johanneischer Theologie*. WUNT 126. Tübingen: Mohr Siebeck, 2000.

————. "Jesus Christus und der Geistparaklet: Eine Studie zur johanneischen Verhältnisbestimmung von Pneumatologie und Christologie." In *Johannesstudien: Untersu-*

*chungen zur Theologie des vierten Evangeliums,* by Otfried Hofius and Hans-Christian Kammler, pp. 87-190. WUNT 88. Tübingen: Mohr Siebeck, 1996.

Kanagaraj, Jey J. "The Implied Ethics of the Fourth Gospel: A Reinterpretation of the Decalogue." *TynBul* 52 (2001): 33-60.

———. "Johannine Jesus, the Supreme Example of Leadership: An Inquiry into John 13:1-20." *Them* 29 (2004): 15-26.

———. *"Mysticism" in the Gospel of John: An Inquiry into Its Background.* JSNTSup 158. Sheffield: Sheffield Academic Press, 1998.

Kangas, Ron. "A Panoramic View of the Gospel of John." *Affirmation & Critique* 9 (2004): 8-25.

Käsemann, Ernst. "Ketzer und Zeuge." *ZTK* 48 (1951): 292-311.

———. *The Testament of Jesus: A Study of the Gospel of John in the Light of Chapter 17.* Translated by Gerhard Krodel. Philadelphia: Fortress, 1968.

Kautsky, Karl. *Foundations of Christianity.* London: Allen & Unwin, 1925 [1908].

Kealy, Sean P. *John's Gospel and the History of Biblical Interpretation.* 2 vols. MBPS 60A, 60B. Lewiston, NY: Mellen, 2002.

Keck, Leander E. "Derivation as Destiny: 'Of-Ness' in Johannine Christology, Anthropology, and Soteriology." In *Exploring the Gospel of John: In Honor of D. Moody Smith,* edited by R. Alan Culpepper and C. Clifton Black, pp. 274-88. Louisville: Westminster John Knox, 1996.

———. "Toward the Renewal of New Testament Theology." *NTS* 32 (1986): 362-77.

Keefer, Kyle. *The Branches of the Gospel of John: The Reception of the Fourth Gospel in the Early Church.* LNTS 332. London: T & T Clark, 2006.

Keener, Craig S. *The Gospel of John: A Commentary.* 2 vols. Peabody, MA: Hendrickson, 2003.

———. "Is Subordination within the Trinity Really Heresy? A Study of John 5:18 in Context." *TJ* 20 (1999): 39-51.

Keith, Chris. "Recent and Previous Research on the *Pericope Adulterae* (John 7:53–8:11)." *CurBR* 6 (2008): 377-404.

Kellum, L. Scott. *The Unity of the Farewell Discourse: The Literary Integrity of John 13:31–16:33.* JSNTSup 256. London: T & T Clark, 2004.

Kelly, J. N. D. *Early Christian Creeds.* 3rd ed. London: Longman, 1972.

———. *Early Christian Doctrines.* 5th ed. London: Adam & Charles Black, 1977.

Kennedy, H. A. A. "The Covenant-Conception in the First Epistle of John." *ExpTim* 28 (1916): 23-26.

Kenney, Garrett C. *Leadership in John: An Analysis of the Situation and Strategy of the Gospel and the Epistles of John.* Lanham, MD: University Press of America, 2000.

Kerber, Daniel. *"No me eligieron ustedes a mí, sino que yo los elegí a ustedes": Estudio exegético teológico sobre al verbo ἐκλέγομαι en el cuarto evangelio.* Montevideo: Facultad de Teología del Uruguay, 2002.

Kerr, Alan R. *The Temple of Jesus' Body: The Temple Theme in the Gospel of John.* JSNTSup 220. London: Sheffield Academic Press, 2002.

Kieffer, René. *Le monde symbolique de Saint Jean.* LD 137. Paris: Cerf, 1989.

Kierspel, Lars. *The Jews and the World in the Fourth Gospel: Parallelism, Function, and Context.* WUNT 2/220. Tübingen: Mohr Siebeck, 2006.

Kilpatrick, G. D. "What John Tells Us about John." In *Studies in John: Presented to Professor J N Sevenster on the Occasion of His Seventieth Birthday*, pp. 75-87. NovTSup 24. Leiden: Brill, 1970.

Kim, Dongsu. *An Exegesis of Apostasy Embedded in John's Narratives of Peter and Judas against the Synoptic Parallels.* SBEC 61. Lewiston, NY: Mellen, 2004.

Kim, Jintae. "The Concept of Atonement in the Gospel of John." *JGRCJ* 6 (2009): 9-27.

Kim, Stephen S. "The Significance of Jesus' Raising Lazarus from the Dead in John 11:1-44." *BSac* 168 (2011): 53-62.

Kinlaw, Pamela E. *The Christ is Jesus: Metamorphosis, Possession, and Johannine Christology.* SBLAB 18. Atlanta: Society of Biblical Literature, 2005.

Kistemaker, Simon J. "The Temple in the Apocalypse." *JETS* 43 (2000): 433-41.

Klassen, William. "Vengeance in the Apocalypse of John." *CBQ* 28 (1966): 300-311.

Klauck, Hans-Josef. "Gemeinde ohne Amt? Erfahrungen mit der Kirche in den johanneischen Schriften." *BZ* 29 (1985): 193-220.

Klein, Hans. "Der Paraklet als Subjekt Prophetischer Rede im Johannesevangelium." *SS* 9 (2011): 173-88.

Klink, Edward W., ed. *The Audience of the Gospels: The Origin and Function of the Gospels in Early Christianity.* LNTS 353. London: T & T Clark, 2010.

———. "Expulsion from the Synagogue? Rethinking a Johannine Anachronism." *TynBul* 59 (2008): 99-118.

———. *The Sheep of the Fold: The Audience and Origin of the Gospel of John.* SNTSMS 141. Cambridge: Cambridge University Press, 2007.

Klos, Herbert. *Die Sakramente im Johannesevangelium.* SBS 46. Stuttgart: Katholisches Bibelwerk, 1970.

Knight, Mark. "*Wirkungsgeschichte*, Reception History, Reception Theory." *JSNT* 33 (2010): 137-46.

Knöppler, Thomas. *Die theologia crucis des Johannesevangeliums: Das Verständnis des Todes Jesu im Rahmen der johanneischen Inkarnations- und Erhöhungschristologie.* WMANT 69. Neukirchen-Vluyn: Neukirchener Verlag, 1994.

———. *Sühne im Neuen Testament: Studien zum urchristlichen Verständnis der Heilsbedeutung des Todes Jesu.* WMANT 88. Neukirchen-Vluyn: Neukirchener Verlag, 2001.

Koester, Craig R. "The Church and Its Witness in the Apocalypse of John." *TTKi* 78 (2007): 266-82.

———. "Jesus' Resurrection, the Signs, and the Dynamics of Faith in the Gospel of John." In *The Resurrection of Jesus in the Gospel of John*, edited by Craig R. Koester and

Reimund Bieringer, pp. 47-74. WUNT 222. Tübingen: Mohr Siebeck, 2008.

———. "Roman Slave Trade and the Critique of Babylon in Revelation 18." *CBQ* 70 (2008): 766-86.

———. "'The Savior of the World' (John 4:42)." *JBL* 109 (1990): 665-80.

———. *Symbolism in the Fourth Gospel: Meaning, Mystery, Community.* 2nd ed. Minneapolis: Fortress, 2003.

———. *The Word of Life: A Theology of John's Gospel.* Grand Rapids: Eerdmans, 2008.

Kollmann, Hanjo-Christoph. *Die Kreuzigung Jesu nach Joh 19,16-22: Ein Beitrag zur Kreuzestheologie des Johannes im Vergleich mit den Synoptikern.* EH 23/710. Frankfurt: Peter Lang, 2000.

Köstenberger, Andreas J. "The Destruction of the Second Temple and the Composition of the Fourth Gospel." In *Challenging Perspectives on the Gospel of John,* edited by John Lierman, pp. 69-108. WUNT 2/219. Tübingen: Mohr Siebeck, 2006.

———. "Early Doubts of the Apostolic Authorship of the Fourth Gospel in the History of Modern Biblical Criticism." In *Studies on John and Gender: A Decade of Scholarship,* pp. 17-47. SBL 38. New York: Peter Lang, 2001.

———. "Jesus as Rabbi in the Fourth Gospel." In *Studies on John and Gender: A Decade of Scholarship,* pp. 65-98. SBL 38. New York: Peter Lang, 2001.

———. "Jesus the Good Shepherd Who Will Also Bring Other Sheep (John 10:16): The Old Testament Background of a Familiar Metaphor." *BBR* 12 (2002): 67-96.

———. *The Missions of Jesus and the Disciples According to the Fourth Gospel: With Implications for the Fourth Gospel's Purpose and the Mission of the Contemporary Church.* Grand Rapids: Eerdmans, 1998.

———. "The Seventh Johannine Sign: A Study in John's Christology." *BBR* 5 (1995): 87-103.

———. *A Theology of John's Gospel and Letters: The Word, the Christ, the Son of God.* BTNT. Grand Rapids: Zondervan, 2009.

Köstenberger, Andreas J., and Stephen O. Stout. "'The Disciple Jesus Loved': Witness, Author, Apostle—A Response to Richard Bauckham's *Jesus and the Eyewitnesses.*" *BBR* 18 (2008): 209-31.

Köstenberger, Andreas J., and Scott R. Swain. *Father, Son and Spirit: The Trinity and John's Gospel.* NSBT 24. Downers Grove, IL: InterVarsity, 2008.

Kovacs, Judith, and Christopher Rowland. *Revelation: The Apocalypse of Jesus Christ.* BBC. Oxford: Blackwell, 2003.

Kowalski, Beate. *Die Rezeption des Propheten Ezechiel in der Offenbarung des Johannes.* SBB 52. Stuttgart: Katholisches Bibelwerk, 2004.

———. "'Lichtfrau, Drache, Zornesschalen . . .': Zur Bedeutung eschatologischer Zeichen in der Offenbarung des Johannes." *ETL* 78 (2002): 358-84.

———. "Thesen zur joh Christologie." *BN* 146 (2010): 107-23.

Kragerud, Alv. *Der Lieblingsjünger im Johannesevangelium: Ein exegetischer Versuch.* Oslo: Osloer Universitätsverlag, 1959.

Kraybill, J. Nelson. *Apocalypse and Allegiance: Worship, Politics, and Devotion in the Book of Revelation*. Grand Rapids: Brazos, 2010.

———. *Imperial Cult and Commerce in John's Apocalypse*. JSNTSup 132. Sheffield: Sheffield Academic Press, 1996.

Kruck, Günter, ed. *Der Johannesprolog*. Darmstadt: Wissenschaftliche Buchgesellschaft, 2009.

Kruse, Colin G. "Sin and Perfection in 1 John." *ABR* 51 (2003): 60-70.

Kuehn, Evan F. "The Johannine Logic of Augustine's Trinity: A Dogmatic Sketch." *TS* 68 (2007): 572-94.

Kügler, Joachim. *Der andere König: Religionsgeschichtliche Perspektiven auf die Christologie des Johannesevangeliums*. SBS 178. Stuttgart: Katholisches Bibelwerk, 1999.

Kuhl, Josef. *Die Sendung Jèsu und der Kirche nach dem Johannes-Evangelium*. SIMSVD 11. St. Augustin: Steyler, 1967.

Kümmel, Werner Georg. *Introduction to the New Testament*. Translated by Howard Clark Kee. Rev. ed. London: SCM Press, 1975.

Kundsin, K. "Charakter und Ursprung der johanneischen Reden." *Latvijas Universitates Raksti (Acta Universitates Latviensis): Teologijas Fakultates Serija* 1, no. 4 (1939): 185-301.

Küng, Hans, and Jürgen Moltmann, eds. *Conflicts about the Holy Spirit*. Concilium 128. New York: Seabury, 1979.

Kysar, Robert. "Community and Gospel: Vectors in Fourth Gospel Criticism." *Int* 31 (1977): 355-66.

———. *The Fourth Evangelist and His Gospel: An Examination of Contemporary Scholarship*. Minneapolis: Augsburg, 1975.

Labahn, Michael. "Between Tradition and Literary Art: The Miracle Tradition in the Fourth Gospel." *Bib* 80 (1999): 178-203.

———. "Controversial Revelation in Deed and Word: The Feeding of the Five Thousand and Jesus' Crossing of the Sea as a 'Prelude' to the Johannine Bread of Life Discourse." *IBS* 22 (2000): 146-81.

———. *Jesus als Lebensspender: Untersuchungen zu einer Geschichte der johanneischen Tradition anhand ihrer Wundergeschichten*. BZNW 98. Berlin: de Gruyter, 1999.

Labahn, Michael, and Manfred Lang. "Johannes und die Synoptiker: Positionen und Impulse seit 1990." In *Kontexte des Johannesevangeliums: Das vierte Evangelium in religions- und traditionsgeschichtlicher Perspektive*, edited by Jörg Frey and Udo Schnelle, pp. 443-515. WUNT 175. Tübingen: Mohr Siebeck, 2004.

Ladd, George Eldon. *A Theology of the New Testament*. Grand Rapids: Eerdmans, 1974.

Lake, Kirsopp. *The Earlier Epistles of St. Paul: Their Motive and Origin*. 2nd ed. London: Rivingtons, 1914.

Lambrecht, Jan. "Final Judgments and Ultimate Blessings: The Climactic Visions of Revelation 20,11–21,8." *Bib* 81 (2000): 362-85.

———. "Jewish Slander: A Note on Revelation 2,9-10." *ETL* 75 (1999): 421-29.

Larsen, Kasper Bro. *Recognizing the Stranger: Recognition Scenes in the Gospel of John.* BIS 93. Leiden: Brill, 2008.

Larsson, Tord. *God in the Fourth Gospel: A Hermeneutical Study of the History of Interpretations.* ConBNT 35. Stockholm: Almqvist & Wiksell, 2001.

Lattke, Michael. "Einheit im Wort: Die spezifische Bedeutung von ἀγάπη, ἀγαπᾶν, und φιλεῖν im Johannesevangelium." Ph.D. diss. University of Freiburg, 1973.

Latz, Andrew Brower. "A Short Note Toward a Theology of Abiding in John's Gospel." *JTI* 4 (2010): 161-68.

Law, Robert. *The Tests of Life: A Study of the First Epistle of St. John.* 3rd ed. Edinburgh: T & T Clark, 1914.

Lazure, Noël. *Les valeurs morales de la théologie johannique.* EBib. Paris: Gabalda, 1965.

Lee, Dorothy. "The Gospel of John and the Five Senses." *JBL* 129 (2010): 115-27.

———. "In the Spirit of Truth: Worship and Prayer in the Gospel of John and the Early Fathers." *VC* 58 (2004): 277-97.

Lee, Edwin Kenneth. *The Religious Thought of St. John.* London: SPCK, 1962.

Le Fort, Pierre. *Les structures de l'Église militante selon Saint Jean: Étude d'ecclésiologie concrète appliquée au IV évangile et aux épîtres johanniques.* NST 25. Geneva: Labor et Fides, 1970.

Leiman, Sid Z. *The Canonization of Hebrew Scripture: The Talmudic and Midrashic Evidence.* TCAAS 47. Hamden, CT: Archon, 1976.

Leinhäupl-Wilke, Andreas. *Rettendes Wissen im Johannesevangelium: Ein Zugang über die narrativen Rahmenteile (John 1,19—2,12—20,1—21,25).* NTAbh 45. Münster: Aschendorff, 2003.

Leuenberger, Martin. "Die personifizierte Weisheit vorweltlichen Ursprungs von Hi 28 bis Joh 1: Ein traditionsgeschichtlicher Strang zwischen den Testamenten." *ZAW* 120 (2008): 366-86.

Leung, Mavis M. "The Roman Empire and John's Passion Narrative in Light of Jewish Royal Messianism." *BSac* 168 (2011): 426-42.

Levering, Matthew. "Predestination in John 13–17? Aquinas' *Commentary on John* and Contemporary Exegesis." *Thomist* 75 (2011): 393-414.

Levieils, Xavier. "Juifs et Grecs dans la communauté johannique." *Bib* 82 (2001): 51-78.

Lewis, F. Warburton. *Disarrangements in the Fourth Gospel.* Cambridge: Cambridge University Press, 1910.

Liebert, Elizabeth. "That You May Believe: The Fourth Gospel and Structural Development Theory." *BTB* 14 (1984): 67-73.

Lierman, John. "The Mosaic Pattern of John's Christology." In *Challenging Perspectives on the Gospel of John*, edited by John Lierman, pp. 210-34. WUNT 2/219. Tübingen: Mohr Siebeck, 2006.

———. *The New Testament Moses: Christian Perceptions of Moses and Israel in the Setting of Jewish Religion.* WUNT 2/173. Tübingen: Mohr Siebeck, 2004.

Lietzmann, Hans. *Die Entstehung der christlichen Liturgie nach den ältesten Quellen.* Darmstadt: Wissenschaftliche Buchgesellschaft, 1963.

Lieu, Judith. *I, II, and III John: A Commentary.* NTL. Louisville: Westminster John Knox, 2008.

———. *The Second and Third Epistles of John: History and Background.* Edited by John Kenneth Riches. SNTW. Edinburgh: T & T Clark, 1986.

———. *The Theology of the Johannine Epistles.* NTT. Cambridge: Cambridge University Press, 1991.

Lightfoot, J. B. *Biblical Essays.* Grand Rapids: Baker Books, 1979.

———. "The Christian Ministry." In *St. Paul's Epistle to the Philippians,* pp. 181-269. 1881. Reprint, Lynn, MA: Hendrickson, 1981.

———. *St. Paul's Epistles to the Colossians and to Philemon.* London: Macmillan, 1879.

Lincoln, Andrew T. "The Beloved Disciple as Eyewitness and the Fourth Gospel as Witness." *JSNT* 85 (2002): 3-26.

———. *Truth on Trial: The Lawsuit Motif in the Fourth Gospel.* Peabody, MA: Hendrickson, 2000.

Lindars, Barnabas. *Behind the Fourth Gospel.* SCC 3. London: SPCK, 1971.

———. "The Fourth Gospel: An Act of Contemplation." In *Studies in the Fourth Gospel,* edited by F. L. Cross, pp. 23-35. London: Mowbray, 1957.

———. *The Gospel of John.* NCB. London: Marshall, Morgan & Scott, 1972.

———. "The Son of Man in the Johannine Christology." In *Christ and the Spirit in the New Testament: In Honour of Charles Francis Digby Moule,* edited by Barnabas Lindars and Stephen Smalley, pp. 43-60. Cambridge: Cambridge University Press, 1973.

Ling, Timothy J. M. *The Judaean Poor and the Fourth Gospel.* SNTSMS 136. Cambridge: Cambridge University Press, 2006.

Lingad, Celestino G. *The Problems of Jewish Christians in the Johannine Community.* TGST 73. Rome: Editrice Pontificia Università Gregoriana, 2001.

Lioy, Dan. *The Book of Revelation in Christological Focus.* SBL 58. New York: Peter Lang, 2003.

———. *The Search for Ultimate Reality: Intertextuality between Genesis and Johannine Prologues.* SBL 93. New York: Peter Lang, 2005.

Llewelyn, Stephen R. "The Use of Sunday for Meetings of Believers in the New Testament." *NovT* 43 (2001): 205-23.

Loader, William R. G. "The Central Structure of Johannine Christology." *NTS* 30 (1984): 188-216.

———. *The Christology of the Fourth Gospel: Structure and Issues.* BBET 23. Frankfurt: Peter Lang, 1989.

———. "Jesus and the Law in John." In *Theology and Christology in the Fourth Gospel:*

*Essays by Members of the SNTS Johannine Writings Seminar,* edited by Gilbert van Belle, Jan G. van der Watt and P. J. Maritz, pp. 135-54. BETL 184. Leuven: Leuven University Press, 2005.

Löfstedt, Torsten. "The Ruler of This World." *SEÅ* 74 (2009): 55-79.

Longenecker, Richard N. *The Christology of Early Jewish Christianity.* SBT 17. Naperville, IL: Allenson, 1970.

Lossky, Vladimir. "The Procession of the Holy Spirit in Orthodox Trinitarian Theology." In *Eastern Orthodox Theology: A Contemporary Reader,* edited by Daniel B. Clendenin, pp. 163-82. Grand Rapids: Baker Books, 1995.

Luther, Martin. *Word and Sacrament I.* Vol. 35 of *Luther's Works.* Edited by Theodore Bachmann. Philadelphia: Fortress, 1960.

Macdonald, Duncan Black. *The Hebrew Philosophical Genius: A Vindication.* Princeton, NJ: Princeton University Press, 1936.

Mach, Michael. "Concepts of Jewish Monotheism during the Hellenistic Period." In *The Jewish Roots of Christological Monotheism: Papers from the St. Andrews Conference on the Historical Origins of the Worship of Jesus,* edited by Carey C. Newman, James R. Davila and Gladys S. Lewis, pp. 21-42. JSJSup 63. Leiden: Brill, 1999.

Mackay, Ian D. *John's Relationship with Mark: An Analysis of John 6 in the Light of Mark 6–8.* WUNT 2/182. Tübingen: Mohr Siebeck, 2004.

MacRae, George. "The Fourth Gospel and *Religionsgeschichte.*" *CBQ* 32 (1970): 13-24.

Maier, Gerhard. *Die Johannesoffenbarung und die Kirche.* WUNT 25. Tübingen: Mohr Siebeck, 1981.

Maier, Harry O. *Apocalypse Recalled: The Book of Revelation after Christendom.* Minneapolis: Fortress, 2002.

Malatesta, Edward. *Interiority and Covenant: A Study of* εἶναι ἐν *and* μένειν ἐν *in the First Letter of Saint John.* AnBib 69. Rome: Biblical Institute Press, 1978.

Maldamé, Jean-Michel. "Quand Jésus guérit: Une lecture théologique de la guérison de l'aveugle-né (Jn 9)." *EV* 112 (2002): 9-15.

Malevez, Léopold. "Nouveau Testament et Théologie fonctionnelle." *RSR* 48 (1960): 258-90.

Manning, Gary T. *Echoes of a Prophet: The Use of Ezekiel in the Gospel of John and in Literature of the Second Temple Period.* JSNTSup 270. London: T & T Clark, 2004.

Manson, T. W. "The Johannine Jesus as Logos." In *A Companion to John: Readings in Johannine Theology (John's Gospel and Epistles),* edited by Michael J. Taylor, pp. 33-58. New York: Alba House, 1970.

Marcato, Giorgio. "Ricerche sulla 'Scuola Giovannea.'" *Ang* 75 (1998): 305-31.

Marchadour, Alain. *Les personnages dans l'evangile de Jean: Miroir pour une christologie narrative.* LB 139. Paris: Cerf, 2004.

Mardaga, Hellen. "The Repetitive Use of ὑψόω in the Fourth Gospel." *CBQ* 74 (2012): 101-17.

Marino, Marcello. *Custodire la Parola: Il verbo* τηρεῖν *nell'Apocalisse alla luce della tradizione giovannea*. SRB 40. Bologna: Dehoniane, 2003.

Marmorstein, Arthur. *The Doctrine of Merits in Old Rabbinic Literature*. New York: Ktav, 1968 [1920].

Marrow, Stanley B. "Κόσμος In John." *CBQ* 64 (2002): 90-102.

Marshall, I. Howard. *The Epistles of John*. NICNT. Grand Rapids: Eerdmans, 1978.

———. *New Testament Theology: Many Witnesses, One Gospel*. Downers Grove, IL: Inter-Varsity Press, 2004.

Martin, Ralph P. *Worship in the Early Church*. Rev. ed. Grand Rapids: Eerdmans, 1974.

Martyn, J. Louis. *History and Theology in the Fourth Gospel*. 2nd ed. Nashville: Abingdon, 1979.

Marulli, Luca. "A Letter of Recommendation? A Closer Look at Third John's 'Rhetorical Argumentation.'" *Bib* 90 (2009): 203-23.

Mathewson, David. "Assessing Old Testament Allusions in the Book of Revelation." *EvQ* 75 (2003): 311-25.

———. "The Destiny of the Nations in Revelation 21:1–22:5: A Reconsideration." *TynBul* 53 (2002): 121-42.

———. "A Note on the Foundation Stones in Revelation 21.14, 19-20." *JSNT* 25 (2003): 487-98.

Matson, Mark A. *In Dialogue with Another Gospel? The Influence of the Fourth Gospel on the Passion Narrative of the Gospel of Luke*. SBLDS 178. Atlanta: Society of Biblical Literature, 2001.

Maxwell, William D. *An Outline of Christian Worship: Its Developments and Forms*. London: Oxford University Press, 1945.

May, Gerhard. *Creatio ex Nihilo: The Doctrine of "Creation Out of Nothing" in Early Christian Thought*. Translated by A. S. Worrall. Edinburgh: T & T Clark, 1994.

Mayo, Philip L. *"Those Who Call Themselves Jews": The Church and Judaism in the Apocalypse of John*. PTMS 60. Eugene, OR: Pickwick, 2006.

McCarthy, Dennis J. *Old Testament Covenant: A Survey of Current Opinions*. Richmond: John Knox, 1972.

McGrath, James F. *John's Apologetic Christology: Legitimation and Development in Johannine Christology*. SNTSMS 111. Cambridge: Cambridge University Press, 2001.

McIlhone, James P. "Jesus as God's Agent in the Fourth Gospel: Implications for Christology, Ecclesiology, and Mission." *CS* 44 (2005): 295-315.

McRay, John. *Archaeology and the New Testament*. Grand Rapids: Baker Books, 1991.

McWhirter, Jocelyn. *The Bridegroom Messiah and the People of God: Marriage in the Fourth Gospel*. SNTSMS 138. Cambridge: Cambridge University Press, 2006.

Mealy, J. Webb. *After the Thousand Years: Resurrection and Judgment in Revelation 20*. JSNTSup. Sheffield: JSOT Press, 1992.

Meeks, Wayne A. "The Divine Agent and His Counterfeit in Philo and the Fourth

Gospel." In *Aspects of Religious Propaganda in Judaism and Early Christianity*, edited by Elisabeth Schüssler Fiorenza, pp. 43-67. Notre Dame: University of Notre Dame Press, 1976.

———. "Equal to God." In *The Conversation Continues: Studies in Paul and John*, edited by Robert T. Fortna and Beverly R. Gaventa, pp. 309-21. Nashville: Abingdon, 1990.

———. "The Man from Heaven in Johannine Sectarianism." *JBL* 91 (1972): 44-72.

———. *The Prophet-King: Moses Traditions and the Johannine Christology*. NovTSup 14. Leiden: Brill, 1967.

Menken, M. J. J. "'Born of God' or 'Begotten by God'? A Translation Problem in the Johannine Writings." *NovT* 51 (2009): 352-68.

———. "Envoys of God's Envoy: On the Johannine Communities." *PIBA* 23 (2000): 45-60.

———. "Observations on the Significance of the Old Testament in the Fourth Gospel." *Neot* 33 (1999): 125-43.

Menoud, P.-H. "L'originalité de la pensée joh." *RTP* 28 (1940): 233-61.

Metzger, Bruce M. *A Textual Commentary on the Greek New Testament*. 2nd ed. Stuttgart: Deutsche Bibelgesellschaft; United Bible Societies, 1994.

Metzner, Rainer. *Das Verständnis der Sünde im Johannesevangelium*. WUNT 122. Tübingen: Mohr Siebeck, 2000.

———. "Vollmacht im Johannesevangelium." *NovT* 45 (2003): 22-44.

Meyer, Annegret. *Kommt und seht: Mystagogie im Johannesevangelium ausgehend von Joh 1,35-51*. FB 103. Würzburg: Echter, 2005.

Meyer, Paul W. "'The Father': The Presentation of God in the Fourth Gospel." In *Exploring the Gospel of John: In Honor of D. Moody Smith*, edited by R. Alan Culpepper and C. Clifton Black, pp. 255-73. Louisville: Westminster John Knox, 1996.

Michaels, J. Ramsey. "Reflections on the Three Epistles of John." In *A Companion to John: Readings in Johannine Theology (John's Gospel and Epistles)*, edited by Michael J. Taylor, pp. 257-71. New York: Alba House, 1970.

Mihalios, Stefanos. *The Danielic Eschatological Hour in the Johannine Literature*. LNTS 436. London: T & T Clark, 2011.

Miller, E. L. "'In the Beginning': A Christological Transparency." *NTS* 45 (1999): 587-92.

———. *Salvation-History in the Prologue of John: The Significance of John 1:3-4*. NovTSup 60. Leiden: Brill, 1989.

Minear, Paul S. "Logos Ecclesiology in John's Gospel." In *Christological Perspectives: Essays in Honor of Harvey K. McArthur*, edited by Robert F. Berkey and Sarah A. Edwards, pp. 95-111. New York: Pilgrim, 1982.

Miranda, Juan P. *Der Vater, der mich gesandt hat: Religionsgeschichtliche Untersuchungen zu den johanneischen Sendungsformeln, zugleich ein Beitrag zur johanneischen Christologie und Ekklesiologie*. EH 23/7. Bern: Peter Lang, 1972.

———. *Die Sendung Jesu im vierten Evangelium: Religions- und theologiegeschichtliche Untersuchungen zu den Sendungsformeln*. SBS 87. Stuttgart: Katholisches Bibelwerk, 1977.

Mitchell, Margaret M. "'Diotrephes Does Not Receive Us': The Lexicographical and Social Context of 3 John 9-10." *JBL* 117 (1998): 299-320.

Miura, Nozomi. "A Typology of Personified Wisdom Hymns." *BTB* 34 (2004): 138-49.

Moloney, Francis J. "The Gospel of John as Scripture." *CBQ* 67 (2005): 454-68.

——. *The Johannine Son of Man.* 2nd ed. BSR 14. Rome: Libreria Ateneo Salesiano, 1978.

Moltmann, Jürgen. "Theological Proposals towards the Resolution of the *Filioque* Controversy." In *Spirit of God, Spirit of Christ: Ecumenical Reflections on the Filioque Controversy,* edited by Lukas Vischer, pp. 164-73. FOP 103. London: SPCK; Geneva: World Council of Churches, 1981.

Moo, Jonathan. "Continuity, Discontinuity, and Hope: The Contribution of New Testament Eschatology to a Distinctively Christian Environmental Ethos." *TynBul* 61 (2010): 21-44.

Moody, Dale. "God's Only Son: The Translation of John 3:16 in the Revised Standard Version." *JBL* 72 (1953): 213-19.

Moore, George Foot. "Intermediaries in Jewish Theology: Memra, Shekinah, Metatron." *HTR* 15 (1922): 41-85.

——. *Judaism in the First Centuries of the Christian Era: The Age of the Tannaim.* 3 vols. Cambridge, MA: Harvard University Press, 1927–1930.

Moore, Hamilton, and Philip McCormick. "Domitian." *IBS* 25 (2003): 74-101.

Morgen, Michèle. "Le (Fils) monogène dans les écrits johanniques: Évolution des traditions et élaboration rédactionnelle." *NTS* 53 (2007): 165-83.

Morris, Leon. *The Apostolic Preaching of the Cross.* 3rd ed. Grand Rapids: Eerdmans, 1965.

——. *The Biblical Doctrine of Judgment.* London: Tyndale, 1960.

——. *The Gospel According to John.* NICNT. Grand Rapids: Eerdmans, 1971.

——. *Jesus Is the Christ: Studies in the Theology of John.* Grand Rapids: Eerdmans, 1989.

——. *The Revelation of St. John.* TNTC. Grand Rapids: Eerdmans, 1969.

——. *Studies in the Fourth Gospel.* Grand Rapids: Eerdmans, 1969.

Morton, Russell. "Glory to God and to the Lamb: John's Use of Jewish and Hellenistic/Roman Themes in Formatting His Theology in Revelation 4–5." *JSNT* 83 (2001): 89-109.

——. *One upon the Throne and the Lamb: A Tradition Historical/Theological Analysis of Revelation 4–5.* SBL 110. New York: Peter Lang, 2007.

——. "Revelation 7:9-17: The Innumerable Crowd before the One upon the Throne and the Lamb." *ATJ* 32 (2000): 1-11.

Mosser, Carl. "The Earliest Patristic Interpretation of Psalm 82, Jewish Antecedents, and the Origin of Christian Deification." *JTS* 56 (2005): 30-74.

Motyer, Stephen. *Your Father the Devil? A New Approach to John and "the Jews."* PBTM. Carlisle: Paternoster, 1997.

Moule, C. F. D. "The Individualism of the Fourth Gospel." *NovT* 5 (1962): 171-90.

——. "A Neglected Factor in the Interpretation of Johannine Eschatology." In *Studies in John: Presented to Professor J. N. Sevenster on the Occasion of His Seventieth Birthday*, pp. 155-60. NovTSup 24. Leiden: Brill, 1970.

Mounce, Robert H. *The Book of Revelation*. NICNT. Grand Rapids: Eerdmans, 1998.

Mowry, Lucetta. "Revelation 4–5 and Early Christian Liturgical Usage." *JBL* 71 (1952): 75-84.

Moyise, Steven. "Does the Author of Revelation Misappropriate the Scriptures?" *AUSS* 40 (2002): 3-21.

———. "Intertextuality and the Use of Scripture in the Book of Revelation." *Scriptura* 84 (2003): 391-401.

———. *The Old Testament in the Book of Revelation*. JSNTSup 115. Sheffield: Sheffield Academic Press, 1995.

———. "The Old Testament in the New: A Reply to Greg Beale." *IBS* 21 (1999): 54-58.

———. "Singing the Song of Moses and the Lamb: John's Dialogical Use of Scripture." *AUSS* 42 (2004): 347-60.

Mühlen, Heribert. "'Wir als wir selbst sind mit euch': Grundverheissung des Neuen Bundes." *TGl* 95 (2005): 48-79.

Müller, Christoph G. "Der Zeuge und das Licht: Joh 1,1–4,3 und das Darstellungsprinzip der σύγκρισις." *Bib* 84 (2003): 479-509.

Müller, J.-J. "Les citations de l'Écriture dans le quatrième Évangile." *FoiVie* 100 (2001): 41-57.

Müller, Mogens. *The Expression "Son of Man" and the Development of Christology: A History of Interpretation*. CIS. London: Equinox, 2008.

Müller, Ulrich B. "Die Heimat des Johannesevangeliums." *ZNW* 97 (2006): 44-63.

Mulzac, Kenneth. "The 'Fall of Babylon' Motif in the Books of Jeremiah and Revelation." *JATS* 8 (1997): 137-49.

Murphy-O'Connor, Jerome. "The Descent from the Cross and the Burial of Jesus (Jn 19:31-42)." *RB* 118 (2011): 522-57.

———. *St. Paul's Corinth: Texts and Archaeology*. GNS 6. Wilmington, DE: Michael Glazier, 1983.

Mussies, Gerard. *The Morphology of Koine Greek as Used in the Apocalypse of St. John: A Study in Bilingualism*. NovTSup 27. Leiden: Brill, 1971.

Mussner, Franz. *Die johanneische Sehweise und die Frage nach dem historischen Jesus*. QD 28. Freiburg: Herder, 1965.

———. *The Historical Jesus in the Gospel of St. John*. Translated by W. J. O'Hara. QD 19. New York: Herder & Herder, 1967.

Naselli, Andrew David, and Philip R. Gons. "Prooftexting the Personality of the Holy Spirit: An Analysis of the Masculine Demonstrative Pronouns in John 14:26, 15:26, and 16:13-14." *DBSJ* 16 (2011): 65-89.

Naylor, Michael. "The Roman Imperial Cult and Revelation." *CurBR* 8 (2010): 207-39.

Need, Stephen W. "Jesus the Bread of God: The Eucharist as Metaphor in John 6." *Theology* 105 (2002): 194-200.

Neirynck, Frans. *Jean et les Synoptiques: Examen critique de l'exégèse de M.-É. Boismard.* BETL 49. Leuven: Leuven University Press, 1979.

Neubrand, Maria. "Das Johannesevangelium und 'die Juden': Antijudaismus im vierten Evangelium." *TGl* 99 (2009): 205-17.

Neusner, Jacob. *Judaism: The Evidence of the Mishnah.* Chicago: University of Chicago Press, 1981.

Newman, Carey C., James R. Davila, and Gladys S. Lewis, eds. *The Jewish Roots of Christological Monotheism: Papers from the St. Andrews Conference on the Historical Origins of the Worship of Jesus.* JSJSup 63. Leiden: Brill, 1999.

Newman, J. Kevin. "Certain Old Testament Parallels in St John's Gospel." *DRev* 121 (2003): 211-24.

Neyrey, Jerome H., and Richard L. Rohrbaugh. "'He Must Increase, I Must Decrease' (John 3:30): A Cultural and Social Interpretation." *CBQ* 63 (2001): 464-83.

Nichols, Stephen J. "Prophecy Makes Strange Bedfellows: On the History of Identifying the Antichrist." *JETS* 44 (2001): 75-85.

Nicholson, Godfrey C. *Death as Departure: The Johannine Descent-Ascent Schema.* SBLDS 63. Chico, CA: Scholars Press, 1983.

Nicklas, Tobias. "Der Ewige spricht in die Zeit—Gotteswort und Menschenwort in der Offenbarung des Johannes." *SS* 9 (2011): 113-22.

———. "Die johanneische 'Tempelreinigung' (John 2,12-22) für Leser der Synoptiker." *TP* 80 (2005): 1-16.

———. "Die Prophetie des Kajaphas: Im Netz johanneischer Ironie." *NTS* 46 (2000): 589-94.

———. "'Gott ist die Liebe' (1 Joh 4,8b)—1 Joh als Knotenpunkt biblischer Theologie." *BL* 79 (2006): 245-48.

Nicol, William. *The Sēmeia in the Fourth Gospel: Tradition and Redaction.* NovTSup 32. Leiden: Brill, 1972.

Nicoll, W. Robertson, ed. *The Expositor's Greek Testament.* 5 vols. London: Hodder & Stoughton, 1897–1910.

Niebuhr, H. Richard. *Christ and Culture.* New York: Harper, 1951.

Nielsen, Helge Kjær. "John's Understanding of the Death of Jesus." In *New Readings in John: Literary and Theological Perspectives; Essays from the Scandinavian Conference on the Fourth Gospel in Aarhus 1997*, edited by Johannes Nissen and Siegfried Pedersen, pp. 232-54. Sheffield: Sheffield Academic Press, 1999.

Nielsen, Jesper Tang. "The Narrative Structures of Glory and Glorification in the Fourth Gospel." *NTS* 56 (2010): 343-66.

———. "Resurrection, Recognition, Reassuring: The Function of Jesus' Resurrection in the Fourth Gospel." In *The Resurrection of Jesus in the Gospel of John*, edited by Craig R. Koester and Reimund Bieringer, pp. 177-208. WUNT 222. Tübingen: Mohr Siebeck, 2008.

Nielsen, Kirsten. "Old Testament Imagery in John." In *New Readings in John: Literary and Theological Perspectives; Essays from the Scandinavian Conference on the Fourth Gospel in Aarhus 1997*, edited by Johannes Nissen and Siegfried Pedersen, pp. 66-82. Sheffield: Sheffield Academic Press, 1999.

Nissen, Johannes. "Community and Ethics in the Gospel of John." In *New Readings in John: Literary and Theological Perspectives; Essays from the Scandinavian Conference on the Fourth Gospel in Aarhus 1997*, edited by Johannes Nissen and Siegfried Pedersen, pp. 194-212. Sheffield: Sheffield Academic Press, 1999.

———. "Mission in the Fourth Gospel: Historical and Hermeneutical Perspectives." In *New Readings in John: Literary and Theological Perspectives; Essays from the Scandinavian Conference on the Fourth Gospel in Aarhus 1997*, edited by Johannes Nissen and Siegfried Pedersen, pp. 213-31. Sheffield: Sheffield Academic Press, 1999.

Noack, Bent. *Zur johanneischen Tradition: Beiträge zur Kritik an der literarkritischen Analyse des vierten Evangeliums*. LSSTS 3. Copenhagen: Rosenkilde & Bagger, 1954.

Nunn, H. P. V. *The Authorship of the Fourth Gospel*. Eton: Alden & Blackwell, 1952.

Obermann, Andreas. *Die christologische Erfüllung der Schrift im Johannesevangelium: Eine Untersuchung zur johanneischen Hermeneutik anhand der Schriftzitate*. WUNT 2/83. Tübingen: Mohr Siebeck, 1996.

O'Brien, Kelli S. "Written That You May Believe: John 20 and Narrative Rhetoric." *CBQ* 67 (2005): 284-302.

O'Day, Gail R. "Jesus as Friend in the Gospel of John." *Int* 58 (2004): 144-57.

O'Donnell, John J. *The Mystery of the Triune God*. New York: Paulist Press, 1989.

O'Grady, John F. "The Good Shepherd and the Vine and the Branches." *BTB* 8 (1977): 86-89.

———. *Individual and Community in John*. Rome: Pontifical Biblical Institute, 1978.

Okorie, Adam M. "The Self-Revelation of Jesus in the 'I Am' Sayings of John's Gospel." *CurTM* 28 (2001): 486-90.

Olsson, Birger. "*Deus Semper Maior*? On God in the Johannine Writings." In *New Readings in John: Literary and Theological Perspectives; Essays from the Scandinavian Conference on the Fourth Gospel in Aarhus 1997*, edited by Johannes Nissen and Siegfried Pedersen, pp. 143-71. Sheffield: Sheffield Academic Press, 1999.

O'Neill, J. C. "How Early Is the Doctrine of *Creatio ex Nihilo*?" *JTS* 53 (2002): 449-65.

———. *The Puzzle of 1 John: A New Examination of Origins*. London: SPCK, 1966.

Onuki, Takashi. *Gemeinde und Welt im Johannesevangelium: Ein Beitrag zur Frage nach der theologischen und pragmatischen Funktion des johanneischen "Dualismus."* WMANT 56. Neukirchen-Vluyn: Neukirchener Verlag, 1984.

O'Rourke, John J. "Hymns of the Apocalypse." *CBQ* 30 (1968): 399-409.

Orphanos, Markos A. "The Procession of the Holy Spirit According to Certain Later Greek Fathers." In *Spirit of God, Spirit of Christ: Ecumenical Reflections on the Filioque Controversy*, edited by Lukas Vischer, pp. 21-45. FOP 103. London: SPCK; Geneva: World Council of Churches, 1981.

Østenstad, Gunnar H. *Patterns of Redemption in the Fourth Gospel: An Experiment in Structural Analysis.* SBEC 38. Lewiston, NY: Mellen, 1998.

Paddison, Angus. "Engaging Scripture: Incarnation and the Gospel of John." *SJT* 60 (2007): 144-60.

Pagels, Elaine H. *The Johannine Gospel in Gnostic Exegesis: Heracleon's Commentary on John.* SBLMS 17. Nashville: Abingdon, 1973.

Painter, John. "Earth Made Whole: John's Rereading of Genesis." In *Word, Theology, and Community in John,* edited by John Painter, R. Alan Culpepper and Fernando F. Segovia, pp. 65-84. St. Louis: Chalice, 2002.

———. *1, 2, and 3 John.* SP 18. Collegeville, MN: Liturgical Press, 2002.

———. *John: Witness and Theologian.* London: SPCK, 1975.

———. "Memory Holds the Key: The Transformation of Memory in the Interface of History and Theology of John." In *Critical Appraisals of Critical Views,* edited by Paul N. Anderson, Felix Just and Tom Thatcher, pp. 229-45. Vol. 1 of *John, Jesus, and History.* SBLSymS 44. Atlanta: Society of Biblical Literature, 2007.

———. "Monotheism and Dualism: John and Qumran." In *Theology and Christology in the Fourth Gospel: Essays by Members of the SNTS Johannine Writings Seminar,* edited by Gilbert van Belle, Jan G. van der Watt and P. J. Maritz, pp. 225-43. BETL 184. Leuven: Leuven University Press, 2005.

———. *The Quest for the Messiah: The History, Literature and Theology of the Johannine Community.* Edinburgh: T & T Clark, 1991.

Pancaro, Severino. *The Law in the Fourth Gospel: The Torah and the Gospel, Moses and Jesus, Judaism and Christianity According to John.* NovTSup 42. Leiden: Brill, 1975.

———. "The Relationship of the Church to Israel in the Gospel of St. John." *NTS* 21 (1975): 396-405.

Park, Soon-Ja. "Jésus en Samarie: Jean 4,27-42." *SB* 97 (2000): 22-36.

———. "L'Entretien avec la Samaritaine: Jn 4,1-26." *SB* 96 (1999): 26-55.

Paroschi, Wilson. *Incarnation and Covenant in the Prologue to the Fourth Gospel (John 1:1-18).* EH 23/820. Frankfurt: Peter Lang, 2006.

Parris, David Paul. *Reception Theory and Biblical Hermeneutics.* Eugene, OR: Pickwick, 2009.

Parsenios, George L. *Departure and Consolation: The Johannine Farewell Discourses in Light of Greco-Roman Literature.* NovTSup 117. Leiden: Brill, 2005.

———. *Rhetoric and Drama in the Johannine Lawsuit Motif.* WUNT 258. Tübingen: Mohr Siebeck, 2010.

Pastorelli, David. *Le Paraclet dans le corpus johannique.* BZNW 142. Berlin: de Gruyter, 2006.

Patfoort, Albert. "Emplois bibliques et patristiques du verbe ἐκπορεύομαι: Une enquête." *RThom* 102 (2002): 63-72.

Pattemore, Stephen. *The People of God in the Apocalypse: Discourse, Structure and Exegesis.* SNTSMS 128. Cambridge: Cambridge University Press, 2004.

Pazdan, Mary Margaret. "Discipleship as the Appropriation of Eschatological Salvation in the Fourth Gospel." Ph.D. diss., University of Toronto, 1982.

Peels, H. G. L. *The Vengeance of God: The Meaning of the Root NQM and the Function of the NQM-Texts in the Context of Divine Revelation in the Old Testament.* OtSt 31. Leiden: Brill, 1995.

Pendrick, Gerard. "Μονογενής." *NTS* 41 (1995): 587-600.

Perry, Peter S. "Critiquing the Excess of Empire: A *Synkrisis* of John of Patmos and Dio of Prusa." *JSNT* 29 (2007): 473-96.

Peters, Olutola K. *The Mandate of the Church in the Apocalypse of John.* SBL 77. New York: Peter Lang, 2005.

Petersen, Silke. *Brot, Licht und Weinstock: Intertextuelle Analysen johanneischer Ich-bin-Worte.* NovTSup 127. Leiden: Brill, 2008.

Pfeifer, Gerhard. *Ursprung und Wesen der Hypostasenvorstellungen im Judentum.* AzTh 31. Stuttgart: Calwer, 1967.

Phelan, John E. "Revelation, Empire, and the Violence of God." *ExAud* 20 (2004): 65-84.

Phillips, Peter M. *The Prologue of the Fourth Gospel: A Sequential Reading.* LNTS 294. London: T & T Clark, 2006.

Pierce, Ronald W. "Covenant Conditionality and a Future for Israel." *JETS* 37 (1994): 27-38.

Piper, Otto A. "The Apocalypse of John and the Liturgy of the Ancient Church." *CH* 20 (1951): 10-22.

Pisano, Ombretta. *La radice e la stirpe di David: Salmi davidici nel libro dell'Apocalisse.* TGST 85. Rome: Editrice Pontificia Università Gregoriana, 2002.

Poirier, John C. "Hanukkah in the Narrative Chronology of the Fourth Gospel." *NTS* 54 (2008): 465-78.

Pollard, T. E. *Johannine Christology and the Early Church.* SNTSMS 13. London: Cambridge University Press, 1970.

Popkes, Enno Edzard. *Die Theologie der Liebe Gottes in den johanneischen Schriften: Zur Semantik der Liebe und zum Motivkreis des Dualismus.* WUNT 2/197. Tübingen: Mohr Siebeck, 2005.

Porsch, Felix. "'Ihr habt den Teufel zum Vater' (Joh 8,44): Antijudaismus im Johannesevangelium?" *BK* 44 (1989): 50-57.

———. *Pneuma und Wort: Ein exegetischer Beitrag zur Pneumatologie des Johannesevangeliums.* FrTS 16. Frankfurt am Main: J. Knecht, 1974.

Porter, Stanley E. "Can Traditional Exegesis Enlighten Literary Analysis of the Fourth Gospel? An Examination of the Old Testament Fulfilment Motif and the Passover Theme." In *The Gospels and the Scriptures of Israel,* edited by Craig A. Evans and W. Richard Stegner, pp. 396-428. JSNTSup 104. Sheffield: Sheffield Academic Press, 1994.

———. "The Language of the Apocalypse in Recent Discussion." *NTS* 35 (1989): 582-603.

Potgieter, S. T. "'n Johannese Ekklesiologie?" *VerbEccl* 23 (2002): 502-15.

Poythress, Vern S. "Johannine Authorship and the Use of Intersentence Conjunctions in the Book of Revelation." *WTJ* 47 (1985): 329-36.

Preisker, Herbert. *Die urchristliche Botschaft von der Liebe Gottes im Lichte der vergleichenden Religionsgeschichte.* AWRBR 5. Giessen: Töpelmann, 1930.

Price, S. R. F. *Rituals and Power: The Roman Imperial Cult in Asia Minor.* Cambridge: Cambridge University Press, 1984.

Prigent, Pierre. *Apocalypse et liturgie.* CahT 52. Neuchâtel: Delachaux et Niestlé, 1964.

Pryor, John W. *John, Evangelist of the Covenant People: The Narrative and Themes of the Fourth Gospel.* Downers Grove, IL: InterVarsity Press, 1992.

Pugliese, Marc A. "How Important is the *Filioque* for Reformed Orthodoxy?" *WJT* 66 (2004): 159-77.

Purvis, James D. "The Fourth Gospel and the Samaritans." *NovT* 17 (1975): 161-98.

Puthussery, Johnson. *Days of Man and God's Day: An Exegetico-Theological Study of ἡμέρα in the Book of Revelation.* TGST 82. Rome: Editrice Pontificia Università Gregoriana, 2002.

Rainbow, Paul A. "Monotheism and Christology in I Corinthians 8.4-6." D.Phil. thesis. University of Oxford, 1987.

———. *The Pith of the Apocalypse: Essential Message and Principles for Interpretation.* Eugene, OR: Wipf & Stock, 2008.

———. *The Way of Salvation: The Role of Christian Obedience in Justification.* Milton Keynes: Paternoster, 2005.

Randall, John F. "The Theme of Unity in John 17:20-23." *ETL* 41 (1965): 373-94.

Rappaport, Angelo S. *Myth and Legend of Ancient Israel.* 3 vols. New York: Ktav, 1966.

Rasimus, Tuomas, ed. *The Legacy of John: Second-Century Reception of the Fourth Gospel.* NovTSup 132. Leiden: Brill, 2010.

Rastoin, Marc. "Encore une fois les 153 poissions (Jn 21,11)." *Bib* 90 (2009): 84-92.

Reim, Günter. *Studien zum alttestamentlichen Hintergrund des Johannesevangeliums.* SNTSMS 22. Cambridge: Cambridge University Press, 1974.

Reinhartz, Adele. *Befriending the Beloved Disciple: A Jewish Reading of the Gospel of John.* New York: Continuum, 2001.

———, ed. *God the Father in the Gospel of John.* Semeia 85. Atlanta: Society of Biblical Literature, 1999.

———. "'Jews' and Jews in the Fourth Gospel." In *Anti-Judaism and the Fourth Gospel: Papers of the Leuven Colloquium, 2000,* edited by Reimund Bieringer, Didier Pollefeyt and Frederique Vandecasteele-Vanneuville, pp. 213-27. JCH 1. Assen: Van Gorcum, 2001.

———. "Judaism in the Gospel of John." *Int* 63 (2009): 382-93.

———. *The Word in the World: The Cosmological Tale in the Fourth Gospel.* SBLMS 45. Atlanta: Scholars Press, 1992.

Rendtorff, Rolf. *The Covenant Formula: An Exegetical and Theological Investigation.* Translated by Margaret Kohl. Edinburgh: T & T Clark, 1998.

Renouard, Christine. "Le personnage de Nicodème comme figure de nouvelle naissance." *ETR* 126 (2004): 577-86.

Rensberger, David. *Johannine Faith and Liberating Community*. Philadelphia: Westminster, 1988.

Reymond, Robert L. *John, Beloved Disciple: A Survey of His Theology*. Fearn: Mentor, 2001.

Reynolds, Benjamin E. *The Apocalyptic Son of Man in the Gospel of John*. WUNT 2/249. Tübingen: Mohr Siebeck, 2008.

———. "The Johannine Son of Man and the Historical Jesus: Shall Ever the Twain Meet? John 9.35 as a Test Case." *JSHJ* 9 (2011): 230-42.

———. "The Use of the Son of Man Idiom in the Gospel of John." In *"Who Is This Son of Man?" The Latest Scholarship on a Puzzling Expression of the Historical Jesus*, edited by Larry W. Hurtado and Paul L. Owen, pp. 101-29. LNTS 390. London: T & T Clark International, 2011.

Reynolds, Edwin. "The Feast of Tabernacles and the Book of Revelation." *AUSS* 38 (2000): 245-68.

Rhea, Robert. *The Johannine Son of Man*. ATANT 76. Zürich: Theologischer Verlag, 1990.

Richards, E. Randolph. *Paul and First-Century Letter Writing: Secretaries, Composition and Collection*. Downers Grove, IL: InterVarsity Press, 2004.

Richey, Lance Byron. *Roman Imperial Ideology and the Gospel of John*. CBQMS 43. Washington, DC: Catholic Biblical Association of America, 2007.

Richter, Georg. "Die Fleischwerdung des Logos im Johannesevangelium." In *Studien Zum Johannesevangelium*, edited by Josef Hainz, pp. 149-98. BU 13. Regensburg: Pustet, 1977.

———. "Die Fußwaschung Joh 13,1-20." In *Studien zum Johannesevangelium*, edited by Josef Hainz, pp. 42-57. BU 13. Regensburg: Pustet, 1977.

Riedl, Johannes. *Das Heilswerk Jesu nach Johannes*. FreiTS 93. Freiburg: Herder, 1973.

Riesner, Rainer. "Versuchung und Verklärung (Lukas 4,1-13; 9,28-36; 10,17-20; 22,39-53 und Johannes 12,20-36)." *TBei* 33 (2002): 197-207.

Ringe, Sharon H. *Wisdom's Friends: Community and Christology in the Fourth Gospel*. Louisville: Westminster John Knox, 1999.

Ringgren, Helmer. *Word and Wisdom: Studies in the Hypostatization of Divine Qualities and Functions in the Ancient Near East*. Lund: Ohlsson, 1947.

Rinke, Johannes. *Kerygma und Autopsie: Der christologische Disput als Spiegel johanneischer Gemeindegeschichte*. HBS 12. Freiburg: Herder, 1997.

Robinson, J. A. T. *Honest to God*. Philadelphia: Westminster, 1963.

———. *The Priority of John*. Edited by J. F. Coakley. London: SCM Press, 1985.

———. *Redating the New Testament*. London: SCM Press, 1976.

———. "The Relation of the Prologue to the Gospel of St. John." *NTS* 9 (1963): 120-29.

Robinson, Joseph Armitage. "The Christian Ministry in the Apostolic and Sub-Apostolic Periods." In *Essays on the Early History of the Church and the Ministry by Various Writers*, edited by H. B. Swete, pp. 57-92. London: Macmillan, 1918.

Robinson, Thomas A. *The Bauer Thesis Examined: The Geography of Heresy in the Early Christian Church*. Lewiston, NY: Mellen, 1988.

Rockwell, Stephen. "Assurance as the Interpretative Key to Understanding the Message of 1 John." *RTR* 69 (2010): 17-33.

Rokeah, David. *Jews, Pagans, and Christians in Conflict*. StPB 33. Jerusalem: Magnes Press, Hebrew University; Leiden: Brill, 1982.

Romanowsky, John W. "'When the Son of Man Is Lifted Up': The Redemptive Power of the Crucifixion in the Gospel of John." *Hor* 32 (2005): 100-116.

Romeo, Joseph A. "Gematria and John 21:11—the Children of God." *JBL* 97 (1978): 263-64.

Ronning, John L. *The Jewish Targums and John's Logos Theology*. Peabody, MA: Hendrickson, 2010.

———. "The *Targum of Isaiah* and the Johannine Literature." *WTJ* 69 (2007): 247-78.

Roose, Hanna. "Joh 20,30f.: Ein (un)passender Schluss? John 9 und 11 als primäre Verweisstellen der Schlussnotiz des Johannesevangeliums." *Bib* 84 (2003): 326-43.

Rordorf, Willy. "Die Hausgemeinde der vorkonstantinischen Zeit." In *Kirche: Tendenzen und Ausblicke*, edited by C. W. Williams, pp. 190-96, 235-37. Berlin: Burckhardthaus-Verlag, 1971.

Rotz, Carol J., and Jan A. du Rand. "The One Who Sits on the Throne: Towards a Theory of Theocentric Characterisation According to the Apocalypse of John." *Neot* 33 (1999): 91-111.

Rowe, C. Kavin. "For Future Generations: Worshipping Jesus and the Integration of the Theological Disciplines." *ProEccl* 17 (2008): 186-209.

Rowland, Christopher. "The Vision of the Risen Christ in Rev. 1.13ff.: The Debt of an Early Christology to an Aspect of Jewish Angelology." *JTS* 31 (1980): 1-11.

Rubel, Georg. *Erkenntnis und Bekenntnis: Der Dialog Als Weg der Wissensvermittlung Im Johannesevangelium*. NTAbh 54. Münster: Aschendorff, 2009.

Ruck-Schröder, Adelheid. *Der Name Gottes und der Name Jesu: Eine neutestamentliche Studie*. WMANT 80. Neukirchen-Vluyn: Neukirchener Verlag, 1999.

Ruckstuhl, Eugen. *Die literarische Einheit des Johannesevangeliums: Der gegenwärtige Stand der einschlägigen Forschungen*. NTOA 5. Freiburg: Universitätsverlag; Göttingen: Vandenhoeck & Ruprecht, 1987.

Ruiz, Miguel Rodriguez. *Der Missionsgedanke des Johannesevangeliums*. FB 55. Würzburg: Echter Verlag, 1987.

Rusam, Dietrich. "Das 'Lamm Gottes' (Joh 1,29.36) und die Deutung des Todes Jesu im Johannesevangelium." *BZ* 49 (2005): 60-80.

Ruschmann, Susanne. *Maria von Magdala im Johannesevangelium: Jüngerin—Zeugin—Lebensbotin*. NTAbh 40. Münster: Aschendorff, 2002.

Rust, Eric C. "Time and Eternity in Biblical Thought." *ThTo* 10 (1953): 327-56.

Sadananda, Daniel Rathnakara. *The Johannine Exegesis of God: An Exploration Into the Johannine Understanding of God.* BZNW 121. Berlin: de Gruyter, 2004.

Salier, Willis Hedley. *The Rhetorical Impact of the Sēmeia in the Gospel of John.* WUNT 2/186. Tübingen: Mohr Siebeck, 2004.

Sals, Ulrike. *Die Biographie der "Hure Babylon": Studien Zur Intertextualität der Babylon-Texte in der Bibel.* FAT 2/6. Tübingen: Mohr Siebeck, 2004.

Salzmann, Jorg Christian. "Jüdische Messiasvorstellungen in Justins Dialog mit Trypho und im Johannesevangelium." *ZNW* 100 (2009): 247-68.

Sandnes, Karl Olav. "Whence and Whither: A Narrative Perspective on Birth ἄνωθεν (John 3,3-8)." *Bib* 86 (2005): 153-73.

Sänger, Dieter, ed. *Das Ezechielbuch in der Johannesoffenbarung.* BTS 76. Neukirchen-Vluyn: Neukirchener Verlag, 2004.

Scarano, Angelo. *Storia dell'interpretazione ed esegesi di 1 Gv 3,18-22.* AnBib 157. Rome: Pontificio Istituto Biblico, 2005.

Schapdick, Stefan. "Autorität ohne Inhalt: Zum Mosebild des Johannesevangeliums." *ZNW* 97 (2006): 177-206.

Schelkle, Karl. "John's Theology of Man and the World." In *A Companion to John: Readings in Johannine Theology (John's Gospel and Epistles),* edited by Michael J. Taylor, pp. 127-40. New York: Alba House, 1970.

Schiffmann, Lawrence H. "The Concept of Covenant in the Qumran Scrolls and Rabbinic Literature." In *The Idea of Biblical Interpretation: Essays in Honor of James L. Kugel,* edited by Hindy Najman and Judith H. Newman, pp. 257-78. JSJSup 83. Leiden: Brill, 2004.

Schimanowski, Gottfried. *Die himmlische Liturgie in der Apokalypse des Johannes: Die frühjüdischen Traditionen in Offenbarung 4-5 unter Einschluss der Hekhalotliteratur.* WUNT 2/154. Tübingen: Mohr Siebeck, 2002.

Schlatter, Adolf. "Die Sprache und Heimat des vierten Evangelisten (1902)." In *Johannes und sein Evangelium,* edited by Karl H. Rengstorf, pp. 28-201. WF 82. Darmstadt: Wissenschaftliche Buchgesellschaft, 1973.

Schlund, Christine. *"Kein Knochen soll gebrochen werden": Studien zu Bedeutung und Funktion des Pesachfests in Texten des frühen Judentums und im Johannesevangelium.* WMANT 107. Neukirchen-Vluyn: Neukirchener Verlag, 2005.

Schmid, Hansjörg. *Gegner im 1. Johannesbrief? Zu Konstruktion und Selbstreferenz im johanneischen Sinnsystem.* BWANT 159. Stuttgart: Kohlhammer, 2002.

———. "How to Read the First Epistle of John Non-Polemically." *Bib* 85 (2004): 24-41.

Schmidt, Daryl D. "Semitisms and Septuagintalisms in the Book of Revelation." *NTS* 37 (1991): 592-603.

Schnabel, Eckhard J. "John and the Future of the Nations." *BBR* 12 (2002): 243-71.

Schnackenburg, Rudolf. "Christian Morality According to John." In *A Companion to*

*John: Readings in Johannine Theology (John's Gospel and Epistles)*, edited by Michael J. Taylor, pp. 187-203. New York: Alba House, 1970.

———. "Der Menschensohn im Johannesevangelium." *NTS* 11 (1965): 123-37.

———. *The Gospel According to St. John*. Translated by Kevin Smyth et al. 3 vols. New York: Herder & Herder; Seabury; Crossroad, 1968–1982.

———. "Is There a Johannine Ecclesiology?" In *A Companion to John: Readings in Johannine Theology (John's Gospel and Epistles)*, edited by Michael J. Taylor, pp. 247-56. New York: Alba House, 1970.

———. *The Johannine Epistles: Introduction and Commentary*. Translated by Reginald Fuller and Ilse Fuller. New York: Crossroad, 1992.

Schneiders, Sandra M. *Written That You May Believe: Encountering Jesus in the Fourth Gospel*. New York: Crossroad, 1999.

Schnelle, Udo. *Antidocetic Christology in the Gospel of John: An Investigation of the Place of the Fourth Gospel in the Johannine School*. Translated by Linda M. Maloney. Minneapolis: Fortress, 1992.

———. "Cross and Resurrection in the Gospel of John." In *The Resurrection of Jesus in the Gospel of John*, edited by Craig R. Koester and Reimund Bieringer, pp. 127-51. WUNT 222. Tübingen: Mohr Siebeck, 2008.

———. *Das Evangelium nach Johannes*. THKNT. Leipzig: Evangelische Verlagsanstalt, 1998.

———. "Recent Views of John's Gospel." *WW* 21 (2001): 486-90.

———. "Trinitarisches Denken im Johannesevangelium." In *Israel und seine Heilstraditionen im Johannesevangelium: Festgabe für Johannes Beutler SJ zum 70. Geburtstag*, edited by Michael Labahn, Klaus Scholtissek, and Angelika Strotmann, pp. 367-86. Paderborn: Schöningh, 2004.

Scholtissek, Klaus. "Das hohepriesterliche Gebet Jesu: Exegetisch-theologische Beobachtungen." *TTZ* 109 (2000): 199-218.

———. "Die Brotrede Jesu in Joh 6,1-71: Exegetische Beobachtungen zu ihrem johanneischen Profil." *ZKT* 123 (2001): 35-55.

———. "Eine Renaissance des Evangeliums nach Johannes: Aktuelle Perspektiven der exegetischen Forschung." *TRev* 97 (2001): 267-88.

———. *In ihm sein und bleiben: Die Sprache der Immanenz in den johanneischen Schriften*. HBS 21. Freiburg: Herder, 2000.

———. "Johannes auslegen I: Forschungsgeschichtliche und methodische Reflexionen." *SNTSU* 24 (1999): 35-84.

———. "Johannes auslegen II: Methodische, hermeneutische und einleitungswissenschaftliche Reflexionen." *SNTSU* 25 (2000): 98-140.

———. "The Johannine Gospel in Recent Research." In *The Face of New Testament Studies: A Survey of Recent Research*, edited by Scot McKnight and Grant Osborne, pp. 444-72. Grand Rapids: Eerdmans, 2004.

———. "Relecture und Réécriture: Neue Paradigmen zu Methode und Inhalt der Johannesauslegung aufgewiesen am Prolog 1,1-18 und der ersten Abschiedsrede 13,31–14,31." *TP* 75 (2000): 1-29.

———. "Relecture—Zu einem neu entdeckten Programmwort der Schriftauslegung." *BL* 70 (1997): 309-15.

Schreiber, Stefan. "Kannte Johannes die Synoptiker? Zur aktuellen Diskussion." *VF* 51 (2006): 7-24.

Schröder, Jörn-Michael. *Das eschatologische Israel im Johannesevangelium: Eine Untersuchung der johanneischen Israel-Konzeption in Joh 2–4 und Joh 6.* NET 3. Tübingen: Francke, 2003.

Schuchard, Bruce G. *Scripture Within Scripture: The Interrelationship of Form and Function in the Explicit Old Testament Citations in the Gospel of John.* SBLDS 133. Atlanta: Scholars Press, 1992.

Schulz, Siegfried. *Untersuchungen zur Menschensohn-Christologie im Johannesevangelium: Zugleich ein Beitrag zur Methodengeschichte der Auslegung des 4. Evangeliums.* Göttingen: Vandenhoeck & Ruprecht, 1957.

Schürer, Emil. *The History of the Jewish People in the Age of Jesus Christ (175 B.C.-A.D. 135).* Revised and edited by Geza Vermes, Fergus Millar and Martin Goodman. 3 vols. in 4. Edinburgh: T & T Clark, 1973–1987.

Schwankl, Otto. *Licht und Finsternis: Ein metaphorisches Paradigma in den johanneischen Schriften.* HBS 5. Freiburg: Herder, 1995.

Schwartz, Eduard. "Aporien im vierten Evangelium." *NKGWG,* part 1 (1907): 342-72; part 2 (1908): 115-48; part 3 (1908): 149-88; part 4 (1908): 497-650.

Schwarz, Günther. "Gen 1:1; 2:2a und Joh 1:1a.3a—ein Versuch." *ZNW* 73 (1982): 136-37.

Schweitzer, Albert. *Von Reimarus zu Wrede: Eine Geschichte der Leben-Jesu-Forschung.* Tübingen: Mohr Siebeck, 1906.

Schweizer, Eduard. *Church Order in the New Testament.* Translated by Frank Clarke. London: SCM Press, 1961.

———. "The Concept of the Church in the Gospel and Epistles of St. John." In *New Testament Essays: Studies in Memory of Thomas Walter Manson, 1893–1958,* edited by A. J. B. Higgins, pp. 230-45. Manchester: Manchester University Press, 1959.

———. *EGO EIMI: Die religionsgeschichtliche Herkunft und theologische Bedeutung der johanneischen Bildreden, zugleich ein Beitrag zur Quellenfrage des vierten Evangeliums.* 2nd ed. FRLANT 38. Göttingen: Vandenhoeck & Ruprecht, 1965.

Schwindt, Rainer. *Geschichte der Herrlichkeit: Eine exegetisch-traditionsgeschichtliche Studie zur paulinischen und johanneischen Christologie.* HBS 50. Freiburg: Herder, 2007.

———. "'Seht das Lamm Gottes, das hinwegnimmt die Sünde der Welt' (Joh 1,29): Zur Frage einer Sühnetheologie im Johannesevangelium." *TTZ* 119 (2010): 193-216.

Scott, Martin. *Sophia and the Johannine Jesus.* JSNTSup 71. Sheffield: JSOT Press, 1992.

Scroggs, Robin. "The Earliest Christian Communities as Sectarian Movement." In *Early Christianity*, edited by Jacob Neusner, pp. 1-23. Vol. 2 of *Christianity, Judaism and Other Greco-Roman Cults: Studies for Morton Smith at Sixty*. SJLA 12. Leiden: Brill, 1975.

Seal, David. "Shouting in the Apocalypse: The Influence of First-Century Acclamations on the Praise Utterances in Revelation 4:8 and 11." *JETS* 51 (2008): 339-52.

Sebastian, Michael R. "Le titre de Rabbi dans la Christologie de l'Évangile de Jean." *BLE* 110 (2009): 363-74.

Seebass, Horst, and Anthony C. Thiselton. "Flesh." *NIDNTT* 1:671-82.

Segal, Alan F. *Two Powers in Heaven: Early Rabbinic Reports About Christianity and Gnosticism*. SJLA 25. Leiden: Brill, 1977.

Segalla, Giuseppe. "Un epilogo necessario (*Gv* 21)." *Teol* 31 (2006): 514-33.

Segovia, Fernando F. "John 1:1-18 as Entrée into Johannine Reality." In *Word, Theology, and Community in John*, edited by John Painter, R. Alan Culpepper and Fernando F. Segovia, pp. 33-64. St. Louis: Chalice, 2002.

———. *Love Relationships in the Johannine Tradition: Agapē/Agapan in I John and the Fourth Gospel*. SBLDS 58. Chico, CA: Scholars Press, 1982.

Sevenster, G. "Remarks on the Humanity of Jesus in the Gospel and Letters of John." In *Studies in John: Presented to Professor J. N. Sevenster on the Occasion of His Seventieth Birthday*, pp. 185-93. NovTSup 24. Leiden: Brill, 1970.

Sevrin, Jean-Marie. "L'intrigue du quatrième évangile, ou la christologie mise en récit." *RTL* 37 (2006): 473-88.

Shelfer, Lochlan. "The Legal Precision of the Term 'παράκλητος.'" *JSNT* 32 (2009): 131-50.

Shepherd, David. "'Do You Love Me?' A Narrative-Critical Reappraisal of ἀγαπάω and φιλέω in John 21:15-17." *JBL* 129 (2010): 777-92.

Shepherd, Massey H. *The Paschal Liturgy and the Apocalypse*. ESW 6. Richmond: John Knox, 1960.

Sidebottom, E. M. *The Christ of the Fourth Gospel in the Light of First-Century Thought*. London: SPCK, 1961.

Siew, Antoninus King Wai. *The War between the Two Beasts and the Two Witnesses: A Chiastic Reading of Revelation 11:1–14:5*. LNTS 283. London: T & T Clark, 2005.

Sim, David C. *Apocalyptic Eschatology in the Gospel of Matthew*. SNTSMS 88. Cambridge: Cambridge University Press, 1996.

Simoens, Yves. *La gloire d'aimer: Structures stylistiques et interprétatives dans le Discours de la Cène (Jn 13–17)*. AnBib 90. Rome: Biblical Institute Press, 1981.

Simon, Lutz. *Petrus und der Lieblingsjünger im Johannesevangelium: Amt und Autorität*. EH 23/498. Frankfurt: Peter Lang, 1994.

Slater, Thomas B. "Context, Christology and Civil Disobedience in John's Apocalypse." *RevExp* 106 (2009): 51-65.

Smalley, Stephen S. "Diversity and Development in John." *NTS* 17 (1970–1971): 276-92.

———. *1-3 John*. WBC 51. Waco, TX: Word, 1984.

———. "The Johannine Son of Man Sayings." *NTS* 15 (1968–1969): 278-301.

———. *John: Evangelist and Interpreter*. Exeter: Paternoster, 1978.

———. "'The Paraclete': Pneumatology in the Johannine Gospel and Apocalypse." In *Exploring the Gospel of John: In Honor of D. Moody Smith*, edited by R. Alan Culpepper and C. Clifton Black, pp. 289-300. Louisville: Westminster John Knox, 1996.

———. "The Testament of Jesus: Another Look." In *Studia Evangelica VI: Papers Presented to the Fourth International Congress on New Testament Studies Held at Oxford, 1969*, edited by Elizabeth A. Livingstone, pp. 495-501. Berlin: Akademie-Verlag, 1973.

Smith, Barry D. "The Chronology of the Last Supper." *WTJ* 53 (1991): 29-45.

Smith, D. Moody. "The Contribution of J. Louis Martyn to the Understanding of the Gospel of John." In *The Conversation Continues: Studies in Paul and John*, edited by Robert T. Fortna and Beverly R. Gaventa, pp. 275-94. Nashville: Abingdon, 1990.

———. "Johannine Christianity." In *Johannine Christianity: Essays on Its Setting, Sources, and Theology*, pp. 1-36. Columbia: University of South Carolina Press, 1984.

———. *Johannine Christianity: Essays on Its Setting, Sources, and Theology*. Columbia: University of South Carolina Press, 1984.

———. "Johannine Studies Since Bultmann." *WW* 21 (2001): 343-51.

———. *John among the Gospels: The Relationship in Twentieth-Century Research*. Minneapolis: Fortress, 1992.

———. "Theology and Ministry in John." In *Johannine Christianity: Essays on Its Setting, Sources, and Theology*, pp. 190-222. Columbia: University of South Carolina Press, 1984.

———. *The Theology of the Gospel of John*. NTT. Cambridge: Cambridge University Press, 1995.

Smith, Ian. "A Rational Choice Model of the Book of Revelation." *JSNT* 85 (2002): 97-116.

Smitmans, Adolf. *Das Weinwunder von Kana: Die Auslegung von Jo 2,1-11 bei den Vätern und heute*. BGBE 6. Tübingen: Mohr Siebeck, 1966.

Snyder, Graydon F. "John 13:16 and the Anti-Petrinism of the Johannine Tradition." *BR* 16 (1971): 5-15.

Söding, Thomas. "Die Wahrheit des Evangeliums: Anmerkungen zur johanneischen Hermeneutik." *ETL* 77 (2001): 318-55.

———. "Gott und das Lamm: Theozentrik und Christologie in der Johannesapokalypse." In *Theologie als Vision: Studien Zur Johannes-Offenbarung*, edited by Knut Backhaus, pp. 77-120. SBS 191. Stuttgart: Katholisches Bibelwerk, 2001.

——— "'Ich und der Vater sind eins' (Joh 10,30): Die johanneische Christologie vor dem Anspruch des Hauptgebotes (Dtn 6,4f)." *ZNW* 93 (2002): 177-99.

———. "Inkarnation und Pascha: Die Geschichte Jesus im Spiegel des Johannesevangeliums." *IKaZ* 32 (2003): 7-18.

———. "Kreuzerhöhung: Zur Deutung des Todes Jesu nach Johannes." *ZTK* 103 (2006): 2-25.

Spaulding, Mary B. *Commemorative Identities: Jewish Social Memory and the Johannine Feast of Booths.* LNTS 396. London: T & T Clark, 2009.

Spencer, Richard A. "Violence and Vengeance in Revelation." *RevExp* 98 (2001): 11-33.

Staley, Jeffrey Lloyd. *The Print's First Kiss: A Rhetorical Investigation of the Implied Reader in the Fourth Gospel.* SBLDS 82. Atlanta: Scholars Press, 1988.

Stare, Mira. *Durch ihn leben: Die Lebensthematik in Joh 6.* NTAbh 49. Münster: Aschendorff, 2004.

Stark, Werner. *Sectarian Religion.* Vol. 2 of *The Sociology of Religion: A Study of Christendom.* MR 2. London: Routledge & Kegan Paul, 1967.

Stauffer, Ethelbert. *New Testament Theology.* Translated by John Marsh. London: SCM Press, 1955.

Steegen, Martijn. "To Worship the Johannine 'Son of Man': John 9,38 as Refocusing on the Father." *Bib* 91 (2010): 534-54.

Stefan, Crinisor. "The Paraclete and Prophecy in the Johannine Community." *Pneuma* 27 (2005): 273-96.

Stemberger, Günter. *La symbolique du bien et du mal selon Saint Jean.* PD. Paris: Seuil, 1970.

Stephens, Mark B. *Annihilation or Renewal? The Meaning and Function of New Creation in the Book of Revelation.* WUNT 2/307. Tübingen: Mohr Siebeck, 2011.

Stettler, Hanna. "Die Gebote Jesu im Johannesevangelium (14,15.21; 15,10)." *Bib* 92 (2011): 554-79.

Stevens, George B. *The Johannine Theology: A Study of the Doctrinal Contents of the Gospels and Epistles of the Apostle John.* New York: Scribner, 1894.

Stevenson, Gregory. *Power and Place: Temple and Identity in the Book of Revelation.* BZNW 107. Berlin: de Gruyter, 2001.

Stibbe, Mark W. G. *John as Storyteller: Narrative Criticism and the Fourth Gospel.* SNTSMS 73. Cambridge University Press, 1992.

———. "Telling the Father's Story: The Gospel of John as Narrative Theology." In *Challenging Perspectives on the Gospel of John,* edited by John Lierman, pp. 170-93. WUNT 2/219. Tübingen: Mohr Siebeck, 2006.

Straub, Esther. *Kritische Theologie ohne ein Wort vom Kreuz: Zum Verhältnis von Joh 1–12 und 13–20.* FRLANT 203. Göttingen: Vandenhoeck & Ruprecht, 2003.

Strauss, David Friedrich. *Das Leben Jesu, kritisch bearbeitet.* 2 vols. Tübingen: Osiander, 1835–1836.

Strecker, Georg. *The Johannine Letters: A Commentary on 1, 2, and 3 John.* Edited by Harold W. Attridge. Translated by Linda M. Maloney. Hermeneia. Minneapolis: Fortress, 1996.

Streeter, B. H. *The Four Gospels: A Study of Origins.* London: Macmillan, 1924.

———. *The Primitive Church*. London: Macmillan, 1929.

Streett, Daniel R. *They Went Out from Us: The Identity of the Opponents in First John*. BZNW 177. Berlin: de Gruyter, 2011.

Stuckenbruck, Loren T. *Angel Veneration and Christology: A Study in Early Judaism and in the Christology of the Apocalypse of John*. WUNT 2/70. Tübingen: Mohr Siebeck, 1995.

Stuckenbruck, Loren T., and Wendy E. S. North, eds. *Early Jewish and Christian Monotheism*. JSNTSup 263. London: T & T Clark, 2004.

Stylianopoulos, Theodore. "The Orthodox Position." In *Conflicts about the Holy Spirit*, edited by Hans Küng and Jürgen Moltmann, pp. 23-30. Concilium 128. New York: Seabury, 1979.

Sullivan, Clayton. *Rethinking Realized Eschatology*. Macon, GA: Mercer University Press, 1988.

Sundberg, Albert C. "Christology in the Fourth Gospel." *BR* 21 (1976): 29-37.

———. "*Isos Tō Theō* Christology in John 5:17-30." *BR* 15 (1970): 19-31.

Tabb, Brian J. "Johannine Fulfillment of Scripture: Continuity and Escalation." *BBR* 21 (2011): 495-505.

Taeger, Jens-Wilhelm. "'Gesiegt! O himmlische Musik des Wortes!' Zur Entfaltung des Siegesmotivs in den johanneischen Schriften." *ZNW* 85 (1994): 23-46.

Talbert, C. H. "The Fourth Gospel's Soteriology between New Birth and Resurrection." *PRSt* 37 (2010): 133-45.

Tasker, R. V. G. "The Biblical Doctrine of the Wrath of God." *Them* 26 (2001): 4-17.

Tasmuth, Randar. "Authority, Authorship, and Apostolicity as a Part of the Johannine Question: The Role of Papias in the Search for the Authoritative Author of the Gospel of John." *ConJ* 33 (2007): 26-42.

Tavo, Felise. "The Ecclesial Notions of the Apocalypse in Recent Studies." *CurBR* 1 (2002): 112-36.

———. *Woman, Mother and Bride: An Exegetical Investigation Into the "Ecclesial" Notions of the Apocalypse*. BibTS 3. Leuven: Peeters, 2007.

Taylor, Michael J., ed. *A Companion to John: Readings in Johannine Theology (John's Gospel and Epistles)*. New York: Alba House, 1977.

Teeple, Howard M. *The Literary Origin of the Gospel of John*. Evanston, IL: Religion and Ethics Institute, 1974.

Thatcher, Tom. *Greater Than Caesar: Christology and Empire in the Fourth Gospel*. Minneapolis: Fortress, 2009.

———. *The Riddles of Jesus in John: A Study in Tradition and Folklore*. SBLMS 53. Atlanta: Society of Biblical Literature, 2000.

———, ed. *What We Have Heard from the Beginning: The Past, Present, and Future of Johannine Studies*. Waco, TX: Baylor University Press, 2007.

———. *Why John Wrote a Gospel: Jesus—Memory—History*. Louisville: Westminster John Knox, 2006.

Theobald, Michael. "Gott, Logos und Pneuma: 'Trinitarische' Rede von Gott im Johannesevangelium." In *Monotheismus und Christologie: Zur Gottesfrage im hellenistischen Judentum und im Urchristentum*, edited by Hans-Josef Klauck, pp. 41-87. QD 138. Freiburg: Herder, 1992.

———. *Herrenworte im Johannesevangelium*. HBS 34. Freiburg: Herder, 2002.

Thettayil, Benny. *In Spirit and Truth: An Exegetical Study of John 4:19-26 and a Theological Investigation of the Replacement Theme in the Fourth Gospel*. CBET 46. Leuven: Peeters, 2007.

Thiselton, Anthony C. "Reception Theory, H. R. Jauss and the Formative Power of Scripture." *SJT* 65 (2012): 289-308.

———. *Thiselton on Hermeneutics: The Collected Works and New Essays of Anthony Thiselton*. ACTR. Aldershot: Ashgate, 2006.

Thomas, John Christopher. *Footwashing in John 13 and the Johannine Community*. JSNTSup 61. Sheffield: Sheffield Academic Press, 1991.

———. "The Fourth Gospel and Rabbinic Judaism." *ZNW* 82 (1991): 159-82.

———. "A Note on the Text of John 13:10." *NovT* 29 (1987): 46-52.

Thompson, Marianne Meye. *The God of the Gospel of John*. Grand Rapids: Eerdmans, 2001.

———. *The Humanity of Jesus in the Fourth Gospel*. Philadelphia: Fortress, 1988.

———. "'The Living Father.'" *Semeia* 85 (1999): 19-31.

Thompson, Steven. *The Apocalypse and Semitic Syntax*. SNTSMS 52. Cambridge: Cambridge University Press, 1985.

Thüsing, Wilhelm. *Die Erhöhung und Verherrlichung Jesu im Johannesevangelium*. 3rd ed. NTAbh 21. Münster: Aschendorff, 1979.

Thyen, Hartwig. "Das Johannesevangelium als literarisches Werk und Buch der Heiligen Schrift." *ZNW* 12 (2009): 54-61.

———. *Studien zum Corpus Iohanneum*. WUNT 214. Tübingen: Mohr Siebeck, 2007.

Tofană, Stelian. "Jesus 'the Prophet' in the Witness and Belief of His Contemporaries According to the Fourth Gospel—a Johannine Theological Perspective." *SS* 7 (2009): 98-115.

Tóth, Franz. *Der Himmlische Kult: Wirklichkeitskonstruktion und Sinnbildung in der Johannesoffenbarung*. ABG 22. Leipzig: Evangelische Verlagsanhalt, 2006.

Trebilco, Paul. "What Shall We Call Each Other? Part Two: The Issue of Self-Designation in the Johannine Letters and Revelation." *TynBul* 54 (2003): 51-73.

Tresmontant, Claude. "Biblical Metaphysics." *CC* 10 (1960): 229-50.

Trumbower, Jeffrey A. *Born from Above: The Anthropology of the Gospel of John*. HUT 39. Tübingen: Mohr Siebeck, 1992.

Tsutserov, Alexander. *Glory, Grace, and Truth: Ratification of the Sinaitic Covenant According to the Gospel of John*. Eugene, OR: Pickwick, 2009.

Turner, Nigel. *Syntax*. Vol. 3 of *A Grammar of New Testament Greek*, by James Hope Moulton. Edinburgh: T & T Clark, 1978.

Tzaferis, Vassilios. "Inscribed 'To God Jesus Christ.'" *BAR* 33, no. 2 (2007): 38-49.

Uebele, Wolfram. *"Viele Verführer sind in die Welt ausgegangen": Die Gegner in den Briefen des Ignatius von Antiochien und in den Johannesbriefen.* BWANT 151. Stuttgart: Kohlhammer, 2001.

Um, Stephen T. *The Theme of Temple Christology in John's Gospel.* LNTS 312. London: T & T Clark, 1988.

Umoh, Camillus. *The Plot to Kill Jesus: A Contextual Study of John 11.47-53.* EH 23/696. Frankfurt: Peter Lang, 2000.

Untergassmair, Franz Georg. *Im Namen Jesu—Der Namensbegriff im Johannesevangelium: Eine exegetisch-religionsgeschichtliche Studie zu den johanneischen Namensaussagen.* FB 13. Stuttgart: Katholisches Bibelwerk, 1974.

Urban, Christina. *Das Menschenbild nach dem Johannesevangelium: Grundlagen johanneischer Anthropologie.* WUNT 2/137. Tübingen: Mohr Siebeck, 2001.

Vahrenhorst, Martin. "Johannes und die Tora: Überlegungen zur Bedeutung der Tora im Johannesevangelium." *KD* 54 (2008): 14-36.

van Belle, Gilbert. "The Death of Jesus and the Literary Unity of the Fourth Gospel." In *The Death of Jesus in the Fourth Gospel*, edited by Gilbert van Belle, pp. 3-64. BETL 200. Leuven: Leuven University Press, 2007.

———. "Repetition, Variation and Amplification: Thomas Popp's Recent Contribution on Johannine Style." *ETL* 79 (2003): 166-78.

———. *The Signs Source in the Fourth Gospel: Historical Survey and Critical Evaluation of the Semeia Hypothesis.* Translated by Peter J. Judge. BETL 116. Leuven: Peeters, 1994.

van Belle, Gilbert, Michael Labahn, and Pieter Maritz, eds. *Repetitions and Variations in the Fourth Gospel: Style, Text, Interpretation.* BETL 223. Leuven: Peeters, 2009.

Vanderlip, D. George. *Christianity According to John.* Philadelphia: Westminster, 1975.

van der Merwe, Dirk G. "The Character of Unity Expected among the Disciples of Jesus, According to John 17:20-23." *APB* 13 (2002): 224-54.

———. "Eschatology in the First Epistle of John: κοινωνία in the *Familia Dei.*" *VerbEccl* 27 (2006): 1045-76.

———. "The Exposition of John 17:6-8: An Exegetical Exercise." *HvTSt* 59 (2003): 169-90.

———. "Family Metaphorics: A Rhetorical Tool in the Epistle of 1 John." *APB* 20 (2009): 89-108.

———. "'Having Fellowship with God' According to 1 John: Dealing with the Intermediation and Environment through Which and in Which It Is Constituted." *AcTS* 8 (2006): 165-92.

———. *"Imitatio Christi* in the Fourth Gospel." *VerbEccl* 22 (2001): 131-48.

———. "The Protection Believers Can Expect from God in the Fulfilment of Their Mission." *SK* 21 (2000): 135-55.

———. "Salvation in the Johannine Epistles." *HvTSt* 60 (2004): 533-54.

———. ""Ὥρα, A Possible Theological Setting for Understanding Johannine Eschatology." *APB* 13 (2002): 255-87.

van der Watt, Jan G. "*Double Entendre* in the Gospel According to John." In *Theology and Christology in the Fourth Gospel: Essays by Members of the SNTS Johannine Writings Seminar*, edited by Gilbert van Belle, Jan G. van der Watt and P. J. Maritz, pp. 463-81. BETL 184. Leuven: Leuven University Press, 2005.

———. "Ethics and Ethos in the Gospel According to John." *ZNW* 97 (2006): 147-76.

———. "The Father Shows the Son Everything: The Imagery of Education in John 5:19-23." *APB* 18 (2007): 263-76.

———. "I Am the Bread of Life: Imagery in John 6:32-51." *AcT* 2 (2007): 186-204.

———. "The Presence of Jesus through the Gospel of John." *Neot* 36 (2002): 89-95.

———. "The Use of αἰώνιος in the Concept ζωὴ αἰώνιος in John's Gospel." *Neot* 33 (1989): 217-28.

van Hartingsveld, Lodewijk. *Die Eschatologie des Johannesevangeliums: eine Auseinandersetzung mit R. Bultmann*. VGTB 36. Assen: Van Gorcum, 1962.

van Rossum, Joost. "The 'Johannine Pentecost': John 20:22 in Modern Exegesis and in Orthodox Theology." *SVTQ* 35 (1991): 149-67.

van Tilborg, Sjef. *Reading John in Ephesus*. NovTSup 83. Leiden: Brill, 1996.

Varghese, Johns. *The Imagery of Love in the Gospel of John*. AnBib 177. Rome: Gregorian and Biblical Press, 2009.

Vawter, Bruce. "John's Doctrine of the Spirit: A Summary View of His Eschatology." In *A Companion to John: Readings in Johannine Theology (John's Gospel and Epistles)*, edited by Michael J. Taylor, pp. 177-85. New York: Alba House, 1970.

Vibert, Simon. "Lives Jesus Changed: Character Studies in John's Gospel." *Anvil* 26 (2009): 7-19.

Vischer, Lukas, ed. *Spirit of God, Spirit of Christ: Ecumenical Reflections on the Filioque Controversy*. FOP 103. Geneva: World Council of Churches, 1981.

Volf, Miroslav. "Johannine Dualism and Contemporary Pluralism." In *The Gospel of John and Christian Theology*, edited by Richard Bauckham and Carl Mosser, pp. 19-52. Grand Rapids: Eerdmans, 2008.

von Rad, Gerhard. *Old Testament Theology*. Translated by D. M. G. Stalker. 2 vols. New York: Harper & Row, 1962–1965.

von Wahlde, Urban C. *The Earliest Version of John's Gospel: Recovering the Gospel of Signs*. Wilmington, DE: Michael Glazier, 1989.

———. *The Gospel and Letters of John*. 3 vols. ECC. Grand Rapids: Eerdmans, 2010.

———. "The Gospel of John and the Presentation of Jews and Judaism." In *Within Context: Essays on Jews and Judaism in the New Testament*, edited by David P. Efroymson, Eugene J. Fisher and Leon Klenicki, pp. 67-84. Philadelphia: American Interfaith Institute, 1993.

———. "He Has Given to the Son to Have Life in Himself (John 5,26)." *Bib* 85 (2004): 409-12.

———. "'The Jews' in the Gospel of John: Fifteen Years of Research (1983–1998)." *ETL* 76 (2000): 30-55.

———. "The Johannine 'Jews': A Critical Survey." *NTS* 28 (1982): 33-60.

———. "The Pool(s) of Bethesda and the Healing in John 5: A Reappraisal of Research and of the Johannine Text." *RB* 116 (2009): 111-36.

Voorwinde, Stephen. *Jesus' Emotions in the Fourth Gospel: Human or Divine?* LNTS 284. London: T & T Clark, 2005.

———. "John's Prologue: Beyond Some Impasses of Twentieth-Century Scholarship." *WTJ* 64 (2002): 15-44.

Vos, Geerhardus. *The Pauline Eschatology.* Princeton, NJ: Princeton University Press, 1930.

Vouga, François. "Antijudaismus im Johannesevangelium?" *TGl* 83 (1993): 81-89.

———. "Erinnerung an Jesus im Johannesevangelium." *ZNT* 10 (2007): 28-37.

Wach, Joachim. *Sociology of Religion.* Chicago: University of Chicago Press, 1944.

Waddell, Robby. *The Spirit of the Book of Revelation.* JPTSup 30. Blandford Forum: Deo, 2006.

Waetjen, Herman C. *The Gospel of the Beloved Disciple: A Work in Two Editions.* London: T & T Clark, 2005.

———. "Logos πρὸς τὸν θεόν and the Objectification of Truth in the Prologue of the Fourth Gospel." *CBQ* 63 (2001): 265-86.

Wainwright, Arthur W. *Mysterious Apocalypse: Interpreting the Book of Revelation.* Nashville: Abingdon, 1993.

Waltke, Bruce K. "The Phenomenon of Conditionality within Unconditional Covenants." In *Israel's Apostasy and Restoration: Essays in Honor of Roland K. Harrison,* edited by Avraham Gileadi, pp. 123-39. Grand Rapids: Baker Books, 1988.

Ware, Timothy. *The Orthodox Church.* Rev. ed. London: Penguin, 1997.

Wead, David W. *The Literary Devices in John's Gospel.* TD 4. Basel: Friedrich Reinhardt Kommissionsverlag, 1970.

Weber, Max. *The Methodology of the Social Sciences.* Translated and edited by Edward A. Shils and Henry A. Finch. Glencoe, IL: Free Press, 1949.

———. *Wirtschaft und Gesellschaft.* Vol. 3 of *Grundriss der Sozialökonomik.* Tübingen: Mohr, 1922.

Webster, Jane S. *Ingesting Jesus: Eating and Drinking in the Gospel of John.* SBLAB 6. Atlanta: Society of Biblical Literature, 2003.

Weidemann, Hans-Ulrich. *Der Tod Jesu im Johannesevangelium: Die erste Abschiedsrede als Schlüsseltext für den Passions- und Osterbericht.* BZNW 122. Berlin: de Gruyter, 2004.

Weiss, Johannes. *Die Predigt Jesu vom Reiche Gottes.* Göttingen: Vandenhoeck & Ruprecht, 1892.

Wengst, Klaus. *Bedrängte Gemeinde und verherrlichter Christus: Der historische Ort des Johannesevangeliums als Schüssel zu seiner Interpretation.* BTS 5. Munich: Kaiser, 1981.

————. *Das Johannesevangelium*. 2 vols. THKNT 4. Stuttgart: Kohlhammer, 2000–2001.

Wenham, John. *Easter Enigma*. CEP. Grand Rapids: Academie Books, 1984.

Werblowsky, R. J. Zwi, and Geoffrey Wigoder, eds. *The Encyclopedia of the Jewish Religion*. New York: Adama, 1986.

Wernle, Paul. *Der Christ und die Sünde bei Paulus*. Leipzig: Mohr Siebeck, 1897.

Westcott, B. F. *The Gospel According to St. John: The Greek Text with Introduction and Notes*. 2 vols. in 1. Grand Rapids: Eerdmans, 1954.

Westermann, Claus. *The Gospel of John in the Light of the Old Testament*. Translated by Siegfried S. Schatzmann. Peabody, MA: Hendrickson, 1998.

Whitacre, Rodney A. *Johannine Polemic: The Role of Tradition and Theology*. SBLDS 67. Chico, CA: Scholars Press, 1982.

White, R. E. O. "'No One Comes to the Father but by Me.'" *ExpTim* 113 (2002): 116-17.

Whiteley, Iwan M. "An Explanation for the Anacoloutha in the Book of Revelation." *FilNeot* 20 (2007): 33-50.

Wilckens, Ulrich. "Christus traditus se ipsum tradens: Zum johanneischen Verständnis des Kreutzestodes Jesu." In *Der Sohn Gottes und Seine Gemeinde: Studien zur Theologie der Johanneischen Schriften*, pp. 29-55. FRLANT 200. Göttingen: Vandenhoeck & Ruprecht, 2003.

————. "Gott, der Drei-Eine: Zur Trinitätstheologie der johanneischen Schriften." In *Der Sohn Gottes und Seine Gemeinde: Studien zur Theologie der Johanneischen Schriften*, pp. 9-28. FRLANT 200. Göttingen: Vandenhoeck & Ruprecht, 2003.

————. "Monotheismus und Christologie." *JBTh* 12 (1997): 87-97.

Wiles, Maurice F. "Eternal Generation." *JTS* 12 (1961): 284-91.

————. *The Spiritual Gospel: The Interpretation of the Fourth Gospel in the Early Church*. Cambridge: Cambridge University Press, 1960.

Wilkens, Wilhelm. *Zeichen und Werke: Ein Beitrag zur Theologie des 4. Evangeliums in Erzählungs- und Redestoff*. ATANT 55. Zürich: Zwingli, 1969.

Willett, Michael E. *Wisdom Christology in the Fourth Gospel*. San Francisco: Mellen Research University Press, 1992.

Williams, Catrin H. *I Am He: The Interpretation of* ʾAnî Hû *in Jewish and Early Christian Literature*. WUNT 2/113. Tübingen: Mohr Siebeck, 2000.

Williams, P. J. "Not the Prologue of John." *JSNT* 33 (2011): 375-86.

Williams, Ronald J. *Hebrew Syntax: An Outline*. 2nd ed. Toronto: University of Toronto Press, 1976.

Wilson, Bryan R., ed. *Patterns of Sectarianism: Organization and Ideology in Social and Religious Movements*. London: Heinemann, 1967.

————. *Religious Sects: A Sociological Study*. WUL. London: Weidenfeld & Nicolson, 1970.

Wilson, Robert McL. "The Early History of the Exegesis of Gen. 1:26." *StPatr* 1 (1957): 420-37.

Windisch, Hans. *Johannes und die Synoptiker: Wollte der vierte Evangelist die älteren Evangelien ergänzen oder ersetzen?* UNT 12. Leipzig: Hinrichs, 1926.

———. *The Spirit-Paraclete in the Fourth Gospel.* Translated by James W. Cox. FBBS 20. Philadelphia: Fortress, 1968.

Witherington, Ben, III. *John's Wisdom: A Commentary on the Fourth Gospel.* Louisville: Westminster John Knox, 1995.

Woll, D. Bruce. *Johannine Christianity in Conflict: Authority, Rank, and Succession in the First Farewell Discourse.* SBLDS 60. Chico, CA: Scholars Press, 1981.

Wrede, William. *The Messianic Secret.* Translated by J. C. G. Greig. Cambridge: James Clarke, 1971.

Wright, John Wesley. "'Blessing, Honor, Glory, and Might, Forever and Ever!' Nicea and the Christology of the Book of Revelation." *WesTJ* 39 (2004): 7-38.

Wright, N. T. "Monotheism, Christology and Ethics: 1 Corinthians 8." In *The Climax of the Covenant: Christ and the Law in Pauline Theology,* pp. 120-36. Minneapolis: Fortress, 1992.

———. *The New Testament and the People of God.* COQG 1. Minneapolis: Fortress, 1992.

———. *Paul: In Fresh Perspective.* Minneapolis: Fortress, 2005.

Wright, William. *Apocryphal Acts of the Apostles: Edited from Syriac Manuscripts in the British Museum and Other Libraries.* 2 vols. London: Williams & Norgate, 1871.

Wyckoff, Eric J. "Jesus in Samaria (John 4:4-42): A Model for Cross-Cultural Ministry." *BTB* 35 (2005): 89-98.

Yamauchi, Edwin M. *Pre-Christian Gnosticism: A Survey of the Proposed Evidences.* Grand Rapids: Eerdmans, 1973.

Yarbro Collins, Adela. "The Worship of Jesus and the Imperial Cult." In *The Jewish Roots of Christological Monotheism: Papers from the St. Andrews Conference on the Historical Origins of the Worship of Jesus,* edited by Carey C. Newman, James R. Davila and Gladys S. Lewis, pp. 234-57. JSJSup 63. Leiden: Brill, 1999.

Yee, Gale A. *Jewish Feasts and the Gospel of John.* ZS. Wilmington, DE: Michael Glazier, 1989.

Yinger, J. Milton. *Religion in the Struggle for Power: A Study in the Sociology of Religion.* Durham, NC: Duke University Press, 1946.

Yinger, Kent L. *Paul, Judaism, and Judgment According to Deeds.* SNTSMS 105. Cambridge: Cambridge University Press, 1999.

Young, Norman H. "C. H. Dodd, 'Hilaskesthai' and His Critics." *EvQ* 48 (1976): 67-78.

———. "'Hilaskesthai' and Related Words in the New Testament." *EvQ* 55 (1983): 169-76.

Zahn, Theodore. *Introduction to the New Testament.* Translated by John Moore Trout et al. 3 vols. New York: Scribner, 1909.

Zangenberg, Jürgen K. *Frühes Christentum in Samarien: Topographische und traditionsgeschichtliche Studien zu den Samarientexten im Johannesevangelium.* TANZ 27. Tübingen: Francke, 1998.

Zeilinger, Franz. *Die sieben Zeichenhandlungen Jesu im Johannesevangelium.* Stuttgart: Kohlhammer, 2011.

Zenger, Erich. "Gott hat niemand je geschaut (Joh 1,18): Die christliche Gottesrede im Angesicht des Judentums." *BK* 65 (2010): 87-93.

Zerwick, Maximilian. *Biblical Greek, Illustrated by Examples.* Edited by Joseph Smith. SPIB 114. Rome: Pontifical Biblical Institute, 1963.

Zimmermann, Ruben. *Christologie der Bilder im Johannesevangelium: Die Christopoetik des vierten Evangeliums unter besonderer Berücksichtigung von Joh 10.* WUNT 171. Tübingen: Mohr Siebeck, 2004.

———. "Nuptial Imagery in the Revelation of John." *Bib* 84 (2003): 153-83.

Zingg, Edith. *Das Reden von Gott als "Vater" im Johannesevangelium.* HBS 48. Freiburg: Herder, 2006.

Zumstein, Jean. "Der Prolog, Schwelle zum vierten Evangelium." In *Der Johannesprolog,* edited by Günter Kruck, pp. 49-75. Darmstadt: Wissenschaftliche Buchgesellschaft, 2009.

———. "Die Sünde im Johannesevangelium." *ZNW* 12 (2009): 27-35.

———. "Dieu est amour." *FoiVie* 99 (2000): 95-106.

———. "Jesus' Resurrection in the Farewell Discourses." In *The Resurrection of Jesus in the Gospel of John,* edited by Craig R. Koester and Reimund Bieringer, pp. 103-26. WUNT 222. Tübingen: Mohr Siebeck, 2008.

———. *Kreative Erinnerung: Relecture und Auslegung im Johannesevangelium.* ATANT 84. Zürich: Theologischer Verlag Zürich, 2004.

———. "Le lavement des pieds (Jean 13,1-20): Un exemple de la conception johannique du pouvoir." *RTP* 132 (2000): 345-60.

———. "L'interpretation johannique de la mort du Christ." In vol. 3 of *The Four Gospels 1992: Festschrift Frans Neirynck,* edited by Frans van Segbroeck et al., pp. 2119-38. BETL 100. Leuven: Leuven University Press, 1992.

# INDEX OF AUTHORS

# INDEX OF SUBJECTS

# INDEX OF
# PRINCIPAL SCRIPTURE PASSAGES